World Wisdom
The Library of Perennial Philosophy

The Library of Perennial Philosophy is dedicated to the exposition of the timeless Truth underlying the diverse religions. This Truth, often referred to as the *Sophia Perennis*—or Perennial Wisdom—finds its expression in the revealed Scriptures as well as the writings of the great sages and the artistic creations of the traditional worlds.

The Perennial Philosophy provides the intellectual principles capable of explaining both the formal contradictions and the transcendent unity of the great religions.

Ranging from the writings of the great sages of the past, to the perennialist authors of our time, each series of our Library has a different focus. As a whole, they express the inner unanimity, transforming radiance, and irreplaceable values of the great spiritual traditions.

Zen Buddhism: A History Volume 1 appears as one of our selections in the Treasures of the World's Religions series.

Treasures of the World's Religions
Series

This series of anthologies presents scriptures and the writings of the great spiritual authorities of the past on fundamental themes. Some titles are devoted to a single spiritual tradition, while others have a unifying topic that touches upon traditions from both the East and West, such as prayer and virtue. Some titles have a companion volume within the Perennial Philosophy series.

NANZAN STUDIES IN RELIGION AND CULTURE
James W. Heisig, General Editor

Heinrich Dumoulin. *Zen Buddhism: A History.* Vol. *1, India and China.* Vol. *2, Japan.* Trans. James Heisig and Paul Knitter (Bloomington: World Wisdom, Inc., 2005, new edition)

Frederick Franck, ed. *The Buddha Eye: An Anthology of the Kyoto School* (Bloomington: World Wisdom, Inc., 2004, new edition)

Frederick Franck. *To Be Human Against All Odds* (Berkeley: Asian Humanities Press, 1991)

Winston L. King. *Death Was His Kōan: The Samurai-Zen of Suzuki Shōsan* (Berkeley: Asian Humanities Press, 1986)

Paul Mommaers and Jan Van Bragt. *Mysticism Buddhist and Christian: Encounters with Jan van Ruusbroec* (New York: Crossroad, 1995)

Robert E. Morrell. *Early Kamakura Buddhism: A Minority Report* (Berkeley: Asian Humanities Press, 1987)

Nagao Gadjin. *The Foundational Standpoint of Mādhyamika Philosophy.* Trans. John Keenan (New York: suny Press, 1989)

Nishida Kitarō. *Intuition and Reflection in Self-Consciousness.* Trans. Valdo Viglielmo et al. (New York: suny Press, 1987)

Nishitani Keiji. *Nishida Kitarō* (Berkeley: University of California Press, 1991)

Nishitani Keiji. *Religion and Nothingness.* Trans. Jan Van Bragt (Berkeley: University of California Press, 1985)

Nishitani Keiji. *The Self-Overcoming of Nihilism.* Trans. Graham Parkes and Setsuko Aihara (New York: suny Press, 1990)

Paul L. Swanson. Foundations of T'ien-T'ai Philosophy: The Flowering of the Two-Truths Theory in Chinese Buddhism (Berkeley: Asian Humanities Press, 1989)

Takeuchi Yoshinori. *The Heart of Buddhism: In Search of the Timeless Spirit of Primitive Buddhism.* Trans. James Heisig (New York: Crossroad, 1983)

Tanabe Hajime. *Philosophy as Metanoetics.* Trans. Takeuchi Yoshinori et al. (Berkeley: University of California Press, 1987)

Taitetsu Unno, ed. *The Religious Philosophy of Nishitani Keiji: Encounter with Emptiness* (Berkeley: Asian Humanities Press, 1990)

Taitetsu Unno and James Heisig, eds. *The Religious Philosophy of Tanabe Hajime: The Metanoetic Imperative* (Berkeley: Asian Humanities Press, 1990)

Hans Waldenfels. *Absolute Nothingness: Foundations for a Buddhist-Christian Dialogue.* Trans. James Heisig (New York: Paulist Press, 1980)

ZEN BUDDHISM:
A History

Volume 1
India and China

Henrich Dumoulin

Translated by
James W. Heisig and Paul Knitter

with an Introduction by
John McRae

World Wisdom

Zen Buddhism: A History
Volume 1: India and China
© 2005 World Wisdom, Inc.

*World Wisdom would like to thank James W. Heisig
for his assitance in making this volume possible*

Most Recent Printing indicated by last digit below:

10 9 8 7 6 5 4 3

Library of Congress Cataloging-in-Publication Data

Dumoulin, Heinrich.
  [Zen. English]
  Zen Buddhism : a history / Henrich Dumoulin ; translated by James W. Heisig and
Paul Knitter.
      v. cm. – (Treasures of the world's religions)
  Includes translations from Chinese texts.
  Translation of: Zen, Geschichts und Gestalt.
  Includes bibliographical references and index.
  Contents: v. 1. India and China – v. 2. Japan
  ISBN-13: 978-0-941532-89-1 (v.1 : pbk. : alk. paper)
  ISBN-10: 0-941532-89-5 (v.1 : pbk. : alk. paper)
  ISBN-13: 978-0-941532-90-7 (v.2 : pbk. : alk. paper)
  ISBN-10: 0-941532-90-9 (v.2 : pbk. : alk. paper) 1. Zen Buddhism–History. I.
Heisig, James W., 1944- II. Knitter, Paul F. III. Title. IV. Series.
  BQ9262.3. D85513 2005
  294.3'927'09–dc22

                                                                          200501887

Printed on acid-free paper in Canada.

For information address World Wisdom, Inc.
P. O. Box 2682, Bloomington, Indiana 47402-2682

www.worldwisdom.com

Contents

Part Two: Origins and Blossoming in China

Foreword to the 1988 Edition

More than fifty years have passed since Zen Buddhism found entry to the West through the pioneering genius of D. T. Suzuki. During the years following World War II one might have suspected that this spontaneous and inflated fascination of the Western mind for an altogether foreign and exotic form of meditation was no more than a temporary fad destined soon to pass away. But now, as we approach the end of the twentieth century, it is clear that Zen has secured for itself a place in the spiritual history of our emerging global community.

The Zen movement has spread wide and deep. The numerous forms of Zen meditation existing and even competing with one another today point to a healthy plurality within the movement, while the depth of its impact is to be seen in the disciples of Zen actively engaged in meditation. The scientific study of religion, which has grown so impressively during this century, has also delved into Zen extensively and intensively within the field of Buddhist studies. Research on Zen, and in particular on the history of Zen, has taken on ever greater importance. The United States and Japan have emerged as the two main poles of Zen research.

Considering these developments, I am especially pleased that this modest work, rooted and nurtured in a Japanese milieu and composed from a Japanese point of view, will now appear in the United States in a translation by close friends and colleagues. A glance through the two volumes of this work will show that for all the Japanese influence, the whole owes a great deal to American scholarship. It is my hope that my efforts will meet a sympathetic and critical audience in North America. At the same time, I must beg the indulgence of my readers, for I am only too aware that the increasing advances being made in the study of Zen Buddhism, especially in the last two decades, and the nearly unsurveyable spectrum of related literary scholarship make for unavoidable lacunae and inadequacies in a work such as this. Specialized research will no doubt have much to add to the general overview presented here. This is all the more welcome since the Zen movement is important not only to the academic community but also to the many men and women whose lives it has enriched. I am grateful to be able to make even a small contribution to this course of events.

In addition, I cannot but express my gratitude to those who organized and collaborated in this English translation. It would not have come about without the efforts of the Nanzan Institute for Religion and Culture in Nagoya and the editor of its *Studies in Religion and Culture*, Professor James Heisig, who took the initiative in the project and invited the able assistance of Professor Paul Knitter of Xavier University. Together they have labored with untiring care to render the German original in a form suited to the English-speaking world and to monitor the many technical details involved in preparing the work for publication. Finally, I wish to thank Macmillan Publishing Company and its publisher Mr. Charles Smith for including this work in its impressive list of scholarly publications.

Tokyo, 4 June 1986   Heinrich Dumoulin

Prologue to the 1988 Edition

It was the American Buddhist Ruth Fuller Sasaki who first urged me to write a history of Zen Buddhism. Having translated into English my earlier studies on the development of the Zen movement in China, studies that she graced with excellent glossaries and indexes, she encouraged me to expand my work and suggested that I put together an overview of the entire history of Zen. With great hesitation I took her advice. The resulting volume, which appeared in 1959 under the title *Zen—Geschichte und Gestalt* (published by Francke as volume 87 of the Dalp series) was, despite its many deficiencies, well received. An English translation followed (*A History of Zen Buddhism*), published by Pantheon in New York and Faber and Faber in London; subsequent paperback editions earned it a certain popularity in colleges throughout North America.

Since both the German and the American editions have long since gone out of print, I suggested to my publishers that a newly revised edition might be in order. They responded favorably to the idea but recommended—and then held firmly to that recommendation—that large sections be reworked. As it turned out, more than half the book was revised, resulting in a considerably larger book. During the nearly thirty years that had elapsed since the book's first publication, an abundance of new and important works on Zen Buddhism had appeared. Clearly a few additions or expanded references would not suffice to incorporate this work into my study. Even though I limited myself to the new literature related to the history of Zen, I ended up writing a new book.

In the course of the rewriting, it has been possible to compare and make use of much source material newly translated into European languages—especially the translations of the *Platform Sūtra of the Sixth Patriarch* by Philip B. Yampolsky and Wing-tsit Chan, as well as translations of the *Discourses of Lin-chi (Rinzairoku)* by Ruth Fuller Sasaki and Paul Demiéville. While the extensive studies of Edward Conze on the Wisdom sūtras and the widely used work of the Dutch scholar Erik Zürcher, *The Buddhist Conquest of China*, have not required that we rethink the foundations of Zen history, they have nonetheless exposed previously neglected roots of the tradition. The voluminous reference work *Zen Dust*, a joint production of Miura Isshū and Ruth Fuller Sasaki, has also been of great help.

Finally, I am indebted to the remarkably productive Zen research that has gone on in Japan since the end of World War II. The works of Yanagida Seizan on the early history of Zen are epoch-making and open up new horizons for Zen scholarship. In addition, many Japanese books on the history of Zen in China, especially the numerous annotated translations of source materials into Japanese, have made accessible a wider range of historical material. Prominent among the standard technical dictionaries on buddhism are the three volumes in modern Japanese of the *Cyclopedia of Zen Learning (Zengaku daijiten)*. As might be expected, the Japanese contribution to Zen research has far surpassed the West in range and value, and has been of great service in my own history of Zen. For all its inadequacies, of which I myself am only too keenly aware, it is my hope that this work will aid both my colleagues and successors in dispelling the darkness that surrounds the origins of Zen and help to reveal a richer picture of its history as a whole.

It only remains for me to fulfill the pleasant duty of thanking all those who have helped me in my studies, especially my researches into the history of Zen. The beginnings of my study of Zen go back to my years as a student at what was then the Imperial University of Tokyo, where for the first time I joined Japanese students in the reading of Zen texts. Furuta Shōkin, together with a colleague who died in the war, introduced me to the kōan collection known as the *Mumonkan*; Furuta was to move on as a scholar of Chinese and Japanese Zen literature and secure an enduring reputation through editing the Japanese works of his teacher and friend, D. T. Suzuki. Long before the "Zen boom" sounded over the West, he encouraged me to explore this extraordinary development within the religious tradition that began with the Buddha. Since my student years I have kept in close contact with Nakamura Hajime, with whom I read the original text of the *Bodhisattvabhūmi* in a seminar directed by our esteemed teacher, Ui Hakuju. After the war we had several occasions to collaborate in international interreligious encounters. From his rich personality and from his broad knowledge and warm tolerance I have gained a deep grasp of his religion. There is not space enough to list the names of all the Japanese Buddhists to whom I am gratefully indebted both personally and academically.

My recent reexploration of the history of Zen owes much to Professor Yanagida Seizan of the University of Kyoto, the world's foremost scholar in the history of Chinese Zen. Professor Yanagida was most generous to me with his time; in long conversations he gave me an abundance of valuable insight, taught me how to make critical use of the rich Zen literature, and provided me with an inside view into his own research. To the best of my ability I have incorporated his personal guidance, as well as his pioneering studies, into my modest work. Another Rinzai master, Professor Nishimura Eshin of Kyoto's Hanazono University, helped me appreciate the peculiarities of Rinzai Zen. Similar assistance regarding the Sōtō school was provided by Professor Kawamura Kōdō of Komazawa University in Tokyo. Professor Yonezawa Hiroshi, a graduate of Sophia University who is currently on the faculty of Bunkyō University in Tokyo, helped me to clarify and work through the new Japanese literature on Zen. Last but not least, I owe a debt of gratitude to the established master of the history of East Asian art, Dietrich Seckel, Professor Emeritus of the University of Heidelberg; as a favor to an old friend, Professor Seckel read through the section on Zen art in the final chapter of this first volume and suggested substantial changes, which I happily accepted.

Mr. Taka Kampachi, a graduate of Sophia University's master of arts program and a doctoral student in its Department of German Literature, assembled the list of Chinese characters and historical tables; whatever inaccuracies remain, however, are my own responsibility. Miss Wada Yūko typed the entire manuscript. To all these collaborators, and to the Institute for Far Eastern Religions of Sophia University—expecially its director, Professor Thomas Immoos, and its secretary, Mrs. Shimozawa Maya—I wish to express my heartfelt thanks. I also owe a debt of gratitude to the Francke Verlag of Bern for the tedious task of typesetting the manuscript and seeing it to publication.

Tokyo, May 1983   HEINRICH DUMOULIN

Linguistic Conventions

The Japanese language forms part of the foundation for this history of Zen, first because Zen came to be known in the West from Japan and in Japanese form, but also because I wrote this book mainly with the aid of Japanese Zen literature. Accordingly, all Zen terms are given in their Japanese form. Even in the case of Chinese titles of Zen works, names of temples, and names of different schools, the Japanese version is often given first; in the list of characters, in the historical tables, and often in the text itself, the Chinese reading is frequently provided in parentheses. Proper names are always given according to the country of origin (Chinese or Japanese) and according to Asian usage, first the family or kinship name is listed and then the personal name. Zen masters are often designated according to the temple or mountain on which their monastery stands; a second name is then added from among their numerous monastic names. In Zen literature one generally finds the full name of the master and then one of the other names, which is freely selected and then used throughout the study. In the list of characters, both names are given in their customary Japanese order.

While most technical terms from Asian languages have been set in italics, the more commonly known Buddhist terms have been rendered in roman type. Japanese words have been transcribed throughout in the now standard Hepburn system as adapted by *Kenkyūsha's New Japanese English Dictionary*. There are no accepted norms for dividing Japanese words or capitalizing titles. The conventions adopted here have been applied consistently; to avoid confusing the reader, quotations and titles that follow other conventions have been adjusted accordingly. In order to facilitate research by those likely to make use of them, Sino-Japanese characters for the technical terms that appear in the text have been supplied in an appendix.

Chinese words have been transcribed in the classical Wade-Giles system of romanization. The adoption of any other of the available methods would have presented insurmountable problems for the general reader not familiar with the underlying principles of transposition. Words of Indic provenance have been typeset uniformly with their diacritical marks. Where such marks are lacking in quotations or titles, they have been supplied for the sake of consistency.

The Sanskrit word *dharma* (Pāli, *dhamma*; Chin., *fa*; Jpn., *hō*), which has found its way into European languages, calls for a brief explanation. We may distinguish three main uses of the term: (1) duty, law, doctrine; (2) thing, element of being; (3) universal Buddha reality (*dharmadhātu*). Not uncommonly, the first and third meanings pass over into one another. The second meaning stems from the Śrāvakayāna philosophy (especially from the *Abhidarmakośa*), but is also present in Zen texts. The capitalized word *Dharma* generally refers to the all-embracing Buddha reality.

A complete bibliography is included at the end of volume 2. Both the glossary of Sino-Japanese characters and the indexes cover only technical terms and the names of individuals and texts. Geographical names have been omitted. In general, Chinese characters have been typeset in their traditional form rather than in their abbreviated Japanese form.

Preface

Zen (Chin., Ch'an, an abbreviation of *ch'an-na,* which transliterates the Sanskrit term *dhyāna* or its Pāli cognate *jhāna,* terms meaning "meditation") is the name of a Mahāyāna Buddhist school of meditation originating in China and characterized by the practice of meditation in the lotus position (Jpn., *zazen;* Chin., *tso-ch'an*) and the use of the kōan (Chin., *kung-an*), as well as by the enlightenment experience of *satori.* Zen schools, Zen practice, and Zen enlightenment occupy a position of great importance in the religious and intellectual history of Asia, and because of its spiritual and human profundity, Zen has also attracted increasing attention in the West. Theoretical and practical interest in Zen has given rise to a vast and varied secondary literature on the subject that, together with the translation of numerous original Zen sources into European languages, has fostered an intense interest in the history of Zen Buddhism.

History is a pretentious science. Caught up in a constant process of change and development, it continually poses new demands on the researcher. Although scientific research into the history of Zen Buddhism is still in its initial stages, it seems to be moving today from a first to a second phase in its development. The first phase was characterized by general works, collections of representative selections from Zen literature, and studies aimed primarily at presenting a general overview of the field. The second phase is deepening our knowledge of Zen history by providing access to a wider range of literature, more penetrating monographs by philosophers and experts in comparative religion, and a more comprehensive perspective.

APPROACH AND LIMITATIONS

For the historian, Zen Buddhism is at once a fascinating and a frustrating subject. The frustrations arise mainly from the difficulty of mastering the connections between the tangle of crisscrossing lines that make up its total picture. This is true both of its external portrait—one thinks of the broad temporal and geographical expanse it covers—and of the complex mosaic of religious, cultural, and psychological factors that make up its internal portrait.

Certain points are more immediately evident. Foremost among them is the fact that the Zen school holds a prominent place within Buddhism itself. Contrary to what some were still arguing at the beginning of this century, Zen is not a mere sideshow but something of far greater moment, a tradition in which aspirations and ideals essential to Buddhism find their fulfillment. To be sure, Zen is deeply rooted in things Buddhist; without Śākyamuni and his enlightenment the Zen way would be simply unimaginable. At the same time, Buddhism owes some of its most noteworthy achievements to Zen. One might well say that without Zen, Buddhism would not be what it is today. Zen represents one of the purest manifestations of the religious essence of Buddhism; it is the fruit and flower of that larger tree.

Zen is most influential in the Mahāyāna countries of East Asia—China (formerly including Vietnam), Korea, and Japan. One can also trace its impact in more southern regions, principally in Tibet, where the singular developments of Lamaism show certain common roots with Zen, and also in the Theravāda countries of Southeast Asia, where Buddhist orthodoxy cannot be fully understood without attention to its contravening heresies. One readily notices the influence of Zen in conversation with progressive Theravāda monks as Zen slowly comes to find its place within the general consciousness of contemporary Buddhism.

We must also acknowledge the thoroughly Asiatic character of Zen. When oriental methods of meditation are treated in the West, Zen is often set alongside Yoga, and not without good reason, for despite the differences scholars are wont to point out, the two schools of meditation display obvious family resemblances.

Yoga and Taoism converge in Zen Buddhism. More accurately, one might say that the Buddhist practice of meditation, which was clearly influenced by Yoga, flowed into the broader stream of ancient Chinese Taoism. External similarities between Buddhism and Taoism do not of themselves, however, permit us to conclude that there was contact between these two traditions from early antiquity. This makes their eventual marriage in Mahāyāna Zen all the more fascinating.

Given the connections and contrasts among the religious paths of Asia, the historian faces difficult and unresolved questions, the implications of which have yet to surface. Connections and correlations can also be expressed in terms of contrasts. Yet for all the religions of Asia have in common, the historian must guard against reduction and simplification.

Above all, a history of Zen Buddhism must seek to clarify the way in which the foundational pillars of Zen are anchored in the religion of the Buddha and in Asian thought. While this obliges the historian to explore beyond the boundaries of the Mahāyāna school of Zen, he must nevertheless never lose sight of the school itself. Certain formidable figures in the history of Zen shine like lighthouses standing tall and strong in the ocean swell. Not only do they illumine and typify the essence of Zen, they also provide a presentiment of the present pluralistic situation of Zen. The particular view of Asian spirituality that Zen offers us is rich in secular, cultural, and especially psychological insights; to overlook these various dimensions would be inexcusable. This means that our historical portrait will also have to include the human, often all too human, element. History deals with human beings, who would not be what they really are without their shadows.

The phenomenon of Zen is thus complex and manifold. Part and parcel of Asian spirituality, it is bound up with numerous other currents and movements. This makes it easy for historians of Zen to cast their nets so far and wide as to lose the focus of their search. This may be why certain Zen enthusiasts have expanded the term Zen to refer to all kinds of psychic phenomena. Certainly one needs to try to view Zen in a broad perspective and to guard against prematurely dismissing possible correlations. Nonetheless, a clear definition of limits is required to ensure that Zen is properly evaluated in religious history. The subject of our study is the Zen school of Mahāyāna Buddhism; whatever can aid us to understand better the origins, development, differentiation, and influence of that school is important. Yet in view of the vastness and wealth that mark the outreach of Zen to broader culture realms, we can venture only a general and clearly demarcated outline of its religious and cultural contacts.

THE THESIS OF D. T. SUZUKI

One of the best-known interpreters of Zen Buddhism, D. T. Suzuki, has presented Zen to the West as an experience that is essentially free of history and metaphysics, superseding all categories and transcending all paradoxes. In *An Introduction to Zen Buddhism* he writes:

> We may say that Christianity is monotheistic and the Vedānta pantheistic; but we cannot make a similar assertion about Zen. Zen is neither monotheistic nor pantheistic; Zen defies all such designations. Hence there is no object in Zen upon which to fix the thought. Zen is a wafting cloud in the sky. No screw fastens it, no string holds it. . . . Zen wants to have one's mind free and unobstructed; even the idea of oneness or allness is a stumbling block and a strangling snare which threatens the original freedom of the spirit.[1]

In his pioneering efforts to clarify the meaning of Zen for the West, Suzuki has consistently guarded against all efforts to place the Zen experience within a philosophical system. He often stresses the essential difference between Zen and Yoga or the yogic forms of meditation within Buddhism. No doubt there is a great deal of valuable historical information in his writings that helps us understand the essence of Zen, and yet at no time does he present his readers with a historical picture of Zen Buddhism. The celebrated Chinese historian and philosopher Hu Shih criticizes his Japanese colleague for not sufficiently recognizing the historical conditioning of Zen:

> I resolutely resist all assertions that it is impossible for human reason to understand and evaluate Zen. . . .
> The Zen movement is an integral component of the history of Chinese Buddhism; and the history of Chinese Buddhism is an integral part of the general religious history of China. Zen can be understood only within its historical context, just as other schools of Chinese philosophy must be studied and understood in their historical contexts.[2]

Like most academic disputes, the controversy between these two Asian scholars was never clearly decided. Undoubtedly Suzuki commands a superior and deeply experiential knowledge of Zen. Since the time of this dispute, many scholars have come to agree that religious experience, especially when it is a question of the experience of higher, transcendent realms, lies beyond metaphysical concepts and cannot be completely grasped from a historical perspective. Zen certainly qualifies as an experience transcending time and space. But even though the Zen experience forever eludes the reach of historical investigation, history has an important role to play in the study of Zen. The abundant historiographical literature that has emerged during the past two decades shows that Suzuki's thesis on the ahistoricity of Zen has not really been accepted. Or perhaps better, it indicates that Suzuki's claim has been understood as it was originally meant—namely, as a warning against those who look to positivistic science for an adequate basis upon which to understand Zen.

History must be conscious of its own limitations. So must metaphysics. Yet neither history nor metaphysics can be excluded from a study of Zen Buddhism. Regarding metaphysics, a statement that Rudolf Otto made in his preface to the first German publication on Zen is to the point: ". . . no mysticism can exist purely in the blue; it invariably rests on a foundation which it mightily seeks to deny but which gives it its special character and an identity different from all other forms of mysticism."[3]

As for history, no one will question the value of establishing the given facts, of clearly reporting what happened, of putting everything in proper context. To explore carefully the origins and historical roots of a phenomenon helps us to understand better its essence. For this reason we must explore the earliest beginnings of Zen. These include, as already noted, ancient Yoga and Taoism, as well as the Buddhist sūtras, and, even more important, the imposing personalities of Zen Buddhism. It is impossible to understand the early development of Zen without a careful study of its different schools and movements. Moreover, the many and varied artistic and cultural expressions of Zen are themselves all vitally dependent on particular cultural and historical contexts.

ASIAN AND WESTERN MODES OF UNDERSTANDING

History seeks to understand. Intellectual history and the history of religions aim to grasp human thinking, feeling, and action in their depths. Of course, such an undertaking can never be accomplished once and for all. The more profoundly one tries to penetrate the human spirit, the more carefully and intelligently one must proceed. The difficulties that mark humanity's efforts to prove its own religious depths must also figure in any account of the differences between East and West, between the cultures of Asia and the cultures of the West. Fortunately, the creative and persevering efforts of contemporary scholarship in Asian studies have, within the favorable conditions provided by the modern world, made possible a new meeting between the two hemispheres. In our day, East and West know incomparably more about each other than they did a mere century ago. At the same time, the accelerated pace of a unified technological civilization is sweeping more and more people into a lifestyle that is principally, if not exclusively, concerned with the external things of life. For a majority of people the inwardness of the human spirit lies out of reach; only a few serious seekers are intent on exploring the deeper regions of the spiritual and religious life.

Confronting the fundamentally different ways of thinking in the East and the West, one can say that the path to deeper mutual understanding is difficult but not impossible. I remain convinced that behind and within all these obvious and undeniable differences is a common ground and a common horizon. Such a conviction, I believe, can stimulate initiatives that are not only exciting and promising but capable of changing the world. In this context, the task of the historian is not only to challenge and encourage but also to admonish and warn. All of this bears so directly on the study of Zen history as to merit a closer look.

Human understanding is not simply a matter of the intellect. It is rather a holistic experience based on the senses, particularly on seeing and hearing. Sight brings into play the special significance of art for deeper human understanding. In this regard, bridges of understanding to the East exist today that were simply not available to earlier generations in the West. Thanks to a highly developed technology in the graphic arts and ready access to well-endowed museums all over the world, a wealth of artworks has become a sort of public legacy in our day. The tourist trade also provides possibilities for travel enabling millions to come into direct contact with the artistic treasures of Asia. Such cultural bridges signal both an opportunity and a responsibility. One's first encounter with the strangeness of another world can touch off an enticing delight in the exotic. Many tourists will remain content with this and draw no further benefit from their encounter with Asian culture. Yet persons for whom the world of the spirit is real will find that this glimpse into a strange new culture will lead them to search more deeply into the riches of Asian art. For them, the initial enchantments are not enough: true art, insofar as it touches the human spirit, moves the spectator to become a participant in an inner experience that seeks to grasp and truly understand the meaning of art.

Zen Buddhism, rich in extraordinary works of art, invites one to an encounter in which the essence of the real is envisioned anew. If we could boldly break with our usual Western way of understanding to grasp the richness of Zen Buddhist art correctly—that is, in a meditative assimilation—we would be in a better position to approach the depths of Zen. For Westerners, art offers an enjoyable and relatively less arduous path to understanding than does meditation. But to pursue it, to explore the richness of Asian and particularly Zen Buddhist art, one must be careful not to become ensnared in making comparisons with Western art. One's primary aim must rather be to discover what the work is trying to say, to uncover its inner meaning. I hope to offer in this book a modest aid to those seeking to approach Asian art in this way.

The primary means of communicating understanding is language. This is why many Westerners interested in the East are laboring strenuously to listen directly to the voice of Eastern wisdom by learning the languages of Asia. Not a few students of Zen struggle with the demanding task of learning a very difficult language, well aware that much of the rich and peculiar spiritual wealth is often veiled behind the garb of bizarre and suggestive Chinese and Japanese linguistic forms. Japanese Zen masters are happy to teach their Western students at least some of the basic Zen vocabulary, whose content they then proceed carefully to unpack. In this way, many Western Zen practitioners have built up a small vocabulary of terms in Asian languages, much like the European lover of the classics who never had the opportunity to study them but who has nonetheless mastered a number of key expressions in Greek.

At the same time, as developments in the contemporary philosophy of language have made abundantly clear, a mere knowledge of language does not suffice. Interpersonal communication, which is the very purpose of language, takes place in understanding what is shared. And that requires interpretation. Hence, hermeneutics has an important role to play in the encounter with the world of Asian spirituality. Literal translation is not enough; nor is a glossary of synonymous concepts and paraphrases. Quite the contrary—in order to clear the way for a better understanding of what is new and different, it is more helpful first to clear one's head of Western linguistic structures. The content of Asian spirituality cannot be reduced to common denominators shared with the West, as anyone who has seriously struggled to understand the East knows only too well. The stark otherness of Asia demands constant caution in the adoption of Western terms. Scholars of course need to make use of such terms, since it is their job to communicate Eastern spirituality to Western languages; yet they can never forget that there are no tidy "equivalencies" between the languages of different cultures, that differing verbal structures cannot be reduced to a common "identical value." Every translation is an interpretation, and therefore no translation is able to guarantee that the full content of a foreign word or expression has been rendered perfectly. It is important, therefore, to take the East itself as one's starting point, to try to enter into the East with as much empathy as possible, to let the East present itself in all its facets. Concrete examples and symbols are of great help in that they appeal to something all human persons have in common. Yet our ability to understand what another culture is saying in its own way will depend on the degree to which we have been able truly to enter into that culture.

The East-West encounter places great demands on the ability of both sides to understand each other. Concretely, the effort invested in understanding Zen is worthwhile not only because of its proven methods of meditation but also because of its power of expression. The Zen literature of eastern Asia bears impressive witness to the ability of Zen to communicate through language as well as through gesture and mien. Religious people around the world have been intrigued by its collections of kōan—one of the most curious forms of world literature, full of riddles and intended puns, ecstatic outbursts, and paradoxes. In these collections, as well as in other utterances of enlightened Zen masters, we find sayings of great verbal power. Hui-neng, Lin-chi, Dōgen, and Hakuin are among the most imposing figures in this regard. In these four giants of Zen history we see an extraordinary power of language—the same penetrating power that shines through in many of the writings of other masters—coupled with penetrating speculative insights. The process of unlocking the world of Zen literature is in full swing. The names of two prominent pioneers in this effort, D. T. Suzuki and Wilhelm Gundert, are indelibly impressed on the history of our times. Although scholars of Zen literature are currently taken up largely with linguistic concerns, they are preparing the way for the further step of penetrating more deeply into questions of content and meaning.

Three great Asian countries have made significant contributions to the history of Zen Buddhism through their religious and cultural achievements. This fact at once creates great problems and also offers greater rewards. The historical approach must give due consideration to the differences between the cultures of India, China, and Japan. While Zen belongs to China and Japan, India is more than a mere background. The important contributions of Yoga and early Buddhism require a selective but sufficiently detailed consideration, though always from the perspective of the main theme of this book.

NOTES

1. Daisetz Teitaro Suzuki, An *Introduction to Zen Buddhism* (New York, 1964), p. 41.

2. Hu Shih, "Ch'an (Zen) Buddhism in China: Its History and Method," *Philosophy East and West* 3 (1953): 3–24. Suzuki's reply ("A Reply to Hu Shih"), printed in the same issue, was reprinted in his *Studies in Zen* (New York, 1975), pp. 135–64, and was preceded by a résumé of Hu Shih's arguments, pp. 129–35. Hu Shih concludes his critique with a citation from Suzuki's *Living by Zen*. In his essay Hu further developed views on the history of Zen in China first set forth in an extensive study entitled "The Development of Zen Buddhism in China," SPSR 15.4(1932): 475–505. *Living by Zen*, first published in 1950, was later reissued in an edition prepared by Christmas Humphreys (London, 1972).

3. S. Ōhasama and A. Faust, *Zen: der lebendige Buddhismus in Japan* (Gotha, 1925), p. ix.

Note to the 2005 Edition

James W. Heisig

The decision to reprint Heinrich Dumoulin's two-volume *Zen Buddhism: A History* was not an easy one to make. Although only fifteen years in print, its publication coincided with an explosion of scholarly work on Zen in the West that exposed it to criticism from the moment it appeared. Indeed, even as I was going through the galley proofs of the first volume on China, the author was mailing me drafts of a Supplement he was composing in the attempt to digest recent research on the Northern School of Chinese Zen and to assess its consequences for his own work. By the time Fr. Dumoulin died in 1995, nearly every section and subsection in the two volumes had become the doctoral specialization of someone somewhere. Among his posthumous papers was discovered a sixty-page draft of an essay on Korean Zen, intended as a Supplement to vol. 2. But given the number of scholars working in the area with a knowledge of the Korean sources—something he himself lacked—I thought it best not to release it for publication. Ten years later I found myself in the still more difficult position of having to decide about how best to honor the crowning achievement of a devoted historian and friend at a time when scholarship has passed much of his life work by.

The enthusiasm of World Wisdom for reprinting the two volumes was easy to understand. The need for a comprehensive history of Zen was obvious and there was no other single work in English, or any other Western language for that matter, capable of meeting that need. Along with a rising level of sophistication among practitioners of Zen, the status of its textual tradition in world intellectual history has continued within academia and without. At the same time, as likely as experts in the field were to share in the scholarly suspicion surrounding the book and to have ceased quoting it as an authoritative text, they were just as likely to have it within arm's reach for confirming a date or checking an obscure reference.

The motives for releasing a new edition were compelling, but so was need for caution. The place the volumes occupied when they were first published is clearly not the place they will occupy in reprint, and it was felt that this needed to be communicated to the majority of readers who, by any reckoning, would not be specialists in Zen historiography. To this end, two Zen scholars with two quite different understandings of Zen studies were invited to prepare introductory essays, John McRae for the volume on *India, China, and Tibet*, and Victor Hori for the volume on *Japan*. Within the context of providing general guidance on how to use Fr. Dumoulin's work, they were encouraged to take issue with one another and to give the reader unfamiliar with such things a general feel for the issues involved and the passion of those involved with them. I would like personally to thank Professors McRae and Hori for consenting to take on the task, and for carrying it out under such peculiar conditions. On reading through their final texts, pared and polished through months of interchange with each other, I cannot help but see Fr. Dumoulin grinning sheepishly at the contrasting opinions his books had provoked, and reaching for a pen to start scrawling down his own thoughts on the matter.

Without the unfailing guidance of Mary-Kathryne Steele and the generous cooperation of Stephen Williams, none of this would have been possible. To both of them, and their co-workers at World Wisdom, my thanks.

Nanzan Institute for Religion and Culture
Nagoya, Japan
4 June 2005

Introduction

John R. McRae

Upon its initial publication in 1988, the English translation of Heinrich Dumoulin's *Zen Buddhism: A History, India and China*, instantly became an indispensable resource for both specialists and the audience of general readers interested in Zen Buddhism. A number of laudable features ensured the book's immediate success. First, especially in tandem with the second volume in the set treating Zen in Japan, the book's coverage was rewardingly comprehensive. For the first time English readers could trace the history of the school from its earliest conceptual and practical beginnings in India, through its formation and evolution as an innovative religious movement in China, and on to its efflorescence in Japan. The comprehensive nature of Dumoulin's coverage derived from his own intellectual vision, his determination to address all aspects of his chosen subject matter, from beginning to end.

Second, within this comprehensive sweep was embodied a most thorough devotion to critical scholarship, with the primary and secondary sources for every issue sifted carefully and evaluated on the basis of relevance, historical implication, and religious meaning. A brief glance at the annotation was enough to convince even the most skeptical reader that the author wrote, not only on the basis of his own scholarship, but after having made an extensive examination of the best secondary scholarship available in Japanese and European languages. Although the author claimed no experiential or sectarian identity as a Zen Buddhist—he remained a committed Christian all his life—this was clearly a book with a certain authority, one that could be trusted to offer the best interpretations possible at the time.

Third, rather than foregrounding the decades of research that went into making his book possible, Father Dumoulin presented the fruits of his analysis in a very accessible narrative. Using a style that, while never flashy, was always readable and workmanlike, Dumoulin outlined the evolution of Zen Buddhism in straightforward and easily comprehensible terms. There was nothing here of the intentionally obfuscatory tone taken in some of D. T. Suzuki's (1870–1966) works on Zen, for example, in which the author's goal was as much to mystify as to explain his subject matter.

Fourth, although Dumoulin did not write in order to inspire the achievement of some state of Buddhist enlightenment in his readers, as a Jesuit he was deeply sensitive to the spiritual dimensions of his subject matter. He was writing history, but at the same time he was clearly deeply moved by the religious insights achieved by different members of the Zen tradition. Indeed, judging by the pages of *Zen*

Buddhism: A History, India and China it would seem that placing these insights within an easily comprehensible framework and bringing them to the attentions of his readers was the primary goal of his many decades of scholarship.

In the background of his *Zen Buddhism: A History, India and China* was a lengthy spiritual and intellectual path.[1] Expected by his family to study law, Dumoulin instead decided to enter the Jesuit novitiate at the age of nineteen. He became interested in matters Japanese during his novitiate years, but was also well educated in western philosophy and world religions. After a doctoral degree in 1929 from the Gregorian University in Rome, he began the formal study of Japanese in a one-year program at the University of Berlin. After this brief intro-duction he began his theological studies for the priesthood, in Holland; in 1933 he was ordained a priest in the Society of Jesus and in 1934 he completed his Licentiate in Theology. He was then sent to England for his tertiate, allowing him to learn spoken English, and then set off via the trans-Siberian railway to Japan in 1935.

When Dumoulin was able to complete his formal study of Japanese in only one year, his intellectual gifts prompted the regional superior, Father Hugo Lassalle (later renowned for promoting Zen meditation among western-ers and in particular for Catholics), to select the young Dumoulin for higher studies. Although law was suggested to him, this was a course of study he had already rejected earlier in his life, and he asked to be allowed to study oriental religions. This unique request was accepted, and in 1936 Dumoulin enrolled at Tokyo Imperial University, the only foreign student in the Department of Religious Studies. In contrast to the Department of Indian and Buddhist Phil-osophy and the Department of Shintō Studies, the broad coverage and (as we would say now) multidisciplinary style of this Department provided a conge-nial home for the extremely well-educated young German scholar. His men-tor was an Old Testament scholar and fluent German speaker named Ishibashi Tomonobu (Chishin) 石橋智信 (1886–1947), who always referred to Dumoulin as "Herr Doktor" and recommended that he study Kamo no Mabuchi 加茂真渕 (1697–1769), an important Shintō revivalist. After some difficulty learning to comprehend the formal language of Japanese professorial lectures, Dumoulin immersed himself in his studies and in 1943 produced a doctoral dissertation on Mabuchi. (The dissertation was defended in 1946.) During this period Dumoulin published a couple of articles and several reviews on subjects relating to Shintō, and beginning in 1942 he taught western philosophy at Sophia University and the Catholic seminary in Tokyo until wartime conditions made this impossible in 1944. He taught at Sophia until his retirement in 1976, and he continued to publish extensively on Shintō, Buddhism in the modern world, and the Buddhist-Christian encounter from the early 1940s until his death.

In 1940 Dumoulin wrote a review of Daisetz Teirarō Suzuki's *Zen Buddhism*

---

1. The following review of Dumoulin's scholarly life is indebted to Heisig 1985 and Watanabe 1985. Note that the latter is selective and does not include any works after 1985.

and Its Influence on Japanese Culture, which he begins with an impressive rehearsal of Suzuki's already very significant contributions to the field. Suggesting that the apparently disconnected essays in the volume actually constitute an integrated thesis, Dumoulin proceeds to refute several of Suzuki's most cherished points. Thus Dumoulin noted that the fondness for simplicity in Japanese art predated the advent of Zen, writing that "The profound influence of Zen on Japanese art is undeniable. However, other equally important factors must not be left out of account" (324). Although Dumoulin allows that Suzuki's work "makes inspiring reading," he "cannot approve of such simplification of facts and developments" (325).

By the erudition of the review, it is clear that Dumoulin had already made substantial studies of the Japanese Zen tradition. In the years that followed his interest in Zen Buddhism was further piqued by two young Zen priests who were fellow-students of his. With them he translated the *Mumonkan* 無門関 into German (1953, revised and republished in 1975), and at the same time he published his first historical account of Chinese Zen. This latter work was *The Development of Chinese Zen After the Sixth Patriarch in the Light of Mumonkan* (1953). In 1959 he finished his history of Zen Buddhism in German, which was published in English four years later as *A History of Zen Buddhism*. The present volume was first published in 1985 in German and in 1988 in English translation, then re-issued in a revised and expanded English version in 1994. It thus represents the fruits of over four decades of in-depth study, if we count from the date of publication of Dumoulin's review of D. T. Suzuki's book.

Before reviewing the different versions of Dumoulin's history of Zen Buddhism, it will be instructive to consider the implications of his other writings on Buddhism and Christianity. For the present purposes, the most salutary impression one gains from *Christianity Meets Buddhism* (1974) is the earnest and equitable fashion in which Dumoulin describes his goals.

The relation between Buddhism and Christianity is regarded here in the light of their encounter and their dialogue, seeking to deepen mutual understanding. This dialogue has been carried on in openness and respect, and has created an atmosphere of mutual interest and growth. And since the plurality of religions is assumed as a fact, committed Buddhists and committed Christians can meet together in dialogue as equitable partners, and seek to understand and to learn from each other. (p. 2)

A few lines below, Dumoulin might well be describing his own attitude toward Buddhism:

The Westerner often finds himself of two minds about Asia and Asian culture: he experiences a strong leaning, and at the same time an inner resistance toward Eastern matters. Far Eastern spirituality enchants him, but appears enigmatic in many respects. The religion of the Buddha seems particularly paradoxical, not so much with regard to its complicated doctrines as to the many faces of its living practice. (pp. 3–4)

And, finally, on the goals of the Buddhist-Christian dialogue itself:

> Unity is not the goal of the dialogue between Christianity and Buddhism, neither syncretistically as an integration of one religion into another, nor as a sublimation of both religions into a higher unity. The goals of the dialogue, to put it simply, are to gain and deepen mutual understanding and cooperation, on the personal level, for the common welfare of mankind. (p. 35)

This fairly captures, I believe, the nobiliy of Dumoulin's scholarly and personal quest. As a committed Catholic, there was never any question of his becoming Buddhist. (He attempted the practice of zazen for a time later in life, but stopped because of the physical strain.) Nor was there any sense that he wrote of Buddhism, and in particular Zen Buddhism, in order either to undercut it or to promote it. Instead, he stood as a wonder-struck outsider to Buddhism, simultaneously baffled and awed by what he saw to be the deep spiritual truths its participants experienced. For Dumoulin the benefits of this deepened personal understanding of Buddhism by Christians and of Christianity by Buddhists were self-evident, and in his *Understanding Buddhism* (1994) he underlines this by writing, "Dialogue has become a necessity not only for harmonious coexistence and cooperation between people of different religious cultures, but for the more basic reason that the questions that haunt people of all cultures cannot be satisfactorily addressed if the interreligious horizon is closed off." (p. 11)

Dumoulin begins his *Understanding Buddhism* with an enumeration of some of the misconceptions Westerners (by which he means Western Christians) have about Buddhism, then defines the goal of his book as "to provide an antidote for these misunderstandings" (p. 1). He writes:

> My hope is that the discussion of the selected key themes will help remove stumbling blocks that have prevented Western and especially Christian inquirers from participating as fully as they might in what I consider to be one of the greatest spiritual and intellectual adventures of our time. (p. 3)

One buddhologist who has reviewed *Understanding Buddhism*, Jan Nattier, was particularly harsh in her assessment of the accuracy of Dumoulin's descriptions of Buddhism. She points out that in working to remove the stumbling blocks just mentioned, Dumoulin "does not hesitate to remake Buddhism itself in order to do so" (Nattier 1996). In declaring such practices as *asubha-bhāvanā* (meditation on the impure, using such objects as human corpses) to be a "sick obsession," in asserting that in Abhidharma scholasticism the sense of *dukkha* or suffering had become "distorted," in relying on discredited scholarship to assert that Buddhism did not deny the reality of a "true self," in favoring knowledge over the defeat of desire as the only means to liberation, and in misrepresenting the vows of Amitābha, Dumoulin commits serious errors in his presentation of Buddhism. Nattier's final conclusion is that *Understanding Buddhism* should not be taken as an objective account of central issues in the Buddhist tradition, but "as a primary source—that is, as an autobiographical essay that reveals how one Christian thinker, aided and abetted by a number of Westernized Japanese Buddhists, has found usable ideas and practices within the Buddhist repertoire."

Our purpose here is to evaluate Dumoulin's research on Chinese Zen Buddhism, and this critical evaluation serves as a useful warning. That is, there is an undeniable nobility in Dumoulin's professed goals; one can only be moved by the sincerity and genuine goodness of his life's mission. However, to what extent did his identity and mission as a Christian get in the way of his under-standing of Buddhism? Or, given that much of of the scholarship on which he constructed his interpretation was done in the first half of the twentieth century, to what extent were his sources for the understanding of Indian and East Asian religions simply too old to support the weight of his massive project as we move forward into the twenty-first century?

It is interesting, for the historian of ideas, to see how Dumoulin's researches on Indian and Chinese Zen Buddhism progressed from *The Development of Chinese Zen* (1953), to *A History of Zen Buddhism* (1963), and finally to *Zen Buddhism: A History, India and China* (1988; revised ed. 1994). The choice of the *Mumonkan* as his initial entrée to Zen studies was as understandable as it was momentous. Far more popular in Japanese Zen than it ever was in China, the *Mumonkan* is a concise yet provocative product of thirteenth-century Sung-dynasty Chinese Zen. Consisting of forty-eight *kōans* or "public cases" presenting encounters between enlightened Zen sages and their interlocutors, this text was in several ways a propitious choice.

Even though Dumoulin had twice abstained from taking up the study of law, here he studied a religious document whose basic format was derived from the legal encounters between judge and plaintiffs. He does not comment on the irony, though, and the forty-one pages of his basic exposition in *The Development of Chinese Zen* represent his first published summary of "The Golden Age of Zen during the T'ang Era," "The Five Houses," and "The Development of Koan Zen in the Sung Era." Thus we see, in his very first significant publication on the history of Chinese Zen, a core group of subjects that was to remain central to his two later volumes. When comparing these three works it becomes apparent that Dumoulin transformed his initial impressions primarily by the addition of new data and new subject matter; even though it would no doubt be a simple matter to detect areas where the *Zen Buddhism: A History, India and China* of 1988 dif-fers substantially from the works of 1953 and 1969, overall there is something of a straight-line progression from one to the other. This is particularly noticeable in the latter two volumes, in which even the language of the 1988 opus is bor-rowed from the 1969 work.

If anything, Dumoulin's contribution to *The Development of Chinese Zen* (49 pages, if we include the bibliography as his) was overshadowed by Ruth Fuller Sasaki's (1892–1967), given her translator's preface of twenty-two pages, primary text citations of thirty-four pages, and character glossaries of forty-five pages. As translator, editor, and publisher (through the First Zen Institute of New York, which she funded), Sasaki's contribution to *The Development of Chinese Zen* was huge. In particular, her decision to include Chinese characters within the text made it a wonderful resource for serious students of the Zen tradition.

Beginning in 1956, well after she translated Dumoulin's treatise on the *Mumonkan*, Ruth Fuller Sasaki put together a team of scholars and practititioners that was going to transform Zen studies in a most fundamental manner. The most important Japanese scholars to participate in this team were Iriya Yoshitaka 入矢義高 (1910–1998), a specialist in Chinese literature who was interested in Chinese Zen texts because of their extensive use of colloquial language, and Yanagida Seizan 柳田聖山 (b. 1922), a specialist in Chinese Zen whom Dumoulin justifiably describes as "the world's foremost scholar in the history of Chinese Zen" (xii). Iriya was famous for his correspondence in Chinese with Hu Shih 胡適 (1891–1962) regarding Zen texts and terminology, and in 1967 Yanagida was to publish his magisterial *Studies in the Historical Works of Early Zen* (Yanagida 1967), which used Dunhuang documents and other sources to examine the emergence and evolution of Chinese Zen during the seventh to tenth centuries.

The most important American scholar to participate in Sasaki's team was Philip B. Yampolsky (1920–1996), whose translation of the *Platform Sūtra of the Sixth Patriarch* (Yampolsky 1967) included a lengthy introduction that was certainly the best single piece of academic writing on Chinese Zen at the time. Other American participants in Sasaki's working group included Burton Watson, later to become the premier translator of Chinese historical and philosophical texts, and the poet Gary Snyder. This team produced a seminal English translation of the *Record of Linji*, the recorded sayings text depicting the great Linji Yixuan (d. 867), as well as a translation of the *Sayings of Layman Pang*, another very lively Song-dynasty text. However, the legacy of the team that Ruth Fuller Sasaki gathered at Daitokuji in Kyoto should not be measured by its immediate output, but by how it served as a catalyst for the thorough re-evaluation of Chinese Zen texts.

Working under Sasaki's autocratic and sometimes idiosyncratic supervision, the members of this team were provided by Sasaki with financial support until her death, when it emerged—very much contrary to their expectations—that her funds had been exhausted. Due to sectarian rivalries, the participants in the team soon found themselves without even access to the extensive library of note cards they had created, the beginnings of a database on Zen terminology, biography, and texts. (This situation festered for so long that, by the time the resources produced under Sasaki's support became available to scholars they were long since obsolete.) Although the situation after Sasaki's death was frustrating, Yanagida and Iriya had forged a partnership that was not to be stopped. With Yanagida at Hanazono College and Iriya at Nagoya and later Kyoto University, they began a joint seminar in Chinese Zen texts that led to a very substantial number of publications and the thorough re-interpretation of Chinese Zen.

Iriya's initial introduction to Zen texts came through his interest in the evolution of colloquial Chinese language, as already mentioned above. Gifted with a prodigious memory and a great thirst for relevant material, he read through the entire corpus of Chinese manuscripts from Dunhuang looking for new data. In this process he encountered Zen texts attributed to Bodhidharma and from the Northern, Southern, and Oxhead schools of Chinese Zen. When he consulted Japanese editions of Zen texts containing similar material, though, he realized that medieval and premodern Japanese Zen teachers had simply not recognized the colloquial Chinese expressions that abound in these texts, let alone understood their actual meaning. Instead, the Japanese Zen tradition had read Chinese texts as best they could from their knowledge of literary Chinese, and the differences between literary and colloquial language often resulted in drastic misinterpretations. To give only one example, it is common even today in Zen monastic training situations for masters to shout "Katz!" at their students. However, the word in question here did not mean "to shout 'katz' loudly," but simply a verb meaning "to shout." It was as if English readers read "he yelled" and took it to mean "he made a loud sound of 'yell'"! (The traditional misreading is given in Dumoulin 1953, 9.) This example may seem trivial, but since errors such as this were compounded the result was substantial.

Iriya and Yanagida edited a series of Chinese Zen texts, translating them into modern Japanese and providing them with substantial annotation explaining their terminology, contents, and implications. They insisted that the Japanese translations not be merely transpositions of the Chinese into formal Japanese grammar, but rather a new style of rendering the colloquial Chinese into fluent modern Japanese. The first text to receive this treatment was, once again, the *Record of Linji,* which Yanagida published in 1961. (In the course of his lengthy career Yanagida has repeatedly reworked his understanding of the *Record of Linji,* to date publishing five separate translations of the text!) The most substantial series edited by Iriya and Yanagida was *Zen no goroku* (Recorded Sayings of Zen), which included their own annotated translations and those of other scholars. Texts published in this series include the *Treatise on the Two Entrances and Four Practices* attributed to Bodhidharma; the first two "transmission of the lamp" historical texts of Zen, both associated with the Northern school; and more than a dozen other volumes. This project, which was initiated in 1969 and saw its final volume appear in 1981 (three volumes of the planned-for twenty will never appear, unfortunately), allowed at last for the study of Chinese Zen texts using sound editions and philological explanations.

At the same time Yanagida was transforming the study of Chinese Zen with his research publications, which were voluminous, insightful, and inventive. In the days before copy machines, let alone computers, he and his wife twice hand-copied the *Anthology of the Patriarchal Hall* (*Tsu-t'ang chi,* or *Sodōshū* in Japanese, a "transmission of the lamp" history from 952 that was preserved along with the printing blocks for the Korean edition of the Chinese Buddhist canon). Unraveling the secrets of the *Anthology of the Patriarchal Hall* became his life's mission, and in order to accomplish it he became the world's leading authority on Zen texts from Dunhuang. Having described his scholarship in detail elsewhere (McRae 1993–94) here I will only point out that his writings explored many facets of Chinese Zen, from the earliest period through its most glorious efflorescence in the Song dynasty. Within this monumental oeuvre, though, it is fair to say that Yanagida considers the Hongzhou school of Mazu Daoyi (709–88) as representing the first emergence of the uniquely "Zen" style of repartée known as "encounter dialogue."[2] For Yanagida, it was with Mazu that Zen came into its maturity, that it developed its most distinctive style of encounter-based spiritual training, and that it came to be embraced most fully by and within Chinese culture.

For some reason Yanagida never had many Japanese students, but he helped train a succession of westerners. Philip Yampolsky introduced me to Yanagida in spring 1973, and I was fortunate enough to work with him for the next two years. For the first year or more of this time I visited him at his house once a week, reading texts and discussing Chinese Zen with him. Those visits are among the most cherished memories of my entire life, because of Yanagida's immense learning, his easy-going manner, and his burning desire to make Zen Buddhism better understood. He never accepted any payment, and yet he welcomed my often foolish questions and strange misreadings with a charming equanimity. Every visit included a cup or two of *matcha,* the bitter green tea used in the tea ceremony and accompanied by a small sweet or two, made either by himself or his wonderful wife. (Mrs. Yanagida became a very prominent tea teacher, and when the two traveled to the United States in 1989 Yanagida was amused that she had over two hundred students attending her classes, while only about thirty or so attended his lectures!)

Just as I was about to leave Japan, Bernard Faure arrived. Yanagida described him as a "young French student," and neither of us realized at the time what a remarkable impact Faure would have on Zen studies. (Faure and I did not meet until years later.) Urs App was the next major western figure to arrive, and this gifted Swiss scholar eventually became Yanagida's closest colleague at Hanazono and the Associate Director of the International Research Institute for Zen Buddhism (IRIZ;; iriz.hanazono.ac.jp). While Yanagida continued to write his essays, articles, and books by hand, he quickly recognized the value of computer technology in the study of such a complicated field as Chinese Zen, and he supported App's innovations in a range of activities in the creation of electronic texts and online databases. Along with Lewis Lancaster, then of the University of California, Berkeley, App and his colleague Christian Wittern (now of the Institute for Humanistic Studies, Kyoto University) played a very significant role in the development of electronic Buddhist texts. In addition to providing invaluable technical assistance to the emerging Chinese Buddhist Electronic Texts Association (CBETA; www.cbeta.org), App and Wittern created an array of databases specifically related to Zen.

---

2. "Encounter dialogue" was my translation of Yanagida's *kien mondō* 機縁問答, not a widely used phrase in Chinese texts but his desriptive for Chinese Zen dialogue. See Yanagida 1983.

It is not clear how much Dumoulin was influenced by these developments. Although he was obviously deeply impressed by reading Yanagida's works, and he was aware of the impact Iriya's reinterpretations of Chinese Zen texts by the rules of colloquial Chinese usage (Dumoulin 1992, 70), Dumoulin was not a regular participant in the seminars held by Iriya and Yanagida over the years. There are no references to Iriya or Yanagida in Dumoulin's A *History of Zen Buddhism* of 1963, which was written (in German in 1959) before Ruth Fuller Sasaki's team had disbanded but well before Yanagida published his *magnum opus* of 1967, and before Yampolsky published his translation and study of the *Platform Sūtra* in the same year. Nor does one see much evidence of the research on Shen-hui and early Zen by Hu Shih, for whom only two articles are listed in the bibliography.

In contrast, Dumoulin's 1963 bibliography includes eleven different citations of articles, translations, and books by D. T. Suzuki, and it is clear from reading the text that Dumoulin had very mixed views of the value of Suzuki's contributions. He wrote, for example, that Suzuki's books were

> distinguished by lively suggestiveness, abundance of material, and absorbing exposition but not by clear order and transparent logic, have contributed to conceptual confusion. Over and over Suzuki stresses the independence and incomparability of Zen as nothing other than personal experience which, in its pure subjectivity, forgoes all sub- and superstructures, appears spontaneously without cause, and is inexpressible in words. Indeed, this experience is so far beyond words that it transcends and embraces all philosophy and theology. All clear delineations vanish in Suzuki's expositions for his European-American audience. (33)

I have already suggested above that explaining Buddhism to a Western Christian audience was Dumoulin's primary intellectual and humanistic goal, and his frustration at Suzuki's impact in making his life's work all the more difficult is almost palpable. In spite of this reaction, Suzuki's influence is nevertheless evident on virtually every page of the first few chapters of Dumoulin's narration, if only in the choice of topics. Suzuki was so prolific and so compelling that his works became an inescapable resource for the Jesuit father, a scholar compelled to consider every facet of the evidence available. Suzuki had effectively set the agenda with his discussions of the perfection of wisdom, emptiness, suchness, and other theoretical issues of Indian Buddhism, and so Dumoulin provided his readers with a more balanced consideration of these same topics.

In the beginning of his treatment of Chinese Zen in his A *History of Zen Buddhism*, and at the very beginning of his *Zen Buddhism: A History, India and China*, Dumoulin introduces the famous 1953 debate between Hu Shih and D. T. Suzuki over the proper way to study Chinese Zen. Although he never seriously critiques Hu Shih's position—a fact to which we will return just below—in each case he uses the occasion to criticize the inherent contradiction and confusing quality of Suzuki's approach. In A *History of Zen Buddhism* he writes:

Suzuki emphasizes the time- and space-transcending character of the Zen experience to which no historical research can have access. But when in the course of his reply, as in all his works, he cites copiously the words and anecdotes of the early Chinese Zen masters, he nonetheless places his reader in a definite intellectual milieu. It is therefore not a matter of indifference in our interpretation of Zen to become acquainted with the Chinese heroes of the T'ang and Sung periods who figure in these anecdotes, and to gain some knowledge of their education and their view of life, together with their customs and ancestral faith. We are thus driven to historical inquiry. (52–53)

It certainly seems fair to think of Father Dumoulin himself as "driven to historical inquiry." In the present volume (see pp. ix–xx) Dumoulin is perhaps more measured in his comments, and he has the benefit of intervening decades of scholarship on mysticism and religious experience. He writes, "But even though the Zen experience forever eludes the reach of historical investigation, history has an important role to play in the study of Zen" (xix–xx). And, only an accomplished intellectual with a profound empathy for religious experience could have put so much meaning into the line, "Human understanding is not simply a matter of the intellect" (xxi).

Nevertheless, Dumoulin battles repeatedly with Suzuki in the early chapters of his book, often countering Suzuki's vague or mistaken explanations explicitly, sometimes merely presenting his own very different style of analysis. Thus Dumoulin corrects Suzuki on the dissociation of Zen and yoga (21); works to include Suzuki's views on *prajñā* and the identity of the bodhisattva (31); strives at the beginning of his chapter, "The Mahāyāna Sūtras and Zen," to counter or correct what he feels are Suzuki's misinterpretations; and critiques the internal contradiction of Suzuki's view of the ahistoricity of Zen (63; this repeats the material from A History of Zen Buddhism, 52–53, introduced just above). Then, suddenly, Suzuki simply disappears from the pages of Dumoulin's exposition: The only substantive references that I can find in the remainder of his book pertain to the psychological process of enlightenment as it is experienced through *kōan* training (254); a textual reference (315); and a term used for "questions about things" in early Zen texts (318–19). The other references to Suzuki are inconsequential citations in the annotation (151 n. 46, 207 n. 49, 263 n. 32 and 49, 292 n. 79 and 81, 293 n. 82, 295 n. 115, 338 n. 113, 122, and 123; 339 n., 129–31 and 136; and 340 n.150).

Dumoulin's treatment of D. T. Suzuki's ideas and contributions is in stark contrast to his response to Hu Shih's ideas. In the debate between Suzuki the experientialist and Hu Shih the historian, Dumoulin attempts to make an even-handed assessment, but he saw himself as a critical historian who focused on the spiritual dimension of mankind. Although I have not encountered any clear statement of this—one suspects Dumoulin would have been too modest to make any claims in this regard—his life mission implies that tried to be better than both Suzuki and Hu, more sensitive to spiritual issues than the former and a better historian than the latter. At the very least, his mission was to perform the best possible historical analysis so as to explore the spiritual dimensions of mankind. In the process, he seems to have overlooked any potential bias that might have crept into his work from his acceptance of Hu Shih's scholarship.

One of the reasons writing this Introduction to Dumoulin's India and China volume has been both delightful and difficult for me individually is the dialogue in which he and I have engaged in print. Most conspicuously, in my recent *Seeing through Zen* (2003, 103–7 and 120) I used poor Father Dumoulin as a foil for trying to change the way scholars think about the Chinese Zen tradition. I criticized his view of the "Golden Age of the T'ang" as romantic, pointing out that the romantic appreciation for one aspect of human culture frequently carries with it a cynical disregard for something else. In this case, the romantic imagination of the great T'ang-dynasty masters—Ma-tsu, Chao-chou, Lin-chi, etc.—allowed the Zen of that period to be put up on a pedestal and idealized as a great efflorescence of human spontaneity and inspired religious behavior. All this would be well and good were it not for the inevitable under-appreciation of the riches of Sung-dynasty Zen in the writings of Dumoulin and others. I argued forcefully that we should look at the myriad developments of Sung-dynasty Zen not in terms of the degeneration of a once-creative tradition, but as the positive ramifications of a strong religious spirit that Zen teachers carried with them into that period. Also, when we consider that Dumoulin only devoted to the discussion of Sung-dynasty Zen about five percent (pp. 123–36 out of 290 pages) of his 1969 history (which treated Indian, China, and Japan in a single volume) and only about fifteen percent of his 1994 history (pp. 243–96 out of 340 pages, or almost double that if we count the volume on Japanese Zen), we are justified in questioning the fairness of his coverage.

Also, Dumoulin was by no means the only source of this bias, only "the most convenient example of a general style of interpretation" (McRae 2003, 120). After mentioning works by Arthur F. Wright, Kenneth K. S. Ch'en, Jacques Gernet, and Wm. Theodore de Bary, I pointed out that

> A number of different historiographical factors have concatenated to cre-
> ate this situation, ranging from Hu Shih's scholarship, Confucian prejudices,
> overemphasis of the novelty of "popular" or vernacular religious develop-
> ments in the post-Song period, and the misapplication of Japanese sectarian
> models to the Chinese subject matter. (120)

Here I would like to focus on only one of these issues, because it will help the reader appreciate the value and limitations of the volume now under consideration: the role of Hu Shih's scholarship in Dumoulin's exposition.

Based on an extensive examination of Hu Shih's research on Shen-hui and early Chinese Zen (McRae 2001), it is now apparent that Hu Shih only studied Shen-hui in order to show how Chinese culture threw off the yoke of Indian cultural imperialism. Hu Shih was motivated by a kind of missionary impulse, to retake Chinese culture for the Chinese, and he saw in Buddhism a foreign power not unlike the imperialist states of the nineteenth and twentieth centuries. Projecting his love for modern China onto the past and working explicitly as an instrumentalist historian (i.e., one who creates an image of a certain past in order to move his readers into a certain understanding of the present), Hu Shih fundamentally misperceived Shen-hui as a revolutionary whose teaching of sudden enlightenment functioned as the key to the elimination of Buddhism from Chinese soil. Hu Shih saw the "Chinese Rennaissance" of the Sung dynasty as the recrudescence of Chinese culture after many centuries of Buddhist domination. My point in critiquing Dumoulin was to show how, if one accepted the idealistic notion of the T'ang-dynasty greats uncritically, one would also be inclined to accept the cynical devaluation of Sung-dynasty Buddhism as degenerate and corrupt.

In fact, as argued in *Seeing through Zen*, the vitality of the Sung-dynasty "climax paradigm" of Zen Buddhism was so apparent that this dualistic notion of T'ang spontaneity and Sung decline simply cannot be sustained. My first "Rule of Zen Studies" reads "It's not true, and therefore it's more important!" precisely in response to Hu Shih's position that Zen texts were 98% false and could therefore be rejected. This is of course not to say that everything that is important in the Chinese (or Japanese) Zen tradition is also false; to assert the converse of the rule would be to do serious violence to its heuristic intent.

Using Dumoulin's writings as a foil for criticism in this way was not in any way disrespectful. Certainly, it is not much different from his own repeated criticisms of Suzuki, a figure toward whom Dumoulin felt both admiration and frustration. My feelings toward Dumoulin are much the same: respect and gratitude toward a great pioneer in our field, but frustration at what I feel are the limitations of his work. For example, I was immensely complimented when Dumoulin relied substantially on my research in writing his *Zen Buddhism in the 20th Century* (Dumoulin 1992, 81 and 160–61), and even more so when he included a "Supplement" on "The Northern School of Chinese Zen" in the 1994 republication of *Zen Buddhism: A History, India and China*, in which he drew heavily on my own work and that of Bernard Faure. Although complimented, nevertheless I cannot overlook Dumoulin's inability to comprehend the full implications of my position regarding the retrospective attribution of texts to the so-called fifth and fourth patriarchs, Hung-jen (601–674) and Tao-hsin (580–651). Where my original point was to suggest that we should not use these texts to produce a set of sequential images of Zen patriarchs, each in perfect succession like a "string of pearls," Dumoulin reduces the relevance of this interpretation to a minor question of textual authenticity (315). It is as if the historical pattern in which he works, in which his goal is to explain the spiritual life of every major Zen patriarch as fully as possible, would not allow him to recognize the full implications of the theory with which he nominally agreed.

It is also frustrating that Dumoulin knows of the proper reading of the verse attributed to Shen-hsiu in the *Platform Sūtra*, but steadfastly refused to consider its implications. In his chapter on the *Platform Sūtra*, Dumoulin quotes the verse attributed to Shen-hsiu as:

The body is the Bodhi tree,
The mind is like a clear mirror.
At all times we must strive to polish it,
And must not let the dust collect. (132)

Although many authors have made this mistake (cf. Yampolsky 1967, 130), this reading is simply incorrect: the second line clearly reads "The mind is like a bright mirror's stand." This might seem at first to make no sense, but without reading it in this fashion the second line of the reply attributed to Hui-neng makes even less sense:

Originally there is no tree of enlightenment,
Nor is there a stand with a clear mirror.
From the beginning not one thing exists;
Where, then, is a grain of dust to cling? (133)

The introductory and concluding chapters of my 1986 book on the Northern school, which Dumoulin uses extensively in his Supplement, are devoted to explaining the meaning of this reference to the mirror's stand and what the implications are for the understanding of the *Platform Sutra* and the evolution of early Zen. Dumoulin even quotes the crucial passage that provides the key to the entire puzzle, a description of votive lamps in Shen-hsiu's *Treatise on the Contemplation of Mind* (*Kanjinron* in Japanese pronunciation), but he was unable to or uninterested in considering its implications so as to reevaluate his interpretation of the *Platform Sutra* and early Zen (326).

Here, because we are both scholars dedicated to the advance of learning, I have commented on Dumoulin's failure to indicate a full appreciation of my work in his 1994 Supplement. In fact, I am told, he was fully cognizant of the broader implications involved, but recognized that he could not respond fully without completely reconceptualizing his entire project. In a sense, the gap between his exposition and the inventive insights of Bernard Faure is even wider; for example, compare the absence of any serious appreciation of Faure's seminal 1983 contribution on the hagiography of Bodhidharma in Dumoulin's Supplement with that in my Seeing through Zen (McRae 2003, 14 and 156 n.14, and 158 n.4). This sort of intellectual leap-frogging is a natural outgrowth of the scholarly process.

Based on all this, how should the reader use this book? It is certainly an excellent reference work—where else could we go to learn the dates of a Zen monk, or to verify the title of a Zen text, or to read the traditional account of an encounter between two sages. It may be many years before we have a similarly comprehensive treatment of the history of Zen Buddhism to consult in English. However, its title notwithstanding, Heinrich Dumoulin's *History of Zen Buddhism: India and China* is actually *not* a history of Zen Buddhism in India and China. It should *not* be used as a guide to the historical development of Zen Buddhism in those countries. It is *not* a reliable source for understanding Zen Buddhism in India and China.

This does not mean that Dumoulin's *History* is without uses—far from it. The reader should simply understand what sort of tool it is and for what purposes it may reasonably be put. Father Dumoulin spent decades laboring to decipher and transmit the legendary accounts of Zen Buddhism, using the best scholarship available to him. His work is a monument to the evolution of the image of Zen Buddhism within twentieth-century scholarship, principally that of Japan, as seen through the eyes of someone consciously striving to make Buddhism comprehensible to a Western Christian audience. Subsequent decades of scholarship have revealed the idealism of his interpretive eye. We have learned that the legendary accounts Dumoulin so painstakingly compiled need to be understood in terms of mythopoeic creation rather than historical narration. We have learned to see the gaps in his story, the romanticism of his perspective. We have learned at least some of the complexities of the evidence he used, and we have become aware of vast quantities of evidence that he was unable to use or in which he was not interested.

The Zen tradition makes much of the ancestors, and for Zen studies Dumoulin is one of the most important patriarchs of recent generations. If I have dismissed the value of his efforts with respect to the purpose for which they were intended, it is only through a deep sense of respect. He made it possible for us to arrive at where we are today, for which we all owe him a debt greater than Mount Sumeru, the king of mountains. We have of course not "arrived" anywhere yet in Zen studies, but Dumoulin's *History* is an appropriate tool for our self-reflection as participants in the study of Zen, and even more broadly as inheritors of the East-West cultural traditions of the twentieth century. To proceed without that self-reflection would be a variation on the "intellectual pathology" which academic students of Zen (but by definition not practititioners) may contract (see McRae 2003, 10).

It is simply that Dumoulin's *History of Zen Buddhism: India and China* can no longer be considered a piece of secondary scholarship. It is now a primary text, a source for us to examine so that we might better understand ourselves. That is, by reading this book we may be able to learn how the field of Zen studies developed over the course of the twentieth century. Rather than swatting ourselves in the head with this rather sizeable tome, we should use it as a treasure trove for the examination of our own intellectual origins.

It is with this in mind that I hold my palms together, in the gesture of respect known as *añjali-mudrā* in Sanskrit and *gasshō* in Japanese.

References Cited

Dumoulin, Heinrich, S.J.

1940   Review of Daisetz Teirarō Suzuki, *Zen Buddhism and Its Influence on Japanese Culture*. *Monumenta Nipponica* 3: 323–25.

1943   *Kamo Mabuchi. Eine Beitrag zur japanischen Religions- und Geistesgeschichte*. Tokyo: Sophia University.

1953 *The Development of Chinese Zen After the Sixth Patriarch in the Light of Mumonkan.* Translated from the German With Additional Notes and Appendices by Ruth Fuller Sasaki. New York: The First Zen Institute of America.

1959 *Zen: Geschichte und Gestalt.* Bern: Francke.

1963 *A History of Zen Buddhism.* New York: Pantheon Books, and London: Faber and Faber.

1974 *Christianity Meets Buddhism.* Translated by John C. Maraldo. LaSalle, Illinois: Open Court Publishing Company.

1992 *Zen Buddhism in the 20th Century.* Translated and adapted from the German by Joseph S. O'Leary. New York and Tokyo: Weatherhill.

1994 *Understanding Buddhism: Key Themes.* Translated and adapted from the German by Joseph S. O'Leary. New York and Tokyo: Weatherhill.

Heisig, James W.

1985 "Editor's Introduction." *Japanese Journal of Religious Studies* 12, nos. 2–3: 109–17.

Hu Shih

1953 "Ch'an (Zen) Buddhism in China: Its History and Method." *Philosophy East and West* 3, no. 1: 3–24.

McRae, John R.

1986 *The Northern School and the Formation of Early Ch'an Buddhism.* Kuroda Institute Studies in East Asian Buddhism, no. 3. Honolulu: University of Hawai'i Press.

1993–94 "Yanagida Seizan's Landmark Works on Chinese Ch'an." *Cahiers d'Extrême-Asie* 7: 51–103.

2001 "Religion as Revolution in Chinese Historiography: Hu Shih (1891–1962) on Shen-hui (684–758)." *Cahiers d'Extrême-Asie* 12: 59–102.

2003 *Seeing through Zen: Encounter, Transformation, and Genealogy in Chinese Zen Buddhism.* Berkeley: University of California Press.

Sasaki, Ruth Fuller, trans.

1975 *The Record of Lin-chi.* Kyoto: Institute for Zen Studies.

Sasaki, Ruth Fuller, Yoshitaka Iriya, and Dana R. Fraser, trans.

1971 *A Man of Zen: The Recorded Sayings of Layman P'ang.* New York: Weatherhill.

Suzuki, D[aisetz] T[eitarō]

1953 "Zen: A Reply to Hu Shih." *Philosophy East and West* 3, no. 1: 25–46.

Watanabe Manabu 渡辺学

1985 "The Works of Heinrich Dumoulin: A Select Bibliography." *Japanese Journal of Religious Studies* 12, nos. 2–3:. 263–71.

Yampolsky, Philip B.

1967 *Platform Sūtra of the Sixth Patriarch: The Text of the Tun-huang Manuscript with Translation, Introduction, and Notes.* New York: Columbia University Press.

Yanagida Seizan

1961 *Kunchū Rinzairoku.* Kyoto: Kichūdō.

1967   *Shoki Zenshū shisho no kenkyū (Studies in the Historical Works of Early Zen)*. Kyoto: Hōzōkan.

1983   "The Development of the 'Recorded Sayings' Texts of the Chinese Ch'an School." Translated by John R. McRae. In Lewis Lancaster and Whalen Lai, eds., *Early Ch'an in China and Tibet*. Berkeley Buddhist Studies, no. 5. Berkeley: Lancaster-Miller Press. Pp. 183–205.

ZEN BUDDHISM: A History

Volume 1
India and China

Part One
Beginnings and Roots in India

1

Śākyamuni,
the Enlightened One

THE FIGURE OF THE BUDDHA

Zen Buddhism traces its origins directly back to Śākyamuni, the founder of the Buddhist religion. One finds the figure of Buddha at the very core of the spiritual tradition that Zen boasts as its own. To claim, however, that the history of Zen really begins with Śākyamuni—a point that will require further explanation—does not entail any claim regarding the historicity of the person of the Buddha or the factual reality of the line of succession that leads back to him. These two claims are in no sense comparable.

Hardly anyone raises doubts any more concerning the historicity of the person of Śākyamuni.[1] Even though the Pāli Canon, which took shape centuries after the entrance of the Buddha into nirvāṇa, contains much that is historically questionable, and even though the historical core of the story of Buddha has been lavishly shrouded with legend and his figure overlaid with ancient myths, we do possess architectural and artistic testimony of great historical value dating back centuries before the common era. Moreover, very shortly after the death of the Buddha, Buddhism developed into a widespread movement, replete with an abundance of monasteries and loyal devotees. The extreme form of historical criticism that arises periodically and was particularly in vogue during the nineteenth century has reached a much more realistic balance in our times. Given the nature of our sources, pure history cannot be distilled from legend. Yet Buddhologists generally agree that there is a sound historical core to events of which we find similar accounts in both the Pāli and the Sanskrit scriptures. Hypotheses reducing the Buddha to a solar myth or a pious legend reconstructed from the deeds of a holy yogi are no longer recognized as tenable.

Zen's claim to trace its tradition back to Śākyamuni is something else again. To locate the figure of Śākyamuni at the beginning of the history of Zen in spite of the absence of any historical evidence requires that we treat the claim as part of the self-understanding of Zen. An historical presentation, however critical, must also take into account the self-understanding of the movement in question, since such self-understanding is rooted in the essence of that movement. The figure of the Buddha stands out preeminently among the defining characteristics of Zen and lives on in the thought, the devotion, and the life of Zen disciples.

It is one thing to sketch the life and actual figure of the Buddha from the reports of the Pāli Canon and other "biographical" sources; it is quite another to bring into focus the defining characteristics that mark the image of the Buddha in the various schools that make up the great diversity of the Buddhist religion. These characteristics may be of a very general nature, but they are nonetheless important for all the traditions within Buddhism. Zen Buddhism is no exception here in bringing into relief certain essentials of the image of the Buddha that are particularly important to the Zen tradition.

This kind of historical approach is possible because the Buddha enjoys a prominent position among the spiritual figures of Asia—the ascetics, the saints, and the sages. He is not an Indian hermit or a spiritual master, nor is he a mystic sage like Yājñavalkya, who helped his followers to the knowledge of a deeper eternal truth. The life and deeds of the Buddha broke through the ancient Vedic traditions of India and opened new horizons. Deeply rooted in the Indian soil from which he sprang, he did not descend from the heavenly heights like an avatar but was born of a noble family of warriors who legend tells us commanded a prosperous estate. Prince Siddhārtha chose to abandon his claim to secular authority and follow the path of religion, and it was in the realm of religion that he distinguished himself in the India of his times. After his experience of enlightenment he was honored with the title of Buddha—the Awakened One. In the mind of his followers, this title bestows a religious rank of universal significance that reaches beyond the Indian motherland.

The figure of the Buddha Śākyamuni was equally received in the cultures of India and East Asia, which, despite the common label of *Asia* devised by the West, are really distinct from one another and should not be conflated. Indeed, India and East Asia are culturally as different from each other as the Germanic-Latin cultures of Europe are different from the cultures of Asia Minor and their Semitic neighbors. The majestic power and warm welcome of the Buddha are felt not only in India and countries strongly influenced by Indian culture—Ceylon (Sri Lanka), Burma, Thailand, for a time Indonesia, and until recently Cambodia and Laos—but also in the East Asian countries of China, Korea, and Japan. The school of Zen Buddhism, which is full of the spirit of China and Japan, is bound essentially to this figure, in whom disciples find the fulfillment of enlightenment, the Exalted One who symbolizes the universality of enlightenment.

The image of the Buddha embodied in Śākyamuni underwent a far-reaching evolution in conjunction with the general development of Buddhist doctrine, practice, and speculation. We shall be examining this process in greater detail insofar as it touches on the history of Zen. At the outset, however, one should bear in mind that all these developments are in some way linked with the historical Buddha and as such inspire a religious reverence in those who profess to follow him. The figure of the Buddha is worthy of respect. Even if Buddhists are trained by their elders, monks, and meditation masters to stress the pure humanity of the historical Śākyamuni, the founder of their religion, and to consign all the other-worldly and supernatural elements of his story to the realm of myth and legend, this does not alter the fact that the highest reverence is given the figure of the Buddha. Although he was human and nothing more, the Buddha remains for his followers a supreme figure. Even students of Zen who have attained a high degree of enlightenment continue to revere Śākyamuni deeply in the belief that his enlightenment far surpasses the experience of all others. The Buddha is worthy of respect, pure and simple. This attitude, common to Buddhism as a whole, has exercised a decided and deep influence on Zen Buddhism as well.

Here Zen Buddhists stand in community with all Buddhists. Given the multiformity of the Buddhist religion, the question naturally arises as to the common bonds that unite the tradition. It is one of the essential functions of the figure of the Buddha to form such a bond; this is particularly important to remember in evaluating Zen Buddhism. Since the advent of the Zen movement in the West it has not been unusual to find scholars of religion distinguishing between "Buddhism" and "Zen Buddhism." This all too readily gives the misleading impression that we can align the two side by side like separate religions— an error equivalent to offering an account of Protestantism and Catholicism without any mention of their common basis in the person of Christ. If we take *Buddhism* as the general term for a particular religious tradition, then Zen is a school within that tradition. Concerning the question of the bonds between this school and its mother religion, we must give attention first of all, though not exclusively, to the image of the Buddha—more specifically, to the image of Śākyamuni, the historical Buddha. It is here that Zen finds its very center, its heart. Not only from textual evidence, of which there is certainly no lack, but also from the statements of authentic Zen masters, and above all from sympathetic acquaintance with Zen disciples, it is clear what the image of the Buddha means for Zen Buddhists.

THE GREAT EXPERIENCE

The strict relationship between Zen Buddhism and the image of Śākyamuni is evident. For Zen Buddhists, the most important element in the wealth of legends about the Buddha is his enlightenment. Among the four great events in the Buddha's life, there is a mutual correspondence between his birth and first sermon on the one hand, and his enlightenment and entrance into nirvāna on the other. But the experience of enlightenment stands clearly at the center. Śākyamuni enters into history as the Enlightened One. As the Buddhist scriptures report, through this overpowering experience he came to understand himself as the holy and supreme Buddha. Throughout Buddhism the powerful confession of faith of his disciple Śāriputra resounds like "the roar of a lion":

> Lord! such faith have I in the Exalted One, that methinks there never has been, nor will there be, nor is there now any other, whether wanderer or brahmin, who is greater and wiser than the Exalted One, that is to say, as regards the higher wisdom.[2]

The report of the Buddha's enlightenment presented in the Pāli Canon cannot lay any claim to historical credibility.[3] Still, the facticity of this experience remains beyond doubt. The Pāli reports do not actually correspond to the Zen view of the Buddha's enlightenment as a sudden, ecstatic breakthrough, like a powerful torrent breaking through a rocky embankment. According to the Pāli tradition, inspired by Yoga, Śākyamuni's great experience unfolded in the course of three watches of the night. Zen literature pays little attention to the details of this report. There is evidence enough in the story of Śākyamuni's life that it was a transforming experience. In any case, Zen Buddhists see in his experience the prototype of the "Great Enlightenment." With what took place there, the Buddha's entrance into nirvāna had in a certain sense already taken place.

That Zen Buddhists show a pious respect for the entire life of the Buddha, with all its legendary elements, is only natural. Zen disciples recognize in the meditative experience of Prince Siddhārtha under the rose-apple tree, an experience that demonstrates the contemplative gifts of the young man, an often overlooked presentiment of the great experience to come. They are deeply moved by the stories of how the Buddha abandoned the home of his parents, leaving behind palace, wife, and child. For Zen, as for all Buddhism, this departure from home into homelessness is an essential condition for following the spiritual path. The futility of all the yogic mortifications to which the ascetic Gautama submitted himself confirms the Zen view that it is impossible to force enlightenment—a conviction, however, that does not exclude either the highly disciplined life of a Zen monastery or the thundering and thrashing met in the Rinzai school of Zen. The various events of the Buddha's life awaken in Zen Buddhists an awe not unlike what we read in the richly anecdotal biographies of Zen masters, and testify to the multitude of paths leading to authentic spiritual awakening.

Individual elements in the story of the Buddha cannot distract the disciple of Zen from the central event of the Buddha's life, his enlightenment. The figure of the lean and frustrated ascetic who, strengthened by a dish of rice given him by a pious woman, sets himself down under the pippala tree (Ficus religiosa) in Uruvelā on the bank of the river Nerañjarā, determined not to move from the lotus position until he tastes of the Great Enlightenment, a figure sitting in unmovable determination who then, like the sea stirred by the sweep of a mighty wave, is caught up in an experience and sinks into unmoved quiet—this is the authentic image of the Buddha. What Śākyamuni experienced at that moment, according to the firm conviction of all Zen Buddhists, was nothing other than the "enlightenment of all the Buddhas and patriarchs," to whom the Zen masters bear witness and of whom Zen literature speaks with the highest reverence.[4] Zen understands itself to be part of the tradition that is rooted in this great experience.

Every experience of enlightenment is ineffable, beyond the grasp of words and concepts. This fundamental fact applies as well to the "Great Experience" of the Buddha. At the same time, we must bear in mind that every experience carries with it its own interpretation, which means that a supreme experience implies an interpretation that embodies a universal view of the world. According to common Buddhist views, the content of the Buddha's enlightenment is preserved in his first sermon at Benares. Delivered on the authority of one who had been enlightened, this sermon embraces the Buddha's religious vision of the world and of life, a vision that was in part new and in part a revision of traditional views in a new and clearer light. The form this sermon takes in the Pāli Canon was determined—to what extent, it cannot be said with certainty—by the transmitters and editors of the Buddha's message. The original words of the Buddha remain unknown; it is enough that the sermon at Benares contains the core of what the newly enlightened Buddha saw.

According to the Zen Buddhist view, the enlightened vision of the Buddha contains the truths that are decisive for every disciple of Zen. In his preaching, the Buddha presented his enlightenment as an experience of existence itself. The Enlightened One saw things as they really are, that is, in their existential reality. Above all, he was moved by suffering (in the broad sense of the term): suffering is rooted in coming to be and passing away, in becoming, or, according to the scholastic term, in "dependent co-origination" (Pāli, paṭicca-samuppāda; Skt., pratītya-samutpāda). This teaching affirms the transitoriness of all the things of the world, an element that is particularly important for Zen Buddhism. Meditating on the enlightened Buddha, disciples of Zen can strengthen their conviction of transitoriness. In this world of becoming (saṃsāra), all things, just as they are, are in an existential state of impermanence. Step by step, aspirants on the path of Zen come to this realization and so share in the Buddha's momentous experience of universal suffering and transitoriness.

Also to be taken into account as part of the content of the Buddha's experience is the saving path of liberation, which the section of the sermon at Benares dealing with the "Truth of the Way" calls the Eightfold Path. There is a fundamental unity between the way of Zen and this original Buddhist path of salvation, which enlightens all living beings caught in the darkness of an existence filled with suffering and offers them the promise of liberation. All things, just as they are, are now transfused with light. If the Zen Buddhist view of the world is by and large an optimistic one, it is because of the glow of hope that emanates from the "Great Experience" of the Buddha and guarantees a happy outcome to those who walk the difficult path of Zen.

THE TRANSMISSION OF ENLIGHTENMENT

Amidst the abundant Zen literature of the Sung period (960–1279) in China we find five chronicles that set forth the meaning of Śākyamuni's experience of enlightenment for Zen Buddhism. The so-called Five Records of the Lamp (Jpn., Gotōroku; Chin., Wu-teng lu)[5] make clear how important it is for Zen that the tradition of the enlightenment be maintained. The "lamp" that is passed from generation to generation is the enlightenment experience, or in broader terms, the mind of Śākyamuni. The five chronicles aim to trace the precise line of transmission from Śākyamuni to their own times. Even though they are only partially helpful as an historical source for the Zen movement in China, they are of the greatest help in clarifying the self-understanding of Zen. Eventually, every later development or offshoot of a religion attempts to demonstrate its ties to its origins. Both orthodoxy and authority are at stake in such efforts, but the Zen school is concerned with more than establishing its institutional legitimacy. It does not wish to be an institution but to lay claim to a spiritual tradition. In the Zen Buddhist view, what is being passed on in Zen is the very essence of Buddhist truth itself. For such a transmission, one may object, names and genealogies are hardly necessary. Every truly enlightened Zen master would agree. Still, Zen does belong to history, and the five chronicles from the Sung period, for all their historical inadequacies, point to one of the essential traits of the way of Zen.

The five chronicles were compiled during the relatively short period of two hundred years. The first of them, known as *The Ching-te Record of the Transmission of the Lamp,* is foundational. Compiled by the Zen monk Tao-yüan of the line of Hōgen, it was presented to Emperor Chen-tsung of the Northern Sung dynasty in the year 1004 and published under imperial patronage in 1011. The chronicle narrates how the enlightened mind of Śākyamuni has been passed on through the centuries right up to the present, first from Śākyamuni himself to his disciple Kāśyapa, or Mahākāśyapa ("the great Kāśyapa"). Śākyamuni is last in a line of seven Buddhas; with Kāśyapa the line of twenty-eight Indian Zen patriarchs begins, ending with Bodhidharma, the first of the Chinese Zen patriarchs. Thus the disciple Kāśyapa, of whom we hear so much in the Pāli Canon,[6] is the first official transmitter of the mind of Śākyamuni. According to tradition, he had married at a young age but then abandoned the world without ever having consummated his marriage. The first time he met the Buddha he threw himself at his feet and was received into the community of disciples and ordained a monk. As a sign of special favor, the Buddha exchanged robes with Kāśyapa. In the Buddhist scriptures Kāśyapa is referred to as the "first of the strict observers of the rule"; he took a leading role in the order.

The second of the Chinese chronicles of the Sung period, *The T'ien-sheng Record of the Widely Extending Lamp,* is the work of an industrious lay disciple of the Rinzai school. Without naming the previous Buddhas, this chronicle begins with Śākyamuni and narrates the memorable event to which the Zen school ascribes its origins. According to this account, once, during his sermon on Vulture Peak, the Exalted One held up a golden lotus blossom to all those assembled. Only Kāśyapa understood, and smiled. According to book 2 of the chronicle, which is probably the earliest version of this well known episode, "the World Honored One thereupon turned to the assembly and said, 'I possess the True Dharma Eye, the Marvelous Mind of Nirvāṇa. I entrust it to Mahākāśyapa.' "

The third chronicle, entitled *The Chien-chung Ching-kuo Supplementary Record of the Lamp,* was completed in 1101 (and published in 1103) by a learned monk of the Ummon school named Fo-kuo Wei-po. The title of book 1, "The True School," reveals the intent of the work: to preserve the unbroken transmission of genuine enlightenment. The line of transmission is traced from Śākyamuni through the twenty-eight Indian and six Chinese patriarchs until around the end of the T'ang period (618–906). The individual narrations are kept short; the episode of the transmission of the mind to Kāśyapa is not portrayed in detail.

What the third chronicle lacks, the fourth supplies. As its title indicates, it presents *A Collection of Essential Material from the Zen Sect's Successive Records of the Lamp.* This chronicle is the work of Hui-weng Wu-ming, a monk in the yogic line of the Rinzai school, and gathers together all available information on the seven Buddhas, then continues with the Indian and Chinese patriarchs and culminates with figures who are contemporaries of the redactor, who completed his task in 1183. Here we find the words Śākyamuni addressed to Kāśyapa in the final elaborated form that was henceforth to be passed on in the Zen schools. In book 1 of the chronicle, we read:

> The World-Honored One spoke: "I possess the True Dharma Eye, the Marvelous Mind of Nirvāṇa, the True Form of the Formless, the Subtle Dharma Gate that does not rest on words or letters but is a special transmission outside of the scriptures. This I entrust to Mahākāśyapa."

The last of the five chronicles, *The Chia-t'ai Comprehensive Record of the Lamp,* was compiled by Lei-an Cheng-shou, a monk of the Ummon school, and completed in 1204. It is an exhaustive account (including short biographies of lay Zen friends, episodes in the lives of Zen devotees, poetry, and prose) focusing primarily on Zen during the Sung period. This record was also counted among the so-called Five Chronicles, all of which narrate the "transmission of the lamp"—Śākyamuni's experience of enlightenment.

The foundational story of Śākyamuni's spiritual transmission to the smiling disciple Kāśyapa has been the common heritage of the Zen movement at least since the time of its normative formulation in the fourth chronicle. The episode owes its place in the life of Zen not least to the form it took as a kōan (apparently based on the version of the fourth chronicle) in one of the most popular and widely used kōan collections, the *Mumonkan.*[7] In his critical commentary, Master Wu-men salts the narrative with a grain of wit:

> Rather strange. What if everyone in the great assembly had smiled— how would the true Dharma Eye have been passed on [in one line of succession]? And if Kāśyapa had not smiled, how would the Dharma Eye have been passed on [at all]? When someone says that the true Dharma Eye can be passed on, it is like the old man with the gold-colored face playing tricks at the village gate. But if someone says that it cannot be passed on, how could it then have been entrusted only to Kāśyapa?[8]

According to tradition, Ānanda, the Buddha's beloved disciple and the second in the line of twenty-eight Zen patriarchs, was able to reach enlightenment only after the death of the Buddha. The transmission of enlightenment to Ānanda also becomes a kōan in the *Mumonkan* collection.[9] The robe that Śākyamuni gave to Kāśyapa with the transmission of his mind also figures in this kōan. Legend has it that Kāśyapa was to take care of the robe and pass it on to the next Buddha, Maitreya. For this reason, Kāśyapa's body was not cremated after his entry into nirvāṇa, as was the custom, but is to be found, dressed in the Buddha's robe, within Mount Kukkuṭapāda, where he awaits the coming of Maitreya.[10]

According to a Sanskrit chronicle, before the "Master of the Dharma" Kāśyapa entered nirvāṇa he passed the Dharma on to Ānanda, indicating that the latter was to choose as his successor Śāṇavāsa,[11] who is listed as third in the line of twenty-eight Indian Zen patriarchs. Some of the following names (Upagupta, Dhītika, Vasumitra) are also found in the early Buddhist lists of Dharma masters.[12] The names of the fourteenth and fifteenth Indian Zen patriarchs, Nāgārjuna and his disciple Kāṇadeva (also called Āryadeva), are also worthy of note for the important position they hold in the spiritual tradition of Zen Buddhism.

The list of twenty-eight Indian Zen patriarchs can certainly make no claim to historical credibility. And yet this unbroken line of spiritual transmission represents an essential element in the self-understanding of Zen. Through the transmission of the experience of enlightenment Śākyamuni remains somehow present in Zen Buddhism.

THE ZEN BUDDHIST VIEW OF ŚĀKYAMUNI

Śākyamuni's experience of enlightenment, passed on from generation to generation, came to occupy a prominent position in Zen Buddhism. Originating some one thousand years after the death of the World Honored One, Zen too inherited accounts of the Buddha's life interwoven with Yoga and blurred by extravagant legends. The yogic elements were particularly strong in those aspects of the story having to do with meditation and with his miraculous powers. According to legend, the Bodhisattva entered his mother's body in "deep awareness" and there rested in the posture of yogic meditation, that is, in the lotus position. His mother, Māyā, herself in a higher state of consciousness, was awestruck. His meditation under the rose-apple tree has already been mentioned. The Buddha's miraculous powers earned him recognition as "the greatest of all yogis."[13] Legends tell of his ability to pass through physical bodies and to read thoughts. He had the spiritual power to cure sickness. His entry into nirvāṇa is depicted as a yogic meditational experience. Yogic elements appear in all of Buddhism, albeit in a variety of different forms. In Zen Buddhism, they may be traced, at least in part, to Śākyamuni's Indian roots, as we shall see in the next chapter.

All forms of Buddhist theory show lines of filiation with Śākyamuni. If there is an original doctrine of Buddhism, variously interpreted by numerous different schools, it is to be found in basic elements common to all its branches. The Chinese Zen patriarchs, however, discovered many departures from the genuine spirit of Śākyamuni in the doctrinal developments that arose in the centuries following the death of the Buddha. But even though they fixed their attention on the "Great Experience" of the Enlightened One, it was through the mediation of the Mahāyāna systems that the essential elements of Śākyamuni's vision became part and parcel of Zen Buddhist thought.

During the flowering of classical Chinese Zen, the figure of Śākyamuni and his experience of enlightenment were not infrequently entangled in paradoxical contradictions, as the various kōan and the collections of sayings of the Chinese Zen masters amply testify. Śākyamuni does not in any way appear in these texts as the great founding figure on whom religious devotion is centered. The dictum from the *Rinzairoku* is well known: "If you meet the Buddha, kill him!"[14] In one of the kōan of the *Mumonkan*, Master Wu-men comments: "For one who has truly grasped Chao-chou's answer, there is no Śākyamuni in the past and in the future no Maitreya."[15] Elsewhere Wu-men states ironically: "The good old Śākya has given us a village comedy."[16] These Zen sources recognize in Śākyamuni a transcending not only of his human person but also of his enlightened Buddhahood. There is something that overreaches the Buddha, as we read in the kōan:

> Master Fa-yen from the East Mountain spoke: "Śākyamuni and Maitreya are but his servants. Now tell me, who is *he?*"

Perhaps the question should read: "*What* is it?" But the commentators use the personal pronoun *he* to explain the Chinese character that literally means "the other," even though they stress that this *he* transcends all duality. Here we have to do with the metaphysical background of Zen Buddhism—that is, the necessity of overcoming all duality. Insofar as any image of the Buddha stands in the way of this, the Buddha must be killed. To speak in this manner of Śākyamuni in no way contradicts what has been said in the earlier sections of this chapter. For Zen, it is the ineffability of the experience that has the last word.

NOTES

1. Śākyamuni, literally the sage *(muni)* from the Śākya tribe, means the Buddha, the Enlightened One; as a young prince living in the home of his parents he was called Siddhārtha; Gotama (Pāli) or Gautama (Sanskrit) is his family name; he is also referred to as Gotama, the ascetic. Tradition is unanimous in attributing to him a lifespan of 80 years. The year of his death is uncertain. His dates are customarily given as 560–480 or 563–483 BCE. Japanese scholars have offered grounds for a later dating. Regarding the dates of the Buddha, see E. Lamotte, *Histoire du bouddhisme indien* (Louvain, 1967), pp. 13ff. M. Winternitz reports in his *Geschichte der indischen Literatur* (Leipzig, 1907–1922) on the controversy related to the year of the Buddha's death (vol. 2, part 2, pp. 2, 357ff). H. Bechert shows an impressive command of the material in his treatment of the problem, arriving at the conclusion: "There is much to be said for the claim that the chronology of Buddhism was first reconstructed . . . during the time of Aśoka or later, and that the death of Buddha . . . is to be set in the first half of the fourth century." See his article "Buddhism," in *Theologische Realenzyklopädie* (Berlin, 1977–) vol. 7, pp. 320–21. See also H. Bechert, "The Date of the Buddha Reconsidered," *Indologica Taiwanensia* 10 (1982): 29–36.

2. *Mahāparinibbāna Suttanta*, 1:16; see *Dialogues of the Buddha*, part II, trans. by T. W. and C. A. F. Rhys Davids (London, 1977), p. 87.

3. H. Oldenberg is of the opinion that "the analysis of the historical critic is unable to return a clear and bold verdict, a decisive Yes or No." *Buddha: His Life, His Doctrine, His Order* (Delhi, 1971), p.108. See also E. J. Thomas's remarks on the historical uncertainty of the Pāli Canon in *The Life of the Buddha as Legend and History* (London, 1927), p. xxiv.

4. The term "enlightenment of all the Buddhas and patriarchs" appears frequently in the work of Dōgen, a Zen master noted for his ties to tradition, and is still to be heard in Zen halls today.

5. These five records are, respectively, the *Keitoku dentōroku* (Chin., *Ching-te ch'uan-teng lu*, CE 1004), T. 2076, vol. 51; the *Tenshō kōtōroku* (Chin., *T'ien-sheng kuang-teng lu*, CE 1036), Z.2B. VIII:4-5. *Kenchū seikoku zokutōroku* (Chin., *Chien-chung ching-kuo hsü-teng lu*, 1101), Z.2B. IX:1-2, *Shūmon rentō eyō* (Chin., *Tsung-men lien-teng hui-yao*, 1182), Z.2B. IX:3-5, *Katai futōroku* (Chin., *Chia-t'ai p'u-teng lu*, 1204), Z.2B. X:1-2. These chronicles lay out the line of tradition; the *Keitoku dentōroku* and *Rentō eyō* begin with the seven Buddhas before Śākyamuni; the *Katai futōroku* begins only with Bodhidharma. On the five chronicles, see also *Zen Dust*, pp. 348–52, 412–13.

6. Basing himself on the original sources, Lamotte gives an extensive account of Kāśyapa (or Mahākāśyapa), who played a leading role in the monastic order. It is said of him that he was "the first of those who observed the strict rule." *Histoire du bouddhisme indien*, p. 19; see also pp. 24, 71, 101, 137. On the successors of the Buddha see pp. 226ff, and the diagrammatic line of succession on p.773.

7. Case 6. The episode is apparently first referred to in the *Tenshō kōtōroku* chronicle. See *Zen Dust*, pp. 151–52.

8. Chinese graphs from the terms *True Dharma Eye* and *Marvelous Mind of Nirvāṇa* form the names of two Japanese Zen temples: Shōgen-ji, erected in Ibuka to the memory of the famous master Kanzan (1277–1360), and the Rinzai temple of Myōshinji in Kyoto. See *Zen Dust*, p. 326.

9. Case 22.

10. See Lamotte, *Histoire du bouddhisme indien*, pp. 227, 230.

11. Lamotte, *Histoire*, pp. 226–27.

12. Lamotte, *Histoire*, p. 773; see also pp. 149–50, 190–92, 203–04, 207, 226–32.

13. The expression is found in a Sanskrit text preserved in Tibetan. It is cited in H. Beckh, *Buddha und seine Lehre* (Stuttgart, 1958), p. 120.

14. *Rinzai eshō goroku* (Chin., *Lin-chi hui-chao yü-lu*), in one book (T. 1985, vol. 47) apparently compiled by the disciple Hui-jan; there is some doubt as to the compiler and the original date of publication. See *Zen Dust*, pp. 346–47.

15. Case 37.

16. Case 42.

17. Case 45. The idea of transcending Śākyamuni is also present in cases 37, 42, and 43 of the *Mumonkan* collection. See the explanation given in my translation of the work: *Mumonkan: Die Schranke ohne Tor* (Mainz, 1975), pp. 133–34, 148ff, 154, 157–58.

2

The Yogic Element in Buddhism

ESSENTIAL CHARACTERISTICS OF YOGA

It is no accident that most studies of Yoga, even the most thorough, do not begin with a definition of Yoga. To capture the essence of a religious phenomenon that is so diverse, so extensive, and so profoundly rich is well-nigh impossible. There is good reason to focus on Patañjali's classical treatment of Yoga. Modern scholars generally trace his main textual source, the *Yoga Sūtra*, back to the second century CE.[1] The origins of Yoga itself stretch back much further, as far as prehistoric times. Excavations of Mohenjo-daro and Harappa (2500–2000 BCE), begun only in this century, have turned up clear indications of the practice of Yoga in these pre-Aryan cities.[2] References to Yoga appear in some of the Upanishads. Subsequent Indian religious beliefs and philosophical systems are permeated by the influence of Yoga. The process by which Yoga has penetrated the most varied and sometimes contradictory forms of intellectual and spiritual life continues into our own times. Westerners are attracted to the integral Yoga of the contemporary thinker and mystic Aurobindo as well as by forms of Christian Yoga. Even today, anyone who has grown up on Indian soil or immigrated to this complex and rich culture comes under the influence of Yoga.

The melding of Yoga with Buddhism—a process that continued through the centuries—represents a landmark on the path of Yoga through the history of India. This phenomenon merits special attention since yogic roots are to be found in the Zen Buddhist school of meditation. Before treating this point in detail, however, it may be helpful to review certain essential elements of Yoga that are important both for Buddhism in general and for Zen in particular.

The Sanskrit root word *yuj*, which means to "place in a yoke," "harness," "bind together," "unite," or "tame," provides a useful starting point for explaining Yoga. The Indians used this word to indicate the many different ways of practicing concentration, meditation, and asceticism, convinced as they were of the need for persistent, methodical efforts in order to reach final liberation through the control of the self and of cosmic powers.

Like the ancient techniques of shamanism, the beginnings of Yoga are shrouded in the darkness of the past. But unlike shamanic techniques, which aim at magical powers and ecstatic states, Yoga uses meditation and structured spiritual exercises in order to free oneself from the conditions of earthly existence. And while primitive shamanic elements have found their way into Yoga in a variety of forms, they have never been essential to the concerns of Yoga. The miraculous powers of the shaman, which yogis are often eager to display, are seen only as side effects. In his classical work on Yoga, Eliade lists four characteristic accomplishments of shamanism, all of which go beyond the laws of nature and all of which he finds present in Yoga.[3] Yet this very fact leads him all the more resolutely to stress "the difference between the Yoga method of meditation and the technique that results in 'shamanic' ecstasy."[4] Shamanic magic is not a constitutive element of Yoga, nor of Buddhism, where one also comes across magico-shamanic phenomena.[5] Just how Zen Buddhism distances itself from the world of magic will be explained later.

Yoga is based on the conviction of a fundamental unity between human beings and the cosmos according to which the individual person is a microcosm, a physical-spiritual whole tied up with the universe and its powers. The interaction between body and spirit conditions the complicated techniques of Yoga and is evident in the basic practices of bodily postures (āsana), rhythmic breathing, (prāṇāyāma), and concentration (dhāraṇā). Any portrayal of Yoga that emphasizes either its physical or spiritual practices one-sidedly misses an essential trait of Yoga—the unity of body and spirit. Only if one gives oneself over to Yoga exercises with all one's bodily and spiritual powers can one attain the goal of Yoga; only then can one achieve control of self and cosmos and here on earth become a jīvanmukta, one freed in this life.

The prominence accorded meditation in the spiritual exercises of Yoga is all the more remarkable in that it was apparently peculiar to Indian spirituality, whence it spread far and wide throughout Asia. While other cultures richly developed their spiritual potential through theoretical speculation and philosophical thought, the Indians preferred the concrete practice of concentration and meditation. Rather than search for knowledge of the world around them, they sought to penetrate the depths of the psyche. On this point the Greeks and Indians parted paths at the earliest stages. In the Indian Vedas, the Indo-Aryan spiritual heritage was "Asianized."[6] According to Eliade, this was due mainly to the influences of the original, pre-Aryan peoples of India. "The absence of the Yoga complex from other Indo-European groups"[7] is a clear indication of the uniqueness of Indian Yoga. The exploration of the way within represents one of the principal defining traits of Yoga.

Another characteristic of Yoga important for understanding Buddhism, and particularly Zen, is its concern with ultimate salvation. The precise definition of this goal requires a thorough study of the whole complex of problems associated with the Yoga tradition. Part of this complex has to do with the relation of Yoga to Buddhism. Thus I shall elaborate a comparison between the final goals of Yoga and Buddhism in the context of the Buddhist notions of nirvāṇa and enlightenment. As a way of salvation, Yoga possesses at its core a religious relevance, albeit one that disappears in many of its peripheral forms. The final goal is attained through a liberating experience, a peculiarity that the Yoga path of salvation shares with Buddhism.

THE PRACTICE OF MEDITATION IN INDIAN BUDDHISM[8]

If it is true that the "first flowering" of Yoga took place during the time of the Buddha,[9] the presence of yogic elements in legends of the Buddha found in the Pāli Canon and in Buddhist history become more believable. Scholars of Buddhism have made the claim that "Yoga is an essential ingredient in the original teaching" of Buddhism,[10] and even refer to Buddhism as "a branch of Yoga."[11] Some have even argued for the exaggerated view that "the whole of Buddhism, through and through, is nothing but Yoga."[12] This claim is true for the concentration techniques in early Buddhism, for nearly all of them show traces of early Yoga traditions and parallels thereto.[13]

In any case, the original form of Buddhism lies in darkness, particularly in regard to what elements it may have taken over from Yoga. Critical research into the sources behind the Pāli Canon and the early Sanskrit texts have yielded no entirely reliable conclusions concerning the teachings and religious practice of precanonical Buddhism. One stands on fairly firm ground in regarding the Four Noble Truths and the Eightfold Path as the heart of primitive Buddhist doctrine. Already in the earliest period, the Four Noble Truths were an object of meditational practice and experience.[14] Buddhist practice clearly differed from Yoga in rejecting all violent physical exertion and asceticism out of fidelity to the "Middle Way" inherited from the Buddha himself.

The sūtras of the Pāli Canon offer abundant descriptive accounts of levels and states of meditation. Despite the many repetitions and partial overlays that make this material so very complex and difficult to summarize, Buddhist scholars have studied and organized it to the point of being able to identify parallels with Yoga.[15] Heiler has painted a coherent general picture for us by placing the four stages of *dhyāna* at the center and then relating all other phenomena to it. But efforts to construct a systematic picture of all the various meditational practices of early Buddhism—for example, the collection of thirty-seven steps that, according to the *Mahāparinibbāna Sutta*, the Buddha is supposed to have presented to his followers as the culmination of his path to enlightenment—do not lead to satisfactory results. In what follows, I shall mention only the most important structural elements and schemata that are related to Yoga.

The Eightfold Path, which forms for the practitioner the practical cornerstone of the Buddha's first sermon, presents the leitmotif of Buddhist life. Its significance extends far beyond the practice of contemplation; Yoga elements in the Eightfold Path are undeniable. The Eightfold Path is open to a variety of interpretations: one can take the first seven steps as preparatory to the final goal of contemplation (*samādhi*), or one might see in the eight steps a well-rounded path to salvation in which each step has its own part to play in the attainment of salvation.[16]

According to a comprehensive formulation in the Pāli Canon, the way of salvation leads from the observance of the rules of morality (*sīla*) to contemplative concentration (*samādhi*), where a salvific knowledge (*paññā*) is achieved that is

bound inseparably with liberation (vimutti).[17] This fourfold formula, which occurs
in many texts and is repeated eight times in the Mahāparinibbāna Sutta, constitutes
a blueprint of the doctrine of salvation in early Buddhism. Contemplative concentration is merely the means and yet occupies the central position. Moral
discipline is directed towards contemplation, which is accompanied by wondrous
powers (iddhi),[18] and the knowledge gained in concentration culminates in liberation. In addition to the well known Five Commandments[19] and numerous
other prescriptions, the moral code of the monastic order requires the celibate
lifestyle of brahmacaryā.[20] Preconditions for attaining concentration are the bri-
dling of the senses, vigilance of the spirit, and constant self-control—all of
which are typical of Yoga.

There are close ties to morality in a method, recommended in the Pāli
Canon, known as the meditation on the four "Immeasurables" (appamaññā),
also referred to as the four "Brahma Abodes" (brahmavihāra) or four "Practices"
(bhāvanā). In this exercise, the monk is said to extend the powers that fill his
heart—benevolence (mettā), compassion (karuṇā), co-rejoicing (muditā), and
equanimity (upekkhā)—

> over one heavenly region, and then over the second, the third, and fourth
> regions, upward and downward, crossways and sideways, completely in every
> direction—pouring out upon the whole world the powers of benevolence
> (of compassion, co-rejoicing, and equanimity) that fill his heart. . . .[21]

This meditational practice is also recommended in the Yoga Sūtra and is most
likely the common legacy of ancient Indian spirituality. It is held in high regard
in Buddhism as an eminent expression of the spirituality of early Buddhism.[22]

Yoga meditation begins with the body. As Heiler notes, "Contemplative
concentration is a purely spiritual activity; the seated posture of the body is only
of auxiliary significance."[23] Yet Buddhism admits of no meditation or state of
higher spiritual consciousness apart from the cross-legged posture (āsana). The
posture of an erect body with legs folded under has been known in India from
time immemorial. The search for its origins takes us to the dim dawn of history,
as is shown by a figure excavated in Mohenjo-daro that most likely depicts a
Yogi.[24] Both the Upanishads and the early Buddhist sūtras tell of ascetics and
disciples of the Buddha seated in meditation in cool groves under shady trees,
there experiencing unity with Brahmā or recognizing the sorrow and vanity of
all earthly things and acquiring a foretaste of the repose of nirvāṇa.

Like regulation of the posture, rhythmic breathing belongs to the ancient
Indian Yoga heritage. Whereas many Yoga practices seek to suppress the awareness of breathing as the last vital function, the "select and joyous" control of
the breath praised in the Buddhist sūtras makes respiration conscious:

> The monk breathes in and out consciously. When he takes a long breath,
> he recognizes, "I am taking a long breath"; and when he exhales slowly,
> he recognizes, "I am exhaling slowly." When he takes a short breath, he

recognizes, "I am taking a short breath"; and when he exhales quickly, he recognizes, "I am exhaling quickly."[25]

Buddhists reject the forced inhibition of breathing practiced in Yoga. At the fourth stage of *dhyāna* breathing becomes imperceptible by itself.

The four contemplative concentrations (Pāli, *jhāna;* Skt., *dhyāna*) and the four infinite states (*arūpa*), which in many instances in the Pāli Canon are joined successively to a ninth stage of the destruction of consciousness and sensation (*nirodha*), form the core of meditational practice in Indian Buddhism.[26] After the conquest of the five hindrances (*nīvaraṇa*) of desire, hatred, sloth, fear, and doubt the ascent through the four stages of concentration begins. In the first stage, that of inner composure and cessation of desire, objects are still represented and a feeling of delight pervades the practitioner. In the second stage release from the outer world is achieved and the consideration of objects disappears, but joy permeates the body. In the third stage this feeling of joy gives way to equanimity, and spiritual concentration is perfected. The fourth and highest of the stages of *dhyāna* is a state of equanimity (*upekkhā*) in which the world has vanished and with it all joy and suffering. In meditation on the infinities the practitioner passes successively through the states of the infinity of space, the infinity of consciousness, nothingness, and the realm beyond consciousness and unconsciousness. The subsequent "destruction of consciousness and sensation" signifies not the final liberation of nirvāṇa but an ecstatic condition.

The four stages of contemplative concentration take priority among the ways of meditation. According to tradition, the Buddha entered from the fourth stage of *dhyāna* into nirvāṇa. This stage opens the door to all the higher spiritual powers that, in Yoga fashion, play an important role in Indian Buddhism. The miraculous powers (*iddhi*) acquired in meditation include extraordinary states of consciousness and such unusual physical abilities as levitation, invisibility, bilocation, the ability to pass through material barriers, or to touch the sun and the moon, clairaudience, and so on.[27] The three cognitions, or knowings (*tevijjā*), that make up knowledge (*paññā*), the third element of the fourfold formula, share this miraculous quality. Those who have achieved knowledge from the fourth stage of *dhyāna* are able to recall their previous existences, to understand the destiny of all beings in the cycle of rebirths, and to know the nature of suffering and how to overcome it. This supreme knowing, which comprises the understanding of all higher levels of Buddhist teaching, gives birth to the condition of sainthood (*arahant;* Skt., *arhat*).

In this connection, mention must be made of two guidelines for meditative concentration that are also reflected in Zen. While the objects considered (*kammaṭṭhāna*)[28] are more directives to psychic technique than to spiritual reflection, they dispose the practitioner seriously for contact with the fundamental truths of the transitoriness of life (*anicca*), the insubstantiality of individual existence (*anattā*), and universal suffering (*dukkha*), dispositions that are prerequisites for success in all Buddhist meditation. Zen has no such detailed considerations, although the Zen novice is taken through exercises that, like the recommendation in the sūtra to fix one's attention on the impurities and ugliness of the body, unmask beauty and bring about an experience of human frailty. The Zen masters speak a great deal about death and renunciation to their disciples so that in grasping these basic truths they may more easily attain enlightenment. The Zen monastery is as much pervaded by an awareness of transitoriness as are the meeting places of the bhikkhu.

The practice of total fixation of the mind known as kasiṇa also leads to the state of concentration. In this exercise an extraordinary degree of concentration is achieved by focusing attention on a physical object. The monks gaze intently at a circle or disk of clay or earth, or at a vessel of water, or at fire, or a treetop swaying in the wind (kasiṇa of the four basic elements: earth, water, fire, and wind), or they focus on a spot of color, space, or light. They gaze until the "sign" of the object has been impressed so deeply on their consciousness that they can see its after-image with their eyes closed as clearly as they had seen it with their eyes open. In Tantric Buddhist meditation the maṇḍala, which may have developed from the kasiṇa, serves a similar function.[29] Zen, too, makes use of symbolic representations of spiritual realities, which are appropriated through concentration that passes through the senses. Among the masters of the Igyō school of Chinese Zen we encounter the practice of "circular figures," which is related to the practice of kasiṇa. Symbolic representations of metaphysical truths also occur frequently in Zen. These images often serve not only as illustrations of abstract truth but also as a means of practicing concentration.

In the two meditational practices just referred to the concern for spiritual centering is evident. This concern, which is so important both in Buddhism and in Yoga, is characterized in early Buddhism by the Pāli word sati (Skt., smṛti), which means "remembrance" but which in the context of meditation takes the sense of "attentiveness," "heed," "awareness," or "keeping in consciousness." Attention to breathing and corporeal processes is crucial. In the stereotypical formula for the fourth stage of dhyāna, sati signifies the "deep consciousness" that has been purified in equanimity. "Attention to the body" (kāyagatā sati) is recommended especially to resist Māra—that is, to pacify unruly influences from the realm of the senses. The relation of such attentiveness to spiritual concentration is illuminating.[30] It enables us to conclude that there is a broad relatedness between the early Buddhist practice of sati and the way Zen seeks to achieve spiritual concentration through the practice of the kōan.

This overview of the practices of contemplative concentration in Indian Buddhism shows the extent to which the influence of Yoga pervades meditational techniques in early Buddhism. Given the uncertainty surrounding historical connections, it is difficult to prove particular cases of direct dependency. The Yoga Sūtra, which is often used as the most reliable textual basis for a comparison between Yoga and the contemplative practices of early Buddhism, is dated several centuries after the beginning of Buddhism. At the time of Śākyamuni and the development of the Buddhist monastic community, Yoga techniques were already widely known and used in the religious life of India. The close ties between Yoga and early Buddhism are generally recognized by Buddhist scholars today. The brief review of these ties presented above should help us better to understand the distinguishing traits of Zen. In the same way, a look at how nirvāṇa relates to the Yoga experience can also help us get a broader perspective on the relationship between enlightenment and salvation in Zen Buddhism.

NIRVĀṆA: THE FINAL GOAL OF THE BUDDHIST WAY[31]

The influence of Yoga is also evident in the early Buddhist notion of nirvāṇa. Etymologically, nirvāṇa has a negative meaning. Derived from the Sanskrit verb *va* (to blow, like the wind) with the negative prefix *nir*, it denotes a motionless rest where no wind blows, where the fire is quenched, the light has been extinguished, the stars have gone out, and the saint has died.[32]

> The subjugation of desire, the subjugation of hatred, the subjugation of perplexity; this, O friend, is called nirvāṇa.[33]

> Dissolved is the body, extinct is perception; the sensations have all vanished away. The conformations have found their repose: the consciousness has sunk to its rest.[34]

The saint vanishes into nirvāṇa, according to the Buddha's famous simile, like an oil lamp sinking in upon itself and expiring when its fuel has been consumed. Such language and images evoke the concepts of emptiness and nothingness.[35]

At the same time, Buddhists have always viewed nirvāṇa as their final goal and prized it as consummate blessedness, supreme happiness, a haven of peace, and an isle of deliverance.[36] Just as the final goal of Yoga—called *kaivalya* in the *Yoga Sūtra*—liberates the yogi from all bonds, ineffable nirvāṇa, cut off from the realms of coming to be and passing away, assures the Buddhist of escape from transitoriness; it is characterized by a snuffing out of all desire for the sensual world (*kāma-taṇhā*), for existence in this changing world (*bhava-taṇhā*), and for self-extinction (*vibhava-taṇhā*). Like the final state of Yoga, nirvāṇa can be reached only by the path of meditation. Early Buddhist doctrine speaks of two kinds of nirvāṇa—a nirvāṇa "in the this-worldly order" (*ditthe dhamme*) and a nirvāṇa without remainder or substrate (*upādhi*), parinirvāṇa (*parinibbāna*). Actually, there is no essential difference between the two. In each case, total liberation is attained: "It is peacefulness, exaltation, . . . the annihilation of all sensual desire, nirvāṇa." Negatively, it is called "extinction"; positively, it is "the realm of the immortal" (*amatā dhātu*).

The final liberation, attained in both Yoga and Buddhism through meditation, is interpreted differently in the systematic thought of the two traditions. Yoga carries with it a rich variety of different religious and philosophical worldviews and thus attributes a variety of meanings to its final state of liberation. The explanation of the final goal presented in the *Yoga Sūtra* is also distinct from that of Buddhist nirvāṇa. The term *kaivalya*, usually translated as "absolute isolation"[37] or "isolation,"[38] or again as "bareness,"[39] or "for-itself existence,"[40] signifies in the Sāṃkhya philosophy, on which the *Yoga Sūtra* rests, the separation of *puruṣa*[41] (spirit, human person, self) from *prakṛti* (nature), as the result of inward-turning efforts at meditation. Yet in spite of its clear dependence on Sāṃkhya, the Yoga system of Patañjali cannot be identified with it.[42]

The canonical scriptures of Buddhism offer little help in clarifying the final goal, nirvāna. It is reported that the Buddha was often asked whether the Perfect One exists or does not exist after death. As was his wont with "metaphysical" questions, the Buddha declined to answer, apparently because the solution to such questions was of no value for the one thing necessary, the attainment of salvation. He has therefore been accused of philosophical agnosticism.[43] It is also possible that the Buddha refused to pronounce on life after death because of the inadequacy of our conceptual language to speak of such matters, because human words cannot make valid statements about what lies beyond—the other shore, the realm of immortality.

To seek to resolve the paradox of the Buddhist doctrine of nirvāna logically is to land oneself either in nihilistic or substantialistic explanations, both of which were explicitly rejected by the Buddha. Śākyamuni renounced as heresy the materialistic-nihilistic ideology (*ucchedavāda*), which does not recognize any liberation, as well as the metaphysical doctrine of substance (*sassatavāda*), which argues for the existence of permanent, indestructible bodies. Was his final word a "Middle Way," as Mahāyāna philosophy was later to teach? We really do not know how Śākyamuni understood nirvāna. Nor do the historical sources at our disposal allow us to unearth the teachings of original Buddhism. According to the explanations of early Buddhist philosophy, which inclines towards skepticism and pessimism, nirvāna connotes primarily, if not exclusively, deliverance from the cycle of the world of becoming and thus escape from this existence subject to the law of karma.

Still, throughout the Pāli Canon mention is made of a higher, ultimate reality lying beyond the reach of all conceptual thought and yet accessible in meditative rapture. For example, we read:

> There is, O disciples, an unborn, an unoriginated, uncreated, unformed. Were there not, O disciples, this unborn, unoriginated, uncreated, unformed, there would be no possible exit from the world of the born, originated, created, formed.[44]

> The great ocean is deep, immeasurable, unfathomable. So also . . . if the existence of the Perfect One be measured by the predicates of corporeal form: he is deep, immeasurable, unfathomable as the great ocean.[45]

Negations here signify complete transcendence of human thought and speech. In the following verses, we can hear the same mystical tones:

> He who has gone to rest, no measure can fathom him.
> There is no word to speak of him.
> What thought could grasp has blown away.
> And every path to speech is barred.[46]

If the word *mysticism* in its broadest sense includes every insight into, knowledge of, or contact with transcendent reality, even the most indirect and incomplete, then we may certainly say that the Buddhist way of salvation, as well as the ancient Indian tradition of the Vedas and the Upanishads, is permeated with mystical qualities. In this sense mysticism is found in almost all the religions of human history, and especially in the spirituality of India, with its strong Yoga influence. From early on Buddhism cultivated the same judicious control of the senses and all cravings that the "Middle Way" between pleasure and austerity urged of its followers, and promoted the resolute struggle for spiritual recollection that is the foundation for further advance. The lack of a corresponding metaphysic is only redressed through the mystically inspired philosophy of Mahāyāna.

THE ROOTS OF ZEN IN YOGA

D. T. Suzuki deserves our gratitude for having stressed the uniqueness of the way of Zen for his Western audience.[47] This he did particularly by disassociating it sharply from Yoga. He felt it necessary to do so because of the way Westerners, even Orientalists and specialists in the history of religions, tend to throw all Asiatic forms of meditation, including Yoga and Zen, into the same pot. But when Suzuki presses the distinction to the point of denying any relationship between these two Far Eastern traditions, some corrective is called for.

The very fact that Zen belongs to Buddhism means that it is related to Yoga, the influence of which pervades the whole of Buddhism. If in the foregoing I have stressed the early Buddhism of India, it was not that I intended to overlook the continued presence of the yogic element in later Mahāyāna Buddhism. Strictly speaking, the origins of the Zen school in Mahāyāna are enough to show its proximity to Yoga.

In addition to these rather abstract arguments, the concrete picture of Zen, with its many congruities with Yoga, makes a strong case for the affinity of these two ways of meditation. Since a clear picture of Zen can only emerge when we explore its development and delve more deeply into its special character, a few brief comments will have to suffice for the time being.

The characteristics of Yoga mentioned in the opening section of this chapter—the consciousness of a cosmic unity, the body-soul totality of the human person, the primacy of meditation, and the experience of liberation—no doubt represent its essential traits and can be found one and all in Zen Buddhism. In Zen they take a particular shape, but as with Yoga we remain in the context of Far Eastern spirituality. For Westerners, this commonality is particularly evident in externals, but this external commonality rightly points to an inner congruency as well. The Zen disciple seated in the lotus position, like the Buddha himself under the pippala tree, resembles a yogin. Like the yogins, practitioners of Zen strive to control their breathing and focus their concentration on one point, not of course in the same way in all the branches of Zen. To be sure, external parallels do not entail full, essential equivalence. Yoga and Zen differ on important points, not only in terms of final goal but also in methods adopted to reach that goal. This should become clearer in later chapters as we take a closer look at the specific form that Zen came to assume.

One final remark regarding the goal of the two traditions, the experience of liberation, is in order. The different interpretations that Yoga and Zen give to this ultimate experience have already been noted. What remains important, however, is that both traditions hold up an *experience* as their final goal. On the basis of the experience attained by their ascent, Eastern spiritualities like to make claims of universal relevance. If we take these claims seriously, not only Yoga and Zen but all genuine experiences that touch the core of the human would be fundamentally identical, differing from each other according to the standpoint they adopt. No doubt, profound experiences touch people at the innermost core of their being. That the East has been prominent in fostering the meditative way of experience—to which the West, alas, has not always paid proper esteem—is also beyond doubt. But in the final analysis, such profound experiences take place in both hemispheres and indeed all over the world. It is crucial that they be interpreted and evaluated correctly. For all their common characteristics, these experiences are articulated variously according to race and culture, time and place. Historical study of the phenomena needs to pay close attention to the causes and circumstances that brought them about, to the particular characteristics and effects they gave rise to. When scholars of Zen examine the Yoga tradition, they find affinities with Zen that to be sure derive from a common human nature and experience, but both traditions—and the experiences they embrace—also demand detailed historical study. The universality of human experience is always relative, and as such allows for ever more comprehensive and ever deeper historical knowledge.

NOTES

1. Although nothing definite is known about Patañjali, the alleged author of the *Yoga Sūtra*, his identification with the second-century BCE grammarian of the same name is no longer regarded as tenable. Scholars now date the former figure sometime between the second and fourth centuries of the common era, a time when Mahāyāna Buddhism was already in full bloom. See J. W. Hauer, *Der Yoga: Ein indischer Weg zum Selbst* (Stuttgart, 1958), pp.228 and 223ff; see also his chapter treating the origins of Yoga in the time of the Vedas, pp.19–95. Mircea Eliade regards "the ascetic practices and contemplative formulas" that Patañjali gathered and classified as something "India had known from time immemorial." *Yoga: Immortality and Freedom* (Princeton, 1973), p.7.

2. On the excavations, culture, and religion in Harappa and Mohenjo-daro, see Eliade, *Yoga*, pp.353–58.

3. These are (1) initiation with symbolic dismemberment, death, and resurrection; (2) mystical journeys as healer and psychopomp; (3) the mastery of fire; and (4) the ability to take on animal forms and make oneself invisible. Eliade, *Yoga*, p.320.

4. Eliade, *Yoga*, p.327.

5. Magical yogic powers are also ascribed to the Buddha, among them the shamanic

"rope trick," the "mango trick," in which a seed placed into the ground suddenly grows into a tree, and the production of "inner heat." Eliade, *Yoga*, pp.321–22, 330ff.

6. Eliade, *Yoga*, p.360.

7. Eliade, *Yoga*, p.360.

8. F. Heiler's *Die buddhistische Versenkung: Eine religionsgeschichtliche Untersuchung* (Munich, 1918) has become more and more important with the passage of time. See also Eliade, *Yoga*, pp. 162–99; J. W. Hauer, *Der Yoga*, pp. 165–81; D. Schlingloff, *Die Religion des Buddhismus* (Berlin, 1962–63), vols. 1 and 2; and other literature cited in subsequent notes to this chapter. All terms included in parentheses are Pāli, unless stated otherwise.

9. Hauer, *Der Yoga*, p. 13; cf. p. 227.

10. As proof of this, E. J. Thomas evinces the fact that superhuman abilities known in Yoga as *vibhūti* are mentioned in the ancient Buddhist formula for confession (*pātimokkha*). See *The History of Buddhist Thought* (London, 1933), p. 17.

11. L. de la Vallée-Poussin, *Nirvāṇa* (Paris, 1925), p. 11.

12. H. Beckh, *Buddha und seine Lehre*, p. 138. J. Wunderli calls Buddhist contemplative concentration "a birth of Yoga" in *Schritte nach innen* (Freiburg, 1975), p. 123.

13. Detailed evidence is presented in Heiler, *Die buddhistische Versenkung*, pp. 44–47. Hauer argues that "the two ways, Yoga and Buddhism . . . [are] . . . different elaborations of one and the same movement" (*Der Yoga*, p. 39). Heiler speaks of the "religious psychotechnique" of Yoga (*Die buddhistische Versenkung*, p. 44). Similarly, L. de la Vallée-Poussin plays down "predominantly psychic and hypnotic Yoga" (*Nirvāṇa*, p. 12). On Buddhism and Yoga, see also A. B. Keith, *Buddhist Philosophy in India and Ceylon* (Oxford, 1923), pp. 143ff.

14. Thomas, *The History of Buddhist Thought*, pp. 42–43; see also pp. 42–57.

15. Of the sources already mentioned, see particularly the works of Heiler, Beckh, Schlingloff, Thomas, and Keith. The *Visuddhimagga* of Buddhaghosa (fifth century CE) offers the most comprehensive presentation of the way of meditation. See Nyanamoli's translation from the Pāli, *The Path of Purification* (2d ed., Colombo, 1964).

16. See Beckh's presentation of the Noble Eightfold Path (*Buddha und seine Lehre*, pp. 144–47). He is of the view that "the first seven steps of the 'Eightfold Path' are only an aid (*parikkhārā*) and prelude to the eighth stage of spiritual contemplation or meditation (*samādhi*)" (p. 145). In contrast, according to the Japanese Buddhologist Ui Hakuju, the Eightfold Path presents a purely ascetic regulation of the course of life, without regard to an experience that transcends the senses. See his *Indo tetsugakushi [History of Indian Philosophy]* (Tokyo, 1935), pp. 99ff.

17. Heiler, *Die buddhistische Versenkung*, p. 5. Beckh sees in the fourfold formula the method of arrangement of the *Dīgha Nikāya* wherein "the entire Buddhist norm is contained in nuce" (*Buddha und seine Lehre*, pp. 45ff).

18. On the connection of *iddhi*, which belongs among the "higher spiritual powers," to meditation, see Eliade, *Yoga*, pp. 177ff, and the relevant sections in Heiler (*Die buddhistische Versenkung*, pp. 31–35) and Beckh (*Buddha und seine Lehre*, pp. 187–92).

19. To the injunctions against killing, theft, unchastity, and deceit is added the prohibition of alcoholic beverages. Originally, this prohibition applied to Buddhist lay men (*upāsaka*) and lay women (*upāsikā*) as well.

20. *Brahmacaryā* is also recommended in the Upanishads and in the *Yoga Sūtra* as helpful

to meditation. On the meaning of the term see Thomas, *The History of Buddhist Thought*, p. 44. Zen masters down to our own times have been aware of the significance of sexual moderation for meditation, though not with the clarity of motivation of which Eliade writes: "Yoga attaches the greatest importance to these 'secret forces of the generative faculty,' which, when they are expended, dissipate the most precious energy, debilitate mental capacity, and make concentration difficult" (*Yoga*, p. 50).

21. As Heiler has noted, the Four Immeasurables, frequently mentioned with other meditation practices (contemplation and states of infinity) as constituting a preliminary stage, should rather be seen as an "autonomous scale of contemplation, parallel to and on a par with the others" (*Die buddhistische Versenkung*, p. 81); they also appear in Yoga. Beckh sees the Immeasurables as the state of mind corresponding to the first injunction against killing, and stresses the proof of compassion (*Buddha und seine Lehre*, pp. 153–54).

22. Schlingloff sees the Immeasurables as the meditative foundations of the Buddhist way of life and closes his work with an account of their development (*Die Religion des Buddhismus*, pp. 92–99). Heiler also draws attention to their particular importance. The Four Immeasurables, he tells us, must become "the innermost possession of the meditator" and "a translucidation, a transformation and fulfillment of one's being at its deepest recesses" (*Die buddhistische Versenkung*, p. 347). Lamotte, however, sees them as no more than a "hors d'oeuvre" to the Buddhist way of salvation (*Histoire du bouddhisme indien*, p. 48). W. L. King, in his *Buddhism and Christianity: Some Bridges of Understanding* (London, 1963, pp. 175ff), and H. de Lubac, in his *Aspects du bouddhisme* (Paris, 1951), evaluate and esteem this Buddhist meditation practice in comparison with the Christian love of neighbor. On this theme, see also my *Begegnung mit dem Buddhismus: Eine Einführung* (Freiburg, 1978), pp. 82–85, 108.

23. Heiler, *Die buddhistische Versenkung*, p. 9.

24. Eliade, *Yoga*, p. 430.

25. Cited in Heiler, *Die buddhistische Versenkung*, p. 9. Controlled breathing (*prāṇāyāma*) is cultivated widely in Yoga, but is also of great importance in Buddhism. According to the Pāli Canon, the practitioner is supposed to "direct attention to each and every breath." See Beckh, *Buddha und seine Lehre*, pp. 164–65. On the meaning of the correlation of breath and posture in Yoga, see Eliade, *Yoga*, pp. 53–59. Eliade sees in the practice a "refusal," whereby the practitioner transcends or oversteps the ordinary, profane, human state of mind.

26. The presentation of the states of contemplation and states of infinity constitutes the core of Heiler's *Die buddhistische Versenkung* (see pp. 9–28). See also the chapter on the hindrances in the first book of the Abhidhamma Piṭaka, the *Dhammasaṅgani*, translated by C. A. F. Rhys Davids as *A Buddhist Manual of Psychological Ethics* (London, 1974), pp. 287–92.

27. The miraculous magical powers (Skt., *siddhi*) play a predominant role in Yoga. On the significance of magical powers in Yoga, see Eliade, *Yoga*, pp. 85–94; regarding the parallels between Buddhism and Yoga, see Hauer, *Der Yoga*, p. 170. See also note 18 to this chapter.

28. The objects considered are described in the *Satipatthāna Sutta*; a list of forty such *kammaṭṭhāna* can be found in the *Visuddhimagga*. See Heiler, *Die buddhistische Versenkung*, pp. 13ff.

29. See H. von Glasenapp, *Buddhistische Mysterien* (Stuttgart, 1940), pp. 107–108.

30. The basic text in the Pāli Canon is the *Satipatthāna Sutta,* available in English trans-lation in *Dialogues of the Buddha [Digha Nikāya],* vol. 2, translated by T. W. and C. A. F. Rhys Davids, Sacred Books of the Buddhists, vol. 3 (1910, reprint, London, 1977). See also the two essays on the text by L. Schmithausen in ZMR 57 (1973): 161–86; 60 (1976): 241–66. *Sati* meditation is still practiced zealously in Theravāda Buddhism. An offshoot is to be seen in the modern Burmese method of meditation. See the "Exkurs über die neue burmesische Meditationsmethode im Vergleich mit dem Zen-Weg" in my *Östliche Meditation und christliche Mystik* (Freiburg and Munich, 1966), pp. 209–16.

31. The literature available in Western languages on nirvāna is immense. A great deal of information and interesting connections are presented in G. R. Welbon's study, *The Buddhist Nirvāna and its Western Interpreters* (Chicago, 1968).

32. On the history and etymology of the term, see Thomas, *The History of Buddhist Thought,* pp. 121–22; de la Vallée-Poussin, *Nirvāna,* p. 54. Welbon (see above, note 31) investigates all the relationships of the word.

33. From the *Samyutta Nikāya,* cited in II. Oldenberg, *Buddha: His Life, His Doctrine, His Order,* p. 264. See also the *Anguttara Nikāya* 3:55, 4:34.

34. From the *Udāna* VIII,9, cited in Oldenberg, *Buddha,* p. 266.

35. The nihilistic interpretation of nirvāna, which was for a time dominant in the West, has only a few remaining proponents today. Nakamura Hajime vigorously stresses the positive character of nirvāna: "Contrary to the prevalent Western opinion about nirvāna, the craving for extinction in the sense of annihilation or nonexistence (*vibhava-tanhā*) was indeed expressly repudiated by the Buddha. . . . It is only by way of expression that nirvāna is negation." See his essay, "The Basic Teachings of Buddhism," in H. Dumoulin, ed., *Buddhism in the Modern World* (New York, 1976), p. 18.

36. Nakamura (ibid., pp. 19–22) has assembled from the Pāli Canon a long string of symbolic expressions that illustrate the blissful happiness of the "ideal state." At the conclusion of his nuanced treatment of nirvāna, Oldenberg (*Buddha,* p. 285) cites the following passage: "He who is permeated by goodness, the monk who adheres to Buddha's teaching, let him turn to the land of peace, where transientness finds an end, to happiness" (*Suttanipāta* 1093, *Dhammapada,* 23, 203, 225, 368).

37. Eliade, *Yoga,* p. 93; see also p. 16.

38. Beckh, *Buddha une seine Lehre,* p. 143.

39. Hauer, *Der Yoga,* p. 108; see also p. 338.

40. Wunderli, *Schritte nach innen,* p. 140.

41. ". . . *purusa* is inexpressible." See Eliade, *Yoga,* p. 16.

42. Hauer locates the cause for the distinction "in the contrast of the profound and immediate experience of Yoga to the speculation of Sāmkhya" (*Der Yoga,* p. 284).

43. See Nakamura's passage on the Buddha's silence regarding metaphysical questions, in "Die Grundlehren des Buddhismus. Ihre Wurzeln in Geschichte und Tradition," in H. Dumoulin, ed., *Buddhismus der Gegenwart* (Freiburg, 1970), p. 10. E. Conze stresses the pragmatic character of Buddhism as a way of salvation in his *Buddhism: Its Essence and Development* (New York, 1975), pp. 15ff; see also pp. 38ff. On how this relates to transcendence, see my *Begegnung mit dem Buddhismus,* pp. 56ff.

44. *Udāna* VIII, 3.

45. *Samyutta Nikāya* IV, pp. 374ff.

46. *Suttanipāta,* p. 1074ff. The oft-cited sayings of the Buddha mentioned in the text

(above, notes 44 and 45) appear in Oldenberg's treatment of the "question as to the ultimate goal" (*Buddha*, pp. 277–85). These well-balanced pages continue to make good reading, and his conclusion rings ever more true: "The faith of ancient Buddhism begs to be treated for what it is and understood in its own terms."

47. In *An Introduction to Zen Buddhism* he notes: "Zen is not the same as *dhyāna*" (p. 32); "Zen is not a system of *dhyāna*" (p. 96); "*dhyāna*, as it is understood by Zen, does not correspond to the practice as carried on in Zen" (p. 40).

3
The Essentials
of Mahāyāna

THE BEGINNINGS OF MAHĀYĀNA

Zen originated in China as a meditation school of Mahāyāna Buddhism, and like so many other Chinese schools of Buddhism, was shaped by the teachings of Mahāyāna. As its name, the "Great Vehicle," indicates, Mahāyāna is characterized by its opposition to the other schools of Buddhism, which came to be known by the rather condescending name given them by the Mahāyānists: the Hīnayāna, or "Small Vehicle." This term, no longer accepted by modern scholars, was applied summarily to the complicated and historically murky formation of sects within early Buddhism.[1] Among the many schools of early Buddhism, two stand out clearly. The Sarvāstivāda, who for a millennium or more carried on vigorously in Northwest India, beyond Gandhāra to Afghanistan in the west and to Kashmir in the east, developed a significant body of literature but has been extinct now for several centuries. The other dominant line, the Theravāda, is centered in Sri Lanka and is found today in most of the countries of Southeast Asia. Claiming the Pāli Canon as its own, Theravāda doctrine is characterized chiefly in the "third basket" of the Buddhist scriptures, the Abhidhamma. The high point of doctrinal development within Theravāda is marked in Buddhaghosa's *Visuddhimagga*, "the greatest and most famous doctrinal book in Pāli," dating from the fifth century CE.[2]

For a long time, Western Buddhist scholarship considered Mahāyāna a later development of Buddhism. Although the Pāli Canon most likely contains the oldest extant Buddhist writings, the beginnings of Mahāyāna doctrine stretch back even farther into Buddhist history, possibly to the time of the formation of the first sects. The enthusiasm of Western scholars for what they considered to be the purely rational and ethically advanced spirituality of the Pāli Canon often led them to look on Mahāyāna as a deviation from, or even a degeneration of, these pure beginnings. It seemed to represent a total break with the past. The Russian scholar Theodore Stcherbatsky depicts the appearance of Mahāyāna in terms of almost dramatic fervor:

> When we see an atheistic, soul-denying philosophic teaching of a path to personal Final Deliverance, consisting in an absolute extinction of life, and a simple worship of the memory of its human founder—when we see it superseded by a magnificent High Church with a Supreme God, surrounded by a numerous pantheon and a host of Saints, a religion highly devotional, highly ceremonious and clerical, with an ideal of Universal Salvation of

all living creatures, a salvation by the divine grace of Buddhas and the Bodhisattvas, a Salvation not in annihilation, but in eternal life—we are fully justified in maintaining that the history of religions has scarcely witnessed such a break between new and old within the pale of what nevertheless continues to claim common descent from the same religious founder.[3]

Such statements express the attitude with which Western scholars were wont to approach Mahāyāna. So clouded by prejudice was such a view that it prevented them from detecting the common life-stream that flows through apparently different forms.

There is no evidence anywhere in the history of Buddhism of a shaking of the foundations that could have brought about a radical upheaval of the sort envisioned by Stcherbatsky. We know of no outstanding personality before the common era who might have founded Mahāyāna. The attempts—largely in vain—during the early councils to bring about a mitigation, and above all a relaxation, of the strict monastic rule can be seen as efforts in the direction of the Mahāyāna reform.[4] During this period there are also signs of early attempts at doctrinal development. Traces of Mahāyāna teachings appear already in the oldest Buddhist scriptures. Contemporary scholarship is inclined to view the transition to Mahāyāna as a gradual process hardly noticed by people at the time.[5] Much of what is new in the Mahāyāna movement was not presented as wholly original thought. It is possible that intellectual and religious influences reached India from the Occident during the period from Alexander to Augustus. And it is clear that Mahāyāna developed in organic connection with the whole of Buddhism, that is, that it originated directly from the early schools of Buddhism as a result of internal division. We know from the sources that the followers of both vehicles lived peacefully for a long time side by side in the same monasteries, observing the same Vinaya discipline. The first Mahāyāna scriptures clearly acknowledged as such date back probably to the first century BCE.[6]

The gradual growth of Mahāyāna thought brought about a pervasive change that affected almost all the basic Buddhist concepts. Nirvāṇa was linked with the vision of the cosmic Buddha and, as the goal of salvation, became equated with the attainment of Buddhahood. Buddha, nirvāṇa, and enlightenment came to express the absolute side of reality, whose manifestation is the world of saṃsāra flowing through the manifold of becoming, in which sentient beings go astray in the search for salvation. The ethical doctrine of the pāramitās ("perfections") was made subservient to the higher wisdom embodied in the bodhisattva. Yet Mahāyāna proper was born only with the proclamation of the "Great Vehicle" in conscious opposition to the inferior "Lesser Vehicle." Significantly, this took place in sūtras claiming the religious authority of the Buddha himself. The power behind the movement stemmed not from philosophical speculation but from the inspiration of spiritual personalities. The sūtras, as the expression of this new religious consciousness, became the movement's directing force.[7]

The Zen school lives in the spiritual world of Mahāyāna. Even though it is contemplative and devoted to the monastic life, it has none of the narrowness of the early Buddhist monastic rule. Religiously, Zen takes its inspiration from the basic ideals of Mahāyāna, despite the fact that as a sign of its final transcendence of everything empirical it sometimes ridicules or even burns the Mahāyāna sūtras. Such apparent frivolity does not alter the fact that Mahāyāna belongs to the inner core of Zen. Let us now turn to some of the essential characteristics that can help clarify Zen's spiritual locus.

THE BODHISATTVA IDEAL

As the religious way of salvation for all sentient beings, Buddhism holds the appropriate vehicle (yāna) to carry them from this sorrowful earthly existence to the yonder shore.[8] The first possibility of salvation is provided by the vehicle of the "hearers" (śrāvaka). Hearers who comprehend the Buddha's teaching and faithfully follow it acquire salvation for themselves through contemplation (samādhi) and become saints (arhats). All the disciples of early Buddhism followed Śākyamuni on this path and entered nirvāṇa. Mention is occasionally made in the Pāli Canon of self-enlightened Buddhas (pratyekabuddhas) who attained perfect Buddhahood through their own power. The third vehicle, that of the bodhisattva, is deemed superior to the other two by Mahāyāna devotees. It alone is called "great" (mahā) and assures all sentient beings of perfect salvation. On the highest authority, the Mahāyāna sūtras reveal the perfection of the bodhisattva vehicle.

Mahāyāna doctrine developed religiously and philosophically around the bodhisattva ideal. The term bodhisattva signifies a "being fixed on (sakta) enlightenment," or simply a "being (sattva) of enlightenment."[9] Although perfectly enlightened and in possession of the omniscience of a Buddha, the bodhisattva forgoes final entrance into nirvāṇa in order to aid sentient beings on their path to enlightenment. Indeed, all sentient beings participate in the Buddha nature and are thus able to achieve perfect enlightenment. The idea of the bodhisattva is thus related to the other basic teaching of Mahāyāna, namely that of the Buddha nature within all living things.

Were the bodhisattva nothing but the image of the perfect follower of the Buddha, the way to enlightenment as a bodhisattva, the "bodhisattva career" (bodhisattvacaryā), could be said to correspond to the Christian way of perfection. But the bodhisattva plays a more far-reaching role in Mahāyāna Buddhism. Because bodhisattvas aid sentient beings on the way to salvation they enjoy a cultic veneration second only to that accorded the Buddha himself. Carried off into the realm of the miraculous, their phenomenal contours often give way to the cosmic.

Total dedication to the law of the Buddha is a condition for becoming a bodhisattva. The bodhisattva career begins with the awakening of the resolve for enlightenment (bodhicitta-utpāda) and the taking of the vow (praṇidhāna) to ascend tirelessly through the perfections of all the stages until supreme enlightenment is attained, in order then to assist all sentient beings in their quest for salvation. The ten stages of the bodhisattva's career are described in various

Mahāyāna scriptures.[10] According to the description provided in the *Daśabhūmika Sūtra*, the level of arhat, at which the four *dhyānas* have been mastered, is reached in the first six stages. From the seventh stage on, it is the bodhisattva who carries on (*dūraṃgamā*). The peculiarity of the bodhisattva career in Mahāyāna is evident in the practice of the ten perfect virtues (*pāramitā*).[11] Originally, only six were mentioned, the first five of which—giving (*dāna*), morality (*śīla*), patience (*kṣānti*), energy (*vīrya*), and meditation (*dhyāna*)—were directed toward the sixth—wisdom (*prajñā*)—as the goal and fruit of all spiritual striving in Mahāyāna. Later, four other perfect virtues were added and the goal became excellence of knowledge (*jñāna*), which connoted intellectual cognition in contrast to the more intuitive, enlightened insight of prajñā.[12] Through the practice of these perfections, the bodhisattva in the seventh stage has entered the sea of omniscience. From there he ascends, through contemplation of the emptiness and unbornness of all things, to the tenth stage, that of the "Dharma clouds" (*dharmameghā*), where he achieves "all forms of contemplation." Seated on a vast lotus flower, he possesses the composure known as "the knowledge of the Omniscient One." The sūtra describes the magnificent scene of his consecration (*abhiṣeka*), where he becomes manifest as a fully enlightened Buddha. At this point, however, he does not enter nirvāṇa, but out of great compassion descends by skillful means (*upāya*) from the Tuṣita heaven back to earth to save all sentient beings.

The concept of the bodhisattva is many-sided and comprehensive. In Theravāda Buddhism the term is applied in a more limited way only to the final stage before attaining perfectly enlightened Buddhahood; it is applied particularly to Śākyamuni during his previous existences and during the time of the ascetic practices that preceded his attainment of the great enlightenment. In contrast, according to the fully formed doctrine of Mahāyāna, the bodhisattva is possessed of perfected enlightenment (*prajñāpāramitā*, literally, "wisdom that has gone beyond").[13] The detailed teaching on the bodhisattva that developed in the Prajñāpāramitā sūtras is already contained in the basic text known as the *Aṣṭasāhasrikā-prajñāpāramitā Sūtra*, which consists of 8,000 *ślokas* (thirty-two-syllable lines) and whose oldest portions date back to 100 BCE.[14] Without perfect enlightenment, as this sūtra states, all virtues and achievements are worthless:

> Even if a bodhisattva, after he has raised his mind to full enlightenment, would, for countless aeons, give gifts, guard his morality, perfect his patience, exert his vigor, and enter the trances, . . . if he is not upheld by perfect wisdom and lacks in skill in means, he is bound to fall on the level of Disciple (*śrāvaka*) or Pratyekabuddha.[15]

The "perfection of wisdom" (*prajñāpāramitā*) cannot be attained without total emptiness of spirit. Unenlightened persons hear talk of "emptiness" and try to express their understanding of it in signs, but the bodhisattva is one who has "gained the path of emptiness" and "coursed in the signless."[16] The perfection of wisdom is beyond all concepts and words. But above all, the bodhisattvas, who "find rest in one thought" (*eka-citta-prasādam*), are freed from all bondage to the ego. Their spirit is hampered neither by the concept of Dharma nor by its non-concept. Bodhisattvas do not grasp at ideas, they cling to nothing; their perfected knowledge is empty. This is the essence of supreme wisdom: "The bodhisattva should stand in perfect wisdom through standing in emptiness."[17]

Although bodhisattvas see through the emptiness of all things, they do not renounce the world, but rather renounce entry into nirvāṇa in order to work for the salvation of all sentient beings. They keep close to the "boundary line of reality" (bhūta-koṭi), without either taking so much as a single step into nirvāna or continuing to cling to the unenlightened restlessness of saṃsāra. Aware of the nothingness of all things and the ultimate irrelevance of every spiritual effort, they nevertheless work ceaselessly for the benefit of all that lives. "This logic of contradiction," D. T. Suzuki says, "is what may be called the dialectics of prajñā."

It is not by chance that Suzuki dedicates the greater part of the third volume of his Essays in Zen Buddhism to a field marked off by the notions of prajñā and the bodhisattva.[18] There he finds the sources of Zen Buddhist enlightenment. For Suzuki, the psychology of the bodhisattva is one of the greatest mysteries in the life of the spirit. He describes its "in-between" attitude in similes and paradoxes reminiscent of Zen literature. The bodhisattva "holds a spade in his hands and yet the tilling of the ground is done by him empty-handed. He is riding on the back of a horse, and yet there is no rider in the saddle and no horse under it. He passes over a bridge, and it is not the water that flows, but the bridge."[19] The bond between enlightened insight (prajñā) and compassion (karuṇā) allows the bodhisattva to strive continually for ever greater insight while at the same time working for the welfare of all sentient beings. Suzuki uses paradox to explain his understanding of this way of life: "It is like a master of archery shooting one arrow after the other into the air: he can keep all the arrows in the air because each one supports the one that went before. He does this for as long as he wishes."[20] In such a description of the bodhisattva way the proximity of prajñā to Zen enlightenment is unmistakable.

The ideal of the bodhisattva stems from the Indian spirit, for which images, desires, wishes, and vows are as much realities as are humans and their deeds. This form—between Buddha and human, neither male nor female—is the product of creative fantasy. With their enlightened insight the bodhisattvas embody the Great Compassion (mahākaruṇā). The attraction this image had for the common people proved enormous. In Mahāyāna Buddhism bodhisattvas became the highly revered divinities of salvation for all errant humankind. Their compassion and miraculous power soon came to be esteemed more highly than the enlightened wisdom that was the source of their salvific acts.

Over the centuries, the concept of the bodhisattva was broadened. In addition to the heavenly enlightened beings, great historical personalities like Nā-gārjuna and Asaṅga were designated and honored as bodhisattvas. In the end all holy, enlightened individuals, lay or monk, were referred to as bodhisattvas because of their great knowledge and compassion. Yet the distinction between these three types of bodhisattvas has remained in religious consciousness. In cultic devotion heavenly enlightened beings and historical personalities do not stand on the same level.

The bodhisattva ideal has wrought a persistent influence on the whole of Buddhism, particularly in Zen, where it has borne rich fruit. Even today, the vows of the bodhisattva play an important role in the life of the Zen disciple. They are pronounced at the very beginning of the journey and repeated constantly throughout the long years of practice:

> However innumerable the sentient beings, I vow to save them all.
> However inexhaustible the passions, I vow to extinguish them all.
> However immeasurable the dharmas, I vow to master them all.
> However incomparable the truth of the Buddha, I vow to attain it.

In the last of the four vows, the initiates bind themselves to supreme enlightenment. By their omniscience, bodhisattvas dwell in the realm of the Absolute. Zen disciples commit themselves to follow the way of the bodhisattva, whose goal is supreme enlightenment. In striving for this goal the image of the bodhisattva is ever before them. Not a few bodhisattvas are mentioned, and their fortunes vividly described, in Mahāyāna literature. The supernatural world is teeming with bodhisattvas and heavenly beings. Zen students are especially familiar with the bodhisattva Mañjuśrī (Jpn., Monju) whose statue is to be found in every Zen hall. The bodhisattvas Avalokiteśvara (Jpn., Kannon), Kṣitigarbha (Jpn., Jizō) and Maitreya (Jpn., Miroku), the Buddha of the future who is still tarrying in the bodhisattva state, hold an important place in Japanese Zen. All these figures are objects of cultic veneration, but more important, they represent for Zen followers the incarnation of the bodhisattva ideal.

BUDDHOLOGY

The image of the bodhisattva represents a new and seminal idea whose roots spread deep and wide in the Mahāyāna tradition. A shift in the understanding of the Buddha and Buddhahood constituted another fundamental innovation. The early embellishment and elevation of the figure of the Buddha arose out of the devotional needs of his disciples; these developments took on doctrinal importance when they gave rise to speculative elaborations concerning the realm of the Absolute.

The first steps toward a Mahāyāna Buddhology can be found among the Mahāsāṃghikas, a progressive sect that had probably broken off from the conservative mainline by the time of the second Buddhist council.[21] Their Buddhology was rooted in the works of the Sarvāstivāda.[22] The docetism implicit in this movement was brought into the open by the Lokottaravāda, an offshoot of the Mahāsāṃghikas.[23] According to this school, the Buddha is not an ordinary human but a supramundane (lokottara) being to whom the laws of this world do not apply. From such a supernaturalized image of the Buddha, there developed a metaphysical Buddhology in which the Buddha's earthly origins were, if not entirely forgotten, at least reduced to an insignificant phase in the endless history of Buddhahood. Emerging originally from the multitude of sentient beings lost and in need of salvation, the Buddha had overstepped the boundary line of the mundane and entered into the realm of absolute reality. He no longer stands on the human side of reality; by nature he is the Absolute. This is the powerful new discovery of Mahāyāna, anticipated religiously by the growing tendency toward ritual worship of the Buddha and philosophically by developments in Indian philosophy. In the Mahāyāna view, the Buddha is all-encompassing. His essence lies in the sphere of ineffable mystery, beyond all propositional statements. The identification of the final state of nirvāṇa with the Buddha follows consistently from Mahāyāna Buddhology. But the world of becoming is also included in the mystery of the Buddha. The enlightened eye sees the universal reality of the Buddha, the unity of saṃsāra and nirvāṇa.

The full expression of this new Buddhology is contained in the doctrine of the three bodies of the Buddha, one of the central tenets of the Mahāyāna.[24] This systematic ordering of diverse and contradictory aspects of the Buddhist vision was given a final form at a rather late date, in the philosophical school of the Yogācāra. The first of the three bodies is commonly referred to as the Apparitional Body (nirmāṇakāya). Later schools distinguish here between the complete apparition of the Perfected One (for example, of Śākyamuni) and partial manifestations (as in the case of the great Buddhist spiritual teachers). Second is the Enjoyment Body (saṃbhogakāya), the idealized, perfected form of the Buddha that invites personification (especially known and revered in this respect is the Buddha Amitābha, Jpn., Amida). Finally, there is the Cosmic Body of the Buddha (dharmakāya), which is none other than the absolute and consummate reality of the Buddha. Clearly, this view of the Buddha satisfies very different perspectives at the same time. The unlimited possibilities for the Perfected One to appear—as unlimited as imagination itself—provide material for a whole pantheon of Buddhas, all of whom, however, are finally united in the one Buddha nature of the dharmakāya. The cultic need for veneration was able to clothe the blessed body of the Buddha in an unspeakable splendor of light and beauty; endow it with infinite wisdom, power, and compassion; and depict his Pure Land as the home of all human yearnings. The metaphysics of this Buddhology is cosmotheistic, and its corresponding anthropology, mystical. The deepest concern of the human individual must be the attainment of the enlightened view, for only the enlightened can grasp the perfect reality that is the Buddha. At the same time, enlightenment signifies the realization of one's own deepest self—the Buddha nature inherent in all sentient beings.

Mahāyāna teaches a unified vision that promises to fulfill in large measure the fundamental longing of the human spirit for unity.[25] Of all the religious practices of Mahāyāna, meditation holds the place of prominence: it alone can aid in realizing the vision of unity. The cultic tendency to veneration of persons, which makes up such a large part of popular piety, is in essence secondary. The meditative element plays a more or less important role in all the schools of the Mahāyāna, including Pure Land Buddhism (the focus of which is faith in the salvific power of the Buddha Amida), in which the invocation of the Buddha's name, ceaselessly repeated, brings about a meditative and spiritual state of mind.[26] The esoteric element is especially evident in Tantrism, while the value of meditation is brought to its greatest development in Zen. In different ways, both Tantrism and Zen are in pursuit of the same goal: the breakthrough to a higher, hidden truth, the knowledge of which transfers the illuminated one into the absolute realm where all is one, and that One is the Buddha.

THE HISTORY OF MAHĀYĀNA BUDDHISM

While there is an impressive number of concise studies on Śākyamuni, early Buddhism, and Theravāda, we lack a comprehensive presentation of Mahāyāna Buddhism as a whole. There are a number of reasons for this. Overshadowed by preferential interest in the Pāli Canon, research into Mahāyāna has moved forward slowly; moreover, the subject matter is extremely complex and difficult. Mahāyāna extends over a broad and widely diverging field whose historical and geographical horizons are not easily presented in an overview.

In fact, researchers have approached Mahāyāna from a variety of different angles and brought clarity to many areas. The material gathered in the process would, if sorted out and organized, suffice at least for a provisional general study of Mahāyāna. But since such a study is unfortunately not yet available, for the time being we shall have to be content with a brief look at some of the results of contemporary research that may aid us in locating Zen within the larger field of Mahāyāna.

First to be noted are the early Buddhist schools whose philosophical elements were a harbinger of later Mahāyāna developments. We have already mentioned the beginnings of these philosophical proposals. At the end of all these developments stand the two great Mahāyāna philosophical systems that have exercised a powerful influence on the whole of Mahāyāna: the school of the "Middle Way" (Mādhyamika) and the "Doctrine of Consciousness" (Vijñānavāda), also called the "Course in Yoga" (Yogācāra). Both philosophical schools are closely linked with the Mahāyāna scriptures and later institutionalized sects. These schools emerged in final form quite late, only after Mahāyāna had been active in different regions for some centuries.

The school of the Middle Way must be viewed as foundational for all of Mahāyāna. In it well advanced, typically Mahāyāna thought was for the first time organized into a system, and as such still exercises a normative influence today. The creation of the system is credited to Nāgārjuna, Mahāyāna Buddhism's greatest thinker, a South Indian said to have lived during the second half of the second century of the common era. In this cursory presentation of Mahāyāna philosophy we can mention only a few of the key ideas of the Middle Way, though Zen masters will often be referring us back to Nārgārjuna and his thought. As its name indicates, this school traces a "middle way" between being and nonbeing, between realism and nihilism. It holds that despite the "emptiness" (śūnyatā) of all existent things in this changing world, and despite the absence of all substance, qualities, essential characteristics, predicates, definitions, and rational conclusions, there remains the ineffable, final Reality, which can be seen only with the eye of wisdom (prajñā). Nārgārjuna's thought is through and through dialectical, and Zen bears the impress of his spirit.

The doctrine of the Vijñānavāda, or Yogācāra, school was fixed in written form by Asaṅga and Vasubandhu (fourth and fifth centuries CE)[27] and can be described as an idealism of consciousness. In this changing world, no thing (dharma) exists outside of consciousness. Psychological analysis leads in Yogācāra thought to the recognition of eight types of consciousness, of which the eighth is a higher-level consciousness, that is used by Zen masters to explain the process of enlightenment. In this "storehouse consciousness" (ālaya-vijñāna) are said to be stored all realities and all impressions; in it is preserved the unity of the processes of consciousness. In its religious practice, this school makes use of Yoga elements; hence its other appellation, the "Course in Yoga." Its tendency to an epistemological idealism has had wide influence on Mahāyāna and especially on the Zen school.

The great Mahāyāna sūtras form the center of Mahāyāna; in them the new religious inspiration is crystallized. A massive and imposing body of literature, the sūtras differ greatly in content, but each and every one of them breathes the spirit of Mahāyāna. These widely scattered writings serve many religious communities. While individual sūtras or groups of sūtras take up particular themes, they concur and overlap at many points. Moreover, one and the same sūtra can give rise to different religious movements. They are often accompanied by explanatory commentaries, or śāstras. Nearly all the sūtras and śāstras of Mahāyāna Buddhism are written in Sanskrit, which means that they originated in Indian Buddhism. Translated into Chinese and Tibetan, these texts had a much more extensive influence in East Asia than in their Indian motherland. A majority of the texts are preserved today only in translation. Often their Indian origin is questionable, and in many cases it is possible that Chinese originals were given Indian origins in order to enhance their authority. In its imposing totality, Mahāyāna literature enjoys high esteem.

The Mahāyāna sūtras and their commentaries include the sūtras and tantras of the esoteric Buddhism of India and the Himalayan countries as well as the Amitābha sūtras of Pure Land Buddhism. The Prajñāpāramitā sūtras mentioned above are basic to all of Mahāyāna, since they not only bestow the authority of the Buddha himself on the school of the Middle Way but have had a definitive influence on many other Mahāyāna schools as well. The Vijñānavāda school also has its own scriptures and treatises, the most important of which are the tracts by the two brothers Asaṅga and Vasubandhu.[28] Important Mahāyāna sūtras are also found in the collections known as the Avataṃsaka ("garland") and Ratnakūṭa ("preciousness") sūtras. The Mahāyāna Mahāparinirvāṇa Sūtra has its counterpart in the Pāli Canon. As important as the entrance of the Buddha into nirvāṇa is for the Buddha's life history, the metaphysics it implies is every bit as important in Mahāyāna thought. The Suvarṇaprabhāsa ("golden ray") Sūtra enjoys special affection among the common people in their cultic practices. Many other Mahāyāna sūtras could be mentioned. In the Buddhism of East

Asia, the "holy book" *par excellence* is the *Saddharmapuṇḍarīka Sūtra* ("lotus of the True Law"), accorded the highest place by some sects and greatly esteemed by all Buddhists.

Many Japanese Buddhist scholars have dedicated their life's work largely to one sūtra. Their contribution to the study of Mahāyāna, together with the painstaking translations done by Western scholars, merit high praise. The sūtras open the way to a total picture of Mahāyāna in all its different branches, but this is an undertaking of gigantic proportions, one that will require the collaboration of generations of scholars to see to completion. We have already noted the special ties that bind particular individual schools and sūtras. Because of the extraordinary significance of the sūtras for the practice of Mahāyāna, these relationships merit special attention. For this reason an entire chapter shall be devoted to the relation of Zen to individual Mahāyāna sūtras. Before that, however, we need to consider yet another path of easy access to Mahāyāna.

In their efforts to form an orderly overview, historians of Mahāyāna will also have to consider—last but not least—the process by which the various branches came to form the Buddhist tree. To be sure, the beginnings of such organization appear late in Buddhist history. In Indian Buddhism, Mahāyāna tendencies developed and gathered ever greater momentum without, it would appear, any deliberate attempt at institutional structuring. With the flowering of Mahāyāna in China there emerged a palette of different Mahāyāna schools, all of which were then transplanted to Japan, where they were further enriched through the Nichiren and other movements. Organizational forms, very loose in the beginning, changed in the course of the centuries. Already in China the different schools led a rather isolated existence, although they knew each other and tried to foster contact, as the various discussions on doctrinal issues show. With the diversification that took place in Japan the schools gradually came to take a clear organizational form. Only in the Edo period (1600–1868) did this organization achieve its final form. The six sects of the Nara period (710–794)— Kusha, Jōjitsu, Sanron, Hossō, Kegon, and Ritsu—somehow manage to continue;[29] the once mighty mountains of the Heian period (794–1175), Hiei and Kōya, with their monastic compounds of the Tendai and Shingon sects respectively, have preserved their prestige; and the typically Japanese Buddhism of the Kamakura period (1185–1333)—beginning with the Amida schools, Zen, and Nichiren—continues to exercise a profound influence on the shape of religious life in Japan. These schools, forged in China (with the exception of the Nichiren sect) and fashioned in Japan, embrace the whole of Mahāyāna, with all its varied contents and forms of religious life. A study of the history of Mahāyāna can begin with these schools but must then trace the elements preserved in them through their many phases of development back to their roots.

In this sense, the Zen school exists as one of many Mahāyāna schools; it understands itself as one of them and seeks to foster continued, at times even intimate, contact with them. The imposing significance of Zen Buddhism in Japan should not lead one to forget the place that Zen occupies within the broad and fertile history of Mahāyāna Buddhism.

NOTES

1. Because of the disparaging connotation of the term, modern Buddhist scholarship avoids as far as possible using the designation *Hīnayāna*. Nearly all recent presentations of Buddhism distinguish between the primitive Buddhism of Śākyamuni and the later developments in the vehicles and schools. C. Regamey treats consecutively precanonical Buddhism, the Lesser Vehicle, and the Great Vehicle. See his "Der Buddhismus Indiens," *Christus und die Religionen der Erde*, vol. 3. (Freiburg, 1951). E. Conze appends to his complete presentation of Buddhism an informative chronological table, "The Main Dates of Buddhist History," in *Buddhism: Its Essence and Development*, pp. 213ff, in which the first entry in the Hīnayāna column is given as 246 BCE. Ui Hakuju offers the following chronology in the abridged edition of his history of Indian philosophy: (1) original Buddhism, to 30 years after the Buddha's entry into nirvāṇa; (2) early Buddhism, to 270 BCE (the consecration of Aśoka); (3) sectarian Buddhism, from 270 until about 100 BCE; and (4) from 100 BCE until 100 CE, Hīnayāna and early Mahāyāna. The entire period belongs to the early development of Buddhism. See his *Indo tetsugakushi*, pp. 188ff.

2. A. Bareau, "Der indische Buddhismus," *Die Religionen Indiens*, vol. 3 (Stuttgart, 1964), p. 82. On the development of the sects in early Buddhism, see E. J. Thomas, *The History of Buddhist Thought*, pp. 37ff and appendix 2 on the eighteen schools, pp. 288–92; M. Walleser, *Die Sekten des alten Buddhismus* (Heidelberg, 1927); and A. Bareau, *Les sectes bouddhiques du Petit Véhicule* (Saigon, 1955). Vasumitra's *Samayabhedoparacanacakra*, a Sautrāntika work treating the eighteen schools, has been translated by Masuda Jiryō as "Origins and Doctrines of Early Indian Buddhist Schools," AM 2 (1925): 1–78.

3. Th. Stcherbatsky, *The Conception of Buddhist Nirvāṇa* (Delhi, 1977), p. 42. O. Rosenberg argues on the contrary that "there is no distinction in fundamental outlook. . . . The distinction rests not in the theory but in the praxis of salvation, in which Mahāyāna allows for a larger number of paths leading to the same goal" (*Die Probleme der buddhistischen Philosophie*, Materialen zur Kunde des Buddhismus, vols. 7 and 8 (Heidelberg, 1924), p. 226.) No doubt there is a consensus between Hīnayāna and Mahāyāna in fundamental outlook, but even so, there are deep-reaching distinctions in theory and praxis that cannot be overlooked. Stcherbatsky's judgment falls wide of the mark when he claims: "For it must be allowed that the Mahāyāna is a truly new religion, so radically different from Early Buddhism that it exhibits as many points of contact with later Brahmanical religions as with its own predecessor" (p. 41).

4. Compare Bareau, "Der indische Buddhismus," pp. 21ff, 69–72; see also his monograph "Les premiers conciles bouddhiques," in AMG 60 (1955).

5. J. Filliozat puts it this way: "The imperceptible transition from the old ideas to those of the Mahāyāna was able to succeed thanks to an advanced, natural development of new speculative ideas in the old schools." See "Der Buddhismus," in *Manuel des études indiennes*, vol. 2 (Hanoi, 1953), p. 564.

6. For example, parts of the Prajñāpāramitā sūtras, concerning which more follows.

7. D. T. Suzuki remarks to the point: "It is to be remembered that the spiritual vitality of Buddhism lies in its sūtras and not in its śāstras so-called, which are philosophical treatises, and this is what we naturally expect of religious literature. Whoever the compilers of the Mahayana sūtras may be, they [the sūtras] are genuine expressions of the deepest spiritual experiences gone through by humanity as typified in this case by Indian minds." See his introduction to Beatrice Lane Suzuki's *Mahāyāna Buddhism* (London, 1948), p. xxx. We shall find this view confirmed in the course of our investigations.

8. Mahāyāna doctrine names the three vehicles: of hearers (śrāvaka), of those awakened for themselves alone (pratyekabuddha), and of enlightened beings (bodhisattva).

9. See Thomas, The History of Buddhist Thought, p. 167.

10. The fullest treatment appears in the Daśabhūmika Sūtra, one of the Avataṃsaka sūtras. A piece of the same title in the Mahāvastu explains the ten stages (bhūmi) of the bodhisattva course from a Theravāda point of view. The two logographs of the title of the Mahāvastu in its Chinese translation literally mean "great deed" or "great event," referring to the enlightenment of Śākyamuni. On the doctrine of the bodhisattva ideal, see the massive Japanese work Daijō bosatsudō no kenkyū [Studies on the Way of the Bodhisattva in Mahāyāna], edited by Nishi Yoshio (Kyoto, 1968). My résumé of the bodhisattva stages follows the description of the Daśabhūmika Sūtra. See Thomas, The History of Buddhist Thought, pp. 205–10. Filliozat ("Der Buddhismus," pp. 571–72) extracts the same stages from the Mahāyāna-sūtrālaṃkāra.

11. There is a list of ten perfect virtues in the Pāli Canon that differs from the ten perfect virtues of Mahāyāna. See Filliozat, "Der Buddhismus," p. 555.

12. See B. L. Suzuki, Mahāyāna Buddhism, p. 60. Compare W. E. Soothill and L. Hodous, A Dictionary of Chinese Buddhist Terms (London, 1937), p. 51. The Chinese characters of the transcription of the two Sanskrit terms point in the same direction.

13. "Wisdom which has gone beyond" is Conze's translation. See his Buddhist Wisdom Books: The Diamond Sūtra, the Heart Sūtra (London, 1970), p. 52.

14. On this sūtra (Aṣṭasāhasrikā-prajñāpāramitā Sūtra), see E. Conze, The Prajñāpāramitā Literature (The Hague, 1960), pp. 51–57.

15. The Perfection of Wisdom in Eight Thousand Lines and its Verse Summary, translated by E. Conze (Bolinas, Cal., 1975), 16:311, p. 196.

16. Conze, The Perfection of Wisdom, 16:310, p. 195.

17. Conze, The Perfection of Wisdom, 2:35, p. 97. Also cited by D. T. Suzuki in his Studies in the Laṅkāvatāra Sūtra (London, 1930), p. 95.

18. Essays II, pp. 75–331; quotation above from p. 322.

19. Following Suzuki's free translation in Essays III, p. 325.

20. Essays III, p. 268.

21. See Thomas, The History of Buddhist Thought, pp. 31ff. In Buddhist scholarship, the view that the transition of Mahāyāna was achieved in the Mahāsāṃghika sect has won qualified recognition. Bareau finds in this school "an ontological doctrine that . . . is close to the doctrine of Mahāyāna. . . ." ("Der indische Buddhismus," p. 93). He believes it possible to establish "the sources of the fundamental essentials of Mahāyāna doctrine" in this group (p. 108).

22. See Bareau, "Der indische Buddhismus," pp. 120–21.

23. In his depiction of the bodhisattva career Thomas calls attention to a fundamental difference between the standpoint of Buddhism and that of Western docetism. He writes: "This is unlike the gnostic docetism which represented the essentially divine as assuming the mere appearance of the human. Indian thought never conceived any fundamental difference in kind between the human and the divine." Thomas applies this insight to Buddhism (The History of Buddhist Thought, p. 203).

24. Nearly all presentations of Mahāyāna Buddhism explain the doctrine of the three bodies (trikāya) of the Buddha; see for example Bareau, Les sectes bouddhiques du Petit Véhicule. pp. 150ff. In a Japanese study entitled "Busshinron no tenkai" ["The Development

of the Doctrine of the Bodies of the Buddha"], R. Habito shows the historical development that led to the identification of the Buddha with the Dharma. According to his thesis, Śākyamuni experienced the Dharma and, as more and more of his disciples came to believe, possessed the Dharma as a "body." In the interpretation of the Mahāsāṃghikas, the aspect of the Dharma emerged strongly in the image of the Buddha. In the Mahāyāna schools, the final form of the doctrine of the three bodies of the Buddha crystallized through an intermediate stage that accepted two Buddha bodies. See Habito's study in SK 52 (1978): 1–21.

25. For this reason, adherents of Mahāyāna describe their doctrine as "deep" in comparison with the "shallow" doctrine of the Hīnayāna. See Ui, Indotetsugakushi, p. 160.

26. Compare Suzuki's studies on "The Kōan Exercise and the Nembutsu" in Essays II, pp. 115–62; see also my Östliche Meditation und christliche Mystik, pp. 204–208.

27. The dates of the brothers Asaṅga and Vasubandhu are not certain. If Asaṅga had Maitreyanātha as his teacher—which would make this latter the school's real founder—then the origins of the school can be placed in the fourth century. See A. Bareau, "Der indische Buddhismus," p. 125. On the origin of the idealism of the Yogācāra school, see L. Schmithausen, "Spirituelle Praxis und philosophische Theorie im Buddhismus," ZMR 57 (1973): 161–86.

28. On the writings of the Yogācāra school, see Bareau, "Der indische Buddhismus," pp. 139ff.

29. The enumeration of the six sects of the Nara period derives from traditional Japanese Buddhist historiography. Actually, these sects were "schools" only in the narrow sense—that is, organizations for studying certain treatises. See W. Gundert, Japanische Religionsgeschichte (Tokyo, 1935), pp. 41–52; cf. pp. 35–36, 38ff.

4

The Mahāyāna
Sūtras and Zen

THE SPIRITUAL AND INTELLECTUAL CONTEXT OF ZEN

The outline of the main elements of Mahāyāna attempted in the previous chapter should help us place Zen, Mahāyāna's meditational school, in its wider context. In stressing the independent development of Zen, D. T. Suzuki has to admit that "undoubtedly the main ideas of Zen are derived from Buddhism, and we cannot but consider it a legitimate development of the latter."[1] Sprung from the native soil of Buddhism and organized into and nurtured through its several branches into a school of its own, the Zen found in the lands of East Asia belongs to Mahāyāna Buddhism.

In order to bring the spiritual and intellectual context of Zen into clearer relief, however, we can focus on the great Mahāyāna sūtras that enjoy a special proximity to Zen. These sūtras give voice to the new spiritual inspiration of Mahāyāna and offer an important stimulus to speculative reflection. Suzuki's early, more academic, writings contain a wealth of material on the relationship between Zen and the Mahāyāna sūtras.[2] At first, Western literature on Zen did not pay sufficient attention to this relationship; for a long time, fascination with the early Chinese masters of whom the chronicles and kōan collections speak overshadowed the Indian sūtras.

The two decisive components of Zen are the Mahāyāna sūtras, which provide its religious-metaphysical roots, and the Chinese spirit, which provides its distinctive dynamism. Any attempt to understand the spiritual environment of Zen must take both elements into account. It was only when the Chinese leaven was added to Mahāyāna Buddhism that the fermentation process began that resulted in Zen. In this chapter we shall examine the significance of certain Mahāyāna sūtras for Zen.

THE SŪTRAS OF PERFECT WISDOM—PRAJÑĀPĀRAMITĀ

We have already touched on the sūtras of Perfect Wisdom (*prajñāpāramitā*) during the course of our review of the main elements of Mahāyāna Buddhism in the previous chapter. The bodhisattva ideal, one of the essential elements of Mahāyāna, is a central theme in these sūtras, which form the foundations of the philosophy of the Middle Way (Mādhyamika). The influence of these sūtras extends throughout virtually the whole of Mahāyāna Buddhism, but these texts have left their strongest stamp on the Zen school.

As their name indicates, these sūtras have to do with Perfect Wisdom and indeed are basically an exaltation of prajñā, revered in these works as the mother of all Buddhas and bodhisattvas, the source of all merits and of final liberation. In the main text, a sūtra of eight thousand lines, wisdom is exalted in a variety of terms and expressions: "worthy of homage," "excellent are all her works," "unstained and the entire world cannot stain her," "she brings light to the blind so that all fear and distress may be forsaken," "in her we can find shelter," "she cannot be crushed," "she is the antidote to birth and death."[3] In these sūtras the significance of wisdom for the pursuit of salvation is evident. It is wisdom that sets the wheel of doctrine in motion. The new doctrine of the Wisdom school is thus considered by Mahāyāna to be the "second turning of the Dharma wheel," second in importance only to the first teachings preached by Śākyamuni.

The Prajñāpāramitā sūtras also set forth the evangel of the Buddha by claiming silence as their highest and most valid expression. Wisdom, all-knowing and all-penetrating, is deep, inconceivable and ineffable, transcending all concepts and words. Most important, wisdom sees through the "emptiness" (Skt., śūnyatā, adj., śūnya; Jpn., kū) of all things (dharma). Everything existing is always "empty." The broad horizon of meaning enveloping this word, which occurs throughout all the sūtras, suggests that in the attempt to grasp its content feeling must take precedence over definition. In the Heart Sūtra, the shortest of the Prajñāpāramitā texts, wisdom is related to the five skandhas, the constitutive elements of human beings, and to all things contained in them. The sūtra is recited daily both in Zen and other Mahāyāna temples, often repeated three times, seven times, or even more. In drawn out, resounding tones the endless chanting echoes through the semidark halls: kū-kū-kū–"empty, empty, empty." Like the Hīnayāna monk meditating on despicable objects (kammatthāna), the ordinary Japanese woman recites the word empty in order to grasp the transience and nothingness of this temporal world—a prerequisite for advance on the religious way of salvation.[4]

The notion of emptiness is not entirely original to the sūtras of Perfect Wisdom. In the Abhidharma, śūnya stands for duḥkha ("suffering" in the most comprehensive sense)[5] and the grasping of "emptiness" is one of the "doors to liberation."[6] In the Wisdom sūtras the stress is put on demonstrating the doctrine of the emptiness of "inherent nature" (svabhāva). Free of all inherent nature and lacking any quality or form, things are "as they are"—they are "empty." Hence, emptiness is the same as "thusness" (tathatā), and because all things are empty, they are also the same. Whatever can be named with words is empty and equal. Sameness (samatā) embraces all material and psychic things as part of the whole world of becoming that stands in opposition to undefinable nirvāṇa. In emptiness, nirvāṇa and saṃsāra are seen to be the same. The identity of emptiness, thusness, and sameness embraces the entire Dharma realm (dharmadhātu). Like the Dharma realm, Perfect Wisdom is unfathomable and indestructible.[7] Here the doctrine on wisdom reaches its culmination.[8]

Of special importance for Zen is the fact that Perfect Wisdom reveals the essence of enlightenment. As a synonym for emptiness and thusness,[9] enlightenment is neither existence nor nonexistence; it cannot be described or explained. "Just the path is enlightenment; just enlightenment is the path."[10]

Although the statements about Perfect Wisdom in the basic early texts of the Prajñāpāramitā literature are open to transcendence, wisdom—even in its identification with emptiness, thusness, sameness, the Dharma realm, and enlightenment—remains in a state of suspension. It touches on the realm of the Absolute and yet is not itself an absolute being. Lamotte sums things up this way in his monumental study and translation of one of the seminal texts of East Asian Buddhism:

> Perfected Wisdom is not a being in the metaphysical order; nor is it a subsistent absolute to which one can adhere. It is rather a spiritual state. . . . Transcending the categories of existence and nonexistence, empty of every quality, Perfect Wisdom can be neither affirmed nor denied: it is excellence in which nothing is lacking. . . ."[11]

The message of the Wisdom sūtras is preeminently religious. But the Prajñāpāramitā movement, which arose in opposition to the early Buddhist philosophical schools,[12] had to bring philosophical reflection into the picture. In addition, the atmosphere in Buddhist monasteries of the time was thick with philosophy. The philosophical school of the Middle Way developed on the foundations of the Prajñāpāramitā sūtras and in its basic content can hardly be distinguished from them. Accordingly, the philosophical tracts need to be read against the background of the sūtras and can aid in a more thorough comprehension of the sacred texts. The religious element in any case remains fundamental and can be attained only through meditation. Still, philosophical reflection can spark religious zeal in meditation, where dialectic and paradox also come into play.

For all the extensive research that has been carried out on the work of Nāgārjuna, the founder and greatest thinker of the school of the Middle Way, much remains obscure to us. There are unresolved problems of textual criticism related to the authorship of Mādhyamika treatises;[13] even texts that are certainly the work of Nāgārjuna, above all the *Mūlamadhyamakakārikā*, contain perplexing verses that complicate the hermeneutical task.[14] If we focus on the doctrinal agreement that exists between the Wisdom sūtras and the tracts of the Mādhyamika we note that both schools characteristically practice the method of didactic negation. By setting up a series of self-contradictory oppositions, Nāgārjuna disproves all conceivable statements, which can be reduced to these four:

All things (*dharma*) exist: affirmation of being, negation of nonbeing

All things (*dharma*) do not exist: affirmation of nonbeing, negation of being

All things (*dharma*) both exist and do not exist: both affirmation and negation

All things (*dharma*) neither exist nor do not exist: neither affirmation nor negation

With the aid of these four alternatives (*catuṣkoṭika:* affirmation, negation, double affirmation, double negation), Nāgārjuna rejects all firm standpoints and traces a middle path between being and nonbeing.[15] Most likely the eight negations, arranged in couplets in Chinese, can also be traced back to Nāgārjuna: neither destruction nor production, neither annihilation nor permanence, neither unity nor difference, neither coming nor going.[16]

Nāgārjuna's method of *reductio ad absurdum (prasaṅga)* borders on a universal skepticism or nihilism.[17] Indeed, his philosophy is often so understood. But modern interpreters unanimously warn against a nihilistic interpretation.[18] Unfortunately, we still lack a truly satisfying exposition of Nāgārjuna's philosophy. Like the Buddha, Nāgārjuna offered no answers to ultimate metaphysical questions. His explanation of the positive statements in his philosophical vocabulary is consistently negative. "Thusness" and "sameness" are identical with "emptiness"; "truth in the highest sense" *(paramārtha-satya)*, which is different from the temporary truth of the phenomenal world *(saṃvṛti-satya)*, is "the unutterable, the unthinkable. . . ."[19] No thinker since has with equal consistency maintained silence about the essence of reality. "This true essence . . . is inexpressible, for the actual essence of things, like nirvāṇa, lies outside the realm of human knowledge and can therefore never be grasped in words."[20]

Perhaps Nāgārjuna's philosophy should be understood in terms of a negative theology. The imbedding of his philosophy in the teachings of the sūtras of Perfect Wisdom lends weight to such an approach. As with Plato, one senses in Nāgārjuna an underlying intuitive experience, even though, unlike the Neoplatonists, he maintained strict silence regarding such experience.[21] This suspicion is supported by the fact that Nāgārjuna is revered in all of Mahāyāna as a great religious figure, in many places as a bodhisattva. Not only Zen, but also the Tantric branch of Buddhism and the devotional communities of Amitābha Buddha count Nāgārjuna among their patriarchs. Although his dialectical legacy is esteemed in the Zen tradition, it is his religious vitality that has had the greater influence.

Among the later Prajñāpāramitā sūtras, Zen gives special importance to the *Diamond Sūtra* and the *Heart Sūtra.* As already mentioned, the *Heart Sūtra* enjoys a place of preeminence in cultic practice. Suzuki takes the magical formula that concludes the sūtra to be a kōan.[22] In the sūtra's short version (the shortest form has only eighteen lines), he finds an introduction to the attainment of enlightenment in the form of a kōan.

The chief reason for the fondness of Zen followers for the *Diamond Sūtra* lies in its liberal use of paradox. In numerous repetitions this sūtra drives home the paradox of "nothingness."

> What has been taught by the Tathāgata as the possession of marks, that is truly a no-possession of no-marks. . . . Hence the Tathāgata is to be seen from no-marks as marks. . . .

> The Tathāgata spoke of the "heap of merit" as a non-heap. . . . For the Tathāgata has taught that the dharmas special to the Buddhas are just not a Buddha's special dharmas. . . .

Just that which the Tathāgata has taught as the wisdom which has gone beyond, just that he has taught as not gone beyond. . . .

The Tathāgata has taught this as the highest (paramā) perfection (pāramitā). And what the Tathāgata teaches as the highest perfection, that also Blessed Buddhas do teach. . . .[23]

The negations of the Diamond Sūtra, like those of Zen in general, are meant to help one acquire intuitive knowledge. W. Gundert explains, from his Zen perspective, that "this kind of negation, which really is the highest form of affirmation, . . . belongs to the style of the sūtras of Perfect Wisdom, especially that of the Diamond Cutter Sūtra, the Vajracchedikā."[24] The Wisdom sūtras are meant to bring one to a religious experience in which one penetrates the emptiness of all things and grasps their suchness, an experience like the dispersing of darkness and the dawning of light. Just as emptiness is ineffable and immeasurable, neither increasing nor decreasing, so does suchness, "that unsurpassable and perfect illumination," neither grow nor diminish.[25] Emptiness, thusness, and Perfect Wisdom stand on a single line, elevated above the process of change and reaching into the realm of transcendence.

Not without reason, the school of Zen considers itself the rightful heir to the teachings of Perfect Wisdom. Hui-neng, the Sixth Patriarch of Zen, was awakened to the Great Enlightenment by a verse in the Diamond Sūtra: "Let your mind take its rise without fixing it anywhere."[26] The Diamond Sūtra remained his favorite ever after.

A kōan in the Mumonkan collection narrates how Te-shan Hsüan-chien, a "seeker after the Tao," traveled to South China with a thick commentary on the Diamond Sūtra under his arm. On the way, he asked an old woman for a bit of refreshment. She set him on the right path by asking: "In the sūtra it is written: 'The past mind is incomprehensible; the present mind is incomprehensible; the future mind is incomprehensible.' Excellent One, which mind is it you wish to refresh?" Te-shan was speechless. During that very night, with Master Lung-t'an, he attained the Great Enlightenment. On the following morning he burned his commentary. What need had he now of scriptures? "Even if one should penetrate all the obscure teachings, it would be like a tiny hair dropped in boundless space. And even if one should grasp the very pivot of the earth, it would be no more than a drop of water cast into the sea."[27] Living experience exceeds all wisdom gained from the sūtras.

In the spiritual and intellectual climate of Zen, negation and paradox were able to flourish. Enlightenment grasps all things "as they are," that is, in their thusness. Zen masters offer invaluable aid in what Suzuki has aptly called "the handling of prajñā."[28]

THE DOCTRINE OF TOTALITY—AVATAMSAKA (HUA-YEN)

Zen owes much of its character and color to the Avatamsaka sūtras and to the Chinese Hua-yen (Jpn., Kegon) school that developed from them. The massive

Avataṃsaka Sūtra (Chin., *Hua-yen ching;* Jpn., *Kegongyō*), known to us today chiefly through three Chinese translations of sixty, eighty, and forty books, respectively, is actually a compilation of several originally independent texts, the earliest of which, the *Daśabhūmika Sūtra,* may date from the first century of the common era. The work of assembling these disparate texts was probably not completed much before the mid-fourth century, or shortly before the transmission of the text to China, where Buddhabhadra and others made the sixty-book translation between the years 418 and 421. It is this text that serves as the scriptural warrant for the Hua-yen school.[29] The second and longer sūtra (eighty books), translated into Chinese by Śikṣānanda (659–699), contains expansions and additions to the recension in sixty books.[30] The forty-book Chinese translation (also known as the *Gaṇḍavyūha Sūtra*) is the work of the Buddhist monk named Prajña. Composed independently of the two previous sūtras, it presents the same basic material as the others and is preserved in its Sanskrit original.[31] The Sanskrit word *avataṃsaka* means "garland" or "wreath"; the name of the Chinese school, Gaṇḍavyūha, is composed of the words *gaṇḍa* (Chin., *hua*) meaning "flower" and *vyūha* (Chin., *yen*) meaning "ornamentation."

The Avataṃsaka sūtras presuppose the work of the two main philosophical schools of Mahāyāna—the school of the Middle Way and the Yogācāra school. The metaphysics of emptiness (*śūnyatā*) and the teaching on "mind only" (*vijñaptimātra*) are integrated into the sūtras. Nevertheless, the Avataṃsaka sūtras preserve their own special message, which has profoundly influenced Zen. Although the Wisdom sūtras and the doctrine of Mind-only led to the formation of different philosophical schools in India, the Avataṃsaka sūtras have really no equivalent in any of the Indian Mahāyāna schools. Only some time after the translation of the basic sūtras did the Hua-yen school take shape in China. The patriarchs of this school were contemporaries of the early Zen movement in China.

The Hua-yen school holds a prominent place in Mahāyāna Buddhism. According to tradition, it was during the first three weeks after attaining the Great Enlightenment that Śākyamuni delivered the sermon recorded in the sūtra. Because his listeners were not able to grasp the deep content of his message he later turned to a style of preaching more accessible to those whose religious capacities were as yet unprepared for more profound teachings. The followers of the Hua-yen school thus characterize their doctrine, in contrast to that of other Buddhist teachings, as the "full" or "perfect" teaching and extol their sūtra as the "king of the sūtras." Suzuki places particular importance on the relationship between Hua-yen and Zen. For him, "Zen is the practical consummation of Buddhist thought in China and the Kegon (Avataṃsaka) is its theoretical culmination." The two are related in such a way that "the philosophy of Zen is Kegon and the teaching of Kegon bears its fruit in the life of Zen."[32]

In their symbol-laden imagery and penetrating comparisons, the Avataṃsaka sūtras are the building stones out of which the richly ornate edifice of Mahāyāna, founded on prajñā-knowledge of emptiness and sameness, in its fully developed form is constructed. The basic idea is one of unity in plurality: All in One, One in All. The All melts into a single whole. There are no divisions in the totality of reality. The Japanese historian of religion Anesaki Masaharu has termed this worldview a "cosmotheism," in that it views the cosmos as holy, as "one bright pearl," the universal reality of the Buddha.[33] The universal Buddhahood of all reality is the religious message of the Avataṃsaka sūtras.

These sūtras contain the highly impressive analogies that have become the common property of Mahāyāna–the drop of water at one with the sea, the grain of sand that contains the universe.

In each dust-mote of these worlds
Are countless worlds and Buddhas . . .
From the tip of each hair of Buddha's body
Are revealed the indescribable Pure Lands . . .
The indescribable infinite Lands
All assemble in a hair's tip [of Buddha].[34]

The sūtra is trying to describe the totally indescribable infinity of the Buddha world and to this end makes use of astronomically large numbers. Reality is ineffable, inconceivable, unimaginable, indescribable. The constant recurrence of these words is meant to convey not only the infinity of time and space but also the ineffability of Buddha knowledge and the realization achieved in *samādhi*. Unlike the Prajñāpāramitā sūtras, the Avataṃsaka sūtras offer a "negative theology" that springs from the richness of the Buddha reality.

An important theme in these sūtras is the relatedness and interpenetration of all levels of reality. One of the best known illustrations of the spatial interpenetration of all things comes from the display the Third Patriarch of Hua-yen, Fa-tsang (643–712) put on for the Empress Wu.[35] Fa-tsang had an entire hall in the imperial palace—the walls, the ceiling, and the floor—covered with mirrors, and in the middle, next to a burning torch, he set the image of the Buddha. The empress viewed the illumined image not only in all the mirrors around the room, but also in the mirrorings of the countless mirrors, and so on in an unending spectacle of mirror images of mirror images. Exuberant but shaken, she grasped the meaning of the symbolic language. Fa-tsang explained to her, however, that even though this analogy of the mirrors captures the infinite interpenetration of all things in space, it does not offer an analogous expression of the mutual interrelatedness of all moments of time, and certainly not of the contemporaneity and mutual inherence of space and time.

Another example from the sūtra is the analogy of Indra's net. A net made of precious pearls hangs over Indra's palace. All the pearls hang together and each reflects the others. In taking hold of one pearl one takes them all; in looking at one pearl one sees them all.[36] Other powerful images illustrate the mutual penetration of all things. This interrelatedness applies not only to the phenomena of the temporal world of saṃsāra but also, given the mutuality of saṃsāra and nirvāṇa, to all of reality.

The Avataṃsaka sūtras depict the universal reality of the Buddha in the figure of a tower that Maitreya, the Buddha of the future, shows to the young pilgrim Sudhana.[37] The tower is an image of the universal Buddha, Vairocana, the Dharma realm (dharmadhātu), and the cosmic body of the Buddha (dharmakāya). Guided by Maitreya, Sudhana is allowed to enter the tower where he sees

> the objects arrayed in such a way that their mutual separateness no more exists, as they are all fused, but each object thereby never loses its individuality, for the image of the Maitreya devotee is reflected in each one of its objects, and this not only in specific quarters, but everywhere all over the Tower, so that there is a thoroughgoing mutual interreflection of images.[38]

Unity in totality allows every individual entity of the phenomenal world its uniqueness without attributing an inherent nature to anything.

The Dharma realm is accessible only through immediate experience. Whoever enters the Buddha tower has achieved perfect enlightenment. As the story of the pilgrimage of Sudhana reveals, the vision experienced in the tower allows the faithful disciple to realize the whole of reality and the full, unlimited power of the Buddha. The dividing line between time and space dissolves. The Enlightened One possesses the universe in a particle of dust and eternity in the present moment. The magnificent structure of Borobudur in Java presents the Buddha world of the Avataṃsaka sūtras.

The Chinese Hua-yen school translated the daring symbolism of the Avataṃsaka sūtras into philosophical concepts. The *Tract on the Meditation of Dharmadhātu*, composed by the First Patriarch, Tu-shun (557–640), marks the high point in the school's speculative metaphysics.[39] The Third Patriarch, Fa-tsang, is considered the second founder of the school. Under his direction the movement grew and earned high and widespread esteem. Tsung-mi (780–841), who appears in the line of succession as the Fifth Patriarch, became one of the better known figures in Chinese Buddhism. On the Zen family tree he is listed as the head of a flourishing Zen school of his time.[40] Pursuing the path of enlightenment, he considered the Kegon teaching the highest expression of the Buddha truth. This is evident in many of his writings, especially in his *Treatise on the Origin of Humanity*, which is still studied zealously today and used as an introduction to Buddhist thought. Fa-yen, the founder of one of the "Five Houses" in Chinese Zen, stressed the basic principle of Kegon metaphysics: sameness in difference and difference in sameness. During the Sung period, the inner affinity of Zen to Kegon led to a complete assimilation of the latter by the Chinese Zen masters. The preference shown the Avataṃsaka sūtras and Kegon metaphysics persists undiminished to this day in Japan.

The peculiar attitude of Zen disciples to nature draws its sustinence from the cosmotheistic worldview set forth so splendidly in the Avataṃsaka sūtras. A religiously rooted conviction about the divine unity of the universe permits one to search for the fulfillment of one's deepest being through fusing with nature. Life in a Zen monastery is immersed in nature. The natural phenomena accompanying the ebb and flow of the seasons lend a rhythm to spiritual events.

With loving devotion the novice watches a hawk circle the mountain peak on whose slope the monastery rests. Every living being, every minute thing is significant, since even the smallest of them contains the mystery in its entirety. Reverence for the sanctity of the universe vibrates through all art influenced by Zen and permeates the whole of ancient Japanese culture. It is from these religious moorings that the Japanese appreciation of nature is to be understood. To be sure, this attitude toward nature harbors inadequacies and limitations that derive, in the final analysis, from its nearly unavoidable tendency toward pessimistic naturalism.

A further relationship between Kegon and Japanese Zen remains to be traced. As already pointed out, the idealistic perspective of Yogācāra philosophy is woven into the sūtras. Buddha is mind. The phenomenal world holds no nature of its own. The reality of all things derives from mind. Zen was able to achieve a high degree of spiritualization in the life of its disciples, something it then passed on to Japanese art and culture. Zen painters never paint material things in their bare materiality. Rather, their delicate ink sketches uncover the spiritual essence without sacrificing the objectivity of their themes. Things thus depicted are illuminated so that their essence—mind or spirit—can shine through, for true reality is a thing of the spirit, and spirit is embodied. Through spiritual insight the oriental mind transcends "objectivity and abstraction, which for us are mutually exclusive opposites or poles of tensions. . . . Thus even in an image cut off from the empirical, phenomenal world, there can be an abundance of concrete reality."[41]

THE RESPONSE OF SILENCE—VIMALAKĪRTI

The *Vimalakīrti Sūtra*, which leads us back to the time of Śākyamuni, presents an engaging expression of the spirit and teaching of Mahāyāna. The central figure of the sūtra is a householder named Vimalakīrti who, though never ordained a monk, attained a high degree of enlightenment in the lay state and led the committed life of a bodhisattva. Whether, as the sūtra claims, Vimalakīrti or his prototype is actually to be counted among the original followers of Śākyamuni we cannot say. The name means "spotless glory." The sūtra paints the ideal picture of a lay bodhisattva and offers a suitable stimulus to lay Buddhism through its appealing depiction of the advantages of the way of the bodhisattva over that of the disciple (*śrāvaka*).

Dating at the latest from the second century of the common era, the *Vimalakīrti Sūtra*—its full title is *Vimalakīrti-nirdeśa Sūtra*, which means "sūtra of the teaching of Vimalakīrti"—is one of the early Mahāyāna sūtras.[42] It may be supposed that at the time of its composition the basic texts of the Prajñāpāramitā corpus were known. The *Vimalakīrti Sūtra* adopts the central insights about emptiness found in the Wisdom sūtras and belongs to the early sources of tradition for the philosophy of the Middle Way. Mind is not understood idealistically, as in the Yogācāra doctrine, but as "no-mind."[43]

The *Vimalakīrti Sūtra* has been translated into Chinese more often than any other sūtra. Particularly notable are the translations of Kumārajīva (350–409) and Hsüan-tsang (600/2–664).[44] While the latter translation is from a recension that reveals the sūtra at its highest stage of development, it was in Kumārajīva's translation that the sūtra was best known in East Asia. In Japan, its most famous interpreter was the Japanese prince regent Shōtoku Taishi (574–622). The sūtra was also often translated into Tibetan, as well as into other Central Asian languages. The short text is known in the West through three or four English translations as well as one in French and one in German.[45]

In China, the *Vimalakīrti Sūtra* belongs to a line of tradition that stretches from the Prajñāpāramitā sūtras to Zen. The sūtra shows a predilection for the use of paradox and negative statements. A number of passages on meditation and enlightened wisdom clearly point in the direction of Zen. The third chapter contains a scene that typifies the teaching of the sūtra. The Buddha proposes to send one of his disciples to Vimalakīrti, who had previously sent five hundred distinguished young men to the master. Meanwhile, Vimalakīrti himself lies at home on a sickbed. His illness, however, is a "skillful means" (*upāya*) to attract many visitors to his house, where he might instruct them. The disciple to be sent is to inquire after the condition of the venerable layman, but one by one candidates for the mission excuse themselves, each relating a previous experience in which Vimalakīrti had embarrassed them for their inadequate understanding of Buddhist doctrine. Motivated by *śūnya* knowledge, Vimalakīrti had explained to the disciples one by one—and this is the essential content of this chapter—the meaning of right meditation, right preaching and teaching, right begging and receiving, the right practice of contrition, and the right way of merit.

The meeting with Śāriputra, the first recorded in the sūtra, is the most important for us. Here Śāriputra relates Vimalakīrti's explanation of the right way of meditation:

> As I was sitting in the forest under a tree in quiet meditation, Vimalakīrti approached me and said: "To sit is not necessarily to meditate. Not to reveal the body in the three worlds (of lust, form, and formlessness), that is meditation. Not to rise up from concentration in which the inner functions are extinguished and yet to conduct oneself worthily, that is meditation. Not to abandon the way of the teaching and yet to go about one's business as usual in the world, that is meditation. Not to give one's spirit abode within or without, that is meditation. Not to allow oneself to be bothered about all sorts of possible bad intentions but rather to practice the thirty-seven aids to enlightenment, that is meditation. Not to cut [off] disturbances and yet to enter nirvāṇa, that is meditation. Anyone who sits thus in meditation receives the seal of the Buddha."[46]

As the sūtra goes on to relate, Śāriputra was speechless and unable to bring himself to answer. In the passage just cited, a contrast is set up between the Mahāyāna form of meditation and that of the Pāli Canon.[47] From the perspective of Zen, a number of the essential characteristics of this new—though perhaps also closer to the original—form of Buddhist meditation are of particular interest.

Of itself, sitting in quiet is not enough. In the dynamic, objectless meditation of Mahāyāna everyday values and activities are bound up with the deepest state of concentration. In referring to the thirty-seven aids toward enlightenment the sūtra shows its ties to tradition, whereas Zen makes a clean sweep here. Most striking of all is the remark at the end of the discussion about not eliminating disturbances. The translations are not in agreement on this passage.[48] According to the clear and unequivocal translation of Kumārajīva, it is not necessary to cleanse the mind of disturbances in order to achieve enlightenment. This is precisely the viewpoint of the Sixth Patriarch of Chinese Zen, Hui-neng, and his disciples. Regarding divergencies of opinion on this question in Chinese Zen, we shall have more to say later.

Vimalakīrti's remarks about the right way of meditation bring us very close to the meditational practices of Zen. At the point where the *Vimalakīrti Sūtra* reaches its climax, the presence of Zen is unmistakable. Mañjuśrī, the bodhisattva of wisdom, asks the assembly of bodhisattvas what it means when a bodhisattva enters the Dharma of nonduality. The ninth chapter describes how thirty-two bodhisattvas tried to come up with an answer, each describing the condition of nonduality in terms of the resolution of a pair of opposites such as arising and dissolving, subject and object, purity and impurity, saṃsāra and nirvāṇa. The bodhisattvas then pose the same question to Mañjuśrī, who replies:

> In my view, there is nothing to say about all things, nothing to explain, nothing to show, nothing to know. Cut off from all questioning and answering—this is to enter into the doctrine of nonduality.[49]

Then he asks Vimalakīrti to state his view: "Vimalakīrti remained silent and spoke not a word." For this the bodhisattva of wisdom praised him saying, "Well done, well done! No signs, nor words—this is indeed to enter into the doctrine of nonduality."[50]

Thus are all Zen masters reluctant to express enlightenment, the condition of nonduality, in words or signs. The singularity of reality, which transcends all objects and is experienced in enlightenment, is inexpressible. In a later chapter, the sūtra speaks of a "pure Buddhaland" in which bodhisattvas "perform their Buddha function through solitude, non-speaking, non-explaining, non-showing, non-knowing, non-doing, and non-creating."[51] The paradox of the bodhisattva life with its characteristic negations hovers over the Zen disciple, pointing the path to enlightenment. As the sūtra says of the bodhisattvas, "stillness is their house."[52] Out of the nonactivity of silence flows their pure activity. The *Vimalakīrti Sūtra*, like the way of Zen, is woven together with prajñā; it is genuine Mahāyāna and therefore close to Zen.

PSYCHOLOGICAL PERSPECTIVES—THE LAŃKĀVATĀRA SŪTRA

In the Chinese historical work *Further Biographies of Eminent Monks* it is reported that Bodhidharma, the founder of Zen in China, gave a copy of the four-volume translation of the *Laṅkāvatāra Sūtra* to his disciple with these words: "As I observe, there are no other sūtras in China but this, take it for your guidance and you will naturally save the world."[53] Most likely he was referring to the translation by Gunabhadra (394–468) in four books, dated 443. Like the entire Bodhidharma tradition, this episode is historically questionable; still, we can presume that already at an early date there was a close relation between Zen disciples and the Laṅkāvatāra Sūtra. Although the Diamond Sūtra replaced the Laṅkāvatāra as the most important scripture in the southern Zen tradition inaugurated by Hui-neng, the Sixth Patriarch of Zen, the sūtra continued to hold pride of place in the northern tradition. Indeed, early histories of the Zen tradition in China sometimes refer to it as the "Laṅkāvatāra school."

D. T. Suzuki, inspired mainly by the close bond between the Laṅkāvatāra Sūtra and Zen, devoted himself to thorough research on this difficult Mahāyāna text, translating the Sanskrit original into English[54] and preparing a comprehensive volume of studies on the sūtra. As Suzuki points out in his foreword, the Laṅkāvatāra Sūtra contains "many difficult and obscure passages," which he was unable to unravel to his own satisfaction.[55] He sees the sūtra as "a memorandum kept by a Mahāyāna master, in which he put down perhaps all the teachings of importance accepted by the Mahāyāna followers of his day," apparently with no attempt to keep them in any order. Changes and additions were introduced by later editors, "giving the text a still more disorderly appearance."[56]

The Laṅkāvatāra Sūtra does indeed contain various doctrinal perspectives, indicating that at the time of its composition divisions among the philosophical schools within Buddhism had not yet been clearly defined. Today the origins of the sūtra are generally placed—without any conclusive evidence—in the second or third centuries of the common era, and South India is regarded as its birthplace.[57] The text contains a preponderance of material that was fashioned into a system by the Yogācāra school. Like this school, the sūtra is characterized by a dominant interest in psychological processes. In what follows, we shall focus on those aspects that show a clear relationship to Zen.

The Laṅkāvatāra Sūtra is "one of the nine principal texts of Mahāyāna in Nepalese Buddhism; in China and Japan it also occupied an important position in the philosophy of Mahāyāna Buddhism."[58] The special interest it takes in the psychological aspects of the process of enlightenment is evident in its preference for terms that describe psychological states and changes in the subject.[59] The sūtra is focused on the doctrine of the "storehouse-consciousness" (ālaya-vijñāna) from which issue the seven other consciousnesses, together accounting for the entire psychic life of the individual in this world of becoming. Identical with the storehouse-consciousness is the impersonal "womb of the Perfected One" (tathāgatagarbha), in which the karmic seeds (bīja) of all past experiences are preserved. When, for reasons that elude explanation, the seeds are set in motion, the unconscious recollection of all activities, which resides in the storehouse of consciousness, works like a delicate fragrance or "impression" (vāsanā) to stimulate the psychic processes. The narcotic effect of this deceptive "fragrance" propels sentient beings in ignorance and desire through the realm of rebirths.

This process of recurring appearances is brought to a halt through a conversion (parāvṛtti) at the root of consciousness that implies liberation rather than destruction. This conversion, one of the key concepts in the sūtra, can be taken as a psychological description of the moment of enlightenment.[60] Mind breaks through the multiplicity of appearances and comprehends the emptiness of all things, grasping thusness (tathatā) and coming into contact with the Unborn (anutpāda). The power by which all this takes place is, according to the Laṅkāvatāra Sūtra, the "noble consciousness" (āryavijñāna), a psychological capacity that performs the same function as prajñā in the Wisdom sūtras. Despite the difference in terminology, however, the teaching of the Laṅkāvatāra Sūtra hardly differs from the Middle Way teachings. The metaphysical aspect is ubiquitous, even if the psychological perspective is preferred. The same storehouse-consciousness contains both an absolute and an evolutionary aspect, and there are numerous expressions for ultimate reality that go beyond the descriptions of psychological phenomena.[61]

When Zen masters attempt to offer their students a psychological explanation of the process of enlightenment they generally return to the teaching on the eight consciousnesses and stress that the decisive transformation takes place on the eighth level, that is, with ālaya consciousness. While there is much that suggests an identification of Zen enlightenment with conversion (parāvṛtti), it is not clear whether the Laṅkāvatāra Sūtra holds to sudden or gradual enlightenment. Most likely, one can find both viewpoints in such a diversely formulated work.[62] In the sūtra, the bodhisattva Mahāmati addresses the following question to Buddha: "When the mind is cleansed by the Buddha of its own outflowings, is it done all at once or by degrees?" Unfortunately, the answer in the text is not clear. The Chinese translations disagree and the Sanskrit original is garbled. According to Suzuki, the answer of the sūtra is "sometimes gradual and sometimes abrupt." In any case, when one experiences inner transformation, the experience will have a suddenness about it. Suzuki writes:

> The process needed by the Buddha for cleansing is sometimes gradual and sometimes abrupt. But the notion of revulsion or up-turning (parāvṛtti) leads us to imagine the process to be abrupt rather than gradual, while in our actual experience of life what the psychologist calls conversion takes place in either way, gradual or abrupt. . . . Psychologically this is a phenomenon suddenly happening in the consciousness. When a man was walking in a certain direction all the time, his steps are all of a sudden made to turn back; he faces now the North instead of the South. This abrupt shift of the vista is a revolution, a revulsion; he is sure to be strongly conscious of the transformation.[63]

The Laṅkāvatāra Sūtra also refers to the "supreme knowledge" (pariniṣpanna) that transcends all duality as a "self-realization" (svasiddhānta).[64] Such a view is also commonly found in Zen. When Zen speaks of enlightenment as "seeing into one's own nature" or "the original countenance one had before one was born," it is clearly referring to an experience of the self. Such an interpretation applies to Chinese Buddhism and the way it identifies one's own nature with the Buddha nature or with the cosmic body of the Buddha.

The Mahāyāna sūtras agree that the highest truth cannot be grasped without inner experience, and all stress, with different degrees of insistence, that all liberating experience bears a suprarational character. But in addition to this, one finds in the Laṅkāvatāra Sūtra an irrationality that bears amazing resemblances to Zen. In the sūtra's second chapter the bodhisattva Mahāmati asks the Buddha to shed light on 108 questions. The questions make up a strange mixture of religious seriousness and nearly absurd platitudes. The Buddha answers with 108 negations only loosely related to the questions. As the beginning of the scene makes it clear that the Buddha is treating the situation as an opportunity to offer "instruction in self-realization," perhaps the questions and answers have a function similar to that of the kōan in Zen practice: to unmask the inadequacy of reason and point the way to experience.[65]

The experiential quality of supreme knowledge is thus linked directly to the ineffability that results when rational thought patterns are overcome. Although suprarationality does not necessarily imply irrationality, the Laṅkāvatāra Sūtra, in stressing the reluctance to use words, seems to move toward the irrational when it reports of Buddha lands in which the Buddha truth is not passed on by words but by a mere gaze or a contraction of the facial muscles, by raising the eyebrows or frowning or smiling, by spitting or winking, or by similar gestures.[66] Zen is well known for having invented a motley collection of such concrete expressions for enlightenment. We read of Zen masters grimacing or lifting a finger or uttering a cry in order to trigger enlightenment in a disciple. In so doing they considered themselves to be in imitation of the Buddha who, in the celebrated sermon on the Vulture Peak, took a flower and held it up to the assembled multitude. Master Wu-men celebrates this episode, to which Zen traces the beginning of the transmission of the supreme truth "without written signs and words," in the following verse:

> As he lifts up the flower
> The serpent appears.
> Kāśyapa twists his face into a smile,
> And humanity and heaven do not know what to do.[67]

The transmission of the supreme truth "without written signs and words" happens in deepest silence. Mute gestures take the place of words.

Zen offers many examples of "body language," but the wordlessness of such language is quite different, as we have already observed, from the sort of ineffable experience to which the mystics testify. In laying so much emphasis on the inadequacy of human words, the mystics do not mean to deny the inner relationship that exists between word and reality. From the viewpoint of Mahāyāna, however, it would appear that language is fundamentally confined to the realm of distinction and therefore bound to fall into error. Suzuki writes: "This relation between words and meaning, or between syllables (akṣara) and reality (tattvam or tathātvam), or between doctrine (deśanā) and truth (siddhānta) is like that between the finger and the moon."[68] In this interpretation of the Laṅkāvatāra Sūtra, the relationship remains an external one. The words of Master Wu-men imply the same externality: "It is like striking at the moon with one's staff, or scratching one's shoe because one's foot itches."[69] One should not press these comparisons. Words and language belong indisputably among the basic values of the human being.

Convinced that there can be no religious experience without some form of religious teaching, I have sought to locate Zen in its spiritual and intellectual environment and to treat some of the Mahāyāna sūtras from which it draws inspiration. Although the Chinese school of Zen began to develop only some centuries after the formative period of these sūtras, in terms of spiritual content Zen is deeply rooted in them. This fact is of the greatest importance for the proper understanding of Zen, for the basic ideas of Mahāyāna are essential to understanding the meaning of Zen enlightenment.

We have been able to examine no more than a small fraction of the extensive Mahāyāna literature, a few sūtras whose influence on Zen is historically certain and clear. If anything, the restricted reach of our treatment points to the magnitude of the scholar's task. These sūtras, which originated in India in the period immediately preceding the dawn of Christianity and during the first centuries of the common era, bear witness to a religious movement the importance of which comes close to that of the first turning of the Dharma wheel by Śākyamuni. Thus far, historical research has been able to ascertain very little about the beginnings of Mahāyāna in India. The Mahāyāna sūtras are complex, enigmatic, richly imaginative, and at the same time speculative texts that reflect a great development in religious history. Through them Mahāyāna radiated in all directions. The interpretations of these texts and their spiritual content vary a great deal and render the situation still more complicated.

My intent in this chapter has been to appeal to the Mahāyāna sūtras to shed light on our understanding of Zen. But the reverse is also true: the particular form that the spiritual legacy of the sūtras has assumed within Zen offers insights into their deeper meaning. This meaning is not always clear; indeed, a diversity of meanings is often possible. Still, the way Zen has come to understand the sūtras deserves our full and careful attention, for disciples of Zen have felt themselves filled with the same spirit that inspired the Mahāyāna sūtras.

NOTES

1. D. T. Suzuki, An Introduction to Zen Buddhism, p. 37.

2. In particular, nearly the entire third volume of his Essays in Zen Buddhism and considerable parts of the first two volumes, as well as his Manual of Zen Buddhism (New

York, 1960), treat this question in detail. During his creative period Suzuki provided extensive analysis of the Laṅkāvatāra Sūtra. (See his Studies in the Laṅkāvatāra Sūtra.)

3. Aṣṭasāhasrikā VII, 170–71; cited in E. Conze, Selected Sayings from the Perfection of Wisdom (London, 1968), pp. 61–62. Conze's books have unlocked the Prajñāpāramitā literature for us. His The Prajñāpāramitā Literature, in which he describes all the texts whose translations exist in Chinese, Tibetan, other Asian languages, and in Western languages, and in which he investigates their origins and historical connections, is fundamental. Conze has translated both The Large Sūtra on Perfect Wisdom (Berkeley, 1975) and parts of the Aṣṭasāhasrikā Sūtra into English, as well as shorter texts: The Short Prajñāpāramitā Texts (London, 1974), Buddhist Wisdom Books: The Diamond Sūtra, the Heart Sūtra, and the Selected Sayings mentioned above. Several of the essays in his Thirty Years of Buddhist Studies (London, 1967) treat the Perfection of Wisdom (pp. 123–209), as do sections of his Buddhist Thought in India (London, 1962). A German translation of sections of the Aṣṭasāhasrikā and the entire Diamond Sūtra was prepared by M. Walleser, Prajñāpāramitā: Die Vollkommenheit der Erkenntnis (Göttingen, 1914). See also the studies of T. Matsumoto, Die Prajñāpāramitā-Literatur (Stuttgart, 1932).

4. I have often been present at the recitation of the Heart Sūtra in Buddhist temples. The kū fills the hall and penetrates to the very bones and marrow of the devout. H. Waldenfels is right to draw attention to the religious aspect of emptiness in his Absolute Nothingness: Foundations for a Buddhist-Christian Dialogue, translated by J. W. Heisig (New York, 1980), pp. 19–23.

5. See Conze, Thirty Years of Buddhist Studies, p. 161.

6. Conze, Thirty Years, p. 128.

7. Conze, Thirty Years, p. 133.

8. See T. R. V. Murti, The Central Philosophy of Buddhism: A Study of the Mādhyamika System (London, 1970), pp. 86, 219–20. See also the two passages of the Aṣṭasāhasrikā cited in Conze, Selected Sayings, p. 93.

9. Conze, Selected Sayings, p. 114.

10. Conze, Selected Sayings, p. 115–16.

11. E. Lamotte, Le traité de la grande vertu de sagesse de Nāgārjuna, vol. 2 (Louvain, 1949), in the résumé of the contents of chapter 17, p. 18.

12. T. Matsumoto points to the teaching of the Sarvāstivādin as the focus of this critique. In his view, "the principle of Prajñāpāramitā doctrine is identical to the essential core of Buddhism, so that its revival is . . . at the same time a revival of Buddhism itself" (Die Prajñāpāramitā-Literatur, p. 27. Cf. F. J. Streng, Emptiness: A Study in Religious Meaning (Nashville, 1967), p. 33.

13. See Murti, The Central Philosophy of Buddhism, pp. 88–91; Streng, Emptiness, pp. 28–29. The original authorship of the Great Treatise on the Perfection of Wisdom (Mahāprajñāpāramitā Śāstra) is still disputed; on this question see M. Saigusa, Studien zum Mahāprajñāpāramitā (upadeśa) Śāstra (Tokyo, 1969), pp. 3–8.

14. K. K. Inada finds Nāgārjuna's stanzas "terse and abstract" in spite of their versification, and speaks of "cryptic strains" in them. See his translation of the Mūlamadhyamakakārikā (Tokyo, 1970), pp. 4–5.

15. For Conze, Nāgārjuna's "argumentation which demolishes all possible alternatives" and in which he "disproves the opponent's thesis, and does not prove any thesis of his own" (the comments are Murti's) shows the radically negative character of his thought

(*Buddhist Thought in India*, p. 241). On the four alternatives, see E. Frauwallner, *Die Philosophie des Buddhismus*, vol. 2 (Berlin, 1969), pp. 194–95.

16. For the pregnant formulation of the eight negations (Jpn., *happu*) in Chinese see J. Takakusu, *The Essentials of Buddhist Philosophy* (Honolulu, 1947), p. 103; see also the entire section, pp. 100–107.

17. "Nāgārjuna and his tradition were criticized by their contemporaries as nihilistic (*nāstika*) but this critique is misguided . . ." With these words Inada comments on the view of the Indian scholar H. Narain who sought to show that the theory of "emptiness" (*śūnyavāda*) is "absolute nihilism" (*Mūlamadhyamakakārikā*, p. 31). J. W. de Jong rejects the nihilistic interpretation of Stcherbatsky, whose translation of the term *śūnya* with the Western notion of "relative" he sees as a "distortion of Buddhist thought." See "The Problem of the Absolute in the Mādhyamika School," in a collection of de Jong's essays entitled *Buddhist Studies*, edited by G. Schopen (Berkeley, 1979), pp. 53–58; the quotation appears on p. 57.

18. Conze likens the intellectual effort of "emptiness" to a "ladder that reaches out into the infinite," and argues that it "embodies an aspiration" and represents a "method which leads to the penetration into true reality" (*Buddhist Thought in India*, p. 243). As a "means," "emptiness" is not only an "in-between" but also an "over-and-beyond."

19. See Murti, *The Central Philosophy of Buddhism*, p. 244. In defense against the nihilistic interpretation of the philosophy of the "Middle Way" he remarks: "Nāgārjuna is emphatic in stating that without the acceptance of the paramārtha (the ultimate reality) there can be no deliverance (Nirvāṇa) from Saṃsāra" (p. 235). De Jong also stresses "the mystical and soteriological character of the philosophy of the Mādhyamikas," noting that "on a philosophical level, they refrain from any a priori whatsoever, but mystical experience leads them to the absolute by way of deliverance." ("The Problem of the Absolute in the Madhyāmika School," p. 58).

20. E. Frauwallner, *Die Philosophie des Buddhismus*, vol. 2, p. 184; see the entire section on Nāgārjuna with citations from the original texts, pp. 170–217.

21. Murti takes this view when he writes that "Paramārtha satya . . . is experienced by the wise in a very intimate way" (*The Central Philosophy of Buddhism*, p. 245).

22. *Essays* III, p. 202.

23. Conze, *Buddhist Wisdom Books*, pp. 28, 39–40, 52–53.

24. *Bi-yän-lu* I, p. 368.

25. Walleser, *Prajñāpāramitā*, p. 112.

26. A free rendition of Suzuki in the light of the Chinese translation. See his *Essays* III, p. 91.

27. *Mumonkan*, case 28.

28. Suzuki gives several examples of this in *Essays* III, pp. 250–55.

29. T. 278, vol. 9; Nj. 87. For a brief but detailed description of Avataṃsaka literature, see *Zen Dust*, pp. 337–41.

30. T. 279, vol. 10; Nj. 88.

31. T. 293, vol. 10; Nj. 89. On the following, see the important studies of Suzuki on the Avataṃsaka sūtras in *Essays* III, pp. 21–214; and G. C. C. Chang, *The Buddhist Teaching of Totality: The Philosophy of Hua Yen* (University Park, 1971).

32. Introduction to Beatrice Lane Suzuki's *Mahāyāna Buddhism*, p. iv.

33. The Japanese term *ikka myōju* is the title of one of the ninety-five books of the

Shōbōgenzō, written by the Japanese Zen master Dōgen. See the English translation of N. Waddell and M. Abe in EB 4 (1971): 108–18.

34. The translation is from Chang, *The Buddhist Teaching of Totality*, p. 5.

35. Chang depicts the scene, *The Buddhist Teaching of Totality*, pp. 22ff.

36. D. T. Suzuki, in the introduction to B. L. Suzuki's *Mahāyāna Buddhism*, p. xxxiv.

37. Suzuki portrays the pilgrimage of Sudhana to the tower of Maitreya in his chapter on the abode of the bodhisattva in *Essays* III, pp. 107–66.

38. *Essays* III, p.148. Suzuki's translation here is free.

39. For an English translation, see Chang, *The Buddhist Teaching of Totality*, pp. 207–23.

40. In the generational line of Ho-tse Shen-hui, a disciple of Hui-neng.

41. D. Sekel, "Interpretation eines Zen-Bildes," NOAG 77 (1955): 47.

42. We are following E. Lamotte's dating here. No Sanskrit text is extant. The oldest Chinese translation presents the basic text of Prajñāpāramitā doctrine. See Lamotte, *L'enseignement de Vimalakīrti* (Louvain, 1962), pp. 66–77.

43. Lamotte, *L'Enseignement de Vimalakīrti*, pp. 56–60.

44. On Chinese translations, see *Zen Dust*, pp. 423–24.

45. An English translation by H. Idumi was serialized in EB (1922–1928); Lu K'uan Yü (C. Luk) based his English translation on Kumārajīva's Chinese (Berkeley, 1972), while R. A. F. Thurman followed the Tibetan throughout in his *The Holy Teaching of Vimalakīrti: A Mahāyāna Scripture* (University Park, 1976). The standard text, however, is E. Lamotte's richly commented and well introduced French translation. A German translation has been prepared by J. Fischer and Y. Yokata under the title, *Vimalakīrti-nirdeśa: Das Sūtra Vimalakīrti* (Tokyo, 1944).

46. This translation is my own, based on the Japanese version edited by Nakamura Hajime, who has followed Kumārajīva's translation. See *Yuimagyō*, in *Butten [Buddhist Texts]* II, Sekai kotenbungaku zenshū, vol. 7 (Tokyo, 1965), p. 12. The thirty-seven aids to enlightenment, already referred to in the opening chapter of the sūtra, are described in detail by Fischer and Yokota, *Vimalakīrti-nirdeśa*, p. 143, note 34.

47. Lamotte draws attention to the traits of Śāriputra's way of meditation as "siesta, repose, retreat, solitude, standing aside from all the noises of the world" (*L'enseignement de Vimalakīrti*, p. 142).

48. Lamotte refers to three different translations. The Tibetan text concurs in the essentials with Kumārajīva's translation. Hsüan-tsang's rendition, which deviates from the others, has clearly been influenced by scholastic theories. (*L'enseignement de Vimalakīrti*, p. 144, text and notes).

49. After Nakamura, *Yuimagyō*, p. 43.

50. After Nakamura, *Yuimagyō*, p. 43.

51. After Nakamura, *Yuimagyō*, p. 49.

52. After Nakamura, *Yuimagyō*, p. 38. The passage opens with the words: "Perfect knowledge is the mother of the bodhisattva, and 'skill-in-means' (*upāya*) the father."

53. See the passage on the *Laṅkāvatāra Sūtra* and Bodhidharma in Suzuki, *Studies in the Laṅkāvatāra Sūtra*, pp. 44–51. Tao-hsüan's *Further Biographies (Hsü kao-seng chuan)* can be found in T. 2060, vol. 50.

54. D. T. Suzuki, *The Laṅkāvatāra Sūtra: A Mahāyāna Text* (London, 1932).

55. Suzuki, *The Laṅkāvatāra Sūtra*, p. v.

56. Suzuki, *The Laṅkāvatāra Sūtra*, p. xi.

57. See *Zen Dust*, p. 372. Suzuki gives a detailed treatment of the three Chinese translations (by Guṇabhadra in four books, 443; Bodhiruci in ten books, c.513; Śikṣānanda et al. in seven books, c. 700–704) and the Tibetan translation. He compares these translations with one another and with the Sanskrit text on which he was working. See *Studies in the Laṅkāvatāra Sūtra*, pp. 3–15.

58. Suzuki, *Studies*, p. 3.

59. Suzuki gives particular attention to Sanskrit combinations using the terms *gocara*, *gatti*, *gatigama*, and *adhigama*, which stress the aspect of experience in enlightenment. *Studies*, p. 422.

60. Suzuki, *Studies*, pp. 97–98, 119, 247–48, 417.

61. See Suzuki, *Studies*, pp. 106, 6–10, 114–42.

62. *Zen Dust*, pp. 190–191.

63. Suzuki, *Studies*, p. 207.

64. Suzuki puts special emphasis on this point, *Studies*, pp. 98ff, 159ff, 418–19, 457; see also his introduction to *The Laṅkāvatāra Sūtra*, p. xxxiii.

65. The 108 questions and 108 negative statements appear in chap. 2, secs. 2 and 3 of Suzuki's translation, pp. 23–33.

66. See Suzuki, *Studies*, p. 107.

67. *Mumonkan*, case 6, p. 53.

68. Suzuki, *Studies*, p. 109.

69. *Mumonkan*, p. 35.

Part Two

Origins and Blossoming in China

5

Preparations in
Chinese Buddhism

THE HISTORICAL UNDERSTANDING OF ZEN

Although the roots of Zen reach back to India, its historical origins are in China. To gain a historical understanding of the movement it is important to have a clear idea of the diversity of the context in which it unfolded. It might seem questionable whether a way of enlightenment is open to historical understanding at all. No doubt the experience of enlightenment itself lies beyond any intellectual categories we may posit for it, but this does not exempt us from the obligation to examine the historical conditions that belong to the phenomenon of Zen as a whole.

In the introduction, mention was made of the controversy between D. T. Suzuki and his Chinese colleague Hu Shih regarding the historical character of the Chinese Zen movement.[1] In the course of their confrontation Suzuki emphatically rejected any historical approach to Zen, arguing that Zen is pure experience and nothing more. Yet when the Japanese scholar himself pursues a careful, scientific study of Zen, and when he cites abundantly from the sayings and anecdotes of the early Chinese masters, Suzuki is in effect placing his readers in a particular intellectual milieu. It can therefore hardly be a matter of indifference to our appreciation of Zen whether or not we try to learn more about these Chinese heroes of the T'ang and Sung periods, whether or not we inquire into their training, education, and worldview, or their customs and ancestral faith. In all this, we are driven to historical inquiry.

Two factors make the historical understanding of Zen particularly difficult. First, Zen appeared on the scene only after a rather long period of development in Chinese Buddhism. During its first four or five centuries Buddhism assumed a variety of forms and tendencies that influenced the entire evolution of Buddhism and its schools in China. The influence of these centuries is present in Zen, even if at times like a hidden undercurrent.

Second, the chronicles regarding the beginning and early development of Zen in China, which have long been held in great esteem, cannot make a strong claim to historical credibility.[2] Written without regard for history, these literary works grew up out of the spirit of Zen and were intended to pass on this spirit. The past is glorified and tailored to fit the ideals of an author of a later period. The historical picture that is drawn by the chronicles, then, requires emendation and elaboration.

Here we shall direct our attention to the early history of Buddhism in China, focusing on the sources of Zen that are evident in these first centuries; we shall also try to acquaint ourselves with figures who can be considered the pioneers and precursors of Zen.

THE RECEPTION OF BUDDHISM IN CHINA

The transplanting of Buddhism from its native soil in India into the culture and life of China may be counted among the most significant events in the history of religions. It meant the introduction of a higher religion—complete with scriptural canon, doctrines, morality, and cult—into a land with an ancient culture of its own. The Buddhist influx into China began during the first century of the common era and so spread that by the fourth century we can speak of a period in which Chinese Buddhism flowered. The enormous task of translating the hundreds of volumes of the Buddhist canon from Pāli and Sanskrit into Chinese testifies to the tremendous diligence of the monks, as well as to their rare ability to feel their way into a foreign culture.

The rapid spread of Buddhism points to a certain perceived superiority of Buddhism over China's popular religion, which had become encrusted with magic and superstition; yet more significantly, Buddhism's persistent influence among all classes of Chinese people, and especially its penetration into the whole of Chinese culture, can be explained only on the basis of an inner affinity with ancient Chinese thought. The relationship of Chinese Buddhism to its Indian counterpart has been variously interpreted. In contrast to contemporary European scholars, who approach the question from an indological point of view and admit only a modicum of originality to Chinese Buddhism, educated Chinese of earlier centuries felt such an inner resonance with Buddhism that they came to consider it, along with Taoism and Confucianism, as a genuine expression of Chinese religiosity.[3]

Given the state of our historical sources, we cannot know in detail just how the widely diversified religion of the Buddha was transplanted into China. Still, modern research into the "Buddhist conquest of China" has opened up a number of valuable perspectives related to our concern.[4] Here we shall pursue the lines that lead specifically to the Zen school.

Meditation has always and everywhere enjoyed a place of prominence in Buddhism. The first Buddhist monks to arrive in China from the regions of India or Central Asia not only brought with them sacred images and books but also their practice of Buddhist meditation. The emphasis on the practice of meditation in Chinese Buddhism is first attested with the arrival in China, probably in the year 148 CE, of An Shih-kao.[5] This "first important known Buddhist translator in China,"[6] taught the familiar methods of meditation found in the Pāli Canon. These in turn were soon mingled with Taoist meditational techniques. Most of the numerous translations attributed to An Shih-kao, deal with meditation (dhyāna) and concentration (samādhi).[7] His translation of the *Sūtra on Concentration by Practicing Respiratory Exercises* explains the ancient yogic and early Buddhist practice of controlling the breath by counting inhalations and exhalations (ānāpānasmṛti).[8] This technique is basic to Zen meditation, and even today Zen novices are generally directed, usually with the aid of a master, to begin their Zen training by learning to sit and count their respiration (Jpn., *sūsokkan*).

Taoism, too, taught breath control as a means to spiritual concentration and longevity. Buddhist meditational texts describing the levels of concentration on the path to composure and liberating knowledge offered further insight. We do not know how seriously the first Chinese Buddhists followed these Indian instructions. What we do know is that they held Buddhist meditation in high esteem. They transliterated the Sanskrit word *dhyāna* with a Chinese character pronounced *ch'an* (archaically, *dian*), or *zen* in Japanese, denoting ceremonial renunciation or release.[9] The form of meditation taught in the Pāli Canon came to be known as "the Zen of the Lesser Vehicle," and that in the Mahāyāna canon "the Zen of the Great Vehicle." Originally the same methods were employed, but, depending on the viewpoint one assumed, the nature of the contemplation was interpreted either in Hīnayāna or Mahāyāna fashion. In this way doctrine influenced both the method and the experience of enlightenment.

The tradition of *dhyāna* is said to represent an unbroken line of transmission in China. Most of the translations of Buddhist texts during the Later Han period (25–220) focus on meditation and concentration. K'ang Seng-hui, a Sogdian and one of the best known Buddhist monks in China during the second half of the third century (he arrived in 247), advanced the cause of the *dhyāna* teachings and composed a commentary to the sūtra on meditation that An Shih-kao had translated.[10] Meditation was practiced by many famous Buddhist monks of the time, not a few of whom retreated to solitude in the mountains. In the Shan Mountains, Buddhist settlers preserved the secrets of the way of Yoga.[11]

Buddhist pioneers in China translated both Hīnayāna and Mahāyāna texts. As in India, both forms of Buddhism existed in China side by side. The first Chinese translations of Mahāyāna texts were begun during the second half of the second century, a process that brought to the fore the affinities between Buddhism and the Chinese worldview. An inclination to the way of negation, a sense of equality and harmony, and a strong feeling for the oneness of reality were elements in Chinese wisdom that also characterized Mahāyāna Buddhism. The use of Taoist terms for Buddhist beliefs and practices not only helped in the difficult task of translation but also brought Buddhist scriptures closer to the Chinese people. But the conformity of word and thought is never complete, and one of the results of using traditional Chinese terms in these translations was that many first-generation Chinese Buddhists misunderstood some important Buddhist teachings.

The wisdom teachings of Lao-tzu and Chuang-tzu—or "philosophical Taoism" as it is called in the European literature in order to distinguish it from "popular Taoism"—provided one of the best bridges of understanding between Chinese thought and Buddhism. During the third century a spiritual movement known as the "Dark Learning" or the "Study of Mystery" (Chin., *hsüan-hsüeh*; Jpn., *gengaku*) came into being. Because of its Taoist elements some refer to this movement as Neo-Taoism;[12] yet, rather than a revival movement carried out by disciples of Taoist wisdom teachings, *hsüan-hsüeh* was a movement of literati who used the *Book of Changes (I-ching)* and the *Book of the Way and the Power (Tao-te ching)*, together with Hsiang Hsiu's *Commentary on Chuang-tzu*, to explore ontological and metaphysical problems. This intellectual ferment mediated a wealth of Chinese terminology to Buddhism through speculations on being (Chin., *yu*; Jpn., *u*), nothingness (Chin., *wu*; Jpn., *mu*), fundamental nonbeing (Chin., *pen-wu*; Jpn., *honmu*), substance (Chin., *t'i*; Jpn., *tai*), and function (Chin., *yung*; Jpn., *yū*), and the reinterpretation of the notion of the "Supreme Ultimate" (Chin., *t'ai-chi*; Jpn., *taikyoku*) and the *ying-yang* polarity (Jpn., *in-yō*). In all this, Buddhists sensed an affinity with their own notions of emptiness, nothingness, and nirvāna, as well as with their speculations on the relationship between the absolute and the phenomenal. Buddhists were especially impressed by the Chinese rejection of duality between being and nonbeing and by their emphasis on the ineffability of reality.

That the Chinese showed a preference for Mahāyāna over Hīnayāna is due principally to the wisdom teachings of the Prajñāpāramitā sūtras, which they found to resonate deeply with their own spiritual heritage. The Buddhist monk Lokakṣema, an Indo-Scythian who came to China between 168 and 188, was the first to translate into Chinese parts of the *Aṣṭasāhasrikā-prajñāpāramitā Sūtra* (in eight thousand lines), one of the basic texts of Prajñāpāramitā literature.[13] About a hundred years later the *Sūtra on the Perfection of Wisdom in 25,000 Lines* (*Pañcaviṃśati-sāhasrikā-prajñāpāramitā Sūtra*) found its way to China from Khotan, a center of Mahāyāna Buddhism in Central Asia. It was mainly through this sūtra that Mahāyāna teachings on wisdom became known in China.[14] The Chinese translations of these two Prajñāpāramitā texts remained the normative sources for Mahāyāna in China even after Dharmarakṣa, an Indo-Scythian and "the greatest Buddhist translator before Kumārajīva,"[15] had produced a second translation. Dharmarakṣa came from Tun-huang and was active during the second half of the third century in Ch'ang-an, maintaining relations with the Buddhist circles of Lo-yang. In these three cities, the *hsüan-hsüeh* movement flourished.

From the third century on the Mahāyāna wisdom teachings predominated among educated Chinese. It was a period that produced many experts in the Prajñāpāramitā sūtras. One Chinese school that followed this line is associated with the name of Chih Min-tu, through whom the philosophy of the Wisdom sūtras acquired great influence in China. He did not understand emptiness in ontological or metaphysical terms but instead as referring to a mind empty of conscious thought.[16] In like manner, the sectarian teachings of Chih Tun (or Chih Tao-lin, 314–366), which showed a marked affinity to Hīnayāna, offered no satisfying explanation of the Wisdom sūtras, for which they were later sharply criticized by Seng-chao, the "first Chinese Mādhyamika specialist."[17]

The first period of Chinese Buddhism comes to an end with two well-known Chinese Buddhist monks, Tao-an (312–385) and Hui-yüan (337–417), both of whom exemplify the Chinese assimilation of Buddhism. Both their careers show the influence of training in the Hīnayāna, and yet both are clearly representatives of Chinese Mahāyāna Buddhism. Tao-an[18] spent his early years in

North China, where he was a disciple of the famous Fo-t'u-teng, also known for his esoteric tendencies. Tao-an's activity reached its high point during his stay in Hsiang-yang (349–365), when a large group of some four hundred or five hundred disciples gathered around him to live a highly disciplined monastic life under his stern guidance. Tao-an knew the old Buddhist forms of meditation and also engaged in devotional practice with his disciples. The product of a classical Chinese education, he rejected the syncretistic method of ko-i (Jpn., kakugi), an exegetical strategy that mixed mundane literature and Buddhist scriptures. Yet he allowed his disciple Hui-yüan to use Taoist concepts to explain Buddhist doctrines.[19] Tao-an wrote a commentary on the *Sūtra on the Perfection of Wisdom in 25,000 Lines*. For him, fundamental nothingness (Chin., *pen-wu*; Jpn., *honmu*) was "the true nature of all phenomena, the absolute underlying worldly truth."[20] This period of assimilation and transition is characterized by an unqualified acceptance of Mahāyāna's wisdom teachings, even though the philosophical systematization of the Mādhyamika school remained alien to the Chinese mind.

Hui-yüan, Tao-an's most prominent pupil, became a monk while remaining a nobleman. Through his efforts Mount Lu on the Yangtze River, a sacred place shrouded in legend, became a celebrated center of the early Buddhist movement in China. Hui-yüan's teaching hardly differed from those of his master, but circumstances forged him into a courageous defender of the Buddhist religion.[21] A fervent devotee of Amitābha Buddha, he was fond of using pictures and visual aids for his meditation. His followers are said to have formed the so-called White Lotus Society. "On the basis of such traditions Hui-yüan is regarded as the founder of the Pure Land School and its First Patriarch."[22] Meditation was practiced assiduously in his circle of followers in the hope of catching a glimpse of the glory of Amitābha and the other-worldly Pure Land through visions and ecstasy. Beyond this, Hui-yüan pursued meditation in order to achieve unity with the Absolute or the source of all things—whether it be called nature, or world-soul, or Buddha. "Meditation cannot reach full quiescence without insight. Insight cannot reflect the depths without meditation."[23] Buddhist and Taoist elements combine in the meditational practice of Hui-yüan. In Taoism the depth of reality is called primordial nothingness; this same reality is grasped by prajñā when it sees through the emptiness of all things. Many philosophical mystics of Chinese Buddhism followed Hui-yüan's practice of reciting the name of Buddha (Jpn., *nembutsu*) at each stage of their spiritual ascent, without sensing any contradiction between metaphysical immersion in absolute emptiness and the highly imaginative, joyful vision of Amitābha.

During this period of assimilation there was steady progress in the adaptation of Buddhist doctrine to Chinese forms of thought, or in the integration of the Chinese way of thinking into the Buddhist religion. Buddhist notions like prajñā, *tathatā* ("thusness"), and *bodhi* ("enlightenment") were sinicized, while Mahāyāna took on the typically Chinese notion of *wu-wei* ("nonaction"). But the deepest roots of this remarkable inner affinity between the basic ideas of Buddhism and Taoism suggest a naturalistic view of the world and of human life that inspires the Mahāyāna sūtras as well as Chuang-tzu, Lao-tzu and other Chinese thinkers. The naturalistic element in Mahāyāna Buddhism found more congenial possibilities for development in the spiritual climate of China than in the country of its origin, India. Where the Indians had been inhibited by their agonizing struggle for salvation, the Chinese, who desired nothing so much as to penetrate the secrets of nature, were attracted to Taoist-Buddhist naturalism.

As already suggested, Taoism played a central role in the reception that China gave to Buddhism. An appreciation of the close relationship between these two religions during the early years of Chinese Buddhism paves the way for understanding how the Taoist influence on Buddhism was later to culminate in the teachings of the Zen school. Legends that link the introduction of Buddhism into China with the symbolic figure of Lao-tzu are of no more than secondary importance.[24] More significant are the lines of contact running between the growing Buddhist movement and the stream of Taoist spirituality that were inaugurated at the end of the Han period. Meditation, in a variety of forms, pervaded religious praxis at all strata, but the most profound influence rested in the spiritual bonds between the Buddhism of the Mahāyāna sūtras and Taoist teachings on wisdom. The "Taoist guise"[25] that Buddhism donned did not remain external but worked deep-reaching changes on Buddhist thought. This encounter with the spiritual heritage of ancient China became a fountainhead that was to nourish the various schools of Chinese Buddhism, all of which were intimately related to one another despite doctrinal differences. With the development of Zen, this spring swelled into a mighty torrent. This does not mean that the origins of the Zen school can be explained simply as a more or less fortuitous blend of Buddhist and Taoist elements. We should rather say that what developed during the T'ang period was a new awareness of the creative energies inherent in Chinese Buddhism, an awareness that grew until it resulted in the formation of the unique meditation school of Mahāyāna that is Zen.

KUMĀRAJĪVA AND THE SCHOOL OF THE "MIDDLE WAY"

The early work of translating Buddhist texts into Chinese culminates in the figure of Kumārajīva (344–409 or 413), whose labors represent a transition to the schools of Chinese Buddhism proper.[26] Born in Kuchā, he entered the Buddhist monastic order in Kashmir and studied the teachings of the Sarvāstivādin for three years. From there he moved to Kashgar, where he assimilated Indian literature and Mahāyāna Buddhism. Shortly thereafter he returned to his native Kuchā and for some twenty years dedicated himself to the study of the Mahāyāna sūtras. By now a well-known scholar, his arrival was awaited in North China but was delayed for some seventeen years owing to local wars that kept him confined in the northwestern border area. After finally reaching Ch'angan, he began what was to be an illustrious career. In the well-equipped translation institute that he founded and headed, numerous Hīnayāna and Mahāyāna works were rendered into Chinese in a mere eight years.[27] But the most imposing scholarly accomplishment of this brilliant man was the translation, in one hundred books, of the commentary on the *Mahāprajñāpāramitā Sūtra* ascribed to Nāgārjuna.[28] The translation of this and other texts of Prajñāpāramitā literature were produced out of his unflagging commitment to the teaching of the Middle Way. Convinced Mahayanist and skilled interpreter of Nāgārjuna that he was, Kumārajīva's energetic and clear-sighted dedication enabled Mahāyāna to gain a conclusive ascendancy in China. His correspondence with Hui-yüan, whose questions about the teachings of Mahāyāna—especially regarding the doctrine of the *dharmakāya*—he tried to answer, shows that even among prominent Chinese Buddhists there was widespread uncertainty about the content of Mahāyāna doctrine at the time.[29]

Another important teacher, Buddhabhadra (359–429), was altogether of another character and inclination than Kumārajīva, enjoying high esteem among his Chinese contemporaries for his miraculous powers.[30] An extraordinary meditation master, he cherished silence and kept his distance from the royal court. On arriving in China, he first lived with Kumārajīva in Ch'ang-an, but soon headed south, where Hui-yüan was glad to offer him hospitality at Mount Lu. By origin and training Buddhabhadra was a Hinayanist. Apparently what drove him from Ch'ang-an was not any doctrinal conflict but the hostility of the monastic community as well as the free lifestyle of Kumārajīva, which he was not able to reconcile with his conception of Buddhist monasticism.[31] Buddhabhadra followed the meditation method of the *Dharmatrāta-dhyāna Sūtra*, which teaches a Hīnayāna style of breath regulation, the contemplation of impurities, concentration on the Four Immeasurables, and fixation on the five elements (*skandha*), the six sense organs (*indriya*), and the twelvefold causal chain.[32] He translated this sūtra into Chinese and lectured on it during his stay at Lu-shan. The distinction between Hīnayāna and Mahāyāna was so vague in the minds of his disciples that in a letter dating from this time he is referred to as a "master of Mahāyāna meditation."[33] Even the sūtra he translated was mistaken as Mahāyanist. This confusion is typical of the ambiguity of this transitional period.

From Lu-shan, Buddhabhadra turned south to the capital city of Chien-k'ang, where he pursued a successful career as a teacher, a master of meditation, and a translator. He did Chinese Buddhism the great service of translating the *Buddhāvatamsaka-nāma-mahāvaipulya Sūtra* (the *Avatamsaka Sūtra*) in sixty books.[34] The translation of this basic text of the Hua-yen school helped Buddhabhadra steer a middle course between Hīnayāna and Mahāyāna. He died in Chien-k'ang in 429. His pupil Hsüan-kao (d. 444) took a position in sharp opposition to the new ideas of Tao-sheng (one of Kumārajīva's disciples) regarding sudden enlightenment. This progressive movement originated in the circle of Kumārajīva's followers, although in later generations proponents of Mahāyāna meditation were also to be found among the followers of Buddhabhadra.[35] This brings us close to the time when Bodhidharma is supposed to have made his appearance in China.

The sūtras of Perfect Wisdom having already found their way into China in the second century, Kumārajīva's translations of the doctrinal tracts (Skt., *śāstra*; Chin., *lun*; Jpn., *ron*) opened the way to a philosophical understanding of the teaching on the Middle Way. Kumārajīva was not a creative thinker, but he was a first-rate translator. As the old Chinese biography says of him, he "loved Mahāyāna and desired to spread it."[36] Through intense study he appropriated the basic Mādhyamika teachings and propagated the Mādhyamika interpretation of Buddhism through his numerous collaborators and students. For all that, he did not establish a "school" in the strict sense of the word. What can be said is that "the history of the Sanron ["three treatise," i.e., Mādhyamika] school begins in China with the advent of the famous Kumārajīva of Kuchā."[37] Kumārajīva translated all three treatises from which the school takes its name: the *Madhyamaka Śāstra* (Chin., *Chung-lun*; Jpn., *Chū-ron*) and *Dvādaśanikāya Śāstra* (Chin., *Shih-erh men lun*; Jpn., *Jūnimon-ron*) of Nāgārjuna, and the *Śata Śāstra* (Chin., *Po-lun*; Jpn., *Hyaku-ron*) of Āryadeva. Some of his disciples had an extraordinary grasp of the Mādhyamika philosophy. Of his some five hundred students, Seng-chao and Tao-sheng are both important for understanding the background of Zen in China.

It is possible that the line of succession of the "School of the Three Treatises" (Chin., San-lun-tsung; Jpn., Sanronshū) begins with Tao-sheng, but more likely that the school "owes its real foundation to Seng-lang's work."[38] In any event, the order of persons and events is not easy to track in the available sources. During the sixth century, the best known representatives of the school are two of the disciples of Seng-lang (d. after 528), Seng-ch'üan and Fa-lang (507–581). Both of them clearly distinguished the Mahāyāna doctrine of emptiness from the nihilistic Hīnayāna doctrine of the *Satyasiddhi Śāstra* (Chin., *Ch'eng-shih lun*; Jpn., *Jōjitsu-ron*). With Chi-tsang (549–623), who composed numerous commentaries on the Mādhyamika scriptures, the first phase of the School of the Three Treatises came to an end.[39] Through the mediation of the school's activity the interpretation of Mahāyāna in terms of the philosophy of the Middle Way was disseminated far and wide. While Kumārajīva cannot be considered its founder in a strict sense, he is clearly the spiritual father of the School of the Three Treatises.[40]

SENG-CHAO

The first great period of Chinese Buddhism—at the turn of the fifth century—produced no more brilliant representative than Seng-chao (384–414), Kumārajīva's brilliant disciple. Of humble origins, Seng-chao entered the school of the celebrated master and zealously embraced the Buddhist path of salvation, mastering the metaphysical speculations of the Middle Way teachings to the point that he was able to combine the wisdom of Chuang-tzu, Lao-tzu, and the Neo-Taoists, with which he had been familiar from childhood, with the Buddhist doctrine of the Great Vehicle. According to the entry on him in *Biographies of Eminent Monks*, he was not satisfied with the wisdom of China alone.[41] After reading the *Tao-te ching* he exclaimed: "This is certainly beautiful, but the realm where our spirit can rest and where earthly pains are overcome has yet to be discovered." The biography goes on to recall how he was filled with joy and wonder as he read the *Vimalakīrti Sūtra* in the old translation (before Kumārajīva). Proclaiming "Now I know where I belong," he thereupon decided to enter the Buddhist monastic order. He sought out Kumārajīva in the city of Ku-tsang, in northwest China, and from there followed him to Ch'ang-an in order to help with the work of translation. The biography points out how he made special efforts to receive personal instruction from the master and thus arrived at the deep understanding that is so evident in his writings.

Among the four essays that make up the collection known as the *Chao-lun (Treatises of Chao)*, which bears an introduction by the editor, the most important is entitled "Prajñā is without Knowledge."[42] It was his first work after helping Kumārajīva translate the *Pañcaviṃśati-sāhasrikā-prajñāpāramitā Sūtra* (403/404) and occupies the third place in the collection. The first two treatises are "Things are without Change" and "The Emptiness of the Nonreal." The fourth essay, "The Namelessness of Nirvāṇa," is only partially the work of Seng-chao. Appended to the treatise on prajñā is an exchange of correspondence with Liu I-min, a lay disciple at Lu-shan. When the *Chao-lun* was brought there by Tao-sheng (408) it was a source of great astonishment to the community. Hui-yüan, the leading Chinese Buddhist of the day, is said to have cried out in excitement, "Truly extraordinary!"[43] The work is unique in that Seng-chao was the first Chinese to capture the quintessence of the Mādhyamika philosophy in a truly Chinese manner, as the words that Kumārajīva is reported to have spoken to his followers testify: "My understanding is not inferior to yours; but your expression is superior."[44] He was referring not so much to the stylistic qualities of Seng-chao's prose as to the way it appropriated Mādhyamika thought to the Chinese intellectual milieu.[45]

In his treatise "Prajñā is without Knowledge," composed in his early youth, Seng-chao has given us a masterpiece of philosophical mysticism. A Chinese interpretation of the Middle Way, the work sets forth the Chinese understanding of basic Mahayana teachings that was to perdure in Chinese Buddhism, particularly in Zen but also in contemporary Japanese philosophy inspired by Zen. According to Seng-chao, prajñā is the wisdom of the wise, a holy wisdom directly related to absolute truth (*paramārtha-satya*), which cannot be an object of ordinary knowledge. Regarding all things (*dharma*) that come to be and pass away according to the chain of causality, prajñā is without knowledge: as the "illuminating power of nonknowing," prajñā enlightens true, nonobjective reality, which is without particular qualities.[46]

Like the Wisdom sūtras, Seng-chao loved negation and paradox. Perfect Wisdom knows and does not know; it is spirit and nonspirit, existence and nonexistence, world and nonworld. True reality is unspeakable; Perfect Wisdom transcends words and concepts.

> Hence the sage is like an empty hollow. He cherishes no knowledge. He dwells in the world of change and utility, yet holds himself to the realm of non-activity (*wu-wei*). He rests within the walls of the nameable, yet lives in the open country of what transcends speech. He is silent and alone,

void and open, where his state of being cannot be clothed in language. Nothing more can be said of him.[47]

In assuming Chinese garb, the Perfect Wisdom of Buddhism, far from sacrificing any of its dialectical acuteness, gained in figurative power. Seng-chao shows how the truth reflects the "ten thousand (myriad) things" like a mirror. The image of the mirror had, of course, already been employed in the Mahāyāna sūtras, but Seng-chao may have had in mind Chuang-tzu's saying: "The Perfect Man employs his mind as a mirror."[48] The comparison of the human mind to a mirror played a role in the competition to determine the successor to the Fifth Patriarch of Chinese Zen and has remained one of the best-loved motifs in Zen literature. Hui-neng, the Sixth Patriarch, introduced into Zen yet another insight that Seng-chao found in the writings of Chuang-tzu. Among the contradictions resolved in the Tao, Chuang-tzu lists the contradiction between true and false. In his commentary on the *Vimalakīrti Sūtra*, Seng-chao, obviously under Chuang-tzu's influence, concludes: "This may be called the state of all pervasiveness without obstructions, and the Buddhist Way of universal equality."[49] Buddhist enlightenment, like the Tao, knows of no extremes—a motif that has been central to Zen since the time of Hui-neng.

One of the Chinese emperors of the Ch'ing dynasty called Seng-chao a "patriarch of the school of meditation."[50] Strictly speaking, the claim may not be entirely appropriate, but the meditative bent of Seng-chao is beyond doubt. He seeks the highest wisdom, which, far from being able to be found in the words of a textbook, lies behind words and must be experienced directly. "The Inscrutable is found in an intuitive experience that opens insight into the Middle Way."[51] We do not know precisely how much progress he made in this line before his untimely death. In his commentary he describes the *samādhi* of *dharmakāya*, giving preference to Mahāyāna forms of meditation over the Hīnayāna practice of concentration. The reprimand that Śāriputra is given in the *Vimalakīrti Sūtra* for practicing Hīnayāna methods of meditation is, according to Seng-chao, "greatly beneficial."[52]

The relationship of Seng-chao to Zen is seen in his orientation to the immediate and experiential perception of absolute truth. Among the commentators on his works are two Zen masters, Hui-teng (before 839), of the Ox-head school, and Te-ch'ing (1546–1623), who is known by the name of his mountain, Han-shan.[53] Te-ch'ing read in Seng-chao's work paradoxical statements that worked like kōan to awaken the experience of enlightenment in him. He records his experience in true Zen style:

> The raging storm which uproots mountains actually is calm; the rushing streams do not flow; the hot air rising from the surface of a lake in the springtime is motionless; sun and moon revolving in their orbits do not turn round.[54]

He describes the excitement he felt when reading the first copy of a new edition of Seng-chao's works in similar terms:

My joy surpassed all bounds. I jumped up and prostrated myself before the image of the Buddha, but—oh wonder!—my body remained motionless. I lifted the curtain and went out to look round. A gust shook the trees in the courtyard and falling leaves whirled in the air. But in my vision not a single leaf moved, and I knew that "the raging storm uprooting mountains is eternally calm."[55]

These passages show the impact that Seng-chao's writings had on later generations of the Zen movement.

Seng-chao is well known among the classical Chinese Zen masters, who often quote from his works. Case 31 in the kōan collection known as the *Hekiganroku* (Chin., *Pi-yen lu*) begins: "With subconscious stirring, images appear; with awareness, ice forms." According to Gundert, these words, taken from Seng-chao's essays, try to reach "the still point that lies before all movements of the spirit, the point at which distinction, Yes and No, has yet to appear."[56] In the fortieth case in the same work, the conversation partner of the famous Zen master Huai-jang (677–744) cites a passage form Seng-chao's "The Namelessness of Nirvāṇa" regarding the oneness of heaven, earth, and humanity.[57] The Zen master Shih-t'ou (700–790) had a powerful experience when he read in the same treatise the words: "Those who understand the world of things in such a way that they see themselves in all these things, they and they alone can be called saints." "The master was so struck," Gundert notes, "that he slammed his fist on the table and exclaimed: 'Saints do not have their own selves, for everything is their self. Who can speak any more of me and you, of myself and yourself!' "[58] The Zen master Ho-shan Wu-yin (891–960) begins an instruction as follows: "One who learns by practice is called a 'hearer.' One who has finished learning is called a 'neighbor.' One who transcended these two we consider in truth to have passed beyond."[59] These statements from the *Treatise on the Priceless Treasure*, a work falsely attributed to Seng-chao,[60] point out the stages on the path to truth. Seng-chao is not explicitly quoted in the *Mumonkan*, but Japanese interpreters see an allusion to the *Treatise on the Priceless Treasure* in one of its kōan.[61]

Seng-chao regards the path of enlightenment as a gradual progression, appealing to the passage from the sūtras: "Three arrows hit the target, three animals cross the river. The hitting and the crossing is the same, but the arrows penetrate in different degrees and the animals are submerged to different depths because they differ in strength."[62] Not only on the way to the truth, but also in its actual comprehension, there are variations and stages of progression. If the knowledge of all earthly things is impossible, "how much less could one in one act measure the infinity of empty space and lift the veil from 'the secret of secrets'."[63]

It is hard to exaggerate the influence of Seng-chao on Chinese Buddhism. In particular, his spirit has left its stamp clearly on Zen, mainly through his description and praise of prajñā as wisdom in all its clarity, "unnameable, undefinable, existent and nonexistent, not real, not unreal,"[64] making its home in the realm of the Absolute. Seng-chao's stress on the cosmic derives to a great

extent from his Chinese heritage. His work represents a convincing statement of the synthesis of Buddhism and the Chinese view of life.

TAO-SHENG

Because of his doctrine of sudden enlightenment, Tao-sheng (ca. 360–434), another of the followers of Kumārajīva, has been called the actual founder of Ch'an.[65] A modification of this claim has it that "ideologically speaking, the origin of the Ch'an school goes back to Tao-sheng."[66] Whatever his role in the actual formation of Zen, there is no denying the importance of his contribution to the religious and philosophical milieu out of which the movement sprang.

Tao-sheng belonged to that early generation of Chinese Buddhists who combined the law of the Buddha with Chinese thought and thus firmly planted the former in Chinese soil. Reared from early youth in a monastery—his first teacher was the monk Fa-t'ai (d.378)—he embraced the teaching of the Buddha wholeheartedly; his *Weltanschauung*, however, was formed by Chinese thought, above all by Lao-tzu and Chuang-tzu. Surrounded by friends, he retained the autonomy of a strong, free spirit. He visited the two main centers of Chinese Buddhism of the time, Mount Lu on the Yangtze River and the northern capital of Ch'ang-an. When he arrived at Lu-shan in 397, he met Saṅghadeva, the Hīnayāna scholar of the Sarvāstivāda school, and studied Abhidharma under him. He did not share the belief of Hui-yüan and his friends in the Western Paradise of Amitābha. He distrusted words and images. He applied the words of Chuang-tzu, "forget the fish-trap and catch the fish,"[67] to the Buddhist way— the fish being reality or the Buddha who cannot be caught definitively in human words. And yet Tao-sheng treasured and esteemed the sūtras, in which "everything has its meaning." "The Buddha does not lie," he said, and thus did not lie when he left behind the medicine of the scriptures in place of himself.[68]

A brief stay in Ch'ang-an (405/6–408) was enough to establish him as one of the four main disciples of Kumārajīva.[69] During these years he took part in the work of translation and, we may suppose, absorbed *śūnyavāda* philosophy under the skillful guidance of the scholarly master of Mādhyamika. His sudden return to Lu-shan in 408 and departure for Chien-k'ang the following year seems to have been brought about by tensions in the monastic community of Ch'ang-an. What he had attained in Ch'ang-an bore fruit in the tireless activity of his later years. His commentaries on the Mahāyāna sūtras occupy the larger part of his literary productions.[70] His treatises *The Non-Meritorious Nature of Good Works* and *Becoming a Buddha through Sudden Enlightenment* were well known.

Tao-sheng's treatise on sudden enlightenment is no longer extant. We know of its contents only through the *Pien-tsung lun* (*Discussion of Characteristic Teachings*), composed by the Buddhist nobleman and poet Hsieh Ling-yün (385–433), who had friendly contact with the monks.[71] The work was composed in the southern capital of Chien-k'ang under the supervision of Tao-sheng, who gave his approval to it. There is, however, good reason to doubt that the work accurately reflects the thought of Tao-sheng.[72] Hsieh Ling-yün contrasts the viewpoint of his friend with, on the one hand, the teaching of the Buddha according to which enlightenment is attained at the end of a long and difficult road and, on the other, a saying of K'ung-tzu (Confucius) regarding his disciple Yen Hui, which he misinterprets in Neo-Taoist terms. In contrast to these authorities, Hsieh Ling-yün presents his friend Tao-sheng as a "Buddhist with a new doctrine" that is supposed to be true, definitive, and superior both to the doctrine of the Buddha and to the wisdom of K'ung-tzu.[73]

What is this "new doctrine"? Or rather, in what sense can the doctrine of sudden enlightenment be regarded as new? Given the divergent and often ambiguous uses to which it would be put in later years, some clarification of this concept is called for at the outset. From its beginnings Buddhism has been a way of enlightenment. In common usage as well as in early Buddhist writings, enlightenment is regarded as a kind of new insight or vision that breaks suddenly upon the inner eye and is appropriated into consciousness. The Buddhist canon has much to say about enlightenment. As the songs of the monks and nuns attest, the Buddha's disciples experienced in different ways the same enlightenment that the Buddha himself had experienced under the pippala tree. The doctrine of enlightenment presented in the Mahāyāna sūtras brings into account the experiential dimension of the discovery of truth. While sudden enlightenment is in no sense foreign to Indian Buddhism, there may be a kernel of truth in the opinion of Hsieh Ling-yün that the Chinese, with their penchant for intuitive comprehension, preferred sudden enlightenment, while the Indians, with their more strongly developed scientific inclination, opted for the gradual way.[74]

It is in fact the case that the Indian Buddhist canon describes the way to the final realization of enlightenment and nirvāṇa in terms of a gradually ascending path. In Abhidharmic Hīnayāna Buddhism, method and system, scheme and analysis cramp the spirit's freedom of movement; yet even there, the uniqueness of the experience that belongs to the nature of enlightenment was never denied explicitly. The stages referred to in the Buddhist scriptures refer mainly to the *way* to knowledge rather than to the *goal*—to the liberating *process* rather than to the liberation itself. The attainment of the goal, the moment of arrival at the conclusion of the journey, is sudden. A further distinction is drawn between the objective and the subjective aspects of apprehending the goal. The goal of the path to salvation is the Absolute, which by its very nature must be grasped as a simple reality, whole and indivisible. In terms of the object, talk of gradual stages of perception is impossible. If there is room for any "more or less," it resides in one's subjective grasp of the object.

Tao-sheng's doctrine of sudden enlightenment applies to the attainment of the goal in both its objective and subjective aspects. Absolute being is by its very nature simple, indivisible, and empty, and can be comprehended only *in toto*. Gradual enlightenment is a metaphysical absurdity. The subjective perception of truth likewise takes place in a single, indivisible act. "The fruit drops when it is ripe"; "The woodcutter halts when only empty space is left"; "When the mountain is climbed, the landscape of the goal appears all at once."[75] This change of view effects a spiritual transformation in which the eye of wisdom is opened to final knowledge. It is as if one were standing before a wall in all one's efforts along the way; the breakthrough itself happens suddenly, without any "more or less."

Such similes make plain the radical distinction between way and goal. Attainment of the goal transcends the categories in effect along the way. In the *Lotus Sūtra*, enlightenment is divided into four stages. Tao-sheng rejects this notion. From the Mahāyāna viewpoint one must say "that these four steps are taken by the believer in one single act of illumination."[76] The Buddha germ must grow in every living being up to that decisive moment when all at once time comes to an end and a new mode of being begins.[77]

Tao-sheng's doctrine sparked vigorous opposition among his contemporaries, and the debate was carried on after his death. In order to understand this whole discussion properly, it is best to recall Tao-sheng's place in the wider spiritual and intellectual context of Chinese Buddhism. His encounters with the *Mahāparinirvāna Sūtra*, the Mahāyāna version of the death of the Buddha, a text that differs entirely from the *Parinibbāna Sutta* of the Pāli Canon, are most important in this regard.[78] It was probably during his stay in Ch'ang-an that Tao-sheng heard of this great Mahāyāna text—little known in China at that time—and came to know of its teaching on the universal Buddha nature and the universal possibility of salvation. On this point, there was much uncertainty among the Buddhist scholars of this period.

Tao-sheng caused no small stir among his fellows when he proposed that even the *icchantika*, that is, those persons given over to sensual desires, can attain salvation.[79] He did not abandon this position, even when an incomplete translation of the Mahāyāna *Nirvāṇa Sūtra*, which denied that the *icchantika* possessed the Buddha nature, was made known.[80] In this inadequate translation Tao-sheng was unable to detect the authentic vision of Mahāyāna. The storm raged on as Tao-sheng pursued his polemic forcefully until he was obliged to leave the capital city in 428 or 429. On Mount Lu he received the news that a second, complete translation of the sūtra (completed by Dharmakṣema between 414 and 421 and brought to Chien-k'ang in 430) had confirmed his views and restored his good name.[81] The integration into Chinese Mahāyāna of this central doctrine of the *Nirvāṇa Sūtra* concerning the universality of the Buddha nature was to have a profound effect on the development of Buddhist thought in China.

The doctrine of the Buddha nature stands in contrast to the negativism of the philosophy of the Middle Way.[82] It signals a highly positive dimension in the religious thought of Mahāyāna. Buddha nature was considered to be identical with the "true self" (Chin., *chen-wo*) and with the *dharmakāya*. All living beings possess this nature and are thus able to attain Buddhahood. The Buddha nature is pure and bright; when it represents the "immortal self" for which the Chinese are always searching, it may be compared with the Ātman of Vedānta.[83] The Buddhist view, however, attributes no substantiality, form, or qualities to Ultimate Reality. It would seem that Tao-sheng saw no contradiction between the notion of the Buddha nature in the *Nirvāṇa Sūtra* and the Mādhyamika philosophy of emptiness that he had embraced during his studies with Kumārajīva. Both perspectives were passed on in Chinese Buddhism; in classical Ch'an they are fused completely.

The idea of Buddha nature or self-nature is endorsed by such eminent Zen masters as Hui-neng and Dōgen. Tao-sheng expressly linked the Buddha nature with sudden enlightenment by seeing the latter as the realization of one's Buddha nature. The affinity to Zen is evident. So far, however, a direct line has not been established between Tao-sheng and the origins of Chinese Zen. Because of his relationship to the *Mahāparinirvāṇa Sūtra,* Tao-sheng may be regarded as one of the spiritual fathers of the Chinese Nirvāṇa school, which was organized into a school only after his death and soon thereafter absorbed into the powerful T'ien-t'ai school.

During this period there was no actual school of sudden enlightenment in China. The line starting with Tao-sheng soon died out with the passing of his two disciples Tao-yu and Fa-yüan (d.489),[84] both of whom worked to promote the teachings of their master. The chief opponent of sudden enlightenment at the time was Hui-kuan (d.443, or at the latest, 447), also a disciple of Kumārajīva. His treatise on gradual enlightenment outlined five periods and seven stages in the doctrinal preaching of the Buddha.[85] Later we hear of a disputation at the court of the emperor Hsiao-wen in 460 between Tao-sheng's disciple Tao-yu and Fa-yao, an advocate of the way of gradual enlightenment.[86] The controversy continued throughout practically the whole of the fifth century. Liebenthal rejects the argument of the Chinese historian T'ang Yung-t'ung that there is a "weak thread" leading from the circle of sudden enlightenment in the fifth century to the beginnings of Zen Buddhism. For him, the conclusion is clear: "There is no historical connection between Tao-sheng and Ch'an Buddhism."[87] This conclusion, as he points out, is supported by the fact that numerous essential characteristics of the Chinese Zen school do not appear in the writings of Tao-sheng.[88]

The early history of Chinese Buddhism provides valuable clues to the circumstances in which Zen originated. Together with the Buddhist Dharma, a broad stream of Indian mysticism, including ancient Yoga traditions, entered the Middle Kingdom. Hīnayāna and Mahāyāna were welcomed indiscriminately with open arms. The fusion of Mahāyāna metaphysics and the Chinese view of life was so complete that the borderlines between influence and originality can no longer be clearly defined. In the wake of the great Indian teachers and translators there followed a generation of independent thinkers who also made significant achievements in the art of meditation. From the school of Kumārajīva came eminent personalities like Seng-chao, whose impact on later Zen masters was probably stronger than anyone else's, and Tao-sheng, of whom the Japanese Buddhologist Ui Hakuju says, "His teaching was to a large degree Zen-like and his influence was very great."[89] We have tried here to pursue a chronological and ideological path to the wellsprings of Zen. This may help compensate for the darkness with which legend has surrounded the original headstream.

NOTES

1. See note 2 of the introduction. The stimulus that Hu Shih has given research into the historical development of Zen is a happy one, though his positions in many cases are unfounded. The inadvertent contribution of Suzuki to the historical understanding of Zen is far more important.

2. See above, chap. 1, note 5.

3. See W. Liebenthal, "Was ist chinesischer Buddhismus?", AS 6 (1952): 116–129.

4. E. Zürcher's standard two-volume work, The Buddhist Conquest of China (Leiden: 1972), treats the first four centuries of the common era; see also K. Ch'en, Buddhism in China. For the approach taken here, see R. H. Robinson, Early Mādhyamika in India and China (Madison, 1967).

5. Ch'en, Buddhism in China, p. 43; Zürcher, The Buddhist Conquest of China, p. 33.

6. Ch'en, Buddhism in China, p. 43.

7. A catalogued list appears in Nj., appendix 2, no. 4; see Zürcher, The Buddhist Conquest of China, p. 33, and Chen, Buddhism in China, pp. 49–50.

8. T. 603, vol. 15. The Chinese title is Ta-an-pan-shou-i-ching (Jpn., Daiampanshuikyō). See Ch'en, Buddhism in China, p. 47, and Zürcher, The Buddhist Conquest of China, p. 53.

9. The Japanese scholar Ui Hakuju believes that the rendering of the Sanskrit word dhyāna with two Chinese characters is a later development. Similar examples show that in early times the final vowel had been eliminated in writing. Hence ch'an is not, as it is often said, an abbreviation of ch'an-na; rather, na is a later and unjustified philological addition. See the preface to Ui's complete one-volume edition of Indo tetsugakushi.

10. See Zürcher, The Buddhist Conquest of China, p. 53.

11. Zürcher, The Buddhist Conquest of China, pp. 140–41, 145–46.

12. See Zürcher, The Buddhist Conquest of China, pp. 86 et passim. W. Liebenthal speaks of Neo-Taoism, for example, in his essay "Chinese Buddhism during the 4th and 5th Century," MN 11 (1955–56): 44–83.

13. On Lokakṣema and his translations, see Zürcher, The Buddhist Conquest of China, p. 35.

14. On the important role of this sūtra in the formation of Buddhist thought in China, see Zürcher, The Buddhist Conquest of China, p. 63.

15. Zürcher, The Buddhist Conquest of China, p. 65.

16. Zürcher, The Buddhist Conquest of China, p. 102.

17. Zürcher, The Buddhist Conquest of China, p. 124.

18. For a report of his life and work, see Zürcher, The Buddhist Conquest of China, pp. 184–204; Ch'en, Buddhism in China, pp. 94–103.

19. See Zürcher, The Buddhist Conquest of China, pp. 184ff, 230.

20. Zürcher, The Buddhist Conquest of China, p. 192.

21. See Zürcher, The Buddhist Conquest of China, pp. 204–39, on the life and work of Hui-yüan. In Buddhism in China, pp. 103–12, Ch'en deals with his resistance to the anti-religious polity of Huan Hsüan.

22. Concerning the term Lotus Society, see Ch'en, Buddhism in China, p. 107.

23. Cited by W. Liebenthal in "Shih Hui-yüan's Buddhism as Set Forth in his Writings," JAOS 70 (1950): 243–259; quotation on p. 249.

24. Zürcher devotes the final chapter of *The Buddhist Conquest of China* (pp. 289–320) to the Buddhist-Taoist conflict of the early period. He reports on the fate of the legend that Lao-tzu, disappointed at the misunderstanding he encountered among his fellow Chinese, left for India and there preached Buddhism. The legend of the "conversion of the barbarians" sparked controversy on both sides. The Taoists considered Buddhism a corrupted form of the Chinese worldview, while the Buddhists saw Taoism as a Buddhist "technique" (*upāya*). On the legend of Lao-tzu's conversion of the barbarians and the opposing Buddhist legend see also W. Eichhorn, *Die Religionen Chinas* (Stuttgart, 1973), pp. 191–92.

25. Zürcher, *The Buddhist Conquest of China*, p.18.

26. On Kumārajīva see the biography in the *Kōsōden*: T.2059, vol. 50, pp. 330a–333a; Ch'en, *Buddhism in China*, pp. 81ff; R. H. Robinson presents a detailed analysis of his method of translating in *Early Mādhyamika in India and China*, pp. 71–95. Liebenthal explains the varying dates of his death (409 and 413) through the established fact that in the year 409 he had suffered an apoplectic stroke and died four years later. He appeals to the study of Tsukamoto Zenryū, "The Dates of Kumārajīva and Seng-chao Reexamined," translated from the Japanese by L. Hurvitz in the *Silver Jubilee Volume of the Jinbun Kagaku Kenkyūsho* (Kyoto, 1954), pp. 568–84. Liebenthal draws the conclusion that Tsukamoto's explanation refrains from drawing. See his *Chao Lun: The Treatises of Seng-chao* (Oxford, 1968), p. 5, n. 17.

27. See the catalog list in Nj., appendix 2, no. 59; cf. R. Robinson, *Early Mādhyamika*, pp. 73–77. A. Wright pays tribute to the center, noting that "the quality and quantity of the translations produced by these men in the space of eight years is truly astounding." See his *Buddhism in Chinese History* (Stanford, 1971), p. 63.

28. T. 1509, vol. 25. The work was completed in the year 405 CE. See E. Conze, *The Prajñāpāramitā Literature*, pp. 41–42, 93–94. Zürcher notes that in this work, "the most comprehensive exposition of the Mādhyamika doctrine," the Chinese found "for the first time a detailed discussion of the nature of the *dharmakāya* and the Buddhology connected with it." (*The Buddhist Conquest of China*, p. 225)

29. Hui-yüan's eighteen letters to Kumārajīva, written between 405 and 409, and their responses are gathered together in the *Ta-sheng ta-i-chang* (Jap., *Daijōdaigishō*, T. 1856, vol. 45). See Zürcher, *The Buddhist Conquest of China*, pp. 226–29.

30. See H. Ui, *Shina bukkyōshi [History of Chinese Buddhism]* (Tokyo, 1936), p. 29; Sakaino Kōyō, *Shina bukkyō seishi [Detailed History of Chinese Buddhism]* (Tokyo, 1935), pp. 502ff. Compare the list of canonical texts translated by Buddhabhadra in Nj., appendix 2, no. 42. According to the biography recorded in the *Kōsōden* (T. 2059, vol. 50, pp. 334b–335c), Buddhabhadra was a disciple of "the great dhyāna master Buddhasena" (cited p. 334c; see the French translation of Robert Shih, *Biographies des moines éminents de Houei-Kiao: Kao seng tchouan.* [Louvain, 1968], p. 91, note 36).

31. Buddhabhadra's sojourn in Ch'ang-an took place from 406 to 411; see the chronology in Liebenthal, *Chao Lun*, p. xii. Ch'en dates the arrival in 408 (*Buddhism in China*, pp. 107–108). The biography of Buddhabhadra tells of a heartfelt sympathy between him and Kumārajīva, and then of a confrontation with one of the latter's students that eventually prompted him to leave Ch'ang-an, taking forty students along with him. See Shih, *Biographies*, pp. 92–95; also Ch'en, pp. 107, 109.

32. Nj. no. 1341.

33. See the reply of Seng-chao to Liu I-min, cited in Liebenthal, *Chao Lun*, p. 90.

34. The Chinese Hua-yen school bases itself on this translation. See *Zen Dust*, pp. 338–339.

35. See Matsumoto Bunsaburō, *Daruma no kenkyū [Studies on Bodhidharma]* (Tokyo, 1942), p. 237. In the second section of his book, Matsumoto presents a detailed but not very reliable account of meditation in China before Bodhidharma.

36. *Kōsōden*, T. 2059, vol. 50, p. 332c. A brief English translation of this biography appears in Liebenthal, *Chao Lun*, pp. 3–4. See also Shih, *Biographies*, pp. 60–81.

37. As reported by Takakusu, *The Essentials of Buddhist Philosophy*, p. 99.

38. Takakusu, *Essentials*, p. 99.

39. Ch'en, *Buddhism in China*, p. 132.

40. The influence of the School of the Three Treatises was greater than Liebenthal seems to appreciate (*Chao Lun*, p. 23). The three treatises, together with the fourth, had a widespread impact on the philosophical worldview of Chinese Mahāyāna Buddhism. The school came as far as Japan, where it is reckoned among the six Buddhist schools of the Nara period (710–794).

41. *Kōsōden*, T. 2059, vol. 50, pp. 365a–366a; English translation in Liebenthal, *Chao Lun*, pp. 6–7; see also the abbreviated version in Fung's *A History of Chinese Philosophy* II, pp. 259–60. Tsukamoto's dating is generally accepted (see note 26 above). A detailed chronology on the life of Seng-chao appears in Liebenthal's work, *Chao-lun* pp. xl–xli. The biography stresses the importance of the *Vimalakīrti Sūtra* for the conversion of Seng-chao. On the influence of this sūtra on Chinese Buddhism in general, see P. Demiéville, "Vimalakīrti en Chine," appendix 2 of Lamotte's *L'enseignement de Vimalakīrti*, pp. 438–455, esp. pp. 440ff; the essay has been reprinted in P. Demiéville, *Choix d'études bouddhiques* (Leiden, 1973), pp. 347–64.

42. T. 1858, vol. 45. The list of available writings of Seng-chao as prepared by Robinson (*Early Mādhyamika*, p. 125) includes fourteen titles. As proof of Seng-chao's importance as a writer, Liebenthal cites the remark of one of the literati of the Ming period: "Among the Chinese (Buddhist) authors, only Seng-chao, Nan-yüeh (Tao-i), and T'ien-t'ai (Chih-i) are first class" (*Chao Lun*, p. vii). Liebenthal's monograph *Chao Lun*, now in its second edition, must count as the authoritative work in a European language on Seng-chao. Of comparable importance is an edited compilation prepared by Tsukamoto Zenryū, *Jōron kenkyū [Studies on the Chao-lun]* (Kyoto, 1955), which includes not only an improved edition of the text with Japanese translation, but also seven essays by the author and six collaborators of his institute.

43. Recounted in the biographical account of the *Kōsōden*, T. 2059, vol. 50, p. 366a. See the translation by Liebenthal, *Chao Lun*, p. 7.

44. See Liebenthal, *Chao Lun*, p. 7.

45. Liebenthal thinks that Mādhyamika underwent a profound transformation in China. He finds "a wall of misunderstanding" (*Chao Lun*, p. 21) between the Indian and Chinese worldviews. "The Chinese Buddhists were all Taoists even if they wrote philosophy" (p. xii); "Seng-chao never fully understood what the Middle Path, propounded in the *kārikās*, meant to Nāgārjuna, its author" (pp. 23–24). Robinson takes the opposite view: "The epistemology, ontology, and theory of language in the *Chao-lun* are thoroughly Mādhyamika" (*Early Mādhyamika*, p. 159). Demiéville praises the philosophical understanding displayed by Seng-chao in his commentary on the *Vimalakīrti Sūtra*—like Tao-sheng, he took part in the translation through Kumārajīva (406)—with these words: "As the commentator Seng-chao understood well, the notion of the unthinkable is central

to the sūtra. All duality is explained as illusory, all logical contradiction is abandoned, the middle is not excluded, the categories of normal thinking are transcended, and all discursive thought is as nothing. The way of liberation passes through the passions. Awakening is rebirth itself. The opposites are reconciled. Truth is 'unthinkable' and proceeds from silence" ("Vimalakīrti en Chine," in Choix d'études bouddhiques, p. 440). This is not the place to enter into the question of the relationship between Indian and Chinese thought. In his writings, Liebenthal has repeatedly stressed the uniquely Chinese nature of Chinese Buddhism. The material he musters in defense of his position merits attention. Even so, Chinese Buddhism, despite its distinctiveness, may be said to have incorporated the essence of Buddhism.

46. See Chinese Philosophy II, pp. 266ff.

47. Chinese Philosophy II, p. 268.

48. Chinese Philosophy II, p. 269, citing from the seventh chapter of his commentary.

49. Chinese Philosophy II, p. 269.

50. From the collection of sayings of Yung-cheng known as the Yü-hsüan yü-lu (1733), as cited in Liebenthal, Chao Lun, p. vii.

51. Liebenthal, Chao Lun, p. 117.

52. See Robinson, Early Mādhyamika, p. 139.

53. On the commentary of Te-ch'ing, see Liebenthal, Chao Lun, pp. 14–15.

54. Liebenthal, Chao Lun, p. 40.

55. Liebenthal, Chao Lun, pp. 40–41.

56. Bi-yän-lu I, p. 507. For an English translation, see K. Sekida, Two Zen Classics: Mumonkan and Hekiganroku (New York, 1977), p. 227. Katō Totsudō notes in his commentary on the work that these words of the kōan came from the treatises of Dharma Master Seng-chao and enjoyed great affection among later generations of Zen. See his Hekiganroku daikōza [Lectures on the Hekiganroku], vol. 5 (Tokyo, 1939), pp. 275–76.

57. Bi-yän-lu II, pp. 142; Sekida, Two Zen Classics, p. 254. Katō (Hekiganroku daikōza, vol. 6, pp. 274–75, 279–80) closes his remarks on the kōan with a detailed treatment of the doctrine of oneness in Mahāyāna Buddhism.

58. Bi-yän-lu II, pp. 154–55.

59. Bi-yän-lu II, case 44, pp. 219–33. As Katō remarks (Hekiganroku daikōza, vol. 7, p. 9), the quotation is traced back to the Treatise on the Priceless Treasure, which is also the source of the first two lines of case 62; see Bi-yän-lu III, pp. 89, 91.

60. Liebenthal surmises that it is the work of a Neo-Taoist of the fifth century (Chao Lun, p. 10); Miura and Sasaki take the probable date of composition to be later (Zen Dust, p. 282).

61. Case 24. See Dumoulin, Mumonkan, pp. 99ff. In his explanation of this kōan, Katō refers to the Treatise on the Priceless Treasure, which he attributes to Seng-chao, and appeals to a dialectics of speech and silence (Hekiganroku daikōza, vol. 14, pp. 194ff). Liebenthal sees in this explanation "no more than another tendency of Japanese commentators to interpret all postures of silence with the aid of Buddhist literature, which is not necessary in every case." See his Wu-men kuan: Zutritt nur durch die Wand (Heidelberg, 1977), pp. 88–89. Elsewhere he notes: "Te-ch'ing . . . was a Ch'an Buddhist. He appreciated the paradoxes in the treatises of Seng-chao as kindred to the problems the Ch'an masters asked their disciples to solve. Indeed, allusions to Seng-chao are com-

mon in Ch'an literature. His influence on this latter form of Buddhism is undeniable" (*Chao Lun*, p. 41).

62. Liebenthal, *Chao Lun*, p. 122.

63. Liebenthal, *Chao Lun*, p. 123.

64. Liebenthal, *Chao Lun*, p. 73.

65. See Hu Shih's "Development of Zen Buddhism in China," in which Tao-sheng is designated the founder of Chinese Zen. According to Hu Shih, Tao-sheng was "a revolutionary thinker" who, under the "nihilistic influence of Lao-tse and Chuang-tse," brought "his destructive criticism" into effect. "Chinese Zen," he argues, "arose not out of Indian yoga or *dhyāna* but as a revolt against it" (SPSR 15 [1932]: 483–84).

Liebenthal's studies on Tao-sheng appeared in "A Biography of Chu Tao-sheng," MN 11 (1955): 44–83, 284–316) and "The World Conception of Chu Tao-sheng," MN 12 (1956): 65–103, 241–68). He approves Hu Shih's research on the history of the origins of Chinese Zen, but does not accept Tao-sheng as the founder of the Zen school.

66. *Chinese Philosophy* II, p. 388. See also Ch'en, *Buddhism in China*, pp. 112–20.

67. *Chinese Philosophy* II, p. 270; cf. Liebenthal, "The World Conception of Chu Tao-sheng," MN 12 (1956): 97.

68. Liebenthal, "World Conception," p. 266; cf. p. 98.

69. In addition to Tao-sheng and Seng-chao, the other main disciples were Hui-jui (378–444?) and Hui-kuan (d.443, or 447 at the latest).

70. A list of his writings is reproduced by Liebenthal, "A Biography of Chu Tao-sheng," pp. 312–16.

71. On Hsieh Ling-yün see the lengthy note by Liebenthal, *Biography*, p. 301–02.

72. Liebenthal, *Biography*, p. 302.

73. See the translation of this passage in *Chinese Philosophy* II, p. 275.

74. *Chinese Philosophy* II, pp. 276–77.

75. These three similes are contained in Liebenthal's translation of texts accompanying the article on the worldview of Tao-sheng, MN 12 (1956): 80, 256–57.

76. Liebenthal, "World Conception," p. 88.

77. Tao-sheng stresses the radical difference between the way and the goal. Enlightenment lies "beyond the confines of being." See *Chinese Philosophy* II, p. 278. Cf. Liebenthal, "World Conception," pp. 86ff.

78. Only fragments of the Sanskrit version of this text remain. The earliest Chinese translation, by Dharmaraksa in two books, was composed in China between 265 and 313 and seems not to have been known by Tao-sheng. The complete translation in forty books, the so-called Northern Text, was compiled by Dharmaksema (?) between 414 and 421 in the northwest capital of Ku-tsang. On the basis of this text Hui-yen and others worked on an improved version that was completed in 453. This latter recension has come to be known as the Southern Text. See *Zen Dust*, pp. 376–77.

79. Liebenthal defines the *icchantika* as "beings who cannot grow and reach consummation in nirvāna because the 'root of the good' (*kuśalamūla*) has been destroyed." He treats the uncertain etymology of the term in an accompanying note ("World Conception," p. 95). According to Miura and Sasaki, the *icchantika* are "persons completely given over to sensual enjoyment, and heretofore considered as forever excluded from attaining Nirvana" (*Zen Dust*, p. 376). They are often likened also to heretics or simply non-Buddhists.

80. This translation, in six books (not mentioned in *Zen Dust*; see note 78 above) was

prepared by Fa-hsien with the aid of Buddhabhadra between 417 and 418. The so-called *icchantika* struggle was unleashed upon his arrival in the capital. See Liebenthal, "Biography," p. 304.

81. The important passage on the universal Buddha nature appears in the twenty-third book of the sūtra.

82. See Ch'en, *Buddhism in China*, pp. 114–15.

83. Liebenthal writes: "In the *Nirvāṇa Sūtra* the final state is described as the blissful and pure life of an everlasting person *(ātman)*" ("Biography," p. 307). Ch'en cites from the second book of the sūtra, in the translation of Dharmakṣema: "That which is without self is life and death; but it is the self that is the Tathāgata. Finite is the *śrāvaka* (hearers, or Hīnayāna followers) and *pratyekabuddha* (Solitary Buddha), but eternal is the Tathāgata's *Dharmakāya*. Pain is the way of the infidels, but joyous is nirvāṇa. Impure are constituted objects, but pure is the true Dharma possessed by the Buddhas and bodhisattvas" (*Buddhism in China*, pp. 114–15).

84. See Liebenthal, "Biography," pp. 310–11, note 110.

85. One can see in this treatise an early attempt at the method of critically distinguishing the stages of doctrine (Jpn., *kyōhan*; Chin., *chiao-p'an*) that were later to play an important role in Mahāyāna Buddhism.

86. See Liebenthal, "Biography," pp. 310–11, note 110.

87. Liebenthal, "Biography," p. 312. The argument he cites is from T'ang Yung-t'ung's two-volume work, *Han Wei liang-Chin Nan-pei-ch'ao fo-chiao shih* (Shanghai, 1938).

88. Liebenthal stresses that in the picture we have of Tao-sheng "essential features, characteristic of Ch'an Buddhism, are absent, above all the emphasis laid on mind, its original, quiet state, and on yogic practice to restore its quietude: non-attachment, non-reasoning, non-purposing" ("World Conception," p. 102). When he goes on to emphasize that the ontology of Zen is grounded in the doctrine of the Middle Way, one is reminded that Tao-sheng also held to the philosophy of emptiness. As Ch'en observes, "To him the ultimate truth or *śūnyatā* of the Prajñā sūtras and Buddha nature of the *Nirvāṇa Sūtra* are the same" (*Buddhism in China*, p. 117). His treatise, *The Non-Meritorious Nature of Good Works*, for example, is stamped with the spirit of prajñā. In judging Tao-sheng, it is important to remember that even though he was no stranger to meditation, he did not function as a *dhyāna* master.

89. Ui, *Shina bukkyōshi*, pp. 59–60.

6

The Early Period

BODHIDHARMA—HISTORY AND LEGEND

Faithful and scholars alike have a heart for exploring origins. But all too often the beginnings of religious movements are shrouded in shadows. Images of founders often get obscured by legend and their supposed teachings detached from the past in order the better to highlight their uniqueness and originality. This is also true of the image of Bodhidharma within the Zen school of meditation. Take for example the famous four-line stanza attributed to Bodhidharma but actually formulated much later, during the T'ang period, when Zen had reached its apogee:

A special transmission outside the scriptures,
Not founded upon words and letters;
By pointing directly to [one's] mind
It lets one see into [one's own true] nature and [thus] attain
Buddhahood.[1]

For later generations these lines represented the quintessence of Zen as embodied in the figure of Bodhidharma. In Zen literature, the question of Bodhidharma's arrival in China from the West (i.e., from India) became synonymous with the meaning of Zen as such, just as the question of "Buddha" was one with the question of ultimate reality. In this sense Bodhidharma stands alongside the Buddha in the mind of his followers.

The stanza contains two pivotal statements around which the entire Bodhidharma legend revolves. The first two lines speak of a spiritual transmission. This is the treasured heritage of Buddhism, the goal of the Buddha's quest: the insight born of enlightenment that he wished to share with all peoples. It is the fundamental conviction of those following the way of Zen that within Buddhism this special transmission has been especially entrusted to the Zen school. The first spiritual transmission, from Śākyamuni to his disciple Kāśyapa, established the Zen patriarchate.[2] Along with the patriarchate, Bodhidharma brought "the seal of the Buddha mind" from its Indian motherland to the Middle Kingdom. In genealogical lists tracing the lineage of Zen from one generation to the next, Bodhidharma is ranked as the twenty-eighth Indian patriarch and the First Patriarch of Zen in China.[3] The story of the patriarchate and the insignia of the patriarch's dignity—the robe and the begging bowl—constitute an important part of the Bodhidharma legend. For indeed, it is legend we are dealing with here, not only because of the total lack of reliable historical data but also because of the very evident motives that lie behind the story.

A further intent of the legendary stanza is to make clear the novelty of Bodhidharma's method of meditation. It tries to show, in as spectacular a manner as possible, that a new beginning has taken place. Lacking previous genealogy in China, the patriarch appears with an originality never before encountered— an originality that colors not only his person but his style of meditating. Of course, the last two lines of the stanza will not strike the reader of Mahāyāna literature as quite so novel.[4] There are solid historical grounds for arguing that Bodhidharma was not really as original as legend would have it. As to the originality that did find expression in Zen—we really do not know when—we shall have more to say later. In the Bodhidharma legend we find the same impulse that is the lifeblood of all legends: to relate something new and unexpected.

Since legends of this sort, in their pure form, belong to the realm of the poetic, they show not only religious concerns but also a creative, artistic imagination. The Bodhidharma legend is no exception, so much so that it is quite impossible to portray it in all its rich detail here.[5]

To sketch but a few of the main elements of the story, Bodhidharma is said to have come from a Brahman family in southern India and may even have been of royal blood. After a long and difficult journey he reached South China. In an encounter with Emperor Wu (502–550), the founder of the Liang dynasty, he pointed to the futility of building Buddhist temples and reciting sūtras. Then he crossed the broad Yangtze River on a reed and for nine years remained seated in meditation before the wall of a monastery until his legs withered away. He bequeathed the seal of the mind—that is, the Zen patriarchate—to his disciple Huik'o. The chronicles report further that his doctrine of a new way to enlightenment aroused harsh opposition. Six times he is said to have miraculously foiled the attempts of his enemies to poison him, and three times to have refused an invitation by the emperor Hsiao-ming to visit the court of the northern kingdom. A later account tells of an official named Sung Yün, who, returning to China from abroad, met Bodhidharma in Central Asia on the very day of Bodhidharma's death. In his hand the patriarch held one of his sandals; the other was found when they opened his grave. Other traditions speak of the patriarch's return to India or of his crossing over to Japan. In several of the accounts, the patriarch's disciples display the general human need to glorify the memory of their dead master.

Is it at all possible to define with any certainty the historical core of the Bodhidharma legend? There are three credible texts from an early period, but all of them differ in content and do little to help determine the sequence of events in the life of the patriarch.

The earliest text is a brief remark by a contemporary, Yang Hsüan-chih, contained in a work on the forty-five temple-monasteries of Lo-yang (c. 547). Paul Pelliot drew attention to this text over fifty years ago.[6] In the temple-monastery of Yung-ning-ssu (Jpn., Einei-ji), Yang Hsüan-chih met a monk from the Western Regions named Bodhidharma, who praised the beauty of the temple, zealously worshiped the Buddha, and claimed to be 150 years old. The text reads as follows:

In those days there was the Śramaṇa Bodhidharma from the western regions, originally a man from Persia (?). He came from rugged countries and was staying in the Middle Land. When he beheld how the golden dome sparkled in the sun, how its light reflected upon the surfaces of the clouds, how the precious bell housed the wind within itself and how its voice rang beyond the heavens, he sang a hymn of praise: "Truly how wonderful it all is!" He said that he was 150 years old and had traveled all countries and visited all regions, but that nothing in Jambudvīpa was comparable with the beauty of this temple, that it surpassed all others, and that there was nothing like it anywhere. With hands clasped, he daily invoked devotedly the name of Buddha.[7]

This rather casual observation does not fit the legendary picture of the enlightened miracle-worker and founder of the Zen tradition. Nor does this widely traveled monk called Bodhidharma look much like the leader of a new school of meditation. No wondrous deeds are recounted and no mention is made of a patriarchate as the vehicle for passing on the mind-seal. It should be remembered that Yang Hsüan-chih's historical account was without ulterior motive; it simply presents a piece of information in passing.

The massive historical opus of Tao-hsüan (d.667), *Further Biographies of Eminent Monks* (Jpn., *Zoku kōsōden*; Chin., *Hsü kao-seng chuan*), is of quite another sort. Its thirty volumes of biographies of holy persons from the beginning of the sixth century to the year 645 constitute a reliable source of historical information. Book 16 contains the first biography of Bodhidharma—a short report on his personality, life, and teaching. The biographical part reads as follows:

Bodhidharma, of South Indian Brahman stock, was a person of wonderful wisdom and penetrating clarity who understood everything he heard. Since his purpose was fixed upon the teaching of Mahāyāna, he quieted his mind in deep concentration. He understood small things as well as things of great moment. He deepened *samādhi*. He pitied this remote corner and guided with the help of the Dharma.

He first arrived at Nan-yüeh during the [Liu] Sung period [420–479]. From there he turned north and came to the Kingdom of Wei. Wherever he stayed he spread the teaching of *dhyāna* [Zen]. With great success he taught far and wide throughout the entire country. But from among those who heard his teaching of enlightenment, he also met with much reproach.

There were Tao-yü and Hui-k'o, who, though young, turned a strong will to matters deep and lofty. When they first met the Master of the Dharma, they comprehended at once where his way led. They served him intimately; they waited upon him and questioned him for four or five years. Touched by their faithfulness, he taught them the true Dharma.

Bodhidharma cultivated the land of Wei with this teaching. Those who recognized the truth followed him and attained enlightenment. His words have been recorded in books and are spread through the world. He claimed to be over 150 years old. He took it as his task to wander and teach. No one knows where he died.[8]

More than a hundred years separate the composition of this biography from the death of Bodhidharma, which clearly makes it a second-hand account. What might Tao-hsüan's sources have been? Most likely he was acquainted with the observations of Yang Hsüan-chih referred to earlier, from which he probably learned the report of Bodhidharma's ripe old age.[9] If he had other reports at his disposal, these have since been lost. His primary source may well have been T'an-lin (fl. 525–543), a disciple of Bodhidharma who is supposed to have edited and written a preface for *Two Entrances and Four Acts*, a work attributed to Bodhidharma. His preface evidently contains some very old materials, for the same biographical notice appears in the *Chronicle of the Laṅkāvatāra Masters* (Jpn., *Ryōga shijiki*; Chin., *Leng-ch'ieh shih-tzu chi*) of Ching-chüeh (683–750), which was found in Tun-huang and dates from between 713 and 716.[10] The treatise reflects conditions existing before the decisive developments that led to the final division between the Northern and Southern schools of Ch'an.

Also stemming from the T'ang period is a nearly identical version of the text of T'an-lin's preface that D. T. Suzuki found among the Tun-huang manuscripts in the National Library of Peking.[11] Suzuki considers this preface by T'an-lin, which was available to Tao-hsüan, the most ancient extant source for the biography of Bodhidharma. Suzuki's claim is strengthened by the verbal congruence between these two different and apparently independent traditions. The possibility of later changes and additions cannot, however, be excluded.[12]

Of the life and personality of T'an-lin we know little. The *Chronicle of the Laṅkāvatāra Masters* provides a fairly credible basis for concluding that he did belong to the circle of Bodhidharma's followers.[13] Although Tao-hsüan does not mention T'an-lin's preface, he does refer in his biography of Hui-k'o to a certain Lin Fa-shih (Dharma Master Lin), who is most likely identical with T'an-lin. About this Lin Fa-shih Tao-hsüan reports that he was a fellow disciple with Hui-k'o under the Zen master Bodhidharma, that he very successfully held lectures on the *Śrīmālādevī-siṃhanāda Sūtra* in Yeh-tu, and that he also wrote a commentary on this same sūtra. During the persecution of Buddhists under the Northern Chou (574) he is said to have helped Hui-k'o hide the sūtras and images of Buddha. He is probably the same T'an-lin who is mentioned during this period as a collaborator in the translation of numerous Buddhist works from the Sanskrit.[14] During his later years this learned monk seems to have lost interest in contemplation. After thieves had cut off one of his arms—he later became known as "one-armed Lin"—he went around wailing and begging at the side of his old friend Hui-k'o, who had suffered the same sad lot but bore it with the indomitable equanimity of a truly enlightened person.

For the most part, T'an-lin's preface is longer and more detailed than Tao-hsüan's report. The following translation follows the text of the *Chronicle of the Laṅkāvatāra Masters*:

The teacher of the Dharma, who came from South India in the Western Regions, the third son of a great Brahman king, possessed wonderful wisdom and penetrating clarity and thoroughly understood everything he heard. Because he fixed his person on the way of Mahāyāna, he laid aside the white dress of the laity and donned the black robes of the monk; he nurtured holiness and quieted his mind in deep concentration. He understood worldly things well and was possessed of both inner and outer clarity; his virtues surpassed the examples of this world. He deplored the decline of right doctrine in the remote corners. Finally, he crossed far over mountain and sea in order to preach [the doctrine] in [the country of] Wei in China. Meditative, spiritual people were converted in their hearts, while resistance arose among many who cherish unenlightened views.

At that time there were only Tao-yü and Hui-k'o. Though both of these śramaṇa were still young in years, they turned their wills to matters deep and lofty. Since they were fortunate enough to encounter the Master of the Dharma, they served him for several years. Reverently did they ask him questions in order to arrive at enlightenment, and carefully did they obey the will of the master. Touched by their faithfulness, the Master of the Dharma taught them the true path.

These four works make up the trusted teaching of the Zen master [Bodhi-] Dharma. The rest—that is, the words and deeds of the master—have been described by T'an-lin and collected in a volume that bears the title *Teaching of [Bodhi-]Dharma*. For all those who sat in meditation, Master Bodhi also offered expositions of the main portions of the *Laṅkāvatāra Sūtra*, which are collected in a volume of twelve or thirteen pages, likewise bearing the title *Teaching of [Bodhi-]Dharma*. These two major works are written in a well-rounded, clear style and are circulated everywhere throughout the kingdom.[15]

Do these three texts—Yang Hsüan-chih's remarks, Tao-hsüan's biography, and T'an-lin's preface—establish the historical existence of Bodhidharma? Not absolutely, but there are good reasons for accepting them as reliable historical testimony. As far as I know, no Japanese historian of Zen has denied the historicity of Bodhidharma.[16] Yanagida ascribes great historical value to the witness of the disciple T'an-lin, but at the same time acknowledges the presence of "many puzzles in the biography of Bodhidharma." Given the present state of the sources, he considers it impossible to compile a reliable account of Bodhidharma's life.[17] In his view, no single founder is responsible for the origins and early development of the Zen movement. Ruth Fuller Sasaki agrees: "Today we know quite clearly that Chinese Ch'an did not originate with an individual Indian teacher and that many of its roots lay deep in native China's thought."[18]

These reports call for further comment. In the description of the Lo-yang temple, Bodhidharma is called a Persian. Given the ambiguity of geographical references in writings of this period, such a statement should not be taken too seriously.[19] Tao-hsüan and T'an-lin speak of Bodhidharma's Indian origins. T'an-lin's account of the third son of a great Brahman king is certainly to be understood as a later addition. And when Tao-hsüan speaks of origins from South Indian Brahman stock, it is not clear whether he is referring to roots in nobility or to India in general as the land of the Brahmans. The two principal sources do not agree concerning the place where Bodhidharma first set foot on Chinese soil. Preferring T'an-lin's report, Yanagida gives some weighty reasons why Bodhidharma must have entered the Middle Kingdom along the northwestern route.[20] This would mean that his activity was confined to a restricted area in North China, and that all other reports of Bodhidharma teaching in North and South China are to be attributed to legends created to emphasize the power and the breadth of his mission. Finally, the information in the last section of T'an-lin's preface about Bodhidharma's concern for the Laṅkāvatāra Sūtra must also be considered a later addition. We shall have more to say later on the relationship between Bodhidharma and this sūtra.

The basic content of these three important historical texts may be summarized as follows: Among the many dhyāna masters who in those days passed across China, there was one named Bodhidharma who was both an ardent advocate of meditation and a pious visitor of temples, and who preached the Dharma and encountered opposition. The earlier sources are silent about the content of his teaching and method of meditation. They say nothing about why he met with resistance. We know of no historically certain events in his life, not even the time and place of his death, although it is generally supposed that he died in 532.[21] Tradition is agreed that Bodhidharma lived to a ripe old age.

THE IMAGE OF BODHIDHARMA IN ZEN HISTORY

The tenuous data that the sources give us about the existence of Bodhidharma cannot really explain the importance he holds for all Zen Buddhists. In the light of these sources, are we even justified in placing Bodhidharma at the beginning of the history of Zen Buddhism in China? Or is he only a legendary person,[22] undeserving of any special attention? Can the history of Zen get along just as well without Bodhidharma?

Certainly we have to admit that the sensational events in Bodhidharma's life are unhistorical and legendary, and yet do they possess a constitutive significance for the development of Zen. In them we see essential elements of Zen that actually existed at the time they were described and transformed into legend. We have already noted two of the central ingredients in the formation of these legends: the transmission of the Buddha mind through the patriarchate and the embodiment of a new method of meditation in Bodhidharma. Both of these factors are inseparably bound to one another and flow together in most of the important legendary accounts. Yanagida calls Bodhidharma an "ideal figure."[23] In fact he symbolized the essence of Zen in the form of an idealized, unreachable model. Followers of Zen can extrapolate from the image of Bodhidharma the inner content of the way to enlightenment.[24]

The Bodhidharma legend developed simultaneously with Zen. The chronicles of the early period touch on different motifs in the legend. Despite the wide divergence in details, the elaborations took shape around a basic core. The legend assumed its standardized, final form in the Southern school amid the divisions and tensions left behind by the stormy eighth century, and it was in this form that it was exported, along with the Zen movement itself, throughout East Asia. The figure of the patriarch was fitted out with stories and sayings to facilitate its inclusion in the golden age of Chinese Zen during the T'ang and Sung periods. [25]

According to the legend, the following conversation took place at Bodhidharma's first meeting with Emperor Wu of the Liang dynasty:

> The emperor asked, "Since ascending to the throne, I have had temples built, sūtras transcribed, and monks ordained. What merit have I gained?"
> The master answered: "No merit at all."
> The emperor replied: "Why no merit at all?"
> The master said: "All these are but impure motives for merit; they mature the paltry fruit of rebirth as a human being or a deva (a god). They are like shadows that follow the form, having no reality of their own."
> The emperor said: "Then of what kind is true merit?"
> He answered: "It is pure knowing, wonderful and perfect. Its essence is emptiness. One cannot gain such merit by worldly means."
> Thereupon the emperor asked: "What is the sacred truth's first principle?"
> The master replied: "Vast emptiness, nothing sacred."
> The emperor said: "Who is this who faces me?"
> The master replied: "I don't know."[26]

The exchange follows the style of a kōan but lacks the typical kōan ending in which the inquirer, a disciple or monk, is brought to an experience of enlightenment. The chronicle states expressly that the emperor did not attain enlightenment as a result of this encounter. The exchange of question and answer is inspired by the Wisdom sūtras, where negation and paradox predominate: prajñā is both merit and non-merit, pure knowledge is empty (śūnya), and so forth. Another version of this particular exchange opens the kōan collection known as the Blue Cliff Records, or Hekiganroku. Openness, unlimited expanse, and nonduality—these are the motifs of the kōan that Hsüeh-tou elevates to cosmic significance in his accompanying verse. Its penultimate stanza ends with the words:

A pure wind invites the universe.
Where will it find an end?[27]

The Bodhidharma legend reaches its high point in the account of Hui-k'o's experience of enlightenment. The historical work of Tao-hsüan testifies to their master-disciple relationship. The chronicles describe in more legendary fashion the dramatic scene in which Hui-k'o is accepted into the circle of disciples. [28]

Bodhidharma was staying in the monastery of Shao-lin-ssu (Jpn., *Shōrin-ji*). Determined to attain the Tao, the highest enlightenment, at any cost, Hui-k'o besieged Bodhidharma day and night with his entreaties. Bodhidharma, however, paid no attention to him. On the 9th of December—the chronicle marks it well—the decisive moment arrived. It was an icy cold winter night. A storm was raging and the wind was whipping the snow about wildly. Moved to compassion, the master looked upon the figure standing there motionless before him in the cold and asked him what he wanted. In so doing, he let him know that one final, decisive effort was needed. Hui-k'o drew out a sharp knife and cut off his left arm at the elbow, presenting it to Bodhidharma. At that the master accepted him as a disciple and gave him a new name, thus designating him as his Dharma heir. With that name he has entered Zen history as the Second Patriarch of Chinese Zen.

This scene, one of the most gripping and powerful in the legend, did not stay locked away in the chronicles but was made into a kōan and used in Zen meditation halls. In simple words, the *Mumonkan* captures its essence:

> Bodhidharma sat in *zazen* facing the wall. The Second Patriarch, who had been standing in the snow, cut off his arm and said, "Your disciple's mind is not yet at peace. I beg you, my teacher, please give it peace." Bodhidharma said, "Bring the mind to me, and I will set it at rest." The Second Patriarch said, "I have searched for the mind, and it is finally unattainable." Bodhidharma said, "I have thoroughly set it at rest for you."[29]

In the kōan, the legend is stylized and reduced to its core. The pacification of the mind (Jpn., *daianjin*, "great inner pacification") is liberation, the goal of Buddhism's path of salvation. Bodhidharma and Hui-k'o, in deep unanimity, are set up as models for the transmission of the Buddha mind.

In Zen Buddhist art the figure of Bodhidharma occupies a place comparable to that of the Buddha himself throughout Buddhist art in general. The "toothless old man" with his large eyes opened wide, has become an archetype capable of unlimited and rich development as an embodiment of the depth and breadth of Zen meditation and enlightenment. But this is a dehistoricized Bodhidharma; historicity is of little significance in the stories that have been passed down. The point at which all the accounts of Bodhidharma crystallize is the legendary story of the quieting of Hui-k'o's mind. The scene has inspired Zen artists to extraordinary feats of creativity in which various motifs of the Bodhidharma legend flow together: Bodhidharma seated motionless for nine years facing the wall or beholding the disciple who brings his own arm as an offering—a bodhisattva emanating both enlightened wisdom and deep compassion.

Attempts to attribute some historical reality to at least parts of this story have not produced any satisfying results.[30] In this episode Bodhidharma is a symbol, an ideal par excellence. The Zen movement of the eighth century drew its inspiration from him at a time when Bodhidharma Zen had reached a high point amid the "forest of masters and disciples." We do not really know at what point in history the style of meditation that Bodhidharma embodies was first developed and accepted. At least the sources that are available today do not offer any clear information. It may have taken place during the time of the early patriarchs, not long after Bodhidharma. Although this period is an historian's twilight zone, it is worth exploring carefully for what it might tell us about this new style of meditation.

Zen tradition attributes six treatises to Bodhidharma. They were later assembled in book form, probably first at the beginning of the Tokugawa period in Japan (1603–1868).[31] Two of the texts, the *The Two Ways of Entrance* (Jpn., *Nishu'nyū*; Chin., *Erh-chung-ju*) and *The Gate of Repose* (Jpn., *Anjin hōmon*; Chin., *An-hsin fa-men*), were found among the Tun-huang manuscripts. The text of *Bodhidharma's Short Treatise on the Four Practices for Entering the Mahāyāna Way*, with the preface by T'an-lin, is the most noteworthy. For a long time it was considered the only authentic writing of Bodhidharma,[32] a view that can no longer be sustained. In its contents, the text is in basic agreement with Mahāyāna teachings of the time. Its form and structure scarcely differ from sections of the *Vajrasamādhi Sūtra* and the *Laṅkāvatāra Sūtra*. The only word that is new and possibly original is *pi-kuan* (Jpn., *hekikan*), which literally means "wall-gaze" or "wall-gazing." In his historical study, Tao-hsüan speaks of a "Mahāyāna wall-contemplation," indicating his familiarity, probably from personal observation, with this form of meditation found among the *dhyāna* masters of his time, especially in the circle of Hui-k'o. If this is all true, it provides us with solid proof of the presence of a new form of meditation already in the seventh century. We may suppose that this "Mahāyāna wall-contemplation" had been practiced even before that, for it corresponds perfectly to none other than the "wall-gazing Brahman" who, according to tradition, was popularly known as Bodhidharma.[33]

The legend also reports a last conversation between Bodhidharma and his disciples shortly before he died:

> Nine years had passed and he [Bodhidharma] now wished to return westward to India. He called his disciples and said: "The time has now come. Why doesn't each of you say what you have attained?"
>
> Then the disciple Tao-fu replied: "As I see it, [the truth] neither adheres to words or letters, nor is it apart from them. It functions as the Way."
>
> The master said: "You have attained my skin."
>
> A nun Tsung-ch'ih said: "As I understand it, [the truth] is like the auspicious glimpse of the Buddha land of Akṣobhya; it is seen once, but not a second time."
>
> The master said: "You have attained my flesh."
>
> Tao-yü said: "The four great elements are originally empty; the five *skandhas* have no existence. As I believe, no Dharma can be grasped."
>
> The master said: "You have attained my bones."
>
> Finally there was Hui-k'o. He bowed respectfully and stood silent.
>
> The master said: "You have attained my marrow."[34]

This conversation, which was also adopted later as a kōan, may well have been modeled on the conversation in the *Vimalakīrti Sūtra* referred to earlier.[35] The basic insights of Mahāyāna philosophy regarding emptiness (*śūnyatā*) and the surpassing of all words and scriptures are acknowledged, and the highest truth is grasped in silence. The episode also served to fortify the position of Hui-k'o over the other disciples and thus paves the way for his succession to the patriarchate. In fact, tradition has it that the transmission of the honors and insignia of the patriarchate took place at the conclusion of this discussion.[36] And so Hui-k'o assumed the role of preserving and passing on intact the true Dharma of enlightenment that Buddha had first entrusted to Kāśyapa. The chronicle follows with the famous verse in which Bodhidharma predicts the future history of Zen in China:

> I came to this land originally to transmit the Dharma
> And to bring deliverance from error.
> A flower opens five petals.
> The fruit ripens of itself.[37]

Bodhidharma's prophecy, already fulfilled at the time it was set in writing, confirms the success of his mission and brings to a close a legend without which it would be altogether impossible to understand the history of Zen.

HUI-K'O AND SENG-TS'AN

The sources for the history of Zen immediately after Bodhidharma are meager. The main font of information remains the historical study of Tao-hsüan, who maintained personal contacts with his contemporaries in the circle of Hui-k'o's disciples. Although belonging himself to the Vinaya school, Tao-hsüan apparently became very interested during the last decades of his life in the aspiring schools of meditation. His historical work includes numerous excursus and addenda that offer important insight into this period.[38] When we come to Hui-k'o, therefore, we stand on solid historical ground.

In Tao-hsüan's history, the biography of Hui-k'o follows immediately upon that of Bodhidharma. Significantly, it is about three times longer.[39] Pared of its legendary accretions, the life of Hui-k'o comes down to a few fairly certain facts. His life spanned the years 484 to 590, if one accepts the legendary length of his apprenticeship under Bodhidharma as nine years. According to the more likely figure of six years given by Tao-hsüan, his dates would be 487 to 493. At the time of his encounter with Bodhidharma, Hui-k'o was a broadly educated man, about forty years old and in the prime of life. As a young man he had studied Taoism and was familiar with the Chinese classics and the philosophical literature of Buddhism. After the death of Bodhidharma he led a hard itinerant life. Tao-hsüan tells of the enmity and persecution that he suffered in Yeh-tu, capital of the eastern half of the kingdom of Wei after its division in 534, through the intrigues of a *dhyāna* master named Tao-heng. During the general Buddhist persecution in the North (574), Hui-k'o fled and hid himself in the mountains near the Yangtze River. But the storm soon blew over and it was possible for him to return to the capital, where he lived another decade before passing away at a ripe old age.[40]

Thus far we have omitted an important element in the Bodhidharma tradition, namely the transmission of the *Laṅkāvatāra Sūtra* from Bodhidharma to Hui-k'o, an event that Tao-hsüan reports in his biography of Hui-k'o. In view of the time span that separates the event from its transcription, the account can lay no great claims to historical reliability. One must also bear in mind that Tao-hsüan's history is not all of a piece, having been adorned with numerous later elaborations. The Chinese scholar Hu Shih was able to uncover a number of contradictions in the voluminous biography of Hui-k'o.[41] Yanagida Seizan, the recognized Japanese authority on the early history of Zen, distinguishes between the basic content of the biography and later additions. He calculates that the second half of the work was written during Tao-hsüan's final years.[42] It includes the names of seven disciples of Hui-k'o who dedicated themselves to meditation and preserved the *Laṅkāvatāra Sūtra*, which they had been given by Bodhidharma as a spiritual testament. Yanagida refers to them as the "Laṅkā masters" or "masters of the *Laṅkāvatāra Sūtra* in the tradition of Bodhidharma."[43] The terms bring together important elements in the Buddhist meditational movement of the time, but how are they to be related? Can one speak of a "Laṅkā" or a "*Laṅkāvatāra Sūtra*" school? Is it right to speak of the Bodhidharma tradition, already at this early stage, as a "Zen school"?

Tao-hsüan uses the term *dhyāna master* (Chin., *ch'an-shih*; Jpn., *zenji*)[44] to refer to any Buddhist monk dedicated to meditation, regardless of origin or orientation; he applies the term not only to Bodhidharma and Hui-k'o and their disciples, but also to monks of other traditions. In his study, Tao-hsüan often reports on *dhyāna* masters without even mentioning their schools. He evidently considers this period of the growth of meditation an important chapter in the history of Buddhism.

In his biography of Fa-ch'ung (587–665?), Tao-hsüan explicitly addresses the question of the relationship between the Zen movement and the *Laṅkāvatāra Sūtra*.[45] Fa-ch'ung was a pioneer for the Laṅkāvatāra movement and maintained close ties with the circle of Hui-k'o's disciples. Most likely Tao-hsüan knew Fa-ch'ung personally. He also knew the third generation follower of Hui-k'o, Hui-man, who with his master Seng-na stands out in the Bodhidharma tradition for zealously promoting the *Laṅkāvatāra Sūtra*. In his biography of Fa-ch'ung, Tao-hsüan describes Fa-ch'ung's active promotion of the *Laṅkāvatāra Sūtra*, which urges the "forgetting of words and thoughts" and seeks to "attain the unattainable," that is, "right insight into the truth."[46] The biography stresses that Hui-k'o was the first to grasp the essence of the *Laṅkāvatāra Sūtra*. In his efforts to preach it, however, he met with opposition from the learned advocates of the Wisdom sūtras, of whom there were many at the time and who rejected his Zen-inspired understanding of Mahāyāna.

The meditational movement of the time, which Tao-hsüan examines in connection with Hui-k'o's disciples, was greatly influenced by the spirit of the *Laṅkāvatāra Sūtra*. Interest focused on the intuitive insight and self-enlightenment urged by the sūtra. One passage in the biography of Hui-k'o, which Suzuki has translated freely, captures the idealistic monism of the sūtra. The passage concludes:

> The deepest truth lies in the principle of identity. It is due to one's ignorance that the maṇi-jewel is taken for a piece of brick, but lo! when one is suddenly awakened to self-enlightenment it is realized that one is in possession of the real jewel. The ignorant and the enlightened are of one essence, they are not really to be separated. We should know that all things are such as they are. When we know that between this body and the one Buddha there is nothing to separate one from the other, what is the use of seeking after nirvāṇa [as something external to ourselves]?[47]

It is impossible to give a clear picture of the method of meditation adopted by the disciples of Hui-k'o and the masters of the Laṅkāvatāra Sūtra. For Tao-hsüan, the unique quality of Bodhidharma's meditation was contained in the word pi-kuan ("wall-gazing"). Pi-kuan meditation, which is quite different from the Indian stages of dhyāna and the "steady gazing" (Skt., śamatha-vipaśyanā; Chin., chih-kuan, Jpn., shikan) of the Tendai (Chin., T'ien-t'ai) school, was worthy of the highest praise. Reviewing the work of Bodhidharma, Tao-hsüan assures his readers: "The merits of Mahāyāna wall-gazing are the highest."[48] But he was not able to explain just what was unique about Bodhidharma's method of meditation, much less to trace the development of this style of meditation among the Laṅkāvatāra masters within the Bodhidharma tradition. In his description of the vigorous activity of the new movement that was developing during Tao-hsüan's final years, Yanagida claims that "the consciousness of the line of patriarchs had not yet reached the surface."[49] Elsewhere he is more specific:

> That we are not able to know the content of Bodhidharma's dhyāna [ch'an, zen] with any clarity is understandable. The treatises on the two entrances and the four acts, which are the only works that are attributed to him, are extremely simple. It is well nigh impossible to decipher the practical differences between his form of meditation and that of the well-known dhyāna masters of his time or to know how his meditation is to be related to the sudden enlightenment that was later called the "highest Mahāyāna Zen."[50]

> It was only later that the fermentation evident in the additional parts of Tao-hsüan's history was brought to completion. After the death of Tao-hsüan the new orientation can be recognized more and more clearly.[51]

In reply to the questions posed above, we may only say that during this early period there was neither a Laṅka school nor a Bodhidharma school of Zen in the strict sense of the term.[52] Only broadly speaking can the meditational movement described in Tao-hsüan's history be called a Zen movement. It was rather the native soil out of which clearly defined Zen schools were to blossom during the eighth century.

Seng-ts'an (d.606), the Third Patriarch in the line of Chinese Zen, is not accorded a separate biography in Tao-hsüan's work. In the biography of Fa-ch'ung his name follows immediately after Hui-k'o's, without any further comment.[53] The names of other disciples follow in turn. Other than this brief mention, we have no certain information regarding Seng-ts'an. The course of his life lies in darkness. According to later chronicles, he served six years under Hui-k'o and received from him the seal of the Dharma. His first encounter with the master is recorded as a kōan-like conversation, obviously a later addition. Because of his great detachment from the world, the epitaph on his tomb compares him to the bodhisattva Vimalakīrti. He is particularly known for his friendliness, magnanimity, and gentleness. The accounts of his final fate do not agree in detail. During the Buddhist persecution of 574 he is said to have fled with Hui-k'o to the mountains and then to have parted company when the latter went to the capital city of Yeh-tu. According to fairly reliable information, he died in the year 606.[54]

Seng-ts'an, who appears in Tao-hsüan's history less frequently than the other disciples of Hui-k'o, may be numbered among the devotees of the Laṅkāvatāra Sūtra. In his biography of Fa-ch'ung, Tao-hsüan lists the names of eight monks, including Seng-ts'an, who he claims discoursed on but did not write about the profound message of the Laṅkāvatāra Sūtra.[55] According to the Account of the Treasure of the Dharma Tradition, a chronicle of the Northern school of Chinese Zen, Hui-k'o passed on the Laṅkāvatāra Sūtra at the end of his life to his disciple Seng-ts'an with these words: "The Dharma that I have received I now pass on to you. In the future you are to explain it to people far and wide."[56]

Tradition has attributed the poem, "Inscribed on the Believing Mind," to Seng-ts'an; if he did not write it, he at least is said to have recited it before his disciples.[57] All of this is highly questionable. Probably composed during the T'ang period, the poem is one of the strongest expressions of Chinese Zen. It is a hymn to the Tao in which the Chinese spirit joins with Buddhist spirituality in praise of the Unfathomable. Taoist influence is evident in the lyricism of the verses, as are the metaphysical notions of emptiness and ultimate unity beyond all opposites that have been the common property of Mahāyāna since the Wisdom sūtras. The language of the poem is at once lofty and powerful. The first stanza, often quoted, reads:

> The Perfect Way knows no difficulties
> Except that it refuses to make preference.
> Only when freed from hate and love
> It reveals itself fully and without disguise.[58]

The hymn closes exalting oneness, where there is no longer you or I, time or space, small or large. The steel-hard final verses of this metaphysical lyric breathe forth controlled, low-keyed excitement:

> In the higher realm of True Suchness
> There is neither "other" nor "self";
> When a direct identification is asked for,
> We can only say, "Not two."
>
> In being not two all is the same,
> All that is is comprehended in it;

The wise in the ten quarters,
They all enter into this absolute faith.

This absolute faith is beyond quickening [time] and extension [space].
One instant is ten thousand years;
No matter how things are conditioned, whether with "to be" or "not to
    be,"
It is manifest everywhere before you.

The infinitely small is as large as large can be,
When external conditions are forgotten;
The infinitely large is as small as small can be,
When objective limits are put out of sight.

TAO-HSIN AND HUNG-JEN

According to the chronicles, five "patriarchs" stand at the beginning of Chinese
Zen history: Bodhidharma, Hui-k'o, Seng-ts'an, Tao-hsin, and Hung-jen. All
the chronicles of both the Northern and Southern schools of Chinese Zen agree
on these five. On the question of the Sixth Patriarch they part ways. According
to the understanding of history found in the chronicles, this unbroken line of
transmission is the foundation of all Zen Buddhism. Yet the sort of literary genre
that characterizes the Zen chronicles offers little assurance of their historical
reliability. For at the same time as they insist on an unbroken line of tradition
as part of orthodoxy, they argue for different points of view, depending on their
orientation and place of origin, and add hagiographical embellishments to edify
the reader. Furthermore, since the records of the chronicles start only at the
beginning of the eighth century, they are of lesser historical importance for the
early phase of Zen history.

   For the historical claims made thus far we have relied on the work of Tao-
hsüan, who was a Buddhist but not a student of Zen. His *Further Biographies of
Eminent Monks* deals with the history of Chinese Buddhism from the early sixth
century to the second half of the seventh century. Unfortunately, his work was
continued only at the beginning of the Sung period (960–1127). To bridge the
320 years that intervene we must rely on historically unreliable chronicles.[59]
Given the tenuous nature of our sources, the sequence of the first five Chinese
Zen patriarchs cannot be determined with full certainty. Tao-hsüan does mention
all five names, and the first three patriarchs, as well as the fourth and fifth, are
related to one another as master and disciple. But there is no information regarding the relation between the Third Patriarch, Seng-ts'an, and the Fourth
Patriarch, Tao-hsin. Only in the Zen chronicles is the succession of all the first
five Chinese Zen patriarchs presented in terms of the master-disciple relationship.
In short, a shadow of historical uncertainty hangs over this rather important
aspect of early Zen history.[60]

   Tao-hsin (580–651), whom the chronicles name as the Fourth Patriarch,
is described as a very strong personality. His biography is a mixture of certain

and dubious assertions. After living for ten years in the monastery of Ta-lin-ssu on Lu-shan, he settled definitively on Mount Shuan-feng.[61] Here, according to the short biography that Tao-hsüan dedicates to him, he spent a very active and profitable thirty years, gathering about five hundred disciples, among them some very famous men.[62] One of his disciples was a certain Hung-jen, whom the Zen chronicles list as the Fifth Patriarch.[63]

At this time, a transformation in lifestyle took place that did a great deal to help Zen to sink roots in Chinese society.[64] In place of the mainly itinerant way of life, there developed forms of stable community life in one location. Zen historians see here the beginning of a development that was to lead to ordered communal life in monasteries during the T'ang and Sung periods. With so many people living together, definite social and institutional changes were bound to arise. The spontaneous alms of the faithful were no longer sufficient to support the monks; local begging excursions were of little help and there were no public funds available. Nothing remained for the monks to do but to go to work themselves. Whether from the very beginning there was specialized work as we find it in later times, permitting some of the monks to devote themselves to meditation while others engaged in housework, administrative duties, or work in the fields, or whether all the exercises and services were shared equally by all, is unclear from the sources. In any event, the preservation of the inner attitude or spirit of Zen in the midst of daily activities was extremely important in the new way of life. Now, not only did sitting in the meditation hall and reciting sūtras have to be performed in the Zen spirit, but the daily duties in house and field were to be undertaken in the same spirit. "Going, standing, sitting, lying," as the four Chinese characters express it succinctly, are all Zen.

This development anticipated later structures in Zen monasteries. The Fourth Patriarch looks like a distant predecessor of later masters who were to facilitate the penetration of Zen into the surrounding culture; he also seems to be a spiritual relative of Dōgen. Still, as the Japanese Buddhist historian Ui Hakuju—himself a member of Dōgen's school and therefore amenable to such comparisons—points out, there are almost no reliable data concerning Tao-hsin.[65]

Concerning his style of meditation, Tao-hsin may be considered the first representative of the phase of Chinese Zen Buddhism known as the "Dharma Gate of the East Mountain," named after the dwelling place of its main representative, Hung-jen. On Mount Lu, Tao-hsin came into contact with exponents of the Prajñāpāramitā sūtras and devotees of Amida Buddha. The contact is mentioned in the biography dedicated to him in the aforementioned *Chronicle of the Laṅkāvatāra Masters.*[66] The text portrays him quoting from the Prajñāpāramitā literature and from a sūtra of the Pure Land school. According to Yanagida, the expression "*samādhi* of one practice" (Chin., *i-hsing san-mei*; Jpn., *ichigyō sammai*), which is already mentioned in one of the Prajñāpāramitā sūtras, expresses the heart of Tao-hsin's Zen style.[67] Similarly, the chronicle reports that Tao-hsin spoke of the identity between mind and Buddha (Jpn., *sokushin sokubutsu*). Even though the tension this set up between the suddenness of enlightenment and the gradual progression of spiritual formation was already present in the sūtras, here it foreshadows the coming split between the Northern and Southern schools of Chinese Zen. The main elements of the doctrine are summed up in a text known as the *Five Gates of Tao-hsin,* which is found in the chronicle of the Laṅkāvatāra masters. The passage reads:

> Let it be known: Buddha is the mind. Outside of the mind there is no Buddha. In short, this includes the following five things:
>
> First: The ground of the mind is essentially one with the Buddha.
>
> Second: The movement of the mind brings forth the treasure of the Dharma. The mind moves yet is ever quiet; it becomes turbid and yet remains such as it is.
>
> Third: The mind is awake and never ceasing; the awakened mind is always present; the Dharma of the awakened mind is without specific form.
>
> Fourth: The body is always empty and quiet; both within and without, it is one and the same; the body is located in the Dharma world, yet is unfettered.
>
> Fifth: Maintaining unity without going astray—dwelling at once in movement and rest, one can see the Buddha nature clearly and enter the gate of *samādhi.* [68]

The text follows the Mahāyāna sūtras in its treatment of the way of enlightenment; its metaphysical content is indebted to the Prajñāpāramitā sūtras and the Yogācāra school. The distinctiveness of Bodhidharma's Zen style is hardly noticeable. Both the Northern and the Southern schools were able to lay claim to the *Five Gates of Tao-hsin* insofar as those committed to a gradual process of realization relied upon the metaphysical statements of the text, while the precursors of sudden enlightenment viewed the sovereignty of prajñā as guaranteeing an enlightenment that can break through unexpectedly and suddenly.

One of the statements of Tao-hsin, reported in a chronicle of the Northern school, marks him clearly as a genuine Zen master. He is said to have delivered the following exhortation to his disciples:

> Sit earnestly in meditation! Sitting in meditation is basic to all else. It is good to sit in meditation for at least thirty-five years, warding off hunger with a little food and keeping the doors [of the senses] closed. Do not read the sūtras, discuss with no one! If you so exercise yourself you will be the first to benefit. Just as a monkey is fully satisfied when it tastes the meat of a nut, few are the persons who bring their sitting in meditation to fulfillment. [69]

The chronicles list Hung-jen (601–674) as Tao-hsin's successor in the patriarchate. He is said to have been accepted into the company of disciples through a kōan conversation, which is hard to imagine since other reports state that he was six years old when he entered the school of the Fourth Patriarch. In any event, he led a long life of tireless practice. The legendary biographies relate how he worked by day and spent the night until dawn sitting in meditation.

Later chronicles speak of his receiving repeated invitations to the imperial court, all of which he firmly declined. To a second envoy he is said to have stated that he would refuse even if he should be executed. Thereupon the emperor praised him—a fitting ending for a legend.

Hung-jen moved his residence to nearby Mount P'ing-jung, also known as the "East Mountain" or the "Mountain of the Fifth Patriarch." Here, with a large group of disciples, he led a community life and practiced meditation according to the methods of his predecessor Tao-hsin. His great concern was to maintain the mind in its original purity. Without excluding the suddenness of enlightenment, he seems to have preferred the gradual, progressive concentration of the mind.

Among the Tun-huang manuscripts, a text bearing the title *Saijōjō-ron* (Chin., *Tsui-shang-ch'en lun*) is attributed to Hung-jen, though its actual authorship is unclear.[70] This short treatise quotes various sūtras and follows the *Amitāyur-dhyāna Sūtra* in advising an upright sitting position with closed eyes and mouth. The sūtra also recommends contemplating the form of the sun and warns against distracting images during nocturnal practices.[71] The visionary meditations of Amida disciples on the Pure Land and on Amida Buddha offer instructions for the control of mind similar to those of Zen meditation. Hung-jen is said to have given the following instructions to his disciples:

> Look to where the horizon disappears beyond the sky and behold the figure *one*. This is a great help. It is good for those beginning to sit in meditation, when they find their mind distracted, to focus their mind on the figure *one*.[72]

The Chinese character for *one* consists of a single horizontal line and, like the contemplation of the form of the sun mentioned in the sūtra, it represents the line beyond the horizon where sky and earth touch. This high regard for the number one, which is characteristic of all spirituality in the Far East, inspired the Mahāyāna exaltation of the single Buddha nature and the "one vehicle." In Zen, the One that is experienced in enlightenment is the nature of the mind itself in its identity with the Buddha nature.[73]

With Hung-jen the early period of Chinese Zen Buddhism comes to an end.[74] The most significant outcome of this period was the clear move beyond Indian *dhyāna* meditation. The central focus of master and disciple alike was the realization of the absolute Buddha reality in the experience of enlightenment. The sūtras continued to be held in high regard and were diligently read, studied, and recited in cultic practices. But it was more in meditation than in study that efforts were made to appropriate the sūtras. Texts from this period give evidence of logical thought schooled in the canonical writings. Paradoxical twists of language are relatively rare, and there is no trace of artificial devices like kōan, shouting, caning, and grimacing. The Zen communities that formed around the two enlightened patriarchs Tao-hsin and Hung-jen came to be known as "The Dharma Gate of the East Mountain" or "The Pure Gate of the East Mountain," and as such were highly esteemed. During the sixty years of monastic communal life an extension of Zen into social life occurred. Increasingly, Zen proved itself to be a formative element in Chinese life and culture.

The rich diversity of spiritual and intellectual elements that flowed together during this early period of Zen Buddhism were the harbinger of conflicts to appear in the following two or three generations. Still, it would have been absolutely impossible to forecast the dramatic nature that these conflicts would assume. Even today, the task of unsnarling that hopeless tangle of unfortunate embroilments, both personal and ideological, is complicated by the obscurity of the historical sources. The period of division between the Northern and Southern schools is one of the darkest in the history of Chinese Zen Buddhism.

NOTES

1. This verse is first found as a fixed formula in the *Sōtei jion* (Chin., *Tsu-t'ing shih-yüan*), dating from 1108. See *Zen Dust*, pp. 228–30; *Essays* I, p. 176.

2. See chapter 1.

3. For relevant Zen chronicles see above, chap. 1, note 5.

4. Miura and Sasaki trace the expression "to see into your own nature and attain Buddhahood" back to a Chinese commentary on the *Nirvāṇa Sūtra* (*Zen Dust*, p. 229).

5. The legend is common to the various Zen chronicles, though different accounts do not agree on all the details. Historical conditions played a formative role in the composition of the various versions.

6. See his *Notes sur quelques artistes des Six Dynasties et des T'ang*, TP 22 (1923): 223ff. Pelliot discovered the remark referred to here in the rather voluminous text of the *Lo-yang ch'ieh-lan-chi* (ca. 547), T. 2092, vol. 51, p. 1000b. See the references in my essay, "Bodhidharma und die Anfänge des Ch'an-Buddhismus," MN 7 (1951): 67–83.

7. See "Bodhidharma und die Anfänge des Ch'an Buddhismus," p. 69.

8. T. 2060, vol. 50, p. 551b,c.

9. In addition to the historical work of Tao-hsüan and the *Lo-yang ch'ieh-lan-chi*, an allusion to Bodhidharma's ripe old age of 150 years is also made in a document found in Tun-huang entitled *Rekidai hōbōki* (Chin., *Li-tai fa-pao-chi*), T. 2075, vol. 51, p. 181a.

10. T. 2837, vol. 85, p. 1285a,b. The text shows minor discrepancies from the historical work of Tao-hsüan, T. 2060, vol. 50, p. 551c. The *Keitoku dentōroku* contains the text under the title "Bodhidharma's Brief Treatise on the Four Works for Entering into the Way of Mahāyāna" (T. 2076, vol. 51, p. 458b,c).

11. This and related materials may be found in the privately published volumes entitled *Kōkan shōshitsu issho oyobi kaisetsu* and *Furoku: Daruma no zempō to shisō oyobi sono ta* (Osaka, 1938). The text of the *Two Entrances* is also to be found in the *Shōshitsu rokumon* (T. 2009).

12. Both H. Ui (*Zenshūshi* I, pp. 2ff) and Suzuki (*Furoku*, p. 4ff, n. 11) juxtapose the report of Tao-hsüan and the preface of T'an-lin in parallel columns in order to point to discrepancies and coincidences between the two.

13. See above note 10.

14. In an essay entitled "Bodhidharma-den no kenkyū" (SK 11 [1932]: 444–58) Hayashi Taiun examines the preface of T'an-lin and tries to discern his identity from it. In his

view, the expert on the Śrīmālādevī-siṃhanāda Sūtra and the collaborator on numerous translations of the time and the disciple of Bodhidharma are one and the same person. In this vein, see also Zenshūshi I, pp. 61–62.

15. T. 2837, vol. 85, pp. 1284c–1285b.

16. Nor does Hu Shih. See his study, "Development of Zen Buddhism in China," pp. 475–505; on Bodhidharma, see pp. 486–87.

17. Chūgoku zenshūshi, p. 12.

18. Chūgoku zenshūshi, pp. 8ff. Sasaki's concurring opinion may be found in her foreword to the unpublished English translation of "Bodhidharma und die Anfänge des Ch'an Buddhismus" (see above, note 6).

19. Ui takes strong issue with the claim that Bodhidharma came from Persia; see Zenshūshi I, pp. 7–8.

20. Chūgoku zenshūshi, p. 12.

21. The inscription on Bodhidharma's tomb, composed by Emperor Wu-ti, gives the date as 536. But according to Hui-k'o's biographical account in the historical work of Tao-hsüan, Bodhidharma passed away before the T'ien-ping period (534–537). See my "Bodhidharma und die Anfänge des Ch'an Buddhismus," p. 82.

22. In his translation of the Mumonkan, W. Liebenthal lists him among the "legendary figures" (Wu-men kuan: Zutritt nur durch die Wand, p. 142).

23. Chūgoku zenshūshi, p. 11. In his view, the legends are an "expression of the idea of Zen at the time of their origination." A similar position is taken by T. Hirata who writes: "In accounts of Bodhidharma later generations forged an image to express the Zen ideal." See his commentary to the Japanese translation of the Mumonkan (Tokyo, 1969), p. 148.

24. Yanagida holds that Bodhidharma's voyage from the West points to the essence of Zen and therefore "must be submitted to unlimited historical examination" (Chūgoku zenshūshi, p. 12).

25. The Bodhidharma legend is found in the chronicles of the Northern and Southern schools of Zen Buddhism as well as in the most important of the kōan collections.

26. Keitoku dentōroku, book 3, T. 2076, vol. 51, p. 219a.

27. Bi-yän-lu I, p. 44.

28. The most detailed picture of the episode, and that on which the account in the text is based, is given in the Keitoku dentōroku, T. 2076, vol. 51, p. 219b.

29. Case 41.

30. Ui resists modern scholars who, in the name of sound human rationality, dismiss a priori the story of Hui-k'o's offering his arm. Such scholars have obviously been unable to imagine the seriousness with which disciples longed for the Dharma in those days (Zenshūshi I, pp. 37–38). Yanagida also defends the possibility of the event (Chūgoku zenshūshi, p. 16).

31. Shōshitsu rokumon (shū) [Bodhidharma's Six Gates]. Shōshitsu (Chin., Shao-shih), the name of the peak of Mount Sung, represents Bodhidharma. See the detailed description of the collection in Zen Dust, pp. 398–99.

32. For an English translation of The Two Ways of Entrance based on the text in the Keitoku dentōroku, see Essays III, pp. 199–204.

33. Yanagida holds that Tao-hsüan grasped how Bodhidharma's "wall-gazing" differed from other Mahayanist methods of meditation (Shoki, pp. 14–15). In this connection, Yanagida speaks of "new activities of Zen followers."

34. *Keitoku dentōroku*, T. 2076, vol. 51, p. 219b,c.

35. See chapter 4.

36. The *Keitoku dentōroku* mentions only the handing over of the robe; the text of the *Denbō shōshūki* (Chin., *Ch'uan-fa cheng-tsung-chi*) names both insignia, namely the robe and the begging bowl (T. 2078, vol. 51, p. 743a).

37. *Keitoku dentōroku*, T. 2076, vol. 51, p. 219c.

38. Tao-hsüan completed his history in 645 and died in 667. A ten-volume appendix compiled during these years was either integrated into his *Zoku kōsōden* or incorporated in a later work, *Sō kōsōden* (*Biographies of Eminent Monks Compiled during the Sung Period*; Chin., *Sung kao-seng-chuan*). T. 2061. See *Shoki*, p. 7.

39. T. 2060, vol. 50, pp. 551c,552a–c.

40. See *Zen Dust*, pp. 240–43, which contains passages from volume 3 of the *Keitoku dentōroku*.

41. See the Japanese summary of the research of Hu Shih on Chinese Zen Buddhism, *Shina zengaku no hensen* [*Transformations in the Study of Chinese Zen*] (Tokyo, 1936), p. 76.

42. *Shoki*, p. 21.

43. *Shoki*, pp. 21ff, 26.

44. "At this time Buddhist monks who gave instruction in meditation were known as *zenji* (*ch'an-shih*) or meditation masters; those who studied and lectured on the scriptures were called *hōshi* (*fa-shih*) or dharma masters. Later, the title 'Zenji', with the meaning of 'Zen Master,' was limited to eminent monks of the Zen sect" (*Zen Dust*, p. 243).

45. *Shoki*, pp. 15, 22ff, 28. See also *Chūgoku zenshūshi*, pp. 18ff. The biography of Fa-ch'ung appears in T. 2060, vol. 50, p. 666; see also Hu Shih, "The Development of Zen Buddhism in China," pp. 488–89.

46. T. 2060, vol. 50, p. 666b.

47. *Essays* I, pp. 194–95.

48. T. 2060, vol. 50, p. 596c.

49. *Shoki*, p. 15.

50. *Shoki*, p. 14.

51. On developments during the final years of Tao-hsüan's life see the detailed account of Yanagida, *Shoki*, p. 15.

52. Ui does not accept the view that "the line of Bodhidharma is identical to the line of the Laṅkā school," although such a school existed (*Zenshūshi* I, p. 25). In a similar vein, see also *Chūgoku zenshūshi*, pp. 16ff; *Shoki*, pp. 14–15. We cannot speak of a Laṅkāvatāra school possessed of a clear self-image at the time of Hui-k'o and his disciples; it is only later that the school comes clearly into its own. Noteworthy in this regard is the remark of Suzuki: "The study of the *Laṅkāvatāra*, as especially related to Zen, was kept up to the time of Fa-ch'ung and Tao-hsüan, who were contemporaries, and this was about the time of Hung-jen, the Fifth Patriarch of Chinese Zen Buddhism. Judging from these historical facts we know that the intellectual study and the practical discipline went on side by side, and that there were as yet none of the clear distinctions which later developed distinguishing Zen after Hui-neng, the Sixth Patriarch, from what preceded him." See his *Studies in the Laṅkāvatāra Sūtra*, p. 54.

53. T. 2060, vol. 50, p. 666b.

54. The year before his death, Fang Kuan (697–763) was commissioned by Shen-hui to compose an epitaph for Seng-ts'an, perhaps in order to compensate for the absence of a

biography by Tao-hsüan. The uncertainty surrounding the grave of the Third Patriarch caused unrest in Zen circles. In a later work, Hōrinden (Chin., Pao-lin chuan), mention is made of the Chinese official Li Ch'ang finding the grave in a spot in Shu-chou (745 or 746). See Yampolsky, pp. 50–51. In consideration of the inscription of Fang Kuan, Tu-ku Chi composed an epitaph for Seng-ts'an that makes use of a tombstone inscription of Hsüeh Tao-heng from the Sui period, since lost. He was obviously influenced by the adherents of the Northern school, since he placed Shen-hsiu and P'u-chi over Hui-neng, a late expression of enmity. On the foregoing, see Shoki, pp. 324–25. See also Yanagida's charts showing diverging inscriptions of the six Chinese Zen patriarchs on p. 324 of this same work. On the traditional biography of Seng-ts'an, see Ui, Zenshūshi, pp. 63ff.

55. T. 2060, vol. 50, p. 666b.

56. Den hōbōki (Chin., Ch'uan fa-pao chi), T. 2838, vol. 85. This text, composed around 713, is a chronicle of the Northern school. See Shoki, pp. 47ff; the comment on the presentation of the Laṅkāvatāra Sūtra is cited on p. 53. In an appendix dealing with sources, Yanagida edits the text of the Den hōbōki (Shoki, p. 565).

57. Shinjinmei (Chin., Hsin-hsin-ming), T. 2010, vol. 48, pp. 376b–377a. The poem is composed of 624 characters. An English translation appears in Essays I, pp. 196–201; for a free German rendering, see S. Ōhasama and A. Faust, Zen: der lebendige Buddhismus in Japan, pp. 64–71. The earliest report on the origin of the song is to be found in the collection of sayings of Pai-chang (720–814). See also Shoki, p. 72.

58. Essays I, pp. 196–97; for final verses, see pp. 200–01.

59. Yanagida speaks repeatedly of the unreliability of the Zen chronicles, though he does not for that reason deny them all historical value. He nuances his position carefully: "The writings on the history of the transmission (of the Buddha mind in Zen [tōshi, literally, "history of the transmission of the lamp"]) do not contain merely historical facts but also an expression of a religious tradition of faith. To speak of them as having been fabricated in this way is still to speak of them as born in history. To treat all transmitted episodes as invention is still to attribute to them the ground of that inventiveness. We must rather conclude, therefore, that the meaning of what is reported here is episodic, even when it touches on historical facticity. To reject these episodes as unhistorical and simply to dismiss them is to disqualify oneself for the reading of the chronicles about the transmission" (Shoki, pp. 17–18). From this follows the necessity of careful examination of all the particular Zen chronicles for their historical relevance (pp. 19–20).

60. The connecting line between Seng-ts'an and Tao-hsin is only established later with Hung-jen's disciple Fa-ju (638–689); Tao-hsüan lists Hung-jen as one of the numerous disciples of Tao-hsin (Shoki, pp. 22, 25, 33ff).

61. The name of a mountain in the modern-day province of Hupei (the name hints at twin peaks). The eastern peak, P'ing-jung, on which Hung-jen established his residence and which is also known as the Mountain of the Yellow Plum (Huang-mei-shan; Jpn., Ōbaizan), is famous in the Zen chronicles as "East Mountain" or the "Mountain of the Fifth Patriarch." See Chūgoku zenshūshi, p. 22; Zenshūshi I, pp. 82–83; Zen Dust, pp. 162, 168, 186.

62. T. 2060, vol. 50, p. 606b. Later accounts such as the Rekidai hōbōki give higher figures (Shoki, p. 35). Tao-hsüan's biography of Tao-hsin (T. 2060, vol. 50, p. 606) belongs to the additional sections of his historical work (see Shoki, p. 63); a somewhat different and later biography can be found in the Den hōbōki (see above, note 56; Shoki, p. 54).

63. The basis for the title of patriarch develops with the uninterrupted line of succession among the disciples of Bodhidharma (see above, note 60).

64. For detailed information, see Zenshūshi 1, pp. 84ff, 87ff; see also Shoki, p. 9.

65. Zenshūshi 1, p. 85.

66. T. 2837, vol. 85, p. 1287.

67. Chūgoku zenshūshi, p. 24. In his presentation, Yanagida follows the chronicle of the Laṅkāvatāra masters. Despite its onesidedness, this text, which dates from the start of the eighth century, is of relative historical value for early Chinese Zen, unlike the chronicles of the Sung period.

68. T. 2837, vol. 85, p. 1288a. I am following Yanagida's rendition of the text into modern Japanese, which involves occasional substitution of the Chinese characters.

69. Cited in Shoki, p. 25. Yanagida refers to this text as "the oldest proof for the practice of meditation in a seated position [zazengi]." Zazengi (Chin., tso-ch'an-i) was later to become a favorite literary genre in Zen Buddhism.

70. T. 2011, vol. 48. The text there appears under the name of Shūshinyō-ron (Chin., Hsiu-hsin-yao lun), a collection of talks by Hung-jen written down by one of the disciples or someone in the circle of Fa-ju's disciples. See Chūgoku zenshūshi, p. 25; Shoki, p. 80.

71. T. 2011, vol. 48, p. 378a,b. Zen masters later speak of the turbidity of illusory thoughts (mōsō) as appearances from the "realm of the devil" (makyō).

72. Cited in Chūgoku zenshūshi, p. 26.

73. Chūgoku zenshūshi, pp. 26–27.

74. Not all followers of the way who gathered about the two masters on the East Mountain may have engaged exclusively in the practice of pure Zen. We know of disciples of Hung-jen who devoted themselves to the recitation of the name of Amitābha (Amida) Buddha. See Zen Dust, p. 175. Hung-jen's biography appears in the Sō kōsōden, T. 2061, vol. 50, p. 754a,b. See note 38 above.

7

The Split between the Northern and Southern Schools

THE "SUDDENNESS" OF THE SOUTH AND "GRADUALNESS" OF THE NORTH

If research into the early period of Chinese Zen is able to confirm the historicity of its "founder," Bodhidharma, it does little to dispel the darkness surrounding his creative accomplishments. Thanks to the principal historical source for this period—the work of Tao-hsüan—we also have important information concerning the first three patriarchs and their succession. The uniqueness of the meditation practiced among Bodhidharma's followers soon became evident. Around the two patriarchs Tao-hsin and Hung-jen, who carried on the Bodhidharma tradition faithfully though not entirely without deviation, the Zen movement of the East Mountain took shape and began to pervade Chinese society. All these developments, however, are no more than the preface to the real history of Zen in China.

Until quite recently the fascinating and dramatic interplay of events that led to the division of Zen has been known only from the perspective of the Southern school. The chronicles of the Southern school offer a reasonable, coherent, and only occasionally contradictory report of the split. Very recently, however, their reliability has been placed in serious question by the discovery of the Tun-huang manuscripts, which at long last let the other side have its say. Today, scholars are busying themselves with the many inconsistencies these new texts have brought to light.

Traditional, semilegendary Zen history summarizes the outcome of these bitter controversies in a formula made up of four characters, pronounced in Japanese *nanton hokuzen* (Chin. *nan-tun pei-chien*, literally, "suddenness of the South, gradualness of the North"). Contrary to first impressions, the formula has little to do with geography. Like the general designations of Mahāyāna ("great vehicle") and Hīnayāna ("little vehicle"), the formula carries with it a value judgement. According to the mainstream of later Zen, not only is sudden enlightenment incomparably superior to gradual experience but it represents true Zen—indeed, it is the very touchstone of authentic Zen. Still, the great importance that later followers of Zen put on history and on the unbroken line of transmission leading back to their founder Bodhidharma should be borne in mind. This was why the five authoritative Zen chronicles of the Sung period constituted the direct historical line supporting the Zen school, which they were convinced represented the culmination not only of Buddhist meditational practices but of the entire Buddhist way.[1]

Resources recently made available present a more differentiated historical picture. The Northern school of Chinese Zen does not at all appear to be the insignificant phenomenon suggested by the legendary story of the young boy Lu and the enlightened verses that enabled him to become the Sixth Patriarch. The Northern movement was held in high regard for many decades after the time of these alleged events. Moreover, it is not at all clear whether the movement's decline was directly precipitated by the well known debate set up by the champion of the Southern school, Shen-hui (670–762)[2] or whether it gradually died off by itself. In any case, in order to understand the history of Zen in China it is essential to examine carefully the origin and development of the Northern school before the beginning of the decisive struggle.

THE NORTHERN SCHOOL

The Northern movement took clear shape as a school only after running into opposition from Shen-hui and his followers.[3] The historical sources inform us that not long after the death of the Fifth Patriarch, Hung-jen, a number of his disciples were carrying on successful activities in the vicinity of the capital cities of Ch'ang-an and Lo-yang. The most notable of them was Fa-ju (638–689), "the first pioneer" and "actual founder" of the Northern school.[4] His own master, Hui-ming, had sent him to the patriarch of the East Mountain in order to learn the true Zen style of meditation. There Fa-ju attained enlightenment with Hung-jen, and Zen literature testifies that he received the Dharma transmission from him.[5] As a disciple, he addressed his master as "patriarch," marking the first clear recognition of the generational line of Bodhidharma Zen. Bridging the gap after the Third Patriarch, Seng-ts'an and the Fourth Patriarch, Tao-hsin, the *Den hōbōki* lists Fa-ju as the Sixth Patriarch and Shen-hsiu (606?–706) as the Seventh Patriarch.[6]

Fa-ju lived for sixteen years with Hung-jen on the East Mountain. After the death of his master, he first traveled south, but then chose to work in the region of Lo-yang. Because of Fa-ju, the monastery of Shao-lin-ssu (Jpn., *Shōrin-ji*, constructed in 496), which is associated with many famous names of Chinese Buddhism and played an important role in the Bodhidharma legend, again rose to prominence. During Fa-ju's short stay at the Shao-lin-ssu, the temple cloister became the center of the growing Zen movement. The chronicles report on the activities of other disciples of Hung-jen and on the spread of Zen in North China. Particular mention is made of Hui-an (584–709), Chih-hsien (609–702), and Hsüan-tse. There is an epitaph for Fa-ju on Mount Sung commemorating the success of his pioneering work.[7]

Fa-ju and his colleagues mark the beginning of the activity of Bodhidharma Zen masters in North China. No doubt the most important personage within the Northern school is Shen-hsiu, a man of high education and widespread notoriety. His epitaph, written by the famous Confucian scholar Ch'ang Yüeh (667–730), definitively swings the patriarchal succession in Shen-hsiu's favor and lists him as the Sixth Patriarch.[8] While this does not necessarily exclude the transmission of the Buddha mind from Hung-jen to Fa-ju, the insertion of Fa-ju into the list of patriarchs never caught on. Furthermore, mention of the "insignia" of the patriarchal rank is a later addition. We may assume that as Shen-hsiu's life drew to a glorious close, he was unquestionably recognized by his school as a patriarch. One of the primary reasons for Shen-hui's attack on Shen-hsiu was to correct this widespread belief, deleting his name from the patriarchal lists and replacing it with the name of Hui-neng.

The sources indicate quite clearly that after Shen-hsiu joined the disciples of Hung-jen at the age of fifty, he came to be highly regarded in the large community of monks on the East Mountain and was even considered first among the disciples. In addition to his thorough knowledge of the Chinese classics and his familiarity with Confucian and Taoist wisdom, he had considerable experience in religious life. He practiced seriously and with success. After receiving the Dharma seal from the Fifth Patriarch he left the East Mountain in order to dedicate himself more thoroughly to the solitary practice of meditation. Later, using the monastery of Yü-ch'uan-ssu (Jpn., Gyokusen-ji) as a base, he did much to spread the practice of Zen meditation. Soon his reputation reached the capital; it was further enhanced when Emperor Wu called him to the capital city of Lo-yang and entrusted himself to Shen-hsiu's guidance as a student of meditation. Thus, at the age of ninety-four, he enjoyed the glow of imperial favor. After his death, Emperor Chung-tsung (705–710) bestowed on him the posthumous title "Zen Master of Deep Penetration" (Daitsū zenji).

For his own teaching, Shen-hsiu took much from his predecessors. Inspired by Tao-hsin's Five Gates, he decided to systematize the work. The core of his teachings, expounded in his treatises on The Beholding Mind and The Gate to the Means of Non-birth of the Great Vehicle, were drawn from Hung-jen's discussions on "preserving the mind."[9] The title of the first treatise, Kanshin-ron (Chin., Kuan-hsin lun), was perhaps selected out of deference to a work of the same name by the great Tendai (T'ien-t'ai) Master, Chih-i (538–597). In the second treatise his dependence on five foundational Mahāyāna sūtras and śāstras is evident: The Essence of Buddha, Entrance into Enlightenment through the Activity of Prajñā, The Wonderful Liberation, The Essence of All Being, and The Unhindered Freedom of All Dharmas.[10] Shen-hsiu delved deeply into Mahāyāna metaphysics. For him, practice was based on doctrine and its aim was to cleanse one's originally pure spiritual nature from all defilements.

Even though Shen-hsiu spent a lifetime studying the Mahāyāna sūtras, nowhere does he explicitly mention the Laṅkāvatāra Sūtra.[11] This in spite of the fact that the sūtra contains the essential elements of the Mahāyāna teaching on meditation—so much so that both those who advocate sudden enlightenment as well as those given to analyzing the conditions of different experiences can appeal to its authority.

The Chronicle of the Laṅkāvatāra Masters lists Shen-hsiu among the advocates of the Laṅkāvatāra Sūtra. This important document of the Northern school stems from Ching-chüeh (683–c. 760), a disciple of two of the more notable disciples of Hung-jen, Shen-hsiu and Hsüan-tse.[12] Right from his first encounter with

Hsüan-tse, who was called to the capital after Shen-hsiu's death, Ching-chüeh felt a strong attraction to this master and shared his predilection for the *Laṅkāvatāra Sūtra*. Composed around 723, the chronicle gathers together a number of different materials to present the *Laṅkāvatāra Sūtra* as the principal sūtra of the Zen movement. It places Guṇabhadra (394–468), to whom we owe the earliest extant Chinese translation of the *Laṅkāvatāra Sūtra*,[13] at the head of a list extending from Bodhidharma and Hui-k'o to Tao-hsin, Hung-jen, and Shen-hsiu, and describes all the patriarchs of the early period as devotees of the *Laṅkāvatāra Sūtra*. The chronicle further establishes a connection with the early masters of the *Laṅkāvatāra Sūtra* mentioned by Tao-hsüan.[14]

The onesided perspective of the chronicle compiled by Ching-chüeh contributed greatly to designating the *Laṅkāvatāra Sūtra* as the normative canonical scripture for the early period of the Zen movement and especially for the Northern school of Chinese Zen.[15] Such a view, however, has no real basis in the historical sources. Certainly, the Mahāyāna sūtras occupied a place of great importance among the followers of Zen, but so did they also among the other schools of Chinese Mahāyāna Buddhism. At the same time, one has to take into account a certain rivalry that led to a relativizing ranking of sūtras according to value or authority. This phenomenon casts a great deal of light on the development of Zen during the early period. Against this background, it remains an open question whether and to what extent the *Laṅkāvatāra Sūtra* enjoyed a privileged position within Chinese Zen. In any case, the radical Zen masters of Hui-neng's school during the eighth and ninth centuries, monks who burned sūtras and rejected all wisdom from them, stand in sharp contrast to the Zen disciples of this early period, especially in the Northern school, who so enthusiastically made use of the sacred texts. Shen-hsiu and his disciples were most definitely influenced by the Mahāyāna sūtras.

Among the disciples of Shen-hsiu, P'u-chi (651–739) and I-fu (658–736) rank as his Dharma heirs. Honored as the "Zen Master of Great Light," P'u-chi's epitaph names him as the Seventh Patriarch. According to other sources, the patriarchate was divided between the two, which would make it appear that there was a lack of strong leadership in the school after the death of Shen-hsiu. No wonder, then, that the lineage of Bodhidharma was soon lost in the Northern school of Chinese Zen.[16]

In hindsight, the importance of the Northern school for the history of Chinese Zen is clear. Far from being an ephemeral phenomenon, for several centuries it embodied the main stream of the Chinese Zen movement.[17] Consider Shen-hsiu and the inscription that the famous Ch'ang Yüeh composed for his tombstone! For East Asian peoples old age is an indication of uncommon wisdom, and Shen-hsiu is said to have lived for more than a century. The epitaph recounts many extraordinary merits and distinctions that were accorded him. Not surprisingly, it praises his broad and deep knowledge and his comprehensive grasp of the Mahāyāna scriptures; it also mentions his special devotion for the *Laṅkāvatāra Sūtra*.[18] The author of his epitaph leaves no doubt that Shen-hsiu was a highly enlightened individual, who "cut off the flow of ideas and put a stop to the rush of imagination, and with all his energy concentrated his mind." He was able to penetrate "into the region where there is no longer any distinction between the sacred and the profane."[19]

During the time in which the Northern school flourished, the Zen movement was viewed very favorably even beyond Buddhist circles. Among the populace, a number of Zen masters were considered to be holy men capable of working miracles.[20] Zen was also esteemed highly in the literary world. Poets such as Wang Wei (700–761) and Tu Fu (712–770) were attracted to silence and praised the Zen way of meditation. The poets seemed to have recognized no distinction between the Northern and the Southern schools, affirming only the incomparable value of a mind that has been cleansed and brought to enlightenment through meditation. Zen even became a special element in T'ang poetry.[21]

Our exploration into the origins and development of the Northern school provides us with background for the decisive turn of events that took place in the eighth century, events many consider to constitute the actual birth of Zen in China.

THE CLAIM OF THE SOUTHERN SCHOOL

The Northern and Southern schools of Chinese Zen Buddhism define themselves in terms of their relation to one another. The Southern school, like the Northern, is not limited by its geographical name. Historically speaking, both schools step onto the stage of Chinese history at the moment when Shen-hui, a disciple of Hui-neng, first hoisted the flag of the Southern school. By laying claim to a line of tradition opposed to that of Shen-hsiu, he effectively introduced the Southern school into the history of Chinese Zen Buddhism. The event took place with full fanfare at the "Great Dharma Assembly" (daihōe) of 15 January 732 in the monastery of Ta-yün-ssu (Jpn., Daiun-ji) in Hua-t'ai (Honan Province), when Shen-hui first sounded the drum of sudden enlightenment.[22]

It may seem strange to take Shen-hui, rather than his master Hui-neng, as the pivotal figure in the story of the split between these two schools of Chinese Zen, since it is Hui-neng who has usually been considered the central figure in the conflict. The main reason for doing so lies, once again, in the particular nature of Zen's historical sources. In fact, the figure of Hui-neng becomes definable historically only through the disciple Shen-hui and his followers. At the same time, the fact remains that the whole phenomenon of the Sixth Patriarch—with all its legends, doctrines, and deeds—represents a turning point for a new and creative phase in the history of Chinese Zen.

Shen-hui was sixty-two or sixty-three years old when he unleashed his broadside against the Northern school. Of his early life we know very little.[23] Tradition has it that in his early years he had read the Chinese classics and the works of Lao-tzu and Chuang-tzu. Together with P'u-chi and I-fu, he practiced meditation for a brief time (699–701) under the direction of the patriarch of the Northern school, Shen-hsiu. When his master was called to the capital city, however, Shen-hui set out southward for the monastic community of Hui-neng in Ts'ao-chi. After remaining there for a number of years he departed on a long pilgrimage, from which he returned just in time to reach Hui-neng on his death-bed (713) and to receive from him the Dharma seal.[24] In obedience to an imperial decree issued in 720, he took up residence in the monastery of Lung-hsing-ssu (Jpn., Ryōkō-ji) in Nan-yang, not far south of the capital city of Lo-yang. In the course of occasional visits to the capital, he engaged in his first confrontations with P'u-chi and I-fu, the disciples of Shen-hsiu who were highly regarded by the imperial court and throughout the city.

The Tun-huang manuscripts have supplied us with the earliest and most reliable account of the Great Dharma Assembly of Hua-t'ai.[25] In an act of daring and courage, Shen-hui called the gathering and opened it to all in order to determine what was true and what false in the two schools. The Northern school was represented by an otherwise unknown Dharma master named Ch'ung-yüan. At the appointed hour, Shen-hui assumed the lion's seat. In his address he reviewed Zen tradition in China, relating how Bodhidharma, a prince from South India, had brought the Zen of the Tathāgata to the Middle Kingdom; how he confronted Emperor Wu with the futility of building temples, constructing images of the Buddha, and copying sūtras; how he passed on the Dharma seal and robe to Hui-k'o in the Shao-lin-ssu monastery; and how this Dharma seal was passed on in an unbroken line down to Hung-jen, who in turn bestowed it on his disciple Hui-neng. The conclusion was clear: as the sixth successor to Bodhidharma, Hui-neng was the true patriarch. The robe that the Southern school possessed offered clear proof that it had preserved the rightful patriarchal succession.

Shen-hui's opening address summarized the essential elements of his attack on the Northern school. First, Bodhidharma introduced the special method of meditation of Tathāgata Zen, that is the transmission of the Buddha mind; his method was not based on the teaching of sūtras. Further, the First Patriarch of Chinese Zen disdained pious practices and did not try to curry favor with the court. But the decisive point was that Bodhidharma's line of succession led to Hui-neng, the master of the Southern school, and that possession of Bodhidharma's robe was guarantee of the unbroken succession. Shen-hui was the first to deliver such a concise line of argument.[26] From the viewpoint of the Southern school, the generational line back to Bodhidharma was more than a mere line of succession based on the master-disciple relationship; it was rather the foundation for the right of the patriarchate to transmit the Buddha mind in an authentic manner. This right is passed on from one generation to the next in a single line and symbolized by the insignia of the office.

Hearing all this for the first time from the mouth of Shen-hui, the representative of the Northern school must have been completely taken aback by the arguments and proofs advanced by the champion of the Southern school.[27] If all this was true, then the Northern school would be no more than a sideline of Bodhidharma Zen. Confused, Ch'ung-yüan asked why there could be only one succession in each generation and whether the transmission of the Dharma was dependent on the transmission of a robe.[28] Shen-hui was ready with his reply. At great length he explained that the Dharma itself was not to be identified with the robe, but that faith in the transmission of the Dharma was tied to faith in the transmission of the robe. He appealed to the story of the gold-embroidered robe that Śākyamuni gave to his disciple Mahākāśyapa. The comparison is far-fetched and unsustainable.[29] Shen-hui mentions Bodhidharma's robe repeatedly in his address. One fragment ends with the assurance:

> The robe is proof of the Dharma, and the Dharma is the doctrine [confirmed by the possession] of the robe. Both Dharma and robe are passed on through each other. There is no other transmission. Without the robe, the Dharma cannot be spread, and without the Dharma, the robe cannot be obtained.

To follow such a path of enlightened knowledge is to enter the cosmic body of Buddha (dharmakāya) and find true liberation.[30]

The accusations that Shen-hui leveled against the Northern school in this Great Dharma Assembly can be reduced to two: first, the Northerners had diverged from the true line of tradition and usurped the patriarchate, and second, they had developed a false notion of enlightenment and true practice. In his opening address, Shen-hui concentrated on the first accusation. The sources tell us that in responding for the Northern school, the disciple Ch'ung-yüan raised a further question about the supposed opposition regarding the path to enlightenment: "Do not both Zen masters Hui-neng and Shen-hsiu originally come from the same school? And since they are fellow students, would not their Zen style be the same?"[31] "In no way!" was Shen-hui's firm reply. Their ways differ inasmuch as Hui-neng teaches the path of sudden enlightenment while Shen-hsiu promotes gradual enlightenment. Shen-hsiu's method of meditation seeks only the concentration and pacification of the mind; by gathering external impressions into itself, the mind is led inward in search of enlightenment. Such a "foolish" approach, according to Shen-hui, contradicts the Mahāyāna tradition as it is authentically expressed in the Vimalakīrti Sutra.[32] True enlightenment, far from being a gradual, progressive process of recollection, is a sudden breakthrough to the no-mind. "Our masters have all taken hold of enlightenment at a single stroke (Jpn., tantō jikinyū) without any talk of steps or progression."[33] Shen-hui vigorously defended this position before the assembly. What was at stake was the final, deepest difference between the two schools.

Because Shen-hui's address is only partially preserved, it is difficult to reconstruct the events at the Great Dharma Assembly of Hua-t'ai in detail. Moreover, there are no reports on the final result or immediate effects of the assembly. Shen-hui continued his campaign against the Northern school, even after moving to Ho-tse-ssu (Jpn., Kataku-ji), the headquarters of his school in Lo-yang (745).[34] A dogged fighter, he carried on his attack one blow at a time, especially in his monthly lectures. Weakened by the death of its two main spokesmen, P'u-chi (739) and I-fu (736), the Northern school could do little to oppose the relentless attacks.

To make matters still worse, Shen-hui and his followers were unscrupulous in their methods of attack, accusing members of the Northern school of plots to steal the patriarchal robe, altering the inscription on Shen-hsiu's tomb, and so forth.[35] Shen-hui reproached P'u-chi for laying claim to the patriarchate by calling himself the "seventh leaf" and for having a monument built for himself on Mount Sung.[36] He also held P'u-chi responsible for having expunged the name of Hui-neng from the Den hōbōki.[37] In these and other still more sweeping accusations, one gets a sense of the overheated, poisoned atmosphere that had been generated. While some of the charges are justified, others need a great deal of qualification.

In this connection, it would be good to have another look at the most controversial point in the unfortunate conflict: the question of the rightful line of succession in Bodhidharma Zen Buddhism. With great care Shen-hui shaped this question into the main brunt of his attack by introducing into the discussion two new considerations, or at least new points of emphasis. On the one hand, he insisted that the authentic line of tradition can be carried on by only one person in each generation, just as there can be only one king per kingdom and only one Buddha per age. On the other, he claimed that as unconditional proof of its authenticity a line of succession must be in possession of Bodhidharma's robe. After the victorious conclusion of the conflict, Shen-hui prepared a list of the names of thirteen patriarchs whom he had determined to be authentic and published it in the Ho-tse-ssu (Jpn., Kataku-ji), located in the capital city of Lo-yang. The list included eight Indian and six Chinese Zen patriarchs. The pivotal point of the list was Bodhidharma, who appears both as the last of the Indian and first of the Chinese patriarchs.[38] The achievement must have deeply satisfied Shen-hui, not only because it enabled him to confirm the position of his faction but also because this "establishment of the true and the false in the two Zen schools" assured that (in Shen-hui's view) the essence of the Buddha mind would be passed on properly.

A bitter change of fortune overtook Shen-hui during his final years. Accused and maligned, he fell from grace at the imperial court and was obliged to leave Lo-yang in 753. Several times he had to change his residence. But the exile did not last long. Dire circumstances brought about by political disturbances resulted in the recall of this brave and influential man to the capital (756), where he was able to provide the government with very helpful services, in return for which he was granted a position of privilege and honor. It seems ironic that one who had so relentlessly criticized masters of the Northern school for carelessly assuming honorific titles and so betraying the true spirit of Bodhidharma should spend his old age basking in the graces of the powers that be. All in all, Shen-hui was an unusual man, possessed of extraordinary energy and ingenuity to the last.[39] What were the motives that drove him? How is he ultimately to be judged?

The Japanese Buddhologist Ui Hakuju, who might be called a member of the Southern school of Zen—if it is still possible after so many centuries to speak of membership in one or the other school—sees in Shen-hui "traits deserving of moral censure and criticism for intolerance."[40] But it will not do simply to condemn Shen-hui outright. Given the climate of Chinese Buddhism at the time, drawing up a list of patriarchs as he did was not so extraordinary. The idea of the transmission of the Dharma is found within all Buddhist schools. The master of Ho-tse ssu was utterly convinced of the exclusive rightness of the Southern school's way to enlightenment, even if in pursuit of his aim he failed in discretion and fell into certain excesses. Instead of judging him, we should try first to acquire a closer and more historical understanding of the man and his times. Even so, much darkness remains, as the bulk of available historical data about the split between the two schools derives from the Southern school and openly champions its cause.

THE OX-HEAD SCHOOL

The "Ox-head school," named after Mount Ox-head (Chin., Niu-t'ou; Jpn., Gozu), located south of Nanking, first appears within Bodhidharma Zen as a school of meditation conscious of its own tradition around the middle of the eighth century.[41] The school took shape after the political disturbances (756–763) that brought Shen-hui to the capital city at the end of his life. The school enjoyed a brief but intense period of activity in the South. The epitaph written by the Chinese literary figure Li Hua (d. 766?) for the famous T'ien-t'ai master Hsüan-lang (673–754) is one of the earliest documents providing information on the lineage of the Ox-head school. Given its rather late date, however, it is unable to lay much claim to historical reliability. The epitaph offers an overview of the history of Bodhidharma Zen, beginning with the Buddha's spiritual transmission to his disciple Mahākāśyapa and recounting how, after twenty-nine generations (not mentioned by name), Bodhidharma had brought Zen to the Middle Kingdom. What is remarkable about the text is that it does not provide a list of succession going back to Bodhidharma but rather explains how Zen broke into three schools, each still thriving at the time of the composition of the epitaph: the Northern school, represented by Shen-hsiu and I-fu; the Southern school of Hui-neng, who is incorrectly described as having received the Dharma from Seng-ts'an; and the Ox-head school. Regarding the latter the text states: "In four generations, [the Dharma] was then passed on to Zen Master Tao-hsin; from Tao-hsin it was given to Zen Master Fa-jung, who lived on Mount Ox-head. His present-day heir is Zen Master Ching-shan."[42]

The text, the earliest written testimony to the Ox-head school, places Fa-jung (594–657) at the beginning and Ching-shan (714–792) at the end of the line. The line of succession within the Ox-head tradition was well defined by the end of the eighth century, perhaps even earlier, by Chih-wei (646–722), whose name appears fifth in the genealogical list.[43] In order to extol its own tradition, the school needed a clear line of succession similar to that of other schools of Chinese Buddhism. It was probably therefore in protest against the dominance of the Northern school at the beginning of the century that it announced its own genealogy. The list of six names was very much according to the fashion of the time. Influence from the Southern school, in the form of both imitation and opposition, is also quite evident. Instead of Shen-hui's eight

Indian Zen patriarchs, the Ox-head school lists twenty-nine Indians in its spiritual lineage. This may be due to the influence of the T'ien-t'ai school, which lists twenty-four Indian *ācaryās* in its lineage.[44]

The epitaph presents Fa-jung as the founder of the Ox-head school, a point on which all the chronicles of the Southern school agree. Tao-hsüan's biography of Fa-jung makes no mention of a relationship with Bodhidharma Zen.[45] That he was a disciple of the Fourth Patriarch, Tao-hsin, is historically questionable. The epitaph of Li Hua is one of the earliest, if not the earliest, proof in support of the claim. In spite of what later Zen writings tell us, the Ox-head school cannot be located within Zen history as the first sideline of Zen after Tao-hsin. Tao-hsüan also devotes a biography to Chih-yen, the second in the lineage of the Gozu line, but there again, no mention is made of any ties to Bodhidharma Zen. The third name on the list is otherwise unknown. There is, however, clear historical evidence of a relationship between Bodhidharma Zen and Fa-chih (635–702), the fourth heir of the Ox-head tradition.[46] He lived with the fifth Chinese Zen patriarch, Hung-jen, on the East Mountain. A devotee of the Buddha Amitābha, he zealously practiced the invocation of the holy name of the Buddha, which was not unusual in the heterogeneous community of Hung-jen.[47] Chih-wei, to whom we referred earlier, was a disciple of Fa-chih and is also said to have spent some time with Hung-jen. It was during the time that Fa-chih and Chih-wei were together on Mount Ox-head that the new school flourished. As a center of the Zen movement, the mountain reached its high point under Chih-wei's two disciples, Hui-chung (683–769) and Hsüan-su. Ching-shan, Hsüan-su's disciple and successor, is mentioned in the epitaph. The school seems to have faded away after eight generations.[48]

The significance of the Ox-head school for the history of Zen lies in the long unrecognized contribution it made to the final form Chinese Zen assumed by the time of the third generation after Hui-neng. Of this we shall have more to say in the next chapter. By distancing itself from the conflict between the Northern and Southern schools, the Ox-head school tried to formulate a third viewpoint. It succeeded, to a certain extent, in striking out on a path of its own between the Northern school's insistence on the need to meditate on the complete teachings of the Mahāyāna sūtras on the one hand, and the Southern school's strict adherence to the wisdom of the Middle Way and rejection of the sūtras as necessary for enlightenment on the other. Fa-jung, whom the school reveres as its founder, had close ties to the School of the Three Treatises (Jpn., Sanron-shū; Chin., San-lun-tsung), and was also influenced by the doctrine of the powerful T'ien-t'ai school. In agreement with the Southern school, he taught that full realization takes place "in the joining of meditational concentration (Skt., *samādhi*; Jpn., *jō*) and enlightened wisdom (Skt., *prajñā*; Jpn., *e*)."[49] His acceptance of the T'ien-t'ai teaching on the universal Buddha nature of all reality, not just of living beings, was roundly rejected by Shen-hui and his followers.

Besides the followers of the Ox-head school, there were others in eighth century China who adhered to neither of the two main schools.[50] In those early

days, organizational requirements were limited to a non-binding decision to un-
dertake community life in a monastery. Many others devoted to meditation and
in search of the way simply traveled around the land on their own. The bitter
conflict occasioned by Shen-hui's attack on the disciples of Shen-hsiu is actually
an exceptional phenomenon, and for that reason all the more remarkable. From
an historical perspective, this split into two enemy camps provoked by differing
views on the essence of practice and enlightenment, is extremely important.
As we shall see in the following chapter, echoes of the conflict were to reverberate
in the divisions that occurred in the so-called Council of Lhasa at the end of
the eighth century.[51]

   T'ang China during the eighth century was going through a time of social
and political agitation. After the period of reconstruction that occurred during
the second half of the century,[57] Chinese Zen would take a new form, a development that will be the subject of chapter 9. Before that, we shall keep to
our present time period, perhaps in defiance of common procedure in historical
studies but out of deference to our sources. After a thorough analysis of the
events surrounding the split between the Northern and Southern schools we
shall step into the historical twilight in search of reasons why the following
generations of Zen accorded the heavily legendary figure of Hui neng such great
prominence and normative authority.

NOTES

1. For these chronicles, see chap. 1, note 5.

2. Shen-hui's dates, which the historical work Sō kōsōden give as 668–760, have been
corrected. See Shoki, pp. 34–35.

3. The ascription "Northern school" (hokushū) was not used by those who belonged
to the school but is a later appellation applied by its opponents. See Chūgoku zenshūshi,
p. 31.

4. Chūgoku zenshūshi, p. 30. Fa-ju is counted among the "ten great disciples" of Hung-
jen. Yanagida treats him in detail in Shoki, pp. 35–41; see also Zengaku daijiten II, p. 1140.

5. This according to the Hō'nyo zenji gyōjō, perhaps compiled by Tu Fei ("Dharma
Master Fei") under the stimulus of Shen-hsiu's disciples P'u-chi and I-fu shortly after Fa-
ju's death. The word fuzoku (explained as "passing on the Great Dharma" in Zengaku
jiten, p. 1234) appears already in Tao-hsüan's biography of Tao-hsin (T. 2060, vol. 50,
p. 606b). The classical term for the "transmission of mind," ishin denshin, is found in
the apocryphal writings of Bodhidharma, and also in important passages of the Sūtra of
the Sixth Patriarch. See the entry on ishin denshin in Zen Dust, pp. 230–31. In the early
texts, the "passing on of the Dharma" or "transmission of mind" is not limited to one
Dharma heir. Yanagida gives a detailed treatment of the Hō'nyo zenji gyōjō (Shoki, pp.
36ff, esp. p. 41), and includes the text and an annotated commentary in an appendix
(pp. 487–89, 490–96). The succession ends with Fa-ju as the sixth member in the line
of transmission.

6. The Den hōbōki takes over the naming of Fa-ju as Hung-jen's successor from the
Hō'nyo zenji gyōjō. In the foreword appeal is made to the "Zen Sūtra" (Jpn., Zengyō; the
full title is Datsumatara zengyō; Chin., Ta-mo-to-lo ch'an-ching; T. 618, vol. 15), a work

attributed to Dharmatrāta but of uncertain origins, in linking Chinese Zen to the names of Indian patriarchs. The text presents brief biographies of the seven Chinese patriarchs. The Bodhidharma legend is also there in its main outlines. The Laṅkāvatāra Sūtra is also cited. Yampolsky rightly notes that the Den hōbōki is particularly illuminating for the state of Zen in China at the start of the eighth century. Clearly it draws attention to the line of generation of the then dominant Northern school and attaches a great importance to it. See Yampolsky, Platform Sūtra, pp. 5ff.; see also Shoki, pp. 48ff.

7. The inscription on the grave is the first sign of Fa-ju's inclusion in the generational line. Its composer is unknown. See Shoki, p. 34.

8. The grave inscription shows a line of succession from Hung-jen to Shen-hsiu (Shoki, pp. 44–45). Yanagida includes the text with commentary in his appendix of sources (pp. 497–516).

9. See Chūgoku zenshūshi, pp. 32ff.

10. Chūgoku zenshūshi, p. 33. In Yanagida's view, the Northern school succeeded in harmonizing Bodhidharma's line of transmission with the doctrinal system of the sūtras, an important cultural and spiritual achievement for the flowering of Zen during the T'ang period, the repercussions of which eventually reached Japan (pp. 33–34).

11. Yanagida takes the point seriously; see Chūgoku zenshūshi, p. 33. The historical work of Tao-hsüan as well as the reports in the Hō'nyo zenji gyōjō and the Den hōbōki also contain no clear statements on a relationship of the sūtra to disciples of Zen in the Northern school; see Shoki, pp. 64–65.

12. See the statements in note 10 of chapter 6. In three sections Yanagida treats the origin and compilation of the Chronicle of the Laṅkāvatāra Masters (Shoki, pp. 58–100). In its composition Ching-chüeh also made use of the Ryōga (butsu) ninbō-shi, written by his master Hsüan-tse. Yanagida surmises an opposition between Hsüan-tse and Ching-chüeh on the one hand and the disciples around Fa-ju on the other. In any case, the chronicle completely omits Fa-ju and treats all important Zen masters as pioneers of the Laṅkāvatāra Sūtra (Shoki, pp. 74ff).

13. See the details on the Laṅkāvatāra Sūtra in chapter 4; on the Chinese translation of Guṇabhadra, see Zen Dust, p. 373.

14. See chapter 6. The Laṅkāvatāra masters are mentioned especially in the biography of Fa-ch'ung, T. 2060, vol. 50, p. 666b.

15. "From the time of the Second Patriarch until that of the Sixth Patriarch, the Laṅkāvatāra Sūtra was widely studied by Zen men. For the Northern School of Zen, the Laṅkā Sūtra remained the preferred text" (Zen Dust, pp. 373–74). The remark needs some qualification; see note 18 below.

16. Miura and Sasaki give the following reasons for this development: "After their deaths [that of the immediate students of Shen-hsiu], however, due to the lack of capable heirs, the continued denunciations of Ho-tse Shen-hui and his followers, and the rise of outstanding masters in the Sixth Patriarch's [i.e., Hui-neng's] line, the Northern School began to decline, and some five generations after Shen-hsiu died out entirely" (Zen Dust, p. 187).

17. Seen in connection with the total history, the Bodhidharma line achieved the highest degree of fame through the "great representative master" Shen-hsiu, as Yanagida stresses repeatedly in his presentation.

18. Yanagida thinks it possible that the remark about Shen-hsiu's reverence for the Laṅkāvatāra Sūtra found its way into the epitaph through the influence of Hsüan-tse (Shoki,

p. 95). The fact that it is cited neither in Tao-hsüan's biography of Tao-hsin nor in the *Shūshinyō-ron* (see chap. 6, note 70) argues against an overly powerful influence of the sūtra (*Shoki*, p. 93). Ching-chüeh, editor of the *Chronicle of the Laṅkāvatāra Masters*, also composed a commentary on the *Heart Sūtra*, one of the Prajñāpāramitā sūtras. In Yanagida's view, it may be that in later years he drew closer to the ideas of the Wisdom school (*Shoki*, pp. 92–93).

19. *Shoki*, p. 499.

20. Belief in such miracles was especially common among the venerators of the *Laṅkāvatāra Sūtra*, but Tao-hsüan was also fond of miracle stories. The miraculous element is already present in the history of the early period of Chinese Zen (for example, in the biography of Tao-hsin). Among the characters of the title accorded Shen-hsiu, "Master of the Great Clarity," is the term *jinzū*, the Sino-Japanese translation of the Pāli word *iddhi*, which means magical or miraculous powers.

21. *Chūgoku zenshūshi*, p. 37. Yanagida devotes a rather long section (pp. 34–37) to the two poets of the T'ang period, Wang-Wei and Tu Fu; see also *Shoki*, pp. 96–97.

22. The dating is Yanagida's. J. Gernet places the event on 23 February 734 in his *Entretiens du Maître de Dhyāna Chen-houei du Ho tsö* (Hanoi, 1949), p. 82.

23. In this connection, see J. Gernet, "Biographie du Maître de Dhyāna Chen-houei du Ho-tsö, JA 249 (1951): 29–60. There is a brief biography of Shen-hui in *Zen Dust*, pp. 192ff; see also the detailed treatment in Ui's chapter "The Rise and Fall of the Kataku School," *Zenshūshi* I, pp. 195–268.

24. According to Gernet, who follows the official biography of Shen-hui recorded in the *Sō kōsōden* (T. 2061, vol. 50, pp. 756–757), Shen-hui's time with Hui-neng covered the years 708 to 713 ("Biographie du Maître de Dhyāna", p. 38). This dating needs correction (see note 2 above). There is much evidence for a somewhat longer stay with Hui-neng.

25. See the foreword of the disciple Tu-ku P'ei to the *Treatise Establishing the True and the False according to the Southern School of Bodhidharma* (Jpn., *Bodaidaruma nanshū teizehiron*). The text was discovered and edited by Hu Shih and included in Gernet's French translation of the discourses of Shen-hui (see note 22) following Hu Shih, book 2. The discourses make up four books. In Hu Shih's opinion, book 3 is also related to the Great Dharma Assembly of Hua-t'ai. See the English translation of W. Liebenthal, "The Sermon of Shen-hui," AM, n.s. 3 (1952): 132:55. For a description of the manuscripts, editions, and translations of the Tun-huang text, see *Zen Dust*, pp. 392–95. Yanagida gives the text of the foreword (*Shoki*, p. 105). He calls the text, which is also known as *Tongo saijōjō-ron* and which summarizes the points of conflict with the Northern school, "a kind of declaration of independence by the Southern school" (p. 103). In the text we repeat the most important points of the opening discourse of Shen-hui.

26. See *Shoki*, p. 106. In both his works, Yanagida presents Shen-hui's case in great detail; Shen-hui has been regarded as the only "inventor" of the story of the insignia of accession to the patriarchate (in particular, the robe); the influence of contemporaries or legend, however, cannot be excluded.

27. Shen-hui had previously argued the claim of the Southern school and disputed with the representative of the Northern school Ch'ung-yüan. See *Chūgoku zenshūshi*, p. 39. Gernet notes that Ch'ung-yüan had held annual discussions with Shen-hui from 731 to 734 (the latter is his date for the "Great Dharma Assembly"). See his *Entretiens du Maître de Dhyāna*, p. 43, note 1.

28. Yanagida cites their exchange in *Shoki*, pp. 106ff.

29. *Shoki*, p. 108. Kāśyapa serves as the first of the "Dharma masters." Legend also recounts that he entered into nirvāṇa wearing Śākyamuni's robe. He is supposed to hand the robe on to Maitreya, the Buddha of the future, at the time of his advent. See E. Lamotte, *Histoire du bouddhisme indien*, p. 227. See also above, chap. 1, note 6.

30. Book 4 in Gernet, *Entretiens du Maître de Dhyāna*, p. 110.

31. Chung-yüan had brought forth this argument already during an earlier discussion in Ryūkō-ji; see *Chūgoku zenshūshi*, p. 39.

32. Shen-hui refers to the famous passage from the *Vimalakīrti Sūtra* to which reference was made earlier (chap. 4, note 46). Yanagida cites the somewhat corrupt passage of the Tun-huang manuscript (*Shoki*, pp. 108–09).

33. Cited in *Shoki*, p. 109.

34. See *Shoki*, p. 148; *Chūgoku zenshūshi*, p. 40. Shen-hui's anger was aimed principally at P'u-chi, whose standing was not weakened by Shen-hui's assault in Hua-t'ai, as the former's summons to the court in Lo-yang demonstrates. His biography, which makes use of the epitaph of Li Yung and draws attention to his great importance, appears in the *Sō kōsōden* (T. 2061, vol. 50, pp. 760c–761b).

35. See *Shoki*, pp. 110–111. An aborted attempt on the robe is described graphically in book 3 of the *Treatise* (*Entretiens*, pp. 95–96).

36. See *Shoki*, p. 111; Gernet, *Entretiens*, pp. 94–95.

37. *Shoki*, p. 111. Shen-hui turned his attention in particular against the *Den hōbōki*, the compilation of which he falsely attributed to P'u-chi. As this work does not mention Hui-neng, one may suppose that he was little known in North China, where the work originated.

38. The theory of the generational line of thirteen Indian and Chinese patriarchs was already included in the *Treatise Establishing the True and the False according to the Southern School of Bodhidharma*. See *Shoki*, pp. 123–124; cf. Gernet, *Entretiens*, book 3, pp. 97–98. The names of the Indian patriarchs given by Shen-hui are the same as those found in the *Zengyō* (see note 6 above) except that Bodhidharma takes the place of Dharmatrāta. We have already seen in the case of the *Den hōbōki* that interest in the line of succession came strongly to the fore in Chinese Zen beginning in the eighth century.

39. Gernet refers to him as a "man of superior moral and physical power" ("Biographie du Maître de Dhyāna," p. 41). Tsung-mi (780–841) extols the courage with which he tackled such formidable opponents as P'u-chi and recounts attempts on his life.

40. *Zenshūshi* I, p. 227.

41. Yanagida treats the Ox-head school in *Shoki*, pp. 126–35, and *Chūgoku zenshūshi*, pp. 45ff (where he includes the names of the six generations). See also the chapter in *Zenshūshi*, pp. 91–134; and *Zen Dust*, p. 175.

42. Cited in *Shoki*, pp. 136–37.

43. *Shoki*, p. 130.

44. Li Hua mentions the twenty-nine generations of Indian Zen patriarchs in an epitaph for the T'ien-t'ai master Hsüan-lang. The importance accredited to Bodhidharma Zen in this epitaph speaks for the manifold close ties between T'ien-t'ai and Zen in the eighth century. Li Hua had many friends in the Buddhist world at the time, including members of the Ox-head school. See, *Shoki*, pp. 132ff, 136ff.

45. Fa-jung's biography and that of his disciple Chih-yen include some additions to the historical work of Tao-hsüan. Yanagida considers any relationship to Bodhidharma Zen uncertain (*Shoki*, p. 128).

46. According to Yanagida, contemporary scholarship has "the strongest historical basis for claiming that the fourth successor, Fa-chih, received the Dharma of Hung-jen on East Mountain" (*Shoki*, pp. 127, 134). According to the biography of Fa-chih in the *Sō kōsōden*, Fa-chih came to Hung-jen at the age of thirteen (other accounts make him thirty years old), became his student, and was counted among the ten great disciples of the Fifth Patriarch. In a repeat visit to East Mountain he was designated by Hung-jen as his successor (T. 2061, vol. 50, p. 757c). This version was taken over by other chronicles (such as the *Keitoku dentōroku*). In contrast, the name of Fa-chih is not mentioned among the ten great disciples of Hung-jen in the *Ryōga (butsu) ninbō-shi* (c. 708). See *Shoki*, pp. 128–29.

47. "The A-mi-t'o [Amitābha] doctrines and practices penetrated into all the other Chinese Buddhist sects" (*Zen Dust*, p. 174ff.). The over five hundred disciples of Hung-jen, as Yanagida observes, were not all necessarily Zen monks (*Shoki*, p. 131).

48. According to Miura and Sasaki, the school lasted for some eight or nine generations (*Zen Dust*, p. 118), although the final name mentioned specifically occurs in the seventh generation (see the table on p. 488).

49. Cited in *Shoki*, pp. 138–39.

50. Examples are given in *Chūgoku zenshushi*, pp. 45ff.

51. One adherent of the Northern school of Zen Buddhism, who nevertheless defended sudden enlightenment, came to Lhasa around the end of the eighth century and there engaged in disputations with Indian Buddhist monks holding the opposite view. Paul Demiéville has translated and commented on this "Council of Lhasa" in his *Le concile de Lhasa: Une controverse sur le quiétisme entre bouddhistes de l'Inde et de la Chine au VIIIème siècle de l'ère chrétienne* (Paris, 1952).

52. The salient political event of the time was the rise of An Lu-shan, who drove the emperor Hsüan-tsung from the capital city of Lo-yang in 756 until order was restored by military intervention.

8

The Sūtra of the Sixth Patriarch

The title of this chapter, chosen with great reservations, points to a truly complex historical phenomenon. What follows has to do not so much with describing the origins and contents of a certain book as with using that book, whose beginnings are obscured by the mists of history and whose contents lead us back to a remote past, to help us form a picture of a new movement that took place within Zen in eighth-century China.

Historically speaking, there is no single creative personality standing at the birth of what we are about to relate, although Zen historiographers mark the start of this new period with the name of the Sixth Patriarch, Hui-neng (638–713). Hui-neng's historicity is beyond question, but a careful examination of the sources tells us that his life was not very different from that of the many other typical Zen masters of his time. The achievement that has been linked with his name—the revolutionary inauguration of a new era within Chinese Zen—far from being the product of a single person, belongs to a complex process extending over decades. That Hui-neng's name came to represent this entire process is, as the Chinese scholar Hu Shih suggests, due primarily (but not exclusively) to the aggressive behavior of his disciple Shen-hui described in the previous chapter. This does not mean that the Zen historian ought simply to substitute Shen-hui's name for Hui-neng's. What we know of Shen-hui and his work would hardly support such a tactic. In addition to the strong influence from Shen-hui and his school, other important currents flowing into the Zen movement of the time are easy to discern. Many of these currents, which first sprang up around Shen-hui, can be traced back to earlier sources, but it was Hui-neng whom the Zen movement of the time elevated and transformed into a symbol of the ideal they were striving for. The figure of the Sixth Patriarch came to embody a comprehensive and inspiring image of the perfection of Zen—what disciples came to call the "Zen of the Patriarchs" (Jpn., soshizen).

This final form of Zen found a fitting and impressive expression in *The Sūtra of the Sixth Patriarch*. The main elements in the Zen movement of the age are constellated in this work. Its privileged position is clear already from the title: in Buddhism the word *sūtra* is commonly reserved for writings representing direct transmissions of the words of the Buddha. The *Sūtra of the Sixth Patriarch* came to occupy a key place among the sacred texts of the Zen school. An early edition of the work discovered in a cave during excavations at Tun-huang in Kansu Province has given scholars invaluable insights into the historical tangle that makes up this new era in Zen's history. At the same time, the discovery has raised a good many unresolved and, at least for the moment, unresolvable questions.

THE TUN-HUANG TEXT AND ITS SOURCES

In the Tun-huang version of the text, the *Sūtra of the Sixth Patriarch* bears the solemn twofold title: *Southern School Sudden Doctrine, Supreme Mahāyāna Great Perfection of Wisdom: The Platform Sūtra preached by the Sixth Patriarch Hui-neng at the Ta-fan Temple in Shao-chou* (Jpn., *Nanshū tongyō saijō daijō makahannya-haramitsu-kyō: Rokuso Enō Daishi Shōshū Daibon-ji ni oite sehō suru no dankyō*; Chin., *Nan-tsung tun-chiao tsui-shang ta-sheng mo-ho-pan-jo po-lo-mi ching: Liu-tsu Hui-neng Ta-shih yü Shao-chou Ta-fan-ssu shih-fa t'an-ching*).[1] In their edition of the manuscript, published under the title *The Platform Sūtra of the Sixth Patriarch Discovered in Tun-huang*, D. T. Suzuki and R. Kōda improved slightly on the Tun-huang manuscript by dividing the relatively short and originally undivided text into fifty-seven sections.[2] Since that time, most translators and commentators have followed their convention.[3] The contents of the book break down into two principal but unequal parts: Hui-neng's lecture, to which is appended an autobiography (secs. 2–11, 12–31, 34–37), and remaining sections dealing with various topics. The first part is the more useful for exploring the sūtra's sources and grasping its message.

The Tun-huang document represents the earliest manuscript yet discovered of the *Sūtra of the Sixth Patriarch*, but is by no means the earliest draft. Experts estimate that the manuscript is in fact a defective copy made sometime between 830 and 860.[4] The version it is based on was completed around the year 820, perhaps earlier; on the basis of comparisons with other known Zen writings, Yanagida argues that the earlier text was composed between 781 and 801.[5] Zen historians have good grounds for claiming that there were still earlier editions of the sūtra.

In the heading and opening section of the text, a disciple named Fa-hai is given as the compiler of the Tun-huang version. He had been charged by the district governor of Shao-chou, Wei Ch'ü, to preserve in writing this important lecture by Hui-neng (sec. 1). The end of the sūtra (sec. 55) reconfirms the fact that Fa-hai copied the lecture, and that the text was then given first to Tao-ts'an and then to his disciple Wu-chen, who (at the time the text was propagated) was still passing on this Dharma.[6] In the sūtra, Fa-hai is said to be one of the ten disciples of Hui-neng (sec. 45) and the chief monk of the community (sec. 55). The last section provides some biographical data that most likely refer to him.[7] As it turns out, every section that mentions Fa-hai is a later addition. His name does not appear in the main body of the sūtra. Nor is he mentioned in other early Zen literature. His collaboration on the Tun-huang text, as well as his very identity, are therefore open to serious doubt.[8]

Thus, the assumption that the disciple Fa-hai recorded his master's lecture soon after the master's death, sometime around 714, breaks down. Yet the Japanese Buddhologist Ui Hakuju adopted this assumption to construct his thesis that the sūtra originated in the circle of Hui-neng's disciples, claiming that the obvious later additions do not lessen the substantial authenticity of the sūtra's teaching. He also concluded that the text in our possession was completed around 820. The Chinese scholar Hu Shih takes a contrary position, arguing that the sūtra originated, in its entirety, among the disciples of Shen-hui.[9] He supports his claim by pointing out the many similarities between statements in the sūtra and passages in Shen-hui's works, in addition to the uncertainty surrounding the supposed compiler, Fa-hai. Still, the possibility that a disciple named Fa-hai did exist and did in fact record his master's lecture cannot be dismissed. We are left with two plausible but irreconcilable alternatives. After reviewing the arguments on both sides, Yampolsky concludes that the problem of the authenticity of the early section cannot be resolved.[10]

In his studies on the early history of Zen, Yanagida sheds some new light on the problem of the "early text of the Platform Sūtra of the Sixth Patriarch" (kohon Rokuso dankyō) and broaches a new solution. Does he succeed in unsnarling the tangle and solving the problem? No doubt he offers new historical perspectives, uncovering long-overlooked connections and offering an impressive overall picture. While it is not possible here to examine all the details of his proposal, we can review its main outlines. Fortunately, Yanagida lightens our task by clearly laying out the steps in his arguments and reviewing his conclusions at several points along the way.

Lost for centuries, discovered in fragmentary condition, and composed of many unequal parts, the Tun-huang manuscript presents historians with a fascinating challenge. It may be assumed that there were earlier versions of the text, especially because of the reports circulating for centuries about repeated alterations in the text.[11] But barring revelations from another happy discovery of ancient manuscripts, nothing definite can be said about these early versions. Regarding the contents of the manuscript, Shen-hui and his school clearly exercised considerable influence. There are also passages that might well stem from other sources, especially the important sections on the "Formless Precepts of the Three Refuges" (secs. 20–26).[12] The receiving of precepts, carried out in solemn ritual, is a central ceremony throughout Buddhism. In the case of Chinese Buddhism, the ceremony was highly esteemed during the T'ang period. Shen-hui's discourses speak of such precepts in an ethical-religious sense, while the "formless precepts" of the Sūtra of the Sixth Patriarch reflect the metaphysics of the Wisdom teachings in the Prajñāpāramitā sūtras.[13] How are we to explain this difference?

This is where Yanagida takes up his proposal. In the discourses of Shen-hui, no mention is made of this new notion of formless precepts, an essential ingredient in the teaching of Hui-neng, evidently because he was not familiar with the idea when composing his lectures.[14] Then how did it find its way into the Platform Sūtra? We recall that the Ox-head school, then in its prime, was a zealous promoter of the Wisdom teachings of the Mādhyamika philosophy. Taking his clue from this fact, Yanagida poses a suggestion: "Might we not resolve the contradiction between the discourses of Shen-hui and the Tun-huang version of the *Platform Sūtra* by considering the tradition of the formless precepts to have come not from the Northern or Southern schools but from the third Zen movement of the time—the Ox-head school?"[15] Pursuing this hypothesis—for that is what he calls it—Yanagida suggests that within the Ox-head school there was an earlier text similar to the *Platform Sūtra*, and that this text was later linked with excerpts from the discourses of Shen-hui. He conjectures that it may well have been "to the mutual advantage of both the Ox-head school and the line of Shen-hui that the present Tun-huang version of the *Platform Sūtra of the Sixth Patriarch* be compiled by the Southern school as one of Hui-neng's lectures."[16]

Yanagida finds his suggestion confirmed by the futility of all efforts to clarify the historically uncertain existence of Fa-hai, the supposed compiler of the Tun-huang version of the *Platform Sūtra*. Moreover, there is little historical support for the account given in Shen-hui's talks of a conversation shortly before Hui-neng's death between the master and a disciple named Fa-hai.[17] The disciple asks about Hui-neng's successor and, more concretely, to whom the patriarchal robe should be given. Refusing to answer, the master rebukes his disciple, adding the prophetic comment that forty years after his death someone would establish the school. The same story is told in the *Platform Sūtra*, except that there the time for the fulfillment of the prophecy is reduced to twenty years.[18] This figure would correspond to the date of the Great Dharma Assembly at Hua-t'ai. Working from a figure of forty years, however, we come close to the turn of events in Shen-hui's life that brought him his final triumph late in life. It was around this time that the disciples of Shen-hui would most likely have fashioned the Tun-huang version of the *Platform Sūtra*.

The conversation between Fa-hai and Hui-neng reported in Shen-hui's discourses does not add substantially to arguments for the existence of the compiler Fa-hai.[19] Both references to this episode were written around the same time, that is, at the end of Shen-hui's life or shortly thereafter. Both give voice to early but historically suspect traditions. At this same time, however, a certain disciple of Hsüan-su (668–752) by the name of Fa-hai was active in the Ox-head school.[20] While it is incorrect to assume that this Fa-hai could have known Hui-neng personally, it is altogether possible that Shen-hui and his disciples maintained contact with Fa-hai.[21] This may be the Fa-hai who, as Shen-hui tells us in his discourses, is mentioned in the biography of Hui-neng.[22] Might this not be how his name found its way into the tradition of the Southern school and eventually into the *Platform Sūtra*? Yanagida considers it possible; in fact, in view of "the mutual influence between the Ox-head school and the Southern school of Shen-hui" he deems it probable.[23] It is thus quite possible that a *Platform Sūtra* of the Ox-head school was transformed into the *Platform Sūtra of the Sixth Patriarch*.[24] The literature of the age shows many cases of changes of name, mistaken identities, conflated and substituted personalities, and other such mutations.

Yanagida schematizes the story of the formation of the *Platform Sūtra of the Sixth Patriarch* in six stages:[25]

1. The earliest layer of the text took form in the Ox-head school; it includes the sections on the formless precepts (secs. 20–26) and the *samādhi* of *prajñā* (secs. 27–30), as well as the section on the seven Buddhas and twenty-eight (or twenty-nine) Indian patriarchs. Fa-hai, the disciple of Hsüan-su may be considered the editor of this stratum.
2. Changes, especially those stressing self-nature and mind-nature, brought the text close to the heterodox notion of an unchanging Absolute, but also prompted critical reactions.
3. During the final year of Shen-hui's life, or immediately after his death, a biography of Hui-neng was composed; as a critical apology against the Ox-head school, it transformed Fa-hai and Wei-ch'ü[26] into disciples of Hui-neng.
4. The earlier text from the Ox-head school was altered by Hui-neng's Southern school; an autobiography of Hui-neng and a report on his ten main disciples were added.
5. A work entitled *Rekidai hōbōki* (Chin., *Li-tai fa-pao chi*), composed before 779, makes mention of an earlier version of the *Platform Sūtra* (from the Ox-head school or another school?).
6. The publication of the Tun-huang version of the *Platform Sūtra of the Sixth Patriarch* took place between the composition of the *Sōkei Daishi betsuden* (781), an important source for the formulation of Hui-neng's biography, and the *Hōrinden* (Chin., *Pao-lin chuan*, 801).

A few comments may help clarify this highly condensed summary. The list of patriarchs given in the Tun-huang version of the *Platform Sūtra* (sec. 51) is not only different from the succession of thirteen patriarchs according to Shen-hui but is based on a different tradition, namely, on the Ox-head school's list of patriarchs preserved in the epitaph written by Li Hua for the T'ien-t'ai master Hsüan-lang.[27] A list of twenty-nine names is first given in the *Rekidai hōbōki*. It was through the Tun-huang version of the *Platform Sūtra* that the number of patriarchs was definitively established at twenty-eight. Since then, the figure of the seven Buddhas and the twenty-eight Indian patriarchs have become fixed in Zen tradition.[28]

In the first two points of his summary, Yanagida touches on important and somewhat problematic themes in Zen teaching, themes we shall take up when considering the doctrinal content of the sūtra. There can be no doubt that the sections in the Tun-huang version of the *Platform Sūtra* dealing with the life of Hui-neng and his disciples stem from the pupils of Shen-hui, as do all references to the controversy with the Northern school.

Yanagida thus presents us with a comprehensive scenario of the origins of the Tun-huang version of the *Platform Sūtra of the Sixth Patriarch* within the Zen movement of the eighth century; his proposal constitutes an impressive alternative to earlier attempts to reconstruct the origins of the sūtra. One might question some of the conclusions of his research, for instance, the attribution of a normative role of the Ox-head school, which has not been clearly established.[29] The extensive data that Yanagida has mustered in support of his thesis rules out simplistic solutions. The most impressive aspect of his new perspective is its depiction of the broad and wide network of relationships that characterized Chinese Zen during the eighth century. The development of the "Zen of the Patriarchs" was a complex process of multiple contacts and exchanges of traditions and viewpoints. It was on the one hand a process of confrontation, conflict, and even condemnation, and on the other, of acceptance, assimilation, and harmonization. The final form that resulted is represented in the *Platform Sūtra of the Sixth Patriarch* in its Tun-huang version.[30] There is no reducing the Zen movement merely to a conflict between the Northern and Southern schools. As we have seen, the Ox-head school played a key role in the development of Zen at this time. In his résumé Yanagida identifies other Zen writings that influenced the formation of the Tun-huang manuscript of the *Platform Sūtra*; these in turn indicate the role of numerous other schools or movements within eighth century Zen.

The *Sōkei daishi betsuden* (an abbreviation of the full original title) was brought to Japan by Saichō (767–822); it originated in the circle of Hsing-t'ao (or Ling-t'ao), a disciple of Hui-neng who tradition tells us watched over the grave of his master in the monastery of Hōrin-ji.[31] The work had a decisive influence on the formation of the legends around the Sixth Patriarch.

The *Reikidai hōbōki* stems from another contemporary Zen school originating with Chih-hsien (609–702), one of the ten disciples of the Fifth Patriarch, Hung-jen.[32] The accounts of Chih-hsien and his successor Ch'u-chi (d. 732) are historically very doubtful. Wu-hsiang (684–762), a Korean, was third in succession; Hui-neng's disciple and great grandson, Ma-tsu Tao-i (709–788), is said to have lived and practiced for some time with him.[33] Wu-hsiang's successor, Wu-chu (714–774), lived in the monastery of Hotō-ji (Chin., Pao-t'ang-ssu) in Szechwan Province, whence the line came to be known as the Hotō (Chin., Pao-t'ang) school. The school boasted possession of the patriarchal robe, which, according to a completely unreliable report, was supposed to have been entrusted to the founder, Chih-hsien, when he was staying at the court of Empress Wu.[34] The Hotō school, known in Zen history through its four representatives, expressly adhered to the teachings of the Southern school, including its sharp rejection of its Northern adversary. At the time the *Rekidai hōbōki* was being written (shortly before the composition of the Tun-huang version of the *Platform Sūtra*), the Sixth Patriarch had already achieved a place of prominence within Zen Buddhism. His image was revered by masters and disciples of various schools and a widespread consensus about his importance was taking shape. Just as the *Sūtra of the Sixth Patriarch* is not the work of a single author, so also its teachings do not reflect the orientation of any one school but rather show elements of all the "Zen of the Patriarchs."[35]

The *Hōrinden* completes the collection of Zen writings of the eighth century. Composed on the threshold of the ninth century, it accurately sums up the events of the past century. A new era was dawning under the sign of the Sixth Patriarch. The Zen movement moved forward committed to the doctrine of sudden enlightenment and grounded in the metaphysics of Mahāyāna as taught in the Prajñāpāramitā sūtras. These aspects of the *Platform Sūtra of the Sixth Patriarch* call for further consideration.

THE BIOGRAPHY OF HUI-NENG

Ascending to the platform, Hui-neng began his weighty discourse in the monastery of Ta-fan (Jpn., Daibon-ji)[36] with a personal introduction. This first part of his presentation, generally referred to as the autobiography (secs. 2–11), does not cover the entire course of his life but simply summarizes the core of the legend of the Sixth Patriarch that took shape during the eighth century. In light of what has been said concerning the origins and sources of the Tun-huang version of the *Platform Sūtra*, it is obvious that Hui-neng's discourse can make no great claims to historical credibility.

How much of the information concerning the life and person of Hui-neng is historically accurate? In view of the available sources, only his name. In the *Chronicle of the Laṅkāvatāra Masters* his name is given as one of the ten disciples of the Fifth Patriarch, Hung-jen.[37] We can deduce his importance from the events of the eighth century. The disciple Hui-neng was certainly regarded highly by his contemporaries. Stories and legends came to surround his name, although the accounts that were passed on did not always agree. In trying to arrive at solid facts regarding dates, places and events, one must bear in mind that one story is just as reliable as another: none of them offers any historical certitude.

The oldest source for the biography of Hui-neng, unfortunately not very reliable, is to be found on an inscription for a memorial pagoda in the Fa-hsing Monastery (Jpn., Hosshō-ji) dated 676.[38] The authors of *Enō kenkyū (Studies on Hui-neng)* regard this inscription as providing our earliest data on Hui-neng and comment:

> The inscription for the Pagoda of the Interment of the Hair commemorates the meeting between Hui-neng and Yin-tsung in the monastery of Fa-hsing and the ceremony of Hui-neng's monastic tonsure. Fa-ts'ai, a monk in the monastery, celebrated this interment on Buddha's birthday and erected the pagoda. Its historical credibility may be considered sound.[39]

Although the inscription itself is not preserved, its text can be found in the collected historical sources from the T'ang period.[40] Yanagida has produced a new edition of the text, which he considers "for the most part credible," adding, however, that "many questions remain regarding the value of the inscription as an historical source."[41] A major difficulty is that the inscription is not mentioned in earlier writings, not even in the *Sō kōsōden*, which frequently refers to such inscriptions.[42] The text refers to the erection of the sacred platform in the monastery by Guṇabhadra and of a prophecy from the year 502 announcing that after 160 years someone would preach the Dharma to a large crowd on this very spot. It goes on to narrate Hui-neng's ordination as a monk by Yin-tsung. A seven-story octagonal pagoda was erected on the very spot where the hair from Hui-neng's tonsure is interred. The inscription bears the name of the otherwise unknown head of the monastery, Fa-ts'ai. If authentic, this is the only source we have that dates back to Hui-neng's lifetime.

All other sources not only date from a later period but can be traced back to the Southern school. This means that the picture they give of Hui-neng as the Sixth Patriarch is an obviously idealized one, legends piled atop one another with no external control. A second source of data on Hui-neng, much later than the pagoda inscription, is an epitaph for Hui-neng composed by the Chinese literary figure Wang Wei at the request of Shen-hui.[43] Although the epitaph itself bears no date, we know for certain that it was written some time after the Great Dharma Assembly of Hua-t'ai in 732, probably during 761, the last year of Wang Wei's life. Its contents rely on biographical information provided by Shen-hui and his disciples. Wang Wei gives the family name of the "Zen Master of Ts'ao-ch'i" as Lu, but does not know his place of birth. As a young man, Lu left the countryside to seek out the Zen master Hung-jen on East Mountain. The latter, impressed by the extraordinary abilities of the disciple, passed on to him the patriarchal robe. Immediately after this, Hui-neng left East Mountain and spent some sixteen years in obscurity among merchants and workers (a piece of information unique to the epitaph). An event of great biographical importance follows: Hui-neng's encounter with the Dharma master Yin-tsung, a teacher of the *Nirvāṇa Sūtra* from whom he received his monastic ordination. After this, Hui-neng began an intensive period of teaching in which he stressed the way of sudden enlightenment and negation as advocated in the Wisdom sūtras. He turned down Empress Wu's invitation to the imperial court.[44] Having predicted his impending death, he took leave of this life amid miraculous signs. His grave is found in Ts'ao-ch'i. A later addition states that Shen-hui was middle-aged when he first met Hui-neng, but this does not accord with Hui-neng's age at the time of his death, as given in the epitaph. The text concludes with a number of verses.

The legendary qualities of Wang Wei's epitaph are undeniable. The story of the bestowal of the robe, a sign of the honor accorded the patriarchate, is an invention of Shen-hui. Later, all the extraordinary characteristics attributed to Hui-neng in this account would be expanded upon and biographical lacunae filled in.

Four other works from the eighth century merit mention in the list of materials pertaining to the biography of Hui-neng.[45] First are the *Discourses of Shen-hui*, together with a short biography of the Sixth Patriarch that is perhaps a later addition to the text of the discourses.[46] Certainly, the *Discourses of Shen-hui* had the strongest overall influence on the tradition of the Southern school. The next source is the *Rekidai hōbōki*, which draws most of its information from the discourses of Shen-hui. The two most important early sources for Hui-neng's biography are the *Sōkei daishi betsuden* (*Special Transmission of the Great Master from Ts'ao-ch'i*) and the autobiography in the Tun-huang text of the *Platform Sūtra of the Sixth Patriarch*. These two sources, differing from the various chronicles of the transmission of the lamp, are in essential agreement and complement each other; they contain the basic materials to be used in the many different versions of the history of Hui-neng that were to follow. For its biographical value, the *Special Transmission* stands first on the list. According to Yanagida, this text "presents the freshest picture of Hui-neng as the founder of the Zen of the Patriarchs and best reflects the new Buddhism that arose after the uproar of An Lu-shan."[47] With distinctive verve, the biography in the *Platform Sūtra* describes the drama of the transmission of the patriarchal honors to Hui-neng.

In all the sources, reports on Hui-neng's origins and early youth are meager and lacking in agreement. In short, choppy sentences, the autobiography moves to the main point. Hui-neng narrates:

> My father was originally an official at Fan-yang. He was [later] dismissed from his post and banished as a commoner to Hsin-chou in Ling-nan. While I was still a child, my father died and my old mother and I, a solitary child, moved to Nan-hai. We suffered extreme poverty and here I sold firewood in the market place. (sec. 2)

This sets the stage for the sūtra. The autobiography tells us how the boy Lu, as he was selling his ware, happened to hear one of his customers read some verses from the *Diamond Sūtra*; his eyes were opened at once and he set out for East Mountain to find the Fifth Patriarch, Hung-jen.

The *Special Transmission* originated among the disciples of Hsing-t'ao, guardian of Hui-neng's grave in Ts'ao-ch'i. In its account of Hui-neng's life, the monastery of Hōrin-ji (Chin., Pao-lin-ssu) plays a central role. After describing the founding of the monastery, the work relates the prophecy of Chih-yao according to which after 170 years the Dharma would experience an incredible increase on this spot; it goes on to mark the favors that the monastery would receive from the imperial court. Regarding Hui-neng's childhood and youth, the work reports only that he was born in Hsin-chou, that his family name was Lu, and that he was orphaned at the age of three. The scene then shifts back to Ts'ao-ch'i, where Hui-neng, now thirty years old, meets a villager named Liu Chih-lüeh who introduces him to a relative of his, a Buddhist nun. A fervent devotee of the *Nirvāṇa Sūtra*, she does a sūtra recitation for him. When she asks him to read, he has to confess that he cannot. "If you can't read the characters, how can you understand the sūtras?" she asked. "The essence of the Buddha nature has nothing to do with deciphering characters," he replied. "What is so strange about someone not being able to read?"[48]

Impressed by the wisdom of the young man, the people of the area urged him to adopt a life of homelessness (Jpn., *shukke*)[49] and to take up abode in Hōrin-ji. After three years of ascetic training, Hui-neng heard of a *dhyāna* master called Yüan. Having sought out the master in his rock cave, he learned how to sit in meditation (*zazen*).[50] Another *dhyāna* master, Hui-chi, recommended that he go to Master Hung-jen on East Mountain, where he could learn the way of Zen. In its description of Hui-neng's visit with Hung-jen, the *Sōkei daishi betsuden* mentions all the important details, including the passing on of the patriarchal honors symbolized in the robe and the begging bowl. Although the account as a whole is straightforward, it applies an imaginative flourish to the account by having Hui-neng wear a heavy stone around his waist when treading rice because he was not heavy enough to do the job. The biography ends with Hui-neng's departure from Hung-jen and the ensuing pursuit by Hui-ming.[51]

The events surrounding Hui-neng's visit to the East Mountain and the transmission of the patriarchate make up the core of the autobiography contained in the *Platform Sūtra of the Sixth Patriarch*. There Hui-neng, having been introduced to the reader in the briefest of terms, is made to set out abruptly on the most important journey of his life. The Tun-huang version does not mention his age; the discourses of Shen-hui and the *Rekidai hōbōki* tell us he was twenty-four. This is the figure used in most of the later chronicles.[52] Hui-neng happens to hear some verses of the *Diamond Sūtra*, which set him off on his quest. During his first visit with the Fifth Patriarch a discussion about the Buddha nature, the central theme of the *Nirvāṇa Sūtra*, takes place. Both of these sūtras are very important in the spiritual evolution of the Sixth Patriarch. Having inquired about Hui-neng's origins and intentions, Hung-jen then informs him coldly that a barbarian from the South could never become a Buddha. The uneducated boy Lu was quick with his response: "Although people from the South and people from the North differ, there is no north and south in Buddha nature" (sec. 3).

Hung-jen immediately sensed the exceptional spiritual energy of this recent arrival from the South; he said nothing and instructed the young man to start working with the other disciples. A lay disciple gave him the job of treading rice. "I did this for eight months," Hui-neng recalls for his audience.

> One day Hung-jen called his disciples together and instructed them: "Each of you write a verse and bring it to me. I will read your verses, and if there is one who is awakened to the cardinal meaning, I will give him the robe and the Dharma and make him the Sixth Patriarch. Hurry, Hurry!" (sec. 4)

The disciples returned to their cells, overwhelmed by the master's request. They agreed to let the first among them, Shen-hsiu, take on the task of composing a verse. Though well-instructed in the sūtras, Shen-hsiu was still far from enlightenment and the master's instructions threw him into a deep anxiety. At length he produced his verses and at midnight wrote them on the middle wall of the south hall:

> The body is the Bodhi tree,
> The mind is like a clear mirror.
> At all times we must strive to polish it,
> And must not let the dust collect. (sec. 6)

Master Hung-jen was the first to see the verses the next morning. Assembling all the monks, he burned incense before the inscription on the wall. The disciples were filled with wonder and considered the question of succession settled. The master, however, called Shen-hsiu aside. Having confirmed his suspicion that Shen-hsiu had written the verses, the master said to him: "This verse you wrote shows that you still have not reached true understanding. You have merely arrived at the front of the gate but have yet to be able to enter it." As the verses make evident, practice can help ordinary persons, but it cannot bring them to perfect enlightenment. "You must enter the gate and see your own original nature. . ." (sec. 7). He left Shen-hsiu to compose further verses. Days passed, but the first monk of the community could not produce a sign of his enlightenment.

Hui-neng was treading rice in the barn when he happened to hear a young monk walk by reciting Shen-hsiu's verses. Immediately he knew that the verses, logically consistent and readily interpreted by resolving the two similes, did not express enlightenment. Dramatizing the illiteracy of the Sixth Patriarch, the sūtra then describes how he was led to the south hall, where he reverenced the verses and asked someone to read them for him. On the spot, his enlightened mind formulated a new stanza expressing true enlightenment. He then requested that his verses be written on the wall of the west hall. The Tun-huang text gives two slightly different versions. The following traditional form is the more accurate:

Originally there is no tree of enlightenment,
Nor is there a stand with a clear mirror.
From the beginning not one thing exists;
Where, then, is a grain of dust to cling?[53]

The admiration of the disciples for these verses of the illiterate peasant was boundless. Still, the master held back his praise. "This is still not complete understanding" (sec. 8). But then at midnight Hung-jen summoned Hui-neng and conferred on him the Dharma of Sudden Enlightenment and the patriarchal robe with the words: "I make you the Sixth Patriarch. The robe is the proof and is to be handed down from generation to generation. My Dharma must be transmitted from mind to mind. You must make people awaken to themselves" (sec. 9). Hung-jen ordered the new patriarch quickly to flee south, and accompanied him to Chiu-chiang Station in Chiang-hsi Province.

The autobiographical report closes with a section on the pursuit by Hui-ming. Various versions are found in Zen literature. The Tun-huang text of the Platform Sūtra stresses the hostile intent of the pursuit, depicting Hui-ming as coarse and violent. However, Hui-ming reached enlightenment on the summit of Mount Ta-yü after Hui-neng had explained the Dharma to him (sec. 11).

According to the Special Transmission, Hung-jen refused to offer any further lectures on doctrine, noting that the Buddha-dharma had left their midst and was heading south. Three days before he died, Hung-jen repeated this declaration and then foretold his coming death. As the report has it, miraculous signs accompanied his passing away. The disciple Hui-ming departed the monastery and met Hui-neng on Mount Ta-yü. There is no report of any hostile intent. On the contrary, he requested instruction from the Sixth Patriarch, who without hesitation handed over to him the robe and begging bowl. Expressing his gratitude, Hui-ming urged Hui-neng to keep moving, for enemies were lying in wait. Hui-ming returned to the Lu-shan, where after three years of practice in a monastery he finally attained enlightenment.[54]

The different biographies give variant accounts of events during the following years. We do not know for sure how many years Hui-neng lived in retreat in South China. Chang Wei reckons sixteen; the *Special Transmission* sets the figure at five. The next notable event in Hui-neng's career is his meeting with Yin-tsung (627–713), a Vinaya master and devotee of the *Nirvāṇa Sūtra*, in the monastery of Chih-chih (Jpn., Seishi-ji). As Hui-neng listened to his lecture on the sūtra, the disciples started arguing among themselves about whether it is the flag of the temple or the wind that is moving, Hui-neng offered the solution: it is the *mind* that is moving.[55] That evening Yin-tsung called him to his room and asked him about the Dharma of Hung-jen. Hui-neng then announced that he had been made the Dharma heir and showed Yin-tsung the patriarchal robe as proof. After Yin-tsung had offered profound reverence, Hui-neng explained to him how the nature of the mind is to be grasped and how the Buddha nature transcends all duality. "The Buddha nature is the Dharma of nonduality." With these words the memorable conversation ended. Deeply moved, Yin-tsung implored the Sixth Patriarch to become his teacher.

Yanagida thinks that this report distorts the real historical situation.[56] The sources tell us that Yin-tsung was a highly esteemed master, revered by the imperial court and recognized as an authority on ritual. In the *Special Transmission* the "wayfarer Lu"—note that he is still a layman—is made to appear his superior:

> How lucky Yin-tsung is! Among those attending his lecture there is one individual who, though an ordinary (unenlightened) man (Jpn., *bonbu*; Skt., *pṛthagjana*), is a bodhisattva of the cosmic Buddha body. The *Nirvāṇa Sūtra* that Yin-tsung explains to the assembly is like brick and stone; what he, the wayfarer Lu, had laid out before him the previous night in his room is like gold and precious jewels.[57]

Such passages are high points in the poetic legend.

In a brief section the *Special Transmission* states that Yin-tsung presided over the giving of the tonsure to Hui-neng; in somewhat greater detail it also reports his monastic ordination in 676 at the hands of a number of high spiritual dignitaries in the monastery of Hosshō-ji. In taking up his mission of preaching, the patriarch was beginning what was to be the final stage of his life. At Hui-neng's wish, Yin-tsung and more than three thousand monks and laity accompanied him on his return to the monastery of Hōrin-ji. There, a large community gathered around the master. We can imagine that for the three or four decades that still remained in his life, he was fully occupied with lectures and the guidance of his disciples.

A significant interruption occurred when the emperor invited Hui-neng to the imperial court; understandably, Hui-neng turned him down. Nonetheless, the patriarch was honored by the court with gifts and a new name for his monastery.[58] In the biographies of previous Zen masters, invitations from the imperial court and discussions with imperial delegates illustrate a twofold attitude toward political power: on the one hand, there is reserve and refusal as proof of the enlightened masters' detachment from all worldly glory, on the other, honors that place them in the social limelight.

In the Tun-huang text of the *Platform Sūtra* we find in addition to the autobiography a final section that supplies further biographical information. After finishing his great lecture Hui-neng returned to Ts'ao-ch'i (sec. 37), where he conducted discussions with some Zen monks who then became his disciples. These included Chih-ch'eng, who had been sent by Shen-hsiu to find out about this Sixth Patriarch and who, upon hearing the master's words, attained enlightenment (sec. 40, 41); Fa-ta, whose knowledge of the *Lotus Sūtra* was elevated to enlightened wisdom through Hui-neng's instruction (sec. 42); Chih-ch'ang, whom the Sixth Patriarch enabled to move beyond the three Buddhist vehicles to grasp the "highest vehicle" (sec. 43); and Shen-hui, who entered the community of Hui-neng's disciples after a kōan-like conversation with the master (sec. 44). From this point on—we do not have an exact date—Shen-hui remained with the Sixth Patriarch until the latter's death. The sūtra lists the names of the ten disciples of Hui-neng. They include, in addition to those just mentioned, Fa-hai, Chih-t'ung, Chih-ch'e, Chih-tao, Fa-chen, and Fa-ju.[59] The number ten reflects the "ten great disciples" of the Fifth Patriarch, Hung-jen. The only one of these disciples to become a well-known personality in Zen history is Shen-hui.

Before he died, Hui-neng made provisions that in the future the transmission of the Dharma should take place through the conferral of copies of the *Platform Sūtra* (sec. 47). He then spoke these moving words of farewell:

> Come close. In the eighth month I intend to leave this world. If any of you have doubts, ask about them quickly, and I shall resolve them for you. I must bring your delusions to an end and make it possible for you to gain peace. After I have gone there will be no one to teach you.

Deeply touched, all the disciples began to cry. Only Shen-hui remained unmoved. Hui-neng turned and spoke to him:

> Shen-hui, you are a young monk, yet you have attained the [status of awakening] in which good and not good are identical, and you are not moved by judgments of praise and blame. You others have not yet understood. . . . You're crying just because you don't know where I'm going. If you knew where I was going you wouldn't be crying. The nature itself is without birth and without destruction, without going and without coming, All of you sit down. I shall give you a verse, the verse of the true-false moving-quiet. . . .

The disciples begged him for these verses. Hui-neng responded with a long hymn (sec. 48) and then recited the enlightened verses of the first six Chinese Zen patriarchs, beginning with the words of Bodhidharma:

> I originally came to China,
> To transmit the teaching and save deluded beings.

One flower opens five petals,
And the fruit ripens of itself. (sec. 49)

When questioned about the genealogy for the transmission of the Dharma, Hui-neng first named the seven Buddhas of the past, then the twenty-eight Indian patriarchs, and finally his predecessors, the five Chinese patriarchs, making himself the fortieth bearer of the Buddha mind. The two groups of verse that follow begin with the well-known words:

Deluded, a Buddha is a sentient being;
Awakened, a sentient being is a Buddha. (sec. 52)

His last words were these:

> Good-bye, all of you. I shall depart from you now. After I am gone, do not weep worldly tears, nor accept condolences, money, and silks from people, nor wear mourning garments. If you did so it would not accord with the sacred Dharma, nor would you be true disciples of mine. Be the same as you would if I were here, and sit all together in meditation. If you are only peacefully calm and quiet, without motion, without stillness, without birth, without destruction, without coming, without going, without judgments of right and wrong, without staying and without going—this then is the Great Way. After I have gone just practice according to the Dharma in the same way that you did on the days that I was with you. Even though I were still to be in this world, if you went against the teachings, there would be no use in my having stayed here.

Hui-neng's death was accompanied by miraculous signs. According to the *Special Transmission*, he died in his parental home in Hsin-chou, which had since been turned into a temple where he had retreated a year before his death. After his death, his body was taken to Ts'ao-ch'i and interred in a specially built pagoda.[60]

The description of Hui-neng's death in the *Platform Sūtra* illustrates the extraordinary reverence and affection his disciples had for him. These pages remind one of the moving descriptions of the Buddha's entrance into nirvāṇa in the Pāli Canon. It is eminently clear that in the biography of Hui-neng Zen Buddhism has fashioned a stirring picture of the ideal Zen master. Where the Bodhidharma legend borders on the realm of fairytale, the history of the Sixth Patriarch remains deeply rooted in the soil of China. All the particular features of the story, whether factual or idealized, are fashioned into a composite whole. First we are shown the strong farm boy whose care for his aged mother manifests the filial piety that is so distinctive of the humanity of his people; then there is the image of the illiterate youth, untouched by book learning, a pure child of nature and at the same time a "seeker after the Tao," the way that leads to enlightenment through the holy words of the Buddha recorded in the sūtras, especially in the *Diamond Sūtra* and *Nirvāṇa Sūtra*. The glorious summit of his life is reached with the revelation of the highest wisdom in the four lines of his enlightenment verse, lines without equal in the history of Zen. The crown of the patriarchate through which the Buddha mind is transmitted comes as a fitting tribute to this "bodhisattva." It is this figure of Hui-neng that Zen has elevated to the stature of the Zen master par excellence. His teachings stand at the source of all the widely diverse currents of Zen Buddhism.

In our search for the materials out of which the legendary biography of the Sixth Patriarch was constructed we looked especially to sources from the eighth century, a period of transition in the history of Chinese Zen. The Tun-huang text of the *Platform Sūtra* formed the foundation for the biography;[61] building on this foundation are elements from the *Special Transmission of the Great Master of Ts'ao-ch'i*, a text that greatly complements the picture of the patriarch's life as recorded in the *Platform Sūtra*. The *Hōrinden*, which contains material from the eighth century and earlier, is unfortunately not preserved in its entirety; the sections with the biography of Hui-neng are missing.[62] The works of Tsung-mi (780–841) offer further valuable material for the early history of Zen.[63] Also deserving of mention is the *Tsu-t'ang chi* (Jpn., *Sodōshū*), compiled by the Chinese monks Ching and Yün in 952 and included in the Koryō edition of the Korean Tripiṭaka (1245).[64] The *Sō kōsōden* contains an outline of the patriarch's life.[65] The *Keitoku dentōroku* (1004), the representative chronicle for the Sung period, brings together the materials of the Hui-neng biography and presents them as valid and genuine accounts for later generations. In classical Zen literature, the dominant influence of Hui-neng is assured. The figure of the Sixth Patriarch embodies the essence of Zen.

SUDDEN ENLIGHTENMENT AS SEEING INTO ONE'S NATURE

Just as we owe much of our knowledge of Hui-neng's biography to Shen-hui and his disciples, so we can turn to the *Discourses of Shen-hui* to appreciate his path to enlightenment. And just as a number of different sources came together to make up the biography, the same is true of the doctrinal passages of the *Platform Sūtra*. Hui-neng's great temple discourse is not in any sense a unified whole cut of a single cloth; it is impossible, moreover, to dismantle it, analyze its content and sources, and then put it back together again. The main doctrinal content of the *Discourses* is hardly original. Indeed, nearly all of its ingredients can already be found in the vast literature of Mahāyāna Buddhism.

In the Tun-huang text of the *Platform Sūtra*, which received its final redaction at the hands of Shen-hui's disciples, great emphasis is placed on opposing Shen-hsiu and the Northern school—or better, what was thought to be the teaching of the Northern school. As recent historical scholarship makes clear, the Northern school was not at all the unified block that Shen-hui's arguments suggest. A doctrine of sudden enlightenment based on the Wisdom teachings was also to be found among the masters and disciples of the Northern school.[66] Because our knowledge of this branch of Zen depends almost exclusively on information from the Southern school, our conclusions have to be drawn with great care and with many qualifications. Although the *Platform Sūtra* does not mention the Great Dharma Assembly of Hua-t'ai, it presupposes this meeting as part of its rejection of the Northern school. At the close of the sūtra, after Hui-neng's temple discourse, the topic is taken up again in a series of slogan-like declarations:

> People in the world all say: "In the South, Neng, in the North, Hsiu," but they do not know the basic reason. . . . The Dharma is one teaching, but people are from the North and the South, so Southern and Northern schools have been established. What is meant by "gradual" and "sudden"? The Dharma itself is the same, but in seeing it there is a slow way and a fast way. Seen slowly, it is the gradual; seen fast it is the sudden [teaching]. Dharma is without sudden or gradual, but some people are keen and others dull; hence the names "sudden" and "gradual." (sec. 39)

This same idea is expressed at the beginning of the sūtra: suddenness and gradualness have no foundation in the Dharma but arise from the spiritual sharpness or dullness of human beings. These human differences make for the different situations from which people approach enlightenment. People who are caught in error will make use of the gradual method, while the enlightened follow the sudden path. This last assertion provides a bit of a problem for interpreters: enlightened persons are not supposed to need practice. Yet Zen includes practice for those who have already been enlightened—practice based on their enlightenment. In the section we are considering, a value judgment about the two different methods is evident. Only in enlightenment, the text concludes, will the differences fade away (sec. 16).

Another passage of the *Platform Sūtra* dealing with the different levels of spiritual capacity among people stresses that even people of "shallow roots," that is, of little talent, possess wisdom (prajñā) and as such do not differ essentially from people of great wisdom. Their unfortunate state is caused by the obstacles they encounter from their erroneous views and deeply-rooted passions. "It is like the times when great clouds cover the sun; unless the wind blows the sun will not appear" (sec. 29). How can such people experience the joy of enlightenment? The sūtra answers:

> There is no large or small in prajñā-wisdom. Because all sentient beings have of themselves deluded minds, they seek the Buddha by external practice and are unable to awaken to their own natures. But even these people of shallow capacity, if they hear the Sudden Doctrine and do not place their trust in external practices but only in their own minds always raise correct views in regard to their own original natures; even these sentient beings, filled with passions and troubles, will at once gain awakening. It is like the great sea which gathers all the flowing streams, and merges together the small waters and the large waters into one. This is seeing into your own nature. (sec. 29)

In opposition to the doctrine of gradual progression, this passage lays out the essential elements that constitute the way of sudden enlightenment. The foundation and core of this way is wisdom (prajñā), which is neither large nor small and is one and the same in all living beings. Before considering different ways of thinking about and articulating wisdom, it is important to point out a fundamental insight essential to all of Mahāyāna and, however variously formulated, common to all the sūtras and śāstras. Reality—be it called "nature," "self-nature," "original nature," "mind nature," "Buddha nature," "Dharma nature," or "thusness"—is one. It is wisdom and light. In order to achieve final liberation, living beings must realize this unity of the real. The beginning and end of the way turn out to be the same. Among all the schools of Mahāyāna Buddhism we find an ultimate consensus regarding this fundamental reality, something like assent to *prima principia* that are beyond question.

Also belonging to the foundations of Mahāyāna is the doctrine on the original purity and equality of this nature and the related doctrine on the identity between nirvāna and samsāra. The philosophical schools of Mahāyāna Buddhism construct their different systems, essentially the same but conceptually diverse, on the basis of the distinction between the noumenal and phenomenal aspects of reality. In Zen, the basic insight of Mahāyāna is expressed in religious praxis, that is, in concrete practice and experience. Even the Northern school does not question any of the fundamental doctrines of Mahāyāna. What is at stake in its conflict with the Southern school is meditational praxis, which is grounded in doctrine and in turn interprets doctrine. The most important point of the controversy deals with the conception and evaluation of error and passion.

In the transitory world of samsāra all living beings are caught up in error and passion, but the passions are not real. On this fundamental point all Zen followers, both in the Northern and in the Southern schools, agree. Passions are hard to grasp and well-nigh impossible to express in words, which is why Buddhists of all orientations are fond of using metaphors to express them. Two such metaphors were mentioned earlier, each stemming from one of the opposing schools. The enlightenment verses of Shen-hsiu, the head of the Northern school, speak of specks of dust clouding a spotless mirror. In the *Platform Sūtra of the Sixth Patriarch* we read of large clouds that by themselves can hide the sun. In both examples we are dealing with metaphors. The reality of passions is not in question. From the Mahāyāna Buddhist point of view, passions are like all phenomena in this world of becoming—empty. And yet they are extremely important for anyone practicing meditation. What attitude should one take to these disturbing factors? How should one look at them? It is in answer to these questions that the Northern and Southern schools part paths.

The position of the Northern school is clearly expressed in Shen-hsiu's metaphor. The mirror of the mind must be wiped clean continually lest the dust of erroneous notions collect on it. This is why one meditates. In such meditation an ongoing process of cleansing takes place until enlightenment is attained. In the *Platform Sūtra of the Sixth Patriarch*, this practice is called "viewing the mind" (Jpn., *kanshin*) or "viewing purity" (Jpn., *kanjō*), obviously alluding to the erroneous methods of meditation in the Northern school (sec. 14). In meditation, one concentrates on the mind as an object in order to perceive its purity. Here the text of the *Platform Sūtra* uses a Chinese character composed of the elements for "eye" and "hand" that here signifies objectivized seeing.[67]

The metaphor of clouds and sun is used twice in the sūtra (secs. 20 and 27). The latter passage has already been referred to. The former carries the imagery further:

> . . . All the dharmas are within your own natures, yet your own natures are always pure. The sun and the moon are always bright, yet if they are covered by clouds, although above they are bright, below they are darkened, and the sun, moon, stars, and planets cannot be seen clearly. But if suddenly the wind of wisdom should blow and roll away the clouds and mists, all forms in the universe appear at once. The purity of the nature of man in this world is like the blue sky; wisdom is like the sun, knowledge like the moon. Although knowledge and wisdom are always clear, if you cling to external environments, the floating clouds of false thoughts will create a cover, and your own natures cannot become clear.

The metaphor of the drifting clouds suggests that all passions are temporary and lacking any real existence in the face of wisdom. As the sun dispels the clouds, so does wisdom disperse the passions. When? Enlightenment breaks through when the time is ripe, just as the fruit drops when it has matured. Why? Here again the question has no logical answer. The experience of enlightenment is not dependent on meditation; there is no causal connection between the two. Meditational practice is neither the cause nor the condition for coming to a realization. Once awakened to wisdom, the mind sees nature (Jpn., *kenshō*), its own nature (*jishō*), which is identical with the Buddha nature (*busshō*).

If meditation is not supposed to cleanse the mind of passions, what purpose does it serve? Does meditation have any function at all or is it a purposeless activity? The question points in fact to the viewpoint of the Southern school, according to which meditation is to be practiced without any purpose, in perfect freedom. The only concern that one meditating need have is to guard against all forms of attachment. As the text just cited states, passions arise when persons cling to external objects. The *Platform Sūtra* warns: "Tao must be something that circulates freely; why should he [the deluded person] impede it? If the mind does not abide in things, the Tao circulates freely; if the mind abides in things, it becomes entangled" (sec. 14).

This understanding of meditation flows from Mahāyāna's central insight regarding the radical equality of all things. Like nirvāna and samsāra, passions and true enlightenment are the same. Meditation is not really different from wisdom. This insight is illustrated in the *Platform Sūtra* in the example of the lamp and the light, an example that makes use of the Chinese notions of substance (*t'i*) and function (*yung*). "The lamp is the substance of light; the light is the function of the lamp" (sec. 15). Here the concepts are stripped of their philosophical relevance. Meditation and wisdom are not two but one, unseparated and inseparable. In its identity with wisdom, meditation enjoys the freedom and spontaneity of the Tao, which is the Chinese equivalent of the Buddhist prajñā.

The understanding of meditation as identical with wisdom stands in sharp contrast to the method of meditation that Shen-hui attributes to the Northern school and harshly criticizes as mere external form. When in his *Discourses* Shen-hui rebukes those of his followers who try to cleanse their minds through concentration, he does so because he is convinced that this will impede the break-through to their self-nature.[68] Did not Vimalikīrti in his sūtra reprimand Śāriputra for going off into the forest to sit in meditation?[69] This reprimand applies to all those who teach others to "sit viewing the mind and viewing purity, not moving and not activating the mind" (sec. 14).

In many passages, the *Platform Sūtra* warns against false practice, especially against clinging to either purity or to emptiness. "When with empty mind one sits in meditation, one can easily cling to indifferent emptiness" (sec. 24).[70] Note also the following passage:

> Self-nature contains the ten thousand things. . . . The deluded person merely recites; the wise man practices with his mind. There are deluded men who make their minds empty and do not think, and to this they give the name of "great." This, too, is wrong. The capacity of the mind is vast and wide, but when there is no practice it is small." (sec. 25)

Consistent with the fundamental Mahāyāna doctrines on no-mind and the identity of meditation with prajñā, the *Platform Sūtra* stresses the spiritual dimension of practice. The intense atmosphere of practice within the Southern school was undeniable. Zen action continued in full swing during the succeeding generations. The high regard accorded the traditional practice of sitting in meditation bore clear witness to an enduring reverence for the legendary founder of Zen, Bodhidharma, the story of whose sitting for nine years facing a wall in meditation belongs to the heart of the Zen myth. According to tradition, Hui-neng himself was sitting in meditation when he entered nirvāṇa.[71]

The concrete phenomena attending the paths to enlightenment according to the teaching on suddenness are not described in the *Platform Sūtra of the Sixth Patriarch*, but all the essential elements regarding practice and enlightenment are there. As an external practice, sitting in meditation is temporary and in the final analysis unimportant. What is crucial is the unattached mind, object-less meditation that clings to nothing. The mind needs no gradual purification since its original purity remains untainted in saṃsāra. The experience takes place in a sudden awakening to wisdom. Meditation and wisdom are identical. No longer caught in the false notions of saṃsāra, wisdom can now shine forth. Enlightened persons know that their light is their own original nature. In Hui-neng's Zen of the Patriarchs, diverse and important currents of Mahāyāna flow together.

THE MAHĀYĀNA DOCTRINES OF NO-MIND
AND THE BUDDHA NATURE

The way of sudden enlightenment in Chinese Zen is rooted in the teachings of the Mahāyāna sūtras and represents their mature fruition. Throughout the various schools of Chinese Buddhism students were reading the sūtras and striving to appropriate their teachings. In the sūtras they would find the central message regarding Buddhahood, yet because the vast Mahāyāna textual corpus is made up of sūtras widely divergent in style and content (the result of the disparate religious viewpoints of the communities that produced them) it was inevitable that differences in the way this message was explained would arise. Then again, divergent philosophical perspectives provoked further interpretative diversity. From school to school, and even within the same school, the scriptures were not infrequently interpreted differently. The strong and progressive Zen movement was no exception. It is helpful to keep this general context in mind when encountering doctrinal nuances which, viewed through the fog of uncertain historical sources, may be difficult to distinguish.

It is a matter of historical fact that from early on many Mahāyāna scriptures were known in the Southern school of Chinese Zen. In the *Platform Sūtra of the Sixth Patriarch* as well as in the writings of Shen-hui and his disciples, two key elements of Mahāyāna thought stand out: the Wisdom teachings of the Prajñāpāramitā sūtras and the doctrine of the Buddha nature central to the *Nirvāṇa Sūtra*. According to tradition, these two pillars of Mahāyāna Buddhism played a decisive role in the life of Hui-neng. The Sixth Patriarch begins his temple discourse by relating how a passage from the *Diamond Sūtra* (one of the Wisdom sūtras), which he happened to hear by pure chance, set him off on the path to enlightenment. The *Special Transmission*, which is so important for the biography of Hui-neng, tells us that the *Nirvāṇa Sūtra* always held first place in the life of the patriarch. The two sūtras stand like twin pillars undergirding Hui-neng's life and forming the foundations for his inner development and for the doctrine of sudden enlightenment. The new path of enlightenment represented by the Zen of the Patriarchs brought these two sūtras, which represent the quintessence of Mahāyāna, to an experiential unity.

Since the time of Hui-neng, the *Diamond Sūtra*, which proclaims the teachings of wisdom in concise and moving terms, has assumed a central place in Chinese Zen Buddhism. Wisdom that sees through emptiness—the emptiness of the phenomenal world, of the empirical ego, of all qualities and forms—and that transcends all words and concepts to press towards nothingness, is the center of all reality. Wisdom (prajñā) and emptiness (śūnyatā) are correlatives expressing one and the same reality in positive and negative terms respectively. The prajñā intuition of emptiness is a seeing, but this seeing is a non-seeing. The Zen masters speak of "no-mind" (Jpn., *mushin*; Chin., *wu-hsin*), or synonymously of non-thinking (Jpn., *munen*; Chin., *wu-nien*).[72]

A passage from the *Platform Sūtra of the Sixth Patriarch* develops this negativity in these terms:

Good friends, in this teaching of mine, from ancient times up to the present, all have set up no-thought [munen] as the main doctrine, non-form [musō] as the substance, and non-abiding [mujū] as the basis. Non-form is to be separated from form even when associated with form. No-thought is not to think even when involved in thought. Non-abiding is the original nature of man. (sec. 17)

All three negations are expressions of "emptiness." Zen Buddhism puts the primary emphasis on munen. No-thought or non-thinking is the core of the doctrine of sudden enlightenment. To begin with, the term denotes the non-clinging of the mind. The mind that does not adhere to anything is free and pure. Hui-neng explains the two terms of the expression:

"No" [mu] is the separation from the dualism that produces the passions. "Thought" [nen] means thinking of the original nature of True Reality; thoughts are the function of true reality. . . . The Vimalakīrti Sūtra says: "Externally, while distinguishing well all the forms of the various dharmas, internally he stands firm within the First Principle." (sec. 17)

In his Discourses Shen-hui explains "no-thought" or "no-mind" in terms of the doctrine of śūnya found in the Wisdom sūtras. Munen exists and does not exist; it is ineffable[73] and inconceivable; at the same time it is the incomprehensible, the non-abiding, the meditation (dhyāna) of the Perfected One (tathāgata).[74] One must let go of the external and the internal, of being and nonbeing in order to attain final equality and to realize that in seeing one's own nature one has reached one's original nature, the Buddha nature.[75] The seeing that accompanies no-thought is the same as the "highest truth" (paramārtha-satya) of the Middle Way (madhyamā pratipad)[76] and the vision of all reality.

The relationship between the "emptiness" (śūnyatā) of the Wisdom sutras and the "no-thought" (munen) of the Zen masters is evident both in their common use of negative statements and in their love of contradiction and paradox. In the philosophical interpretation of "emptiness" offered by the Mādhyamika school, the element of relativity is central. As the commentaries explain, there is smallness only because there is largeness, darkness only because there is light, permanence only because there is impermanence.[77] The center is defined by limits and opposites. Shen-hui makes use of this method of relative opposites in his Discourses, and one section in the Platform Sūtra of the Sixth Patriarch (sec. 46) lines up some thirty-six opposites. Soon after Hui-neng, this capacity for playing with paradox reached a high level of sophistication.

This discussion should make it clear that the munen of which the Zen masters speak is not to be understood primarily in a psychological sense. Their aim was neither to disengage rational thought and imagination nor to cultivate a psychic state of passivity, both of which have more in common with the aims of the dust-cleaning meditation of the Northern school. In his Discourses, Shen-hui expressly interprets the classical image of the mirror—which actually goes back to Chuang-tzu—to mean that the mirror of truth shines continuously, whether or not there happens to be any object in front of it.[78] Neither external passions nor psychic changes can influence no-thought. No-thought is not to be identified with the unconscious of modern psychology.[79] The identification of no-thought with seeing into one's self-nature, with penetrating all things (dharma), and finally with attaining the Buddha nature clearly implies that munen reaches to the realm of the Absolute and brings liberation. The soteriological content of munen is evident in the Platform Sutra of the Sixth Patriarch:

> If you know your original mind, this then is deliverance. Once you have attained deliverance, this then is the prajñā samādhi. If you have awakened to the prajñā samādhi, this then is no-thought. What is no-thought? The Dharma of no-thought means: even though you see all things, you do not attach to them. . . . This is the prajñā samādhi, and being free and having achieved release is known as the practice of no-thought. . . . If you awaken to the Dharma of no-thought, you will penetrate into all things thoroughly, and will see the realm of the Buddha. If you awaken to the sudden doctrine of no-thought, you will have reached the status of the Buddha. (sec. 31)

The Platform Sutra frequently uses the word "nature." In addition to standing on its own—as in the expression "seeing into nature" (kenshō)—it appears in "one's own nature," "self-nature" (jishō), "original nature" (honshō), "wisdom nature" (chieshō), "Dharma nature" (hosshō), and "Buddha nature" (busshō). Insofar as Hui-neng's teaching on sudden enlightenment has appropriated the doctrine of the Buddha nature, it is well integrated into Mahāyāna thought. The doctrine concerning the Buddha nature of all living beings is the central message of the important Nirvāṇa Sūtra. As mentioned earlier, the Special Transmission relates that this was the first Mahāyāna scripture that Hui-neng encountered. The Platform Sutra tells us that Hui-neng always preferred the Diamond Sūtra, but the autobiographical section reports a conversation between the Fifth Patriarch, Hung-jen, and the boy Lu in which the expression Buddha nature comes up rather unexpectedly (sec. 3).

Although the Platform Sutra does not develop the doctrine of the Buddha nature in detail, Shen-hui does. In his Discourses he refers to the Nirvāṇa Sūtra to explain how the Buddha nature is unborn and indestructible. He cites the words of the sūtra: "Because it [the Buddha nature] is neither empirically perceptible nor transempirical, neither long nor short, neither high nor low, neither caused nor destructible, one can call it constant."[80] This statement and others like it have been interpreted in different ways. The Southern school attributes reality but not substantiality to the Buddha nature, as it does to self-nature. The Platform Sutra has this to say of self-nature: "If you give rise to thoughts from your self-nature, then, although you see, hear, perceive, and know, you are not stained by the manifold environments and are always free" (sec. 17). Neither the Buddha nature nor self-nature nor no-thought (munen) can be conceived of in terms of some basic substance that differs from the phenomena of the world. The point is made very clearly in a doctrinal discourse by National Teacher (kuo-shih) Nan-yang Hui-chung, as reported in the Zen chronicle *Keitoku den-tōroku*.[81]

The chronicle reports how once the National Teacher Hui-chung questioned a Zen guest from the South on what kind of teachings he had been studying. The guest explained the doctrine, widespread throughout the South, of the distinction between indestructible nature and corruptible body. "The body," the Zen disciple went on, "is born and then passes away, like a dragon that changes its skeletal structure, or a snake that slips off its skin, or a man who leaves his house. The body is changeable; nature is unchangeable." Hearing this, the master was horrified. Were these not the views of the heretic Śreṇika? This "heretic" or "misleader" plays a specific role in Buddhist literature as the embodiment of belief in an indestructible nature that inhabits the body like a soul.[82] This belief, which has its roots in Indian philosophy, distinguishes between body and soul, between the phenomenal world and nature or substance, and finally, in Buddhist terms, between nirvāṇa and saṃsāra. Hui-chung replied that during his wide travels throughout the land he had encountered numerous advocates of this erroneous doctrine, which runs so contrary to the authentic doctrine of the *Platform Sūtra*, and went on to complain that because of so many changes and additions, the true message of the *Platform Sūtra of the Sixth Patriarch* had been lost. His criticisms were evidently aimed at an erroneous (and evidently widespread) understanding of the Buddha nature that was at odds with the teachings of the Wisdom sūtras.

We do not know who was responsible for the changes and additions mentioned by the National Teacher.[83] Centuries later, a Korean Zen master would teach that the body is born and passes away, while the mind knows neither birth nor death, appealing in defense of his position to the *Platform Sūtra*, perhaps to the following passage later added to the text: "The self-nature of thusness stirs up thoughts, eyes, ears, nose, tongue do not think. The nature of thusness is able to stir up thoughts; without thusness, eyes, ears, color and voice disappear immediately."[84]

According to the *Keitoku dentōroku*, the Zen master Chih-tao, who had spent ten years of his life studying the *Nirvāṇa Sūtra*, tried to convince the Sixth Patriarch of this same understanding of the Buddha nature. "All living beings," he argued, "have two bodies, the material body [Skt., *rūpakāya*; Jpn., *shikishin*] and the Dharma body [Skt., *dharmakāya*; Jpn., *hosshin*]. The material body is impermanent; it is born and it dies. The Dharma body is permanent, without knowing or perceiving." Yanagida translates the meaning of the last part of this citation in modern terms to read "The Dharma body . . . transcends knowing and perceiving."[85] In defense of his view Chih-tao appeals to the *Nirvāṇa Sūtra*. But the Sixth Patriarch sharply rebukes him, a son of the Buddha, for teaching with the heretics "that there is yet another special Dharma body outside the material body" and for seeking another nirvāṇa apart from saṃsāra.

The Southern school of Chinese Zen, which the Sixth Patriarch represents, endorsed the doctrine of the Buddha nature but insisted strongly on the identity of reality. The Buddha nature is not something like an essential, enduring inner substance that is passed on in the cycle of reincarnation. Zen excludes any interpretation of the Buddha nature that would try to introduce duality into reality. Through the Buddha nature, reality itself takes on a glow of transcendent splendor.

The Buddha nature, like its counterpart prajñā, transcends all opposites, even the opposition between good and evil. The Sixth Patriarch is said to have declared: "Do not think about good and evil!"[86] This statement has nothing to do with amorality. What is intended is a transcending of all duality, an overcoming of all discursive thought. Zen is no exception to the generally accepted ethics of Mahāyāna. Yanagida cites the following verses from the *Platform Sūtra*:

If you are a person who truly practices the Way,
Do not look at the ignorance of the world,
For if you see the wrong of people in the world,
Being wrong yourself, *you* will be evil. (sec. 36)

He sees in them a reflection of the simple ethical charge of the *Dhammapada*:

If a man sees the sins of others,
And forever thinks of their faults,
His own sins increase for ever
And far off is he from the end of his faults.[87]

A moral connotation is also evident in the passage of the *Platform Sūtra* on contrition (Jpn., *sange*, sec. 22).[88]

According to the *Nirvāṇa Sūtra*, the Buddha nature embraces all living beings, but not lifeless things. Yet already among its earliest interpreters there were those who suggested that the sūtra implied that the Buddha nature should be extended to all of reality. The ensuing controversy over the universality of the Buddha nature ranges widely over Chinese Buddhism. Within Zen, too, there are staunch advocates on both sides of the question. In opposition to the position of Master Yüan of the Ox-head school, Shen-hui expressed the more conservative view: "The Buddha nature is present in all living beings, but not in lifeless things." He defends his position by arguing that lifeless things have no part in the Dharma body and in prajñā.[89] In the period after Hui-neng, the generally accepted Zen view was that the Buddha nature is unrestrictedly universal.[90]

Not a few Zen masters prefer to use the term *Buddha nature* to describe ultimate reality, and as such introduce it into the concrete cultivation of enlightenment. An early instance of the dialectical use of the Buddha nature—similar to later kōan usage—is a discussion reported to have taken place at the first meeting between the Sixth Patriarch and Shen-hui when the latter was thirteen years old. This episode, mentioned for the first time in the *Special Transmission*,[91] clearly represents a later addition by the school of Shen-hui. As the story goes, Hui-neng was lecturing to a group of disciples, among them Shen-hui.

He opens the Dharma Gate and speaks: "I have a Dharma that has neither name nor letters, neither eye nor ear, neither body nor intention, neither words nor signs, neither head nor tail, neither inside nor outside nor middle; it neither goes nor comes, is neither blue nor yellow nor red nor white nor black; it is not and it is not not; it is neither cause nor fruit."

He then asks the assembly: "What is it?" No one could answer, until the thirteen-year-old novice from the monastery of Kataku-ji stood up and spoke:

"It is the original ground of the Buddha."

"How can it be the original ground of Buddha?" asked the master. He received a prompt reply:

"The original ground is the original nature of all the Buddhas."

"I just told you that it [the Dharma] has no name and no letters. How can you name it the Buddha nature?"

"The Buddha nature has neither name nor letters. But because the master has asked, names and letters arose. And yet, when named, it is without name and letters."

With that the master gave the novice a good slap and dispersed the assembly.[92] But a second act follows, at night. The model for nocturnal meetings was suggested, of course, by Hui-neng's secret induction into the line of succession of the patriarchs by Hung-jen. In the same way, Hui-neng calls the young lad during the night in order to ask him whether the Buddha nature had felt the slap. Not the Buddha nature, the boy replied, but he himself had felt the pain. The story closes with the report that upon hearing the words of the master, Shen-hui attained samādhi.[93]

The essence of this story is also found in the Platform Sūtra of the Sixth Patriarch (sec. 44). Shen-hui arrived from Nan-yang; nothing is said about his age. The conversation is shortened. Hui-neng slapped Shen-hui three times and asked whether it hurt. "It hurts and it also didn't hurt," was his reply. The conversation is made to focus on "self-nature"—not on Buddha nature as in the Special Transmission or on "mind-nature" as in the rest of the conversation. All these expressions are basically synonymous.

As already stated, the doctrine of the Buddha nature is fully integrated into Hui-neng's way of sudden enlightenment, in accord with the needs and desires of Zen students of the time. Yanagida's remark is illuminating: "However original Hui-neng's teaching on self-nature may have been, it never could have come about had not the doctrine of the Buddha nature been spread throughout South China and had not the doctrinal foundations already been laid in the Nirvāṇa Sūtra."[94] Yanagida also surmises the distant influence of Tao-sheng in the doctrine of sudden enlightenment. Be that as it may, there is no doubt that in the Chinese Buddhism of the Southern school a number of distinct doctrinal currents flowed together in almost perfect harmony.

The complex structure of Mahāyāna, which is the genuine form of Chinese Buddhism, also absorbed the ancient Chinese wisdom of the Tao. Without the Tao, the many expressions that the Mahāyāna Buddhists used for ultimate reality could never have touched the hearts of the Chinese. A conversation recorded in the *Discourses* of Shen-hui makes clear just how close Mahāyāna Buddhism is to Taoism. Asked why the Buddhist monks at the imperial court speak only about causality and not about spontaneity, while the Taoist monks speak only about spontaneity and seem to be ignorant of causality, Shen-hui replied, "For Buddhists, spontaneity is the fundamental nature of all things." And he quoted for the Taoists the well-known chapter of the *Tao-te ching* that describes the origin of all things from the ineffable Tao. Gernet comments appropriately: "One could hardly have put it better: Taoists are unconsciously Buddhists, and the Buddhists their close relatives."[95]

The upheaval and transformation that Chinese Zen underwent during the eighth century is a highly involved phenomenon, both regarding the events and the conceptual background. Historical study of this period must include more than its central personality Hui-neng and the text of the *Platform Sūtra* linked to his name, however important each of these may be. It is impossible to sort out all the events, clarify all the influential factors, and untangle all the knots in the story. Riddles and contradictions remain, and the various phases of the story overlap at every turn. In the end, however, the outcome is clear and its main contours and impact were to determine the subsequent life of Zen both in China and other lands.

Our historical account looks on Hui-neng, the Sixth Patriarch, as a religious founder and father, and views the *Platform Sūtra* that bears his name as pivotal. If from now on the transmission of the Dharma or of the seal of the patriarchs takes place not just through the passing on of the insignia of the robe and begging bowl but also, as the *Platform Sūtra* instructs (sec. 38), through passing on the text of the sūtra, this must be understood as more than a symbolic gesture. In this sūtra, the spirit and form of Zen are established for all future generations. The North-South conflict, resolved through the victory of the Southern school, will also reemerge in different forms. It embodies a conflict within human nature that is of enduring significance for the religious history of humanity.

NOTES

1. T. 2007. The manuscript discovered in 1907 is currently listed as sec. 5475 in the Stein Collection of the British Museum in London.

2. *Tonkō shutsudo rokuso dankyō* (Tokyo, 1934). A further edition by Ui Hakuju appeared in *Zenshūshi kenkyū* II, pp. 117–71. Complete English translations were published by Wing-tsit Chan, *The Platform Sūtra* (New York, 1963) and Yampolsky. The latter is used for direct quotations in the text.

3. Allusions in the text follow the same conventions, as do the translations of Wing-tsit Chan and Yampolsky.

4. Yampolsky, pp. 89–90.

5. Namely, between the date of composition of the *Sōkei daishi betsuden* (781) and the *Hōrinden* (801); see *Shoki*, p. 254.

6. There is a lack of clear information on Wu-chen; see Yampolsky, pp. 90–91.

7. At least it seemed to the compiler of the Zen chronicle, the *Keitoku dentōroku*, that the data supplied in sec. 57 applied to Fa-hai. See Yampolsky, p. 64.

8. See *Shoki*, pp. 188ff. The dating of the Hui-neng biography in Shen-hui's discourse is uncertain (see note 46 below). Yanagida surmises that the disciple Fa-hai referred to in the *Platform Sūtra of the Sixth Patriarch* and in the preface later appended to it is the same as a certain Fa-hai of the Ox-head school, a disciple of Hsüan-su (668–752). His biography appears in the *Biographies of Eminent Monks Compiled during the Sung Period*, T. 2061, vol. 50, pp. 738c–739a. Yanagida shows how the *Brief Discourses*, attributed to Hui-neng's disciple Fa-hai, actually presupposes later Zen writings and was first found in the Yüan text of the *Platform Sūtra of the Sixth Patriarch* (*Shoki*, pp. 205, 209). There are two editions of the Yüan text. The edition of Te-i (1290) places Fa-hai's preface after a foreword by Te-i and immediately before the main text; the edition prepared in 1291 by Tsung-pao (T. 2008, vol. 48) begins with a foreword by Te-i and appends six epilogues to the main text, the first of which is Fa-hai's preface. Yanagida gives a detailed account of the "so-called *Brief Discourses*" (*Shoki*, pp. 205–209). The foreword has been translated into English by Lu K'uan Yü (Charles Luk) in his *Ch'an and Zen Teaching* (London, 1962), vol. 3, pp. 15–18, which also includes a complete translation of the Yüan text of the *Platform Sūtra*, and by Yampolsky (pp. 60–63) after the text contained in the collection of T'ang documents, *Ch'üan T'ang wen* (Taipei, 1961). Yampolsky also considers it "of extremely late origin" (p. 63).

9. Hu Shih later modified his position; see *Shoki*, p. 134, note 1.

10. Yampolsky, p. 97.

11. Yanagida devotes four parts of a chapter to the problem in *Shoki*, pp. 148–212. One argument for an earlier composition of the sūtra is the saying of National Teacher Nan-yang Hui-chung reported in the *Keitoku dentōroku*, which will be taken up in the final part of this chapter. Another, more obscure, indication is found in the epitaph for E-hu Ta-i composed by Wei Ch'u-hou (773–828). See Yampolsky, p. 98.

12. Yanagida raises the question of the origins of these various pieces which are not to be found in the early Shen-hui. See *Shoki*, pp. 151ff.

13. In his early years in Nan-yang, Shen-hui taught an ethic in the style of traditional sūtra doctrine: avoiding all evil, doing the good, purifying one's intentions. See *Shoki*, pp. 149–150; concerning the "formless precepts" of the *Platform Sūtra*, see *Shoki*, p. 256.

14. See *Shoki*, pp. 154ff.

15. *Shoki*, p. 154.

16. *Shoki*, pp. 183–84.

17. In the appended biography of Hui-neng (see notes 8 and 46 of this chapter). This conversation is a later addition, as the question regarding the robe shows; see *Shoki*, p. 190.

18. Sec. 49. In the *Sōkei daishi betsuden* (section 36, see note 31 below) and the *Keitoku dentōroku* (vol. 5, biography of Hui-neng) the time span is given as seventy years.

19. The *Keitoku dentōroku* lists Fa-hai among the thirteen disciples of Hui-neng (the *Platform Sūtra* mentions ten by name, sec. 45), but adds little to the *Platform Sūtra*. See *Shoki*, pp. 195–196. Tsung-mi (780–841) mentions a disciple of Shen-hui named Fa-hai in his *Ch'an-men shih-tzu ch'eng-hsi-t'u*. See *Shoki*, p. 202.

20. The dates of this Fa-hai are unknown. From the dates of another known disciple of Hsüan-su named Fa-ch'in (or Tao-ch'in, 714–792) we can calculate the dates of Fa-

hai with some probability. Yanagida rejects the idea that Fa-hai visited Hui-neng but considers it probable that he was known to Shen-hui or at least to his disciples (*Shoki*, p. 202).

21. On relationships between the Buddhist schools and masters in southern China, see *Shoki*, pp. 195–209.

22. Yanagida first sets this out as a hypothesis and then proceeds to indicate arguments in its favor (*Shoki*, pp. 183, 189ff).

23. *Shoki*, p. 191.

24. *Shoki*, p. 204. This is the result of Yanagida's research based on his hypothesis.

25. *Shoki*, pp. 253–54.

26. According to the *Rekidai hōbōki*, Wei Ch'ü composed an inscription for the Sixth Patriarch that was later effaced. The *Platform Sūtra* mentions the establishment of a memorial stone for Hui-neng by the governor of Shao-chou District, Wei Ch'ü (sec. 54). See Yampolsky, pp. 182–83.

27. See note 44 to chap. 7.

28. Yampolsky gives a detailed account of the various forms that the list of patriarchs has taken and their development; see his tables on pp. 8–9, 102.

29. Yanagida himself continually stresses the hypothetical nature of his results. His composite picture illustrates in compelling fashion the network of connections between Buddhist schools during this lively period of upheaval.

30. In the fourth chapter of his work, Yanagida treats "The Advance of the Transmission of the Lamp in the Zen of the Patriarchs."

31. The book is no longer accessible in China. The *Sō kōsōden* and the *Keitoku dentōroku* list the compiler as Ling-t'ao. The abbreviated title is found in the Japanese edition of 1762 (see Yampolsky, p. 70). A new and meticulous redaction of the work was published in 1978 by the Association for the Study of the History of Zen in Tokyo's Komazawa University under the title *Enō kenkyū*. The work bears the subtitle "Basic Biographical and Textual Studies of Hui-neng" and contains some fifty sections running to over 680 pages. The quotations that follow have been translated and numbered according to this edition. This rather early text can lay no more claim to historicity than the other sources for the biography of Hui-neng.

32. Regarding the origins of the *Rekidai hōbōki* (cf. chap. 6, note 9) and the school of Chih-hsien, see Yanagida's treatment in four sections (*Shoki*, pp. 278–334). The *Rekidai hōbōki* probably dates from not long after the death of Wu-chu (714–774), the fourth in the line of succession after Chih-hsien, with whom the second half of the work is concerned.

33. *Shoki*, p. 283.

34. *Shoki*, pp. 281, 285. Yampolsky treats the school of Chih-hsien and relates the story of the robe (p. 93).

35. One can also speak of this as the "Southern school" in the broad sense.

36. The site of the monastery cannot be ascertained. See Yamolsky, p. 93, on attempts to research the question.

37. On the chronicle, see chap. 6, note 10 and chap. 7, note 12.

38. *Kuang-hsiao ssu i-fa t'a-chi* (Jpn., *Kōkō-ji eihatsu tōki*).

39. *Enō kenkyū*, p. 95.

40. *Ch'üan T'ang wen*, chap. 912, XIX, 11996.

41. *Shoki,* p. 212; cf. p. 206. The text is contained in an appendix, pp. 535–38. Yanagida notes that a new pagoda was erected on the same spot in 1636, but nothing is known of Fa-ts'ai.

42. This leads Yampolsky to doubt the historical value of the inscription. He concludes "that it is of late origin, and not of sufficient historical validity to be used as a source for Hui-neng's biography" (p. 65).

43. Yanagida has edited and annotated the text in *Shoki,* pp. 539–58. Yampolsky (pp. 66ff) comments at length on the inscription.

44. The invitation of Empress Wu or Emperor Chung-tsung mentioned in the early inscription at Hosshō-ji is supposed to have been arranged by Shen-hsiu and Hui-an. Yampolsky demonstrates the improbability of the report (p. 65; cf. p. 31).

45. *Enō kenkyū* begins the study of Hui-neng's biography with a list of eighteen fundamental texts and their investigation (pp. 84–93).

46. There is some literature regarding the *Discourses of Shen-hui* (Chin., *Shen-hui yü-lu;* Jpn., *Jinne goroku*). First are the translations of Gernet into French and of Liebenthal into English (see chap. 7, notes 22 and 25) According to Yanagida, who relies on Hu Shih, the oldest text found in Tun-huang is MS 6557 of the Stein Collection (British Museum, London), followed by MS 3047 in the Pelliot Collection (Bibliothèque Nationale, Paris), and M. Ishii's photocopied manuscript with appendixes (the generational line of the patriarchs and a biography of Hui-neng). MS 3047 was critically edited by Hu Shih (1930), and the Ishii text by Suzuki and Kōda (1934). Concerning the editions of and literature on the *Discourses,* see *Zen Dust,* pp. 392ff. After an impressive investigation of the data, Yampolsky dates the work of Shen-hui between 732 and 756, without however excluding the possibility of later alterations and improvements by Shen-hui's disciples. A duplicate of the Ishii text bears the date 791 (see Yampolsky pp. 67–68, note 24). Yanagida considers material contained in Shen-hui's *Discourses* to represent the oldest material on the biography of Hui-neng (see *Shoki,* pp. 185–88).

47. *Shoki,* p. 248.

48. Sec. 12, *Enō kenkyū,* p. 31.

49. This expression, translated from early Buddhist scriptures, is still used in Japan.

50. In the early scriptures, the expressions *zazen* and its equivalent *zenjō* indicate meditation in general.

51. Sec. 12, *Enō kenkyū,* pp. 26–27. The episode of Hui-ming's pursuit is also mentioned in case 23 of the *Mumonkan.* See note 54 below.

52. See the detailed chronological table in *Enō kenkyū,* pp. 631–46, which includes the dates of Hui-neng's life and indicates the relevant literature.

53. The stanza is given in this form in all the later texts of the *Platform Sūtra of the Sixth Patriarch.* In this connection we may mention two texts from the Sung period: the Kōshō-ji text, so called from the monastery where it was discovered in Kyoto (edited by Suzuki and Kōda under the title *Kōshōji-bon rokuso dankyō*) and the Daijō-ji text, found in the temple of Daijō-ji in Kaga (now Kanazawa) and published by Komazawa University in Tokyo. The Yüan text (see note 8 above) is a standard text from a later period. Only the Tun-huang text introduces another form by reproducing two versions:

> *Bodhi originally has no tree,*
> *The mirror also has no stand.*
> *Buddha nature is always clean and pure;*
> *Where is there room for dust?*

And the slightly variant version:

> The mind is the Bodhi tree,
> The body is the mirror stand.
> The mirror is originally clean and pure;
> Where can it be stained by dust?

The differences between the three versifications strike one at once. In the stanzas of the Tun-huang text "nothingness," Zen's all-important negation, is missing. Yanagida draws attention to the similarity of the two versions in the Tun-huang manuscript to Shen-hsiu's verses and considers the transformation of the third line into a radically negative statement significant (Shoki, p. 262). Suzuki translates the line: "From the first, not a thing is." See Suzuki's The Zen Doctrine of No-Mind (London, 1969), p. 22.

54. Sec. 23, Enō kenkyū, pp. 36–37. According to the Tun-huang text of the Platform Sūtra, Hui-ming was a man of rough and robust temperament who at first menaced Hui-neng but achieved enlightenment after receiving the Dharma from him. In case 22 of the Mumonkan the monk Hui-ming comes to enlightenment during a conversation with the Sixth Patriarch. in the Discourses of Shen-hui, the legendary story of Hui-ming's pursuit is related. The biography of another Hui-ming is included in the Sō kōsōden (T. 2061, vol. 50, p. 756b). Yanagida surmises that actors of the early legend often take on the names of persons from a later age known to Shen-hui, like a "shadow" cast back into the past. See Shoki, pp. 191, 198ff.

55. Sec. 25, Enō kenkyū, p. 38. The episode is the basis for case 29 in the Mumonkan.

56. On this question, see Shoki, pp. 225ff.

57. Sec. 26, Enō kenkyū, p. 40.

58. Yanagida refers to the frequent alterations of the names of monasteries as a "speciality" of the "special transmission." The name of Hōrin-ji was first changed to Chūkō-ji (Chin., Chung-hsing-ssu), and then to Hōsen-ji (Chin., Fa-ch'üan-ssu) through the emperor's intervention. Hui-neng's former residence in Hsin-chou was elevated to the rank of a temple with the name Kokuon-ji (Chin., Kuo-en-ssu). See sec. 32, 33, Enō kenkyū, p. 48. For further details, see Shoki, pp. 232ff.

59. Sec. 45. The list begins with Fa-hai (on whom see above) and ends with Shen-hui. We lack biographical data on the eight intervening names. See Yampolsky, p. 170; see also pp. 163, 165, 168.

60. Sec. 38ff, Enō kenkyū, pp. 50f.

61. In the translation of the corrupted portions of the text Yampolsky and Chang appeal also to later textual forms for help, especially the Kōshō-ji manuscript.

62. The text, dated 801, presents, as Yanagida notes in the concluding chapter of his work on the early history of Zen Buddhism in China, "the perfection of the Zen of the Patriarchs" (Shoki, pp. 351–418). Compiled by an unknown monk named Chih-chü, the Hōrinden gathers together much material and "has won general recognition" as "the official version of Ch'an." Thus writes Yampolsky in his description of the contents of the ten books, of which only seven are extant (namely, 1–6, and 8; see pp. 47–51). The work fixes once and for all the line of the seven Buddhas and the twenty-eight Indian patriarchs. Hui-neng's biography is included in the undiscovered final book. A manuscript of book 6 held in a Japanese monastery has been verified by Tokiwa Daijō and reported on in his book Shina bukkyō no kenkyū [Studies on Buddhism in China], vol. 2 (Tokyo, 1941, pp. 203–326. Yanagida organized a mimeographed edition of the discovered sections of the Hōrinden.

63. He is the fifth successor of Shen-hui in the Ho-tse (Jpn., Kataku) school of Zen. Among his numerous writings the well known *Zenmon shishi shōshūzu* (see note 19 above) as well as the *Ch'an-yüan chu-ch'üan-chi tu-hsü* (Jpn., *Zengen shosenshū tojo*; T. 2015, vol. 48) are especially important for the history of Zen. Japanese editions with commentary of both works have been published by Ui.

64. In Korean, *Chodangchip*. The text was complete prior to its transmission to Korea. As the earliest extant historiography of Zen in China, it contains important material for the history of Zen that is not preserved in the Chinese chronicles. See also *Zen Dust*, pp. 352–53.

65. T. 2061, vol. 50, pp. 754b–755c.

66. Fa-ju, see chap. 7, note 4 and accompanying text. Hu Shih treats Chinese Zen from Bodhidhama to Shen-hsiu and P'u-ch'i as a unified Laṅkāvatāra school.

67. See D. T. Suzuki, *The Zen Doctrine of No-Mind*, p. 25.

68. See J. Gernet, *Entretiens du Maître de Dhyāna Chen-houei*, pp. 45–46.

69. See chap. 4, note 46 and accompanying text. Note the expressed connection between the Tun-huang text of the *Platform Sūtra* (sec. 14) and this famous passage from the *Vimalakīrti Sūtra*.

70. The sūtra warns against attachment to purity (sec. 18).

71. Sec. 38, *Enō kenkyū*, p. 50.

72. Suzuki takes the two terms as synonymous (*The Zen Doctrine of No-Mind*, p. 29). Gernet also treats *munen* as the equivalent of *mushin* when this latter is used to translate the Sanskrit terms *acitta* or *acittaka*. He translates *munen* as "absence de pensée" (*Entretiens*, p. 12, note 5). Compare the passage in "No-Mind: The Response to Mu," in Thomas Kasulis's *Zen Action—Zen Person* (Honolulu, 1981), pp. 43–48.

73. Gernet, *Entretiens*, p. 31; cf. p. 48, note 2.

74. *Entretiens*, p. 55.

75. *Entretiens*, p. 55.

76. *Entretiens*, p. 43.

77. *Entretiens*, pp. 23–24. Gernet appeals to a passage in the *Mahāprajñāpāramitā Śāstra* (see the French translation of Lamotte, *Le traité*, vol. 2, pp. 727–28) as well as to Taoist thought. The reference is to M. Granet, *La pensée chinoise* (Paris, 1934), pp. 526–27.

78. See Gernet, *Entretiens*, p. 32, note 4 on the meaning of the mirror motif among Taoist philosophers and related literature. See also note 72 above.

79. Suzuki stresses that "Hui-neng's Unconscious is . . . fundamentally different from the psychologist's unconscious. It has a metaphysical connotation." See *The Zen Doctrine of No-Mind*, p. 60; cf. pp. 56ff.

80. Gernet, *Entretiens*, p. 20.

81. Book 28, T. 2076, vol. 51, p. 437c; cf. *Shoki*, pp. 161ff.

82. The Chinese characters for heretic, *wai-tao* (Jpn., *gedō*), literally mean "outside the Way," a term used to describe the teachings of a non-Buddhist. Dōgen confronts the issues raised by "Śrenika the heretic" (Jpn., Senni-gedō) in the section of his *Shōbōgenzō* dealing with the Buddha nature (*busshō*).

83. According to Yanagida, Chih-tao, a disciple of Hui-neng, could have effected alterations in the *Platform Sūtra* (*Shoki*, p. 165).

84. Cited in *Shoki*, p. 163.

85. *Keitoku dentōroku*, book 5, T. 2076, vol. 51, p. 239b; see *Shoki*, pp. 164–65.

86. He is supposed to have spoken these words to Hui-ming in explaining the Dharma to him. The quotation is not included in the Tun-huang manuscript but only in later editions of the *Platform Sūtra*. It appears in the title and more clearly in the example of case 23 of the *Mumonkan* (pp. 95–96).

87. *The Dhammapada*, trans. by Juan Mascaró (Hardmondsworth, 1973), sec. 253, pp. 71–72, see *Shoki*, pp. 272ff.

88. See my essay on contrition and confessional rites in *Festschrift Gershom Scholem* (Jerusalem, 1967), pp. 117–128. Of the supplementary literature cited there, I would single out S. Dutt, *Early Buddhist Monachism* (London, 1960) and M. W. de Visser, *Ancient Buddhism in Japan*, vol. 1 (Leiden, 1935).

89. Gernet, *Entretiens*, p. 66. The phrase appears in a conversation with Yüan, a master of the Ox-head school, in reference to the *Nirvāṇa Sūtra*; cf. *Shoki*, pp. 167ff.

90. This is the final position arrived at by Dōgen in his treatment of the Buddha nature (see note 82).

91. Tsung-mi also relates the visit of the thirteen-year old Shen-hui to Hui-neng. See Gernet, "Biographie du Maître Chen-houei du Ho-tsö," pp. 34–38.

92. Sec. 29, *Enō kenkyū*, pp. 42–43.

93. The Tun-huang manuscript of the *Platform Sūtra* recounts the first encounter and the conversation of Shen-hui with Hui-neng (sec. 44). Shen-hui's age is not mentioned, nor is mention made of his experiencing enlightenment. The text states only that after the conversation he attended his master until his death.

94. *Shoki*, pp. 166–67.

95. Cited in Gernet's biography of Shen-hui, "Biographie," p. 32, note 4. For the quotation from the *Discourses* see Gernet, *Entretiens*, p. 72.

9

The Zen Movement after Hui-neng

THE BEGINNINGS OF THE "ZEN OF THE PATRIARCHS"

The conflict between the Northern and Southern schools, which had fairly well worked itself out by the middle of the eighth century, left no lasting wounds on Chinese Zen. Already during the lifetime of the Southern school's chief combatant, Shen-hui, the storm that had raged so fiercely during the Great Dharma Assembly of Hua-t'ai had quieted. Meanwhile, the unrest brought about by the revolt of An Lu-shan (755–763) spelled a new social situation for the T'ang dynasty. With Shen-hui's death, the polemics came to an end. Other Zen schools appeared and a "new Buddhism" took shape. Yanagida sees as characteristic of this new development a relaxing of traditional institutional structures, a loosening of metropolitan controls, a geographical diffusion across the entire country, a deeper penetration among the common people, and in general a widespread process of inculturation.[1] The various Buddhist schools developed better relationships with each other, as seen in the ties between the four major currents of Chinese Buddhism: exoteric doctrine (as exemplified by the T'ien-t'ai teachings), esoteric ritual (Tantric rites), meditation (ch'an), and monastic discipline (lü), all of which were brought to Japan by Saichō (767–822), the founder of Japanese Tendai Buddhism.

At the turn of the eighth century the effects of this transitional period in Chinese Buddhism began to assume greater definition. In Zen, the figure of the Sixth Patriarch, Hui-neng, was definitively established as the principal unifying factor. "When you say Zen, everything rests on Ts'ao-ch'i," wrote Liu Tsung-yüan (773–819) in an epitaph for the Sixth Patriarch (815), whom he honored with the posthumous title of "Zen Master of the Great Mirror" (Jpn., Daikan zenji; Chin., Ta-chien ch'an-shih).[2] All the followers of Zen gathered under the banner of Hui-neng. Here again, Saichō offers a good example. During his short stay in China (804 to 805) this intellectually gifted Buddhist monk studied just about every important Buddhist movement in the Middle Kingdom. Although he sat in meditation with the Northern school, he recognized and revered the Sixth Patriarch. Along with many other valued writings, he brought the patriarch's biography, the Sōkei daishi betsuden, to Japan. During a visit to Mount Gozu, he also established personal contact with the Zen of the Southern school.[3]

At this time Zen disciples who considered themselves followers of the Sixth Patriarch and his way of sudden enlightenment were spread throughout the land. Their movement, the "Zen of the Patriarchs" (Jpn., soshizen; Chin., tsu-shih ch'an), traced its origins to the founder of Chinese Zen, Bodhidharma. Their name, which of course came later, indicates their conviction that the transmission of the Buddha mind, so essential to Zen, extends back to Bodhidharma and finally to the Buddha Śākyamuni. This new name contrasts to the "Zen of the Perfected One (Skt., *tathāgata*)," as we see in the answer the Zen master Yang-shan Hui-chi (807–883) gave to his young colleague Hsiang-yen Chih-hsien: "You have indeed grasped the Zen of the Perfected One, but not even in your dreams have you yet seen the Zen of the Patriarchs."[4]

This later report clearly holds the Zen of the Patriarchs high above the Zen of the Perfected One; such a subordination harks back to the conflict that Shen-hui fomented between the Northern and Southern schools by giving the primacy to Bodhidharma's path of enlightenment and referring to it as the Zen of the Perfected One (Jpn., *nyoraizen*). The term refers to the chapter in the *Laṅkāvatāra Sūtra* on "concentrations" (*dhyāna*), in which the highest form of concentration—that which takes place on the "level of Buddhahood"—is called the "concentration of the Perfected One."[5] As the preface by the disciple Tu-ku P'ei tells us, Shen-hui explained to the Dharma Assembly of Hua-t'ai that Bodhidharma, the third son of an Indian king, had entered *samādhi* and attained the Zen of the Perfected One.[6] The reference is clearly to the fourth and highest level of concentration mentioned in the *Laṅkāvatāra Sūtra*.

This ranking of Bodhidharma's way of enlightenment as the Zen of the Perfected One is built into Shen-hui's attack on the Northern school. Even if Bodhidharma had actually studied the Wisdom tradition through the *Laṅkāvatāra Sūtra*, this practice had in Shen-hui's judgment been carried to an intolerable extreme in the Northern school and had thus perverted the authentic Zen way. Shen-hui did not go so far as to set the Zen of the Perfected One in opposition to the Zen of the Patriarchs. On the contrary, he actually spoke highly of the Zen of the Perfected One:

> Allowing both being and nonbeing, forgetting the Middle Way—this is no-thinking (*munen*). No-thinking is the one thought; the one thought is to know all; to know all is the deepest Perfect Wisdom (*prajñāpāramitā*), the deepest Perfect Wisdom is the Zen of the Perfected One (*nyoraizen*).[7]

Thus, far from trying to set up a conflict between the Zen of the Patriarchs and the Zen of the Perfected One, Shen-hui's aim was to place the figure of Hui-neng on the same symbolic level as that of the founder, Bodhidharma.

Unlike the title *Zen of the Perfected One*, the term *Zen of the Patriarchs* cannot appeal to the sūtras for support. It derives obviously from the image of the patriarchs (*soshi*). The word *patriarch* itself is a relatively late development, first appearing in the context of the "transmission of the lamp." Yanagida finds the first reference to patriarchs in the work *Hō'nyo zenji gyōjō*, which was composed not long after the death of Zen Master Fa-ju of the Northern school.[8] It seems that the Northern school placed special value on the genealogy of the transmission of the Buddha mind, counting from one to six or seven transmitters and referring to the patriarchs as "Dharma treasures." The graph for *patriarch* is also used to refer to a Buddha.[9] The Buddha's dignity is further elevated by including *patriarch* among his many honorific titles.

The highly publicized conflict over the sixth member in Bodhidharma's succession did much to place the patriarchate in still more illustrious relief. After the victory of the Southern school at the Great Dharma Assembly of Hui-t'ai, Hui-neng became the patriarch par excellence and entered the history of Zen as the "Sixth Patriarch." If all of Chinese Zen at the turn of the eighth century bore some relation to Hui-neng, it was the Zen of the Patriarchs that unified the different schools. In the *Hōrinden,* a work that draws the curtain on one age and opens the way to a new one, the ideal image of the patriarch is described in these terms:

> One who does not hate in the face of evil, nor rejoice in the face of good, abandons foolishness and yet does not seek Wisdom, leaves behind confusion but does not desire enlightenment, attains the Great Way and transcends distinctions, achieves liberation through the Buddha mind and does not cling to the distinction between the sacred and the profane—such a superior person I call a patriarch.[10]

The writings of the time refer to Bodhidharma as a patriarch and even as the "First Patriarch." That the legendary figure of the founder came to take second place to the growing popularity of the Sixth Patriarch was inevitable. Later generations would underscore the preeminence of Hui-neng by contrasting the Zen of the Patriarchs with the Zen of the Perfected One.[11]

To understand the Zen of the Patriarchs fully one should consider the different meanings attached to the appellation "the Southern school." First of all, the term recalls Shen-hui's struggle against the deviants of what he called the "Northern school." We have already seen how the masters active in northern China at the time, especially around the capital cities Lo-yang and Ch'ang-an, did not consider themselves a special school, and most assuredly did not think of themselves as a *Northern school* standing opposed to a "Southern school."[12] Shen-hui coined the expression *Northern school* only because these deviants—concretely Shen-hsiu and especially his disciple P'u-chi—happened to live in the North, while Hui-neng was located in the South.

Shen-hui used the term *Southern school* in a twofold sense: first, to identify Hui-neng's teachings in the struggle against the "enemy" position in the North, and second, with an entirely different connotation, to identify Bodhidharma's way of meditation. He complained that his authentic Zen is no longer grasped by many of his contemporaries. He attributed absolute validity to this "authentic gate of the Southern school of Bodhidharma."[13] This understanding of the "Southern school" predates the doctrinal debates over the sudden enlightenment of the South and the gradual enlightenment of the North. In the preface to his commentary on the *Heart Sūtra* (one of the Prajñāpāramitā sūtras), the compiler of the *Chronicle of the Laṅkāvatāra Masters,* Ching-chüeh, cited a statement of Li Chih-fei according to which Guṇabhadra is supposed to have used the term

Southern school to refer to the Laṅkā tradition that had been passed on to Bodhidharma. The commentary bears the date 727—five years before the Dharma Assembly in Hui-t'ai. It is impossible to verify Li Chih-fei's statement, but it is certainly of earlier origin.[14]

This close bond between the Laṅkā tradition and the Wisdom sūtras mentioned in Ching-chüeh's preface is noteworthy. His preference was clearly for the *Laṅkāvatāra Sūtra*; indeed, it may have been because of him and his followers that Shen-hui came to identify Bodhidharma's method of meditation with the Zen of the Perfected One referred to in the *Laṅkāvatāra Sūtra*.[15] Shen-hui's claim is without historical foundations. It is true that many teachings of the Mahāyāna sūtras are fused in Zen. A good example of how the *Laṅkāvatāra Sūtra* could be read from the perspective of the Wisdom sūtras is found in the teachings of the eminent Laṅkāvatāra master Fa-ch'ung (587–665?), who had close ties to Zen. Much more concerned with the spirit than with the letter of the sūtras, Fa-ch'ung was a person of extraordinary hermeneutical gifts. As Tao-hsüan tells us in his biography of Fa-ch'ung, the master would "pick out precisely the right passage from the sūtra without expanding on its literal meaning and then would guide his partner in a manner suited to the time and place, for the central meaning of different passages is always the same." To students who were concerned only with literal meanings he would say, "The true meaning of the words is reason."[16]

Through personal relationships Fa-ch'ung was closely associated with the flourishing School of the Three Treatises (Jpn., Sanron-shū; Chin., San-lun tsung). Many of the members of this school—all of them experts in the Wisdom sūtras—were close to the meditational movement of Zen. In fact, there was "a kind of family relationship" between the "view of emptiness in the Wisdom sūtras" and the "tradition of the *Laṅkāvatāra Sūtra*."[17] Many contemporary Zen masters took their inspiration from this current of thought. Fa-ch'ung represents the "unified view of living Laṅkā, Sanron, and Zen."[18] The School of the Three Treatises was also often referred to as a "Southern school." Clearly, the term here carried different connotations.[19] Just as the expression "Perfect Wisdom" (*prajñāpāramitā*) stands for the essence of Mahāyāna thought, so does the designation "Southern school" represent the leading Mahayanist way of enlightenment. This was the sense of the term that Shen-hui picked up and linked with his "doctrine of suddenness" in opposition to the "doctrine of gradualness" that he attributed to the Northern school. Hui-neng then became an integrating figure as his followers formed the nucleus of the Southern school, which during the latter half of the eighth century was no longer understood in geographical terms or as denoting one of two rival positions; instead, it came to represent the vanguard of the Zen of the Patriarchs.

The Zen masters of the T'ang period led the Zen of the Patriarchs into the golden age of its development no longer as a special school but as the authentic expression of the Zen movement of the Sixth Patriarch. While the main themes of the Mahāyāna sūtras were preserved, the method of meditation, no longer determined by the sūtras nor dependent on texts and the printed word, was concerned solely with passing on the Buddha mind. Well-versed in the Tao, the masters radiated enthusiasm. Wherever "no-thought" (*munen*) broke through negation and paradox into enlightenment, there was the Zen of the Patriarchs.

SCHOOLS AND CURRENTS

In his study of Zen movements at the beginning of the ninth century, Tsung-mi, one of the best known Buddhists of his time, names seven schools of varying importance; their number is an indication of the imbalance and division that marked the context within Zen during the eighth century.[20] Some brief comments on these seven schools may help clarify the situation and at the same time introduce the subject of this section. Though we will rearrange Tsung-mi's listing of the schools somewhat, we may begin, as he does, with the Northern school of Shen-hsiu and P'u-chi. As the report tells us, this school, for all the opposition it occasioned, survived into the ninth century. The representative figure of its eighth generation is Master Hung-cheng. There are also names of those who brought the Ox-head school into its eighth generation. In addition, Tsung-mi mentions two other schools, one descended from Chih-hsien and associated with Ch'u-chi and Wu-hsiang, the other descended from Hui-an and represented by the Dharma heirs Ch'en Ch'u-chang and Wu-chu. There is some overlap between these two schools, as evidenced by the fact that other sources place Wu-chu among the successors of Wu-hsiang.[21] Regarding the school of a certain Hsüan-shih, we know nothing besides its name.

The Ho-tse (Jpn., Kataku) school, to which Tsung-mi himself belongs, deserves special mention. Since it originated with Shen-hui, the defender of Hui-neng, one might expect it later to have become a dominant influence. This was not at all the case. There are no names of note among the direct disciples of Shen-hui. Even Tsung-mi's membership in Shen-hui's lineage is questionable, although this scholar is considered to be the Fifth Patriarch of the Hua-yen (Kegon) school.[22] His views strayed from the orthodox Zen of the Patriarchs, for even though he clearly rejected Shen-hsiu's doctrine of gradual enlightenment, his own method of meditation was not really faithful to the no-thinking (*munen*) of Hui-neng. His own ideal was a blend of the "round" (Jpn., *en*; Chin., *yüan*) and the "sudden," (Jpn., *ton*; Chin., *tun*) based on the totalistic metaphysics of Kegon and the Southern school's way of sudden enlightenment. With Tsung-mi the Kataku school disappears. It is only with great reservations that it can be reckoned part of the Southern school.

Tsung-mi's list also includes the school of Hui-neng's disciple, Nan-yüeh Huai-jang (677–744). The third-generation leader of this school is the great Ma-tsu Tao-i (709–788). Alongside of him Zen literature places Shih-t'ou Hsi-ch'ien (700–791), whose teacher, Ch'ing-yüan Hsing-ssu (660–740), was also a pupil of Hui-neng. Tsung-mi does not mention him, however. Zen history provides little detail about these two transitional names, Nan-yüeh Huai-jang and Ch'ing-yüan Hsing-ssu. Their main function seems to have been to maintain the line of succession back to the Sixth Patriarch.

In the picture that Tsung-mi paints of the Zen movement at the beginning of the ninth century, the disciples of the Sixth Patriarch who figured prominently in the *Platform Sūtra*, the *Discourses of Shen-hui*, and the late *Keitoku dentōroku* recede into the background. Besides Shen-hui, only Nan-yüeh Huai-jang, the master of Ma-tsu, is mentioned. But there is also, as we noted, Ching-yüan Hsing-ssu, the teacher of Shih-t'ou, the head of the first line in the second generation. Thus Zen tradition recognizes "five great masters of the school" of Hui-neng (Jpn., *godaishūshō*)—the three already mentioned, plus Nan-yang Hui-chung (d.775) and Yung-chia Hsüan-chüeh (665–713).

There is solid historical information on Nan-yang Hui-chung, also called National Teacher Chung in order to distinguish him from other masters of the same name.[23] He was a man of mild temperament who had devoted himself to sitting in Zen meditation already from an early age. Under the guidance of Hui-neng he attained his Great Experience and then retreated into the solitude of the mountains for some forty years. Later he moved to Nan-yang. After being summoned to the capital by Emperor Su-tsung in 761, he spent the final years of his long life (we do not know exactly how long) close to the court, where he gave occasional lectures. The next emperor, Tai-tsung, bestowed on him the title "National Teacher of Two Emperors."

National Teacher Chung occupies a fitting and important position in Zen literature. The chronicles and kōan collections record the glories of his life. Best known perhaps is the story of the "seamless pagoda," which constitutes case 18 of the *Hekiganroku*.[24] Emperor Tai-tsung—the story confuses him with Su-tsung, but the commentary points out the mistake—asks the gray-haired master, who is perhaps paying him his last visit, what he can do for him when he is a hundred years old. Hui-chung responds directly: "Build the old monk a seamless pagoda!" Taking the reply literally, the emperor inquired about the construction plans. The monk remained silent for a while and then asked: "Do you understand?" The emperor did not, since his mind was functioning at a lower spiritual level. So the National Teacher told him that his disciple Tan-yüan would explain it all to him. The second act conveys the emperor's conversation with the disciple Tan-yüan, who in four verses explains the meaning of the seamless pagoda:

> South of Hsiang and north of Tang,
> In between, gold abounds,
> The ferryboat under the shadowless tree,
> No holy one in the emerald palace you see.[25]

The seamless pagoda—pagodas generally consist of levels and symbolize the cosmos—is full of mystery. From Hunan, Hsiang points south and Tang points north. How can the pagoda lie farther south and farther north? Spatially, it is situated everywhere, and nowhere. It is as precious as pure gold—as precious as the Buddha reality. And the ferryboat under the shadowless tree probably points to the Great Vehicle (Mahāyāna). But within the pagoda, there is nothing special—no holy one in the emerald palace.[26]

The cosmic dimensions of this powerful image are clear. One thinks of Maitreya's tower in the *Avataṃsaka Sūtra*. The song brings the mystery into full light:

A seamless pagoda, difficult to describe.
The blue dragon does not thrive in a placid lake.
It rises to the furthest heights and grows to the greatest breadth.
It shows itself ever and again to all, at every moment.[27]

In Zen tradition, the figure of the National Teacher is tied inseparably to the vision of the seamless pagoda.

Yung-chia Hsüan-chüch, the last of the five great masters of the school of the Sixth Patriarch, is known mainly from a poetic work attributed to him entitled *Shōdōka*, or "Hymn on the Experience of Truth" (the "truth" referred to here is the Tao).[28] Its origins are completely uncertain, though it probably dates from a later period. There is also a variant on the title, "Song of the Buddha Nature of the Highest Vehicle" (Jpn., *Saijōjō busshō-ka*).[29] The song presents the basic ideas of the *Platform Sūtra of the Sixth Patriarch*; already in the opening stanza the passions are identified with the Buddha nature. Hui-neng's famous line, "From the beginning, not one thing exists," appears twice. Moreover, the realization of the Tao through Wisdom (prajñā) takes place suddenly. Throughout the poem, the metaphysical background of the Wisdom sūtras is evident.

THE TWO MAIN LINES OF CHINESE ZEN

In the center of the new Zen movement stand two masters, Ma-tsu and Shih-t'ou, both belonging to the third generation after Hui-neng. The Zen chronicles describe the new surge of energy in moving terms: "West of the river the great Solitary One (Ma-tsu) is the master. South of the lake, Stone-head (Shih-t'ou) is the master. People gather there in crowds. Whoever has not seen the two great masters is regarded as an ignoramus."[30] During the late T'ang period the pivot of the Zen movement shifted from the cities to the countryside.

The two main lines of Chinese Zen Buddhism derive from Mat-su and Shih-t'ou. While it is clear that Chinese Zen in no sense began at this time, it is also true that Zen as we know it today first took a clearly defined form during the third generation after Hui-neng, particularly in the movement that took shape among the people who flocked to these two great masters in the provinces of Chiang-hsi ("west of the river") and Hunan ("south of the lake"). With this Zen movement we are on firmer historical footings. This is not to say that the chronicles and collections of sayings and kōan are not generously sprinkled with legend. The critical overview offered here is open to further research, the results of which will no doubt add, and perhaps also change, much of the overall picture of Zen history.

Ma-tsu is the only Chinese Zen master after Hui-neng to bear the title "Patriarch" (Chin., *tsu*; Jpn., *so*)—namely, the "Patriarch from the House of Ma" (*ma* meaning "horse"). His appearance in the history of Zen was announced by a prophecy whose words play on his name.[31] In a broad-ranging prophecy given to Bodhidharma by his patriarchal predecessor, Prajñātāra, the twenty-seventh Indian Zen patriarch, Ma-tsu and his teacher Huai-jang are mentioned. The verse dedicated to Ma-tsu speaks of a horse that will trample the world under its feet. We also have enlightenment verses attributed to Ma-tsu, an epitaph by Ch'üan Te-yü (759–818) recounts his main achievements. Although Zen literature has woven numerous legends around the figure of Ma-tsu, the main historical outlines are clear. A number of problems remain, however, for con-structing a complete biography.

The two earliest biographies of Ma-tsu are found in the *Sodōshū*[32] and the *Sō kōsōden (Biographies of Eminent Monks Compiled during the Sung Period)*,[33] both of which stem from the second half of the tenth century. The compilers of these works were too far removed from the time of Ma-tsu to have been able to have recourse to firsthand accounts of Ma-tsu, even indirectly. The *Sodōshū* also labors under the same lack of historical consciousness that characterizes the Chinese Zen chronicles in general. The Sung collection of biographies, which brings together a wide spread of historical materials for the years 667 to 987, reports on Ma-tsu as follows:

> The monk Tao-i of the Ma family came from Han-chou. . . . From the time of his youth he despised the dust of the earth, renounced all clinging and dependency, and yearned for the freedom of the itinerant life. He received his tonsure from Master T'ang of the region of Tzu and the monastic precepts from the Vinaya master Yüan in the region of Yü. . . .[34]

These biographical reports of the historical work of the Sung period are important. There are no other references to the Vinaya master Yüan. Yanagida identifies Master T'ang as Ch'u-chi (d.732 or 734) of the T'ang family, the Dharma heir of Chih-hsien, the founder of the school named after Szechwan Province, where the *Rekidai hōbōki* chronicle originated.[35] Based on these sources, Ma-tsu took his first steps in the monastic life under the guidance of Ch'u-chi and came to know Ch'u-chi's successor Wu-hsiang (from Korea, family name Kim). These two disciples, together with a third monk, cared for Ch'u-chi during his final years. Under the direction of Wu-hsiang, Ma-tsu dedicated himself to the practice of meditation, which explains why Tsung-mi describes him as the disciple of Wu-hsiang.[36] But Ma-tsu did not become Wu-hsiang's successor. While the epitaph mentioned above refers to the fact that Ma-tsu began his monastic life in the region of Tzu, it makes no mention of Ch'u-chi.[37]

The genealogy of the Szechwan school, as clearly reported in the *Rekidai hōbōki*, runs from Chih-hsien to Ch'u-chi to Wu-hsiang to Wu-chu. This latter did not, however, practice under Wu-hsiang.[38] Ma-tsu stands as successor to Nan-yüeh Huai-jang, through whom he is linked to Hui-neng. Tsung-mi reports that Ma-tsu had resided earlier with Wu-hsiang but in the course of his travels ended up with Nan-yüeh, the great lover of solitude who recognized Ma-tsu's extraordinary fervor and welcomed him as a disciple. The epitaph, the early biographies, and all later Zen literature confirm the line of succession leading from the Sixth Patriarch by way of Nan-yüeh Huai-jang to Ma-tsu Tao-i.

Ma-tsu is the dominant figure in early Zen. The principal stage of his activity was Chiang-hsi (Kiangsi) Province. Crowds of disciples streamed after him and he often changed location. With him begins the mainstream of Chinese Zen, out of which would arise the powerful Rinzai school. He was the first to make use of shouting (Chin., ho; Jpn., katsu) as a means of fostering enlightenment, a means later made famous by Lin-chi (Jpn., Rinzai). With Ma-tsu paradox is mixed with rudeness. On one occasion, at the conclusion of a paradoxical dialogue, he suddenly grabbed the nose of his disciple Pai-chang and twisted it so violently that the disciple cried out in pain—and attained enlightenment. The chronicle describes his rough and robust personality in these terms: "His appearance was remarkable. His stride was like a bull's and his gaze like a tiger's. If stretched out, his tongue reached up over his nose; on the soles of his feet were imprinted two circular marks."[39]

In contrast to the passive style of meditation practiced in the Northern school, Ma-tsu promoted the dynamic Zen of the Sixth Patriarch; his teacher, Nan-yüeh Huai-jang, had convinced him of the futility of simply sitting in meditation. The chronicle reports:

> He [Ma-tsu] was residing in the monastery of Dembō-in where he sat constantly in meditation. The master, aware that he was a vessel of the Dharma, went to him and asked, "Virtuous one, for what purpose are you sitting in meditation?"
>
> Tao-i answered: "I wish to become a Buddha."
>
> Thereupon the master picked up a tile and started rubbing it on a stone in front of the hermitage.
>
> Tao-i asked: "What is the Master doing?"
>
> The master replied: "I am polishing [this tile] to make a mirror."
>
> "How can you make a mirror by polishing a tile?" exclaimed Tao-i.
>
> "And how can you make a Buddha by practicing zazen?" countered the master.[40]

The meaning of the exchange is clear: the mind is originally clean; to meditate in order to cleanse it of dust is as useless as rubbing a tile to make a mirror of it.

The originally pure mind is one with the Buddha. This conviction constitutes the heart of Ma-tsu's teaching. In the Sodōshū he is made to speak words recalling Bodhidharma and the Laṅkāvatāra Sūtra:

> All of you should believe that your mind is Buddha. This mind is nothing other than the Buddha. At one time, the great master Bodhidharma came from India, passed on this highest Dharma of the One Mind, and thus opened the way to enlightenment. He often quoted words from the Laṅkāvatāra Sūtra and appealed to the minds of all living beings. . . .[41]

The *Keitoku dentōroku* formulates the heart of Ma-tsu's message as follows:

Apart from the mind there is no Buddha, apart from the Buddha there is no mind. Do not cling to good; do not reject evil! If you cling to neither purity nor defilement you come to know the emptiness of the nature of sin. At no moment can you grasp it, since it possesses no self-nature. Therefore the Three Worlds are only mind. The universe and all phenomena bear the seal of the One Dharma.[42]

Ma-tsu's teaching on the identity of the mind with the Buddha and on the transcendence of mind-Buddha-reality becomes concrete in practice. In two cases of the *Mumonkan* he gives two different answers to the same question, "What is the Buddha?" He replies first, "The mind is the Buddha" (case 30), and again, "Neither mind nor Buddha" (case 33). The first answer expresses the mind-quality of the Buddha reality; because of its affirmative form it might be misunderstood as a philosophical sentence. Thus, it needs to be complemented by the negative statement "Neither mind nor Buddha" in order to help the student break through to transobjective truth. In the kōan of the *Mumonkan* Ma-tsu adopts the dialectical language of the Wisdom sūtras, though as the earlier citation makes clear, he also held the *Laṅkāvatāra Sūtra* in high regard.[43] In these references one can also hear traces of Consciousness-only (i.e., Yogācāra) doctrine.[44] The multifaceted language of Ma-tsu, then, reflects many aspects of the metaphysics of the Mahāyāna sūtras.

In one of his lectures, the disciple Nan-ch'üan P'u-yüan (748–834) reveals the Taoist tinge of his master's views. After the kōan about mind and Buddha, the disciple comments:

During the *kalpa* of emptiness, there are no names. Since Buddha's appearance in the world, there are names. Humans comprehend on the basis of external signs. . . . The Great Tao is totally without any thing sacred or profane. What has a name is subject to limitation. Therefore the old man from Kiangsi [Ma-tsu] said: "This is not mind, this is not Buddha, this is not a thing."[45]

Ma-tsu is one of the greatest Zen masters of the T'ang period. As his death approached the superior of the monastery visited him to see how he was doing. Ma-tsu said to him: "Sun-faced Buddha—Moon-faced Buddha," enigmatic words that were made into a kōan in the *Hekiganroku* and are still used today for practice.[46] As to the origin of the expression, Gundert refers to a statement in the seventh part of a Buddha-name sūtra, which was used in confession or penance rituals and which runs as follows:

Then I saw a Buddha named Moon-face. The lifespan of this Buddha with the face of a moon was only one day and one night. Then I saw another Buddha pass by the honorable one with the moon face; his name was Sun-face. The life span of this Buddha with the face of the sun amounted to one thousand eight hundred years.[47]

Whether long or short, the lifetime of a Buddha is immeasurable. The time references given by the sūtra may originate from the basic Buddhist experience of the radical impermanence of the empirical world; they also reflect a ray of the Buddha light from "the other shore." But such explanations are alien to the spirit of Zen. The kōan acquires its depth from the ineffability of truth and its human warmth from the figure of the gray-haired Master Ma, who used the words for a death verse. His experience of enlightenment taught him that this mind, together with its distortions, is Buddha.

Shih-t'ou Hsi-chien, from whom the second main line of Chinese Zen during the T'ang period proceeds, stands in a direct line of succession to Hui-neng because of his little known teacher, Ch'ing-yüan Hsing-ssu. Early biographies of Shih-t'ou can be found in the Sodōshū[48] and in the Biographies of Eminent Monks Compiled during the Sung Period.[49] Endowed with a keen intelligence and a quiet self-confidence, he felt attracted to the spiritual life already as a young man. His birthplace is given as Kao-yao in Tuan-chou, not far from Ts'ao-ch'i, the residence of the Sixth Patriarch, to whom he is said to have paid a visit as a small boy. Legend has it that he was present at the death of Hui-neng in 713. Shih t'ou was an adult when he received monastic orders in the monastery of Rafuzan (Chin., Lo-fu-shan, in the province of Kuang-tung, 728). Not long thereafter he sought out the Zen Master Ch'ing-yüan Hsing-ssu, who was directing a group of disciples in the way of sudden enlightenment in Chiang-hsi. "I have many horned cattle, but one unicorn is enough," said the master as he soon recognized the special qualities of his new pupil. With Ch'ing-yüan, Shih-t'ou attained enlightenment and the Dharma seal, thus taking third position in the generational line of Hui-neng.

After his enlightenment, Shih-t'ou took up residence in Hunan Province (742). According to tradition, he built himself a small hut on a large flat rock, whence he became popularly known as "Stone head" (Chin., Shih-t'ou, Jpn., Sekitō). This is the name he has carried throughout Zen history. He spent twenty-three years in his secluded mountain hut, meditating by himself and instructing a growing band of disciples. At the urging of his disciples he later moved to Liang-tuan in T'an-chou (Hunan Province), where a new Zen center grew up around him (764). His fame spread and attracted many disciples. According to unverified reports, he returned to his beloved mountains, where he passed the final period of his long life.

The Keitoku dentōroku recounts how once in a lecture to his disciples Shih-t'ou appealed to the Buddhas of the previous age who had passed on the Dharma. The following excerpt captures the quintessence of his lecture:

> This very mind, just this is Buddha. Mind, Buddha, and sentient beings, perfect wisdom and the defiling passions—these are but different names for one and the same substance. . . . Know that its substance is apart from extinction and permanence, and that its nature is neither stained nor pure; know that it is absolutely still and completely whole, and that [in it] secular and sacred are exactly the same. . . .

With that a disciple named Tao-wu asked the master, "Who obtained the essential teaching of Ts'ao-ch'i [namely, the doctrine of Hui-neng]?"

> The master said, "He who understands Buddha-dharma obtained it."
>
> "Did you obtain it, Master?" Tao-wu asked. "I don't understand Buddha-dharma," Shih-t'ou replied.
>
> "What about emancipation?" asked another monk.
>
> "Who binds you?" said the master.
>
> "What about the Pure Land?"
>
> "Who defiles you?" was the reply.
>
> "What about nirvāṇa?"
>
> "Who puts you in saṃsāra [birth-and-death]," was Shih-t'ou's reply.[50]

The final book of the *Keitoku dentōroku* contains two doctrinal poems attributed to Shih-t'ou, the *Sandōkai* (Chin., *Ts'an-t'ung-ch'i*), "In Praise of Equality,"[51] and the *Sōanka* (Chin., *Ts'ao-an-ko*), or "Song from a Grass Hut."[52] The faintly Taoist tone of the *Sandōkai* inspired the dialectical thinking of later masters. In the thought games and word plays of Shih-t'ou we may have the roots of the "Five Ranks" system later developed in the Sōtō school.[53]

Ma-tsu and Shih-t'ou usually stand alongside each other in Zen literature as fathers of the two main lines of Chinese Zen. Both were equally renowned, although they differed considerably in talent and temperament. Ma-tsu's popularity derived greatly from his spontaneity and roughness, while Shih-t'ou was known as a quiet, penetrating thinker. The unending streams of disciples that flowed to the centers opened by these two masters helped fashion the Zen of the Sixth Patriarch into the most significant movement within medieval Chinese Buddhism.

STRANGE WORDS AND EXTRAORDINARY ACTIONS

"Strange words and extraordinary actions" (*kigen kikō*),[54] an expression first used by the *Keitoku dentōroku* to describe Ma-tsu's Zen style, aptly characterizes the Zen masters of the late T'ang period—those enlightened disciples who spread across the expanse of China to carry on the succession and heritage of Ma-tsu and Shih-t'ou. Swept up in a period of flourishing growth and spiritual enthusiasm, these original Zen masters expressed their inexpressible experiences in ever new ways and paradoxical twists. The originality of their language contrasts sharply with the monotony of their content. These vigorous and exuberant monks rejected all methods in order that they might be borne along freely by the storm of the spirit. Endowed with an amazing facility at speaking, they enriched religious vocabulary with new terms that mock reason and defy translation.

The rich, overflowing stream of events during those days was captured in the expression "the age of Zen activity" (Jpn., *zenki no jidai*), which indicates the talents, industry and quality of the Zen masters as well as the progressive dynamic of the Zen spirit. Indeed, during this period Zen reached heights never before or since realized. It was the "golden age of Zen," when the spiritual energy unleashed by Ma-tsu and Shih-t'ou spread over the face of China.[55]

Our description of this period can only single out a few of its aspects. This should be sufficient, given the general familiarity of Western readers with this period, thanks mainly to D. T. Suzuki's predilection for the impressive figures of the T'ang period who are given special attention in the kōan collections. In what follows, we will briefly consider the words and deeds of some of the prominent masters of the time.

Looking back to the school of Ma-tsu's disciple Nan-ch'üan, we meet the brilliant Chao-chou Ts'ung-shen (778–897), who surpassed all his contemporaries in his spontaneous, creative powers of inventiveness."[56] He is responsible for the rather grotesque note sounded in the story "Nan-ch'üan kills a cat":

> Once the monks of the Eastern Hall were disputing about a cat. Nan-ch'üan, holding up the cat, said, "Monks, if you can say a word of Zen, I will spare the cat. If you cannot, I will kill it!" No monk could answer. Nan-ch'üan finally killed the cat. In the evening, when Chao-chou came back, Nan-ch'üan told him of the incident. Chao-chou took off his sandal, put it on his head, and walked off. Nan-ch'üan said, "If you had been there, I could have saved the cat!"[57]

Zen writings report many of Chao-chou's paradoxical statements and strange deeds. Often he seemed to push incongruity to the extreme. "A monk once asked Chao-chou, 'When the entire body crumbles and scatters, there is one thing, eternal, spiritual. What of it?' The master replied: 'The wind is rising again this morning.' "[58] Or again: "A monk asked Chao-chou, 'The ten-thousand dharmas return to the One. Where does the One return?' The master replied: 'While I was staying at Ch'ing-chou I made a hemp that weighed seven pounds.' "[59] Such answers to metaphysical questions are meant to manifest the inadequacy of all words to express reality.

Another exchange reveals genuine profundity: "A monk asked Chao-chou, 'If a poor man comes, what should one give him?' The master answered, 'He lacks nothing.' "[60] In a similar vein we have the answer he gave a monk who requested instruction about enlightenment: "Wash your bowls."[61] Enlightenment can come about through the everyday things of life. Consider the concrete answer he gives to the question, "What is Chao-chou?" (Chao-chou is the name of the small town not far from Peking where the master spent his old age and from which he is named, which loads the question with a double entendre.) His answer was this: "The East Gate, the West Gate, the North Gate, the South Gate." The small town is described, just as it is, as open on all sides. From answers such as these we catch a glimpse of the master's uniqueness.[62]

If Chinese Buddhism was greatly affected by its encounter with Taoism, the interpenetration of the two religions culminates in the Zen movement of the T'ang period. Imbued with a sense of new freedom after the struggles and conflicts of the eighth century, and convinced of the surpassing value of sudden enlightenment, the disciples of the Zen movement were able to absorb the innate naturalness of their Taoist heritage. Chao-chou embodies this natural quality with his inimitable spontaneity. The Mumonkan illustrates this through a simple kōan whose deep meaning can easily be overlooked.[63] Chao-chou asks his master,

Nan-ch'üan, about the Tao. The master replies: "Ordinary mind is Tao." Full of youthful enthusiasm, the disciple asks further how to direct himself toward the Tao, and is given the instruction, "If you try to direct yourself toward it, you go away from it." Chao-chou counters, "If we do not try, how can we know that it is Tao?" Nan-ch'üan's reply captures the essence common to the Tao and Zen:

> Tao does not belong to knowing or to not-knowing. Knowing is illusion, not-knowing is blankness. If you really attain to Tao of no-doubt, it is like the great void, so vast and boundless. How, then, can there be right and wrong in the Tao?

"At these words," the narration concludes, "Chao-chou was suddenly enlightened."

The title of this kōan reads "Ordinary Mind is Tao." There is no doubt about the meaning of the Tao or "Way." It is the same as Buddha and Buddha nature—the Ultimate. The word *mind* plays an important role in Zen Buddhism and its understanding can occasion certain problems. The Chinese graph *hsin* (Jpn., *shin*) serves to translate the Sanskrit term *citta*. A very important concept in the philosophical literature of Buddhism, *citta* admits of different meanings according to the system in whose context it appears. Thus, within the idealistic Yogācāra strain of Buddhist philosophy, the Chinese character might be translated "consciousness." The influence of the Mahāyāna sūtras on classical Zen is not to be overlooked, for it is always present whether in the foreground or background. At the same time, the Zen masters do not feel bound to the wisdom of the sūtras since they consider themselves to possess a mind-transmission independent of scriptures and written words. This is the context in which the conversation between Chao-chou and Nan-ch'üan takes place. Zen masters have little interest in philosophical theories; for them the Tao is not an abstract absolute but belongs to the "everyday" as the mind at work in daily life. "Is not everything that one does from morning to night, just as one does it, the Way?" asks a Japanese Zen master.[64] The Tao is "intentionless," transcending knowing and not-knowing; it is "like the great void, vast and boundless." Buddhist enlightenment and Taoist wisdom come together here. In the kōan regarding the Buddha nature of a dog, Chao-chou shows Buddhist enlightenment with his transobjective reply "Mu."[65] The same insight is conveyed in these verses from the second kōan in the *Hekiganroku*:

> The real Way is not difficult.
> It only abhors choice and attachment.[66]

To convey the content of Chao-chou's enlightenment tradition has used the expression "the nonduality of the great Tao" (*funi daidō*). Like the Buddha nature, the nonduality of the Tao is inexpressible.

Another typical figure among the Zen masters of the T'ang period is Te-shan Hsüan-chien (782–865) from the line of Shih-t'ou Hsi-chien. He came from the North and was very well versed in Buddhist studies, especially in the teaching of Perfect Wisdom (*prajñāpāramitā*). Reports of flourishing Zen life in the South tormented him with doubts. Was it not presumptuous and offensive to neglect the study of the sūtras and to aspire to Buddhahood simply by seeing into one's own nature? Full of righteous indignation he set out for the South to combat these frivolous innovations. On the way he met an old woman who gave his trust in sūtra knowledge its first jolt and directed him to Master Lung-t'an Ch'ung-hsin. The eye of enlightenment opened for him at the moment the master blew out a candle and dark night surrounded him. The next day Te-shan burned the commentary to the Diamond Sūtra that he had been carrying around in a box.[67]

Later, numerous disciples gathered around Te-shan. In the training of his disciples he made much use of the stick. He never ascended the platform in the Zen hall without his short staff, which he brandished in the air shouting, "If you can speak, thirty blows! If you cannot speak, thirty blows!"[68] Sticks and shouts, first used by Ma-tsu, came to play an important role for Te-shan and other Zen masters of the T'ang period. The blows were intended as a practical incentive or skillful means (Skt., upāya; Jpn., hōben) and were to become standard parts of Zen practice.

Te-shan enjoyed great popularity and attracted a large following. He captured the essence of Zen in penetrating words:

He said to the assembly: "When there is nothing more within you, do not engage in useless seeking. What is found by useless seeking is no gain. When your mind is without anything and you are no-minds, then you are free and spiritual, empty and marvelous."[69]

He described the ideal of enlightened persons as follows:

They fear not birth and death (saṃsāra). They have no need of attaining nirvāṇa or proving enlightenment. They are just ordinary people, who have nothing further to do.[70]

This is a variation on the theme of the identity of the ordinary mind and Tao and opens a way to his favorite motif of seeking enlightenment in everyday life.

Yen-t'ou Ch'üan-huo (828–887) and Hsüeh-feng I-ts'un (822–908) are among Te-shan's more prominent disciples. Together they appear with their master in a delightful kōan story in which the disciples are making fun of their master, but the master ends up with the last word, proving that he has the deepest and most penetrating insight.[71] Toward the end of the T'ang period, a widely influential Zen center formed around Hsüeh-feng. His disciple, Ch'ang-ch'ing Hui-leng (854–932), whose activity extended into the next period, was also a highly esteemed master. He had a rather strict teacher who made him practice sitting in meditation for two and a half years. After an extraordinary experience he exclaimed, "Today I clearly see the ice within the fire."[72] Rigorous ascetic practice was in no sense foreign to the Zen masters after Hui-neng. After Hsüeh-feng the line of succession proceeds to the schools of Ummon and Hōgen, both of whom belong to the "Five Houses."

The "strange and extraordinary" aspects to the words and deeds of this period are expressed graphically in the "violence" to which the particularly strict

Master Chü-chih was prone. From his master, T'ien-lung, he had learned the so-called one-finger Zen. In place of instruction, Chü-chih would guide his disciples to enlightenment merely by lifting a finger. Now it happened that one day a disciple imitated him. Replying to a question from a visitor, he merely raised a finger the way he had seen his master do. When Chü-chih learned of this, he cut off the disciple's finger with a knife. Crying out in pain, the disciple ran away. But the master called him back. The young man turned around and saw the master lifting his finger. At that moment he was enlightened and realized that simple imitation is not enough. The experience must blossom from within.[73]

MONASTIC LIFE

All life requires form, and if that life is genuine it will create suitable forms for itself. During the golden age of Zen in the T'ang period, the monastic rule of Pai-chang (720–814) was developed to regulate the life of Zen monks. In India, "a robe and a bowl on a stone under a tree" was adequate to the meager needs of the mendicant. In China, however, with its more rigorous climate and different customs, such simplicity did not suffice.[74] For this reason, already in the early years of Chinese Zen, Tao-hsin had set up certain rules for the life of his five hundred disciples. These stipulated, among other things, that they should do manual work in order to support their daily needs. Thus we saw Hui-neng, a newcomer from the South, engaged for eight months in splitting wood and treading the rice mill in the monastery of the Fifth Patriarch Hung-jen. He was not the only member of the community to serve the common good by manual labor. Mention is made in the chronicles of rice-planting, farming, and bamboo-cutting, along with other activities. Begging, too, was not entirely abandoned; it remained as a reminder of the renunciation of property, one of the spiritual foundations of Buddhist monasticism. The monks even renounced the communal possession of land in order to forsake all covetousness.[75]

Pai-chang was the first to lay out a clearly formulated rule for Zen monks, thereby securing Zen's independence from other Buddhist schools. Prior to Pai-chang, Zen monks lived for the most part in monasteries of the Vinaya school (Jpn., Risshū) of Chinese Mahāyāna. Even though many of them often had to live in special areas of these monasteries, they all followed the rule of the Vinaya school and consequently, adhered to the Vinaya of the Dharmaguptakas, an Indian Buddhist sect. Drawing on the traditions of Hīnayāna Vinaya and Mahāyāna Vinaya, Pai-chang created a new rule adapted to Zen in which something of the simple, rigorous spirit of the ancient Buddhist monastic community (saṅgha) lived on. The Pure Rule of Pai-chang (Jpn., Hyakujō shingi; Chin., Pai-chang ch'ing-kuei) included the basic Buddhist commandments—namely, the five injunctions against killing, stealing, unchastity, lying, and alcoholic drink—as well as additional injunctions against any luxury. The original manuscript of the rule is not preserved. A later, more comprehensive, and probably greatly expanded version dating from the Yüan period deals in detail with offices and ceremonies in Zen monasteries.[76] It contains prayer formulas that come from Chen-yen (Chinese Tantric) Buddhism. Whether this influence was already present during the time of Pai-chang cannot be established, given the late edition of the only extant text. A large number of technical expressions used in Zen for cultic buildings and articles as well as for hierarchical ranks within the community, appear for the first time in Pai-chang's rule.

The new rule was practiced in the monastery that Pai-chang himself had established, Daichijushō-zenji (Chin., Ta-chih shou-sheng ch'an-ssu). In the layout of the monastery, a special monks' hall (Jpn., sōdō) was added, independent of the Buddha hall.[77] This innovation made possible the Zen monk's much-lauded "life on a straw mat."[78] During periods of ascetic practice the monks would sleep on the same straw mat on which they sat in meditation and on which, according to defined ritual, they took their meals. Both the lifestyle that Pai-chang spelled out as well as the architectural form of his monastery became models for later Zen monasteries. The service he rendered the monastic community life of Zen earned him the epithet, "The Patriarch Who Created the Forest" (referring to the community of disciples).

No one recognized more clearly or lived out more convincingly the incomparable value of manual labor within the framework of Zen life than Pai-chang. His rule favors the place of manual labor in the life of the monk. His own terse saying in this regard is hard to forget: "A day without work—a day without eating." Nothing was closer to his heart than to see his monks working, and in this regard he himself offered the best example. When in his old age the monks took away his garden tools in order to spare his dwindling strength, he was true to his own directives and refused to eat until they would return his tools to him. In the daily order of the monastery, work periods for the monks from early in the morning until late at night were clearly regulated within a general schedule that alternated between meditation, worship, and manual labor. The visitor to today's Japanese Zen monastery is deeply impressed by the order, cleanliness, and religious discipline found there. The Chinese rules were not introduced into Japan in full, and changes were made during the centuries, but most of what can be seen today goes back to the rule of Master Pai-chang. For the rest, the historical sources paint a sympathetic picture of his personality, showing him as simple and unpretentious in his words, kind and cheerful in his dealings, industrious and energetic in his labors.

External work and administrative chores all too easily lead to spiritual laxity and neglect of meditation. New worldly attachments may become real obstacles on the way to enlightenment. Pai-chang was aware of these dangers and sought to combat them. The inner freedom from all attachments—the theme of the second kōan in the Mumonkan, in which Pai-chang figures prominently—was the favorite topic of his teaching.[79] "To cling to nothing, to crave for nothing"—this is the basic principle he inculcated in his disciples.

When you forget the good and the non-good, the worldly life and the religious life, and all other dharmas, and permit no thought relating to them to arise, and when you abandon body and mind, then you attain complete freedom. When the mind is like wood or stone, there is nothing to discriminate.[80]

Thus Pai-chang, through his Zen rules, passed on the spirit of his master Ma-tsu, in the rigors of whose school he had been trained. Through these rules he also safeguarded practitioners of meditation against a life given to idleness and lacking in restraint, which spells the ruin of spiritual freedom.

In the Zen chronicles and kōan collections mention is made of many other masters active during this early period. Their distinctive characteristics are described traditionally by means of the kōan-like dialogues that they were all fond of. A proper treatment of this broad historical period would require naming these spiritual leaders. But before this chapter closes, we should refer to one interesting figure among the disciples of Ma-tsu, a certain Ta-chu Hui-hai, whose treatise on sudden enlightenment stands as one of the most important works in all of Chinese Buddhist literature. After a short stay with the great Ma-tsu, Ta-chu Hui-hai returned to his hometown of Yüeh-chou to care for his first teacher, who was growing feeble with age. While there he completed a manuscript on sudden enlightenment and sent it to Ma-tsu who read it with amazement and is said to have exclaimed: "In Yüeh-chou there is a great pearl, the perfect and bright luminance of which penetrates everywhere without hindrance."[81] Subsequently, Hui-hai was known as Ta-chu, which means "great pearl." His treatise, the *Tun-wu ju-tao yao-men lun*, was edited by Miao-hsieh (n.d.) and first appeared in 1373. Deeply rooted in Mahāyāna thought, this work is full of insights and citations from Buddhist scriptures. It has earned Ta-chu Hui-hai a lasting place in the history of Zen Buddhism.

The Chinese Zen Buddhist movement during the T'ang period can be reckoned among the most amazing phenomena in the history of religions. The mixing of Buddhist and Taoist elements resulted in a contribution to religious history that was both unique and enriching. Zen disciples burn Buddha images and sūtras, laugh in the face of inquirers or suddenly shout at them, and indulge in a thousand follies. Though they may behave like fools and possess nothing, they feel themselves true kings in the liberating energy of enlightenment. They know no fear, for they desire nothing and have nothing to lose. The adaptation of Indian Buddhist teachings to the Chinese character was fully achieved; Indian metaphysics melded with Chinese ways of thinking and adapted to Chinese linguistic patterns. Strange things went on daily in the Zen temples, yet the movement itself kept well within the bounds of Buddhism. At first sight, some of its iconoclastic gestures may seem bewildering, but the burning of the Buddha image and sūtras does not imply any attack on the holy man from the Śākya tribe or on his doctrine. In fact, the term *iconoclasm* is not really suited to what we are talking about. The Zen monks were not persistent fanatics who went about destroying images and sacred texts. If anything, they were caught up in a light-hearted play resulting from their own experience and symbolizing their unimaginable freedom. Once the intoxication of their game was over, they assembled again before the Buddha image for the reading of the sūtras.

Wherever great masters offered guidance, they could count on the unconditioned response of their disciples, no matter how harsh the masters might be. Masters and disciples speak and act like religious persons on a pilgrimage to the absolute, in search of what is supreme and ultimate. The figure of Lin-chi, the subject of the next chapter, may be considered the culmination of this Zen movement.

NOTES

1. On this and the following, see *Shoki*, pp. 215–16.

2. Cited in *Shoki*, p. 216. The epitaph appears in the *Ch'üan T'ang wen*, chap. 587, XII, 7535.

3. *Shoki*, pp. 216, 218 (note 8); cf. p. 173.

4. From the collections of sayings of Kuei-shan Ling-yu, T. 1989, vol. 47, p. 580b,c. On the Zen of the Patriarchs (*soshizen*), see the first section of chap. 4 of Yanagida's *Shoki*, pp. 213–218. The term *tathāgata-dhyāna* (Jpn., *nyoraizen*) is apparently taken from the *Laṅkāvatāra Sūtra*. Yanagida is of the opinion, however, that the thesis asserting a connection between Bodhidharma's Zen and the *nyoraizen* of the *Laṅkāvatāra Sūtra* is based upon a false conclusion (*Shoki*, p. 317, note 1). Shen-hui seems to be the first to have proclaimed an identity between the meditation of Bodhidharma and the *tathāgata-dhyāna* of the *Laṅkāvatāra Sūtra* and to have made Bodhidharma a patriarch of *nyoraizen*, which he explains in the sense of the doctrine of Perfect Wisdom (see note 7 below and its accompanying text).

5. *Shoki*, p. 106; cf. pp. 103ff and 452. See also *Chūgoku zenshūshi*, p. 46.

6. J. Gernet, *Entretiens du Maître de Dhyāna Chen-houei du Ho-tsö* pp. 82–83; see also *Shoki*, p. 104.

7. Cited in *Shoki*, p. 151; cf. Gernet, *Entretiens*, pp. 55–56.

8. See *Shoki*, p. 214.

9. *Shoki*, p. 490; cf. p. 41.

10. *Shoki*, p. 215 (see above, chapter 8, note 62).

11. See the earlier quotation, note 4. The saying is typical and is often cited in later Zen literature. See for example the *Keitoku dentōroku*, T. 2076, vol. 51, p. 283b.

12. See the section on the Northern school in chap. 7 above.

13. *Shoki*, p. 110; see the section on the Southern school (*Nanshū to wa nani ka*) in chap. 3, pp. 117–127.

14. *Shoki*, pp. 117ff.

15. This is Yanagida's view. On Ching-chüeh and the *Chronicle of the Laṅkāvatāra Masters*, see the section on the Northern school in chap. 7 above.

16. T. 2060, vol. 50, p. 666b; see *Shoki*, pp. 118–19.

17. *Shoki*, p. 120.

18. *Shoki*, p. 122.

19. On the relationship between the "Southern school" and the doctrine of Wisdom, see *Shoki*, pp. 119–25.

20. In the *Yüan-chüeh ching ta-shu ch'ao* (Jpn., *Engakugyō daishoshō*; Z. 1. 14.3.277b–280a), summarized by Yampolsky, pp. 46–47.

21. Yampolsky names the school of Chih-hsien the "school in Szechwan" after Szechwan Province (p. 46). The *Rekidai hōbōki* treats this school in great detail (see above, chap. 8, note 32 and accompanying text).

22. Yanagida offers another possibility of Tsung-mi's genealogy, which has Tsung-mi descending not from the well-known Shen-hui of the Ho-tse school but from another Buddhist monk of the same name. Tsung-mi himself traced his descent back to the famous disciple of Hui-neng. See *Shoki*, p. 336. On the ties between Zen and Kegon in Tsung-mi's doctrine, see pp. 426ff, 456.

23. See the brief biography in *Zen Dust*, pp. 266–268. Early biographies appear in the *Sō kōsōden* (T. 2061, vol. 50, pp. 762b–763b) and the *Sodōshū* (see above, chap. 8, notes 11 and 81.)

24. Another kōan concerning National Teacher Chung appears in case 17 of the *Mumonkan*.

25. Cited in the translation of K. Sekida, *Two Zen Classics*, p. 194.

26. See Gundert's detailed and penetrating explanation of this example in his *Bi-yän-lu* I, pp. 333ff.

27. From the German translation of Gundert, *Bi-yän-lu* I, p. 326.

28. T. 2014; see also the final book of the *Keitoku dentōroku*, T. 2076, vol. 51, pp. 460a–461b. A free German translation with notes has been published by S. Ohasama and A. Faust in their *Zen: Der lebendige Buddhismus in Japan*, pp. 71–91; see also D. T. Suzuki's English rendering in *Manual of Zen Buddhism*, pp. 106–21, and W. Liebenthal's more scientific translation, introduction, and commentary in MS 6 (1941):1–39. Finally, an English translation with commentary was also published by Charles Luk (Lu K'uan Yü) in his *Ch'an and Zen Teaching*, pp. 103–45.

29. *Shoki*, p. 466. The expression "Highest Vehicle," which Zen lays claim to, signifies the surpassing of the difference between the "Great" and "Small" Vehicles.

30. *Sō kōsōden*, T. 2061, vol. 50, p. 764a (in the biography of Shih-t'ou). The passage is also included in the *Keitoku dentōroku* (vol. 6).

31. This comprehensive prophecy contains a number of important names from the early history of Zen, among which are included the names of Ma-tsu and Shih-t'ou. See the *Sodōshū*, cited in *Shoki*, pp. 356ff; for an English translation see J. C. H. Wu, *The Golden Age of Zen* (Taipei, 1967), p. 91.

32. See the mimeographed edition (Kyoto, n.d.), vol. 4, pp. 33–44, compiled in 952; see note 64 of chap. 8 above.

33. T. 2061, vol. 50, p. 766a–c. The *Sō kōsōden* compiled by Tsan-ning (919–1001) is an important historical source, containing biographies of 532 Buddhist monks and mentioning an additional 125.

34. *Sō kōsoden*, T. 2061, vol. 50, p. 766a. I am following the Japanese translation of Yanagida here (*Shoki*, p. 336).

35. *Shoki*, p. 337.

36. *Engakukyō daishōshō*; see *Shoki*, p. 338. Wu-hsiang and Ma-tsu are also introduced together in a list in the *Keitoku dentōroku*.

37. *Shoki*, p. 337. The epitaph of Ch'üan Te-yü is also presented in *Ch'üan Tang wen*, chap. 501, XI, 6466–6467.

38. Tsung-mi presents a different line of succession; the data in the *Rekidai hōbōki* are more reliable, according to Yanagida (*Shoki*, pp. 283–84).

39. *Keitoku dentōroku* (vol. 6), T. 2076, vol. 51, p. 245c.

40. *Keitoku dentōroku* (vol. 5), T. 2076, vol. 51, p. 240c.

41. Cited in *Shoki*, p. 410.

42. *Keitoku dentōroku* (vol. 6), T. 2076, vol. 51, p. 246a.

43. Relying on the *Laṅkāvatāra Sūtra*, Ma-tsu makes "the spirit of Buddha's words into the doctrine and the non-door into the door of the Dharma," thus using the sūtra in a completely original way. See *Shoki*, pp. 408, 410.

44. See the citation (above, note 42) on the identity of the Three Worlds with mind, and the universe with the One Dharma. This contrasts with the famous case 73 of the *Hekiganroku*, in which a monk asks Master Ma, "Independent of the four propositions and transcending the hundred negations, tell me plainly the meaning of Bodhidharma's coming from the West." Ma-tsu replies in typical kōan fashion: "Ts'ang's head is white, Hai's head is black." This saying on the "black" and "white" of the two monks' heads is one of the pearls of Zen literature.

45. The collected sayings of Zen Master Nan-chüan P'u-yüan are contained in the *Kosonshuku goroku* (Chin., *Ku-tsun-su yü-lu*), compiled by Chüeh-hsin during the Sung period. See my *The Development of Chinese Zen*, (New York, 1953), pp. 56–57.

46. In Gundert's view this conversation, recorded in case 3, took place in the final days of Ma-tsu's life. See his *Bi-yän-lu* I, p. 95.

47. *Bi-yän-lu* I, p. 97. See Gundert's detailed account of the case and its verse, pp. 95–101.

48. Vol. 1, pp. 147–55 (see note 32 above).

49. T. 2061, vol. 50, pp. 763c–764a. A brief biography of Shih-t'ou is included in *Zen Dust*, pp. 300ff.

50. *Keitoku dentōroku* (vol. 14), T. 2076, vol. 51, p. 309b. The English translation is adapted from *Zen Dust*, pp. 301–02.

51. *Keitoku dentōroku* (vol. 30), T. 2076, vol. 51, p. 459b.

52. *Keitoku dentōroku* (vol. 30), T. 2076, vol. 51, p. 461c.

53. See *Zen Dust*, p. 302. On the "Five Ranks" see chap. 11 below. The two doctrinal poems document Shih-t'ou's fondness for mountain solitude. In the *Sandōkai* he refers to the Buddha as "the Great Solitary" (*daisen*). This line also gave rise to two other poetic works. The first is the *Rakudōka* (*Song of Delighting in the Way*), composed by Tao-wu Yüan-chih (769–835), a disciple of Shih-t'ou's Dharma successor Yüeh-shan Wei-yen (751–834). The term *rakudōka* is also used for this genre of Zen poem. Second, in the same circles the verses of the *Hōkyō zammai-ka* (*Song on the Samādhi of the Jewel Mirror*) were composed and circulated. These verses have been linked to the name of Yün-yen T'an-sheng (780–841), another disciple of Yüeh-shan, from whom the line leads to the founders of the Sōtō (Chin., Ts'ao-tung) school. See *Chūgoku zenshūshi*, pp. 60–61. The men in the Shih-t'ou line show a tendency towards solitude and mountain seclusion. Yanagida gives this as a characteristic of this line in comparison to that of Ma-tsu, whom he sees as having developed a community lifestyle (Pai-chang); see *Chūgoku zenshūshi*, pp. 60–61, *Shoki*, pp. 480–81.

54. See *The Development of Chinese Zen*, pp. 10, 53.

55. I owe the fitting characterization of the T'ang period as the "golden age of Zen" to Ruth Fuller Sasaki (*The Development of Chinese Zen*, p. 3). An idea of the widely ramified generational lines of Zen masters during those days can be gathered from the tables included at the end of this volume. See also the historical section of the introduction to my translation of the *Mumonkan*, pp. 12ff.

56. The collection of the sayings of Chao-chou (Jpn., *Jōshū Shinsai zenji goroku* or simply *Jōshū roku*) in two volumes (date unknown) is included in the *Kosonshuku goroku* (see note 45 above). It is preceded by a brief biography. See *Zen Dust*, p. 344.

57. *Mumonkan*, case 7.

58. From the collected sayings of Chao-chou; see *The Development of Chinese Zen*, pp. 12, 59.

59. *The Development of Chinese Zen*, pp. 12, 60.

60. *The Development of Chinese Zen*, pp. 12, 61.

61. *Mumonkan*, case 7; Shibayama, *Zen Comments on the Mumonkan* (New York, 1974), p. 67.

62. *Hekiganroku*, case 9, Sekida, *Two Zen Classics*, p. 192. On this case, which bears the title "Chao-chou's Four Gates," see *Bi-yän-lu* I, pp. 199–209.

63. Case 19, Shibayama, *Zen Comments*, p. 140; Dumoulin, *Development of Chinese Zen*, pp. 84–86.

64. From the *Zen no shinzui—Mumonkan*, a commentary to the *Mumonkan* by Yasutani Hakuun (Tokyo, 1965), p. 145. Cited in the German edition of the *Mumonkan*, p. 85.

65. *Mumonkan*, case 2.

66. Sekida, *Two Zen Classics*, p. 150.

67. *Mumonkan*, case 28.

68. *Gotō egen* (vol. 7); see *The Development of Chinese Zen*, pp. 8, 47.

69. *Rentō eyō*; see *The Development of Chinese Zen*, pp. 8–9, 48.

70. *The Development of Chinese Zen*, pp. 9, 49.

71. *Mumonkan*, case 13.

72. Cited in the biography included in *Zen Dust*, pp. 291–94.

73. *Mumonkan*, case 3.

74. See the essay by Nakamura Hajime, "Zen ni okeru seisan to kinrō no mondai" ["The Question of Production and Labor in Zen"], ZB 1(1955): 27–35, 7–17.

75. Nakamura finds an irony in the fact that precisely the Chinese Zen monks, who were the most advanced in forsaking formalism in all things, should have developed a productive, socially advanced life in a community of work. He values the worth of monastic life and solves the moral question implied by early Buddhist proscriptions against such agricultural work by seeing it as Zen practice. See his "Zen ni okeru seisan to kinrō no mondai," pp. 33ff.

76. T. 2025, vol. 48. On Pai-chang's writings see the introduction to Yi T'ao-t'ien's translation, "Records of the Life of Ch'an Master Pai-chang Huai-hai," EB 8 (1975): 42–73. The early edition of the rules of Pai-chang is mentioned in the epitaph that Ch'en Hsü composed for Pai-chang (ibid., pp. 42–43). Vol. 6 of the *Keitoku dentōroku* contains a remark of Pai-chang's to the effect that he was aware of no innovation in his rule that departed from traditional Mahāyāna or Hīnayāna Vinaya, and had no intention of inventing something entirely new but only to pass on the spirit of the past. See T. 2076, vol. 51, p. 251a, cited in *Chūgoku zenshūshi*, pp. 59–60.

77. It is possible that Hui-chung (683–769), the sixth successor in the Ox-head school, had already constructed a Dharma hall, although this would not have corresponded fully to the monks' hall or meditation hall, as such halls are known in Zen. See *Shoki*, pp. 480ff. and the accompanying notes. The monks' hall was overseen by an elder, virtuous monk (Jpn., *chōrō*) who was regarded by the disciples as a "living Buddha." See *Chūgoku zenshūshi*, p. 60.

78. See D. T. Suzuki, *The Training of the Zen Buddhist Monk* (New York, 1965), and more recently E. Nishimura, *Unsui: A Diary of Zen Monastic Life* (Honolulu, 1973).

79. The case treats the question as to whether one who has been enlightened is still bound by (the law of) cause and effect. The head of the monastery had once responded in the negative to a disciple who asked this question, and subsequently was made to live as a fox for five hundred years. Pai-chang retorted to this former monk, who, though a fox, attended an assembly of the monks in the form of an old man, that one cannot obscure causation; with this, the old man achieved enlightenment and was released from his existence as a fox. The two answers, the monk's "not bound" and Pai-chang's "not obscure," both represent one aspect of reality, according to the explanation of the Zen master. One who is truly enlightened, even though not bound by the law of karma, lives freely in the world of becoming according to the law of karma. See the explanatory comments in the German translation, pp. 40–44.

80. *Keitoku dentōroku* (vol. 6), T. 2076, vol. 51, p. 250a. The most important collection of discourses of Pai-chang in existence, *Hyakujō kōroku*, is included in book 3 of the *Record of the Four Houses* (see below, chap. 10, note 2). Yi T'ao-t'ien lists the collections that contain material on Pai-chang and translates selected texts into English ("Records of the Life of Ch'an Master Pai-chang Huai-hai," pp. 44–45). Pai-chang appears there as a "religious genius" (p. 46), and together with Hsi-t'ang Chih-ts'ang and Nan-ch'üan P'u-yüan, "two other advanced disciples," is said to constitute the core of Ma-tsu's circle (p. 47). Yi T'ao-t'ien also translates a text in which Pai-chang figures as Ma-tsu's Dharma heir, as Zen tradition holds. This does not contradict the *yessen* relationship (see note 1 of the following chapter). Yi T'ao-t'ien musters numerous impressive texts showing what a remarkable personality Pai-chang was.

81. Cited in *Zen Dust*, p. 414. For the treatise "On the Essentials for Entering Tao through Sudden Enlightenment" (Jpn., *Tongo nyūdō yōmon-ron*; Chin., *Tun-wu ju-tao yao-men lun*), as well as further biographical details on Ta-chu Hui-hai and a description of his work, see pp. 413ff. See also the English translation by John Blofeld, *The Zen Teaching of Hui Hai on Sudden Illumination* (London, 1962).

10

Lin-chi

THE GENERATIONAL LINE

The dominant figures in the Zen movement after Hui-neng are Ma-tsu, Pai-chang, Huang-po Hsi-yün (d.850), and Lin-chi I-hsüan (d.866). Standing in a direct master-disciple relationship to each other, these four individuals help us focus the core of the "Zen of the Patriarchs": the transmission of the Buddha mind outside the scriptures and sudden enlightenment through seeing into one's own nature and becoming a Buddha. It is customary in Zen literature to treat together the four generations extending from Ma-tsu by way of Pai-chang and Huang-po to Lin-chi. In these masters the Zen brought to China by Bodhidharma and given definitive form by Hui-neng reached what was to be at once both its high point and its consummation.[1]

As already pointed out, the decisive events in the Zen movement run parallel with important sociopolitical changes. Beginning in the middle of the eighth century, a "new Buddhism" arose that transformed the Indian religion into a completely Chinese religion. Although this development permeated the whole of Zen after Hui-neng, it was particularly evident in the line of generation leading to Lin-chi. The four generations are represented in Zen literature by "collected sayings" (Jpn., *goroku*), a literary genre in which the typically Chinese character of the Zen of the Patriarchs is strongly evident. In these texts, consisting of stories, discourses, and sayings, the heritage of India melded into the common language of China. To be sure, the paradox and dialectic of the Wisdom sūtras remained, but reality was communicated now not by what could be thought but by what could be grasped tangibly and physically. The collected sayings of masters Ma-tsu, Pai-chang, Huang-po, and Lin-chi were gathered together in one volume called *The Collection of Four Houses* (Jpn., *Shike goroku*; Chin., *Ssu-chia yü lu*) or, according to its alternative title, *The Collection of the Four Houses of Ma-tsu* (Jpn., *Baso shikeroku*; Chin., *Ma-tsu ssu-chia lu*).[2] This work testifies to the close unity among the four members of this line of succession.

Pai-chang discovered the golden rule that has been confirmed by experience and passed down through Zen tradition: "One whose insight is the same as his teacher's lacks half of his teacher's power. Only one whose insight surpasses his teacher's is worthy to be his heir."[3] Zen recognizes the imperative to development innate in the human. Of course, not all stages of Zen's growth have embraced this imperative equally well. Zen history, like all history, has its high points and its low points. But the four generations that span this great century of Chinese Zen Buddhism are a prime example of what the transmission of mind in Zen really means and what it can achieve.

The four generations are linked not only by external master-disciple bonds but also by a deeply spiritual relationship. Ma-tsu found an expression for this relationship when he uttered his first thunderous "*ho!*", which following generations took up and passed on. Pai-chang told his disciple Huang-po the story of how the master's vocal explosion so shook and shattered him that he remained deaf for three days.[4] Huang-po passed on this powerful method of prodding students to his disciple Lin-chi, in whose school "shouting"—the Japanese pronounce the Chinese character *katsu*—continues to echo loudly. However one pronounces it, the shout symbolizes a continuous line of succession up to Lin-chi and his school.

The school of the Zen of the Patriarchs refers to itself simply as the Zen school. All four masters used this name to describe the meditational path of sudden enlightenment they were passing on, convinced that it represented the transmission of the Buddha mind that had come to the Middle Kingdom through Bodhidharma. For the great Master Ma, the words and mind of Buddha were what is essential. His Dharma heir, Pai-chang, assured the continuance of this precious tradition by giving structure to the religious life of the community. Thanks to his guidance, Huang-po attained the deep insight by which he was able to guide his disciple Lin-chi. And with Lin-chi Chinese Zen attained its unsurpassed zenith.

FROM THE LIFE OF LIN-CHI

Numerous biographical collections within Zen literature report on the life and activity of Lin-chi.[5] The small volume of the "collected sayings" or "discourses" of Zen Master Lin-chi Hui-chao from Chen-chou (Jpn., *Chinjū Rinzai Eshō zenji goroku*; Chin., *Chen-chou Lin-chi Hui-chao ch'an-shih yü-lu*) counts among the classical works of Zen Buddhism, indeed, among the classics of world religious literature. We have neither the date nor a copy of its first edition. The Zen monk Yüan-chüeh Tsung-yen put together a later, modified edition, which contains a preface by the courtier Ma Fang, dated 1120. It must have been around this time that a new edition was prepared that would be the form in which the work was passed down as part of Buddhist literature. The disciple San-sheng Hui-jan is named as compiler on the title page of this edition, although he otherwise scarcely appears in the life of the master. It is not certain whether it was this disciple who actually copied down the discourses of Lin-chi. The context in which the first copy was made is not known.[6] An early text found in the Zen chronicle *Tenshō kōtōroku* (Chin., *T'ien-sheng kuang-teng lu*; 1036), one of the five important chronicles of the Sung period, includes the full text of the *Rinzairoku*. Differing significantly from the earlier version, the 1120 text contains eight additions and is completely restructured to give the work a quite different character.[7] While the earlier version is more biographical, the later modified text resembles the "collected sayings" of the Sung period. At the time of this later redaction, the Rinzai school was in full bloom, and the modifications reflect the concerns of the period.

As it stands, the work is divided into three parts of differing lengths. Part 1, "Discourses," contains the main body of the text and consists of discourses and sayings (Jpn., *Goroku*). It begins with a discourse by Lin-chi from the platform of the Dharma hall in the presence of the district governor, Wang. Passages in the form of questions and answers follow, which are followed in turn by longer discourses. Part 2, "Critical Examinations," (Jpn., *Kamben*) is made up of questions and answers (with the exception of secs. 1 and 23) that aim at authentic existence. Part 3, "Record of Pilgrimages" (Jpn., *Anroku*) begins with an account of Lin-chi's enlightenment and ends with a "memorial inscription" (*tōki*) or "short biography" (*ryakuden*), which is a later addition of Tsung-yen.

The first lines of the memorial inscription offer some basic, historically reliable facts concerning Lin-chi's life. The text begins as follows:[8]

> The Master's name as a monk was I-hsüan. He was a native of the prefecture of Nan-hua in the province of Ts'ao. His family name was Hsing. As a child he was exceptionally brilliant, and when he became older, he was known for his filial piety. After shaving his head and receiving the full commandments he frequented lecture halls; he mastered the Vinaya and made a wide study of the sūtras and śāstras.
>
> Suddenly [one day] he said with a sigh: "These are prescriptions for the salvation of the world, not the principle of the transmission outside the scriptures." Then he changed his robe and traveled on a pilgrimage. ("Record of Pilgrimages," sec. 22)

In typical monastic style and stereotypical language the text lauds the talents and virtues of the young boy. Not surprisingly, he entered the religious life at an early age. What his "assumption of homelessness" really meant would become clear to him later. In his discourses he speaks repeatedly of the "true homelessness" of the Buddhist monk achieved through radical renunciation and the abandonment of all craving. The full consequences of his decision to enter the monastery became clear to the young man only after he had taken his first steps on the way to enlightenment. He clarified for his audience the stages he went through:

> Take me, for example: in bygone days I devoted myself to the Vinaya and also delved into the sūtras and śāstras. Later, when I realized that they were medicines for salvation and displays of doctrines in written words, I once and for all threw them away and, searching for the Way, I practiced meditation. Still later I met great teachers. Then it was, with my Dharma Eye becoming clear, that I could discern all the old teachers under heaven and tell the false ones from the true. It is not that I understood from the moment I was born of my mother, but that, after exhaustive investigation and grinding discipline, in an instant I knew of myself. ("Discourses," sec. 18)

Lin-chi's great teachers in Zen were masters Huang-po and Ta-yü. Yanagida dates Lin-chi's first meeting with Huang-po between 836 and 841, when he was 26 years old.[9] Lin-chi's date of birth is uncertain, somewhere between 810 and

815. If he followed the customs of the time and entered the monastery when he was twenty, then Yanagida's calculations would be just about correct. At that time, Huang-po Hsi-yün lived in the monastery of Daian-ji (Chin., Ta-an ssu) in the provincial capital of Hung-chou. A high official, P'ei Hsiu (797–870), an ardent admirer and zealous student of Huang-po, later built the master a monastery in the western part of Hung-chou Province, on what was called Mount Huang-po, after the best known of the master's names.[10] Tradition was later to ascribe this, incorrectly, as the site of Lin-chi's Great Enlightenment. Not far from the monastery, Ta-yü lived in a hermitage.

There are two versions of the story of Lin-chi's enlightenment. The more dramatic one, which is also the version sanctioned by tradition, is found in the *Rinzairoku*.[11] An alternate account appears in the *Sodōshū*. According to the *Rinzairoku*, the entire event took place in three phases, each in a different setting as noted in the translation that follows. We present the narration here in its entirety:

[1] When Lin-chi was one of the assembly of monks under Huang-po, he was plain and direct in his behavior. The head monk praised him saying: "Though he's a youngster, he's different from the other monks." So he asked: "Shang-tso, how long have you been here?"

"Three years," replied Lin-chi.

"Have you ever asked for instruction?"

"No, I've never asked for instruction. I don't know what to ask," replied Lin-chi.

"Why don't you go ask the head *ho-shang* of this temple just what the cardinal principle of the Buddha-dharma is?" said the head monk.

Lin-chi went and asked. Before he had finished speaking Huang-po hit him. Lin-chi came back. "How did your question go?" asked the head monk.

"Before I had finished speaking the master hit me. I don't understand," said Lin-chi.

"Then go and ask him again," said the head monk.

So Lin-chi went and asked, and again Huang-po hit him. Thus Lin-chi asked the same question three times and was hit three times.

Lin-chi came back and said to the head monk: "It was so kind of you to send me to question the master. Three times I asked him and three times I was hit by him. I regret that some obstruction caused by my own past karma prevents me from grasping his profound meaning. I'm going away for awhile."

The head monk said: "If you are going away, you should go take your leave of the master." Lin-chi bowed low and withdrew.

The head monk went to the master's quarters before Lin-chi and said: "The young man who has been questioning you is a man of Dharma. If he comes to take his leave, please handle him expediently. In the future, with training, he is sure to become a great tree which will provide cool shade for the people of the world."

Lin-chi came to take his leave. Huang-po said: "You mustn't go anywhere else but to Ta-yü's place by the river in Kao-an. He's sure to explain things for you."

[2] Lin-chi arrived at Ta-yü's temple. Ta-yü said: "Where have you come from?"

"I have come from Huang-po's place," replied Lin-chi.

"What did Huang-po have to say?" asked Ta-yü.

"Three times I asked him just what the cardinal principle of the Buddha-dharma was and three times he hit me. I don't know whether I was at fault or not."

"Huang-po is such a grandmother that he utterly exhausted himself with your troubles!" said Ta-yü. "And now you come here asking whether you were at fault or not!"

At these words Lin-chi attained Great Enlightenment. "Ah, there isn't so much to Huang-po's Buddha-dharma!" he cried.

Ta-yü grabbed hold of Lin-chi and said: "You bed-wetting little devil! You just finished asking whether you were at fault or not, and now you say, 'There isn't so much to Huang-po's Buddha-dharma.' What did you just see? Speak, speak!"

Lin-chi jabbed Ta-yü in the side three times. Shoving him away, Ta-yü said: "You have Huang-po for a teacher. It's not my business."

[3] Lin-chi left Ta-yü and returned to Huang-po. Huang-po saw him coming and said: "What a fellow! Coming and going, coming and going—when will it end!"

"It's all due to your grandmotherly kindness," Lin-chi said, and then presented the customary gift and stood waiting.

"Where have you been?" asked Huang-po

"Recently you deigned to favor me by sending me to see Ta-yü," said Lin-chi.

"What did Ta-yü have to say?" asked Huang-po.

Lin-chi then related what had happened. Huang-po said: "How I'd like to catch that fellow and give him a good dose of the stick!"

"Why say you'd 'like to'? Take it right now!" said Lin-chi and immediately gave Huang-po a slap.

"You lunatic!" cried Huang-po. "Coming back here and pulling the tiger's whiskers."

Lin-chi gave a shout.

"Attendant, get this lunatic out of here and take him to the monks' hall," said Huang-po.

Although embellished with extra details and stylized for use as a kōan, this account of Lin-chi's great experience belongs among the most famous cases of enlightenment in Zen history. During the first stage, Lin-chi's repeated failure turns his doubt to painful despair. There seems to be no way out. No matter what he does, he gets hit. Certainly, no words can give the answer to the question about the nature of reality. The master's answers only drive him deeper into darkness. During the second stage, the answer breaks through suddenly. At a rather insignificant remark from Ta-yü, Lin-chi awakens to the Great Experience. In the third stage, in typical Zen fashion, Huang-po tests the experience by trying to undermine it. And here the full force of the experience comes through: Lin-chi strikes out and screams. In the years ahead he would prove to be a master of using this same method with his own students.

The *Rinzairoku* follows the account with a discussion between Zen masters Kuei-shan Ling-yu (771–853) and Yang-shan Hui-chi (807–883) regarding why there were two masters involved in Lin-chi's enlightenment. It reads:

> Later, Kuei-shan, telling the story to Yang-shan, asked: "On that occasion did Lin-chi get help from Ta-yü or Huang-po?"
>
> "He not only rode on the tiger's head but also seized its tail," replied Yang-shan.[12]

The import of Yang-shan's cryptic comment is that Lin-chi was able to appropriate the spirit and teachings of both masters. This throws some light on why Ta-yü, after receiving three blows to the ribs from the disciple he had just helped to enlightenment, dismisses him so quickly. "Your teacher is Huang-po. I have nothing to do with it all." Ōmori Sōgen, a contemporary Japanese Zen master, has high praise for Ta-yü for not claiming the newly enlightened disciple for himself but sending him back to his first master.[13] In any case, Lin-chi remained Huang-po's disciple and became the Dharma heir in his line of succession. For later generations of the Rinzai school, this bond between Huang-po and Lin-chi is indispensible to understanding the history of their school.

In marked contrast the other, less dramatic, version of Lin-chi's enlightenment, contained in the *Sodōshū*,[14] recounts that it was after a much more general and mild suggestion from Huang-po that Lin-chi visited Ta-yü in his hermitage. During the night Lin-chi demonstrated his profound knowledge of the sūtras, only to be driven away by the master's blows the next morning. Huang-po listened to Lin-chi's report of his experience and encouraged him to go back and try again. He was greeted with the words: "So you're not yet ashamed of yourself! Why have you come back?" And with this, Ta-yü took up his staff. One of his particularly sharp blows suddenly brought Lin-chi to enlightenment, but the master did not notice the change in the disciple and threw him out the door. Lin-chi went back to tell Huang-po about the blows and about his happy experience. Ten days later he returned to Ta-yü, who was just about to start swinging when Lin-chi grabbed his staff and began hitting the master. Ta-yü was overjoyed to see that the disciple had reached enlightenment.

We cannot tell which of the two versions is historically more correct. The Rinzai school prefers the version in the *Rinzairoku*. The *Sodōshū* account adds that he spent more than ten years with Ta-yü until the master died. The passage closes with these words:

[Lin-chi] I-hsüan spread the message in the area of Chen-chou. He received the Dharma from Huang-po and always praised Ta-yü. For his method of teaching, he used shouts and blows with his staff.[15]

The detailed account of the experience of enlightenment that appears in part 3 of the *Record of Lin-chi* is followed by brief reports of encounters, sometimes with Huang-po and sometimes with other Zen masters with whom Lin-chi carried on discussions. But given the lack of all chronological sequence, the record has little biographical value. The "Record of Pilgrimages" ends with a conversation that Lin-chi had with his disciple San-sheng shortly before he died (sec. 21). The information in the *Sodōshū* regarding Lin-chi's ten-year stay with Ta-yü deserves to be taken seriously. Yanagida tries to blend the different accounts by affirming Lin-chi's stay with Ta-yü and at the same time pointing out the "probability" of frequent visits to Huang-po.[16] During the Buddhist persecution under Emperor Wu-tsung in 845, Lin-chi could surely have taken refuge in the hermitage of Ta-yü. The year of Ta-yü's death is not known, but it seems likely that he passed away soon after the persecution had subsided. After that, Lin-chi probably spent a few years with Huang-po. Yanagida suggests that Lin-chi's final departure from his master took place in 849 or 850.[17] The *Keitoku dentōroku* offers a moving description of this farewell. "In the future, you'll cut off the tongue of every man in the world," says the master, and with these words of encouragement the disciple took his leave.[18] Almost ten years had passed since his enlightenment. Lin-chi was in the prime of life.

The biographies like to divide the lives of Zen masters into three parts. First there is a period of practice leading to enlightenment, followed perhaps by some additional practice. Then comes a time of traveling to visit Buddhist centers and consult with well-known Zen masters. Finally, there are the years of the master's own teaching activity, which are dedicated mainly to guiding disciples along the path to enlightenment. The Zen sources report on Lin-chi's travels through China and his visits with enlightened masters but do not allow us to fix his exact itinerary. According to the *Keitoku dentōroku*, he first made a pilgrimage to the memorial tower of Bodhidharma in Hunan. He finally settled down in the regional capital of Chen-chou, located in Ho-pei Province in northern China.

Thus began the third phase of Lin-chi's life. He was now head of a small monastery located on the banks of the Hu-t'o River and called Rinzai-in (Chin., Lin-chi yüan, "monastery overlooking the ford"). It is in connection with the name of this monastery that the monk I-hsüan would be remembered throughout Zen history. The setting of his brief activity was modest—in no way comparable to the magnificent monastic complexes in the capital cities of Ch'ang-an and Lo-yang that had been the centers of Zen activity during the first half of the T'ang period, nor to the so-called "Five Mountains and Ten Temples" of the Sung period of which we shall speak later. The number of Lin-chi's followers was limited. Nowhere in the Zen records is there any mention of a "forest of disciples" gathering about him. Itinerant monks and pious pilgrims on their way to the nearby shrine of the bodhisattva Mañjuśrī on Mount Wu-t'ai may have increased the number of those who came to hear his talks. Citizens from the city and officials from the local government may also have attended. Yet from the number of renowned Zen masters who came to visit Lin-chi during the ten years of his activity there, we know that this small monastery soon came to be an important center of the contemporary Zen movement. Among the visitors was the brilliant Zen master Chao-chou Ts'ung-shen (778–897).[19] Lin-chi had previously visited the well-known master Te-shan Hsüan-chien.[20] The *Biographies of Eminent Monks Compiled during the Sung Period* places Lin-chi and Te-shan together, even though they belong to different lines of succession.[21]

Lin-chi had come to the monastery of Rinzai-in at the invitation of a "man from Chao," whom Yanagida identifies as Governor Wang of the Chen-chou region.[22] We know of three members of the Wang family who followed each other in governing the area of Ch'eng-te to which Chen-chou belongs. Lin-chi's patron and friend was probably the third member of the family, Wang Shao-i (who died the same year as Lin-chi, 866). Part 1 of the *Rinzairoku* relates how Lin-chi ascended the platform of the Dharma Hall in the presence of Governor Wang. It seems there were close bonds between the two, which is an important factor in understanding Lin-chi's personality. During the second half of the T'ang period, the administrators of the northern provinces assumed a high degree of independence. Lin-chi carried out his activity in an atmosphere of unrestricted freedom.[23]

A certain monk of Rinzai-in named P'u-hua was very helpful to the newly arrived Lin-chi. According to a prophecy of Yang-shan, this monk was supposed to be of assistance to Lin-chi in Rinzai-in:

> Later on you'll go to the north and there'll be a place for you to stay. . . .
> Afterward there'll be a man to help you, my venerable brother. He'll have a head but no tail, a beginning but no end. ("Record of Pilgrimages," sec. 8)

The memorial inscription sees Yang-shan's prophecy fulfilled in the eccentric monk P'u-hua, who pretended to be crazy, mixed among the people, and then one day disappeared without a trace ("Record of Pilgrimages," sec. 24).[24]

The *Record of Lin-chi* mentions only a handful of Lin-chi's disciples. The name of his Dharma heir, Hsing-hua Ts'un-chiang, (830–888) appears at the end of the memorial inscription. Hsing-hua had come to Lin-chi in 861, attained enlightenment, set off on a long pilgrimage, and then returned to serve Lin-chi until the master's death.[25] The *Record* further states that Lin-chi spoke his last words to the disciple San-sheng Hui-jan, who is supposed to have compiled the work. In his typical rough style, the master's last words were "this blind ass!" ("Record of Pilgrimages," sec. 21). At the end of the memorial inscription the name of the otherwise unknown disciple Pao-shou Yen-chao is mentioned. Equally unknown are two other disciples mentioned in the "Critical Examinations," Ta-chüeh, who is listed as the disciple of Lin-chi or Huang-po, and Ting Shang-tso, known as "Ting of the Upper Seat."[26] The disciple Lo-p'u (834–

898), who is named in several of the stories recorded in the *Rinzairoku*, went south and changed over to the line of succession of Ch'ing-yüan (Shih-t'ou).[27] The earlier *Sodōshū* refers to Ts'un-chiang, and Pao-shou, as well as to a disciple named Kuan-hsi Chih-hsien (d.895) who became a follower of Lin-chi during the master's final years.[28] The long lists of disciples of Lin-chi given in the Zen chronicles of the Sung period lack historical reliability, their obvious aim being to extol the importance of Lin-chi and the school that had meantime reached full flower.

There is a scarcity of data regarding Lin-chi's final years and death. The biographies say nothing at all. Only the memorial inscription, included in the *Rinzairoku* as a later addition, reports that he traveled south and died in the region of Ta-ming. The details are uncertain, but the substance of the report seems accurate. An epitaph composed by the scholar Kung-ch'eng I (dates uncertain), written for Lin-chi's successor Hsing-hua Ts'un-chiang, and preserved in the documents from the T'ang period, informs us that during a trip through southern China this disciple received the surprising news that Master Lin-chi was on his way to P'u-chou at the invitation of Lord Chiang (District Commander Chiang Shen of Ho-chung).[29] Ts'un-chiang, immediately changed course and met the master before he arrived at P'u-chou. But Chiang Shen, most likely having received new orders, was no longer there. Without further delay, Lin-chi, Ts'un-chiang, and other companions set off again. On their way they met Ho Hung-ching, a messenger of the governor of Wei-chou, who invited them to the residence of his lord. Thus Lin-chi came to spend the last months of his life in a monastery of Wei-chou, greatly revered, surrounded by many visitors, and under the special care of his disciple Ts'un-chiang.[30] The memorial inscription reports his death with the simple words:

> Suddenly one day, the master, although not ill, adjusted his robes, sat erect, and when his dialogue with San-sheng was finished, quietly passed away. It was on the tenth of the first month in the eighth year of Hsien-t'ung of the T'ang dynasty [18 February 867].

His final conversation with San-sheng immediately precedes the memorial inscription in the *Rinzairoku* ("Report of Pilgrimages," sec. 22). Since it appears nowhere else, the whole account must be considered highly dubious. Both early Zen chronicles, the *Sodōshū* and the *Keitoku dentōroku*, fix the date of Lin-chi's death at 27 May 866. This latter dating seems preferable.[31] According to the memorial inscription, his body was interred in a pagoda. The epitaph for Ts'un-chiang, however, reports that this disciple was able to perform ritual cremation for his master.[32] By imperial decree, Lin-chi received the posthumous title of "Zen Master of Illuminating Wisdom." (Jpn., *Eshō zenji*; Chin., *Hui-chao ch'an-shih*).

Lin-chi's life began and ended in northern China. From the time of the uprising of An Lu-shan (755–762) until the end of the T'ang period and afterward, the northern provinces were plagued by internal unrest and constant threats from the barbarians beyond the northern borders. In such an invigorating climate,

Lin-chi's personality grew strong. No external luster surrounded his life. Even the quiet glow of old age so common among Zen masters was denied him. He was only about fifty-five when he died. His true greatness came to light only in later generations.

Lin-chi's successors—Hsing-hua Ts'un-chiang, Nan-yüan Hui-yung (d.930), Feng-hsüeh Yen-chao (896–973), Shou-shan Sheng-nien (926–993), and Fen-yang Shan-chao (947–1024)—had to struggle against great difficulties to keep their master's spirit alive and to pass on his tradition. Only in the seventh generation, with Shih-shuang Ch'u-yüan (986–1039), did Lin-chi's line of succession come to southern China where, in the prosperous province of Hunan, it spread quickly and surpassed all other Zen schools. The Rinzai school, which grew vigorously during the Sung period, revered Lin-chi as its founder and patriarch. Little wonder that they glorified him in every way imaginable. We may regret the overzealous idealizing and mythologizing of this hardy man who loved solitude, preferring to view him in his original, unpolished authenticity. As a religious founder, Lin-chi lives on in his school; almost all our knowledge about him we owe to his disciples.

Without the Rinzai school, the vitally important text of the *Rinzairoku* would have been unthinkable. Although members of the school polished and partially altered it, the edition we have today, an authentic work from the Sung period, provides us with the master's discourses and conversations as directly recorded by his disciples. Despite the glosses, we can discern much that is original and genuine.[33] The powerful influence that this work has continued to exercise on the entire Zen movement is evident in our own time. In what follows, we shall consider some of the important themes in this *Record of Lin-chi*.

THEMES FROM THE *RINZAIROKU*

The first major section of the *Rinzairoku* contains twenty-two discourses delivered by Lin-chi, mainly to his disciples, during his ten years in Rinzai-in. In them the master answers questions from his disciples about the Zen way, and these answers often turn into discourses of their own. The talks recorded are based on notes taken by the disciples. Despite later changes and additions, the master's sharp tongue comes through clearly. As is usually the case with such texts, it is impossible to distinguish with certainty between original passages and later interpolations. A number of sentences and some whole passages are so reworked and labored that one can readily identify them as additions from the Sung period.

During the ninth and tenth centuries, within the literary genre of "discourses" or "collected sayings" to which the *Rinzairoku* belongs, a new literary movement arose. Reacting against the cold forms of classicism, it turned to popular, even vulgar, forms of expression.[34] This movement made use of colloquial language, giving voice to popular sentiments that had long been mute. The edition of the *Rinzairoku* that we have today may not be the earliest example of such literature within Zen writings, but it is certainly the most significant and influential. Its language is self-willed and rich in coarse expressions that defy translation into Western languages. Only very recently have we had translations of exceptional quality[35] that communicate the content of the work, and yet they are still not able to catch the totally unique style of the master as he responds to his disciples, sometimes with touching tenderness, sometimes with crude reprimand.

As would be expected, Lin-chi's discourses do not rest on a logically structured system. Although a powerful thinker and lover of dialectics, Lin-chi never draws the line of thought in his conversations to a compelling conclusion. Whatever he says is merely implicit and fragmentary. "The whole in the fragment"—this characteristic of Chinese-Japanese *goroku* literature is especially evident in Lin-chi. As for their philosophical significance, his discourses are grounded in the Mahāyāna sūtras. While his thought is imbued with the spirit of Mahāyāna, his way of expressing himself is unusual, original, sometimes shocking, and always suited to lay bare new aspects of reality. A single passage will frequently contain a variety of themes, all of them pressing upon the disciples and stirring them profoundly. We can imagine the master, with his piercing eyes opened wide (as he is presented in Zen art) watching his audience and not allowing them for a moment to wander from his gaze.

THE QUEST FOR THE HUMAN

The fundamental theme of Lin-chi's discourses is the human. Some have spoken of Lin-chi's "humanism"[36] or of a Far Eastern version of humanism.[37] This much is certain: Lin-chi is first and foremost concerned weith the human, the individual. If we wish to transpose the term humanism to Asia and apply it to the thought of Lin-chi, then we must also bear in mind the special, indeed the unique, content of what Lin-chi has to say about the human. The human is nearly always his concern. A synopsis of all the Chinese characters he uses shows that of the total 1336 characters in the text, the graph for "human being" appears 196 times. Prescinding from characters that are used frequently without any special significance on their own, there are only two other graphs—both of them expressing negation—that are used more frequently than this.[38] But more is at stake than textual statistics. In the discourses of Lin-chi, the human is dominant, as we can see more clearly if we compare his views to those of the surrounding intellectual milieu of his time.

In Chinese thought the human is a center point, one of the three "basic energies." The central place that ethics and social concerns hold in the Chinese classics is well known. An early expression of this characteristic can be seen in the genre of the dialogue (for example, the conversations of Kung-tzu), which may be considered a distant predecessor of the Zen *goroku* style. During the same period when the Zen movement was flourishing, a school of thought within Confucianism, associated with the names of the intellectuals Han Yü (768–824) and Li Ao (d.c. 844), began to give new and compelling attention to the human being. While Han Yü dedicated himself intently to the problem of the person within a general study of nature, Li Ao sought to recover and reformulate the classical image of the human. Despite their fundamental opposition to Buddhism, both these thinkers came very close to Buddhist views, especially in their regard for the Way, or Tao, and in their concern to lead a life according to this Way. Although this new orientation within Confucianism had an obvious impact on the Buddhism of the time, there are no direct links to Lin-chi and the school of Ma-tsu.

Buddhism from its very beginnings has always been concerned with the human being. The basic experience of Śākyamuni, in which all Buddhists have their roots, was an existential human experience, and as such was transmitted and perpetuated in all forms of Buddhism. As Buddhism developed from the Mahāyāna sūtras to Chinese Zen, the anthropological component took on different forms in the different schools. During the second half of the T'ang period, Tsung-mi became for that epoch the main representative of Buddhism's concern for the human. His *Treatise on the Origins of the Human* (Jpn., *Gennin-ron*; Chin., *Yüan-jen lun*) represents the Buddhist refutation, or actual rejection of the works of the Confucian Han Yü, who had used the term "origins" (*yüan*) in the title of his work (820). Tsung-mi's study is still much in use in Japan as an introduction to Mahāyāna teachings.[39]

In his opening chapter, Tsung-mi sets forth what he considers to be the strange and false views of Confucianism and Taoism. He then points out four imperfect doctrines within Buddhism, in order finally to single out the Kegon school (Chin., Hua-yen) as the "supreme vehicle." In this fivefold scheme, belief in karma as the ground (*nindengyō*) for being born as a human being or as a heavenly being (Skt., *deva*) is considered to be inferior to the teachings of the Hīnayāna, or "small vehicle" (Jpn., *shōjō*). He criticizes two initial developments in Mahāyāna, the idealistic doctrine of consciousness (Skt., *vijñānavāda*; Jpn., *hossō*) and Nāgārjuna's philosophy of the Middle Way (Jpn., *hasō*, literally "the destruction of the *dharma-lakṣana*"). The Consciousness-only school (Skt., Vijñaptimātra; Jpn., Yuishiki) was considered by Tsung-mi for several reasons to constitute a preliminary stage of Mahāyāna. With regard to Nāgārjuna's philosophy, Tsung-mi emphasizes the negative aspect of the proof for the emptiness of all things. Only in the unified vision of Kegon does the perfect form of Mahāyāna emerge.

As its title indicates, Tsung-mi's *Gennin-ron* deals with the origins or foundations of the human. Nevertheless, it is difficult to locate a specifically anthropological perspective in the work. Without analyzing the human being according to the Buddhist categories of living beings, Tsung-mi establishes the Buddha nature or Buddha mind as the foundation—and one may say the goal—of humanity.

No mention is made in this work of Zen, but in Tsung-mi's *Zengen shozenshū tojo* (Chin., Ch'an-yüan chu-ch'üan-chi tu-hsü) he distinguishes three Zen schools: at the bottom level, the Northern school of Shen-hsiu; next the line of Ma-tsu from the Southern school, as represented by Huang-po and Lin-chi; and finally the Kataku school, which traces its lineage back to Shen-hui. Tsung-mi declares himself a member of this latter.[40] According to him, the last two schools propose different views of human being and human conduct. True to the traditional views of the sūtras, Tsung-mi takes human conduct to be grounded in an abstract nature, and he criticizes the Ma-tsu school for not recognizing such a ground. Significantly, he uses the same arguments against Ma-tsu and his disciples that he had used against Taoism.[41] No doubt he is correct on some points, but his overall critique is flawed.

For Lin-chi, the question concerning the human being is not a question of human nature. Without denying the metaphysical views of the Mahāyāna sūtras he abhors all philosophical abstractions. His sole concern is with the concrete individual. His "true human" lives bodily in the here and now, just as the Buddha and the patriarchs did. Mahāyāna teachings, especially those of the Kegon school, are translated into concrete terms.

THE TRUE HUMAN OF NO RANK

Lin-chi sought the "true human" not in the Buddhas and patriarchs of the past, and not in an ideal still to be realized in the future, but in the here and now, in the disciples seated before him listening to his discourses. As he told them:

> Nowadays he who studies Buddha-dharma must seek true insight. Gaining true insight, he is not affected by birth-and-death, but freely goes or stays. he need not seek that which is excellent—that which is excellent will come of itself.
>
> Followers of the Way, the eminent predecessors we have had from of old all had their own ways of saving men. As for me, what I want to point out to you is that you must not accept the deluding views of others. If you want to act, then act. Don't hesitate.
>
> Students today can't get anywhere: what ails you? Lack of faith in yourself is what ails you. If you lack faith in yourself you'll keep on tumbling along, bewilderingly following after all kinds of circumstances, be taken by these myriad circumstances through transformation after transformation, and never be yourself.
>
> Bring to rest the thoughts of the ceaselessly seeking mind and you'll not differ from the Patriarch-Buddha. Do you want to know the Patriarch-Buddha? He is none other than you who stand before me listening to my discourse. Since you students lack faith in yourself, you run around seeking something outside. Even if through seeking you find something, that something will be nothing more than elaborate descriptions in written words; in the end you will fail to gain the mind of the Living Patriarch. Make no mistake, worthy Ch'an men! If you don't meet [Him] here and now, you'll go on transmigrating through the three realms[42] for myriads of kalpas and thousands of lives and, held in the clutch of agreeable circumstances, be born in the womb of an ass or a cow.
>
> Followers of the Way, as I see it we are not different from Śākya. What do we lack for our manifold activities today? The six rays' divine light never ceases to shine.[43] See it this way, and you'll be a man who has nothing to do his whole life long [buji no hito].[44] ("Discourses," sec. 10)

In lucid, simple words, this long passage from Lin-chi's discourses makes clear the heart of his message. It also shows how he uses language, how he explains important details and hints at related topics. In the center of it all is his message about the Patriarch-Buddha.[45] To their faces Lin-chi tells his disciples: you are the Patriarch-Buddha. His message shocks them, as they strain to listen more closely. Even the reader of the *Rinzairoku* might be taken aback, wondering what it really means. One thing is clear, Lin-chi is not preaching anything new. In a quite unusual form never before adopted he is expressing one of the fundamental doctrines of Mahāyāna. If all living beings—or more radically, the entire universe—is Buddha nature (Lin-chi prefers the more concrete expressions *Buddha* or *Patriarch-Buddha*),[46] then so are the disciples who are sitting here in the meditation hall listening to their master's lecture. They are, just as they are, the Patriarch-Buddha, "the living Patriarch (Jpn., *kassō*)."[47] They lack nothing. "What do we lack for our manifold activities today?" This simple sentence comes up again and again, in different forms, throughout Lin-chi's talks; it expresses the powerful truth of the universal Buddha nature, in which nothing is missing. The disciples have but one thing to do: believe in themselves. Only then will they give up the restless running around against which Lin-chi warns. They should not delay. Often, in order to strengthen this admonition, Lin-chi uses "body language"—blows from his staff and thundering shouts. One of the purposes, though not the only one, of these "violent" displays is to shock the disciples out of their hesitating doubts.

In the passage quoted above, there is no talk of enlightened wisdom or miraculous powers. The disciples to whom Lin-chi is speaking show no such abilities. They are "ordinary people." This is a central theme in Lin-chi's discourses. With it, he stands in fidelity to Ma-tsu's tradition, which stresses that the ordinary mind is the Way and describes the disciple searching for the Way as one who

> makes use of his past karma; accepting things as they come he puts on his clothes; when he wants to walk he walks, when he wants to sit he sits; he never has a single thought of seeking Buddhahood. Why is this so? A man of old said:
>
> > If you create karma trying to seek Buddha,
> > Buddha will become a great precursor of birth-and-death.
>
> Virtuous monks, time is precious. Yet you try by hurrying hither and thither to learn meditation, to study the Way, to accept names, to accept phrases, to seek Buddha, to seek a patriarch, to seek a good teacher, and try to speculate.
>
> Make no mistake, followers of the Way! After all, you do have a father and a mother. What more would you seek? Try turning your own light inward upon yourselves! A man of old said:
>
> > Yajñadatta [thought he had] lost his head,
> > But when his seeking mind came to rest, he was at ease (*buji*)[48]
>
> Virtuous monks, just be ordinary. Don't put on airs. . . . ("Discourses," sec. 10)

The "ordinary human" is the "true human" who in all life's situations, no matter what the external or internal circumstances, remains simple, natural, and direct, who without pretense or ambitions for what is out of the ordinary lives "at ease" in the present moment. In a famous passage that many consider to be the culmination of his discourses, Lin-chi described this "true human." The master ascended the platform and spoke:

> On your lump of red flesh is a true man without rank who is always going in and out of the face of every one of you. Those who have not yet proved him, look, look! ("Discourses," sec. 3)[49]

A kōan-like scene follows this discourse. A monk asks further questions about the true human. Lin-chi rushes down from his platform, takes hold of the monk and cries: "Speak! Speak!" The monk hesitates. The master pushes him aside: "The true man without rank—what kind of shit-wiping stick is he!"[50] And with that he withdraws into his quarters.

The expression "true human" (Chin., chen-jen; Jpn., shinnin) is of Taoist origin. In no way is the true human anything special. Such a one has no rank. In ancient China everyone had a rank within the hierarchy of society, which meant that a human without rank was a marginal figure.[51] Such individuals, equipped with the "facial gates" of their sense organs—flesh and blood human beings—are the Buddha. In proclaiming this central message of Mahāyāna so clearly, the text translates it into anthropological terms. The way it is preached is pregnant, shocking, original. From all sides, Lin-chi describes the "true human of no rank." With this inimitable metaphor he clarifies the unique quality of the Zen way.

CHARACTERISTICS OF THE "TRUE HUMAN"

The true human is best characterized negatively—as not only "without rank" but also "without qualities,"[52] depending on nothing, without clothes, indescribable, and indefinable. Lin-chi continues:

> He is without form, without characteristics, without root, without source, and without any dwelling place, yet is brisk and lively (Jpn., kappatsu patsuji).[53] As for all his manifold responsive activities, the place where they are carried on is, in fact, no-place. Therefore, when you look for him, he retreats farther and farther; when you seek him, he turns more and more the other way: this is called the "Mystery." ("Discourses," sec. 14)

This passage is taken from a discourse that, appealing to the Wisdom sūtras, urges the disciples to behold the emptiness of all things and to cling to nothing.

> There is only the man of the Way, listening to my discourse, dependent upon nothing—he it is who is the mother of all Buddhas. Therefore Buddhas are born from non-dependence. . . . [Those who are] dependent fall into causation; they don't escape the round of birth-and-death in the three realms. ("Discourses," sec. 14)

Such statements show Lin-chi's Buddhist roots, but the Chinese quality of his thought is also clearly present. His discourses are by no means restricted by the limits of Mahāyāna. The true human, characterized by a lack of characteristics, is lively and dynamic. Yanagida attributes great importance to the authentically Chinese expression *huo-p'o-p'o-ti* (Jpn., *kappatsu patsuji.*) The term can be found also in the writings of the Sung Neo-Confucian scholars the brothers Ch'eng, who used the graph suggesting the image of a fish as a symbol of the human's natural vitality.[54] In his discourses, Lin-chi asks his listeners: "Do you know who it is who right now is running around searching this way?" He answers the question himself: "He is brisk and lively, with no roots at all" (sec. 18). That is, there is nothing to hold or hinder such a one. The ring of Lin-chi's language and its images projects the concrete, free human.

This free human, attuned to nature, stands in stark contrast to the static purity of the ideal human being defended by the Northern school of Chinese Zen. Imitating Shen-hui and using words almost identical to his, Lin-chi rejected this school of meditation. He sharply attacked deluded monks who,

> . . . having stuffed themselves with food, sit down to meditate and practice contemplation: arresting the flow of thought they don't let it rise; they hate noise and seek stillness. This is the method of the heretics. A patriarch said: "If you stop the mind to look at stillness, arouse the mind to illumine outside, control the mind to clarify inside, concentrate the mind to enter *samādhi*—all such [practices] as these are artificial striving." ("Discourses," sec. 17)

The one who is truly free clings neither to motion nor to motionlessness, both of which still belong to the realm of rebirth and are without self-nature. An independent follower of the Way "utilizes motion and utilizes motionlessness" (sec. 18). In solitary freedom, the disciple transcends the three realms and the ten thousand things (*dharma*) of the empirical world. Lin-chi explains:

> Followers of the Way, true Buddha has no figure, true Dharma has no form. All you are doing is fashioning models and creating patterns out of illusory transformations. Anything you may find through seeking will be only a wild fox spirit; it certainly won't be true Buddha. It will be the understanding of a heretic.
>
> The true student of the Way has nothing to do with Buddhas, nothing to do with bodhisattvas or arhats. Nor has he anything to do with what is held to be excellent in the three realms. Having transcended these, in solitary freedom, he is not bound by things. Though heaven and earth were to turn upside down I wouldn't have a doubt; though all the Buddhas of the ten directions were to manifest themselves before me, I wouldn't have any joy; though the three hells were to suddenly yawn at my feet, I wouldn't have any fear. Why is this so? Because as I see it, all dharmas are empty forms; when transformation takes place they are existent, when transformation does not take place they are nonexistent. The three realms are mind only, the ten thousand dharmas are consciousness only. . . .[55]

Only you, the follower of the Way right now before my eyes listening to my discourse, [only you] enter fire and are not burned, enter water and are not drowned. . . . How can this be? There are no dharmas to be disliked.

If you love the sacred and hate the secular
You'll float and sink in the birth-and-death sea.
The passions exist dependent on mind:
Have no-mind, and how can they bind you?
Without troubling to discriminate or cling to forms
You'll attain the Way naturally in a moment of time.[56]

But if you try to get understanding by hurrying along this byway and that (*hahaji*), after three *asaṃkhyeya* kalpas you'll still end up in the round of birth-and-death. Better take your ease (*buji*) sitting cross-legged on the corner of a meditation chair in a monastery. ("Discourses," sec. 18)

This text, given almost in its entirety, contains Mahāyāna teachings as well as Taoist elements from the words of Chuang-tzu.[57] With powerful images the discourse depicts the freedom of the human when identified with the Buddha. Let the world—what is meant is of course the changing world of *saṃsāra*—fall apart together with all Buddhas, bodhisattvas, arhats who may be caught in this world of becoming. Still the disciples of the Way, these truly free humans, would go through fire and water, clinging to nothing, transcending every distinction. Like the Patriarch-Buddha himself,[58] they cannot be distinguished from the "true Buddha" and from the "true Dharma."

In this fragment, too, Lin-chi presents the whole. The freedom of the true human resounds through the entire passage as its main motif. Two aspects of the motif are noteworthy. Lin-chi makes use of the completely free and detached condition of the disciples sitting before him in order to describe the state of enlightenment, without actually using the word *enlightenment*. He avoided it because it was unnecessary for what he wished to communicate. In earlier times the word may have been overused, even worn out and misused. What is more, Lin-chi did not care for the abstract terms that were usually employed to express the experience of enlightenment. The term *kenshō*, for example, which is still used today to designate seeing one's own nature, nowhere appears in his discourses.[59] And yet in describing a spiritual state of total freedom, a state beyond all distinctions, he is speaking of the selfsame state that Zen masters would call enlightenment.

What is more, in the passage quoted above, the true Buddha and the true Dharma are clearly elevated above all the phenomena of the empirical world. Demiéville comments: "The true Buddha must be conceived of as an absolute removed from every empirical designation."[60] On the other hand, all the Buddhas, bodhisattvas, and arhats that are part of the rich symbolism of Buddhist scripture belong to the empirical world; like all phenomena they are "empty" and without a self-nature. Lin-chi criticized those who made the Buddha into a miraculous being endowed with extraordinary signs, dwelling in a supernatural but still tangible state of bliss and enjoying the fruits of asceticism practiced in previous lives.[61] Such images are illusions and distractions from the true Zen way. As such, they need to be cleared away.

Lin-chi's aim was to uproot and destroy, once and for all, anything that might stand as an obstacle to the Zen disciple's realization. This is the intent behind the following oft-quoted and oft-misunderstood passage:

> Followers of the Way, if you want insight into Dharma as is, just don't be taken in by the deluded views of others. Whatever you encounter, either within or without, slay it at once: on meeting a Buddha slay the Buddha, on meeting a patriarch slay the patriarch, on meeting an arhat slay the arhat, on meeting your parents slay your parents, on meeting your kinsman slay your kinsman, and you attain emancipation. By not cleaving to things you freely pass through. . . . ("Discourses," sec. 18)

These statements sound blasphemous, and to be sure they stirred up opposition from all sides. Chinese and Japanese Confucians reacted strongly against this blatant attack on filial piety.[62] With their intentional provocation, these admonitions easily offend normal human sensitivities and raise doubts about their author's ethical and religious integrity. Lin-chi upset in order to set loose. All the phenomena of this empirical world must be killed. Mother and father and relatives are consigned to the level of the empirical. The image is clearly metaphorical. In another passage from the *Rinzairoku*, which rings as no less blasphemous, Lin-chi tells his monks that they cannot attain liberation until they have committed the five great sins: "Killing the father, slaying the mother, shedding the blood of a Buddha, destroying the harmony of the *saṅgha*, and burning the scriptures." Following analogous interpretations from the Buddhist canon, he goes on to explain that the father symbolizes ignorance, the mother carnal desires, and so forth. In short, the five great sins must be understood in the context of liberation.[63]

Lin-chi went to extremes in order to assure "the fully free dynamism of the naked human."[64] In order to possess this freedom the disciples must believe in themselves, reject all self-doubt, and become people of sound, hard resolve who are "masters everywhere."[65]

> Just make yourself master of every situation, and wherever you stand is the true [place]. No matter what circumstances come they cannot dislodge you [from where you stand]. Even though you bear the remaining influences of past delusions or the karma from [having committed] the five heinous crimes, these of themselves become the ocean of emancipation. (Discourses," sec. 12)[66]

This passage is not a casual comment but the core of a particular experience. The true human is free in any life-situation and can play with any event or context. Lin-chi used the example of garments that one doffs and dons:

> There is the robe of purity, the robe of Birthlessness, the robe of Bodhi, the robe of Nirvāṇa, the Patriarch-robe, and the Buddha-robe. Virtuous monks, as for spoken words and written phrases, they're all but a trans-

formation of robes. . . . [Even] mental activities . . . are robes. . . . Much better do nothing (Chin., *wu-shih*, Jpn., *buji*). (sec. 18)

The true and free disciple is detached from all change of garments, even when it has to do with "holy things." Indeed, he or she transcends the distinction between sacred and secular. It is here that the famous dialectical schemata for practice belong. These practices appear in the *Rinzairoku;* indeed Lin-chi may be considered their spiritual father. In any case, it was only within his school that they attained the perfected form in which they were passed on in later tradition. Similar models are found in the other schools of the "Five Houses," which will be taken up in the following chapter.

DISCIPLES OF THE TAO

In the *Record of Lin-chi* the master avails himself of various names to address his disciples, referring to them as "pupils" or "students" (Jpn., *gakusha, gakudōnin*), as "virtuous" or "of great virtue" (Jpn., *daitoku*), as "people of the Way" (Jpn., *dōnin*), and most often by a phrase that means something like "those who follow the Way," "those who adhere to the Way," or "learners of the Way" (Jpn., *dōryū*; Chin., *tao liu*). Translators trying to render these forms of address into a foreign language, even into Japanese, frequently find themselves at a loss for proper equivalents.[67] In fact, there seems to be no major distinction between the expressions, as they all clearly refer to practicing, searching, learning disciples who receive instruction from their master.

To judge from the frequency with which he uses the expression and the special weight it seems to carry in certain passages, we may conclude that Lin-chi had a special preference for the appellation *dōryū*. When translated as "disciples of the Tao," the expression carries a deep meaning. The Tao—the Unnamed, the Mother of all extolled in the book of wisdom by Lao-tzu—is the center of Chinese thought. It was well known to Lin-chi, especially from his study of Chuang-tzu's philosophy. Used as a form of address, it points to the religious dimension of his Zen. There is no proof for this, of course; it is a question of feeling. Linchi's way of interacting with his disciples—his unique master-disciple relationship—reflects an important aspect of his Zen way.

Lin-chi spared no effort in guiding his students, the disciples of the Way, in a manner suited to each of them. His harsh, aggressive style, his coarse reprimands, his frightening shouts, the painful blows he occasionally meted out, always at the right moment—all of this belongs to the classical image of the Chinese Zen master. At the same time, his discourses stirred his disciples to deep reflection and placed lofty demands on their spiritual ideals. Together with his disciples, he lived the life of a Buddhist monk in the rigorous spirit of the Vinaya, most likely according to the rule that Pai-chang had drawn up.

In his talks, Lin-chi stressed the monastic character of Zen. His disciples had to be monks. The Japanese word for monk here is *shukke*, literally "those who have left home," or as the Pāli Canon has it, "those who have left home for homelessness."[68]

Without diluting its original meaning, Lin-chi gave the term his own interpretation. We listen as he voices the complaint that among the students of the time there were so few monks who had really left home and achieved true insight.

> Students nowadays know nothing of Dharma. They are just like sheep that take into their mouths whatever their noses happen to hit against. They neither discriminate between master and slave, nor distinguish host from guest. Such as these, having entered the Way with crooked motives, readily enter bustling places. They cannot be called true renouncers of home—on the contrary—they're in fact true householders.
>
> Now he who is a renouncer of home must, acquiring the usual and true insight, distinguish between Buddha and Māra, between the true and the false, the secular and the sacred. If he can do this, then he may be called a true renouncer of home. But if he cannot distinguish Māra from Buddha, then he has only left one house to enter another. He may be dubbed a karma-creating sentient being, but he cannot be called a true renouncer of home. ("Discourses," sec. 12)

Lin-chi made it unmistakably clear that to leave one's home does not mean exchanging one house for another, or leaving the comforts of one family in order to settle down comfortably in another house called "homelessness." Such monks as these there are, and Lin-chi compared them to sheep sniffing around with their noses, every bit as ignorant and full of craving as worldings who have never left their homes. The ability to make distinctions that Lin-chi required of his disciples did not imply dualistic thinking: it meant simply seeing things as they really are. This ability helps students detach themselves from all clinging and advance on the path to liberation.

Although Lin-chi did not describe the path to enlightenment in detail, he did emphasize that the decisive breakthrough takes place of a sudden, in a single moment. He appeals to his own experience, which he mentions often in his discourses but never describes fully. One brief account ends with the phrase, "in an instant I knew of myself" ("Discourses," sec. 18). Lin-chi distanced himself from all forms of Buddhist meditation that proposed a gradual progression and that tried to explain this process rationally.

> For the Ch'an school, understanding is not thus—it is instantaneous, now, not a matter of time! All that I teach is just temporary medicine to cure a corresponding illness. Indeed, no real Dharma exists. He who understands this is a true renouncer of home; he may spend a million gold coins a day.[69] ("Discourses," sec. 13)

"Attainment is attained instantly" (ibid.). Lin-chi clearly endorsed the school of sudden enlightenment. Holding to his disdain for the theoretical, he never described this experience, nor did he try to explain its nature. As Lin-chi understood it, enlightenment is to be found in the daily activity of the true, ordinary human who is living enlightenment. Thus he tells his disciples:

> There're a bunch of students who seek Mañjuśrī on Wu-t'ai-shan.[70] Wrong from the start! There's no Mañjuśrī on Wu-tai-shan. Do you want to know

Mañjuśrī? Your activity right now, never changing, nowhere faltering—*this* is the living Mañjuśrī. ("Discourses," sec. 15)

One of the most important passages in the *Rinzairoku* speaks of three classes of students. Not content merely with these three, Lin-chi added a fourth, giving us what may be the most impressive picture we have of his idea of the unified, limitless activity of the enlightened human in the here and now of the present, an activity that leaves no trace and yet marks a culmination:

> But should a man of extraordinary understanding come, I[71] would act with my whole body[72] and not categorize him. Virtuous monks, when a student has reached this point, his manifest power is impenetrable to any wind and swifter than a spark from flint or a flash of lightening. The moment a student blinks his eyes, he's already way off. The moment he tries to think, he's already differed. The moment he arouses a thought, he's already deviated. But for the man who understands, it's always right here before his eyes. ("Discourses," sec. 18)

Enlightenment is present here and now in what the disciple is doing. It is new at every moment, complete and unrestricted. Always and everywhere, disciples can enter any realm they wish. As Yanagida comments, the word *enter* is one of the characteristic expressions that Lin-chi uses in different contexts to indicate both setting out on the Way of enlightenment or realization as well as entrance into the world of diversity.[73]

> Followers of the Way, in an instant you enter the Lotus World, the Land of Vairocana, the Land of Emancipation, the Land of Supernatural Powers, the Land of Purity, and the Dharmadhātu; you enter the dirty and the pure, the secular and the sacred, the Realm of Hungry Ghosts, and the Realm of Beasts. Yet however far and wide you may search, nowhere will you see any birth or death; there will only be empty names. ("Discourses," sec. 18)

With slight variations, the same theme reappears later in response to the rhetorical question: "What is lacking in your present responsive activity?" ("Discourses," sec. 16).[74] Activity must respond to things continually, as they arise. In order to respond properly to each new circumstance, disciples require an insight beyond their native gifts. . It is here that the question of practice arises.[75]

According to Lin-chi's anthropology, human beings possess the "Dharma Eye" (Jpn., *dōgen*, literally "eye of the Way") by which they can distinguish true from false. This eye, however, is clouded by numerous distortions, many of them caused by people themselves. Lin-chi knew this from his own experience. In a biographical comment, he described how as a youth "with a burning belly and a turbulent mind, I ran around inquiring about the Way" ("Discourses," sec. 22). Although his encounters with famous teachers were a great help, he still had to supply his own "exhaustive investigation and grinding discipline" ("Discourses," sec. 18). His Dharma Eye began to clear (*dōgen bunmyō*) so that he could distinguish true from false. "It is not that I understood from the moment

I was born of my mother" (ibid.). This experience had a great impact on his own teachings. Again and again he reminds his disciples that only through practice can ordinary people—human beings "born from mothers"—attain true insight.

Possessed of the precious gift of the Dharma Eye, one must practice in order to remove the obstacles that cloud its clear vision. Restlessness, doubt, and clinging all impede the free activity of the Dharma Eye. Lin-chi therefore admonishes his disciples:

> Virtuous monks, don't use your minds mistakenly. The great sea does not detain dead bodies. But all you do is rush about the world carrying them on your shoulders. You yourselves raise the obstructions that impede your minds. When the sun above has no clouds, the bright heavens shine everywhere. When there is no cataract on the eye, there are no [imaginary] flowers in the sky. ("Discourses," sec. 22)

Practice is the first duty of the disciples; the responsibility for carrying it out is entirely theirs. Lin-chi warns against relying on external authorities. Even the words of old and revered monks should not be followed blindly; under no circumstances should you go through your lives "betraying your own two eyes."[76] Lin-chi instilled in his followers a critical spirit. He also had high praise for the pioneers of the Zen way who opened new vistas, applying to them the saying, "The lion's one roar splits the jackals' skulls,"[77] recalling the lion's roar of the enlightened one from the tribe of the Śākya.

Lin-chi's disciples were urged to practice; indeed it was an unconditional requirement. While such practice was demanding, especially when directed at maintaining an inner attitude of total detachment, it was also meant to be easy, simple, and natural. Lin-chi explicitly rejected the *zazen* meditation of the Northern school. This is not to say that he and his disciples followed the Sixth Patriarch and his school in rejecting such meditation altogether. To sit in meditation was part and parcel of all Zen practice at the time. It was simply that Lin-chi did not adopt such practice as part of his method, refusing as he did any cause and effect relationship between meditation and enlightenment.

Much less can study of the sūtras lead to enlightenment. Although Lin-chi himself was well-versed in the sūtras, he was emphatic in his disdain for learning:

> Virtuous monks, make no mistake. I don't care if you understand the sūtras and śāstras, if you are a king or a high minister, if you are as eloquent as a rushing torrent, or if you are clever or wise. I only want you to have true insight.
>
> Followers of the Way, even though you could master a hundred sūtras and śāstras, you're not as good as a teacher who has nothing to do (*buji*). If you do master them, you'll regard others with contempt. Warring *asuras* and men's egotistical *avidyā* increase the karma that leads to hell. ("Discourses," sec. 22)[78]

As proof of all this, Lin-chi told the story of the monk who understood the twelvefold teaching and still fell living into hell.

To counteract scriptural pedantry as well as a crippling preoccupation with method Lin-chi recommends a free-flowing, relaxed way of life. To urge such a lifestyle he makes ready use of Taoist sayings. The previously mentioned warning against exaggerated study of the scriptures ends as follows: "It's better to do nothing and take it easy." He then recites the following verses:

When hunger comes, I eat my rice.
When sleep comes I close my eyes.
Fools laugh at me, but
The wise man understands.[79]

The two last verses appear in an earlier discourse in which Lin-chi makes it clear that the Buddha-dharma does not require any special strain; it suffices to be "ordinary" and "not have anything to do." The "true human of no rank" follows the way of the "ordinary mind" and is a "disciple of the Tao."

LIN CHI AND HIS SCHOOL

The figure of Lin-chi is inseparable from his school, mainly because his individuality as a Zen master is intelligible only in the context of the school that developed from him. All the discourses and stories from his life were elaborated by generations of disciples before taking final literary form. The Rinzai school considers itself to stand in a direct line of inheritance from Lin-chi, who stamped this school with the seal of his own individuality. Like no other Zen school, this main current of Chinese Zen Buddhist tradition feels indebted to its founder.

Lin-chi's extraordinary significance for Zen history is due in part to the role his school played in the Chinese Buddhism of the Sung period (960–1279). The first generations after Lin-chi eked out a rather modest existence in northern China and in the region of the Yellow River. According to early literary testimony from the tenth century to the time of the *Keitoku dentōroku* (1004), the Rinzai school in no way stood out from the other trees of the dense "Zen forest" of the time. During the brief interval before the appearance of the *Tenshō kōtōroku* in 1036, all of this changed.[80] Bringing together all the discourses and kōan-like sayings of the master in their rich abundance, this chronicle became the definitive apologia for Lin-chi and his school. Throughout the work, its compiler Li Tsun-hsü (d. 1038), a lay disciple of the Rinzai school, shows himself to be a fervent devotee of Lin-chi. Married to a princess of the imperial family from the Northern Sung dynasty and a man of high social standing, Li was unfaltering in devoting his entire political and social prestige to the service of the Rinzai school. That the school grew so vigorously during this period is due mainly to his efforts, as recorded in the *Tenshō kōtōroku*. The popularity of the school added lustre to the image of its founder, whose fame spread throughout China during the following centuries. The story of his growing fame is recorded in the different phases of the history of the Rinzai school.

For all that, Lin-chi's place of prominence in the history of Chinese Zen does not derive primarily from the role of his school. All the sources agree that he was an exceptional person and an imposing figure. The *Rinzairoku*, though clearly a literary work, is not mere poetry. While Lin-chi resolutely planted Zen in the soil of China, and while he enabled his disciples to become "ordinary," he himself stands as a figure of uncanny concreteness and vitality, firmly situated in the here and now. The Zen movement of the T'ang period abounds in figures of great masters, most of them clearly above the average norm of Zen masters. With no intention of comparing them or ranking them relative to one another, we cannot but acknowledge that Lin-chi towers above the rest. He wears almost the entire wardrobe of qualities befitting a master. The unique history of his enlightenment, the numerous paradoxical, spirited sayings that flowed from his lips—these have all been recorded in Zen literature. Above all, one is taken by the commanding directness with which he addresses his disciples, his rigorous, pressing admonitions that make no concession to human weakness, and yet, through it all, a human warmth that pervades his being. The exceptional intellectual powers of this Zen master, who has been called "a type of Chinese Socrates,"[81] are evident in his discourses; with a bold sense of adventure he turned his powers to translating the world view of Hua-yen (Kegon) and the Wisdom sūtras into ordinary language and so opened up previously unconceived possibilities for everyday life.

With all these achievements and qualities, Lin-chi stands out as a religious figure. His taunting, unspiritual, even grotesque ways of expressing himself—hardly what one would expect of a monk or abbot—do not obscure the deeply religious content of his message. Raised in the strenuous style of the Vinaya, this homeless monk attained the fullness of spiritual freedom and was able to express with his whole personality and his whole body the truth that possessed him so completely. According to the eminent Sinologist and humanist Paul Demiéville, Lin-chi embodies "a Chinese humanism, the humanism of a Chinese Buddhist, perhaps more Chinese than humanist"[82]—a Buddhism aware of transcendence. For Lin-chi there exists an Unnamed that no eye has seen, no ear has heard, and because of which human beings lack nothing. Lin-chi has his religious roots in the mother soil of Buddhism. "His thought (*pensée*) remains religious, soteriological, aimed at the salvation of the individual, at 'liberation' as the Buddhists put it."[83]

With a founder so clearly ranking among the most outstanding religious spirits of humanity, it is not surprising that his school would endure after him. Chinese Buddhism reached its zenith in Lin-chi and the masters of the T'ang period related to him. In the years to come major achievements would be preserved, but rationalization, systematization, and a preponderance of method, organization, and institutionalization would bring an ebb to this tide. The spiritual storm would lose its original vigor.

NOTES

1. The special meaning of the four generations stands out clearly in the history of Chinese Zen. Yanagida gives an account of these four and stresses that in the collected sayings (goroku) they each refer to their own positions as the "Zen school" (Shoki, pp. 430–32, 456). The four generations stand in a direct master-disciple relationship to one another, even though the representatives of the lines are not always the main disciples of the preceding master. This kind of succession, which appears also in other cases in Zen transmission, is designated through the Sino-Japanese term tesson and means, according to the 1934 Haga edition of the Kanwa shindaijiten (p. 651), kyōdai no unda otoko no ko, oi no ko, almost equal to "nephew." Thus the line of Hui-neng is not carried on by his chief disciple Shen-hui but passes by way of a less known disciple Nan-yüeh Huai-jang to his disciple Ma-tsu. In similar fashion, it is not Ma-tsu's main disciple Hsi-t'ang Chih-ts'ang (735–814), three of whose disciples were Korean, but Pai-chang who succeeds to the Dharma inheritance. From there the line skips over the main disciple Kuei-shan Ling-yu (771–835) and passes on to another disciple or "nephew," Huang-po, and thence directly to Lin-chi. Yanagida gives extensive treatment of this tesson in his essay, "Shinzoku chōshi no keifu" ["New Researches on the Genealogical Transmission of the Lamp"], Zengaku kenkyū [Studies in Zen] 95 (1978): 1–39.

2. The date of origin and name of the compiler are unknown. A description of the six-volume work appears in Zen Dust, pp. 406–07

3. Bi-yän-lu I, p. 224. According to the Keitoku dentōroku (T. 2076, vol. 51, p. 249c), Pai-chang spoke these words upon receiving the Dharma from Huang-po. In the Rinzairoku the idea is put in the mouth of Kuei-shan, the main disciple of Pai-chang. See "Record of Pilgrimages," sec. 9.

4. See Bi-yän-lu I, p. 224. The Chinese character means something like crying out, shout, or the like. How the Chinese came to articulate this "untranslatable exclamatory shout" (Zen Dust, p. 83) we do not know. The character is read katsu in Japanese, corresponding to the sound of a cry, and pronounced monosyllabically as katt or khāt.

5. Yanagida cites the following works by way of introduction to his English biography of Lin-chi: Sodōshū, Keitoku dentōroku, Sō Tenshō kōtōroku, Denbō shojuki, and Goto egen. See "The Life of Lin-chi I-hsüan," EB 5 (1972): 70.

6. Yanagida deals with the question of the origin of the text of the Rinzairoku in the introduction to his annotated edition of the work, published in the Butten kōza series (Tokyo, 1972). He had previously published an edition of the text with commentary as Kunchū Rinzairoku (Kyoto, 1962). Both editions rely upon the text of 1120. Yanagida considers as certain the existence of an earlier text. The introduction takes up the most important text-critical questions (pp. 9–29). For the text (with variants) see T. 1985, vol. 47.

7. Regarding the discrepancies in ordering and additions to the final version of the Rinzairoku in comparison with the text that appears in the Tenshō kōtōroku, see Rinzairoku, pp. 15ff. The compiler of the final text of 1120, Yüan-chüeh Tsung-yen of the Ummon school, is representative of the style of the Sung period. It is to his activity that the present form of the Rinzairoku, which makes it a typical "collection of sayings" of the Sung period, can be traced.

8. The details as well as the following quotation from the Rinzairoku are drawn from the English edition prepared by Ruth Fuller Sasaki, The Recorded Sayings of Ch'an Master

Lin-chi Hui-chao of Chen Prefecture. The numbering of the passages differs somewhat from the English translation of Irmgard Schloegel, *The Zen Teaching of Rinzai* (Berkeley, 1976). Both translations rely on work done on the text in the circle of Ruth Fuller Sasaki. The equally reliable French translation of Paul Demiéville, *Entretiens de Lin-tsi* is remarkable for its fine commentary. There is no German translation. The passages appearing in the text follow the English translation *(Record of Lin-chi)* and are numbered accordingly.

9. Cited in "The Life of Lin-chi I-hsüan," p. 74. Ta-yü is listed in the *Keitoku dentōroku* as a disciple of Chih-ch'ang Kuei-tsung, one of the disciples of Ma-tsu. Huang-po, whose importance is comparable to that of Pai-chang, stands in the first line of the early Zen masters. A collection of his discourses known as the *Enryōroku* (Chin., *Wan-ling lu*), compiled by his disciples into one volume (three volumes in the edition of the Sung period) report on his Zen style. The final edition of the work forms the fifth book of *the Collection of the Four Houses* (see note 2 above). Miura and Sasaki treat the *Enryōroku* in *Zen Dust*, pp. 362–63. For an English translation, see John Blofeld, *The Zen Teaching of Huang Po* (London, 1958).

10. "The Life of Lin-chi I-hsüan," p. 74.

11. From the beginning of the third part of "Record of Pilgrimages," sec. 1. The story of enlightenment is related in rather similar terms in the *Keitoku dentōroku* and in the *Tenshō kōtōroku*, but is placed at the beginning of the account of Lin-chi and recounted in the third person. There disciples or contemporaries speak of Lin-chi, thus providing the stylistic form of part 2 and 3 of the *Rinzairoku*.

12. Kuei-shan (771–853) and Yang-shan (807–883), from the line of Ma-tsu, are recognized as founders of the Igyō school. In the context of the *Rinzairoku*, the two famous contemporaries testify to the transmission of the Dharma in the line of Huang-po and Ma-tsu to Lin-chi, who thus belongs to the Southern school. Witness to these circumstances is important because the long residence of the master and his disciple in northern China might prompt neglect of the Rinzai school in the southern part of the country, the center of Zen's activity. See *Rinzairoku*, p. 237.

13. *Rinzairoku kōwa* (Tokyo, 1980), p. 310. This edition includes the Chinese text, a Japanese translation, and helpful explanations for each section.

14. Yanagida offers a Japanese translation of the entire passage in his *Rinzairoku*, pp. 238–239; see also his résumé in "The Life of Lin-chi I-hsüan," p. 76.

15. *Rinzairoku*, p. 239.

16. See "The Life of Lin-chi I-hsüan," p. 77.

17. *Rinzairoku*, p. 300. Yanagida places his departure "soon after the end of the persecution."

18. "The Life of Lin-chi I-hsüan," p. 78.

19. The encounter is reported in part 2 of the *Rinzairoku*, "Critical Examinations," sec. 17. The conversation unfolds in kōan-like fashion:

> Chao-chou while on a pilgrimage came to see Lin-chi. The master happened to be washing his feet when they met.
> Chao-chou asked: "What is the purpose of the Patriarch's coming from the West?"
> "I just happen to be washing my feet," replied the master.
> Chao-chou came closer and gave the appearance of cocking his ear. The master said: "Now I'm going to pour out a second dipper of dirty water."
> Chao-chou departed.

The question about the meaning of Bodhidharma's coming from the West is a favorite kōan topic; see cases 5 and 37 of the *Mumonkan*.

20. See Yanagida, "The Life of Lin-chi I-hsüan," p. 85.

21. "The Life of Lin-chi I-hsüan," p. 85. Yanagida refers to a sermon of Te-shan and compares it to similar discourses of Lin-chi. It is recorded in the *Rinzairoku* that Lin-chi sent his disciple Lo-p'u to Te-shan to inquire after the latter. See "Critical Examinations," sec. 1.

22. See "The Life of Lin-chi I-hsüan," pp. 79ff.

23. See *Rinzairoku*, pp. 285ff.

24. In the notes to Sasaki's English translation P'u-hua is certified as a disciple of P'an-shan Pao-chi from the circle of Ma-tsu's disciples. He attracted attention by his eccentric manner and was revered as a patriarch of a P'u-hua school. See *Record of Lin-chi*, p. 82, note 177. P'u-hua appears in the "Critical Examinations," secs. 3–6.

25. See Yanagida, "The Life of Lin-chi I-hsüan," pp. 88ff. Yanagida relies on the historically reliable epitaph composed by Kung-cheng for details about Hsing-hua Ts'un-chiang.

26. Nothing further is known of Ta-chüeh (*Record of Lin-chi*, p. 84, note 193); Ting belongs to Lin-chi's disciples (p. 84, note 196). The conversation between Ting Shang-tso and Lin-chi constitutes case 32 of the *Hekiganroku*

27. See Yanagida, "The Life of Lin-chi I-hsüan," pp. 86. He appears in the *Rinzairoku*, "Critical Examinations," sec. 10, 11, 14.

28. "The Life of Lin-chi I-hsüan," p. 87.

29. For a detailed account see "The Life of Lin-chi I-hsüan," pp. 88–89.

30. Yanagida shows how the apparently contradictory data from the epitaph for Hsing-hua Ts'un-chiang and the memorial inscription are not entirely irreconcilable. "The Life of Lin-chi I-hsüan," pp. 88–93

31. "The Life of Lin-chi I-hsüan," p. 93.

32. "The Life of Lin-chi I-hsüan," p. 93

33. The text of the *Rinzairoku*, as Yanagida notes, has been polished in the edition of Yüan-chüeh Tsung-yen (1120) and formalized in the style of the Sung period, a style much opposed to the tastes of Lin-chi himself (*Rinzairoku*, p. 15). Nevertheless, Tsung-yen deserves merit "as the first to have fixed the text of the *Rinzairoku*." "A careful reading of his work is essential for advancing the study of Lin-chi and the *Rinzairoku*" (*Rinzairoku*, p. 25).

34. On the form of the *goroku* and attempts to translate them into Japanese, see *Rinzairoku*, pp. 10ff; on the meaning of *goroku* in Chinese and Buddhist literature, see Yanagida's detailed account (*Rinzairoku*, pp. 310–13). Yanagida remarks there, "*goroku* are fragmentary reports of particular conversations of real persons." The dialogue form corresponds to the character of the Chinese people and as such is already present in classical Chinese literature. The theme of the conversation in the *goroku* is incidental and takes form on the spot, though it always involves a confrontation with a concrete partner. What makes the *goroku* in Zen distinctive is the way they reflect the multiformity of life in the Zen monastery. Composed in the idiom of their environment, they require no particular knowledge of the reader and are thus able to extend beyond the confines of the monastery and its community to the wider reaches of society.

Japanese scholars have done considerable philological research into the common Chinese idiom of that time. Particularly deserving of mention in this regard is Iriya Yoshitaka. Demiéville attributes the linguistic peculiarity of these texts to the way they transform the living word into written form—"an important achievement in the history of literature: the written transformation of the common Chinese idiom, which is as different from the written idiom as the romance languages are from medieval Latin or as spoken Hindi is from Sanskrit. This accounts for the aggressive vulgarities and highly idiomatic expressions so common in Lin-chi, . . . which, however, are often lost because of our inadequate understanding of the spoken language of the T'ang period." (*Entretiens de Lin-tsi*, p. 10).

35. See note 8 above.

36. *Entretiens de Lin-tsi*, p. 18. See also his article "Les entretiens de Lin-tsi", in Demiéville's *Choix d'études bouddhiques*, pp. 436–55.

37. According to Yanagida, it is a humanism according to which "the meaning of life for all people is found in the absolute, unconditioned worth of the human being—the human being understood not as a specially selected, superhuman individual endowed with extraordinary talents but as the general, ordinary person of the everyday world." This is the "Far Eastern type" of humanism of the ordinary individual that Lin-chi sets forth. See *Rinzairoku*, pp. 284–85.

38. *Rinzairoku*, pp. 314–315.

39. Nj., 1594; T. 1886, vol. 45. Concerning its origin and date (neither of which are certain!), see *Rinzairoku*, pp. 291ff. Professor Ui Hakuju held a series of conferences on this text for a closed audience in the Zen temple Kichijō-ji in Tokyo during 1937 and 1938, which I was able to attend together with two Japanese fellow students. Together we prepared a German translation that was subsequently published as resource material in MN 1 (1938): 350–77. The translation is inadequate and contains errors. A partial translation may also be found in *The Buddhist Tradition*, edited by Wm. Theodore de Bary, et al. (New York, 1969), pp. 179–96. Tsung-mi's erudition contrasts sharply with the concrete vitality of Lin-chi.

40. T. 2015. Tsung-mi often mentions the Gozu (Niu-t'ou) school in addition to the Northern and Southern schools. On differences within the Southern school, see *Rinzairoku*, p. 296.

41. *Rinzairoku*, p. 299.

42. The text here makes reference to the realms of desire (*kāma-dhātu*), of forms (*rūpa-dhātu*), and of formlessness (*arūpya-dhātu*), in which sentient beings are reborn while living in saṃsāra.

43. This is a reference to the intellectual light that shines forth from the six sense organs.

44. Chin, *wu-shih*. The expression is related to the famous *wu-wei* ("non-doing, non-action") from Taoist wisdom. Demiéville translates "un homme sans affaires" (*Entretiens de Lin-tsi*, p. 56); Sasaki, whose translation we are following here, also describes the term as "a man who has nothing to do his whole life long" (*Record of Lin-chi*, p. 8).

45. The expression can also mean "patriarchs and Buddhas," but in Lin-chi it seems to have the sense of "Patriarch-Buddha," namely, a living Buddha or living patriarch. The "true human" is "Buddha" and "Patriarch."

46. Lin-chi goes a step beyond Dōgen, who in the chapter of his *Shōbō genzō* on Buddha nature asserts that living beings not only possess Buddha nature but *are* Buddha nature. Instead of the Buddha nature, Lin-chi speaks of the Patriarch-Buddha.

47. See *Rinzairoku*, pp. 323–24.

48. As an apocryphal sūtra recounts, Yajñadatta looked at his beautiful countenance in a mirror. It suddenly disappeared and he set off in search of his head. The sūtra explains that the image in the mirror is the product of his illusory powers of imagining. Our true countenance is "wondrous awakening." ' See Demiéville, *Entretiens de Lin-tsi*, pp. 66–67. Allusions to this story appear several times in the *Rinzairoku*.

49. The designation "true human" (Jpn., *shinnin*; Chin., *chen-jen*) is Taoist in origin. The true human is "without rank" because he or she occupies no place in the hierarchy of Chinese society. D. T. Suzuki ascribes great significance to Lin-chi's "true human of no rank." See his contribution to Fromm, Suzuki, de Martino, *Zen Buddhism and Psychoanalysis* (New York, 1960), pp. 32–33, and his essay "Rinzai no kihon shisō" ["The Fundamental Ideas of Lin-chi"], in volume 3 of the Japanese edition of his collected works (Tokyo; 1968). Suzuki speaks in this connection of the "real Self" as "a kind of metaphysical self in opposition to the psychological or ethical self." Izutsu Toshihiku pursues the philosophical implications of this in his book *Toward a Philosophy of Zen Buddhism* (Teheran, 1977), especially in the opening essay "The True Man Without Any Rank: The Problem of Field Awareness in Zen," pp. 3–62. Thomas Kasulis takes up Lin-chi's term in a section on "The True Person of No Status" in his book *Zen Action—Zen Person*, pp. 51–52. He renders *shinnin* as "true person," observing in a note that he has slightly amended the translation borrowed from Suzuki, who explains the "true man of no rank" when speaking of Rinzai's view "of the man, or person or self" (p. 32). At the conclusion of his work, Kasulis explains his own idea of "Zen person," which he takes to be inseparable from that of "Zen action" (pp. 153–54). We prefer to translate "the true human," using the word "human," as modern dictionaries suggest, as a noun.

50. See case 21 of the *Mumonkan*. The expression "shit-stick" is put in the mouth of Yün-men (see my German translation, p. 90). Liebenthal cites the *Rinzairoku* in his translation (pp. 82–83). Since Lin-chi lived nearly a century before Yün-men, it is probable that he was the first to use the term. Still it is not certain where the priority lies since the text of the *Rinzairoku* that has come down to us today first appeared in 1120 as the redaction of a member of the Yün-men (Jap., Ummon) school. See note 7 above.

51. See *Entretiens de Lin-tsi*, p. 32.

52. Demiéville alludes to *Der Mann ohne Eigenschaften*, a famous novel of the Austrian poet Robert Musil, who was quite familiar with Lao-tzu. See *Entretiens de Lin-tsi*, p. 32.

53. The key graph in the expression *p'o* (read *hatsu* in Japanese) has three forms in Chinese, depending on whether "hand", "water", or "fish" appears as its radical element (see *Rinzairoku*, p. 331). Demiéville translates "like the fish that leaps in the water" ("comme le poisson qui saute dans l'eau"), *Entretiens de Lin-tsi*, p. 82.

54. See *Rinzairoku*, pp. 331–32. Yanagida refers to the use of the expression among the Neo-Confucians of the Sung period. In the *Chu-tzu yü-lei* (*Classified Conversations of Master Chu*, 1270) the two Ch'eng brothers are mentioned and the expression *kappatsu patsuchi* appears several times.

55. The final sentence is a well-known axiom of the Vijñānavāda school. Demiéville remarks: "What an admission of 'idealistic' belief in the style of the school of Vijñaptimātra! This formulation was often cited by the masters at the end of the T'ang period" (*Entretiens de Lin-tsi*, p. 111). In the philosophical view of the Zen masters we see an unmistakable tendency to epistemological idealism. See Ma-tsu on the identity of mind and Buddha (*sokushin sokubutsu*), above, chap. 9, notes 41 and 42.

56. Verses from the "Mahāyāna-Lobhymnen" ' of Pao-chih (418–514); cf. *Record*, secs. 67, 80, 115.

57. See *Entretiens de Lin-tsi*, p. 111; see also the section on Lin-chi and Chuang-tsu in *Rinzairoku*, pp. 308–09.

58. See the citation from sec. 10 of the "Discourses" cited earlier, and sec. 19.

59. *Rinzairoku*, p. 319, 331.

60. *Entretiens de Lin-tsi*, p. 106.

61. See for example "Discourses," sec. 18.

62. On the reaction in China, see *Entretiens de Lin-tsi*, p. 118. During the Edo period (1600–1868) Japanese Confucians frequently accused the Buddhists of lacking filial piety.

63. "Discourses," sec. 22. Compare Demiéville's commentary, *Entretiens de Lin-tsi*, pp. 157ff. The text of the *Rinzairoku* seems to allude to a passage in the *Vimalakīrti Sūtra*. Lin-chi was still more influenced by the early pioneer of the Prajñāpāramitā sūtras in China, Seng-chao. The paradoxical twist of the text on the five great sins as well as that on killing the Buddha and patriarchs must have been influenced by the use of paradox in the Mādhayamika philosophy.

64. *Rinzairoku*, p. 332. Yanagida takes this "nakedness" (*hadaka*)—a spirit of complete carefreeness, independence, and detachment—to be "a mark of Rinzai Zen," which is "Buddhism of the free human," a "completely naked religion" (p. 301).

65. "Discourses," sec. 16.

66. This passage also has the ring of an expression used by Seng-chao; see *Entretiens de Lin-tsi*, p. 73. On the five great sins, see the text accompanying note 63 above.

67. Demiéville renders *dōryū* as "adeptes". The word *ryū* literally means "flowing," in the sense of a "school" or "adherents to an intellectual current." In ancient Chinese literature it designates various schools, including the Taoists. See Demiéville, *Entretiens de Lin-tsi*, p. 57. The expression *daitoku* that appears so frequently in Lin-chi's discourses (Demiéville renders it "Venerables") stems from Indian Buddhism and corresponds to the Sanskrit term *bhadanta* ("great virtue"); see *Entretiens de Lin-tsi*, pp. 57–58.

68. Skt., *pravrajita*.

69. A common turn of phrase at the time of Lin-chi. See *Entretiens de Lin-tsi*, p. 78.

70. Lin-chi's monastery was located on a pilgrimage path that led to the sacred site of the bodhisattva of wisdom, Mañjuśrī, on Mount Wu-t'ai. This brought numerous visitors to the monastery.

71. Lin-chi often refers to himself as a "mountain monk." Sasaki, like many other translators, simply renders the term as "I" so as not to break the flow of the text. Unfortunately, this translation also eliminates part of the stylistic appeal.

72. When words do not suffice, Lin-chi has recourse to "holistic" demonstrations that employ both psychic and physical powers, including shouting and beatings.

73. Yanagida speaks of an "entry" in two successive sections, *Rinzairoku*, pp. 384–87. True insight, which indicates much less the achievement of an experience of enlightenment than a spiritual state of being enlightened, allows one to "enter into" all of reality and see through the emptiness of all things (*Rinzairoku*, p. 388).

74. Yanagida explains that one who responds to circumstances reaches fulfillment. See *Rinzairoku*, p. 305.

75. For the following, see Yanagida's commentary on the expression *dōgen bunmyō* ("clearing of the Dharma Eye"), *Rinzairoku*, pp. 338–41.

76. "Discourses," sec. 17.

77. "Discourses," sec. 17.

78. The world of the *asura* (demons or titans) is one of the six forms of existence in the cycle of rebirths.

79. The verse comes from the *Rakudōka* (*Song of Delighting in the Way*) by a disciple of P'u-chi of the Northern school; it is not to be confused with the *Rakudōka* referred to in note 53 of chap. 9. See *Record of Lin-chi*, p. 81, note 161 and p. 73, note 76.

80. The Rinzai school was brought to southern China by the sixth representative of the line, Fen-yang Shan-chao (947–1024), of which more shall be said in the following chapter. On the *Tenshō kōtōroku*, see *Zen Dust*, p. 412.

81. *Entretiens de Lin-tsi*, p. 18. He praises Lin-chi as "one of the strongest minds in all of Chinese Buddhism, indeed, in all of Chinese religion"; see also p. 436, note 36.

82. *Entretiens de Lin-tsi*, p. 455.

83. *Entretiens de Lin-tsi*, p. 450.

11

Characteristics of the Five Houses

THE PERSECUTION OF BUDDHISM

The two preceding chapters on the Zen movement from Hui-neng to Lin-chi and beyond lead us deep into the second half of the ninth century. The most significant event of the century, the persecution of Buddhism under Emperor Wu-tsung (841–846),[1] occurred a few decades earlier (845), and thus did not have a great impact on the history of Zen. It is, however, important to have a look at Wu-tsung's persecution, if not because of its influence on the development of Zen, then because it helps us appreciate the unique place that Zen holds within Chinese Buddhism. It is commonly held among historians that Zen was the only Buddhist school of the time to survive this storm of persecution without serious damage, a fact that should give us some idea of the vitality of the movement in China during the T'ang period.

Although there had already been limited forms of repression against the new religion in previous centuries, the extent and intensity of Emperor Wu-tsung's campaign against the Buddhists earned for it the name of "the great persecution."[2] This persecution was unleashed through the bitter hatred of an emperor, himself a fanatical Taoist, determined to drive Buddhism from his land. To be sure, already deeply rooted animosities against the Buddhist religion also played a role in these events. Despite centuries of effort to adapt to Chinese thought and customs, at the time of its greatest flourishing in the middle of the T'ang period, Buddhism was still considered a strange and foreign religion by many Chinese, especially by the Confucian intellectuals, who represented the greater part of influential government officialdom.[3]

For many Chinese, the greatest source of scandal in Buddhism was the monastic practice of celibacy it had imported from India. Buddhists seemed to oppose the Chinese family system and ignore filial piety, the first commandment of Confucian ethics. In addition there were the offensive side effects of monastic institutions—in particular, the dispensation from taxes and social service. Whatever fascination these new teachings might have for the Chinese mind, what good were they if they damaged the social fabric of the country? Economic factors also played a clear and determinative role in sustaining the persecution, as the Buddhist community, with the fortunate exception of Zen, contributed little of economic benefit to Chinese society. Zen monks worked their farmlands and cultivated their fields productively; if the information we have about East Mountain is correct, they were doing so already from their early years in China.

The underlying causes of the persecution, then, had long been forming around more general cultural, religious, and socioeconomic issues, and it was on this basis that Emperor Wu-tsung began his attack. Initially the emperor expressed his displeasure by showing clear preference for Taoist clerical dignitaries over their Buddhist counterparts. The first patently hostile measures began in 842 and were aimed primarily at secularizing monks and nuns and confiscating Buddhist properties. Members of monastic communities considered "irregular" were forced to leave their monasteries and return to lay life. These "irregularities" could include evasion of military service, a criminal record before entering religious life, practice of forbidden magic, or even failure to observe the rules of the monastery. Private possessions inconsistent with the monastic commitment to poverty were confiscated, and the freedom of movement of religious persons was restricted. Such measures prompted not a few monks and nuns to abandon religious life of their own accord and return to their families. While the hostility of these gestures was obvious, such persecutions had taken place before without really placing Buddhism in any serious danger. Moreover, some of the measures taken during the first phase of the persecution were not without justification.

In fall of 844 the second phase of the persecution began. Decree after decree aimed at the destruction of the Buddhist religion as a monastic institution was issued. All the small monastic communities throughout the land were unconditionally dissolved and their membership forced to return to lay life (with the exception of older members who were given shelter in official government monasteries). Those most affected by this purge were the younger monks and nuns (at first those under forty, later those under fifty years of age). These monks were not allowed into the government monasteries but were laicized and obliged to pay taxes. In many places, Buddhist monuments, holy scriptures, and images were destroyed. These actions began in the capital, Ch'ang-an, and then spread to other large cities and beyond until they affected the entire country. Just how thoroughgoing these measures were is difficult to say. An official document from the eighth month of the year 845 reads:

> More than 4,600 monasteries are being destroyed throughout the empire; more than 260,000 monks and nuns are being returned to lay life and being subjected to the double tax; more than 40,000 temples and shrines are being destroyed; several tens of millions of ch'ing of fertile lands and fine fields are being confiscated; 150,000 slaves are being taken over to become payers of the double tax.[5]

The document ends with the remark that all this was but the beginning of the reform. The storm was not to rage for long, however. When Emperor Wu-tsung died in the third month of the following year his successor immediately changed and softened these harsh policies. The short duration of the persecution is one reason why Zen suffered so little. The greatest damage was done in the major cities and in the northern provinces. Located principally in the South and in the countryside, the Zen movement was fortunate to find itself far from the fray. Moreover, Zen monasteries struck a rather unimposing image in the eyes of the religious powers. The Zen masters of the T'ang period kept their distance from the imperial court and were not at all engaged in academic or public activities that might have attracted attention. As a result, they were able to sustain their minor losses without consequence.

The Buddhist persecution during the T'ang period signaled a turning point in the history of Chinese Buddhism. The main thrust of the persecution lasted only about a year. How was it possible that in such a short period the broadly based institution of Buddhism could suffer wounds that would leave it permanently crippled? One would have thought that after the storm had subsided the numerous temples and monasteries so beloved by the people would have had the strength to renew themselves. Or had Buddhism—despite its beautiful façade and imposing edifices, its complicated doctrinal systems and impressive rituals—been dealt a blow that exhausted its inner energies? Was there more to the picture than the external damage that was so evident, especially in certain monasteries and convents? Did the debilitation and devastation reach into the very marrow of Buddhism?

A look at the Zen movement, which at that very time was thriving in its rural setting and unhampered in its activities, confirms these suspicions.[6] Within its hard outer shell a seed was ready to burst forth with new life. The persecution of the T'ang period, along with the unrest during the period of the Five Dynasties (907–960), formed a backdrop to the splendid growth that Zen experienced during the Sung period, a time in which Chinese culture, enriched in many ways by Zen Buddhism, was undergoing widespread and exuberant growth.

THE "FIVE HOUSES"

During the second half of the T'ang period and the period of the Five Dynasties, family traditions took shape within the Zen movement that would come to be known in Zen history as the "Five Houses." The term was first used by Fa-yen Wen-i (885–958), who mentions four of the houses in his treatise *Shamon Jikki-ron* (Chin., *Tsung-men shih-kuei lun*):

> When Ts'ao-tung [Jpn., Sōtō] knocks, the answer comes immediately; Lin-chi [Jpn., Rinzai] is like the breath of people calling each other; Yün-men [Jpn., Ummon] is the meeting of box and lid; the unity of light and dark, square and circle in Kuei-yang [Jpn., Igyō] is the edge that cuts the stream. All of them are the echo of a voice from the valley; their agreement is as tight as fingers clasped together.[7]

Though certain features of four houses are given here—the house of Fa-yen would complete the list—these are hardly what we would call their defining characteristics.[8]

To begin with, any attempt to determine a time frame for the Five Houses runs into insurmountable problems. In their life and work, some of the founding fathers of the houses belong to the Zen movement of the T'ang period, which is the fountainhead of Chinese Zen. It was only in the later chronicles that they came to be classified as the Five Houses. Furthermore, by the beginning of the

Sung period (perhaps earlier in the case of the House of Kuei-yang) three of the houses had already dissolved. Only the rival traditions of Lin-chi and Ts'ao-tung continued strongly throughout the Sung period. The survival of the Five Houses is captured in the popular expression "The Five Houses and the Seven Schools," the latter indicating the two new lines of Yang-ch'i (Jpn., Yōgi) and Huang-lung (Jpn., Ōryū) that arose in Lin-chi's school at the beginning of the Sung period. Chronologically, the Five Houses link the Zen masters of the T'ang period with the Zen movement of the Sung period.

The Zen chronicles of the Sung period offer abundant materials on the Five Houses. The most significant source of information, the *Ninden gammoku* (Chin., *Jen-t'ien yen-mu*), was compiled by Hui-yen Chih-chao, a monk of the school of Lin-chi who specialized in the history of the Five Houses.[9] Understandably, he places the House of Lin-chi on the top of his list and devotes two of his six volumes to it; treatments of the houses of Yün-men, Ts'ao-tung, Kuei-yang, and Fa-yen follow. The sequence of course varies throughout Zen literature. The ordering we shall be following is based on the fact that the House of Kuei-yang is the earliest and, like the House of Lin-chi, belongs to the line of Ma-tsu, while the houses of Ts'ao-tung, Yün-men, and Fa-yen fall in the tradition of Shih-t'ou, the other great disciple in the third generation after Hui-neng. The House of Fa-yen was the last to develop and may have been the least significant of the five.

It is important to bear in mind that these "houses" do not signify different schools or orientations but rather different family traditions or styles that developed naturally among the masters and then were given preference in a circle of disciples. The style marking the two houses that were strongly influenced by the tradition of Ma-tsu is called "great potential—great action" (Jpn., *daiki daiyū*; Chin., *tai-chi ta-yung*). A great potential will necessarily break forth in sudden, grotesque, but always meaningful action. Thus in the House of Kuei-yang there developed different forms of expression, from simple kōan stories to easily understood symbolism. The possibilities of expression were even richer in the House of Lin-chi, which made abundant use of dialectical formulas. The House of Ts'ao-tung is famous for the precision and care with which all things were done. This house developed the important formula of the "Five Ranks." The metaphor of the box and the lid alluded to above nicely fits the style of the House of Yün-men. In the methods of the House of Fa-yen, psychological concerns are blended with the worldview of Kegon.

The following presentation will review the differences in Zen practice within the Five Houses, differences that—and this should be stressed—did not diminish the inner cohesion of the Zen movement after Hui-neng.

KUEI-YANG: EXPERIENCE IN ACTION

Life in a Zen monastery centers around experience—the sudden, direct encounter with reality. The faculty for such experience can announce itself in a thousand different ways and can be expressed in forms that are convincing, often shocking, and at times profoundly penetrating. The House of Kuei-yang offers a broad, impressive selection of such expressions. Its particular style, however, gives clear preference to action and silence over words.

The House of Kuei-yang took its name from the two mountains Kuei (Hunan Province) and Yang (Chiang-hsi Province), where the temples of its founders were located. Kuei-shan Ling-yu (771–853) was appointed head of the new Ta-kuei Monastery by his master, Pai-chang, in a rather unusual way. The master placed a water jug in front of the disciples and asked: "If you can't call this a water jug, what do you call it?" Kuei-shan kicked over the water jug and walked away. The wordless gesture revealed his enlightened state.[10]

The most prominent of Kuei-shan's disciples were Yang-shan Hui-chi (807–883) and Hsiang-yen Chih-hsien (d. 898), both of whom were deeply bound to their master and were as brothers to each other. Indeed, the chronicles praise the familial atmosphere in the House of Kuei-yang. This particular trait is evident in the story of Hsiang-yen's enlightenment, which for a number of reasons ranks among the most famous Zen stories. Master Kuei-shan questioned Hsiang-yen about his original being before his birth. Unable to answer, he implored his master for help, only to be told that he must find the answer for himself. In vain Hsiang-yen searched through the scriptures. Finally, he burned all his books and withdrew into solitude in order to devote himself entirely to this question. One day, while weeding the garden, he heard the clatter of a falling tile. The startling sound awakened him to enlightenment.[11]

According to the report of the chronicle, Hsiang-yen returned to his hut, washed, burned incense, and bowed in the direction of Master Kuei-shan's dwelling. Then to record his enlightenment, he composed the following lines:

With one stroke, all previous knowledge is forgotten.
No cultivation is needed for this.
This occurrence reveals the ancient way
And is free from the track of quiescence.
No trace is left anywhere.
Whatever I hear and see does not conform to rules.
All those who are enlightened
Proclaim this to be the greatest action.[12]

These verses are found among the collected sayings of Kuei-shan, together with two other stanzas that Hsiang-yen composed on the same occasion.[13] His fellow disciple and brother in the Dharma, Yang-shan, criticized the first stanza for being too dependent on the master's style and not directly expressive of personal experience. So Hsiang-yen composed these lines:

My poverty of last year was not real poverty.
This year it is want indeed.
In last year's poverty there was room for a piercing gimlet.
In this year's poverty even the gimlet is no more.[14]

Perhaps Hsiang-yen was thinking of the philosophical notion of "emptiness" from the Wisdom sūtras. In any case, this was the occasion on which Yang-shan is said to have spoken the famous line: "You may have grasped the Zen of the Perfected One, but not even in a dream have you seen the Zen of the Patriarchs."[15] In response, the following verse poured forth from Hsiang-yen's lips:

I have my secret
And look at you with twinkling eye.
If you do not understand this
Do not call yourself a monk.

As the Chinese author Chang Chung-yüan correctly explains, these three poems indicate different levels of inner realization.[16] While the first poem describes the experience in artistically stylized form, the second evinces signs of an intellectual belaboring. In the third poem, the allusion to the twinkling eye as an expression of an inner state is authentic Zen. With great joy Yang-shan reports to Master Kuei-shan that Brother Hsiang-yen has grasped the Zen of the Patriarchs.

The Zen style of the House of Kuei-yang is characterized by action and silence, both of them intimately bound up with one another. This is evident in Yang-shan's first meeting with the master. When asked who he was, he simply walked through the hall from west to east and then stopped, without saying a word.[17] Movement from west to east symbolizes the transition from bodily ability or potentiality to function or action.[18] Or again, when asked where he had just come from, Yang-shan replied, "From the fields." And when Kuei-shan wanted to know how many people were there, Yang-shan drove his mattock into the ground and stood motionless. Kuei-shan continued: "Today there are many people on the southern mountain cutting grass." Yang-shan took up his mattock and left.[19] Action and silence flow together to give expression to experience. Kuei-shan respected this style of his disciple Yang-shan and held it in high regard, referring to it as "swordplay."[20]

The relation between substance (potentiality) and function is illustrated in a quaint conversation between the master and his disciple during the tea harvest.[21] Kuei-shan said to Yang-shan: "All day I have been listening to your voice as we picked tea leaves, but I have not yet seen you yourself. Show me your real self." Yang-shan shook the tea tree. The master commented, "You have achieved the function but not the substance." When Yang-shan asked his master what he himself had achieved, the master remained silent. Thereupon Yang-shan remarked, "You, Master, have achieved the substance but not the function." What this exchange implies is the unity of potentiality and action, substance and function.

Kuei-shan and Yang-shan exemplify what Zen calls the practice of the enlightened. Both have effected a breakthrough; both have attained the enlightenment experience and live in contact with the realm of the transcendent. As they go about their daily rounds of work and monastic duties, both their silence and their words manifest a state of enlightenment.

Like Kuei-shan and Yang-shan, Hsiang-yen is numbered among the illustrious masters of his time and is also the subject of many well-known stories, perhaps the most popular being the account of the "Man up in a Tree." A man hanging by his teeth from a branch high up in a tree is asked why Bodhidharma came from the West. With graphic precision, the scene depicts the hopelessness of the human condition and was taken up into the *Mumonkan* as a kōan for use in Zen practice.[22]

The House of Kuei-yang contains a treasury of valuable traditions. One of these is the use of "perfect marks" (Jpn., *ensō*; Chin., *yüan-hsiang*), or more concretely, "circular figures." The circle is one of the eternal forms revered by peoples of all times and cultures, symbolizing the admired and longed-for perfection of being. The image seems first to have been used in Zen by National Teacher Nan-yang Hui-chung, a disciple of Hui-neng. The *Keitoku dentōroku* tells of a disciple who, upon returning to Master Nan-yang after a pilgrimage, drew a circular figure on the ground in front of the master, bowed, and stood there waiting. "The master spoke: 'Do you want to become a Buddha or not?' [The disciple] replied, 'I cannot rub my eyes.' The master said, 'I am not equal to you.' The disciple did not answer."[23] In this exchange, master and disciple alike display great modesty, the disciple because he cannot clear the illusion from his eyes, and the master because he places himself in a position inferior to his disciple. And in the middle of the whole episode lies the circle.

In a passage dealing with Kuei-shan, the chronicle reports a similar encounter:

> The master asked a newly arrived monk what his name was. The monk said, "Yüeh-lun [Full Moon]." The master than drew a circle in the air with his hand. "How do you compare with this?" he asked. The monk replied, "Master, if you ask me in such a way, a great many people will not agree with you." Then the master said, "As for me, this is my way. What is yours?" The monk said, "Do you still see Yüeh-lun?" The master answered, "You can say it your way, but there are a great many people here who do not agree with you."[24]

Circles and full moons express perfect enlightenment, the original face one had before one was born, or the cosmic Buddha body. The disciples know full well that they are far from such perfection. This may also be the reason why Zen masters are wont to draw the circle, the most enduring and pervasive of all Zen symbols, whose form they dash off with incomparable skill and always in such a way that the powerful brush stroke never returns precisely to the point where it began. Does this mean that in every expression there must always remain room for imperfection?

According to the chronicles, Yang-shan seems more than anyone to have cultivated the symbolic use of the circle. The *Ninden gammoku* relates that Tan-yüan Ying-chen, the Dharma heir of National Teacher Nan-yang Hui-chung, had transmitted to Yang-shan the method of ninety-seven circles, by means of which the latter attained enlightenment. A detailed explanation of the circular figures is also given, including specific information on characters and hatch-marks to be set inside the circles to give them their specific meanings.[25]

In the section on Yang-shan, the *Keitoku dentōroku* reports: "As the master sat there with eyes closed, a monk came and stood quietly by his side. The master opened his eyes and drew a circle on the ground. Within the circle he wrote the character for water, then looked back at the monk. The monk said nothing."[26] By tracing the character of one of the four elements within the circle, the master specified the nature of the circle. A few lines further, but not necessarily in the same context as the preceding episode, the chronicle has a paragraph on divination, something highly esteemed in China:

> Once the master asked a monk what he knew besides Buddhism. The monk said that he understood the divination techniques in the *Book of Changes*. The master lifted his fan and asked, "Which one among the sixty-four hexagrams is this one?" The monk was unable to reply. The master answered for him, "It is the great potentiality of thunder and lightning and now it is transformed into the destruction of earth and fire."[27]

Throughout Mahāyāna Buddhism the symbolism of the circle has taken on a variety of different forms. One can hardly speak of dependencies here. Zen is no stranger to the symbol. It was used as a means of promoting enlightenment. The practice of the circle was developed particularly in the Kegon school.[28] We cannot know for certain precisely how Yang-shan and his disciples used and interpreted circles. At a later stage in Zen history circles must have enjoyed widespread use, so much so that they met with opposition. Even as a "preliminary artificial means" (Skt., *upāya-kauśalya;* Jpn., *hōben*), it was argued, circles can be harmful because they veil the true nature of reality—the absolute emptiness and formlessness of all things. The symbol of the circle was not recognized as a legitimate way for striving toward Zen enlightenment.

In early source materials, the House of Kuei-yang is presented as authentic Zen. Its founder, Kuei-shan, depicted the ideal of the enlightened person in Taoist tones that were familiar to the masters of the late T'ang period, especially to Lin-chi: "Like autumn waters, clear and still, pure and undisturbed, unmoving" [Chin., *wu-wei;* Jpn., *mui*], quiet and deep, unhindered, such a person is called a person of the Tao, a person without trouble [Chin., *wu-shih;* Jpn., *buji*]."[29]

LIN-CHI: THREEFOLD AND FOURFOLD FORMULAS

If it is difficult neatly to locate the period of the Five Houses within the history of Chinese Zen Buddhism, there are even greater problems with situating the school of Lin-chi (Jpn., Rinzai). Its founder, Lin-chi, was prominent within the Zen movement during the T'ang period. During the Sung period, the growth of the Rinzai school in southern China represented a whole new phase within Zen. The time between, covering several generations of Zen, lies in darkness. The successors of Lin-chi from the third to the sixth generation carried on the spirit of their founder in northern China without attracting much attention. The special traits of this school—shouting and beating—were the direct inheritance of the peculiar style of its founder. In the previous chapter we tried to communicate something of the essence of Lin-chi's Zen, basing ourselves primarily on the classic work of the school, the *Rinzairoku*. Although this work is imbued with the spirit of Lin-chi, it did not take final shape until many years after his death. The many dialectical and didactic formulas scattered throughout the text were probably editorial glosses added during the tenth and eleventh centuries in the House of Lin-chi. It seems that Feng-hsüeh Yen-chao (896–973) and Fen-yang Shan-chao (947–1024) devoted extensive energies to work on these texts. It is further possible that many of the texts are of later origin. In any case, the threefold and fourfold formulas are distinctive of the House of Lin-chi.

The most important dialectical formula in the House of Lin-chi, "the four alternatives" (Jpn., *shiryōken*; Chin., *ssu-liao-chien*), describes four positions regarding the subject-object relationship. Lin-chi is said to have presented the following at one of his evening conferences:

> Sometimes I take away man and do not take away the surroundings; sometimes I take away the surroundings and do not take away man; sometimes I take away both man and the surroundings; sometimes I take away neither man nor the surroundings.[30]

These four alternatives or positions regarding subject and object represent an ascending grasp of reality. The formula is based on the well-known four propositions of Indian Buddhist logic: being, nonbeing, neither being nor nonbeing, both being and nonbeing (Skt., *catuṣkoṭikā*; Jpn., *shiku fumbetsu*; Chin., *ssu-chü fen-pieh*). In terms of content, they correspond to the four levels of reality (Skt., *dharmadhātu*; Jpn., *hokkai*) in the Kegon school.[31] In the first and second stages illusion is overcome first by the subject and then by the object. That is to say, all clinging to subjective intellectual perception and to the objective world is repudiated.[32] The third stage negates both subject and object, but differentiation still obtains. This posture of negation corresponds to the state of consciousness achieved in extreme concentration. Only in the fourth stage, which affirms the transcendence of the opposition between subject and object, does all confrontation between subject and object cease. Reality is comprehended in its ultimate oneness. In this formula the philosophy of the Middle Way Madhyamika and the metaphysics of the Kegon school flow together.

Questioned further by one of his monks, Lin-chi offered a concrete metaphor for each of the four statements. His image for the first reads:

> The spring sun comes forth covering the earth with brocade;
> A child's hair hangs down, white as silken strands.

Nature expands. The white hair of a child implies a paradox. The second image is different:

> Mandates of the sovereign are spread through the world;
> The general has laid the dust of battle beyond the frontiers.[33]

With his own home not far from the border, Lin-chi had an existential feel for such imagery. He continues with the third image:

No news from Ping and Fen,
Isolated away from everywhere.

Ping and Feng were names of distant regions. In the third stage, concentration is a matter of total seclusion. Finally comes the fourth and crowning image:

The sovereign ascends [his throne in] the jeweled palace;
Aged rustics are singing.

On the highest level of consciousness one sees reality as perfect and all-encompassing. The metaphor is reminiscent of the tenth image in the famous Oxherding pictures, in which the enlightened person, sharing what has been given him, enters the marketplace and stands in the middle of life in all its reality. Typical of Zen. the addition of these colorful images lends concreteness to the four abstract statements of the dialectical formula. The formula not only aids in instruction but also in practice; like a kōan, it can stir the searching mind.

Another fourfold formula in the *Rinzairoku* deals with conversations or encounters between guest and host, or between student and teacher.[34] Its purpose is to teach the proper way to converse.[35] For Lin-chi the proper didactic procedure in conversational intercourse was most important. In his opening remarks he speaks of the many different and strange situations that can develop during practice:

Followers of the Way, the view of the Ch'an school is that the sequence of death and life is orderly.[36] The student of Ch'an must examine [this] most carefully.

When host and guest meet they vie with one another in discussion. At times, in response to something, they may manifest a form; at times they may act with their whole body;[37] or they may, by picking up a tricky device, [make a display of] joy or anger; or they may reveal half of the body;[38] or again, they may ride upon a lion [Mañjuśrī] or mount upon a lordly elephant [like the bodhisattva Samantabhadra].[39]

Four conversations follow illustrating (1) the superiority of the student or (2) of the teacher, (3) the equality of both partners in control of the situation, or (4) a student-like state of confusion on both sides. The text reads:

1. A true student gives a shout, and to start with holds out a sticky lacquer tray. The teacher, not discerning that this is an objective circumstance,[40] goes after it and performs a lot of antics with it. The student again shouts but still the teacher is unwilling to let go. This is a disease of the vitals that no doctoring can cure: it is called "the guest examines the host."

2. Sometimes a teacher will proffer nothing, but the instant a student asks a question, robs him of it. The student, having been robbed, resists to the death and will not let go: this is called "the host examines the guest."

3. Sometimes a student comes forth before a teacher in conformity with a state of purity. The teacher, discerning that this is an objective circumstance, seizes it and flings it into a pit.[41] "What an excellent teacher!" exclaims the student, and the teacher replies, "Bah! You can't tell good from bad!" Thereupon the student makes a deep bow: this is called "the host examines the host."

4. Or again, a student will appear before a teacher wearing a cangue and bound with chains. The teacher fastens on still more chains and cangues for him.[42] The student is so delighted that he can't tell what is what:[43] This is called "the guest examines the guest."

Lin-chi closes the discourse with this admonition:

> Virtuous monks, all the examples I have brought before you serve to distinguish demons and point out heretics, thus making it possible for you to know what is erroneous and what is correct.

This guest-host pattern was highly valued in the Rinzai school; it illustrates the teaching methods that were in vogue when the *Discourses of Lin-chi* were redacted and that were to be used in years to come. We really do not know whether the formula, as seen in the text cited above, can be traced back to Lin-chi or not. In the opinion of Demiéville, the four conversational alternatives "smack of the scholasticism of the Sung period."[44] Yanagida argues that another guest-host formula in the text, similar but more complicated in its propositional style, was a later addition.[45]

In the first book of the *Ninden gammoku*, which deals with Lin-chi, the master makes use of a formula that does not occur in the *Rinzairoku* to describe the fourfold pattern of relationships obtaining between light and activity (Jpn., shishōyū). Sometimes light precedes activity; sometimes activity precedes light; sometimes light and activity are simultaneous, sometimes they are not.[46]

Lin-chi's "four types of shouting" (Jpn., shikatsu), listed in the *Rinzairoku* ("Critical Examination," sec. 20), are most likely a later addition.[47] The well-known passage reads:

> Sometimes a shout is like the jeweled sword of the Vajra King; sometimes a shout is like the golden-haired lion crouching on the ground; sometimes a shout is like a weed-tipped fishing pole; sometimes a shout doesn't function as a shout.[48]

In each of the four types of shouting we see characteristics of enlightenment. The sword cuts through all false notions. The lion crouched in ambush suddenly pounces on its prey. Just as a weed-tipped pole is used to probe fish from the bottom and attract them, so does the master use shouting to test his students.[49] Paradox and transcending power are manifest in the fourth roar.

Lin-chi's much-discussed threefold formula, known as the "Three Statements" (Jpn., sanku), appears in the *Rinzairoku* in conjunction with two other threefold formulas, the "Three Mysteries" (Jpn., sangen) and the "Three Essentials" (Jpn., *sanyō*). None of these is explained ("Discourses," sec. 9). After the proclamation of the Three Statements, the master adds only this: "Each statement must comprise the gates of the Three Mysteries, and the gate of each mystery must comprise the Three Essentials." The textual data at our disposal do not allow for much clarification here. The English, French, and Japanese translations show a wide divergence of interpretation. As Ruth Fuller Sasaki rightly observes, "This is one of Lin-chi's most enigmatic discourses. . . . The exact meaning of Lin-chi's 'Three Statements' is not clear." She reports further that the Three Statements, the Three Mysteries, and the Three Essentials are interpreted variously as the Buddha, the Dharma, and the Tao (Way); or as the three Buddha bodies—*dharmakāya, saṃbhogakāya, nirmāṇakāya*—or as the three principles of Chinese Buddhist philosophy—*li* ("principle"), *chih* ("wisdom"), and *yung* ("functioning").[50] Yanagida concludes that "the meaning of the Three Mysteries and the Three Essentials is not very clear," pointing out numerous attempts at explanation in later Zen literature.[51] Demiéville finds the Three Statements "richly mysterious."[52]

To single out these formulas and make them too central would be to paint a false picture of the House of Lin-chi. For while Lin-chi, with his grounding in Mahāyāna metaphysics and his well-honed speculative powers, delighted in dialectical statements, his primary concern was concrete realization and experience. The formulas were but an aid to practice. In a sense, they were a bridge between the spontaneous outbursts of the Zen masters of the T'ang period and the highly stylized kōan practice of the Sung period. Given the state of the historical sources, it is not possible to define the individual phases of this development. After becoming the most influential school of its time, the House of Lin-chi contributed significantly to the spiritual awakening that occurred during the Sung period and that was in fact the last high point of Chinese culture to be influenced decisively by Buddhism.

TS'AO-TUNG: "THE FIVE RANKS"

The House of Ts'ao-tung (Jpn., Sōtō) takes its name from an abbreviated combination of the graphs of its two founders, Tung-shan Liang-chieh (807–869) and Ts'ao-shan Pen-chi (840–901), each of whom received their names from the mountains on which their respective monasteries stood.[53] We do not know for sure when the house first took this name, though there are indications that it was soon after the death of Ts'ao-shan. Like the House of Lin-chi, it survived to develop into one of the most important schools or sects of Chinese Zen Buddhism.

Tung-shan was not yet ten years old when he left his parental home for a local temple to begin what was to be a restless monastic life. During his study of fundamental Buddhist teachings he demonstrated such extraordinary intellectual acumen that his teacher decided to send him to the experienced master Ling-mo (747–818), one of the many disciples of Ma-tsu. Ordained at the age of twenty, he studied for a short time with the two famous masters Nan-ch'üan

P'u-yüan (748–835) and Kuei-shan Ling-yu (771–853) before becoming a disciple of Yün-yen T'an-sheng (780–841), whose line of succession he carried on. Through Master Yün-yen he was able to "comprehend the sermons of inanimate things," which in Zen does not refer to the miraculous powers of Buddhist saints, who are said to hear with their eyes and see with their ears, but to knowledge of the undifferentiated identity of animate and inanimate beings in the unity of Buddhahood. Many of the exchanges between Tung-shan and his master have been preserved in Zen literature.

After these years of study, Tung-shan visited the temples of China where he became acquainted with the leading representatives of the age. These encounters with Zen masters from various traditions gave him a broad appreciation of the rich diversity of Zen doctrine and method at the time. His long years of wandering came to an end when he entered the monastery on Mount Tung at the age of fifty-two to devote himself totally to the guidance of his disciples, among whom Ts'ao-shan and Yün-chü Tao-ying (d. 902) were the most distinguished.

Tung-shang is a typical representative of southern Chinese Zen. Born south of the Yangtze River (in Chekiang Province), he spent his entire life in southern China, whose gentle climate gave his personality a different quality from that of Lin-chi, who was reared in rough northern climes. A person of literary gifts, he was fond of teaching through the medium of poetry. He shared this love of poetry with his master, Yün-yen, who asked him at the time of his departure:

"When will you return here?"

"When Your Reverence has a dwelling place, then I'll come."

"Once you have gone it will be difficult for us to meet," said the master.

"It will be difficult not to meet," returned Liang-chieh.

Then Liang-chieh said, "Your Reverence, a hundred years from now, if someone were to ask me, 'Can you draw a portrait of your master?' how should I reply?"

"Only answer him, 'Just *this* it is'," said Yün-yen.

Liang-chieh remained silent for a time. Then Yün-yen said, "In undertaking this matter you must investigate minutely." Liang-chieh still had some doubts.

Later, when Liang-chieh was crossing a stream, he saw his reflection in the water, and [at that moment] completely realized the meaning of [Yün-yen's] words. He composed this verse:

Seeking it from others is forbidden.
For thus it becomes further and further estranged.
Now that I go my way entirely alone,
There is nowhere I cannot meet it.
Now it is just what I am,
Now I am not what it is.
Thus must one understand,
Then one accords with True Suchness.[54]

In poetic style typical of Tung-shan, these verses express the Mahāyāna view of the oneness and equality of reality and the self. Tung-shan also put into verse the well-known formula of the Five Ranks (Jpn., *goi*; Chin., *wu-wei*),[55] which his master Yün-yen is supposed to have entrusted to him as a secret teaching.[56] Among the disciples of Tung-shan, it was Ts'ao-shan who preserved this precious teaching, elaborating and perfecting it in the process. His character and interests being totally different from those of his fellow disciple Yün-chü, Ts'ao-chan loved to study. From early youth he became acquainted with the teachings of Confucianism and continued his studies even after entering the Buddhist monastic life with parental permission at the age of eighteen. His time of study with Tung-shan was brief (probably from 865 to 868). Only two conversations with his master have been handed down, one dating from the time of his arrival and the other from his departure. He traveled little. For thirty-five years he dwelled in quiet contemplation in the two monasteries at Ts'ao-shan and Ho-yü-shan, where he applied his keen mind to penetrating the meaning of the Five Ranks. The chronicles list the names of nineteen of his disciples. Within four generations, however, his line had become extinct.

Yün-chü, the other important disciple of Tung-shan, had little or no interest in the dialectic of the Five Ranks. He directed his efforts toward the immediate experience of enlightenment, which he incarnated in an exemplary ethical life. Before devoting himself to Zen, he had studied the monastic discipline (Vinaya). He came to Tung-shan two years before the arrival of his colleague Ts'ao-shan but remained in training under the master longer, as numerous records of their conversations attest. Yün-chü enjoyed higher esteem than any of Tung-shan's disciples. The many excellent students later to emerge from his school establish him as one of the most important and influential figures of the age. Thanks to his disciples and spiritual heirs, the Ts'ao-tung school was carried on in China and its line of tradition transmitted to Japan.

The Five Ranks of the House of Ts'ao-tung represent the most important dialectical formula in all of Zen Buddhism. Master Hakuin sees in it the "main principle of Buddhism and the essential road of *sanzen* [Zen practice]."[57] In contradistinction to the other fivefold formulas in Buddhist philosophy based on ontological-psychological analysis—one thinks of the *Abhidharmakośa* or the doctrine of *vijñaptimātra*—all five ranks of Ts'ao-tung express various aspects of one and the same thing: the fundamental identity of the Absolute (or universal One) and the relative (or phenomenal many). The formula of the Five Ranks originated in Mahāyāna metaphysics but was given a Chinese form. Given its affinity with the *I Ching* (*Book of Changes*), we may speak of it as an expression of Chinese philosophy. The basic concepts stem from Tung-shan, who in turn was building on foundations laid by Shih-t'ou and other Zen masters of the T'ang period. But it was Ts'ao-shan who grasped the core of the master's teaching and gave it its final form.

The classical statement of the fivefold formula appears in five stanzas that can be traced back to Tung-shan and Ts'ao-shan.[58] The first line of every stanza is composed of three Chinese graphs that serve as a title or indication of the essential content of the rank in question. This is the work of Tung-shan, who may have received the formulations verbally from his master Yün-yen. The next three lines make use of poetic metaphors to present the meaning of the rank. On the basis of recent research, we can attribute them to Ts'ao-shan. Since each of the stanzas expresses the same view of enlightenment from a different perspective, one may also speak of them as "Five Ranks."[59]

The two key concepts in the fivefold formula—*cheng* and *p'ien*, in Japanese, *shō* and *hen*—signify literally, "the straight" and "the bent." They refer to what is absolute, one, identical, universal, and noumenal set up in tension with what is relative, manifold, different, particular, and phenomenal. They are related to the corresponding notions of *li* (Jpn., *ri*; absolute principle) and *shih* (Jpn., *ji*; appearance) in Chinese philosophy, and are also referred to as the dark and the light, depicted respectively by a black circle ● and a white circle ○. Tung-shan explains "the straight" as follows: "There is one thing: above, it supports heaven; below, it upholds earth. It is black like lacquer, perpetually in movement and activity."[60] The straight is also the foundation of heaven and earth and of all being. But this absolute is dynamic, constantly in motion. The perceiving mind cannot lay hold of the straight and grasp it as an object. In Buddhist terminology, it is the true emptiness, without duality, of which the metaphysics of Perfect Wisdom (*prajñāpāramitā*) speaks.

The absolute becomes manifest in appearances, in "the bent" or light. Absolute and phenomenal cannot be separated; they are identical, one. The absolute is the absolute in relation to the relative, and the relative is relative in relation to the absolute. Therefore, the relative-phenomenal is also called "marvelous being" (Jpn., *myōu*) because it is inseparable from "true emptiness" (Jpn., *shinkū*). The saying "the marvelous being of true emptiness" or "the true emptiness of marvelous being" expresses the quintessence of the enlightened view of reality.

The following translation of the five stanzas can give only an approximate sense of their deep meaning:

1. The Bent within the Straight [Jpn., *shōchūhen*]:
   In the third watch of the night
   Before the moon appears,
   No wonder when we meet
   There is no recognition!
   Still cherished in my heart
   Is the beauty of earlier days.

2. The Straight within the Bent [Jpn., *henchūshō*]:
   A sleepy-eyed grandam
   Encounters herself in an old mirror.
   Clearly she sees a face,
   But it doesn't resemble hers at all.
   Too bad, with a muddled head,
   She tries to recognize her reflection!

3. The Coming from within the Straight [Jpn., *shōchūrai*]:
   Within nothingness there is a path
   Leading away from the dusts of the world.
   Even if you observe the taboo
   On the present emperor's name,
   You will surpass that eloquent one of yore
   who silenced every tongue.

4. The Arrival at the Middle of the Bent [Jpn., *henchūshi*]:
   When two blades cross points,
   There's no need to withdraw.
   The master swordsman
   Is like the lotus blooming in the fire.
   Such a man has in and of himself
   A heaven-soaring spirit.

5. Unity Attained [Jpn., *kenchūtō*]:
   Who dares to equal him
   Who falls into neither being nor non-being!
   All men want to leave
   The current of ordinary life,
   But he, after all, comes back
   To sit among the coals and ashes.[61]

Two approaches stand out from the vast literature aimed at interpreting the meaning of the Five Ranks. One is primarily concerned with the philosophical content of the formula, the other with its psychological and literary meaning. Ever since Hakuin used the text of the Five Ranks to conclude the final version of his system of kōan, its dialectical formula has been considered the crowning achievement of literature on the kōan.[62]

Given the close historical connections between the Chinese Zen Buddhism of the Five Ranks and the worldview of the Kegon school, the insights of this latter may aid us in understanding the spiritual meaning of the fivefold formula of the House of Ts'ao-tung.[63] The teaching of the four Dharma realms (Jpn., *shi hokkai*) attributed to the Kegon patriarch Ch'eng-kuan (737–838) provides a direct point of entry. The central notions in this teaching, *shih* (appearance) and *li* (principle), correspond to the key words *p'ien* (the bent, off-center) and *cheng* (the straight, true). The basic thesis, that there is a mutual penetration of all things in the whole of reality, is the same in both positions. The difference is that the Kegon school takes a more philosophical approach, while Zen disciples seek realization through practice. In neither case should the thesis be understood statically. Each of the formulations attempts to present the flowing stream of reality by stressing a different aspect of it.

Kegon philosophy begins with the realm of *shih* (Jpn., *ji hokkai*), in which all things (Skt., *dharma*) exist in mutual dependence through the causal efficacy of the Dharma realm (Jpn., *hokkai engi*). In the second realm, *li* (Jpn., *ri hokkai*),

the principle or absolute, is the reality of all things. In comparing the four
Dharma realms with the Five Ranks, we find that the first two ranks correspond
to the first Dharma realm of *shih*.[64] The identity of the straight (absolute) and
the bent (relative) acknowledged in the first two ranks of the Zen formulation
is considered under two aspects. First, multiplicity is seen in sameness; all diverse
things and events are in their essence the same, formless and empty. Emptiness
is undisturbed by any subjective element. Already on this first level, an enlightened viewpoint is present. But Zen practice, of necessity, presses on. The second
aspect of the Five Ranks sees the whole in every individual thing; that is, the
multiplicity of things is penetrated by the essential principle. The Japanese Buddhologist Katō Totsudō explains both the distinction and the connection between
the ranks:

> While on the first rank, the vast multiplicity of things appears to be con-
> tained within the natural law of true being-as-it-is, from this perspective
> [the second level] the law of being-as-it-is is seen to be active in every
> individual thing in the world of appearances. If the first rank approaches
> the world of appearances from their true nature, the second uses appearances
> to arrive at their true nature.[65]

The bipolarity of the two ranks is clearly expressed in symbolic imagery: the
first rank is represented by a circle with its top half darkened ◒ and the second
by a circle with the bottom half darkened ◓.

The third of the Five Ranks—"Coming from within the Straight"—corresponds to the second realm in the Kegon scheme, that of *li*. The relative is
not mentioned. The absolute stands in its naked absoluteness. At the same
time, the potentiality of the absolute for the relative is expressed in the graph
for "middle" or "in." The absolute is pregnant with all possibility, like the seed
prior to the first sprouting of its germ. The title and verse of this level admit
of different interpretations.[66] In focusing attention on the absolute's transcendence of all opposition, all the opposites are removed at this level. "Fire and ice
stand alongside each other in a common absoluteness, spring flowers bloom in
the fall, the cow . . . made of mud . . . can low, . . . the wooden horse whin-
nies."[67] Yet even in this perspective the absolute retains its potential for relating
to the relative. The dynamic significance of the graph *lai* ("coming, emerging")
is of critical importance for fully understanding this third rank. The absolute is
posed, as it were, on the verge of entering the world of appearances. "Arriving
at Sameness is not a final state; this 'Arriving at Sameness' demands a simultaneous 'Leaving Sameness'; thus a dynamic circle of movement between arriving
at and departing from sameness should take place."[68] This interpenetration is
confirmed by other possible translations of the title line. "The Coming from
within the Straight" stresses the dynamic element. "Sameness in the Middle"[69]
emphasizes the absolute's transcendence of all opposites. However it is interpreted, the radical absolute of the third rank is bound inseparably to potentiality.
Its symbolic representation is a blackened circle (the absolute) surrounded by a
white circle (potency) ◉.

Textual traditions offer two variants for the title of the fourth rank; both of them make good sense. We adopted the reading *henchūshi*, "Arrival at the Middle of the Bent." The alternative reading, *kenchūshi*, "Arriving in Mutual Integration," has sameness and difference arriving together. The advantage of this latter title is that it corresponds neatly to the third Dharma realm of the Kegon schema, the realm of the "uninhibited interpenetration of *li* and *shih*" (Jpn., *riji muge hokkai*).

The reading *henchūshi* focuses on the diversity of the ten thousand things. It is characteristic of Mahāyāna thought to mark off the boundaries of the world of diversity in this way. Again, Katō Totsudō states it well:

> The point here is to take life in all its rich variety just as it is, with its ten thousand opposites, and to go along with whatever circumstances require, embracing things after their own inclination or according to chance, letting things be rather than getting in their way, and thus allowing each and every thing, each and every appearance, to pursue a meaning and purpose distinct from my own.[70]

The term *li* (absolute) does not appear in the title line of the fourth rank, but is certainly present in its content. Just as the absolute cannot exist without a potentiality for the relative, so the relative cannot exist without the absolute. By viewing phenomena, mutual conditions, and powers in their own relative form, we see the absolute revealed in pure relativity. Tung-shan likens this process to two fencers with swords bared, neither of whom can force the other to yield; or again, to the lotus blossom unharmed in the midst of the flames. In the symbolism of this rank, the relative is located as the middle of the absolute ○.

In the original rendering of the title line, "Arrival at the Middle of the Bent," the relationship of opposition between the third and fourth ranks is evident. Even though the title lines of each mention only one pole explicitly—either the absolute or the relative—the other is clearly implied. This device serves to preserve the full force of the formula's symmetry.[71] The second, middle graph of all the title lines is the same: *chū*. In the first two ranks it is translated simply as "in," signifying the mutual penetration of the relative and the absolute. In the next two ranks it is better rendered as "middle," since the sense is that both poles exhibit a dynamic that transcends opposition.

The fifth rank crowns the entire schema, pointing to the oneness of unrestricted interpenetration in a freedom that surpasses all opposition. This rank corresponds to the highest Dharma realm in the Kegon scheme, namely, the realm of the mutual penetration of *li* and *shih*. The fifth rank also corresponds to the fourth Dharma realm of the unrestricted interpenetration of all phenomena (Jpn., *jiji muge hokkai*). Here the Kegon worldview that lives within Zen comes fully into its own: the "harmonious interplay between particularities and also between each particularity and universality creates a luminous universe."[72] The stanza of the fifth rank indicates a "return to fusion."[73] The one "who falls into neither being nor nonbeing"—the enlightened individual—"comes back to sit among the coals and ashes." The symbol of this fifth rank is the darkened circle ●.

The basic formula of the Five Ranks underwent certain changes within the House of Ts'ao-tung, without however in any way diminishing its dialectical character. The dialectic between the two poles, *li* and *shih*, remained intact. In his research of this question, Alfonso Verdu examines the important concrete changes expressed in the following three formulas: the "Five Ranks of Merit" (Chin., *kung-hsün wu-wei*; Jpn., *kōkun goi no ju*), the "Five Ranks Regarding Lord and Vassal" (Chin., *chün-ch'en wu-wei*; Jpn., *kunshin goi*), and the "Secret Meaning of the Five Ranks" (Chin., *wu-wei chih-chüeh*; Jpn., *goi shiketsu*), which is linked to the formula of the "Manifestation of the Mystery of the Five Ranks" (Chin., *wu-wei hsien-chüeh*; Jpn., *goi kenketsu*).[74]

The formula of the "Five Ranks of Merit," which is attributed to the old Master Tung-shan, introduces a new perspective by thematizing an ethical, ascetical development that differs from the noetic orientation of the basic formula. In any case, it is uncertain whether the insights of full enlightenment are present already on the earlier ranks or only on the fifth rank of perfection.

The formula of the "Five Ranks Regarding Lord and Vassal" is preceded by a lengthy explanatory commentary by Ts'ao-shan. As symbols of the "straight" and the "bent," lord and vassal represent respectively the absolute element of reality (*li*) and the phenomenal element (*shih*). The third rank of the formula is described as "the lord alone" and the fourth as "the vassal alone." The opposition between these two ranks supports the *henchūshi* reading of the fourth rank even though the word for the absolute is not actually used. Later, the fourth rank was given various interpretations by different commentators.

The third formula is simpler in its dialectical structure. The middle ranks (the third and fourth) are without potentiality; they indicate simply sameness and diversity. All fivefold formulas of ranks or states lead to the same goal—perfect unity in total interpenetration. "This is the Hua-yen world of *li-shih wu-ai* (Jpn., *riji muge*)," Verdu concludes, "where the 'form' is equally the void as the void is the 'form.' Word and nonword are but the discriminative mind—aspects of perfect identity in itself."[75]

This Chinese predilection for formulas and numerical schemes accompanied by diagrams and figures is by no means limited to Zen or even Buddhism in general, but reaches back to early Chinese antiquity. The principal symbol for the Five Ranks—light and dark in the form of circles, where light signifies the phenomenal world and dark the noumenal world—is also to be found among the scholars of the Kegon school.[76] The real roots of the diagrams, however, are to be found in the *Book of Changes*, which had been analyzed for several generations and applied in a variety of ways. It seems that in the case of the Five Ranks, Ts'ao-shan, who composed the poetic verses, also drew the diagrams. Such symbols formed an important part of Zen history, responding to the need for visible signs or images, a need that was especially strong during the Sung period and was to lead to the remarkable artistic accomplishments of Japanese Zen.

The influence of the Five Ranks extended beyond the House of Ts'ao-tung. The eminent Rinzai master Fen-yang Shan-chao (947–1024) was the first in the House of Lin-chi to make use of the Five Ranks of the House of Ts'ao-tung.

The explanatory verses he composed are included in his kōan collection, which makes up the second volume of the three-volume *Fun'yōroku*, edited by his disciple Shih-shuang Ch'u-yüan (986–1039).[77] This work represents the first significant kōan collection in Chinese literature.

Little is known of Ts'ao-shan's disciples. His line disappeared in the fourth or fifth generation. Yün-chü Tao-ying and his immediate followers carried on the House of Ts'ao-tung but showed little interest in the Five Ranks. Only with the revival of the school in the twelfth century did disciples again give attention to the importance of the fivefold formula.[78] From this developed a number of commentaries of mixed value.[79] The Five Ranks became part of the general Zen heritage.

YÜN-MEN: "THE ONE-WORD BARRIERS"

Like the House of Ts'ao-tung, the houses of Yün-men and Fa-yen belong to the main line of Shih-t'ou, within which divisions had begun already during the first generation after Shih-t'ou. While the House of Ts'ao-tung was formed around the disciple Yüeh-shan Wei-yen, a second line traced its way via T'ien-huang Tao-wu (748–807), Lung-t'an Ch'ung-hsin, and Te-shan Hsüan-chien (782–865) down to the famous master Hsüeh-feng I-ts'un (822–908), a prominent figure at the end of the T'ang period. To Hsüeh-feng the two houses of Yün-men and Fa-yen are indebted for their common origin. Together they typify the Zen movement during the Five Dynasties period (907–960) and form a bridge to the following Sung dynasty.

During the period of the Five Dynasties, the North was torn by the ravages of war while the South enjoyed peace and order. Many of the politically independent provinces set themselves up as small kingdoms and enjoyed a general state of well-being that often included a highly developed intellectual culture. For the houses of Yün-men and Fa-yen there were numerous advantages to such a social and political situation. Yet despite all they had in common, the two developed their own distinct characteristics.

Yün-men Wen-yen (864–949) was one of the most eminent Zen personalities of his time.[80] He holds an important place within Zen literature and has been the subject of many stories in the Zen chronicles and the kōan collections (eighteen related cases appear in the *Hekiganroku* alone, five in the *Mumonkan*). Born in Chia-hsing (southwest of Shanghai), Yün-men entered religious life at an early age, studying and observing the Buddhist monastic rule (Vinaya) until, driven by the desire for higher wisdom, he took up the itinerant life. He attained enlightenment while with Ch'en Tsun-su (Mu-chou Tao-tsung or Tao-ming), an eccentric disciple of Huang-po who practiced an extremely rigorous form of Zen in Mu-chou. Three times Yün-men asked his master for instruction in the highest truth. The third time, Mu-chou (so called because of his place of residence) threw him out of the gate and shut it so suddenly and with such force that it caught Yün-men's leg and broke it. In the extreme pain Yün-men attained enlightenment.

Mu-chou sent him to Hsüeh-feng, the most illustrious Zen master of the time.[81] After spending a number of years with this master, Yün-men became his Dharma heir. He then set out as a wandering monk, visiting a number of well-known Zen masters until he ended up in Shao-chou, a southern city in Kuang-tung Province where a viceroy from the family of Liu had assumed control after the fall of the T'ang dynasty. The powerful Liu gave full protection to Yün-men. Following the death of the abbot Ju-min, the prince decreed that Yün-men become head of the Reiju-in monastery (Chin., Ling-shu-yüan). Later, another ruler from the Liu family built him the monastery of Kōtaizen-in (Chin., Kuang-t'ai ch'an-yüan) on Mount Yün-men. This accounts for his name: the geographical name of the mountain was extended to the monastery and the founding abbot, who then passed into Zen history as Master Yün-men. The region ruled by the family of Liu in South China and known as the Kingdom of Nan-han became the site of important cultural and artistic developments. In such a milieu, the House of Yün-men flourished and produced some of the most lofty artistic works of Chinese Zen.

On Mount Yün-men the master gathered a large number of disciples and guided them on the path toward enlightenment. Just as he himself had to pay a great price to attain enlightenment, his disciples were not spared the same demands. It was part of his regular practice to strike them with his staff and frighten them with sudden shouts. His special style consisting of short, sharp answers came to be known as the "one word barriers."[82] Zen literature abounds in such "one-word" retorts, especially in the collected sayings of Yün-men (Jpn., Ummonroku)[83] and in the Ninden gammoku. Consider the following exchanges:

"What is Zen?"—"That's it."
"What is the way?"—"Grab it."[84]
"What is Yün-men's sword?"—"Patriarch."[85]

Or again, to a monk who asks about a sword so sharp that it would cut a hair blown across its blade, the only reply given is "Bones."[86]

The following three examples are taken from the Ninden gammoku:

"What is the eye of the True Dharma?"—"Everywhere."

"He who kills his father and kills his mother confesses before the Buddha. But where shall one confess who kills the Buddha and the patriarchs?"—"Obvious."

"What is the meaning of the Patriarch's coming from the West?"—"Master."

Not all the answers consist of one graph; sometimes there are two, three, or more. But the answers are always extremely pregnant and incisive. What is more, the same question may occasion different answers.

The breadth and heart of Yün-men's pithy retorts stand out clearly in the contrast between a case from the Mumonkan:

"What is the Buddha?"—"A shit-stick."[87]

and one from the collected sayings of Yün-men:

"What is the pure Dharma body?"—"A flowerbed of peonies."[88]

The last example reflects Yün-men's aesthetic sense in his ability to see the purity of the cosmos in the beauty of nature. All the same, the genuine Zen master makes no difference between "pure" and "impure." When talking about the Buddha nature of reality, Yün-men can find expressions whose concreteness are in no sense inferior to those of Lin-chi.

Yün-men's curt answers were meant to aid practice, to spur insight, and thus to promote realization. Not only his punchy one-syllable retorts, but also his more extended conversations and stories came to be used as kōan. Yün-men discovered the classical mode of expression for the eternal Now of time-transcending enlightenment. The sixth example in the *Hekiganroku* illustrates the point well:

> Yün-men addressed the assembly and said: "I am not asking you about the days before the fifteenth of the month. But what about after the fifteenth? Come and give me a word about those days."
> And he himself gave the answer for them: "Every day is a good day."[89]

This kōan has received many different interpretations. Certainly, its main message is clear and speaks to everyone, not just to students of Zen. But the story also touches on a deeper, veiled mystery—the mystery of time. The Japanese Zen master Yasutani Hakuun explained that the previous fifteen days signify the time of practice from the first awakening of the desire for truth until the time of ultimate comprehension in experience. The Now of enlightenment is as perfect as the full moon at the halfway mark of its cycle. Just as the moon wanes and becomes dark, so during the fifteen days following enlightenment the consciousness of the awakening, which still lingers in the mind as a residue, fades and disappears. Enlightenment then means "every day," and the "every day" means enlightenment. Hence the very distinction between before and after is rendered useless. Reality is one single Now. This Now or today is every day. "Every day is a good day." A good day is nothing special.[90] Gundert ponders, "is there, in the grayness of an ordinary everyday that contains nothing special, something very special? And again, might this something very special not itself be everyday?"[91] One has the sense that this kōan is a pearl of great price.

Tung-shan Shou-ch'u (d. 900) is the best known of Yün-men's disciples. Continuing his master's use of "one word barriers," he distinguished between "dead words" that contain rational intention and "living words" that are not bound by reason.[92] His best-known short answer has been preserved in case 18 of the *Mumonkan*. To a monk who asks him, "What is the Buddha?", he replies: "Three pounds of flax." The moment of Tung-shan's enlightenment also came to be the subject of a kōan. The *Mumonkan* relates the story as follows in case 15:

> When Tung-shan came to have an interview with Yün-men, Yün-men asked, "Where have you been recently?" "At Ch'a-tu, Master," Tung-shan replied. "Where did you stay during the last *ge* [retreat] period?" "At Paotzu of Hunan," replied Tung-shan. "When did you leave there?" "On the

twenty-fifth of August," Tung-shan answered. Yün-men exclaimed, "I give you sixty blows with my stick!" The next day Tung-shan came up again and asked the master, "Yesterday you gave me sixty blows with your stick. I do not know where my fault was." Yün-men cried out, "You rice bag! Have you been prowling about like that from Chiang-hsi to Hunan?" At this Tung-shan was enlightened.

Whether Tung-shan actually received these blows is not clear from the wording of the text. Commentators disagree on the point. The editor of the work, Wu-men Hui-k'ai (1183–1260), however, criticizes Yün-men's gentle handling of Tung-shan and attributes the fall of the House of Yün-men to such manifestations of weakness.[93]

The House of Yün-men made a considerable contribution to Chinese culture. Its founder, Yün-men, has been called the "most eloquent of the Ch'an masters."[94] Paradoxically, this master had a great fear of words, and yet thanks to his enlightenment he could "stand unharmed in the midst of flames."[95] From him emanated the "light" of which he said, "all people have it within themselves, but when they seek after it, it is all darkness."[96] In this ever-present, dynamic light one finds the secret of Yün-men's powerful language. During the early Sung period, the House of Yün-men flourished, and together with the House of Lin-chi exercised a considerable influence on the upper classes of Chinese society.

The highpoint of this development comes with Hsüeh-tou Ch'ung-hsien (980–1052), the poet of the hundred verses of the *Hekiganroku.*[97] His own master and Yün-men's successor, Chih-men Kuang-tsu (d. 1031), was also a poet. We have already noted how the Rinzai master Fen-yang used poetry to express enlightened wisdom. Hsüeh-tou surpassed all of these poetic predecessors. As a master, he enjoyed great popularity and attracted many disciples. Among his works is a collection of some 250 poems.[98] His work reached its highest level in the verses that he composed for cases he himself had selected, mostly from the *Keitoku dentōroku* and the collected sayings of Yün-men. His goal was to forge the essence of the masters' words and deeds into poetic form. In this way, he laid the foundations for the *Hekiganroku*, which, in the words of a Chinese Zen disciple, represents "the foremost scripture containing the beliefs of our faith."[99] In this kōan collection we have the epitome of poetic achievement in Zen literature. Through his writings, Hsüeh-tou contributed to the restoration of the House of Yün-men, which had fallen into a state of decline at the time.[100] The house did not survive, however, as an independent school; during the Sung period it was absorbed into the powerful Rinzai school.

FA-YEN: THE INTERPENETRATION OF ATTRIBUTES

The House of Fa-yen, the last of the Five Houses, was short-lived. The name Fa-yen derives from the posthumous title its founder was given by his friend and patron, Prince Li Ching (916–961), a local lord in South China. Fa-yen Wen-i (885–958), the founder of the last of the Five Houses, centered his activity in a politically and culturally important center in the South, located on the site of present-day Nan-ching. Many disciples came to the monastery of Seiryō-ji (Chin., Ch'in-liang-ssu) to hear this master so well versed in both the Chinese and Buddhist classics; with confidence they entrusted themselves to his sure and gentle guidance. His psychological insight and clever versatility were widely reputed.

Despite his high intellectual cultivation, Fa-yen adopted an authentically Zen style and passed it on as such to his followers. While he did not pounce upon his students and strike them with his staff, he did give them answers of extraordinary precision and power. His favorite method was pure Zen—simply to repeat the words of a question or remark, without any explanation. An illustration from the *Keitoku dentōroku* gives an idea of the method at work. Fa-yen asked his companion, Shao-hsiu, what this saying of the ancients meant: "A slight differentiation causes a separation as between heaven and earth." Shao-hsiu replied: "A slight differentiation causes a separation as between heaven and earth." The master asked: "How can your interpretation hold good?" Shao-hsiu asked: "What is yours?" The master replied: "A slight differentiation causes a separation between heaven and earth."[101] Numerous such examples have come down to us in the writings of Zen, as well as a large number of striking answers in the typical Zen style. For example:

> "What should one do during the twelve hours of the day and night?"—
> "Every step should tread on this question."[102]

In offering his students such teachings and responses, Master Fa-yen stood in the best of Zen tradition.

In the House of Fa-yen, the Kegon worldview occupied an even more prominent place than it did in other Zen schools. The master studied Kegon scriptures intensively, and had his disciples read the works of the patriarchs Tu-shun (557–640) and Fa-tsang (643–712). Fa-yen well understood the interpenetration of the six attributes of being: totality and differentiation, sameness and difference, becoming and passing away. These attributes, illustrated by a circle, represent aspects of reality that are neither identical nor different. Fa-yen explains:

> The meaning of the six attributes of Kegon is that within sameness there is difference. For difference to be different from sameness is in no way the intention of all the Buddhas. The intention of all the Buddhas is both totality and differentiation. How can there be both sameness and difference? When a male body enters *samādhi*, a female body is indifferent to it. When there is indifference terms are transcended. When the ten thousand appearances are utterly bright, there is neither reality [*li*; Jpn., *ri*] nor appearance [*shih*; Jpn., *ji*].[103]

By contemplating a circle in which the six attributes are written, one can come to an experience of this doctrine of oneness.

The basic insight of the Kegon school concerning "difference in sameness" and "sameness in difference" is illustrated in an episode from the life of Fa-yen, recorded in characteristic Zen style, that was later to become a famous kōan in the *Mumonkan* collection:

> The monks gathered in the hall to hear the great Fa-yen of Ch'ing-liang give *teishō* [instruction in Dharma] before the midday meal. Fa-yen pointed to the bamboo blinds. At this two monks went to the blinds and rolled them up alike. Fa-yen said, "One has it; the other has not." (case 26)

Wu-men comments that the master may have failed—a comment intended to push students more deeply into the kōan's meaning. If the surface of the episode communicates "difference in sameness," its underside contains "sameness in difference." What matters is that one overcomes duality. [104]

Fa-yen carried on the methods of the T'ang Zen masters. He loved paradoxes and aimed at inducing sudden enlightenment. Thus his bonds with the heritage of the Zen tradition are undeniable. Moreover, a brief overview of his school reveals that it planted the seeds for later developments in Chinese Zen Buddhism.

Fa-yen's Dharma heir, T'ien-t'ai Te-shao (891–971), continued to guide the House of Fa-yen, but not along a straight Zen line. After he had achieved enlightenment and acquired a significant following, he turned to the teachings of the T'ien-t'ai school, which, after the confusion of the time of the Five Dynasties, had suffered considerable decline in popularity. Enjoying the favor of the local prince, T'ien-t'ai Te-shao was appointed to the office of regional teacher in the southern princedom of Wu-yüeh, a center and catalyst for cultural development during the Sung period. [105] His two disciples, Yung-ming Yen-shou (904–975) and Tao-yüan (dates unknown), played important roles, in very different ways, in subsequent Zen history.

Yung-ming introduced a development that truly bore fruit only later. [106] This "famous and enthusiastic syncretist" [107] was ahead of his time in attempting a comprehensive synthesis of all Buddhist teachings. This he proposed in his extensive work, the *Sugyōroku* (Chin., *Tsung-ching lu*). He recited the *Lotus Sūtra* and combined the recitation of the name of Amitābha Buddha (Jpn., *nembutsu*; Chin., *nien-fo*) with his Zen practice. Listed as the first patriarch of the Pure Land school during the Sung period, the magnanimous and learned Yung-ming may be considered the pioneer of the unification movement between Zen and the *nembutsu* tradition, a movement that later was to gain the upper hand in Chinese Buddhism. [108]

Tao-yüan's work, on the other hand, was to become a cornerstone in the history of genuine Chinese Zen. The chronicle he compiled, the *Keitoku dentōroku*, marks, with its extensive account of all the Zen masters and their projects, the close of a certain period in the history of the formation and expansion of Zen in China. At the same time, it provided a wealth of materials that laid the foundations for the so-called kōan-Zen that was soon to develop. Most of the kōan in the collections stem from Tao-yüan's chronicle either directly or indirectly. Unfortunately, we know very little of his activity. In the House of Fa-yen, especially through Fa-yen's work, the *Shūmon jikki-ron*, the period of the Five Houses was brought to clear self-consciousness. Fa-yen proved to be such a convincing advocate for his house that even the preeminent Confucian Chu Hsi, otherwise no friend of Buddhism, could offer him nothing but unequivocal praise.[109]

The roots of the Five Houses of Chinese Zen reach back to the era of transition during the second half of the T'ang period. This was the time of the great and original Zen masters, in whose lineage the Five Houses were formed. Without introducing any essential changes, the houses articulated particularities and differences that would influence the further development of Zen history. The Five Houses also formed a bridge to the second flowering of Chinese Zen during the Sung period.

NOTES

1. See K. Ch'en, *Buddhism in China*, pp. 226–233. E. Reischauer recounts how the important Japanese Buddhist monk Ennin (793–864) experienced the persecution of Buddhism during his travels in China. See his *Ennin's Travels in T'ang China* (New York, 1955), especially the chapter "The Persecution of Buddhism," pp. 217–71.

2. Reischauer (*Ennin's Travels*, chap. 7) mentions four persecutions and on the basis of official reports details the disturbances of the great persecution of 845.

3. Typical here is the memorial inscription of the eminent literary figure Han Yü dating from 819. Reischauer reproduces the document completely (*Ennin's Travels*, pp. 221–24) and Ch'en cites the important passages (*Buddhism in China*, pp. 225–26).

4. Reischauer gives particular weight to the economic factor in his presentation.

5. Reischauer, *Ennin's Travels*, p. 227.

6. Yanagida contrasts Ennin's laments with the short report in the Zen chronicle *Sodōshū*. See *Chūgoku zenshūshi*, pp. 66–67.

7. Cited in *Chūgoku zenshūshi*, p. 84. The name of the houses in the text will be given in Chinese since it is only in China that these lines were considered "houses."

8. The Five Houses are clearly mentioned by name in the *Dembō shōshūki* (Chin., Ch'uan-fa cheng-tsung chi) of Ch'i-sung, published in 1064 (T. 2078). Biographies of the masters of the Five Houses are included in the *Keitoku dentōroku* and other Zen chronicles.

9. T. 2006. The foreword is dated 1188. See *Zen Dust*, p. 365. A detailed report on the Five Houses is contained in the last of the great Zen chronicles, *Gotō egen* (Chin., Wu-teng hui-yüan), or *A Compendium of the Five Lamps*, in twenty books, published in 1253. A text known as *Goke shōshūsan* (Chin., Wu-chia cheng-tsung tsan), *In Praise of the Five Houses of the True School*, compiled by Hsi-sou Shao-t'an (completed in 1254), contains seventy-four biographies of the masters of the Five Houses. The *Goke goroku* (Chin., Wu-chia yü-lu) or *Record of the Five Houses*, published in 1632, deals exclusively with the Five Houses. In Japan, Tōrei Enji (1721–1792) published a work known as the *Goke sanshō yōromon* (*A Detailed Study of the Fundamental Principles of the Five Houses*). See the entries on this literature in *Zen Dust*, pp. 359–60, 426–30. See also Lu K'uan Yü (Charles Luk), *Ch'an and Zen Teaching* and Chang Chung-yuan, *Original Teachings of Ch'an Buddhism* (New York, 1969). Both books draw a great deal of material from the Chinese Zen chronicles.

10. This story is recorded in the *Mumonkan*, case 40. Kuei-shan was clearly in the enlightened state at the time of the event.

11. The story of Hsing-yen's enlightenment, translated from the Keitoku dentōroku, book 11, is repeated in Chang Chung-yuan, Original Teachings of Ch'an Buddhism, pp. 219–23. The realization of enlightenment through an unexpected noise appears frequently in reports of enlightenment.

12. Chang Chung-yuan, Original Teachings of Ch'an Buddhism, p. 189.

13. Kuei-shan's collected sayings are contained in T. 1989; for these three stanzas see vol. 47, p. 580b,c. The first and second stanza are also to be found in the Keitoku dentōroku; see Chang, Original Teachings, pp. 220 and 215.

14. Chang, Original Teachings, p. 190.

15. See above, chap. 9, note 4.

16. Chang, Original Teachings of Ch'an Buddhism, pp. 189–90.

17. Keitoku dentōroku, T. 2076, vol. 51, p. 284a.

18. See Lu K'uan Yü, Ch'an and Zen Teaching, p. 69, note 2.

19. Lu K'uan Yü, Ch'an and Zen Teaching, p. 71. Of the numerous examples of silent action showing enlightenment that are related in the chronicles, the image of silently raising a fan is frequently used.

20. See Chang Chung-yuan, Original Teachings of Ch'an Buddhism, pp. 196ff.

21. This episode is also related in book 11 of the Keitoku dentōroku; see Chang's explanation, Original Teachings, p. 188, and Lu K'uan Yü, Ch'an and Zen Teaching, p. 62.

22. Case 5.

23. Book 6, T. 2076, vol. 51, p. 246b.

24. Book 9, T. 2076, vol. 51, p. 256b. There are numerous nuances possible in the translation of this text. See Chang Chung-yuan, Original Teachings of Ch'an Buddhism, pp. 205–06; Lu K'uan Yü, Ch'an and Zen Teaching, p. 65. The latter sees in the circle and the globe of the moon the symbol of the cosmic Buddha body or dharmakāya (Ch'an and Zen Teaching, note 1).

25. T. 2006, vol. 48, pp. 321c–322b.

26. Book 11, T. 2076, vol. 51, p. 283b.

27. T. 2076, vol. 48, p. 283. Cited in Chang Chung-yuan, Original Teachings of Ch'an Buddhism, p. 216.

28. See the entry on the image of the circle, "Ensō," in Mochizuki, Bukkyō daijiten, vol. 1, pp. 306–307. Later the practice was much used in esoteric Buddhism (mikkyō).

29. From the collected sayings of Kuei-shan Ling-yu, T. 1989, vol. 47, p. 577b,c.

30. "Discourse," sec. 10. See the English translation of Ruth Fuller Sasaki, Record of Lin-chi, p. 6.

31. See the entry on "Shihokkai" in Mochizuki, Bukkyō daijiten, vol. 2, pp. 1993–1994.

32. See Demiéville's commentary on the formula in his French translation, Entretiens de Lin-tsi, pp. 52ff.

33. The Chinese original is unclear. I cite here the translation of Sasaki (Record of Lin-chi, p. 6). Demiéville interprets the sentence differently (Entretiens de Lin-tsi, p. 51). Japanese translators waver in their interpretations.

34. The metaphor of guest and host appears several times in the Rinzairoku, beginning with "Discourse," sec. 4. Sasaki refers to it as a "teaching device" (Record of Lin-chi, p. 68, note 27).

35. The formula ("Discourse," sec. 18) normally bears the title "The Four Situations of Guest and Host." Demiéville speaks of "four cases of consultation between visitor and host" (*Entretiens de Lin-tsi*, pp. 112, 126). The text shifts over to describing the partners as "learner" or "student" (Jpn., *gakunin*) and "teacher." This latter is referred to by the term *zenchishiki* (Skt., *kalyāna-mitra*), an expression from ancient Buddhist literature signifying a good friend or a friend who leads one to the good. In Zen, this is the relationship of master to disciple. The option of translating the term as "teacher" stresses the didactic element.

36. Demiéville refers to a saying of K'ung-tzu praising orderliness in conversation (*Entretiens de Lin-tsi*, p. 127).

37. Demiéville offers two possible explanations—either that it refers to the engagement of the whole person or that it has to do with physical actions of all sorts, like striking, suddenly standing up from a seated position, and so forth. (*Entretiens de Lin-tsi*, p. 127).

38. According to Sasaki, a Zen master bares half the body "when, through cryptic words or gestures, he partially discloses a profound truth in such a way as to obscure it from any but one with a truly perceptive eye" (*Record of Lin-chi*, p. 77, note 117).

39. *Record of Lin-chi*, p. 27.

40. Jpn., *kyō*, an object that possesses no reality. The teacher literally grabs the bait.

41. Gundert translates the phrase as referring to the student (*Bi-yän-lu* II, p. 111). The text is not specific and allows for the translation of Sasaki (whom Demiéville follows), according to which it is not a person but a "thing" that is cast into the pit.

42. The translation of Akizuki Ryōmin reads "handcuffs and foot-shackles." See his translation, with commentary, of the *Rinzairoku*, vol. 10 of *Zen no goroku* (Tokyo, 1967), p. 112.

43. This phrase is open to a variety of interpretations and translations. While we have preserved the phrasing of Sasaki, Gundert reads "the one cannot distinguish the other" (*Bi-yän-lu* II, p. 111).

44. *Entretiens de Lin-tsi*, p. 127.

45. Demiéville (*Entretiens de Lin-tsi*, p. 113) sides with Yanagida here.

46. T. 2006, vol. 48, 304b.

47. Demiéville (*Entretiens de Lin-tsi*, p. 196) appeals to Yanagida in making this claim.

48. *Record of Lin-chi*, p. 47.

49. This is Sasaki's interpretation of this difficult metaphor (*Record of Lin-chi*, p. 84, note 200).

50. *Record of Lin-chi*, pp. 69–70, notes 37 and 41.

51. *Rinzairoku*, p. 67.

52. *Entretiens de Lin-tsi*, p. 44. Although Demiéville sees the formulas as an "object of endless exegesis," he takes issue with certain of the interpretations.

53. A second possible explanation has it that the first character (*ts'ao*) derives from Ts'ao-ch'i, the name of the residence of the Sixth Patriarch, Hui-neng. The choice of the character would thus express the school's origins from the Sixth Patriarch (*Zen Dust*, p. 166); see also their detailed entry on Tung-shan Liang-chieh, pp. 296–99.

54. *Keitoku dentōroku*, book 15, T. 2076, vol. 51, p. 321c. The translation cited (with slight adjustments) appears in *Zen Dust*, pp. 306–07. See also the translation of Chang Chung-yuan, *Original Teachings of Ch'an Buddhism*, pp. 59–60, and Lu K'uan Yü, *Ch'an and Zen Teaching*, pp. 131–32. Yanagida presents the text in the version found in the

collections of sayings of Tung-shan (T. 1986, vol. 47, p. 508a,b); see his *Rinzairoku*, p. 78. The mirror image in the water is a "he" insofar as it indicates the self and an "it" insofar as it is something external and objective that serves as an impetus.

55. See the poetic text *Hōkyō zammai* (Chin., *Pao-ching san-mei*) at the end of the collected sayings of Tung-shan (Chin., *Tung-shan Liang-chieh ch'an-shih yü-lu*; Jpn., *Tōzan Ryōkai zenji goroku*), T. 1987, vol. 47, p. 515a,b. The verse on the Five Ranks is found in this work (p. 525c), in the collection of sayings of the disciple Ts'ao-shan (Chin., *Fu-chou Ts'ao-shan Pen-chi ch'an-shih yü-lu*; Jpn., *Bushū Sōzan Honjaku zenji goroku*), T. 1987, vol. 47, p. 532c–533a), and in the *Ninden gammoku* (Chin., *Jen-t'ien yen-mu*) T. 2006, vol. 48, p. 314c. The latter source likewise contains a longer poem, also entitled *Hōkyō zammai* (p. 321a,b).

56. It is possible that he had received this in turn from his master, Yüeh-shan Wei-yen, a direct disciple of Shih-t'ou.

57. The Japanese Rinzai master Hakuin recognized the paramount significance of the Five Ranks. A translation of his commentary, from which the citation in the text is taken, can be found in *Zen Dust*, pp. 63–67. A study by A. Verdu, *Dialectical Aspects in Buddhist Thought: Studies in Sino-Japanese Mahāyāna Idealism* (Kansas City, 1974), offers a penetrating account of the Five Ranks in the Sōtō school (pp. 115–87). As he explains, the dialectic of the Five Ranks needs to be understood from the point of view of the metaphysics of the Mahāyāna schools and Kegon philosophy. He points to a structural parallel between the fivefold schemata in Kegon and the Five Ranks. He locates the peculiarity of the latter in the fact that "they represent an attempt to visualize explicitly the five perspective moments that are implicitly identical for the enlightened mind" (pp. 117). As Verdu shows in his study, this accounts for the predominant significance of the dialectical element in Zen realization.

58. The Five Ranks were recorded by Ts'ao-shan Pen-chi, a disciple of Tung-shan, in the form in which they were handed down (see *Zen Dust*, pp. 309–10). According to one tradition, Tung-shan had already received the poem from his master, Yün-yen; it is also variously ascribed to either Tung-shan or Yün-yen's master, Yüeh-shan. See note 303 to the text of the *Ninden gammoku* in the collection *Kokuyaku Issaikyō; shoshūbu*, vol. 6, (Tokyo, 1937), p. 365. This brings the text close to Shih-t'ou. Neither Yün-yen nor Yüeh-shan left behind writings, as Miura and Sasaki have noted (*Zen Dust*, p. 307).

59. This is the convention that Miura and Sasaki follow (*Zen Dust*, p. 309). Gundert uses the similar term, "die Fünf Standorte" (*Bi-yän-lu* II, pp. 193, 206ff). Chang Chung-yuan speaks of them as the "Five Relations between Particularity and Universality" (*Original Teachings of Ch'an Buddhism*, p. 46), and Verdu generally refers to them as the "Five Degrees Dialectic of the Sōtō Zen School" (*Dialectical Aspects in Buddhist Thought*, p. 115). Ryosuke Ohashi and Hans Brockard's German translation of S. Hisamatsu's structural analysis of the text adopts the phrase "Fünf Stände" (*Die Fünf Stände von Zen-Meister Tosan Ryokai* [Pfullingen, 1980]). In German, the term "die Fünf Stufen" is most common.

60. From the collection of Tsung-shan's saying, cited in my *The Development of Chinese Zen*, pp. 26, 74.

61. [After the English translation of Sasaki and Miura (*Zen Dust*, pp. 67–72), with some adjustments. The author uses the terms *das Gerade* and *das Gekrümmte*, while Sasaki and Miura prefer "the True" and "the Apparent" to render Chinese characters that suggest a contrast between "the true" and "the off-center." We have kept the imagery of the German contrast.—*Translators.*]

62. The literature related to these verses has had a long history of its own. The free, poetic translation of Gundert (Bi-yän-lu II, pp. 206ff) is exemplary. Ryosuke Ohashi and Hans Brockard, editors of the German translation of Hisamatsu's work on the Five Ranks, have labored greatly at its literary form; their translation of the headings of the five stanzas is as follows: "In the Straight the Bent" "In the Bent the Straight," "Departing from the Straight," "Arriving at the Coherent," "Homecoming in the Coherent" (see note 59 above, pp. 9–10).

63. See Chang Chung-yuan's summary essay, "Interfusion of Universality and Particularity," Original Teachings of Ch'an Buddhism, pp. 41–57.

64. See the table in Chang, Original Teachings of Ch'an Buddhism, p. 53.

65. Cited in Bi-yän-lu II, pp. 208–209.

66. See Verdu's explanation of the third stanza in the appendix on the Five Ranks in his book Abstraktion und Intuition als Wege zur Wahrheit in Yoga und Zen (Munich, 1965), pp. 268ff.

67. Verdu, Abstraktion und Intuition, p. 287.

68. Verdu, Abstraktion und Intuition, p. 288, note 1.

69. Verdu, Abstraktion und Intuition, p. 287. Verdu puts the accent on the dynamic element in his later work, translating it as "Coming from the midst of equality" (Dialectical Aspects in Buddhist Thought, p. 124) Ōhasama and Faust, Zen: der lebendige Buddhismus in Japan, render the line "Stepping out of sameness" (p. 125).

70. Cited from Gundert, Bi-yän-lu II, pp. 210–11.

71. Gundert stresses the fact that the fourth rank stands "diametrically opposed" to the third (Bi-yän-lu II, p. 210). Miura and Sasaki praise "the total inclusiveness, perfect symmetry, and matchless beauty" of the formula (Zen Dust, p. 63).

72. Chang Chung-yuan, Original Teachings of Ch'an Buddhism, p. 42.

73. Ohasama and Faust, Zen, p. 125.

74. See the Chinese text of the formula of the "Five Ranks of Merit" in T. 1986, vol. 47, p. 525c (cf. p. 516a). For "Five Ranks Regarding Lord and Vassal, see T. 1987, vol. 47, p. 527a; for "Secret Meaning of the Five Ranks," see pp. 533b,c; for "Manifestation of the Mystery of the Five Ranks," see p. 531b. See also Verdu, Dialectical Aspects in Buddhist Thought, pp. 140–77, 182–87. The dialectical formulas are practiced as kōan to this day. This is not to say that the practitioner is thereby made conscious of the high-level dialectic contained there. The formulas open a way to learning how to resolve all opposition and make the practitioners experience their own transcendent nature.

75. Verdu, Dialectical Aspects, p. 177.

76. See H. Nakamura, Ways of Thinking of Eastern Peoples: India, China, Tibet, Japan (Honolulu, 1964), pp. 182ff. Nakamura treats the symbolic representations of various Buddhist schools and draws special attention to Zen Buddhism and the Five Ranks. Like the I Ching (Book of Changes), Buddhist diagrams had an influence on the Neo-Confucianism of the Sung period. Verdu, especially in his Dialectical Aspects in Buddhist Thought, illustrates the dialectic of Mahāyāna and the Five Ranks through numerous diagrams and drawings.

77. T. 1992, vol. 47; see Zen Dust, pp. 355–56.

78. Verdu cites explanations of the two Sōtō masters Chi-yin Hui-hung (12th century) and Yung-chüeh Yüan-hsien (1578–1657) in his analysis of the Five Ranks. In one passage he treats an interpretation of the Five Ranks made by Chi-yin on the basis of the Hōkyō

zammai and Yüan-hsien's attempt at a refutation (*Dialectical Aspects in Buddhist Thought*, pp. 130–39).

79. Hakuin criticized the "perversion of the Five Ranks" through "the piling up of entanglement upon entanglement" (see *Zen Dust*, p. 64).

80. See the brief biographical sketch in *Zen Dust*, pp. 160–61.

81. The houses of Yün-men and Fa-yen have their common point of origin in Hsüeh-feng I-tsun (822–908). Chang Chung-yuan has translated his biography from book 16 of the *Keitoku dentōroku* (*Original Teachings of Ch'an Buddhism*, pp. 275–82).

82. The cry "*kan!*" is written with a character meaning "barrier" and differs from the *katsu* that subsequently became common.

83. The complete title of the collection is *Ummon Kyōshin zenji kōroku* (T. 1988; Chin., *Yün-men K'uang-chen ch'an-shih kuang-lu*) or *Ummon Ōsho kōroku*, commonly abbreviated as *Ummonroku* (Chin., *Yün-men lu*). It includes three books and was first published in 1076.

84. *Ummonroku*, T. 1988, vol. 47, p. 546c.

85. *Ummonroku*, p. 546a.

86. *Ummonroku*, p. 546a. The following three examples in the text come from book 2 of the *Ninden gammoku*. See T. 2006, vol. 48, p. 312c.

87. Case 21. The same phrase occurs in the *Rinzairoku*. Regarding which was first, see above, chap. 10, note 50.

88. T. 1988, vol. 47, p. 552c.

89. Case 6. See K. Sekida, *Two Zen Classics*, p. 161.

90. From a lecture, though it is possible that Yasutani is relying on earlier authors.

91. *Bi-yän-lu* 1, p. 161.

92. See Chang Chung-yuan, *Original Teachings of Ch'an Buddhism*, p. 271.

93. *Mumonkan*, case 15. For the explanation of the kōan, see Dumoulin, *Mumonkan*, pp. 73ff.

94. J.C.H. Wu, *The Golden Age of Zen*, p. 213.

95. Wu, *The Golden Age of Zen*, p. 214.

96. *Hekiganroku*, case 86. See *Zengaku daijiten* 1, p. 78.

97. See the brief biography in *Zen Dust*, pp. 159–160; Gundert, *Bi-yän-lu* 1, pp. 11–14.

98. Known in Japanese as the *Soeishū*.

99. Cited in Gundert, *Bi-yän-lu* 1, p. 96.

100. See *Zen Dust*, pp. 159–160. Also belonging to the House of Yün-men is Ch'i-sung (1007–1072), the famous compiler of the text of the *Dembō shōshūki* (Chin., *Ch'uan-fa cheng-tsung chi*), which appeared in 1064 (T. 2078, vol. 51). The work presents the Zen school that carries on the Dharma of Bodhidharma as the "true school." Ch'i-sung also wrote a commentary on the Confucian classic *Chung-yung* (*Doctrine of the Mean*), see T. 2115, vol. 52.

101. T. 2076, vol. 51, p. 399b. The translation used here is by Lu K'uan Yü, *Ch'an and Zen Teaching*, p. 224. Chang Chung-yuan offers an alternate rendition of the passage (*Original Teachings of Ch'an Buddhism*, p. 246). The famous word-play on the "pointing of the finger" and the "moon" appears in the same source: "The monk asked the master: 'I asked about the pointing; why did you speak of the moon?' The master replied, 'Because

you asked about pointing.' " T. 2076, vol. 51, p. 398c; translation from Lu K'uan Yü, p. 219. See also Chang, p. 242.

102. T. 2076, vol. 51, p. 399a.

103. *Ninden gammoku*, book 4, T. 2006, vol. 48, p. 324a. A circle with the six attributes is worked into the text.

104. Case 26. See the comment of Wu-men and the verse, as well as the notes to the German translation (*Mumonkan*, pp. 104–105). Chang Chung-yuan writes in connection with this kōan that for Zen "opposites are natural phenomena," and that the dichotomy between them is to be transcended in order to arrive at nonduality (*Original Teachings of Ch'an Buddhism*, p. 233).

105. See Yanagida, *Rinzairoku*, pp. 89–90.

106. On Yung-ming see Chang Chung-yuan, *Original Teachings of Ch'an Buddhism*, pp. 250–253 (an English translation of the passage on Yung-ming in the *Keitoku dentōroku*, book 26); see also Wu, *The Golden Age of Zen*, pp. 240–41.

107. *Zen Dust*, p. 175. Wu is of the opinion that syncretism accelerated the downfall of the House of Fa-yen (*The Golden Age of Zen*, p. 241).

108. See Ch'en, *Buddhism in China*, pp. 404–05.

109. Proof by way of direct citation is to be found in Wu, *The Golden Age of Zen*, pp. 242–45.

12

The Sung Period: A Time of Maturation

ZEN AND THE SPIRIT OF THE AGE

The Sung period ranks among the most culturally developed epochs in Chinese history. After the country had recovered, relatively quickly, from the disturbances of the transitional period of the Five Dynasties, the founder of the Sung dynasty, Emperor (former General) Chao K'uang-yin led the kingdom he had conquered and unified into a time of renewed and flourishing growth. To do this, he had to absorb certain losses. The extensive political power of the T'ang period could not be regained. While the emperors of the T'ang had received foreign emissaries and their gifts, the China of the Sung had to pay tribute to the ever-lurking military might of the Khitan state of Liao. The Sung period divides into two parts, known as the Northern Sung (960–1126) and the Southern Sung (1127–1279). During the Southern Sung, the brother of the emperor (who, with his father, Hui-tsung, had been captured in the North) carried on the Sung rule with his followers in the South. The loss of the northern provinces did little damage to the kingdom's cultural well-being; political losses were compensated for by economic growth and an intellectual renewal.

During the Sung period, Chinese civilization attained heights it had known before only during the time of classical antiquity. One may properly speak of a "renaissance," since the general cultural growth was accelerated by a return to the classics. The sciences flourished and a general spirit of inquiry reaped a rich harvest of new knowledge, which in turn fed the fine arts and was illumined by them.

The dominant intellectual movement of the time, known in the West as Neo-Confucianism, contributed to this renaissance by adopting the naturalistic and rationalistic orientation of the classics to confront modernity. The golden age of Buddhism, whose numerous schools had attracted large segments of the Chinese population for half a century with their metaphysical speculations, elaborate rituals, and mysticism, was clearly over. While it is true that the Neo-Confucians of the Sung period found valuable insights in Mahāyāna metaphysics and incorporated some of them into their own systems, for the most part they rejected Buddhism despite the profound stimulus it had provided to Chinese thought.

After Emperor Wu-tsung's great persecution (845), Buddhism lived on in only two movements, the meditational school of Zen and the mainly popular school of the Pure Land. To the Zen monasteries of this period fell the responsibility of representing the Buddhist heritage at a higher level, and from them

flowed intellectual and artistic currents greatly enhancing the culture of the
Sung period. In its response to the "spirit of the times," Zen was also able to
define its own self-image.

Prior to the Sung period, Zen consisted mainly of the Five Houses. The
houses of Kuei-yang and Fa-yen did not survive into the new epoch. During the
second half of the Sung period, the masters of the Yün-men line received greater
recognition. Hsüeh-tou Ch'ung-hsien and Ch'i-sung are among the most highly
esteemed masters of their time.[1] The House of Ts'ao-tung, which had declined
rapidly after its great achievements during the T'ang period, seemed to have a
very dubious existence at the beginning of the Sung period; as the period progressed, however, the Ts'ao-tung line revived.

It was the House of Lin-chi that was dominant among Zen schools during
the Sung period. This house, which was to continue in Japan as the Rinzai
school, entered the Sung period under the leadership of Fen-yang Shan-chao
(947–1024). His successor was Shih-shuang Ch'u-yüan (986–1039), whose two
disciples Yang-ch'i Fang-hui (992–1049) and Huang-lung Hui-nan (1002–1069)
established the two lines that have made up the Rinzai school since the Sung
period.

The reduction of the Zen movement to two or three schools in no way
affected the number of its adherents. On the contrary, as the Rinzai school
quickly covered the land with its monasteries, the number of Zen monks grew
markedly. But this growth in numbers was not always accompanied by a growth
in the depth and authenticity of religious experience. Indeed, the rapid outer
growth occasioned an inner decline that, in the end, brought the very existence
of Zen itself into crisis. The development of the kōan as a methodical way to
enlightenment was intended as a way out of this crisis of inward impoverishment
masked by outward splendor.

Bodhidharma and the great masters of the T'ang era had avoided the capital
and steadfastly resisted the overtures of the imperial court. But during the Sung
period Zen monasteries maintained friendly relations with the court, were often
involved in political affairs, and became focal points in social and cultural life.
As the number of Zen disciples grew, their quality necessarily declined. The
danger of numbers was all the greater since up to this time Zen had known
neither doctrine nor systematic exercises but had been concerned only with
transmitting the Buddha mind through direct experience.

Another danger of the time was an intellectualism that developed more
strongly than ever and, encouraged by certain syncretistic tendencies inherent
in Buddhism as a whole, aimed at a blending of Zen with other sects. Admittedly,
many of the masters of the T'ang period were well versed in the sūtras and
śāstras, but they saw liberation as coming only from experience and instilled in
their disciples the conviction that the experience of enlightenment was superior
to all knowledge of the sūtras. During the Sung period, however, many tried
to forge a union between sūtra knowledge and Zen enlightenment.

As long as it was only a question of the *Avataṃsaka Sūtra*, the danger was
not serious, inasmuch as that sūtra has an intimate relationship to Zen and holds

the key to its distinctive worldview. But efforts toward rapprochement with the highly differentiated and theoretical doctrine of the T'ien-t'ai school were unacceptable to Zen.[2] In confrontation with this school, Zen opposition to sūtra Buddhism occasionally led to the extreme of rejecting all sacred writings. Then too, at first glance, the idea of ties between Zen and Amida Buddhism may seem surprising, given the fundamental differences that separate the two traditions. Here again one senses how deeply Zen is rooted in basic Buddhist tradition—a tradition that may be transcended in enlightenment but never denied.

The Sung period reflects China's traditional love for the written word. Indeed the wealth of distinguished literature that it produced is one of its hallmarks. Zen was unable to extricate itself from this influence. During the Sung period Zen produced the library of important works that give authentic expression to its view of reality. These works present us, as it were, with the paradox of the mystic writ large. Just as the mystic, overwhelmed by the ineffability of his mystical experience, still feels the need to give this experience ever new expressions, so did the Zen of the Sung period, despite its occasional iconoclastic tendencies, give China its richest indigenous expression of Buddhist literature. Genuine Zen literature consists of chronicles, which serve to maintain the tradition, and collections of sayings and kōan, which reveal the exemplary power of the words and deeds of the ancients. On occasion, Zen followers have also written commentaries on the Buddhist sūtras and the classics. Although authentic Zen writings unceasingly affirm the inadequacy of all human words, they also betray their authors' love of the literary. Many of these works not only teach and inspire, they also lay claim on the reader with their beauty and style.

The later phase of the Sung period was a time of general social and cultural decadence and Zen was not exempt from this tendency. No longer do we meet any of the great, creative personalities whose numbers had populated the "Zen forest" during the T'ang period. The catchword of the Sung period was method and system, and the principal importance of this concern was the way it fostered the use of Zen kōan.

KŌAN PRACTICE AND KŌAN COLLECTIONS

Although the practice of using kōan took clear shape during the Sung period, its origins lie further back in Zen history. The "paradoxical words and strange deeds" of the Zen masters of the T'ang period, which were assembled in the Zen chronicles and collected sayings of the Sung period, provide the basic materials for all the classic kōan cases. The historical sources for the kōan are late and rather unreliable; with great literary freedom their authors took up the disconcerting answers and antics of Zen adepts and transformed these words and stories into what we have today—kōan cases and specific aids on the way to enlightenment.

Literally, the word kōan (Chin., *kung-an*) is a combination of graphs that signifies "public notice" or "public announcement." A kōan, therefore, presents a challenge and an invitation to take seriously what has been announced, to ponder it and respond to it. But the special character of this "announcement" confronts the listener or reader with a perplexing puzzle. One becomes confused, and the more one tries to come up with an answer and search for a solution, the more confused one gets. The essence of the kōan is to be rationally unresolvable and thus to point to what is arational. The kōan urges us to abandon our rational thought structures and step beyond our usual state of consciousness in order to press into new and unknown dimensions. This is the common purpose of all kōan, no matter how much they may differ in content or literary form.

We may begin our résumé of the history of kōan practice with the Rinzai master Nan-yüan Hui-yung (d. 930), who was in fact the first to use kōan, confronting his disciples with the words of the early masters in order to bring them to sudden enlightenment. Around this time, or perhaps somewhat later, Zen followers began to gather together the many stories about those early inventive and highly esteemed masters who could bring their students to enlightenment with a word or blow or bizarre gesture. These stories were then arranged in order, provided with clarifying commentaries, and adorned with verse.

The earliest kōan collection is found in the writings of Fen-yang Shan-chao,[3] who did much to revive the spirit of Lin-chi, the founder of his school. The chronicles describe him as an imposing, expansive personality. Among the many students who entrusted themselves to his guidance was Shih-shuang (Tz'u-ming) Ch'u-yüan,[4] who was put through a hard program of training before being named Fen-yang's Dharma heir. Fen-yang's writings were edited by Shih-shuang in a three-volume work entitled *Fun'yōroku* (Chin., *Fen-yang lu*). The work details his devoted discipleship as a follower of his great model, Lin-chi.

Fen-yang's writings are replete with paradoxical and dialectical statements and many other motifs from the *Rinzairoku*. The first book is composed of lectures and practical admonitions, and the third of religious poems and verse. In the second book we find three groups of one hundred kōan each, the most important of which is the first series, which offers one hundred kōan cases from the ancients (Jpn., *juko*), complete with commentaries and verses by Fen-yang. In these stories we hear from Bodhidharma, from the Sixth Patriarch, and from many well-known Zen masters of the T'ang period. The second series is made up of one hundred kōan-questions called *kitsumon* (Chin., *chieh-wen*), which were formulated by Fen-yang himself and clearly show his creative gifts. In the last hundred examples Fen-yang offers his own particular answers (Jpn., *betsugo*) to riddles of earlier times.[5] We should not be surprised to find such a large number of cases at the very beginning of the development of kōan practice. It is estimated that there are in all some 1,700 kōan within the Zen tradition. Nor is it unusual to hear that Master Fen-yang composed so many of them himself. Even today, Zen masters continue to come up with new kōan based on their own experience and dealings with their disciples.

Under Fen-yang's successor, Shih-shuang, the Rinzai school grew in popular esteem and the master himself was highly respected at the imperial court. The *Tenshō kōtōroku*, a work compiled by the nobleman Li Tsun-hsü that laid the foundations for the golden age of Rinzai in the Sung empire, appeared during his lifetime (1036).[6] It is counted among the five authoritative Zen chronicles of the Sung period and contains much kōan material. Shin-shuang's disciples Yang-ch'i and Huang-lung carried on the transmission of the spirit and teachings of Lin-chi faithfully.

Huang-lung Hui-nan, who gathered a dense "forest" of disciples about him, was distinguished by his ingenious use of paradox, as his well-known "three barriers" (Jpn., sankan) show. The following play of question and answer was later passed on as a kōan:

> Question: "All people have their own native place owing to the causal nexus. Where is your native place?"
> Answer: "Early in the morning I ate white rice gruel; now I feel hungry again."
> Question: "In what way do my hands resemble the Buddha's hands?"
> Answer: "Playing the lute in the moonlight."
> Question: "In what way do my feet resemble the feet of a donkey?"
> Answer: "When the heron stands in the snow, its color is not the same."[7]

Although important masters such as Hui-t'ang Tsu-hsin (1025–1100) and Tou-shuai Ts'ung-yüeh (1044–1092)[8] number among the followers of Huang-lung, this branch of Zen disappeared in China before the end of the Sung period. It was brought to Japan by the Japanese Buddhist monk Eisai (1141–1215).

It was in Yang-ch'i's line of the Rinzai school that Zen experienced its greatest development in China. A mild-mannered man who attracted many disciples, Yang-ch'i Fang-hui is the subject of many traditional stories. His second-generation disciple, Wu-tsu Fa-yen (1024–1104) holds a place of prominence.[9] Under him and his immediate successors, the use of the kōan during the Sung period reached its high point.

The first part of Fa-yen's name, Wu-tsu (which has often led to his being confused with another master of the same name), literally means "fifth patriarch." It was given him because he had lived for over thirty years on the famous East Mountain in the region of the Yellow Plum—which also came to be called the "Mountain of the Fifth Patriarch" after the death of the Fifth Patriarch, Hung-jen. Here he carried out his teaching in authentic Zen style. The four kōan in the Mumonkan that deal with him all have a distinctive flavor. In one, he places the student in a typical kōan situation in which there is no exit:

> If you meet a man of Tao on the way, greet him neither with words nor with silence. Now tell me, how will you greet him? (case 36).

Or:

> Even Śākya and Maitreya are his slaves. Who is his?
> (case 45).

The answer could be: "the true human of no rank." He also gives his students this precious case to grapple with:

> To give an example, it is like a buffalo passing through a window. Its head, horns, and four legs have all passed through. Why is it that its tail cannot? (case 38).

A question based on a folk legend invites the student to metaphysical reflection:

Ch'ien-nü and her soul are separated: which is the true one? (case 35).

With Wu-tsu Fa-yen we are truly in the middle of the world of the kōan.

Fa-yen's main disciple, Yüan-wu K'o-ch'in (1063–1135), was a central figure in the kōan Zen of the Sung period.[10] Raised in a Confucian family, from early youth Yüan-wu displayed a strong intellectual curiosity and a phenomenal memory. After studying the Buddhist scriptures in a local Buddhist temple he decided to become a monk and set out on a long pilgrimage that ended at the feet of Master Wu-tsu Fa-yen. But he was only able to entrust himself fully to the master after an initial failure in which a serious sickness, foretold by the master, had broken his proud self-confidence. Under Wu-tsu's guidance he achieved an extraordinarily powerful and enduring experience of enlightenment.

After a short period of temple service, Yüan-wu returned to his home in Szechwan to care for his aged and ailing mother. We later meet him in the monastery of Reisen-in (Chin., Ling-ch'üan-yüan), where he was delivering lectures on sayings and stories from the ancients; the examples he used were to become the core of the famous Hekiganroku collection. He attracted many disciples and won the favor of the Northern Sung emperor Hui-tsung (r. 1101–1125), a lover of art but politically weak. The emperor gave him the purple robe and the title "Zen Master of the Buddha Fruit" (Jpn., Bukka zenji; Chin., Fo-kuo ch'an-shih). When the northern kingdom fell, he escaped to the South where he lived for a time with his disciple and Dharma heir Ta-hui Tsung-kao (1089–1163) in the monastery of Shinnyo-in (Chin., Chen-ju-yüan). There the young Hung-chih Cheng-chüeh (1091–1157) of the Sōtō school visited him to pay his respects and receive instruction. On this occasion, the young guest may have also met Ta-hui, with whom he was later to have a formidable confrontation.

Yüan-wu was also highly regarded by Emperor Kao-tsung (r. 1127–1162) of the Southern Sung, who honored him with the title "Zen Master of Full Enlightenment" (Jpn., Engo zenji; Chin., Yüan-wu ch'an-shih), the title by which he is known in Zen history. He passed his final years surrounded by his disciples in a local monastery in Szechwan. When he was preparing for death he wrote the following lines at the request of his disciples:

My work slipped off into the night,
For you no pretty song took flight.
The hour is here; I must away.
Fare ye well! Take care aright![11]

Yüan-wu K'o-ch'in never matched the creative originality of the great Zen masters of the T'ang period, but his own special gifts found a fitting outlet in the kōan collection that he co-authored and brought to completion, the Hekiganroku, or Blue Cliff Record.[12] He recognized the high quality of the cases and verses that Hsüeh-tou of the friendly House of Yün-men had gathered and used them as the foundation for his own collection. From the thorough and intensive way in which he assembled and interpreted these cases, the most significant collection of kōan in all of Zen took shape. The collection contains a hundred cases. The two basic texts—the cases (either episodes or accounts of experiences of enlightenment) and the verses—were drawn from Hsüeh-tou. To these Yüan-wu added notes and a commentary for each text. Thus a kōan case from the *Hekiganroku* collection consists of seven parts: an introduction, case, notes, commentary on the case, verse, notes, and commentary on the verse.

In the verses, Hsüeh-tou shows himself to be a highly gifted poet. Yüan-wu's notes are pointed, often ironic, and always right on the mark; they stir one's interest and attention. The selection of one hundred cases is exquisite. In the rich variety of their content and expression they present the essence of Zen. No systematic ordering is intended, as that might cramp the free movement of the spirit. At the beginning, a few representative pieces are offered: Bodhidharma's meeting with Emperor Wu, culminating in Hsüeh-tou's verse, "Holy truth—open expanse!" (case 1); Chao-chou's remark on the opening verse of the *Shinjinmei*, "The real Way is not difficult. It only abhors choice and attachment" (case 2); and the third case concerning the great master of the T'ang period, Ma-tsu. To read the *Blue Cliff Record* in its given sequence and be guided by the spirit and imagination of the lively commentary Gundert has provided is to find a sure, albeit not easy, entrance into one of the foremost examples of religious world literature.

What happened to the *Hekiganroku* in China is not entirely clear. It met with great acclaim when it was first published during the lifetime of Yüan-wu (1128), only later to fall prey to the fanatical zeal of his successor, Ta-hui Tsung-kao, who burned every copy of the work he could find and destroyed the printer's blocks. As a result, the work fell out of use until some two hundred years later, when the lay Buddhist Chang Ming-yüan gathered together all available copies and brought out a new edition in 1300. It is not known precisely what motivated Ta-hui to act as he did. Miura and Sasaki surmise that he was afraid the work made things too clear and thus would present an obstacle to Zen practice.[13] Gundert also excludes any "base motivation" and blames Ta-hui's decision on an unruly, unbridled temperament. As we have seen, "opposition to written tradition . . . is rooted in the essence of Zen."[14] Perhaps it was the work's own "beauty of expression" that had destined it to the flames.[15] In any case, the whole event, difficult as it is to understand, underlines the fact that Zen allows no written work, no matter how profound and polished, to take the place of practice and experience. The eventual republication of the *Hekiganroku* gave rise to a long string of commentaries in both Chinese and Japanese.

Our knowledge of kōan practice in the Sōtō school is limited. The dialectical design of the Five Ranks was taken over into the kōan method and increasingly employed in Zen practice. The line of Ts'ao-shan Pen-chi, in which the Five Ranks came to full expression, had disappeared early on. The Sōtō school was carried on under the direction of Tung-shan's disciple, Yün-chü Tao-ying (d. 902), though tradition has it that his master had not entrusted him with the Five Ranks. Yün-chü was named after the mountain location of the monastery where he was active for more than thirty years within a large community of followers. Cases of enlightenment played an important role in the guidance he provided his disciples. We do not know whether his early successors in the Sōtō school took a stance against the use of kōan. The Sōtō masters T'ou-tzu I-ch'ing (1032–1082) and Tan-hsia Tzu-ch'un (d. 1119) both edited kōan collections of one hundred cases.[16]

During the Sung period it was Hung-chih Cheng-chüeh (1091–1157) who put the Sōtō school in the limelight. Hung-chih's visit to Yüan-wu, mentioned above, suggests that at least in his early years he was not opposed to the kōan practice of the Rinzai school. As a master he earned recognition and attracted a large following. Because of his success in restoring religious discipline after the decline it had suffered during the disturbances of the previous century, he came to be known as the "Patriarch of the Renewal of Mount T'ien-t'ung." He lived on this mountain for some thirty years,[17] and for this reason the sources sometimes call ihim T'ien-t'ung Cheng-chüeh. His literary gifts are evident in his two collections from the ancients, each a hundred cases with accompanying verses, Juko hyakusoku (Chin., Sung-ku pai-tse) and Nenko hyakusoku (Chin., Nien-ku pai-tse), both of which enjoyed great popularity in his school.[18] His understanding of Zen practice differed from that of his colleague from the Rinzai school Ta-hui Tsung-kao, who engaged him in a rather bitter controversy. The question whether Cheng-chüeh's views disagreed only with those of his opponent or whether he was also in opposition to the great masters of the T'ang period remains moot.

The second largest kōan collection of the Sung period is known by its abbreviated title, the Shōyōroku (Chin., Ts'ung-jung lu). It appeared about one hundred years after the Hekiganroku and was modeled after it.[19] The work was assembled by the Sōtō master Wan-sung Hsing-hsiu (1166–1246), a member of the line of Yün-chü but not a direct successor to Hung-chih. The basis of his work was a group of one hundred cases and verses from Hung-chih Cheng-chüeh's Juko hyakusoku. He lectured on Hung-chih's work at the small monastery of Shōyō-an, the "Hermitage of Composure." Between the text of the cases and their verses he inserted intermediary notes, giving a fivefold structure to each kōan. Five cases were taken from sūtras, but the greater part of the collection is made up of cases from the masters of the T'ang period and from the Five Houses. The same names and sometimes the same episodes and words found in other kōan collections appear in Wansung's collection. Often the Keitoku dentōroku serves him as a source. Wansung's rather formidable volume first appeared in 1224, nearly a century after the Hekiganroku. The cases of the Shōyōroku have become part of Zen's kōan tradition.

The Mumonkan, a collection of "forty-eight cases of enlightenment of the Buddhas and patriarchs," appeared at the end of the Sung period (1229) and represents the most mature of the kōan collections.[20] This volume has its own independent character, different from every other in the genre. With an evident disregard for literary quality, the cases use short, unembellished sentences to enter directly into what is essential, to what makes the kōan what it is. Each case consists of only three parts (in addition to the title): the text of the case, a critical commentary by Master Wu-men, and the verse, which is less a poem than a simple pair of loosely linked lines. The main contents of the kōan are given clear and thematic expression. Many of the episodes, conversations, and dicta appearing in the forty-eight cases are very well-known in Zen history.

The *Mumonkan* is the work of a single editor, Master Wu-men Hui-k'ai (1183–1260), a successor of Wu-tsu Fa-yen from the Yang-ch'i line of the Rinzai school. He does not, however, belong to the well-known line carried on by Wu-tsu Fa-yen's famous successors Yüan-wu K'o-ch'in and Ta-hui Tsung-kao, but to an historically somewhat obscure branch referred to in the *Mumonkan* only through mention of Yüeh-an Shan-kuo,[21] whose eyes, Master Wu-men tells us, were like meteors and whose acts like lightning (case 8).

In Wu-men Hui-k'ai, the Dharma heir of Yüeh-lin Shih-kuan (1143–1217), we have another powerful thirteenth-century representative of Lin-chi's Chinese Zen. Wu-men's practice was shaped through and through by the use of kōan. The intensity of his own enlightenment is evident in the following verses composed in the afterglow of his experience:

A thunderclap under a clear blue sky!
All beings on earth have opened their eyes.
Everything under the sun has bowed at once.
Mount Sumeru jumps up and dances the *san-t'ai*.[22]

His work is the direct expression of his own experience. In his foreword he testifies to the close bond between this sacred text and his personal life:

> In the summer of the first year of Shao-ting [1228], I, Hui-k'ai, was the head of the monks at Lung-hsiang in Tung-chia. The monks begged me for instruction. Finally I took up the kōan of ancient masters and used them as brickbats to knock at the gate in guiding the monks in accordance with their capabilities and types. I have noted down these kōan and they have now unwittingly become quite a collection. There are now forty-eight of them, which I have not arranged in any order. I will call the collection the *Mumonkan*, "The Gateless Barrier."[23]

In his postscript, Wu-men Hui-k'ai explains his title, *The Gateless Barrier*, by appealing to the Zen master Hsüan-sha Shih-pei (835–908), a disciple of the famous Hsüeh-feng I-ts'un at the end of the T'ang period. "Have you not heard," he writes, "what Hsüan-sha said, 'No-gate is the gate of emancipation; no-mind is the mind of the man of Tao'?"[24] Emancipation and selflessness are the two terms that best characterize the religious efforts of Zen masters in their approach to the *Mumonkan* collection. To the Zen student, seeking enlightenment by selfless, spontaneous practice, they show the no-gate that leads to emancipation. Hui-k'ai was in the prime of his life when the *Mumonkan* was first published. His biography reports his later residence in various monasteries. He received numerous tokens of esteem from the emperor of the Southern Sung dynasty, including the title "Zen Master of the Buddha Eye."

A rich and concentrated masterpiece, the *Mumonkan* has also met with extraordinary success and received widespread attention in the West.[25] Although the *Mumonkan* differs markedly from the *Hekiganroku*, both collections are considered the primary representative expressions of the Zen kōan.[26] The difficult task of translation is aided by detailed Japanese commentaries that clarify complex expressions or popular usages. Given their deep linguistic roots in China, these collections stand as a challenge and opportunity for professional Sinologists— at least for those who have not limited their scholarship to the Chinese classics.[27] Japanese Zen masters make rather free use of the kōan, according to their particular understanding of Zen.[28] More than any other writings in Zen literature, these kōan texts have been approached and analyzed from a vast array of perspectives and have presented scholars with the challenge of deepening and enriching our understanding of the Zen experience.

ASPECTS OF THE KŌAN METHOD

In assessing kōan practice, one should keep in mind that one is dealing with a method that leads to enlightenment, not with enlightenment itself. In this regard it is worth recalling the distinction that the Japanese Buddhist scholar Ui Hakuju, commenting on the development of Zen, drew between "doctrine" and "aids" on the way to enlightenment. "Doctrine" he takes to refer to the theoretical material of the sūtras, while "aids" refers to the paradoxical words and actions, the beatings and shoutings, and the kōan method.[29] He finds both elements present in Zen from the beginning. Prior to Ma-tsu and the great masters of the T'ang period more emphasis was placed on doctrine and less on aids, but the opposite became the case as time went on. According to Ui, however, it would be misleading to judge Zen on the basis of the relationship of these two elements, since both have no more than a relative value in the Zen scheme of things. The importance of the aids is often inflated among followers of Zen precisely because they are so distinctively Zen. This easily leads to a depreciation of basic Buddhist teachings. Finally, Ui points out that the two elements are by no means mutually exclusive, but that each actually conditions the other: aids are rooted in Buddhist doctrine and presuppose it, while many doctrinal statements are used as kōan exercises.

Kōan practice became an essential element of Zen self-understanding. Far from being just one practice alongside many others, kōan practice is as important as "sitting in meditation" (*zazen*). Not a few Zen masters, both past and present, have argued that without kōan practice it is impossible to come to deeper realization. But although kōan practice belongs to the essence of Zen, this practice did not develop with the T'ang masters but during the Sung period, when there were already signs that the energy of the Zen movement had begun to decline. If the early Zen masters had reached enlightenment spontaneously out of their own original insights, Zen now had a suitable and effective method by which anyone could attain enlightenment with relative certainty. D. T. Suzuki's assessment of this development is most perceptive:

Aristocratic Zen was now turned into a democratic, systematized, and to a certain extent, mechanized Zen. No doubt it meant to that extent a deterioration; but without this innovation, Zen might have died out a long time before. To my mind it was the technique of the kōan exercise that saved Zen as a unique heritage of Far Eastern culture.[30]

The usual way to answer the question of what a kōan is is to offer a few typical examples. In the preceding pages, we have already met with kōan of different kinds—cases of enlightenment, conversations, strange happenings, paradoxical sayings of the Zen masters, as well as dialectical formulas—and have pointed out the kōan-like features of these various literary forms. The function of a kōan is to serve as a means on the way to enlightenment. They are not ends in themselves, nor do they make any claim to express the inexpressible. As Master Wu-men remarks in his preface to the Mumonkan, kōan are like "bricks to bang on the door with."[31] This functional character of the kōan does not preclude the possibility of defining them; it only makes clear that it is their function that is decisive, and that this can be expressed in many different ways.

The procedure is more or less as follows: The master gives the student a kōan to think about, resolve, and then report back on to the master. Concentration intensifies as the student first tries to solve the kōan intellectually. This initial effort proves impossible, however, for a kōan cannot be solved rationally. Indeed, it is a kind of spoof on the human intellect. Concentration and irrationality—these two elements constitute the characteristic psychic situation that engulfs the student wrestling with a kōan. As this persistent effort to concentrate intellectually becomes unbearable, anxiety sets in. The entirety of one's consciousness and psychic life is now filled with one thought. The exertion of the search is like wrestling with a deadly enemy or trying to make one's way through a ring of flames.[32] Such assaults on the fortress of human reason inevitably give rise to a distrust of all rational perception. This gnawing doubt, combined with the futile search for a way out, creates a state of extreme and intense yearning for deliverance. The state may persist for days, weeks, or even years; eventually, the tension has to break.

This psychic process may be compared to shooting an arrow from a tightly drawn bow. In his renowned Zen in the Art of Archery, Eugen Herrigel gives the process a fitting psychological description. He explains his problem to the master:

When I have drawn the bow, the moment comes when I feel: unless the shot comes at once I shan't be able to endure the tension. And what happens then? Merely that I get out of breath. So I must loose the shot whether I want to or not, because I can't wait for it any longer.

To this the master replies:

The right shot at the right moment does not come because you do not let go of yourself. You do not wait for fulfillment, but brace yourself for failure. So long as that is so, you have no choice but to call forth something yourself that ought to happen independently of you, and so long as you call it forth your hand will not open in the right way—like the hand of a child. Your hand does not burst open like the skin of a ripe fruit.[33]

As in archery so also in the kōan exercise, everything depends on the proper attitude. Only when the attentive mind is relaxed, free from purpose and ego, and fully devoted to the task can it open up of itself.

In his early works Suzuki describes this psychological process in terms of the law of accumulation, saturation, and explosion.[34] Although the psychological concept underlying this model may be partly outdated, it helps to clarify the process and to reveal the danger inherent in it. Accumulation and saturation, when they are in a state of high tension, can by themselves do great harm. An even greater danger is that of premature explosion, more like the detonation of a bomb than the opening of the skin of a ripe fruit. There are plentiful examples from the past and the present showing how the practice of kōan can lead to a bad end. It is not without good reason that Zen masters sound their warnings. The suppression of reason can throw one's psychic life out of balance. As with the therapeutic processes of modern psychiatry, the inviolable dignity of the person sets limits to the use of the kōan. The two processes are not dissimilar. In the Zen practice called "private interview" (dokusan), in which the student makes a progress report to the master, situations may arise that are like those that can take place in the psychotherapist's office. The student utters broken, incoherent words and gives expression to other spontaneous reactions.[35]

The structure of the kōan led C. G. Jung to identify the "great liberation" in Zen with the emancipation of the unconscious.[36] Under the enormous psychological strain of trying to force a solution for the insoluble kōan, enlightenment is experienced as the dawn of a new reality in which the boundaries between the conscious and the unconscious disappear, so that conscious and unconscious alike are laid open. The Zen disciple realizes the totality of human nature in its primal unity, prior to all discrimination and division. Jung's analysis can shed light on the psychological structure of kōan practice.

It was especially because of its psychological implications that the kōan method of Zen stirred up great interest when it became known in the West. There is ample support for such psychological interpretations in the history of Zen during the T'ang and the Sung periods. Of course, we cannot be sure just how much the Zen masters themselves recognized or intended the psychological effects of their methods. Their main concern was to bring their disciples to a genuine experience, and that experience necessarily implied a break with the student's ordinary state of consciousness. The masters knew only too well that their students were imprisoned by the world of things around them, rendering homage to a naive realism and convinced that the knowing subject perceives and knows the world of objects. The jolt produced by the kōan can shake students from this state of consciousness and propel them into a sudden awakening that will help them move from a world of multiplicity to a world of oneness. In their essence, therefore, the kōan are grounded in Mahāyāna's unitive vision of reality.

The connection between kōan and Mahāyāna, clear from the beginning, was later elaborated and illuminated by the systematization of the cases into categories in the school of Hakuin (1685–1768). In this regard, Ruth Fuller Sasaki has observed:

> The kōan is not a conundrum to be solved by a nimble wit. It is not a verbal psychiatric device for shocking the disintegrated ego of a student into some kind of stability. Nor, in my opinion, is it ever a paradoxical statement except to those who view it from outside. When the kōan is resolved it is realized to be a simple and clear statement made from the state of consciousness which it has helped to awaken.[37]

This state of consciousness grasps the unity of reality as Mahāyāna understands it. The purpose of practice is to clear away every trace of duality. All the kōan are meant to serve this same purpose. Thus the metaphysical and religious role of the kōan in Zen Buddhism is every bit as important as its psychological structure.

During the early period of Zen history there was no established method for using kōan. In the reports that have come down to us from the Sung period there are indications of beginnings, and even of well-formed patterns, of stylization. We can notice, for instance, differences in accent corresponding to the different styles of the various masters. A frequent practice was to determine some kind of device that would serve as a focus for the practitioner's attention and energies. The kōan would be compressed, as it were, into a single word, which the students would then take along wherever they went, constantly mulling it over in their consciousness. The classical example of this is the word *nothing* (Jpn., *mu*; Chin., *wu*) in the first case in the *Mumonkan*, a word that was meant to lead the student beyond objective reasoning and toward ultimate unity.

The dialogue between master and disciple—an indication of their close relationship—also plays an important role in Zen Buddhism. This relationship represents an integral part of Asian religious culture in general. In India, the spiritual guide or guru exercised great influence; in ancient China, there was the teacher of wisdom, who was also the teacher of practical living. All this indicates that from the beginnings of Zen Buddhism a close master-disciple relationship was fostered. This relationship became especially evident in the development of methods for kōan practice during the Sung period. Since the time of Hakuin and his disciples, the "private interview" or institutionalized conversation between master and disciple known as *sanzen* in the Rinzai sect and later also as *dokusan*, also became part of standard kōan practice.[38] The interview was surrounded with much ceremony, and during special periods of practice would take place once a day, sometimes more. In these private interviews students would give an account of their experiences, both positive and negative. Hence, they served as a preventive device against dangerous deviations.

Martin Buber was strongly impressed by the master-disciple relationship in Zen and gave special attention to those kōan that centered around some form of interaction between master and disciple. The depth of insight that he perceived in these kōan allowed him, he felt, to compare them to the "legendary anecdotes" of Hasidism.[39] The similarity is really only external. The main concern of the kōan is concentration, irrationality, and nonduality, while Jewish rabbis seek to make their students aware of another, hidden Thou. The literary genre and aims are completely different.[40]

The use of kōan in Zen Buddhism is a unique phenomenon in the history of religion; nothing like it exists in other religious traditions. Developed in China, kōan testify to an authentically Chinese mentality, particularly in the way they are rooted in real life. If Zen can be called the Chinese expression of Buddhism, then kōan are the most Chinese dimension of Zen. There are of course different ways to understand the practice of the kōan, just as individual kōan allow for different interpretations. Witness the Zen practitioners of the Sung period themselves, whose whole lives revolved around the kōan and who contended fiercely with one another regarding their proper use.

THE TWO MAINSTREAMS OF ZEN

Two focal figures mark the middle of the Sung period: Ta-hui Tsung-kao,[41] Yüan-wu's Dharma heir who was the staunch defender of authentic kōan practice in the Rinzai school, and Hung-chih Cheng-chüeh,[42] who guided the Sōtō school on its path of enlightenment. Though friends, the two men differed in their notion of what constituted proper Zen practice. Hung-chih was possessed of considerable poetic talent and produced an important literary work. He loved sitting in meditation and committed himself zealously to the practice. The kōan collection he edited indicated that he both knew and valued kōan practice,[43] though in his preaching and writing he urged a form of practice that scarcely mentions the kōan. As his method grew in popularity and began to attract a large following, it aroused the opposition of Ta-hui, who warned against this "heterodoxy" that he called "silent-illumination Zen" (Jpn., mokushō zen; Chin., mo-chao ch'an). On Ta-hui's lips the words had a contemptuous ring to them, since as a follower of Lin-chi he rejected all forms of sitting motionless in silence.

Hung-chih responded to the attack. In a short, perceptive work of only 288 characters, entitled The Seal of Silent Illumination (Jpn., Mokushōmei; Chin., Mo-chao ming),[44] he disclosed the true meaning of his Zen way. In his view, silent illumination was the most authentic expression of the tradition that had come down from the Buddhas and the patriarchs: To one who forgets words in silence reality is clearly revealed.[45] Already in this sentence, taken from the beginning of the work, we meet the characters for "silence" and "illumination." Silence is the stillness that grounds the enlightened mind, whose natural ability to "shine" is revealed in silence. Reality reveals itself to those sitting in silent meditation without leading them to look on things as objects of intellection. Enlightenment is like the mirror-quality of the enlightened and resplendent Buddha mind:

> One who has attained silent enlightenment belongs to the house of our tradition; silent enlightenment ascends to the heights and penetrates deep into the abyss.[46]

Ta-hui was resolute in his opposition:

> Recently a type of heterodox Zen (Jpn., *jazen*) has grown up in the forest
> of Zen. By confusing the sickness with the remedy, they have denied the
> experience of enlightenment. These people think that the experience of
> enlightenment is but an artificial superstructure meant to attract, so they
> give it a secondary position, like branches or leaves on the tree. Because
> they have not experienced enlightenment, they think others have not either.
> Stubbornly they contend that an empty silence and a musty state of un-
> consciousness is the original realm of the absolute. To eat their rice twice
> a day and to sit without thoughts in meditation is what they call complete
> peace.[47]

In this well-known passage, which is clearly leveled against Hung-chih's
"silent-illumination Zen," Ta-hui singles out for criticism the passivity of what
he sees as a totally false form of practice. Zen practitioners should not, he argued,
pass their days in lifelessness like "cold ashes or a withered tree." The emptiness
of Zen meditation is not a dead, lifeless emptiness. As much as he could, Hung-
chih rejected these unjust accusations. In the heat of argument, he disdainfully
referred to the one-sided practice of Ta-hui as "kōan-gazing Zen" (Jpn., *kanna-
zen*; Chin., *k'an-hua ch'an*).[48] Both epithets, "silent-illumination Zen" and "kōan-
gazing Zen," though devised as detractions, eventually found their way into
history as designations for the two sharply opposing positions.

The heart of the controversy was the kōan. For Ta-hui, kōan practice was
required of each and every Zen student as the surest path to the attainment of
enlightenment, and he urged his students to persevere zealously in their practice
of the kōan:

> Just steadily go on with your kōan every moment of your life. If a thought
> rises, do not attempt to suppress it by conscious effort, only renew the
> attempt to keep the kōan before the mind. Whether walking or sitting, let
> your attention be fixed upon it without interruption! When you begin to
> find it entirely devoid of flavor, the final moment is approaching, do not
> let it slip out of your grasp. When all of a sudden something flashes out in
> your mind, its light will illumine the entire universe and you will see the
> spiritual land of the Enlightened One fully revealed at the point of a single
> hair, and the great wheel of the Dharma revolving in a single grain of
> dust.[49]

No other Chinese Zen Master understood so completely or promoted so
vigorously the use of kōan as Ta-hui. Kōan were the pivot around which all his
teaching revolved. For Ta-hui, the kōan really allows doubt to break through:

> The thousand and ten thousand doubts that well up in your breast are really
> only one doubt, all of them burst open when doubt is resolved in the kōan.
> As long as the kōan is not resolved, you must occupy yourself with it to
> the utmost. If you give up on your kōan and stir up another doubt about

a word of scripture or about a sūtra teaching or about a kōan of the ancients, or if you allow a doubt about worldly matters to come up—all this means to be joined to the evil spirit. You should not too easily agree with a kōan solution that you have discovered, nor should you think about it further and make distinctions. Fasten your attention to where discursive thinking cannot reach. Make sure that you do not allow your mind to run off, like an old mouse that ran into the horn of an ox.[50]

Enlightenment draws meaning and value from doubt:

Many students today do not doubt themselves, but they doubt others. And so it is said: "Within great doubt there necessarily exists great enlightenment."[51]

What is important for the kōan is not literary beauty or deep intellectual paradox. The kōan makes its central point through doubt. Doubt bores into the mind of the practitioner and leads to enlightenment.

Ta-hui preferred the kōan on "nothing," which in his view was able to cultivate doubt better than any other kōan. He warns against the conscious desire for enlightenment and presses for the removal of all imagination and discursive thought, in order then to recommend expressly the kōan on "nothing":

A monk once asked Master Chao-chou, "Has a dog the Buddha nature or not?" Chao-chou said, "Mu!" (Chin., *wu*).

Ta-hui explains:

This one character is the rod by which many false images and ideas are destroyed in their very foundations. To it you should add no judgments about being or non-being, no arguments, no bodily gestures like raising your eyebrows or blinking your eyes. Words have no place here. Neither should you throw this character away into the nothingness of emptiness, or seek it in the comings and goings of the mind, or try to trace its origins in the scriptures. You must only earnestly and continually stir it [this kōan] around the clock. Sitting or lying, walking or standing, you must give yourself over to it constantly. "Does a dog have the Buddha-nature? The answer: "Mu." Without withdrawing from everyday life, keep trying, keeping looking at this kōan![52]

In stressing the intense practice of the kōan on Mu, Ta-hui appealed to Wu-tsu Fa-yen, the teacher of his own master, Yüan-wu K'o-ch'in. Ta-hui looked back to this pioneer of rigorous kōan practice after having burned the *Hekiganroku*, the work of his own master. Most likely he destroyed the text because he found that its literary beauty was preventing students from the painful struggle with the kōan on nothingness, which for him was the only true kōan.[53]

That this kōan about the absolute nothingness of the Buddha nature that transcends being and nonbeing assumed such an important place in Zen history is due in no small measure to the simple fact that Wu-men Hui-k'ai placed it first in the *Mumonkan*. As mentioned in his preface and postscript, Master Wu-men strongly desired to transcend by negation. This opening kōan, which he entitled "Chao-chou's Dog," is one of the few kōan to which he appended a long commentary. In a powerful demonstration of his own understanding of the kōan, Wu-men locates the essence of the kōan in its ability to stir up doubt. The character *mu* is, as he explains, "the gateless barrier of the Zen school." "Do you not wish to pass through this barrier?" If so,

> then concentrate yourself into this "Mu," with your 360 bones and 84,000 pores, making your whole body one great inquiry. Day and night work intently at it. Do not attempt nihilistic or dualistic interpretations. It is like having bolted a red hot iron ball. You try to vomit it but cannot. . . .
>
> Now, how should one strive? With might and main work at this "Mu," and be "Mu." If you do not stop or waver in your striving, then behold, when the Dharma candle is lighted, darkness is at once enlightened.[54]

Ta-hui's teaching that doubt is an essential element of the kōan remained normative throughout Chinese Zen from the end of the Sung period. Kao-feng Yüan-miao (1238–1295), a respected master from the Yang-ch'i line of the Rinzai school who was active well into the Yüan period (1260–1368), described this sense of doubt in his highly acclaimed text *The Essentials of Zen*.[55] The three essential features are "a great root of faith" (Jpn., *daishinkon*), "a great tenacity of purpose" (Jpn., *daifunshi*), and "a great feeling of doubt" (Jpn., *daigijō*). He compares this feeling to the anxiety of a criminal who is in suspense as to whether the heinous crime will be found out or not. All three essential features are indispensable for success in Zen practice.

The Rinzai school dominated Chinese Zen during the Sung period. By the end of the era it had absorbed all the other houses and lesser movements with the exception of the Sōtō school, where the influence of Hung-chih survived. Historians of Zen Buddhism usually focus on the opposition between Hung-chih's "silent-illumination Zen" and Ta-hui's "kōan-gazing Zen." It is easy to look on the controversy as a continuation of the conflict between the Northern and Southern schools. Indeed, many of the passages in Ta-hui's abusive attacks against the quiet sitting practiced by the disciples of silent illumination are reminiscent of Shen-hui's assaults on the "quietism" of the Northern school. Yet there are serious problems with an approach that tries to divide the whole of Zen history from the time of Bodhidharma to the present into two main opposing orientations. The facts of the matter are much more nuanced.

In the first place, the sources at our disposal are too slanted to supply us with certain knowledge of the teachings and practices of the Northern school. At the same time, our understanding of the Zen school during the Sung period is incomparably clearer and more complete. Hung-chih's position aligns him with the House of Ts'ao-tung, whose founders—Tung-shan, Ts'ao-shan, and Yün-chü—support the Sōtō school. These three masters in turn stand in a continuous line with the great masters of the T'ang period. According to its own self-understanding, the Sōtō school belongs to the Southern school of Chinese Zen and, like all Zen schools, reveres the Sixth Patriarch, Hui-neng. Hung-chih's "silent-illumination Zen" is well rooted in authentic Zen tradition.

The differences in concrete practice between the Rinzai and Sōtō schools are undeniable, and they come up again and again both in the controversy between Hung-chih and Ta-hui and in subsequent tensions. The Rinzai adherents reproach the Sōtō school for its tendencies towards passivity. Only to sit in meditation, they say, dulls the mind into inactivity and engulfs it in a sleepy twilight. This may happen, counter the Sōtō adherents, but is it necessarily the case? Authentic Sōtō teachers cultivate an extremely alert and objectless form of meditation. Moreover, kōan are used in the Sōtō school, albeit not in the same dynamic style as in the Rinzai school. The manner of meditation in Sōtō is more calm, but it certainly does not exclude the experience of enlightenment.

The second criticism that Ta-hui directed against Hung-chih has to do with the experience of enlightenment in Zen (Jpn., satori). The Rinzai school aims at a sudden experience that effects a profoundly reorienting conversion. The quickest and surest way to this kind of experience is through the extreme tension-in-doubt produced by the kōan exercise. Both kōan and satori, say the Rinzai followers, are neglected by the Sōtō school. The criticism is not entirely fair. Sōtō also recognizes sudden enlightenment, for which kōan practice can be extremely helpful; not a few of its masters underwent powerful, shattering experiences. And yet, both satori and kōan practice are understood differently. For the Sōtō school the practice of zazen is primary. In addition it speaks of a quiet experience of depth that is carried through one's daily activities and is in no way inferior to sudden satori. The most outstanding example of this approach of the Sōtō school is Dōgen (1200–1253), the Japanese Zen master who experienced the great enlightenment personally, saw the figure of Buddha during zazen, and taught how to bring this experience into one's everyday life. Far removed from any kind of quietistic passivity, Dōgen was given over constantly to a transcending denial by which he strove for an ever more perfect realization of the absolute.

Despite all the differences and contradictions, the two schools of "silent-illumination Zen" (mokushō-zen) and "kōan-gazing Zen" (kanna-zen) considered one another genuine forms of Zen Buddhism. Documents from the time tell us of friendly, cordial relations between Hung-chih and Ta-hui. When Hung-chih died in the monastery of Mount T'ien-t'ung, which through his persevering efforts had become one of the important centers of Zen Buddhist monasticism, Ta-hui hastened to attend the funeral rites of his deserving colleague, and we can be certain that Hung-chih would not have hesitated to show the same respects to Ta-hui.

In the two movements represented by Hung-chih and Ta-hui we have the two main currents of Zen that were to be transplanted from China to Japan. One bridge reached from Ta-hui, Hui-k'ai, and Kao-feng to the Japanese Rinzai school, where, half a millennium later, Hakuin would be drawn to the teaching on the Great Doubt and the Great Enlightenment and would give kōan practice its definitive form. The other bridge stretched from Hung-chih to Dōgen, who, while wrapped up in his study and trying to lay the foundations for the school of Zen he so highly esteemed, would awaken to the Great Experience under his master, T'ien-t'ung Ju-ching (1163–1228).

In one form or another, tendencies to pluralism are present in every period of the Zen movement. Sometimes they are precipitated by the special personalities of influential masters; often they are the result of particular group orientations or historical circumstances. An incredibly rich variety of practices and types of experience have developed over the ages. That development carries on and is especially productive in our own times; there is no telling where it will lead in the future. But towering over this variegated landscape of the history of Zen are the schools of Rinzai and Sōtō, embodied in the two great figures of Lin-chi and Dōgen. Numerous further developments and new forms fall more or less into one or the other of these two most important expressions of Zen. The divergence, rooted in China, was to become still more pronounced and colorful in the Zen Buddhism of Japan.

NOTES

1. On Hsüeh-tou Ch'ung-hsien, see above, chap. 11, note 98; on Ch'i-sung, see the final section of that chapter.

2. Such efforts were found especially in the House of Fa-yen. See chap. 11, note 105 as well as the final section of that chapter.

3. See the biography of Fen-yang in Zen Dust, pp. 158–59.

4. See the brief biography of Shih-shuang Ch'u-yüan in Zen Dust, pp. 212–13.

5. See the description of the kōan collection in Zen Dust, pp. 335ff.

6. See the section "Lin-chi and his School" in chap. 10; Zen Dust, p. 412.

7. Ninden gammoku, vol. 2; T. 2006, vol. 48, p. 310b. The compiler of the six-volume work (published in 1188) is Hui-yen Chih-chao of the Yang-ch'i line. See Zen Dust, p. 365.

8. See the short biography in Zen Dust, pp. 265–66; see also case 47 of the Mumonkan, "Tou-shuai's Three Barriers."

9. See the biography in Zen Dust, pp. 283ff.; see also my introduction to the German translation of the Mumonkan.

10. See the brief biography in Zen Dust, pp. 161ff.

11. Versified from the German translation of Gundert, Bi-yän-lu I, p. 20.

12. T. 2003, vol. 48. The full title reads Bukka Engo zenji Hekiganroku (Chin., Fo-kuo Yüan-wu ch'an-shih Pi-yen-lu), and comprises 10 volumes. The German translation by W. Gundert in 3 volumes covers sixty-eight of the one hundred cases with explanation; ten cases are covered in S. Ohasama and A. Faust, Zen: Der lebendige Buddhismus in Japan. A three-volume English translation of the work was prepared by T. and J. C. Cleary (London, 1977), and a one-volume edition with commentary by K. Sekida, Two Zen Classics.

13. Zen Dust, p. 357.

14. *Bi-yän-lu* I, p. 24. Suzuki thinks that Ta-hui burned the *Hekiganroku* because he felt "that it was not doing any good to the truthful understanding of Zen. While it is not quite clear what he actually did, the book apparently stopped circulating." *Essays* II, p. 218.

15. This is the view of the Clearys in the introduction to vol. 2 of their translation (see note 12 above), p. xxii.

16. See *Zen Dust*, pp. 171–72.

17. For a brief biography of Hung-chih Cheng-chüeh, see *Zen Dust*, pp. 170–71. Cf. *Zengaku daijiten*, vol. 1., p. 532.

18. The two collections were taken up into the comprehensive nine-volume collection of Hung-chih, *Wanshi zenji kōroku* (Chin., *Hung-chih ch'an-shih kuang-lu*), compiled by the disciples of Hung-chih. They can be found in volumes 2 and 3 of the work, T. 2001, vol. 48; cf. *Zen Dust*, pp. 171–72.

19. T. 2004, vol. 48; regarding this collection, see *Zen Dust*, pp. 425–26.

20. T. 2005, vol. 48. German translations include W. Liebenthal's *Wu-men kuan*, with introduction and notes, and my *Mumonkan: Die Schranke ohne Tor: Meister Wu-men's Sammlung der achtundvierzig Kōan*. English translations include Zenkei Shibayama, *Zen Comments on the Mumonkan*; Kōun Yamada, *Gateless Gate* (Los Angeles, 1979), Katsuki Sekida, *Two Zen Classics*; R. H. Blyth, *Zen and Zen Classics*; vol. 4 (Tokyo, Hokuseidō, 1966); N. Senzaki and Paul Reps, *Zen Flesh, Zen Bones* (Tokyo, 1957); and Sōhaku Ogata, *Zen for the West* (London, 1959), pp. 79–134. A short biography of Wu-men Hui-k'ai is included in *Zen Dust*, pp. 203ff. See also the historical introduction to my translation, pp. 12–32, as well as the list of Japanese commentaries (p. 171), which has in the meantime increased by several titles.

21. See my *Mumonkan*, pp. 57–58; see also p. 17.

22. The *san-t'ai* is a Chinese folk dance. These lines appear in the late Zen chronicle, *Gotō gentō* (Chin., *Wu-teng yen-t'ung*), on which see *Zen Dust*, pp. 430–32.

23. Shibayama, *Zen Comments on the Mumonkan*, p. 9.

24. As Liebenthal points out, by using the expression *mumon* ("no-gate") Master Wu-men was criticizing expressions such as the "gate to *samādhi*," "kinds of emptiness," or "medicines," which were discussed in Chinese Buddhism during the T'ang period and later. Paradoxically, no door but the no-door leads to emancipation. See Liebenthal, *Wu-men-kuan*, pp. 20ff.

25. Witness the uncommonly large number of translations in Western languages. Most recently, Ban Tetsugyū published a modern Japanese edition of the text under the title *Gendai Mumonkan* (Tokyo, 1980). In this comprehensive work of 699 pages, the famous contemporary Zen master attempts to show the timeliness of the kōan collection in readable Japanese.

26. Ōhasama and Faust, *Zen*, and Suzuki, *Essays* III, place the two collections alongside one another.

27. The translation of Liebenthal, a skilled Sinologist who uses only Chinese sources, is distinguished for the fragrance of native Chinese soil that pervades it.

28. Numerous examples of this can be found in the writings of Zenkei Shibayama, Kōun Yamada, Tetsugyū Ban, and others.

29. See his *Zenshūshi* III, pp. 308–20.

30. *Essays* II, pp. 90–91.

31. Dumoulin, *Mumonkan*, p. 35.

32. See Suzuki, *Essays* II, pp. 71–72.

33. E. Herrigel, *Zen in the Art of Archery* (New York, 1971), pp. 33–34.

34. In his early phase, Suzuki's psychological interests came to the fore. His essay on kōan practice in *Essays* II is typical in this regard.

35. Dynamic situations appear in the stories of enlightenment of the early Zen masters, for example of Lin-chi. It is only in later times that we find reports of "private interviews."

36. See his introduction to Suzuki's *Introduction to Zen Buddhism*, also included in C. G. Jung, *Collected Works*, vol. 11 (London, 1969), pp. 538–57.

37. These remarks appear in her foreword (pp. xi–xii) to *The Zen Kōan*, by Isshū Miura and R. F. Sasaki (New York, 1965). The foreword, which also appears in *Zen Dust*, has been altered there and the passage cited omitted. Even though the passage does not completely solve the problem of the kōan, it is worthy of note.

38. See *Zen Dust*, pp. 15, 28ff.

39. See his *Schriften zum Chassidismus*, vol. 3 of his collected works (Munich, 1963), pp. 993ff; also pp. 883–94.

40. See the confrontation between Gershom Scholem and Martin Buber, especially the former's *Judaica* (Frankfurt, 1963), pp. 205–06.

41. See the brief biography in *Zen Dust*, pp. 163ff.

42. See notes 17 and 18 above.

43. Regarding the two kōan collections he compiled, see note 18 above.

44. Included in T. 2001, vol. 48, pp. 100a,b. The text has been reprinted almost in its entirety in Mochizuki's *Bukkyō daijiten*, vol. 5, p. 4870. Nukariya Kaiten includes the text of the *Mokushōmei* in his section on Hung-chih. See his *Zengaku shisōshi [A History of Zen Thought]* (Tokyo, 1923), vol. 2, pp. 355–62.

45. From the *Mokushōmei*. As Nara Yasuaki states, the zazen of the Sōtō school, in contrast to Indian *dhyāna*, is objectless and timeless. "The self is in the here and now in its 'suchness.' Practice that truly makes central this sort of letting go of the self in its suchness was called in China 'silent illumination Zen' *(mokushō zen).*" Dogen's zazen, according to Nara, is to be understood in terms of the silent illumination of Hung-chih Cheng-chüeh. See his section on the Sōtō school in *Zenshū [The Zen School]*, vol. 6 of a series of studies on Japanese Buddhism called *Nihon bukkyō kiso kōza* (Tokyo, 1979), p. 55.

46. From the *Mokushōmei*.

47. From the collection of sayings of Ta-hui, *Daie goroku* (Chin., *Ta-hui yü-lu*), T. 1998, vol. 47, p. 901c. A description of the thirty-volume collection appears in *Zen Dust*, pp. 409–10. Yanagida has translated this famous passage into Japanese in his *Chūgoku zenshūshi*, pp. 99–100. See also the rather free translation of Suzuki in *Essays* II, p. 25–26.

48. The compound *kanna* is made up of *kan*, which means seeing; and *na*, which is the same as *wa*, an abbreviation for *watō*, another name for kōan. See my *The Development of Chinese Zen*, p. 40.

49. Cited from *Essays* II, pp. 103–04, 333–34.

50. Cited from his collected sayings, T. 1998, vol. 47, p. 930a; a Japanese translation appears in *Chūgoku zenshūshi*, p. 99. See Suzuki's free translation in *Essays* II, pp. 333–34.

51. T. 1998 vol. 47, p. 886a; *Chūgoku zenshūshi*, p. 100; see also *Essays* II, pp. 102–04.

52. T. 1998 vol. 47, p. 921c; *Chūgoku zenshūshi*, pp. 101–02.

53. Yanagida cites a passage from the collected sayings of Wu-tsu (Jpn., *Goso Hōen goroku*; Chin., *Wu-tsu Fa-yen yü-lu*; T. 1995, vol. 47) in which the master speaks to his disciples like this: "How do you really practice the kōan usually? I believe it is enough to repeat *mu* over and over earnestly. Once you have appropriated this one simple character, no one in the world can take it from you. Is there one among you who can do this? If so, let him step forth and answer! I demand of you neither that you say 'yes' [being] nor that you say 'no' [nonbeing]. Nor do I demand that you say 'neither being nor nonbeing.' What do you answer now?" Cited in *Chūgoku zenshūshi*, pp. 102; T. 1995, vol. 47, p. 665b.

54. Shibayama, *Zen Comments on the Mumonkan*, p. 38.

55. See *Chūgoku zenshūshi*, pp. 103–04. For an English rendering of the passage on the three essentials of Zen, see *Zen Dust*, pp. 246–47. The expression "ball of doubt" (Jpn., *gidan*; Chin., *i-t'uan*), one of Zen's favorites, appears already in the enlightenment verses of Lo-han Kuei-ch'en (867–928), whose disciple Fa-yen Wen-i founded the House of Fa-yen. At the moment of enlightenment, Lo-han Kuei-ch'en writes, "My ball of doubt, fright-shattered, fell to the ground with a crash." (*Zen Dust*, p. 247).

13

Developments in Culture and Society

THE "FIVE MOUNTAINS" AND "TEN TEMPLES"

Zen Buddhism reached the heights of its cultural development during the time of the Northern and Southern Sung dynasties (960–1126, 1127–1279). Across the land Zen monasteries housed large communities of monks and attracted visitors in considerable numbers. Religious practice, as we have seen, was characterized principally by the use of kōan. Both because of their religious influence on the people and because of their cultural significance, the monasteries enjoyed the favor of the imperial court and the ruling classes. Already from its early history, Chinese Buddhism had maintained contact with imperial circles. From the time of the Six Dynasties (265–580) through the short period of the Sui (581–618) and up to the middle of the T'ang period (618–907), the protection and control of political powers aided the widespread and vigorous development of the schools of T'ien-t'ai, San-lun, and Hua-yen, as well as that of esoteric Buddhism and Amitābha piety. The unrest brought about by the rebellion of An Lu-shan, however, greatly weakened these schools, until almost a century later they were practically wiped out in the general Buddhist persecution of 845. In the case of Zen, only rarely during its early history do we hear of special relationships between the imperial court and individual Zen monks or their communities, as for example during the conflict between the Northern and Southern schools. The Zen of the Patriarchs managed very well without political patronage, and the illustrious masters of the second half of the T'ang period promoted an authentic Zen movement out of their own dynamism.

With the onset of the Sung period things changed. As the number of monasteries and monks increased, the good graces and help of the court became much desired commodities.[1] Already during the period of the Northern Sung dynasty, organizational regulations were issued granting special privileges to certain monasteries in the imperial city and other important cities. Country temples clustered around the urban centers. With the downfall of the Northern Sung dynasty, Ta-hui and his master, Yüan-wu, moved from monasteries in the North to those in the South. The leading figure in Zen Buddhism during the period of the Southern Sung dynasty, Ta-hui, came to enjoy considerable influence at the imperial court.

At this time Zen attained a politically privileged position that, although it provided a great deal of security, also meant some degree of state control. The privileges were part of an arrangement unique in the history of Zen—the legal establishment of the so-called Five Mountains and Ten Temples (Jpn., *gozan jissetsu*).[2] Yanagida cites the description of a monk from the Ming period:

> For anyone who wanted to learn Zen during the early days of the Sui and T'ang dynasties, there were no places specially set aside for practice. Residences were rented from the Vinaya monasteries. During the time of the Northern Sung dynasty some very impressive Zen monasteries were built, but as yet there was no grading of monasteries, even though the monasteries in the capital cities enjoyed special privileges. Gradation began during the period of the Southern Sung Dynasty, when the system of the Five Mountains and Ten Temples was established.[3]

The privileged temple complexes, together with their smaller ancillary monasteries, all belonged to the Yang-ch'i line of the Rinzai school. The classification and ranking of the monasteries brought many advantages; given the large number of monks involved, it also brought with it many unhappy consequences. The strong institutionalization was bound to damage the spirit of Zen. The deterioration that characterized much of the Sung period in general was not without its impact on the quality of Zen life. All this does not, however, diminish the fact that the cultural achievements of the Sung period are among the greatest in the history of China, and that through its openness to the spirit of the times, Zen made a definite contribution to these achievements.

ZEN BUDDHISM AND THE NEO-CONFUCIANS

As we have already seen, China's acceptance of Buddhism—one of the most extraordinary and fascinating phenomena in the history of religion—was facilitated, if not actually brought about, by an extraordinary convergence of Chinese spirituality and this newly arrived religion from India. The fundamental orientation of the two ancient traditions was different, but a deeper, hidden affinity united them and promoted the relatively speedy integration of Buddhism into the spiritual universe of China. Of course, not all the contents of Buddhism could be absorbed in the same way. As it turned out, the Mahāyāna expression of Buddhism was much closer to Chinese thought and sensitivities than was the more complicated and diversified "Small Vehicle" (Hīnayāna).

The centuries-long process of transplantation naturally wrought far-reaching changes within Buddhism. The first generations of indigenous Buddhists initiated a process of sinicization of Buddhism that was completed in the great Chinese schools of Mahāyāna between the fifth and ninth centuries. For a brief period Buddhism was the leading influence in Chinese religious life. Before the end of the T'ang period the splendor of the achievement had faded, paving the way for a second important encounter between Chinese tradition and Buddhism during the Sung period. If China's first acceptance of Buddhist ideas and values was to a great extent made possible by the wisdom teachings of Lao-tzu, it was the Neo-Confucians who opened the way to the second exchange. It may seem strange that a fruitful exchange between two religious traditions as dissimilar as are Confucianism and Buddhism should have ever come about, given the completely different worlds to which the two religious movements appear to belong. These basic differences have frequently been pointed out and amply described by scholars of Chinese culture.[4] Nevertheless, a genuine encounter between these two traditions did take place during the Sung period, which means that advantages accrued to both sides. In order to understand this remarkable occurrence we need to consider two fundamental changes that had taken place during the course of the centuries and that had altered the relationship between Confucianism and Buddhism.

We have already pointed out that during the first stage of its implantation in China, Buddhism met with great sympathy and understanding from the followers of the Tao. The Confucians, meanwhile, convinced that this foreign religion could in no way adapt to the soul of China, regarded Buddhism with strong reservations if not downright hostility. But can the Buddhism of the Sung period be called a foreign religion in China? After centuries of sinicization, had not Chinese Buddhism become something genuinely new? The Zen schools of Mahāyāna, as we have tried to make clear, represent a thoroughly Chinese form of Buddhism. The spiritual roots of the great Mahāyāna sūtras were no small aid in developing the Chinese character of Zen, which is closely tied to the metaphysics of the typically Chinese school of Hua-yen. In Hua-yen the sinicization of Mahāyāna teachings reached its zenith. Hence the Zen Buddhists with whom the Neo-Confucians came into contact were authentically Chinese in their thoughts and feelings. They were Chinese Buddhists, steeped in the spirit of Hua-yen philosophy—very different from the Buddhist disciples of the Pāli Canon.

The second shift that deserves our attention has to do with the spiritual climate of China. Just as Buddhism for its part had to go through a process of change after its arrival in the Middle Kingdom, so did tradition-bound Chinese beliefs and attitudes experience needs that to some extent were caused, or at least occasioned, by Buddhist influence. These needs, which may well be characterized as metaphysical, had long been ignored by Confucianism. Now, challenged by the successful growth of Mahāyāna thought in their own midst, Confucians finally began to make room for metaphysical concerns.

Confucians of the T'ang period, especially Han Yü (768–824) and Li Ao (d. 844), can be considered the precursors of Neo-Confucianism.[5] Consistent with their Confucian bent, both thinkers were opponents of Buddhism, although Han Yü was not without praise for his Buddhist friends. Moreover, because of his mystical leanings, he preferred the Mencius among the classics. Li Ao was greatly taken up with anthropological questions, and in his philosophical explanation of the relation between human nature and human feelings he arrived at conclusions carrying an undeniably Buddhist tinge. In his treatment of the philosopher, Fung Yu-lan points out clear Buddhist influences.[6] If Li Ao complained that his fellow scholars were all "steeped in Taoism or Buddhism," it was because they were pursuing metaphysical interests. Li Ao and his school were convinced that such pressing metaphysical questions—including the "burning question" about attaining Buddhahood—could be properly answered by Confucianism. Fung Yu-lan's comment on this conviction is to the point: "Their [the Neo-Confucians'] aim was to induce men to follow a Confucian type of training which would make of them 'Confucian Buddhas.' "[7]

To try to understand this metaphysical shift within Neo-Confucianism without recognizing the influence of Buddhism would be as misguided as trying to understand the development of Zen without considering the metaphysical foundations of the Mahāyāna sūtras. If the predecessors of Neo-Confucian philosophy were influenced by the surrounding world of Mahāyāna, the main Buddhist influence during the Sung period came from Zen. At some time in their lives all the significant Neo-Confucian thinkers during the Sung period had more or less strong contacts with Zen Buddhists.

In the West, the new direction taken by Confucians during the Sung period is called Neo-Confucianism. In China, it goes by the name School of the Study of the Tao.[8] The Western name stresses the bonds with Master K'ung and early Confucians, while the traditional term stresses its roots in the mainstream of Chinese religion. Certainly, the stimuli coming from both Taoism and Buddhism made essential contributions to the new school. As Fung Yu-lan puts it: "Neo-Confucianism . . . started through the combination of Confucianism with Buddhism."[9] The contacts between the new religious movement and Buddhism are therefore beyond question, or more precisely, there are individual threads in the fabric of Neo-Confucianism that clearly link the new philosophers to particular elements within Zen Buddhism.

We will consider five thinkers who are known as "the five philosophers" of the Sung period: Chou Tun-i (1017–1073), Chang Tsai (1020–1077), Ch'eng Hao (1032–1085), Ch'eng I (1033–1108), and Chu Hsi (1130–1200).[10] We shall begin with Chou Tun-i, who is called the founder of the new Confucian philosophy of the Sung period.[11] While his philosophy takes as its starting point the ancient Book of Changes, his diagram of "the Supreme Ultimate" (t'ai-chi) rests on Taoist foundations.[12] There are clear Buddhist influences in his thought, especially in the way he turned to Zen to satisfy his metaphysical appetites. Our sources preserve the names of five Zen masters with whom he maintained an acquaintance.[13] Although some would call him "a great admirer of Buddhism,"[14] the younger Ch'eng referred to him as a "poor Zen fellow."[15] Regarding his great love of nature, the story is told that he refused to cut the grass in front of his window because he felt an affinity with all living beings.[16]

The biography of Chang Tsai, a relative of the Ch'eng brothers, reports that he studied Buddhism and Taoism for many years. We may assume that he also learned about Zen, although there is no explicit proof of this. We may also assume that his troubled complaints against "the extraordinary power of attraction of Buddhist theories" grew out of concrete experiences and encounters.[17] The most acute danger would certainly have arisen from the flourishing Zen movement. Chang Tsai fought resolutely against Buddhist teachings, which he felt were rife with pessimism and nihilism. It was certainly the Buddhists he had in mind when he wrote, "As for those who speak about nirvāṇa, they mean by this a departure [from the universe] which leads to no return."[18] Firmly opposed to anything that would jeopardize the will to life, he was true to the Confucian motto: "In life I shall serve unresistingly, and when death comes, I shall be at peace."[19] His staunch stand against Buddhism certainly must have influenced the Ch'eng brothers.

During his years of study, the elder Ch'eng Hao, known posthumously as Ming-tao,[20] had closer contacts with Zen than any other Neo-Confucian thinker. When he was fifteen or sixteen his father sent him and his younger brother to the school of Chou Tun-i. He was deeply impressed by the famous scholar, an impression that stayed with him for life but that did not diminish his openness to Zen. Imbued with a religious nature and intuitive powers, he found much in Zen that attracted him. His contacts with Zen were of academic value to him, but also had a fundamental importance for his life. There are clear indications that he studied Buddhism and Taoism for about ten years. Among the Mahāyāna sūtras that he studied, the *Avataṃsaka Sūtra* and the *Nirvāṇa Sūtra* are mentioned by name. Zen also occupied a place in his studies. Unfortunately, we do not know the names of his teachers, although it is a simple matter to make reliable conjectures, for there was no lack of capable teachers in Zen Buddhism at that time. Later, some of Ch'eng Hao's students turned to Zen. We should also mention some of Ch'eng Hao's more personal contacts with Zen. At the death of his mother, he participated in a funeral service at a Zen temple and went away with a lasting impression of the dignified seriousness of Zen religious attitudes. He was a frequent visitor to Zen temples, and we may suppose—though not with certainty—that he also took part in meditation exercises. A lengthy discussion on the Tao that was held by the two Ch'eng brothers and their uncle Chang Tsai in a Buddhist monastery confirmed the participants in their adherence to the teachings of Confucius.[21]

In the philosophical work for which the two brothers are listed as co-authors, "it is difficult to establish differences between their teachings."[22] They agreed essentially in their philosophies," especially regarding "Principle," or *li*. "It was the Ch'eng brothers' own idea to make Principle the central focus of their philosophy."[23] Ch'eng Hao's famous dictum, "The sage conforms to Principle,"[24] captures succinctly the conviction of both brothers. Yet there *were* differences between them, however secondary. Wing-tsit Chan points to a difference of emphasis regarding Principle. While Ch'eng I stressed that one Principle manifests itself in different ways, Ch'eng Hao placed greater emphasis on "the idea of production and reproduction as the chief characteristic of the universe. He saw the spirit of life in all things."[25] In this context, Wing-tsit Chan clarifies the proximity of Ch'eng Hao to Buddhism: "Like the Buddhists, he [Ch'eng Hao] almost exclusively emphasizes the mind. To him, 'Principle and the mind are one.' "[26]

According to Ch'eng Hao, every opposition between the internal and the external must be set aside. Wing-tsit Chan thinks that a method calling for the

overcoming of all duality automatically leads to quietism. Whether this stress on nonduality derives from the influence of Chou Tun-i or of Zen Buddhism is a moot question. Wing-tsit Chan continues:

> We must not forget, however, that he [Ch'eng Hao] looked upon Chou Tun-i's doctrine of tranquility as unbalanced and substituted for it seriousness. Moreover, to him the universe is a great current of production. Whatever quietism there is in him, then, is not Buddhist emptiness and silence but a vital, if gentle and quiet, process.[27]

These comments throw considerable light on the perennial, animated debate regarding quietistic or dynamic forms of meditation within Zen, about which we have had much to say in the course of this volume. The Buddhist overtones in the picture of the universe as a process of constant becoming are evident. For the Zen Buddhists of the Rinzai school, who most likely were Ch'eng Hao's dialogue partners, "emptiness" is identical with the vital and dynamic stream of becoming that makes up reality.

As Fung Yu-lan has shown, Ch'eng Hao stands at the origins of a movement that Neo-Confucianists called the "School of the Study of Mind." The school's actual founder is Lu Chiu-yüan (Lu Hsiang-shan, 1139–1193), who developed his own philosophical position through his conflicts with Chu Hsi.[28] Ch'eng Hao's leanings towards a theory of intuitive knowledge prepared the way for this school, also known as the Idealistic school. The precursor of another tradition, known as the Rationalistic school, which took shape under Chu Hsi was the younger brother Ch'eng I, who, like Neo-Confucians in general, was much influenced by Buddhism in his concern for final metaphysical truth. Very different from his older brother in both temperament and thought, Ch'eng I remained faithful to essential Confucian concerns and pursued an ethical ideal. He was also a hardheaded logician and lover of precise analysis. To his students he was a demanding teacher who commanded respect, but in the end had to accept the fact, to his great disappointment, that "nearly all his students had succumbed, at least temporarily, to the charm of foreign teachings."[29]

In his early years Ch'eng I had acquired a sound grasp of Taoist and Buddhist teachings from his first teacher, Chou Tun-i, and, probably together with his older brother, from Taoist and Buddhist teachers themselves. In his writings he set himself up as an opponent of Buddhism and Taoism. Despite the value he recognized in Buddhism, his final verdict was negative:

> The doctrines of the Buddhists cannot indeed be said to lack wisdom, for they have pressed far into what is lofty and profound. And yet, in the final analysis, they fall into the pattern of egotism and self-seeking. Why do I say this? Within the universe, where there is life there is death, and where there is joy there is sorrow. But wherever Buddhism is, there we must look for unreasonableness. In its talk of escaping from life and death, and of gaining surcease from suffering, it reverts in the end to egotism.[30]

If we give credence to what the Buddhist sources tell us, Ch'eng I in his later years maintained both written and personal contacts with Zen Buddhists, especially with the famous master Hui-t'ang Tsu-hsin (1025–1100) and his Dharma heir Ling-yüan Wei-ch'ing (d. 1117) from the Huang-lung line of the Rinzai school.[31] Under these masters he is said to have taken up Zen practice. It is even reported that in meditation he adopted a posture of *seiza* (Chin., *ching-tso*) different from the usual position of *zazen* (Chin., *tso-ch'an*). We find this form of meditation in other Neo-Confucians, even in Chu Hsi.[32]

Several decades separate the death of the younger Ch'eng and the thinker who brought Neo-Confucian philosophy to full bloom, Chu Hsi. The intervening years were bridged by the disciples of the Ch'eng brothers, who formed the Ch'eng school. Among the numerous disciples of Ch'eng I, four are usually singled out, three of whom Chu Hsi tells us specifically took up the study of Zen Buddhism.[33] These three representatives of the Ch'eng school—Hsieh Liang-tso (1050–1103), Yang Shih (1053–1135), and Yu Tso (1053–1123)—did not make any significant contribution to the development of Neo-Confucianism, but they give a clear indication of the kind of relationship existing at the time between Neo-Confucians and Zen Buddhists.

Hsieh Liang-tso studied with the Ch'eng brothers and was greatly encouraged to meditate by the elder brother. He also engaged in lengthy and deep conversations with Zen masters whom Ch'eng I had already known, especially with Hui-t'ang Tsu-hsin. Yang Shih, a man of strong and reliable character, was praised highly by Chu Hsi.[34] He maintained close relations with the Zen master Tung-lin Ch'ang-tsung (1025–1091), with whom he was fond of discussing nature and mind, the two topics that were dearest to his heart. He greatly revered the teaching of Mencius on the original goodness of human nature, a viewpoint on which Neo-Confucians and Zen Buddhists are in full agreement. Yu Tso received his philosophical training mainly from the younger Ch'eng, devoting himself in later years to the study of Zen. He is said to have had contacts with the Zen master K'ai-fu Tao-ning (1053–1113), a disciple of the famous Wu-tsu Fa-yen from the Yang-ch'i line.

Through its love of meditation and its concern for human contacts, the Ch'eng school created a climate of rapprochement between the two leading spiritual movements of the time. As they looked inward, these Neo-Confucians attempted to understand nature and mind; they read Buddhist writings and in their dealings with Zen masters found themselves greatly enriched. And yet they remained faithful to the philosophical principles of Neo-Confucianism laid out so clearly by the Ch'eng brothers. They also continued to voice criticisms of Buddhism.[35]

With Chu Hsi the philosophy of the Sung period reached full flower. A systematic thinker and eminent scholar of the classics, he gathered together the main insights of the four Confucianist philosophers of the eleventh century whom he recognized as authentic, and on this basis constructed a statement of Confucianist teachings that has remained normative through the centuries and has been used as the official text for state examinations.[36] He has been called a second Confucius,[37] not only because of his complete assimilation of the intellectual heritage of China but also because of the synthesis he achieved between that legacy and the creative impulses of the early phase of Neo-Confucianism. His intellectual roots were in the Ch'eng school, but the Buddhist, especially the Zen Buddhist, elements that were part of the atmosphere of the Sung period also had an impact on his thinking.

It is said that as a boy Chu Hsi had a Zen master as his teacher of Confucianism—none other than the famous Yüan-wu K'o-ch'in.[38] The historical grounds for the claim are flimsy, but we do know that in his early years Chu Hsi was a zealous student of Buddhism and gained a solid knowledge of Mahāyāna teachings through wide reading in Buddhist literature. The main ingredients of this study, which went on for about ten years, included not only Chu Hsi's own reading and direct tutelage under teachers with Buddhist leanings, but also personal acquaintance with Zen Buddhists.[39] Foremost among his acquaintances in the world of Zen was Ta-hui's Dharma heir, K'ai-hsi Tao-ch'ien. Chu Hsi's relation with this master is historically well grounded.[40] We do not know, however, whether or not he was personally acquainted with the famous Ta-hui Tsung-kao himself.[41] In any case, he certainly would have been able to learn Ta-hui's brand of Zen through the master's disciple. It is also possible that he practiced meditation under Tao-ch'ien's guidance and even came to some kind of enlightenment experience.[42]

When Chu Hsi entered the school of Li T'ung (or, Li Yen-p'ing, 1088–1158),[43] who was once a fellow student of Chu's then deceased father, his intellectual development took a sharp turn. Through his own teacher, Lo Ts'ung-yen (1072–1135), Li T'ung was linked with Yang Shih, a representative of the Ch'eng school. A confirmed Confucian, Li T'ung guided the young student, whose devotion to him was wholehearted, away from the enticements of Buddhism and back, with full resolve, into the fold of Confucianism. There were, nonetheless, elements in Li T'ung's own intellectual and personal life that may be called Zen-like. He meditated regularly in the seiza position and sought to purify his mind. These attitudes and practices he passed on to his student Chu Hsi. The great philosopher's own leanings towards meditation are well known, and Zen-like elements marked his lifestyle even in his later years, when he was carrying on a resolute and sharp polemic against Buddhism and Zen Buddhism. Throughout his life Chu Hsi cherished the quiet of meditation and led a simple, monastic way of life.[44]

Throughout his intellectual labors, Chu Hsi remained an unremitting and effective adversary of Buddhism. As mentioned, his knowledge of Buddhism was based not only on books but on personal contacts, especially with Zen Buddhists from among the followers of Ta-hui. It is not at all clear that he fostered a personal animosity towards Buddhists. We do know that he spoke with respect of great Zen masters of the T'ang period like Lin-chi. His summary of the history of Buddhism in China is telling:

Buddhism was introduced in the reign of Ming-ti of the Han dynasty. Prince Ying of Ch'u devoted himself to it, but understanding was deficient. In the time of the Chin and Southern Sung Dynasties, the doctrines of Buddhism spread far and wide. Those who were interested in the new religion first made use of the terms familiar to Lao-tzu and Chuang-tzu. . . . When Bodhidharma came to China between 516 and 534, the other schools seemed to have waned. His new method of teaching Buddhism was to concentrate on the mind without using a textbook. During these periods Confucianism was never studied and was forgotten. The superficiality of the school of Lao-tzu gave Bodhidharma a great opportunity to spread his teaching. He talked in such a clever way that nobody could compete with him. The intelligentsia were fascinated by him. I have seen many portraits of patriarchs of the Ch'an school and they seem to be truly extraordinary personalities.[45]

From these brief comments, it is clear that for Chu Hsi, Buddhism was mainly the Zen school of Bodhidharma. He does not mention the great Mahāyāna systems of T'ien-t'ai, Chen-yen, Pure Land, and so forth, even though he was well acquainted with all of their sūtras. His acquaintance with Buddhism came mainly through the Rinzai school,[46] whose stress on mental concentration he found reminiscent of the teaching of Bodhidharma. It is at this point that he takes up his critique.

For the Buddhists, Chu Hsi argued, mind is only consciousness. Insofar as they thus identify mind with nature, they rob it of its reality:

The Buddhists only grind and rub this mind away down to its finest essence, as if it were a lump of something. Having scraped off one layer of skin, they then scrape off another, until they have scraped to a place where they can no longer scrape. And when they have thus ground away until they have reached the mind's innermost essence, they then hold this to be the nature.[47]

The Buddhist teaching on the identity of nature and the mind, understood in terms of the theory of "consciousness-only," stands in contradiction to Chu Hsi's fundamental notion of the one Principle (li) common to the universe and human nature. "To Chu Hsi, mind is the function of human nature, and human nature is identical with Principle."[48] Principle is concrete reality.

For Chu Hsi, to philosophize meant "the investigation of things" (Chin., ko wu; Jpn., kakubutsu),[49] not "to ground the mind" or to plumb the depth of emptiness. His realism in no way corresponded to the Buddhist metaphysics of "emptiness." Yet the world of Principle is, as he saw it, "pure, empty, and vast. . . . [It] holds no determined place; it has no shape or body." Accordingly, he even admitted that "the Buddhists may have a certain justification for their doctrine of 'emptiness.' "[50] But in his own philosophical position there was no room for the Buddhist view. He contrasts the two perspectives in these terms:

Those [the Buddhists] take the view that the mind is "empty" and has no Principle. These [the Confucianists] hold the view that although mind itself may be "empty," all the myriad different Principles are complete within it.[51]

Li exists in every single thing as the spiritual principle united with material ether *(ch'i)*; in the human person, *li* is nature. Far from being confined to the cosmos, it is also the principle of the formless metaphysical world; it is reason and embraces ethical energies.

A word should be added about Chu Hsi's Confucian contemporary, the philosopher Lu Chiu-yüan.[52] Chu Hsi located his colleague's philosophical views right next to Zen Buddhism and railed against him as harshly as he did against the Zen people. Lu Chiu-yüan's unusual proximity to Zen was due not to any direct or indirect influence of Zen, but to his own early and intimate experience. If we can rely on the biographical data, the gifted Lu Chiu-yüan had begun to ponder the mysteries of existence as a young boy of three, four, or five. He was only eight when he read the *Analects* (Chin., *Lun-yü*; Jpn., *Rongo*) of Confucius. At the age of thirteen he had a kind of unitive vision in which he grasped the identity of the self with all things and the identity of human nature with the universe.[53] While his temperament inclined him against Ch'eng I's way of thinking, he felt a strong attraction to the ideas of the elder Ch'eng. And thus while Chu Hsi pursued, and perfected, the views of Ch'eng I, Lu Chiu-yüan carried on the vision of Ch'eng Hao. During the Ming period (1368–1644) Lu Chiu-yüan's philosophy was taken up again by Wang Yang-ming (or Wang Shou-jen, 1472–1529). The two contrasting orientations are thus known as the Ch'eng-Chu school and the Lu-Wang school.[54]

Mind occupied the central place in Lu Chiu-yüan's thought. His concern was not to analyze things but to comprehend mind. For him mind, which is one and the same in humans and in the universe, is identical with the Tao.[55] While Chu Hsi's philosophy explained reality through neatly distinguished concepts such as Principle *(li)*, matter or ether *(ch'i)*, nature *(hsing)*, and mind *(hsin)*, for Lu Chiu-yüan everything comes together in a single mind. Chu Hsi found this kind of thinking confused. In his opinion, philosophy is not even possible without Principle and conceptual diversity. In a particularly noteworthy passage he criticizes Lu Chiu-yüan, and his most important disciple, Yang Chien (1140–1226), as well as Buddhists and Zen Buddhists, not so much through philosophical arguments as through a lucid characterization of a totally different spiritual and intellectual disposition. He writes:

> Lu Chiu-yüan teaches his pupils to devote themselves to meditation in order to keep the mind to themselves. There is no work to be done in the line of reading, debating, or research. Lu's way is rather simple and direct, so the younger generation is attracted by him. . . . Mind according to Lu consists of sensitivity, responsiveness, and consciousness. . . . If mind in its nature consists merely in sensitivity, responsiveness, and consciousness, then its function is indistinguishable from what can be done by animals. . . . This is what is called by Shun "the mind of man," but not "the mind of Tao." Lu mixes the two, thus committing the same error as Kao-tzu [a philosopher who argued with Mencius] who maintained that nature is born in man. . . . The error is also similar to that of the Buddhists who hold that any sentient being partakes of Buddhahood; or to that of the Ch'an

followers, who believe that water-carrying and wood-cutting are a part of meditation. This same confusion, in the thought of Yang Chien, results in a mixture of mind with human nature, and of the physical with the metaphysical. Yang Chien supposes that heaven (t'ien), Way (tao), or Power (te), though differing in name, are the same thing. This mixing or confusing indicates that the school of Lu neglects the step of investigation of things, or of knowledge-seeking. In other words, it keeps a weighing machine without marks on it, or a measuring-stick without a division of inches.[56]

Despite such stark philosophical differences, the two thinkers maintained friendly relations. After a meeting in the Temple of Goose Lake in 1175, Lu Chiu-yüan composed the following lines:

A child knows how to love and also to respect others as it grows.
The mind is handed down by the sages.
When there is such a foundation, one can build a house on it . . .
Too much interest in commentaries leads one to a thorny path.
Too much attention to questions of detail and to subtleties
Causes one to lose oneself as if in the sea.[57]

And again:

Work easy and simple is in the end lasting and great.
Activities involved and complicated are in the end aimless and
inconclusive.[58]

Chu Hsi could not fully accept these verses. The two men were worlds apart. Lu Chiu-yüan's easygoing approach to life had a Taoist tinge to it and was very close to Zen. Confucians frequently reproached him for his Zen leanings and he was even accused of being a Zen disciple disguised as a Confucian. Is there anything to these criticisms?

The foundation of Lu Chiu-yüan's philosophy is his doctrine of mind. If mind and universe are one, if mind is identical to the Tao, and if human nature is original mind, it is indeed difficult to distinguish his views from those of Zen masters. The only difference is that the Zen masters usually speak of Buddha or Buddha nature instead of the Tao. In Zen, the Tao is the same as the Buddha. The influence of Buddhism, especially of Zen Buddhism, on Lu Chiu-yüan is therefore evident. Regarding his notion of "original mind," however, Lu refers explicitly to Mencius, one of his favorite authorities, whom he cites even more often than he does Confucius. When his disciple Yang Chien asked him about the original mind, he responded: "This knowing mind is your original mind."[59] The fundamental difference between this statement and the viewpoint of Zen is evident.

Lu Chiu-yüan had a high regard for intuitive inner experience. He "advocated the simple, easy, and direct method of recovering one's original good nature."[60] Chu Hsi's words stand in stark contradiction: "Knowledge of Tao cannot be attained by sudden conversion. It proceeds step by step, from the rudimentary to the profound, from the near to the remote."[61] Chu Hsi probably had his counterpart, Lu Chiu-yüan, in mind when he pronounced these words. It is by no means clear, however, that Lu accepted the Zen teaching on sudden enlightenment. He did have dealings with Zen Buddhists, but we know the name of only one Zen Master, Fo-chao Te-kuang (1121–1203), a disciple of Ta-hui, with whom he had some brief contact when he was already fifty years old. It may have been Fo-chao who introduced him to the practice of Zen.[62]

No other Neo-Confucianist thinker during the Sung period stands as close to the teaching of Zen Buddhism as does Lu Chiu-yüan. He was led in this direction both by historical circumstances and by his own temperament. But for all that, he was firmly positioned in the Confucian tradition, which at that time was undergoing a process of revitalization under pressure from Buddhist metaphysics. In spite of all his Buddhist and Zen-like qualities, he remains through and through Confucian.[63] This is most evident in his strong criticism of Buddhist ethics. The following excerpt reproduces the essence of a lengthy passage from his works cited by Wing-tsit Chan:

> I use the two words, righteousness and profit, to distinguish between Confucianism and Buddhism. I also use the terms "public-spiritedness" and "selfishness," but actually they mean righteousness and profit. The Confucianists consider man, living in the world, as more intelligent than the myriad things. . . . This is the basis on which Confucian doctrines have been founded. Therefore we call them righteous and public-spirited. Buddhists, on the other hand, consider man, living in the world, as consisting of a chain of birth and death, a wheel of transmigration, and afflictions resulting from passions. . . . This is the basis on which Buddhist doctrines are founded. Therefore we call them profit-seeking and selfish. It is precisely because of righteousness and public-spiritedness that we Confucianists are engaged in putting the world in order, and because of their desire for profit and selfishness that the Buddhists withdraw from the world. . . . Now, those who follow Buddhism are all human beings. As they are human beings, how can they cast aside our Confucian humanity and righteousness? Although they renounced the family, they still want to repay the Four Kindnesses (of parents, the king, teachers, and benefactors). Thus in their daily life they of course sometimes preserve this principle which is rooted in the human mind and cannot be obliterated. However, their doctrines did not arise in order to preserve it. . . . The Buddhists pity people because they have not escaped the wheel of transmigration but continue in the chain of birth and death, regarding them as floating and sinking in the sea of life and death. Do sages and worthies in Confucianism merely float and sink in this sea of life and death of theirs? Our sages and worthies are free from that which the Buddhists pity. . . . From the point of view of the origin of their respective doctrines, we see that the distinction between the Confucianists and the Buddhists as one for public-spiritedness and righteousness and the other for selfishness and profit is perfectly clear and that they are absolutely incompatible.[64]

There is a fundamental accusation within this text and it resounds through all Confucian criticism of Buddhism. We hear it again and again: Buddhists take an attitude toward this world that is at once incorrect and harmful; their world-negating ethic blinds them to the social virtues and thus undermines the foundations of human community. Such negative attitudes, Confucians claim, are rooted in Buddhist doctrine, especially in the dominant popular understanding of the cycle of rebirth. Thus in his critique of Buddhism, Lu Chiu-yüan was in complete agreement with Chu Hsi and the entire Neo-Confucian movement of his time. Japanese Confucianists of the Edo period (1603–1867) were later to level the same criticisms against Buddhism.[65]

The encounter between Zen Buddhism and Confucianism during the Sung period was more than an interesting historical episode. It also marked the final stage of Zen's vitality in China. Through their many contacts with Zen, the Neo-Confucians recognized much that was stimulating and creative in the vitality that Zen brought to the religious atmosphere of China. But they did not permit this positive influence to lead to any essential changes in their own worldview. Neo-Confucians were indebted to Buddhism for their own energetic exploration of new metaphysical terrain, but they used these discoveries to build a new and more relevant Confucian system that was to hold religious and intellectual ascendency in China for centuries to come. Unable to compete with this newly established Confucianism, Buddhism descended to the level of popular religiosity. In its encounter with Confucianism, the depths of Zen's spirituality and the power of its meditational experience were esteemed as never before, but ultimately the friendly relations between Zen Buddhists and Neo-Confucians in China did not bear lasting fruit. More positive results were to come from the continuation of the exchange in Japan.

ZEN ART

Zen art came to full flower only in Japan, though much of its artistic exuberance during the Muromachi period (1336–1573) had its roots in China.

The graphs of the Chinese language provided the material for the development of the art of calligraphy. Zen monks carefully nurtured this art and raised it to new heights of perfection by applying the powers of concentration gained in meditation. Calligraphy was one of the earliest of China's artistic achievements and was later carried on successfully in Japan as well.

During the Sung period ink painting attained what art historians acknowledge to have been its zenith. The Japanese were to imitate but never to surpass it.[66] Ink painting no more owes its origins to Zen Buddhism than does landscape painting, yet as Zen Buddhists began to move up in Chinese society during the Sung period, as they frequented the imperial court and had contact with leading artists of the time, their painters found themselves specially drawn to ink painting. Zen artists were impressed by its technical quality and felt an inner affinity with its form of artistic expression.

Dietrich Seckel captures the core of this affinity between Zen and ink painting when he speaks of Zen ink painting as a "document of a spiritual tradition" and a "testimony to personally gained vision and insight."[67] With brush and ink, Zen painters were able to give visual form to the tradition that enabled them to see through and step beyond the phenomenal world. They did this by depicting episodes, anecdotal events, and inspiring examples from Zen history— scenes all the more powerful for their real-life images of leading Zen personalities, patriarchs, and masters. All of this flowed out of the artists' own experience and conviction of the richness and depth of their own tradition.

Not all the ink paintings of the Sung period were done by Zen Buddhists, nor were all the Zen ink paintings done by Zen monks. Zen Buddhist ink painting also includes works by artists who were close to or inspired by Zen. Thomas Hoover singles out three clearly distinguishable themes in Chinese Zen painting: 1) the "Zen-in-action paintings" (Jpn., zenkiga), whose themes were made up of parables, situations, and special events in the history of Zen; 2) portraiture; and 3) landscape.[68]

One of the oldest known Zen Buddhist ink paintings belongs to the first group.[69] It depicts Zen's Second Patriarch, Hui-k'o, not posed solemnly for a portrait but "as he was putting his mind in order"—that is, engaged in a typical Zen activity. The artist, Shih K'o, lived and worked toward the end of the period of the Five Dynasties or at the beginning of the Sung period. His biography tells us that he turned down a position at the official academy of painting because he preferred a free and unfettered life. One may conclude that his selection of a typical Zen theme was more than an arbitrary choice; it shows how much he himself was filled with the spirit of Zen.

Liang K'ai, who lived during the first half of the thirteenth century and belonged to the official academy of painting, was also acquainted with Zen. He and the Zen monk Mu-ch'i, who lived toward the end of the Sung period, are considered the foremost Zen painters of the period. His work was especially appreciated in Japan. His ink-painting, "Śākyamuni Descending the Mountain," one of the earliest examples of this favorite scene, is known for "its mastery of composition, in which there are no weak spots and whose pervasive asymmetry rests on a hidden balance that finds its axis around the central figure."[70] The work may be included in the class of "Zen-in-action paintings." In it the enlightened Buddha, his robes stirred by a gust of wind, stands beside a rock wall silent and collected, gazing ahead, resolutely facing the work he is about to begin. Another action-painting of Liang K'ai's, "The Sixth Patriarch Cutting Bamboo," is drawn in a different, more humorous vein. It depicts the patriarch in the midst of his daily work, an inviting example for all.[71] In these lighter action-paintings the exemplary character of the subject figures frequently in the theme.

Chih-weng, probably a monk and disciple of the Zen master Yen-ch'i Kuang-wen (d. 1263), also paints the Sixth Patriarch in action as a young layman going out to cut wood.[72] In another work entitled "The Moment of Enlightenment"[73] a figure sits in front of the master, listens to his words, and is enlightened.

According to tradition, the fortunate person is a layman. Important events from Zen history are also presented in ink paintings such as Li Yao-fu's "Bodhidharma on a Reed," which shows the patriarch crossing the Yangtze River;[74] "The Sixth Patriarch Tearing the Scroll," by Liang K'ai;[75] and "Tan-hsia Burning a Wooden Image of the Buddha," by a non-Chinese artist known as Indra.[76] A robust humor saturates the many pictures of the two vagabonds so popular among Zen followers, Han-shan and Shih-te (Jpn., Kanzan and Jittoku), who lived during the T'ang period. Paintings of the two were transported to Japan, where they came to enjoy widespread popularity.[77] The same lighthearted human touch is found in paintings depicting the mendicant monk Pu-tai (Jpn., Hotei), whose rotund figure beams with friendliness.[78] Zen is at home both with quiet folly and gusty laughter. Thanks to Taoist influences, such qualities flourished in China.

The famous Oxherding pictures also originated in China. In the form of an extended parable they present the phases in the process of enlightenment—in other words, the Zen event par excellence. There are four different well-known sets of the pictures. The most enriching is the series of ten pictures drawn by Master K'uo-an Shih-yüan (Jpn., Kakuan Shion), who flourished around 1150. These pictures, passed down in a copy made by the famous Japanese Zen painter Shubun (d. ca. 1460),[79] illustrate the essence of Zen. The ox and the oxherd, two separate entities in the beginning, gradually become one. The ox signifies one's own deep self, while the oxherd symbolizes the human being as such. The progression of pictures unfolds as follows:

The oxherd has lost his ox and stands alone on the vast pasture (first picture); but can the human being lose its self? He searches and catches sight of the tracks of the ox (second picture); there is a mediatory assistance, in which religious things like sūtras and monasteries also play a part. Following the tracks, he finds the ox (third picture); but this is still a distant, intellectual knowledge or intuition of the ox. With fervent effort he tames the beast (fourth picture) and sets it out to pasture under careful surveillance (fifth picture). These two stages comprise practice in the Zen hall, the severe and painful practice until enlightenment is grasped, and the irrevocable practice of the enlightened one. The practitioner finds complete certainty; already the oxherd straddles the back of the ox and rides home triumphantly, playing the flute (sixth picture); the joy of the oxherd and the head of the ox, no longer bent on craving for grass, intimate the perfect freedom attained. Now the two have become one; the oxherd in his freedom no longer has need for the "ox" and forgets it, just as the trap and the net become useless after the hare and the fish are caught in the famous parable of Chuang-tzu. The oxherd stands alone without the ox (seventh picture). Now both oxherd and ox have disappeared in the securing, embracing nothingness of a circle (eighth picture). When the oxherd reappears, everything around him is just as it is (ninth picture)—the everyday life of the enlightened one. And the oxherd enters the town and the marketplace and bestows goodness to all about him (tenth picture).[80]

The symbolism is understood differently in another series of oxherding pictures that first consisted of the five pictures of the Zen master Ch'ing-chü (Jpn., Seikyo) and were later completed with a sixth picture by Master Tzu-te (Jpn., Jitoku, twelfth century). Recently the Zen master Shibayama Zenkei has made this series of Oxherding pictures available to the West.[81] Here the symbolism revolves around the change of coloring from light to dark. According to Shibayama's interpretation, the ox is "the thoroughly pure and immaculately white Ox," "the eternal Mind-Ox that could never be defiled in black or go astray in the wilderness."[82] Through ignorance, delusion, and disappointments it falls into the deplorable state signified by the dark color. The gradual lightening of its color in the process of being tamed indicates the awakening to one's true self and to one's original mind-nature. Aiding this process are "the tether of faith" and the "rod of striving," whose blows drive the ox-mind along. All the pictures are encircled to indicate the spiritual nature of the process. The story unfolds as follows:

THE FIRST PICTURE: THE AWAKENING OF FAITH

An instruction is given for the first time by a good teacher,
    and faith is awakened.
A thought of faith once awakened
    is the basis of the way forever.
A spot of white is therefore observed on the ox head.

THE SECOND PICTURE: FIRST ENTERING

Faith, already awakened,
    is refined at every moment.
Suddenly come to an insight,
    joy springs up in the mind.
First it starts from the top;
    therefore the head is now completely white.

THE THIRD PICTURE: NOT THOROUGHLY GENUINE YET

An insight has already been attained
    and is gradually refined.
The wisdom is bright and clear,
    but is still not quite genuine yet.
Half of the body is now white.

THE FOURTH PICTURE: THE TRUE MIND

Delusions no longer prevail;
    just one true mind.
Pure, immaculate, serene;
    the whole body is thoroughly white.

THE FIFTH PICTURE: BOTH FORGOTTEN

Both the man and the Dharma are forgotten
    and the boy and the ox are asleep.

Forever transcending all the forms,
   there is only the great Void.
This is called the Great Emancipation,
   and the Life of the Buddhas and Patriarchs.

THE SIXTH PICTURE: PLAYING

The source of life is extinguished,
   and from the death he revives;
Assuming any shape according to the conditions
   and playing around in whatever places he finds himself in
His personality has been changed,
   but what he does it not different.[83]

In the second series, a number of new themes are evident, especially the symbolism of color. The empty circle is common to both series. The sixth picture, "Playing," refers back to the last picture of K'uo-an's series. The path ends in the emancipation of enlightenment. The parable of the ox and the oxherd is representative of the flourishing Zen movement of the Sung period; the pictures were to be drawn over and over again, first in China and then in Japan, with relatively few and minor differences.

The second group of Zen Buddhist paintings during the Sung period, the portraitures, shows the seriousness of contemporary Zen religiosity.[84] Although portrait paintings of high quality were to be found in other Buddhist schools of China, it was Zen that brought this art form to its highest and widest development, especially during the period of the Southern Sung and Yüan dynasties. Like the chronicles and the generational tables, these portraits of patriarchs and masters are an expression of the consciousness of history that characterized the Zen movement in its maturity. This consciousness is especially present in the so-called generational portraits (Jpn., *resso-zo*), cycles of patriarchs or masters, one following the other either in a single composite picture or in a series of pictures. The first six Chinese patriarchs were favored subjects in this form.[85] The line of portraits, of course, extended beyond Hui-neng and Lin-chi into the Sung period. The patriarchs and masters were revered as bearers of a historical tradition—namely, the transmission of the Buddha mind apart from writing and scriptures, which constitutes the essence of Zen. The portraits illustrated the stories of the chronicles and focused on one or other important moment or period in Zen history. In this way, the historical past took on meaning for the present moment. In viewing these paintings Zen students could feel themselves part of the vast history of past generations.

For individual Zen followers, historical tradition became concrete in their personal relation with the master. Accordingly, the master-disciple relationship also had an important role to play in the origins and development of Zen portraiture.[86] Many of the portraits bear the master's writing (Jpn., *jisan*), such as a seal (Jpn., *inka*), confirming the enlightened maturity of the disciple. In these portraits, the master was able, as it were, to give himself to his disciples and abide with them. Here the personal dimension of the portraits, which was already present in the historical motivation, comes to the fore. For Zen, history is carried forward by concrete persons who act, make impressions, and exercise influence. The Zen painters attempted to make these revered patriarchs and masters visually present in their personal, as well as in their idealized, uniqueness; and they did this not only out of a sense of historical consciousness but also out of a deep sense of gratitude for all that they, the artists, had received from these enlightened guides. By means of Zen Buddhist portraiture, "the historical personality and the individual person came to occupy a focal point for thought and activity throughout the Zen movement."[87]

Among the portraits of Zen masters during the southern Sung and Yüan periods, some by Chinese and some by Japanese artists, the best known are the portraits of Hsü-t'ang Chih-yü (1185–1269), Wu-chun Shih-fan (1177–1249), and Chung-feng Ming-pen (1263–1323).[88] All three belonged to the same line of succession originating from the lesser known Hu-ch'iu Shao-lung (1077–1136), a disciple of Yüan-wu K'o-ch'in; it was known as the Mi-an line, after the representative of its third generation, Mi-an Hsien-chieh (1118–1186). Throughout the thirteenth and fourteenth centuries, the activity of this line was well known. Masters such as the three just mentioned were to provide the foundations for the bridge being built to Japan. Hsü-t'ang, "one of the most imposing personalities of Chinese Ch'an during the thirteenth century,"[89] is known from a number of excellent self-portraits that can be found today in the two monasteries of Myōshin-ji and Daitoku-ji in Kyoto.[90] He appointed as his official successor his Japanese disciple, Nampo Jōmyō (better known by his honorific title of Daiō Kokushi, 1235–1309), who passed his final days as abbot of the monastery of Kenchō-ji in Kamakura. A collection of the discourses of Hsü-t'ang entitled *Kidō oshō goroku* (Chin., *Hsü-t'ang ho-shang yü-lu*) contains kōan material that is still used today in the Rinzai school.[91]

Master Wu-chun Shih-fan, a contemporary of Hsü-t'ang, also contributed significantly to the transplanting of Zen to Japan, mainly through his Japanese disciple Enni Ben'en (1201–1280), one of the principal founding figures during the Kamakura period (1185–1333). Wu-chun was a disciple of P'o-an Tsu-hsien (1136–1211), who was the principal representative of the Mi-an branch of the Yang-ch'i line of the Rinzai school. The earliest portrait of Wu-chun, an anonymous work done with brush and color on silk, is considered "the best . . . and perhaps the most beautiful of Chinese portraits."[92] It is preserved in the monastery of Tōfuku-ji in Kyoto. This portrait of Wu-chun, together with another from the same early period, is widely known and has been reproduced many times.

Chung-feng Ming-pen brings us into the Yüan period, during which Zen painting continued to flourish and cultural exchanges with the imperial court and the intelligentsia made great advances.[93] Chung-feng was a close friend of well-known contemporaries such as the poet Feng Tzu-chen (1257–1327) and the painter Chao Meng-fu (1254–1322). He was also an eccentric who led a free-wheeling, unconventional life. Drawings depict him as a full-bodied man with a sluggish bearing.[94] Among his disciples were a number of Japanese students who were instrumental in bringing Zen to their homeland. Later we shall have more to say about the important process of Zen's migration to Japan.

Art historians point out the relationship between the Zen Buddhist portraits of patriarchs and masters and paintings of arhats (Chin., lo-han; Jpn., rakan), those early Buddhist saints who reached their goal through a rigorous monastic life and who were also so beloved to Zen followers.[95] If this relationship is valid, it is based on the way the Zen Buddhists accentuated the human qualities of these saints and revered them as model religious personalities, just as they revered their own masters. As Seckel observes, the arhats served "as the original model of the Zen student and so became favorite objects for Zen art. . . . They embody and exemplify inwardly free and spiritually strong persons attempting to move directly from this present world of saṃsāric cycles into the transcendent world of nirvāṇa."[96] Numerous paintings of arhats from the T'ang period and even more from the Sung period have come down to us. Zen artists were fond of presenting them in groups of sixteen, eighteen, or even five hundred; this genre of Zen painting was also later brought to Japan. A symbol of the homo religiosus,[97] the arhat embodies the religious commitment of Zen students striving to live up to this lofty ideal.

In their landscapes, the third category of Zen painting, Zen artists revealed their closest bonds to the contemporary artists of the Sung period. After achieving a definite form during the T'ang period, landscape painting flourished during the Sung. Many excellent studies have analyzed the characteristics of this art form and recognized its masterful techniques. During the Sung period, under the leadership of academic painters, precise rules for landscape painting were established.[98] Zen artists came to exercise a formative influence on academic artists who opened themselves enthusiastically to the inspiration of Zen. This is particularly clear in the case of two leading artists, Ma Yüan (1190–1224) and Hsia Kuei (c. 1180–1230), whose works are classified as Zen painting in Japan. Monochrome ink painting reached its culmination in China in the Zen monk Mu-ch'i (c. 1210–c. 1288), whose best paintings are contained today in Japanese collections. According to Seckel, his "Kaki Fruits" is a picture "full of an incredible silence that says everything . . . It may be the purest and most radical Zen picture there is."[99]

It was in painting that Zen art, both in China and Japan, reached its high-water mark. Artist monks were often the reason why certain Zen monasteries became centers of the spiritual life. Simply stated, Zen Buddhist ink painting points to transcendence. The multidimensionality suggested by the ink shades and simple strokes ranging from hair-thin threads to excessively thick and heavy lines, lets the viewer know that all knowledge is but the foreground of something deeper and greater. The ink paintings are indeed what Seckel calls, with Karl Jaspers, "ciphers of transcendence." Simple concrete things become transparent to a timeless present and an absolute reality. These Zen paintings, Seckel feels, bring the viewer

to a limit beyond which nothing can be said. Perhaps the essential achievement of these paintings is to make visible and conscious the ontological limits of the phenomenal world and so to suggest that these limits can be transcended . . . Here we are pushed to our final limits, in order that we

might glimpse the reality of that which is limitless and beyond all objec-
tification. . . .

Through its empirical grasp of the actual by means of personal and unique
statements, Zen ink-painting seeks to reach beyond both the personal and
the actual into the sphere of the transcendent. . . .[100]

SYNCRETISTIC TENDENCIES AND DECLINE

The Zen movement was hardly discernible as such in its beginnings. However
one tells the story of those early years, one cannot but depict Zen as an unas-
suming group tucked away in a secluded corner of the welter of often quite
imposing Buddhist schools. With Hui-neng it found its proper identity and entered its first golden age. Its defining characteristics quickly made themselves
known. The Sung period may be regarded as a second golden age. Even though
it was during this period that the signs of Zen's decline also began to appear,
the openings to culture and the world that took place during the Sung period
do not themselves necessarily signal a decline. The growing openness to new
contributions from outside influences served a healthy spiritual need. One should
try to understand these changing circumstances and developments with as little
prejudice as possible.

What was really taking place at this stage in the history of Zen became
clear for the first time in the person of Kuei-feng Tsung-mi.[101] During the T'ang
period he exemplified not only the bonds between Zen and the Kegon (Hua-
yen) school but also, and of more profound importance, the readiness of learned
Zen followers to recognize the validity of knowledge based on the written word.
As a young man, Tsung-mi steeped himself in the study of Chinese philosophy,
especially Confucianism. At the age of twenty-seven he met a Zen monk from
the Kataku school[102] and decided to join the seekers after truth in this school.
In no time he was ordained by a Vinaya master. His decisive experience of Zen
did not, however, take place during meditation but was occasioned by the chance
reading of a sūtra text. A passage from the Engaku-kyō (Chin., Yüan-chüeh ching;
Skt., *Purṇa-buddha Sūtra)[103] shook him deeply and brought him to tears. His
painful search, certainly a totally personal but at the same time fundamentally
intellectual search, was satisfied. As he wrote: "This text is rich in literary content, broad in its philosophical meaning. Truly it is not mixed with superficial
elegance, but as it indicates the substance and makes people surrender to the
incitement of Buddhism, no other text is comparable to the Yüan-chüeh ching."[104]

As his life history makes clear, Tsung-mi was more concerned with broad-
ening and deepening his knowledge than he was with deepening his Zen experience. His study of the sūtras opened his eyes to the vast vistas of the Kegon
teachings. As we know from his correspondence with the fourth Kegon patriarch,
Ch'eng-kuan, himself a central figure in Chinese Buddhism at the time, Tsung-
mi was the patriarch's disciple and later became his successor. The breadth of
his research ranged over virtually all the main branches of Buddhism of his age.
He was a prolific writer whose works include commentaries on the Diamond

Sūtra of the Prajñāpāramitā literature and on one of the basic texts of the Yogācāra tradition,[105] a lengthy commentary on the Sūtra of Perfect Enlightenment,[106] a study on the Vinaya and on the Ullambana rites, and reflections on a favorite text of his, The Awakening of Faith in Mahāyāna (Jpn., Daijō kishin-ron; Skt., Mahāyāna-śraddha-utpāda-śāstra; Chin., Ta-sheng ch'i-hsin lun).[107]

His literary works testify to his basic conviction of an underlying unity between Zen and the teachings of the sūtras. In his view, Zen's way of enlightenment needs the metaphysical foundations provided by the scriptures. Clearly such a claim conflicts with Zen's insistence on the transmission of mind from Bodhidharma and Hui-neng to the Zen masters of the T'ang period. Little wonder, then, that "from the moment Tsung-mi departed from Ch'an practice and entered into scholarly investigations and comparative studies, he was the target of criticism."[108] Although he belonged to the Kataku school, which was to fade away soon after his death, he cannot be considered a Zen master. He is a much better representative of Chinese Mahāyāna, the highest intellectual expression of which is to be seen in Kegon. Tsung-mi himself made no significant contribution to Kegon philosophy. His was not a very creative mind. We should rather speak of him as an individual of solid and wide learning, tolerant and kind, a seeker of harmony and synthesis. The Chinese Buddhist syncretists who followed him had good reason to appeal to him for support; he had an equalizing effect within Buddhism and always demonstrated a friendly attitude toward other worldviews such as Confucianism and Taoism.

Tsung-mi's assessment of the Zen schools needs to be understood from his own perspective. For him, the many different tendencies and lines in the Zen world were basically the same. In his major work on the origins of Zen he stresses the points of convergence between Zen and the sūtras and śāstras.[109] Nevertheless, he was convinced that the highest form of Buddhism resides in the all-embracing teachings of Kegon. In an interesting short piece, Gennin-ron (Chin., Yüan-jen lun) he describes Kegon as the fifth and last level of doctrine, one that "leads all other, imperfect teachings back to their true foundations."[110]

Tsung-mi's spiritual heirs during the Sung period were no match for the vision and dynamism of this great advocate of syncretism. T'ien-t'ai Te-shao, the successor to the founder of the House of Fa-yen, maintained contact with T'ien-t'ai (Tendai) Buddhists. From Mount T'ien-t'ai, the center of the once mighty Tendai school, he worked not only for the expansion of his own Zen school but also for the revival of Tendai.[111] His two disciples broke off in different directions. Tao-yüan, the editor of the most famous of all Zen chronicles, the Keitoku dentōroku, remained faithful to the tradition of the old masters and is today numbered among the main redactors of orthodox Zen history; his fellow disciple, Yung-ming Yen-shou, became one of the most influential contributors to the syncretistic movement within Zen during the Sung period. As Yanagida points out, he endorsed Tsung-mi's insistence on the compatibility of Zen and the study of the sūtras.[112] His proclamation of the unity between doctrine and Zen (Jpn., kyōzen itchi) elicited supporting echoes from several quarters and became a popular motto during this period. Yung-ming compiled the hundred-volume Sugyōroku (Chin., Tsung-ching lu), which offered a systematic overview of syncretistic teachings.[113] Not a few Zen masters during the Sung period turned to the study of the Mahāyāna sūtras, especially to the metaphysical achievements of the two schools of Kegon and Tendai, to satisfy their intellectual needs.

Yung-ming's syncretism went as far as to advocate the religious practice of the *nembutsu* (Chin., *nien-fo*) or invocation of the name of Amitābha Buddha. This was by no means a complete innovation, since three disciples of the Fifth Patriarch—Fa-chih (635–702) and his disciple Chih-wei (646–722), the fourth and fifth patriarchs of the Ox-head school, as well as Chih-shen (609–702)— had already practiced the *nembutsu* in addition to Zen meditation. The Ox-head school soon died out, and nothing further was heard of combining the practice of Zen with the *nembutsu* during the T'ang period.[114]

During the Sung period, sometimes with the support of the masters and sometimes against their opposition, the *nembutsu* made greater and greater inroads into Zen monasteries. This process of mixing religious practices continued through the Yüan period and came to term during the Ming dynasty. The simultaneous practice of Zen and the *nembutsu* became a matter of common practice. In trying to judge this whole development, we must not forget the inner affinities of the two practices. The psychological effects of the meditative repetition of the holy name are close to the effects of Zen meditation.[115]

Ch'i-sung (1007–1072) of the House of Yün-men, represents another dimension of the interreligious exchange going on at this time. We have already considered the impact of the Zen experience on Neo-Confucian philosophy, but at the same time the reverse is also true: Neo-Confucianism was having its influence on Zen. Ch'i-sung, known mainly for his *Transmission of the Dharma in the True School* (Jpn., *Dembō shōshūki*; Chin., *Ch'uan-fa cheng-tsung chi*),[116] devoted himself zealously to the study of Confucianism and composed a work on the *Doctrine of the Mean* (Chin., *Chung-yung*), one of the four Confucian classics.[117] Not a few Zen masters of those days took great interest in Confucian spirituality; later in Japan, Confucian ethics were to be largely integrated into Zen Buddhism.

In China, the syncretistic tendencies and movements during the Sung period went on to meet with widespread success. Within Zen Buddhism, the Yang-ch'i line of the Rinzai school absorbed all other schools and lines—including, during the Ming period, the Sōtō school. In Zen monasteries, the invocation of Amitābha was practiced in combination with sitting in meditation. Moreover, during the Ming period we see a complete fusing of all Chinese Buddhists schools and sects. The more intellectually oriented schools of Kegon and Tendai as well as the Vinaya school were all cast in the same mold, the shape of which was determined principally by Zen and the *nembutsu*. Well-known Zen masters contributed to this unification. One of the most effective was the respected monk Lien-chi Chu-hung (1535–1615) who, after being admitted to monastic life by a Zen master, preached the dual practice of Zen and the *nembutsu*.[118] This highly educated man left behind many writings. Han-shan Te-ch'ing (1546–1623), the best known Zen master at the end of the Ming period, also combined Zen practice with devotion to Amitābha Buddha, who, it is said, appeared to him while he was invoking the holy name.[119]

This syncretistic blending, which affected all schools and sects of Chinese Buddhism, has to be understood against the background of the tendency to harmony that characterizes all of China's religious history. The notion of the unity of the three doctrines (sankyō itchi)—namely, the three great religious currents of Confucianism, Taoism, and Buddhism—was known in China "from ancient times."[120] A wall painting depicts the three saints, Confucius, Lao-tzu, and Śākyamuni. Talk of the unity of all three religions "enjoyed widespread popularity among Zen followers from the middle of the T'ang period."[121] Also stemming from this period is Tsung-mi's claim: "Confucius, Lao-tzu, and Śākya-Buddha were all perfect sages."[122] His vision reached beyond Buddhism to embrace the other two great religions of China as well.[123]

During the Ming period at the latest, the history of Zen in China as the story of the transmission of the mind from Bodhidharma outside of all scriptures drew to a close. After the Sung period there were indeed first-rate Zen masters directing their disciples along the proven path to Zen enlightenment. Some of them have already been mentioned. But decline was also evident. Lacking genuinely creative figures, the movement began to stagnate. The political and social explanations that historians give for the general decline of Buddhism in China apply in large part also to Zen.[124] In later popular Buddhist religion, which consisted mainly of the Amida cult, Zen—by nature somewhat elitist—was able to carry on only at the cost of denying some of its elements.

That Zen nevertheless continued to be a vital force within Buddhism is due to its timely transmission from China to foreign lands. Yanagida closes his overview of the history of the Zen school in China with a brief section on what he calls "Zen flying overseas."[125] Actually, of the three countries he mentions, only Japan is separated from the Chinese mainland by water; Korea and Vietnam belong with China to the Asian continent. In these two neighboring lands, Zen, together with other forms of Buddhism, took root and met with some success, especially during the Sung period. Incomparably more extensive and more enduring was the impact of the Zen movement in Japan. Here Zen was to have a second history in no sense inferior to the history it had known in China, and here in our own times it was to reach out to the world beyond Japan's shores. The history of Zen in Japan calls for a special and careful treatment of its own.

NOTES

1. See Buddhism in China, p. 403; Chūgoku zenshūzhi, p. 95.

2. The Five Mountains or monasteries are prefigured in the five monastic sites of India tied up with Śākyamuni the Buddha. Lists of the Five Mountains and Ten Temples, with geographic details, are to be found in Mochizuki, Bukkyō daijiten, vol. 2, pp. 1182–1183; and Zengaku daijiten, vol. 1, p. 340. On the Five Mountains see W. E. Soothill and L. Hodous, A Dictionary of Chinese Buddhist Terms, p. 117. Yanagida also presents the names of the Five Mountains and Ten Temples, arguing that systematic state controls reached their high point during the Yüan period; see his Chūgoku zenshūshi, pp. 96–97. Mochizuki gives gozan jūsastu as an alternative reading of the characters in Japanese.

3. See *Chūgoku zenshūshi*, p. 97. The monk in question is Sung-lien (1310–1381).

4. Olaf Graf writes in his work, *Tao und Jen: Sein und Sollen im sungchinesischen Monismus* (Wiesbaden, 1970): "If ever a people was caught up in this-worldly realism and thus by nature lacked any entry into the views and lifestyle that mark the spirituality of the Śūnyavādin or Mādhyamikavādin, it was the Chinese in general and the Confucian world in particular" (p. 227). He appeals to Max Walleser's view that "it is hard to imagine an encounter between two spiritual worlds more incongruous than those of India and China" (p. 227). In the meeting of Sung Confucianism and Buddhism, above all with Zen Buddhism, Graf judges that the Neo-Confucians experienced a "decisive stimulus," even though their reaction "in the long run . . . was more negatively defensive" (p. 228).

5. According to Fung Yu-lan, Han Yü "may justly be regarded as the first real protagonist of later Neo-Confucianism." See his *Chinese Philosophy* II, pp. 408–09; see also sections on Han Yü and Li Ao, pp. 408–422. Clarence Burton Day includes Li Ao "among the forerunners of Neo-Confucianism"; see his *The Philosophers of China* (New York, 1962), p. 185.

6. *Chinese Philosophy* II, pp. 423–24, 414.

7. *Chinese Philosophy* II, p. 419. The whole passage deserves attention.

8. *Chinese Philosophy* II, p. 407.

9. *Chinese Philosophy* II, p. 424.

10. A sixth name was Shao Yung (1011–1077), whom Fung Yu-lan treats in detail (*Chinese Philosophy* II, pp. 451–476). The Neo-Confucian philosophy of the Sung period is treated in all standard works on the history of Chinese philosophy. Aside from the significant work of Fung Yu-Lan, particularly important are the two volumes of Carsun Chang's *The Development of Neo-Confucian Thought* (New Haven, 1963) and Wing-tsit Chan's *A Source Book in Chinese Philosophy* (Princeton, 1963). Graf refers to Chan as "the best living authority on Sung philosophy and its literature" (*Tao und Jen*, p. 358); Graf's own work deserves attention. Several works in Japanese treat Neo-Confucian philosophy and its relationship to Buddhism. As Wing-tsit Chan notes, Japanese authors tend to overemphasize the similarities between the two (*A Source Book in Chinese Philosophy*, p. 577). For our treatment of the question, the recently published book by Kusumoto Bun'yū, *Sōdai jugaku no zenshisō kenkyū [Studies on Zen Thought in the Confucianism of the Sung Period]* has proved helpful. Kusumoto illumines the situation from the Zen Buddhist point of view and uses a large number of Buddhist sources (not all of which are completely reliable).

11. Carsun Chang's estimation of Chou Tun-i as founder of a new philosophy in the Sung period (*The Development of Neo-Confucian Thought*, vol. 1, pp. 140–41, 158) is, in Graf's view, "too high" (*Tao und Jen*, p. 6). Wing-tsit Chan is of the same opinion (*A Source Book in Chinese Philosophy*, p. 461). See also C. Burton Day, *The Philosophers of China*, p. 186.

12. Carsun Chang supports the view that the diagram was first drawn in the Taoist school; see *The Development of Neo-Confucian Thought*, pp. 141–42. Fung Yu-lan also speaks of the Taoist origins of the diagram in his *Chinese Philosophy* II, pp. 438ff.

13. See *Sōdai jugaku*, pp. 76–97.

14. Wing-tsit Chan, *A Source Book in Chinese Philosophy*, p. 462.

15. Chin., *ch'iung-ch'an-k'o*; Jpn., *kyūzenkaku*. See Chan, *A Source Book in Chinese Philosophy*, p. 462.

16. Chan, *A Source Book in Chinese Philosophy*, p. 435. Fung Yu-lan adopts the anecdote from J. P. Bruce, *Chu Hsi and His Masters* (London, 1923).

17. See Graf, *Tao und Jen*, p. 212. Graf cites from Chang Tsai's work *On the Discrimination of False Teachings* the surprising remark: "Whoever wants to study Buddhist doctrine thoroughly in order to discern what is false there will certainly become a disciple of the Buddha long before reaching that goal through an exhaustive study of this doctrine."

18. *Chinese Philosophy* II, p. 497.

19. *Chinese Philosophy* II, p. 496. Cited from the *Western Inscription* of Chang Tsai.

20. See the detailed chapter in Kusumoto on Ch'eng Ming-tao's career and relationship to Zen (*Sōdai jugaku*, pp. 132–150). His presentation was prepared with critical attention to the central message of his sources. There follows a still more detailed account the "Thought of Ming-tao and Zen," strongly colored by the standpoint of the editor (pp. 150–95).

21. According to Kusumoto (*Sōdai jugaku*, pp. 140–41), it was held in a Zen monastery.

22. Graf, *Tao und Jen*, p. 8. Graf stresses that the brothers "were one in heart and soul" (p. 9). The actual work, *Erh-Ch'eng i-shu [Surviving Works of the Two Ch'eng]* is listed under joint authorship and contained pieces by both of the brothers.

23. Wing-tsit Chan, *A Source Book in Chinese Philosophy*, pp. 518ff., cited on p. 521.

24. Cited in *Chinese Philosophy* II, p. 509.

25. *A Source Book in Chinese Philosophy*, p. 521.

26. *A Source Book in Chinese Philosophy*, p. 522.

27. *A Source Book in Chinese Philosophy*, p. 522.

28. See *Chinese Philosophy* II, p. 500. Fung Yu-lan sets the School of the Study of Mind (*hsin-hsüeh*; Jpn., *shingaku*) in contrast to Chu Hsi's School of the Study of Principle (*li hsüeh*; Jpn., *rigaku*), thus tracing different schools back to the brothers Ch'eng. According to Carsun Chang, "Fung's propensity to exaggerate the doctrinal differences between the Ch'eng brothers leads to . . . considerable misinterpretation" (*The Development of Neo-Confucian Thought*, p. 193). Graf sees no distinction in their philosophical standpoints, but does admit "differences in temperament" (*Tao und Jen*, p. 8). The controversy is significant for us insofar as Fung brings out clearly the greater intellectual proximity of the elder Ch'eng to Buddhism.

29. Graf, *Tao und Jen*, p. 212. Kusumoto reports of disciples of the Ch'eng brothers who at least occasionally turned to Zen (*Sōdai jugaku*, pp. 146–47, 261–17).

30. *Chinese Philosophy* II, p. 509.

31. Kusumoto treats the relations of Ch'eng I to Zen masters in detail; see *Sōdai jugaku*, pp. 204–11.

32. Concerning Ch'eng I's zealous meditation in the *seiza* posture, *Sōdai jugaku*, p. 216. See also *The Development of Chinese Zen*, p. 34, note 71. Regarding "the important role of *seiza* in the Neo-Confucian tradition," see J. Gernet's essay, "Techniques de recueillement, religion et philosophie: à propos du *jingzuo (seiza)* Néo-Confucéen," in *Bulletin de l'École Française d'Extrême-Orient* 69 (1981): 289–305. The Neo-Confucians repudiated Buddhism, including Zen Buddhism, but this does not alter the "central role" that "the practice of concentration played both in Neo-Confucianism and in Buddhism" (p. 298). *Seiza*, as Gernet argues, is "in principle the practice of concentration to which the monks devoted themselves most frequently." Here we have "a typical Neo-Confucian combination of borrowing and repudiation" (pp. 292, 298).

33. See the three names in Carsun Chang (*The Development of Neo-Confucian Thought*, p. 236) and Kusumoto (*Sōdai jugaku*, p. 286). Chang gives as a fourth name that of Lu Ta-lin, while Kusumoto lists two other names. See also Kusumoto's chapter on the Ch'eng

brothers (*Sōdai jugaku*, pp. 286–312) for material related to the following sections of the text.

34. Cited in *Sōdai jugaku*, p. 301.

35. Conversions to Zen Buddhism took place, but the three principal disciples of the Ch'eng school preferred to remain faithful to the Neo-Confucian principles of their teachers.

36. He established the orthodox line of succession of Neo-Confucian thinkers and defined the Four Books. See Wing-tsit Chan, *A Source Book in Chinese Philosophy*, p. 589.

37. Carsun Chang, *The Development of Neo-Confucian Thought*, p. 245. Scholars of the history of Chinese philosophy are unanimous on the outstanding qualities of Chu Hsi.

38. Kusumoto appeals to Buddhist sources for this information; see *Sōdai jugaku*, p. 333.

39. Kusumoto (*Sōdai jugaku*, pp. 334ff) names three: Hu Chi-hsi (1086–1162), Liu Pai-shui (1091–1149), and Liu P'ing-shan (1101–1147). On Chu Hsi's study of Buddhism see Graf, *Tao und Jen*, p. 212. Heinrich Hackmann also speaks of Chu Hsi's study of Buddhism and Taoism, to which Hu Chi-hsi and Liu P'ing-shan, friends of his father, led him. "In particular, the second of these . . . thought he had found in Buddhist philosophers a welcome addition to Confucian teachings." See his *Chinesische Philosophie* (Munich, 1927) pp. 324–25.

40. See the quotation from Chu Hsi's works in Kusumoto, *Sōdai jugaku*, pp. 340–41. Araki Kengo also considers this relationship an established fact; see his *Bukkyō to jukyō* (Kyoto, 1976), p. 194.

41. An exchange between Ta-hui and Chu-Hsi, reported in the foreword to Ta-hui's collected sayings, is legendary according to Araki (*Bukkyō to jukyō*, pp. 194–95).

42. This is the view of Kusumoto, *Sōdai jugaku*, p. 336.

43. There is no agreement on dating Chu Hsi's study under Li T'ung. According to Wing-tsit Chan, it began in 1160 (*A Source Book in Chinese Philosophy*, p. 558). Carsun Chang argues that Chu Hsi studied for ten years under Li T'ung until the death of the latter in 1163 (*The Development of Neo-Confucian Thought*, p. 247). Hackmann also fixes the death of Li T'ung at 1163, and claims that the study could already have begun in 1151 (*Chinesische Philosophie*, p. 325).

44. Kusumoto distinguishes five stages in the career of Chu Hsi. His opposition to Buddhism was most vociferous during his prime (between the ages of 24 and 42 or 43). In his late years after his rejection of Buddhism, he may have come to a more careful consideration of Buddhism, especially of Zen Buddhism. In a lengthy section of his chapter on Chu Hsi, Kusumoto strives to lay out all the amicable contacts Chu Hsi had with Zen during his life, particularly in his old age (*Sōdai jugaku*, pp. 349–56). Gernet cites a description of meditation in the seated position by Chu Hsi and makes mention of a text in which the philosopher offers concrete suggestions for practice ("Techniques de recueillement," pp. 292–93). At the same time, Chu Hsi warned that substituting Zen Buddhist *zazen* for the Neo-Confucian *seiza* could easily bring Buddhism's quietistic tendencies into Confucianism (p. 294).

45. Cited in Carsun Chang, *The Development of Neo-Confucian Thought*, pp. 276–77.

46. For Chu Hsi's sharp critique against Ta-hui, see Araki, *Bukkyō to jukyō*, pp. 194ff, 288.

47. Cited in *Chinese Philosophy* II, pp. 569–70. See Carsun Chang, *The Development of Neo-Confucian Thought*, pp. 277–78.

48. Wing-tsit Chan, *A Source Book in Chinese Philosophy*, pp. 572–73.

49. See *Chinese Philosophy* II, p. 529.

50. *Chinese Philosophy* II, p. 568.

51. *Chinese Philosophy* II, p. 568.

52. All histories of Chinese philosophy treat Lu Chiu-yüan (*Chinese Philosophy* II, pp. 572–79). Carsun Chang includes a chapter on the controversy between Chu Hsi and Lu Chiu-yüan (*The Development of Neo-Confucian Thought*, pp. 285–307), as does Julia Ching in her book *To Acquire Wisdom: The Way of Wang Yang-ming* (New York, 1976), pp. 12–19. In his chapter on Lu Chiu-yüan, Kusumoto treats his relations to Zen Buddhism at length (*Sōdai jugaku*, pp. 399–458).

53. Olaf Graf writes: "That Lu Hsiang-shan at thirteen years of age should already have wrestled with the problem of the reality of the external world and arrived at a conclusion that some 600 years later Kant, approaching the question from another perspective, would propose and seek to give a solid basis to, is indeed something unique in the history of philosophy" (*Tao und Jen*, p. 344). In the case of the intuitively gifted Lu Chiu-yüan, it is less a question of a rational solution than of an intellectual vision.

54. See *Chinese Philosophy* II, p. 500; see note 28 above.

55. Fung Yu-lan cites Lu Chiu-yüan: "The universe is my mind, and my mind is the universe"; and "The universe has never limited and separated itself from man, but it is man who limits and separates himself from the universe" (*Chinese Philosophy* II, pp. 587,575).

56. Cited in Carsun Chang, *The Development of Neo-Confucian Thought*, pp. 296–97.

57. *The Development of Neo-Confucian Thought*, pp. 297–29; see also Julia Ching's essay "The Goose Lake Monastery Debate (1175)," *Journal of Chinese Philosophy* 1 (1974): 161–78.

58. *Chinese Philosophy* II, p. 579.

59. Carsun Chang, *The Development of Neo-Confucian Thought*, p. 287. Wing-tsit Chan stresses the difference between the philosophical statements of Lu Chiu-yüan and the spontaneous experiences of the Zen masters: "His doctrine of mind, for example, has none of the profound mystery of Zen. He stressed thinking, doubt, and judgment, and that is a far cry from Zen" (*A Source Book in Chinese Philosophy*, p. 577).

60. *A Source Book in Chinese Philosophy*, p. 573.

61. See Carsun Chang, *The Development of Neo-Confucian Thought*, p. 301.

62. This is Kusumoto's conjecture, *Sōdai jugaku*, pp. 401–02, 423.

63. See Carsun Chang, *The Development of Neo-Confucian Thought*, pp. 301ff; cf. Wing-tsit Chan, *A Source Book in Chinese Philosophy*, p. 577.

64. Wing-tsit Chan, *A Source Book in Chinese Philosophy*, pp. 575ff.

65. For example, Ogyū Sorai and Dazai Shundai. See my *Kamo Mabuchi: Ein Beitrag zur japanischen Religions- und Geistesgeschichte* (Tokyo, 1943), pp. 158–59.

66. On the following, see the foundational studies of D. Seckel, *Buddhistische Kunst Ostasiens* (Stuttgart, 1957) and *The Art of Buddhism* (New York, 1963). See also K. Brasch, *Zenga [Zen Painting]* (Tokyo, 1961), Yasuichi Awakawa, *Zen Painting* (Tokyo, 1970), O. Kümmel, *Die Kunst Ostasiens* (Berlin, 1921), and Thomas Hoover, *Zen Culture* (London, 1978).

67. *Buddhistische Kunst Ostasiens,* p. 228. This work contains an impressive chapter on the art of Zen Buddhism. Seckel singles out Chinese painting of the Sung period and Japanese painting of the Muromachi period as the two high-water marks of Zen painting.

68. Hoover, *Zen Culture,* p. 116.

69. See Awakawa, *Zen Painting,* plates 1,2; See p. 181 on the painter Shih K'o.

70. Seckel has devoted an entire study to this picture, "Shākyamunis Rückkehr aus den Bergen: Zur Deutung des Gemäldes von Liang K'ai," AS 19 (1965): 35–72. The passage cited is on p. 37.

71. In Awakawa, *Zen Painting,* plates 5 and 6.

72. *Zen Painting,* plate 15; on the painter Chih-weng, see p. 174.

73. *Zen Painting,* plate 14. "When that layman asked the master to teach him the inmost secret of Zen, he received the reply, 'The clouds are in the heaven and the water is in the bottle'—whereupon he instantly perceived the truth" (p. 61).

74. *Zen Painting,* plate 17. The inscription (Jpn., *san*) on the picture comes from the famous Zen monk I-shan I-ning (1247–1317) and reads: "Below the feet it is deep and transparent" (p. 64).

75. The picture is reproduced in *Essays* II, p. 224.

76. *Essays* II, plate 2 following p. 225. On the painter Indra (Chin., Yin-t'o-lo; origins uncertain, probably India or central Asia), whose works already place him in the Yüan period (middle fourteenth century), see Awakawa, *Zen Painting,* p. 184.

77. Han-shan was a poet and is often depicted with a writing scroll; his friend Shih-te, who helped in the monastery kitchen, is pictured with a broom. See Seckel, *Buddhistische Kunst Ostasiens,* p. 238, plate 145. See also the reproductions in Awakawa, *Zen Painting,* plates 21, 95, and 96.

78. Pu-tai was also an historical personality; see Seckel, *Buddhistische Kunst Ostasiens,* pp. 238–239, plate 144; Awakawa, *Zen Painting,* plates 22 and 97.

79. The oxherding pictures were first introduced to the West by D. T. Suzuki in *Essays in Zen Buddhism* I, pp. 249–366. The reproductions were prepared by the Zen abbot Seki Seisetsu of Tenryū-ji in Kyoto. Suzuki reproduced the drawings in their original form in his *Manual of Zen Buddhism,* pp. 128ff. The series is best known in Germany through the book *Der Ochs und sein Hirte,* later translated into English as *The Ox and His Herdsman* (Tokyo, 1969). The work contains an explanation by Master Daizōkutsu R. Ōtsu and Japanese drawings from the fifteenth century. It was translated by Tsujimura Kōichi and Hartmut Buchner. The same set of pictures is contained in Paul Reps, *Zen Flesh, Zen Bones: A Collection of Zen and Pre-Zen Writings,* pp. 165–87. (The ox in the pictures is actually a water-buffalo; the character is better translated as cow, but the pictures are now known in the West as the "Oxherding" pictures.)

80. See my *Zen Enlightenment: Origins and Meaning,* translated by John C. Maraldo (New York, 1979), p. 155.

81. Shibayama Zenkei, *A Flower Does not Talk* (Rutland, 1975), pp. 152–203. In his *Manual of Zen Buddhism* Suzuki introduces a set of ten pictures (pp. 135–44) that follows a Chinese edition with a foreword from the year 1585 based on the pictures of Ch'ing-chü and Tzu-te (see Suzuki's "Preliminary," pp. 127–29). This set ends with the circle. Four of the pictures are included in the series of six pictures that Shibayama reproduces. The latter presents a brief biography of Tzu-te (Jpn., Jitoku), pp. 167–68, and mentions the "Ten White Ox Pictures" by an unknown artist (p. 157).

82. Suzuki, Manual of Zen Buddhism, pp. 158–59.

83. From Shibayama's A Flower Does not Talk, pp. 170, 175, 181, 187, 193, 199.

84. On the following see the excellent work by H. Brinker, Die zen-buddhistische Bildnismalerei in China und Japan von den Anfängen bis zum Ende des 16 Jahrhunderts: Eine Untersuchung zur Ikonographie, Typen- und Entwicklungsgeschichte (Wiesbaden, 1973). See also the section on "Portrait Art in Zen Buddhism" in my essay, "The Person in Buddhism: Religious and Artistic Aspects," translated by Jan Van Bragt, Japanese Journal of Religious Studies 11.2-3 (1984): 143–67. Hoover says of Zen Buddhist portraitures that "they must be ranked among the world's finest portraits" (Zen Culture, p. 116).

85. See Brinker, Zen-buddhistische Bildnismalerei, pp. 65ff, 101ff.

86. Seckel writes: "The portraits of Arhats, patriarchs and priests were promoted with great vigour by adherents of the Ch'an (Zen) school, which attached great importance to deeply religious personages, to contact between masters and pupils, and to the handing on of traditions 'from spirit to spirit' " (The Art of Buddhism, p. 254; see also his Buddhistische Kunst Ostasiens, p. 239).

87. Brinker, Zen-buddhistische Bildnismalerei, p. 18.

88. Brinker gives particular attention in the fourth part of his study to portraits of the Chinese masters Wu-chun Shih-fan (pp. 160–163) and Chung-feng Ming-pen (pp. 163–66). He explains several of the outstanding drawings of Hsü-t'ang Chih-yü (plates 46, 47; cf. plates 26, 27).

89. Brinker, Zen-buddhistische Bildnismalerei, p. 117.

90. Brinker, Zen-buddhistische Bildnismalerei, plate 46 (in Myōshin-ji) and 47 (in Daitoku-ji). A brief biography of Hsü-t'ang is included in Zen Dust, pp. 206–07.

91. T. 2000, vol. 47; for a description of the ten-volume collection, see Zen Dust, pp. 361–62.

92. Cited in Brinker, Zen-buddhistische Bildnismalerei, p. 160. A brief biography of Wu-chun Shih-fan is included. Brinker explains in detail the outstanding portrait of the master (plate 99) and some copies of the work (plates 100–03, pp. 160–63).

93. For biographical details on Chung-feng Ming-pen, see Brinker, pp. 163ff. Ruth Fuller Sasaki cites a noteworthy explanation of the meaning of the word kōan from the discourses of Chung-feng. Just as the public hearing of court cases assures due legal process, Chung-feng argues, so "the kōan do not represent the private opinions of a single man, but rather the highest principle . . . [which] accords with the spiritual source, tallies with the mysterious meaning, destroys birth-and-death, and transcends the passions. It cannot be understood by logic; it cannot be transmitted in words; it cannot be explained in writing; it cannot be measured by reason. . . . The so-called venerable masters of Zen are the chief officials to the public law courts of the monastic community, as it were, and their words on the transmission of Zen and their collections of sayings are the case records of points that have been vigorously advocated. . . . The word kung or 'public,' means that the kōan put a stop to private understanding; the word an, or 'case records,' means that they are guaranteed to accord with the Buddhas and patriarchs. . . ." The text ends praising the kōan as "a torch of wisdom that lights up the darkness of feeling and discrimination." The detailed citation from the discourse of Chung-feng (Chin., Chung-feng ho-shang kuang-lu; Jpn., Chūhō oshō kōroku) was first published in her essay "The History of the Kōan in Rinzai Zen" (see chap. 12, note 36) and then again in Zen Dust, pp. 4–7.

94. Brinker, Zen-buddhistische Bildnismalerei, plates 104–06.

95. The tradition of arhat pictures predates the Zen school. According to Seckel (*Buddhistische Kunst Ostasiens*, p. 237; *The Art of Buddhism*, pp. 250ff), it contains Taoist elements. See also Brinker, *Zen-buddhistische Bildnismalerei*, p. 61; Brasch, *Zenga*, pp. 14–15. In Zen art, the category corresponding to the arhat tradition is the Bodhidharma motif.

96. Seckel, *Buddhistische Kunst Ostasiens*, p. 237.

97. Seckel writes: "The manner of expression . . . hits directly at the essential core of personal spirit and gives deeply impressive pictures of the inwardly liberated, spiritually powerful *homo religiosus*, often rising to the level of the numinously grotesque" (*Buddhistische Kunst Ostasiens*, p. 237). See his *The Art of Buddhism*, p. 248.

98. Hoover, *Zen Culture*, p. 132.

99. Seckel, *Buddhistische Kunst Ostasiens*, pp. 253–54. See his detailed interpretation of the picture in his *Einführung in die Kunst Ostasiens* (Munich, 1960), pp. 345ff.

100. Seckel, *Einführung in die Kunst Ostasiens*, pp. 246, 248–49, 251.

101. For the following see also Jan Yün-hua, "Tsung-mi: His Analysis of Ch'an Buddhism," TP 58 (1972): 1–54; see also part 2 of A. Verdu, *Dialectical Aspects in Buddhist Thought: Studies in Sino-Japanese Mahāyāna Idealism*, pp. 77–113.

102. Tao-yüan. On the Kataku school and Tsung-mi, see chap. 9, notes 20–22 and accompanying text. The genealogical line of Tsung-mi there is not completely clear. Jan Yün-hua rejects the line of succession mentioned there, which Yanagida treats as possible; see the excursus in "Tsung-mi: His Analysis of Ch'an Buddhism," pp. 9–10.

103. T. 842, vol. 17. It is not certain whether a Sanskrit original lies behind the Chinese text. This sūtra, important to Chinese Buddhism, was taken over into Kegon teachings by Tsung-mi. See Jan Yün-hua, "Tsung-mi," p. 8. The sūtra is listed as apocryphal in the index prepared by Paul Demiéville, Hubert Durt, and Anna Seidel for the *Taishō daizōkyō, Répertoire du Canon Bouddhique Sino-Japonais* (Paris, 1978), p. 78.

104. Cited in Jan Yün-hua, "Tsung-mi," p. 9. The Chinese characters on which the translation is based are given there. The final two characters are given in the title of the sūtra that is praised in the saying.

105. *Trimśikā-vijñaptimātra-kārikā*; Tsung-mi's commentary on the work is not available; see Jan Yün-hua, "Tsung-mi," p. 13.

106. In 12 books; see above, chap. 9, note 20.

107. T. 1666, vol. 32; English translation by D. T. Suzuki, *Aśvaghoṣa on the Awakening of Faith* (Chicago, 1900) and Yoshito S. Hakeda, *Aśvaghoṣa: The Awakening of Faith* (New York, 1967).

108. This is the conclusion to which Jan Yün-hua arrives at the end of his study, "Tsung-mi," p. 36.

109. *Zengen-shozenshū tojo* (Chin., *Ch'an-yüan chu-ch'üan-chi tu-hsü*), T. 2015, vol. 48; Japanese translation by Ui Hakuju (Tokyo, 1943). Detailed analysis of the formulas and terms of the work are given by Verdu, *Dialectical Aspects in Buddhist Thought*, pp. 79–103. For a critical discussion, see Jeffrey L. Broughton's "Kuei-feng Tsung-mi: The Convergence of Ch'an and the Scriptures" (Ph.D. diss., Columbia University, 1975).

110. Verdu also analyzes the *Gennin-ron* (*Dialectical Aspects*, pp. 103–06; see also notes 103 and 106 on p. 113). See note 39 and the accompanying text to chap. 10 above.

111. *Chūgoku zenshūshi*, p. 89.

112. *Chūgoku zenshūshi*. Yanagida draws attention to the relationship to Tsung-mi.

113. T. 2106, vol. 48; Nj. 1489. Nanjō translates the title *Records as the Mirror of the (Dhyāna) School*.

114. Concerning the invocation of the name (Jpn., *nembutsu;* Chin., *nien-fo*) in the Pure Land (Chin., Ching-t'u; Jpn., Jōdo) school and its adoption in Zen Buddhism, see *Zen Dust*, pp. 172–76.

115. Suzuki has often made this point; see for example the second half of his essay on the practice of the kōan in chapter 8 of *An Introduction to Zen Buddhism*.

116. T. 2078, vol. 51. In the title Zen is referred to as the "true school" for the first time. Later this name would be given as a title to the Rinzai school, apparently by Emperor Kao-tsung of the Southern Sung dynasty.

117. See *Chinese Philosophy* II, p. 424.

118. According to the biography in Mochizuki's *Bukkyō daijiten*, vol. 3, pp. 2455–56, Lien-ch'ih Chu-hung (Jpn., Renchi Shukō) entered monastic life under a Zen master, practiced the *nembutsu* zealously, spread the double practice of Zen meditation and invocation of the name (which led him to put great stress on the doctrine of the Pure Land) and compiled numerous works. In the *Zengaku daijiten* he is referred to as a representative of the combination of Zen and Amidism (Jpn., *zenjō itchi*) who knew Confucianism and worked for the spread of Zen (vol. 1, p. 503). According to Ch'en he edited the *Tzu-chih lu* (Jpn., *Jichiroku*), which Japanese sources also ascribe to him. Ch'en once refers to him as a Buddhist monk (*Buddhism in China*, p. 437) and later as one of the outstanding clerics of the Ming dynasty (p. 443). In both contexts he speaks of his active life (pp. 437–38, 443–47). According to Y. H. Ku's accurately compiled *History of Zen* (Philadelphia, 1979), Lien-chi Chih-hung was a great friend of Han-shan Te-ch'ing. Since the latter was a Zen master, we may also reckon Chu-hung as belonging to Zen Buddhism (p. 87). For a full treatment of Chu-hung's life and thought, see Yü Chun-fang's *The Renewal of Buddhism in China. Chu-hung and the Late Ming Synthesis* (New York, 1981).

119. Lu K'uan Yü (Charles Luk) has translated a commentary on the *Diamond Sūtra* and Master Han-shan's "A Straight Talk on the *Heart Sūtra*" in *Ch'an and Zen Teaching*, pp. 146–220. See also Ch'en, *Buddhism in China*, pp. 446–47; Ku, *History of Zen*, p. 87.

120. According to the article in Mochizuki's *Bukkyō daijiten* on *sankyozu* ("diagram of the three teachings"), vol. 3, p. 1479.

121. *Bukkyō daijiten*, vol. 3, p. 1479.

122. Cited by Jan Yün-hua, "Tsung-mi," p. 22.

123. Tsung-mi not only had a profound understanding of the non-Buddhist religions of China but was drawn to study them. "I am interested in comparative studies by natural inclination," he remarked of himself (Jan Yün-hua, "Tsung-mi," p. 35). Thus he drew Confucianism and Taoism into a synthetic vision of religion that he laid out in his *Gennin-ron* (*Treatise on the Origin of Humanity*). Even though Tsung-mi believed that Confucian and Taoist teachings say nothing about human origins, he devoted the first section of his work to them before going on to the five stages of doctrine within Buddhism. In Verdu's view, Tsung-mi refracts the stages of the history of Buddhist ideas "through the well known dialectical transition from negation to the negation of negation" (*Dialectical Aspects in Buddhist Thought*, p. 103.) Tsung-mi stands out as an ecumenical and dialectical thinker.

124. In the final section of his *Buddhism in China*, which deals with the decline of Buddhism (pp. 389–408), Ch'en first describes the moral decadence and worldliness within

monastic religion. Dependence on the regime led to the sale of monastic certification and titles. The critical stance of Neo-Confucian philosophy, above all the strong aggressions of the greatest thinker of the age, Chu Hsi, inflicted heavy casualties on Buddhism. To that we must add the signs of internal weakening, above all that produced by syncretistic tendencies such as those we discussed in the Zen school. Yanagida (*Chūgoku zenshūshi*, pp. 104–05) brings out the adverse political circumstances in the Yüan, Ming, and Ch'ing dynasties. Among the aberrations of Zen Buddhism that were brought over from China to Japan one has to count not only syncretistic tendencies and but also transgressions of Buddhist precepts and monastic customs.

125. *Chūgoku zenshūshi*, pp. 104ff.

Epilogue

In treating the period that begins where we have left off, Japanese historians marvel at the Buddhist monks who "longed for the Dharma and traveled to the Kingdom of the Sung" (Jpn., *guhō nyūsō*). These two elements—the Dharma and the travels to the land of the Sung—fittingly express the bonds that Buddhism forged between Japan and China. Japanese Buddhist monks set out for China to wander its vast expanse in search of the true path of the Buddha. The perilous sea voyage was fraught with hardships, but this did not deter them from their resolve. During the Middle Ages, a trip to China was a bold undertaking indeed, requiring great courage and endurance. We shall never know how many ships were destroyed by sudden typhoons or how many pilgrims went to a watery grave. The diary of the Tendai monk Ennin gives harrowing accounts of crises at sea and life and death adventures. With the Dharma ever before their eyes, these monks were driven by a spirit of religious determination.

Together with the founder, Buddha, and the religious community (Skt., *saṅgha;* Jpn., *sō,* literally "monk"), the Dharma numbers among the "Three Jewels" (Skt., *triratna;* Jpn., *sambō*) and constitutes the inner core of Buddhism. It is not just a body of teaching but a wisdom and a Way, an enlightened understanding. When the Japanese Buddhist monks set off to Sung China in quest of the Dharma, it was probably Zen they had in mind as the embodiment of the flowering of Buddhism in the Middle Kingdom. The Japanese found the true Dharma in the practice and life of the Zen masters and their rigorous monastic communities, and hence braved the voyage from their island home to the main land in order to build bridges for Zen Buddhism to make its way to Japan. The Dharma of the Sung period, namely Chinese Zen, was the pivot for the historical turn of Zen to Japan.

The phrase *guhō nyūsō,* whose four Chinese graphs signify "longing for the Dharma—entrance into the land of the Sung," not only points to an important event in the history of Zen but also signals essential traits of the Zen path to enlightenment. The image of these Japanese Buddhist monks driven by their desire for the Dharma to make their way to the land of the Sung directs us to China, the birthplace of Zen Buddhism, where Zen attained a spiritual and cultural high point never to be equalled. I would like to offer some personal comments on the significance of this fact by way of conclusion to the present volume.

Let us first return where we began. When the Japanese monks set out for the Middle Kingdom on what was for them a pilgrimage to their origins, what attracted them to Chinese Zen was not its cultural or artistic achievements or even its special method of meditation, but the simple fact that it was the place where the Dharma could be found. It is in this light that the history of Chinese

Zen Buddhism can best be studied. The lifeblood of this extraordinarily rich and bewilderingly diverse history is its awareness of being the bearer of the true Dharma through the centuries. The Chinese Zen Buddhists considered themselves the direct successors of the founder, Śākyamuni, who according to tradition transmitted his mind to his disciple Kāśyapa, the First Patriarch of Indian Zen. According to Zen self-understanding, the Indian and Chinese patriarchs, together with all their followers, are heirs of the Dharma. In Zen literature, even mere disciples who followed a valid line of tradition and experienced enlightenment under their master are called Dharma heirs.

It is also important to remember that the implanting of Buddhism in China produced a typically Chinese form of Buddhism that was found in all the Chinese schools and was not inferior to Indian forms. This typically Chinese Buddhism is particularly evident in Zen, the most successful of all the schools in terms of adaptation to Chinese culture. The uniqueness of Chinese Buddhism resulted on the one hand from the influx of ancient Chinese ideas, especially the wisdom of Taoism, and on the other hand from the influence of Mahāyāna teachings from India. The specific religiosity of Mahāyāna as it is expressed forcefully in the Mahāyāna sūtras comprehends transcendence and soteriology. These two essential traits are clearly taken up by Zen, especially at the high points of its development in China—in the *Platform Sūtra of the Sixth Patriarch*, in the creativity of the masters of the T'ang period, in the prominent figure of Lin-chi. These landmark figures in the history of Chinese Zen were deeply rooted in the great Mahāyāna sūtras; by their activities the religious message of the sūtras found Chinese expression.

Throughout Buddhism, transcendence is referred to mainly by way of negation. This is as true of the early forms of Buddhism in India as it is of East Asian Buddhism, as true of the fundamental Mahāyāna sūtras as it is of Zen. Chinese Zen's approach to negation differs from that of speculative Indian thought. Although the *mu* that resounds through the Zen halls of East Asia echos the *neti neti* of the Upanishadic sage Yājñavalkya and the emptiness (*śūnyatā*) of the philosophers of the Middle Way, in China this expression is always a concrete utterance of practitioners seeking radically to empty their psychological faculties of all ego. Clearly, this belongs to the tradition of the negative way, since disciples engaged in this practice press ever more deeply into "nothingness" until it embraces them completely. The Zen experience can best be described in purely negative terms, like the highest wisdom (*paramārtha*) of Mādhyamika. Enlightened verses and kōan-like conversations in Zen often show linguistic similarity, if not basic agreement with, formulations from Nāgārjuna's Middle Way. Thus the whole range of arguments used to locate transcendence in Mādhyamika philosophy can well apply to Zen. In their practice and in their way of life, Zen disciples are directed towards transcendence; in their experience transcendence is more clearly present than it is in the realm of the mental operations of Mahāyāna philosophy. Authentic Mahāyāna, however, is never lacking in the experiential dimension.

Zen disciples follow the path of the pilgrim toward salvation as searchers after the absolute. A variant of the expression alluded to earlier, *guhō*, "longing for the Dharma," is *gudō*, "longing for the Way." The Way that Buddhists long for is clearly Buddha's Way of salvation, which leads to final liberation. Chinese Buddhists, whose masters used to call their adherents "searchers after the Way" (*dōryū*), feel bound to follow the path of Buddha. Zen Buddhist monastic life, developed in China since the T'ang period, joins monastic discipline with inner freedom. It is principally because of this ideal of freedom that Zen has attracted the interest of the West. The seriousness of the Zen way is missed when this freedom is conflated with a sense of extravagance or caprice or even with licentiousness. The intent of Zen disciples is always a religious one. Under the rigorous guidance of their master, they seek to live that essential freedom proper to being human, as it has been understood in the Buddhist teachings on salvation.

The articulation of soteriology in Chinese Zen accounts in no small measure for the attraction that many feel to the Zen way of life. The lifestyle is beautifully exemplified in P'ang Yün, a Buddhist layman and follower of Zen during the T'ang period.[1] Little is known of his childhood and early youth. Although educated, he did not follow his father into the highly esteemed life of a public official. He remained a layman, married, and had two children, a son and a daughter. This did not deter him, however, from following his religious and poetic inclinations. Seeking out the acquaintance of several Zen masters—including the two most illustrious masters of his age, Shih-t'ou and Ma-tsu—he practiced and attained a number of enlightened experiences. Under Ma-tsu he attained the Great Enlightenment, which left its deep impression on him. On the occasion he composed the following verses:

[People of] the ten directions are the same one assembly—
Each and every one learns *wu-wei*.
This is the very place to select Buddha;
Empty-minded having passed the exam, I return.

The eminent scholars of Zen Ruth Fuller Sasaki, Iriya Yoshitaka, and Dana R. Fraser, translators of the English edition of the sayings of the layman P'ang, offer a commentary on these verses. Noteworthy is their explanation of *wu-wei* in the second verse:

Wu-wei in Buddhism means "the Unconditioned," and in Taoism "non-doing," the effortless, purposeless action that flows from accord with the Tao. Both meanings are probably intended.[2]

According to these scholars, P'ang touched the Unconditioned, the realm of the Absolute.

P'ang is extolled in Zen literature as another Vimalakīrti—a householder who ascended to the highest levels of wisdom. As is reported, he refused to exchange his white layman's robe for the black robe of the monk. During his later years, after giving away his house and losing all his other possessions in a ship that sank to the bottom of a river, he traveled the land visiting temple monasteries together with his beloved daughter Ling-chao, who earned the two a frugal living by weaving bamboo. P'ang left behind some three hundred poems, only some of which survive. There are also many recorded conversations with Zen followers that testify to his high degree of enlightenment. The chronicle gives a moving report of his death:

> The Layman was about to die. He spoke to Ling-chao, saying: "See how high the sun is and report to me when it's noon."
> Ling-chao quickly responded: "The sun has already reached the zenith, and there's an eclipse." While the Layman went to the door to look out, Ling-chao seated herself in her father's chair and, putting her palms together reverently, passed away.
> The Layman smiled and said: "My daughter has anticipated me."
> He postponed [his going] for seven days.[3]

The chronicle goes on to record his final words: "All is like shadows and echoes." After recounting his request that he be cremated and his ashes scattered over the rivers and lakes, the chronicle concludes by reporting how the monks and lay people mourned and proclaimed that "the Zen adherent Layman P'ang was indeed a Vimalikīrti."

Figures like the layman P'ang do not fit any category; they are simply part of the treasure of Zen. We will meet others like him in our treatment of Japanese Zen in the second volume of this work.

The Zen disciples who traveled to Sung China in search of the Dharma link the Japanese Zen schools with those of China. The bonds between the cultures and religions of the two countries, evident in many different respects, are indissoluble in the case of Zen Buddhism. Chinese Zen contains all the elements that were to develop in the Japanese environment and that are still preserved in Japan, while only documents and relics of more historical interest remain as a testimony to Chinese Ch'an. Japanese Zen cannot cut itself off from its bonds with China. By nature it rests on Chinese foundations. This Chinese influence on Japanese Zen is no less strong today than when Zen first came from China to Japan to plant its seeds in new soil.

NOTES

1. A collection of P'ang's sayings (*P'ang chü-shih yü-lu*; Jpn., *Hō koji goroku*) was probably compiled shortly after his death (August, 808) by his friend Yü Ti, governor of Hsiang-yang, a man sympathetic to the Zen movement. Toward the end of his life P'ang stopped in the vicinity of Hsiang-yang. The earliest extant text of the collection (in 3 books) dates from the Ming period. The wooden tablets on which it is printed bear the date 1637 but do not contain all three-hundred poems attributed to P'ang. Roughly identical to the Ming edition are three Japanese editions, also on wooden tablets, dated 1652, 1668, and c. 1692. The text is included in the *Dainihon zokuzōkyō* (Z. II, 25,1, pp. 28–41. An English translation of selections of the text is contained in *The Recorded Sayings of Layman P'ang: A Ninth-Century Classic* (New York, 1971). The translation from the

Chinese was prepared by Ruth Fuller Sasaki, Yoshitaka Iriya, and Dana R. Fraser. The book's introduction (pp. 11–36) relates P'ang's life as well as the origin and editing of the collection.

2. *The Recorded Sayings of Layman P'ang*, p. 27.

3. *The Recorded Sayings of Layman P'ang*, pp. 75–76.

The Northern School
of Chinese Zen

It was only decades after the discovery of the manuscripts at Tun-huang early in this century that their contents began to find their way, piece by piece, into historical studies of early Chinese Buddhism. They have been found to contain important information about the uncertainties surrounding the textual sources from the Sung period; about documented events surrounding the conflict between the Northern and Southern schools of Zen; about the origins of the *Platform Sūtra*; and finally, about the development of the Northern school, from its roots in the East Mountain school to its demise during the tenth century. At the time I was working on my *Zen Buddhism: A History*, I was unable to take this information fully into consideration. In the meantime, Western scholars have produced a wealth of material, based on the work of Yanagida Seizan, which now permits me to append a condensed overview. I am further indebted to Professor Yanagida for his friendly advice and extensive bibliographical assistance. In addition, I found the work of John R. McRae and Bernard Faure particularly helpful in composing this supplement. In the interest of overall readability, a certain amount of overlap was unavoidable. For this I beg the reader's indulgence.

PREPARATIONS IN CHINESE BUDDHISM

The Mahāyāna sūtras—in particular the Wisdom (*prajñāpāramitā*) sūtras, the Avataṃsaka (Chin., Hua-yen; Jpn., Kegon) sūtras, the *Vimalakīrti Sūtra*, and the *Laṅkāvatāra Sūtra*—form the spiritual background of the Zen movement in China. Chinese Buddhists with experience in meditation, scholars, and devotees of these sūtras prepared the way for Zen in the spiritual life of China. Seng-chao (384–414) and Tao-sheng (360–434) embodied the essential elements of Zen in the early years. The actual founding of the Zen School is attributed to Bodhidharma (d. 532). The masters of *dhyāna* (meditation) in the first phase of Chinese Buddhism

---

* As in the main text, Chinese works are identified by their original title, but thereafter generally referred to by their Japanese pronunciation. Chinese characters not included in the original glossary at the end of this volume have been inserted directly into the text. Likewise bibliographical entries not given in the comprehensive listing at the end of volume 2 have been supplied with Chinese characters in the notes where necessary. —*J. W. Heisig*

were followers of Hīnayāna (or more correctly, Śrāvakayāna) Buddhism. Buddhabhadra (359–429), the most important meditation master of those early days, bridged the transition from Hīnayāna to Mahāyāna. His disciples included Mahāyāna Buddhists. According to the historical sources, meditation masters were more active in north China than in the south; and yogic powers and magic practices played a large role in the north. These are questions that need further research.[1]

As recent studies have shown, the meditation masters Seng-ch'ou 僧稠 (480–560)[2] and T'an-ch'ien 曇遷 (542–607)[3] deserve to be singled out as forerunners of Bodhidharma. Seng-ch'ou is accorded a lengthy biography in the *Further Biographies of Famous Monks* (Chin., *Hsü kao seng chuan*; Jpn., *Zoku kōsōden*)[4] and the names of his teachers and disciples are known. After several unsuccessful attempts, Seng-ch'ou found a method of meditation that suited him and helped him to reach a high degree of spiritual concentration and detachment from the things of the world. He remained for a long time in the monastery of Shao-lin ssu (Jpn., Shōrin-ji). There he composed the *Chih kuan fa* 止觀法 (Jpn., *Shikanhō*), two chapters on methods of concentration for meditation, and disciplined himself to the Zen-like saying of the Indian Master Buddha: "The highest principle is not for words, and the mind of the sage is unhindered."[5]

Although the meditation methods of Seng-ch'ou contained both Hīnayāna and Mahāyāna elements, he himself professed to belong to the Mahāyāna tradition. Two of his manuscripts treat "Methods for Stilling the Mind" and "The Spiritual Practice of Mahāyāna." He recommends sitting in the lotus position for control of the body and inwardness, and as conducive to mental concentration. He describes the strenuous demands that meditation makes on consciousness in these terms: "When the mind and objects are all made to vanish, concentration and peace are achieved spontaneously."[6] His words point to the object-free meditation which the Zen masters will later characterize in the expression "without thought, without representation" 無念無相 (Jpn., *munen musō*).

In one manuscript he describes the "no-mind" achieved in meditation (Jpn., *mushin*):

> All external conditions have no immutable forms of their own. Right and wrong, becoming and disbecoming are all only from the mind. If one is able to attain no-mind, he will not be hindered by dharma.... If one's mind does not mind anything, who will distinguish right from wrong? If rights and wrongs are all negated, all forms of things will be peaceful forever. Because dharmas and the ten thousand delusions are all like the Principle of Suchness.[7]

Yung-ming (904–975) of the Fa-yen house of the Southern school of Zen cites this passage in his well-known syncretistic collection *Tsung-ching lu* 宗鏡録 (Jpn., *Shūkyōroku*). Seng-ch'ou was not unknown in Zen circles. Later Zen monks were fond of using his image for the immediacy of experience: "It is like drinking; only the drinker knows how cold or hot the water is."[8] His recommendation that meditation be done in the cross-legged position brings him close to Zen. He was criticized by adherents of sudden-enlightenment for teaching gradual, progressive advance in religious practice.

In his biography of Seng-ch'ou, Tao-hsüan compares him to his contemporary Bodhidharma, to the disadvantage of the latter.[9] Because of the relations he enjoyed with the ruling powers and the temples he founded, Seng-ch'ou enjoyed a higher status in Chinese society than the itinerant monk Bodhidharma, who came from a foreign land and whom Tao-hsüan made into the representative of a "School of Emptiness," a vague description that apparently referred to his relation to the Wisdom sūtras. In any case, Seng-ch'ou and Bodhidharma both belonged to the flourishing meditation movement of sixth-century China.

In this context, the eminent meditation master T'an-chien, who lived shortly after the time of Bodhidharma, merits attention less for his proximity to Zen meditation than to his significance in the intellectual life of his time and its resultant web of relations to the Zen school.[10] He integrated important elements of Chinese spirituality into the praxis of meditation, but more worthy of note is his loyalty to Taoism from the time of his youth. From the time of the earliest reception of Zen in the West, its Taoist impact was noted and stressed to the detriment of its Buddhist roots. Advocates of this view find support in T'an-ch'ien. But for all his knowledge of and admiration for Lao-tzu and Chuang-tzu, in the final analysis T'an-ch'ien remained Buddhist. Devoted to scholarly research, he studied the Mahāyāna sūtras zealously and acquired a good knowledge of the *Avataṃsaka Sūtra* and the *Laṅkāvatāra Sūtra*, which are closest to Zen, as well as the *Treatise on the Awakening of Faith in Mahāyāna*.[11] He made the *Mahāyānasaṃgraha* of Asaṅga, a summa of Yogācāra philosophy, the focal point of a school. The fact that T'an-ch'ien did not receive the recognition that his scientific achievement merited is attributed by Whalen Lai to the reservations that his Buddhist contemporaries had towards the Taoist elements of his work. Lai quotes the Japanese Buddhologist Kamara Shigeo:

> However, in the early Ch'an tradition there was a conscious effort to dissociate Ch'an from Lao-Chuang, an awareness that the [Buddhist] dharma was unique and a critical spirit directed against the limitations of Taoism.[12]

T'an-ch'ien left behind an essay in which he tries to reconcile the views of Taoist philosophy with Buddhism. In doing so, he makes use of paradoxes from the writings of Chuang-tzu. Might this not be a forerunner of the richly paradoxical language of classical Chinese Ch'an?

THE EARLY PERIOD

Concerning the legends and biographies of Bodhidharma, there are no new sources that expand or enrich our previous knowledge in any essential form. The only transmitted document from the sixth century—the age of Bodhidharma—makes mention of a pious itinerant monk of that name who admired the splendor of a temple in the capital city of Lo-yang, but the question of whether this monk is identical with the first Chinese Zen patriarch remains moot.[13] The biography of Bodhidharma by Tao-hsüan (d. 667) that appears in the three-volume historical work, *Further Biographies of Famous Monks*, contains the earliest extant references to the arrival of Bodhidharma and his work in China. Tao-hsüan refers to Bodhidharma's distinctive form of meditation as "Mahāyāna wall-gazing" (Chin., *pi-kuan*; Jpn., *hekikan*) without explaining what the term means. An enigmatic allusion to *pi-kuan* also appears in a short biography of Bodhidharma by his disciple T'an-lin (506–574), to whom we owe the most important part of the early written transmission of the patriarch.

As scholars have made clear, we possess no genuine writings of Bodhidharma himself. Still, three of the six treatises that had long been attributed to him were discovered among the Tun-huang manuscripts, namely *Verses on the Heart Sūtra* 心經頌 (Chin., *Hsin-ching sung*; Jpn., *Shingyōju*), *Two Ways of Entrance* (Chin., *Erh-chung-ju*; Jpn., *Nishu'nyū*), and *The Gate of Repose* (Chin., *An-hsin fa-men*; Jpn., *Anjin hōmon*). These latter two texts appear originally to have been part of a single text.[14]

The treatise on the two ways of entrance belongs to the oldest strata of the early period. It deals with the two entrances of principle 理 (Chin., *li*; Jpn., *ri*) and practice 行 (Chin., *hsing*; Jpn., *gyō*) and the four practices (Chin., *ssu-hsing*; Jpn., *shigyō*), as evidenced in its fuller title, *Treatise on the Two Ways of Entrance and the Four Practices* 二入四行論 (Chin., *Erh-ju ssu-hsing lun*; Jpn., *Ni'nyūshigyōron*). It was edited by T'an-lin and is rich in information about the early Zen movement at the turn of the seventh century.

The expression *pi-kuan* has been interpreted variously in the history of Zen.[15] Serious Zen disciples rejected the popular sense of gazing at an actual material wall. Zen masters of later centuries saw it as an expression of the awakened spiritual state, hard as stone. Tan-lin's interpretation in the treatise on the four entrances merits preferential attention: "Entering into principle (*li*) is the same as the calming of the mind, and the calming of the mind is *pi-kuan*.[16] This interpretation combines two statements. First, it speaks of entrance into principle, where principle is one of the two entrances to enlightenment, the other being praxis. Principle, or *li*, represents a central idea of Chinese philosophy—the essence or ground of reality—taken over into Buddhism. Tao-sheng, a monk who labored in the early phase of Kumārajīva's translation work at the suitable transposition of Indian Mahāyāna concepts into Chinese, links *li* to the Buddhist expression for ultimate reality.[17] The enlightened arrives at the essential realm where the mind is free. The two entrances through principle and practice are bound inextricably with one another.

Through the four practices of Bodhidharma Zen, enlightened wall-gazing enters into everyday life. It presupposes the general Buddhist form of *satipatthāna* (Skt., *smṛtyupasthāna*; Jpn., 四念處 *shinenjo*) meditation that had come over from India. Seng-ch'ou and other early Chinese meditation masters adopted ancient Indian exercises that Bodhidharma raised to the level of Mahāyāna in the four practices. Tan-lin's book on Bodhidharma, easy to understand and definitive for Buddhist readers, explains the practices in the context of Buddhist doctrine.[18]

In the first exercise, the one who practices overcomes the karmically determined feelings of hatred and other passions carried over from previous existences. In the second, one submits to one's circumstances (Skt., *pratyaya*; Jpn., 縁 *en*). In the third one asks for nothing since all things are empty (Skt., *śūnya*; Jpn., *kū*). And in the fourth, one finds oneself in harmony with the Dharma. In this way the four practices are made understandable so that the Buddhist can easily dedicate himself to them and follow them from the initial stages to the heights of enlightenment. Whereas the entrance into principle takes place all of a sudden, the entrance into practical exercise proceeds one step at a time; but this latter also belongs to the realm of enlightenment because of the essential ties that bind the two entrances together.

The calming of the mind, the second element in the definition of wall-gazing, recalls the story of the enlightenment of Hui-k'o. According to the transmission, Hui-k'o called upon Bodhidharma, who was seated in meditation, and asked him how he might calm his mind. Bodhidharma turned to him and said, "Bring me your mind and I will set it free." Hui-k'o replied that, try as he might, he could not find it. At this Bodhidharma spoke again, "Your mind is freed." As Yanagida notes, this exchange, the oldest of its kind in Zen history to come down to us, has a contemporary ring to it.[19]

> Hui-k'o had asked Bodhidharma for a method to free the mind, not for an ontological principle.... Bodhidharma sets the mind of Hui-k'o free. How? By what means? He does not attempt a momentary soothing but brings the mind of his interlocutor firmly into view in an original and fundamental sense. Though freed, there is no mind that has been freed; though sought, there is no mind to be found. The mind is beyond grasp....[20]

This first kōan prefigures the essence and formation of the Zen school. For Yanagida, it is important that Bodhidharma's answer be understood correctly and fully. The patriarch knows of no way to the liberation of the mind but can only claim, "The mind is freed." The mind is freed here and now; it is the original, pure mind, the true self and Buddha-nature.[21]

Thus presented, Bodhidharma's method of meditation is the translation into praxis of the Mahāyāna doctrine of the wisdom (*prajñāpāramitā*) sūtras, the *Vimalakīrti Sūtra*, and the treatise of Seng-chao.[22] This line of tradition leads to the classical Chinese Zen of the schools of Ma-tsu and Shih-t'ou.

The facts in the manuscripts discovered at Tun-huang cannot always be fixed precisely, but we do know that the Bodhidharma treatise on *Two Ways of Entrance* was known to Tao-hsüan at the time he composed his biography of Bodhidharma. His concluding comment, "His [Bodhidharma's] words are inscribed in books and spread through the world," does not contradict Zen's basic disavowal of any authoritative text, but harmonizes with the conception, still current today, that the writings are records of oral instructions. In this sense T'an-lin explains the entrance through principle as "grasping what is essential on the basis of the teaching."[23] The teaching, as Yanagida clarifies, refers to the teachings of the sūtras. All the sūtras are like fingers pointing to the moon. If the words that Bodhidharma the master speaks to his restless disciple are like the words of the Buddha, then Bodhidharma himself is like the finger. The enlightened one must forget both the sūtras and the finger.[24]

In addition to the work on the two entrances, there are two unsigned, unaddressed letters that serve as Bodhidharma texts. The authorship of the letters is uncertain. Yanagida argues on plausible though not compelling grounds for the authorship of T'an-lin, to whom the first appendix of the Bodhidharma treatise is also ascribed.[25] This appendix lays out the principal motivations of Mahāyāna, beginning with emptiness (śūnyatā) and ending with perfect virtue (pāramitā). The Dharma master referred to in the appendix as Tripitaka is Bodhidharma.[26] The text is presented as the message of Bodhidharma, to whom the same honor is accorded as to Buddha.

The second appendix of the Bodhidharma treatise offers early signs of the typically Zen literary genre of the question-answer dialogue (mondō) out of which the kōan developed. Numerous unknown Zen disciples, whose names have long remained unverifiable, show up as dialogue partners. Apparently they include also disciples of the second and third generation after Bodhidharma, who would have practiced Zen in China in the first half of the seventh century. Outstanding among them is Yüan, a figure who appears in no less than thirteen dialogues speaking a new and powerful language; fully three hundred years before Ma-tsu and Lin-chi, Yüan "denies the system of Buddhist doctrine itself."[27] He also anticipates Shen-hui's critique of the Northern school. According to the view of this disciple, the style of Bodhidharma that his contemporaries attacked corresponds to the true doctrine of the Buddha.

The brief third appendix, a manuscript of later date, introduces exchanges between dialogue partners, some of whom are known to have been disciples of the fourth and fifth patriarchs.[28]

It is possible, therefore, to recognize two lines of tradition in the early Zen movement after Bodhidharma. One line leads from the ambiguous term pi-kuan to the dialogue exchanges (mondō) found in collections of sayings (goroku), the forerunners of the kōan so characteristic of the Southern school. The other line, which hinges on the strict ties of early Zen to the Laṅkāvatāra Sūtra, proceeds from the communication of Tao-hsüan in the biography of Hui-k'o, according to which Bodhidharma handed over the four volumes of this sūtra to Hui-k'o saying, "I have observed in this land of China there is only this sūtra. If you depend upon this sūtra, you will be able to save the world."[29] In his historical work, Tao-hsüan assigns a great importance to the Laṅkāvatāra Sūtra for the meditation movement in the China of his day and age. To be sure, the eight Laṅkā masters listed in his biography of Fa-ch'ung (587–665?) form a distinct line from the circle of Bodhidharma's disciples. Even though the Treatise on the Two Entrances and the Four Practices "does not touch particularly on the Laṅkāvatāra Sūtra,"[30] Yanagida notes that "the relationship of Hui-k'o to the doctrine of the *Laṅkāvatāra Sūtra* is certain," citing passages in the second and third appendices to support this view.[31]

The tendency in the Bodhidharma transmission to favor the *Laṅkāvatāra Sūtra* leads directly to the Northern school. The two oldest chronicles of Chinese Zen history, the *Leng-ch'ieh shih-tzu chi* (Jpn., *Ryōga shikiji*), edited by Ching-chüeh (683–ca. 750), and the *Ch'üan fa-pao chi* (Jpn., *Den hōbōki*), compiled by Tu-fei—both of which arose in the Northern school independently of one another during the early years of the reign of the emperor Hsüan-tsung (713–755)—demonstrate a close relationship to the *Laṅkāvatāra Sūtra.*[32] The *Leng-ch'ieh shih-tzu chi* takes its name from the *Laṅkāvatāra Sūtra* and gives Guṇabhadra (394–468), the translator of the sūtra into Chinese, as the teacher of Bodhidharma at the head of Chinese Zen's line of transmission. The two chronicles take differing positions towards the Bodhidharma treatise. The *Ch'üan fa-pao chi* rejects it as unauthentic,[33] while the *Leng-ch'ieh shih-tzu chi* provides it with additions and takes it up in the text.

Consciousness of a unique line of transmission of Bodhidharma Zen, which is not yet demonstrable in the Bodhidharma treatise, grew during the seventh century and must have taken shape on the East Mountain prior to the death of the Fourth Patriarch, Tao-hsin (580–651).[34] The earliest indication appears in the epitaph for Fa-ju (638–689), one of the outstanding disciples of the Fifth Patriarch, Hung-jen (601–674). The author of the epitaph is not known, but the list comprises six names: after Bodhidharma and Hui-k'o follow Seng-ts'an, Tao-hsin, Hung-jen, and Fa-ju. The *Ch'üan fa-pao chi* takes this list over and adds as a seventh name that of Shen-hsiu (606?–706). In an epitaph for Shen-hsiu, his name is made to take the place of Fa-ju's. The *Leng-ch'ieh shih-tzu chi* omits Fa-ju and ends after Shen-hsiu with the name of his disciple P'u-chi (651–739). These indications from the Northern school argue for the succession of the Third Patriarch, Seng-ts'an (d. 606), which has been thrown into doubt because of lacunae in the historical work of Tao-hsüan. Still, the matter cannot be settled with certainty.

The information contained in the Tun-huang manuscripts permits a more accurate representation of the earliest period of Bodhidharma Zen. The Bodhidharma treatise gives us brief glimpses of the important beginnings of different accents in Zen up until the middle of the seventh century, accents that came into their own during the eighth century and led to explosions that are well enough known. The decades of activity of the Zen patriarchs of East Mountain were part of the incubation period during which distinct and contradictory positions took clear shape.

THE PATRIARCHS OF EAST MOUNTAIN

The characteristic traits of the new period of Zen history that begins with the residence of the patriarchs on East Mountain, namely the establishment of a life-style with monastic rule, are well known. The study of the Tun-huang texts permits us to bring this story into sharper relief, making visible the relation between the legendary beginnings of Chinese Zen and the mutually competing later forms.

Although the meaning of the mythical figure of the founder Bodhidharma for the basic thematic outlines of the Zen way can to some extent be unlocked for historical understanding through the Bodhidharma treatise, a sustained study of the text awaits future research.

TAO-HSIN (580–651), THE FOURTH PATRIARCH

The Zen chronicles refer to two writings of the Fourth Patriarch, Tao-hsin: a no-longer extant text on the Bodhisattva precepts and a text known as *Fundamental Expedient Teachings for Reposing the Mind That Attains Enlightenment* 入道安心要方 便法門 (Chin., *Ju-tao an-hsin yao fang-pien fa-men;* Jpn., *Nyūdō anjin yō hōben hōmon*), which has been taken up into the *Leng-ch'ieh shih-tzu chi*.[35] The tendencies of the Bodhidharma treatise reappear in this important treatise, as we see already from the title. The glyph meaning "entrance" or "entry" (Chin., *erh ju;* Jpn., *ni nyū*) that is used in the title *Two Ways of Entrance* also shows up in the subtitle of the Tao-hsin text. In both cases it refers to entry into the way of Zen. Tao-hsin speaks in his text often of "entering," as at the conclusion of a central passage on the five Dharma gates: "….enter into the gate of meditation"; or again later in the explanation of the practice of meditation: "achieve entrance into the uncreated, correct truth" or "entrance into the correct principle (*li*) of the Unborn."[36] As Tao-hsin remarks in other passages, principle must agree with practice (*hsing;* Jpn., *gyō*), an assertion that, as David Chappell observes, "echoes the thought of Bodhidharma."[37]

The expression *shou-i pu-i* 守一不移 (Jpn., *shuichi fui*), which appears at the height of the passage on the five Dharma gates, was originally Taoist and found its way into Buddhism from Chinese meditation masters. The English rendering "Maintaining the One without Wavering" brings the Taoist origins into clear relief.[38] "The One" of Lao-tzu, a key term in Chinese intellectual history, recalls for Mahāyāna Buddhists their fundamental notion of reality as based in the wisdom sūtras. Tao-hsin cites these sūtras and many other Mahāyāna texts. As a young man he had taken up the worldview of emptiness (*śūnyatā*). He spent more than ten years (613–624) in the temple monastery of Ta-lin on Mount Lu, which had been founded by Chih-k'ai 智鍇 (533–610), an adherent of the San-lun (Jpn., *Sanron*) school and disciple of the T'ien-t'ai (Jpn., Tendai) Patriarch Chih-i (538–597). It is not certain whether Tao-hsin had met Chih-k'ai personally, but the monastery was doubtless imbued with the Mādhyamika spirit.[39] In his treatise Tao-hsin speaks again and again of the "pure and empty mind" that the practitioner must preserve and foster.

Tao-hsin's proximity to T'ien-t'ai goes as far back as his student years in the monastery of Ta-lin. In T'ien-t'ai, theoretical doctrine, which takes on an important place in the axioms of the wisdom sūtras, is bound essentially to the practice of meditation, which takes precedence. The combination of doctrine and praxis was Tao-hsin's ideal. The way that he pointed to was based on doctrinal principles, but the goal can be reached only through intensive exercise. One of the pillars is the "*Samādhi* of One Practice" (Chin., *i-hsing san-mei;* Jpn., *ichigyō sanmai*), which, in his words, "means that the mind aware of the Buddha is the Buddha." Elsewhere we are told that "fixing your awareness on ultimate reality is called *i-hsing san-mei*."[40] The *samādhi* of one practice—also known as the "*samādhi* of one-ness" (Yampolsky) or the "calmness in which one realizes that all dharmas are the same" (Wing-tsit Chan),[41] is one of the four *samādhis* that Chih-i treats in his foundational *Mo-ho chih-kuan* 摩訶止觀 (Jpn., *Makashikan*; T. 1911) as the stages leading up to perfect enlightenment.[42] Tao-hsin was also familiar with the term *chih-kuan* (Jpn., *shikan*), central to T'ien-t'ai meditation, though he may have owed this to the well-known "Treatise on the Awakening of Faith in Mahāyāna" (Skt., *Mahāyāna-śraddhotpāda-śastra*; Chin., *Ta-cheng ch'i-hsin lun*; Jpn., *Daijōkishinron*).[43] Be that as it may, the close relationship of Tao-hsin to T'ien-t'ai comes forth clearly in his treatise.

The strong influence of T'ien-t'ai relies in turn on the wide-ranging acceptance of nearly all important elements of Mahāyāna, which at the time of the founder Chih-i had not only gained access into the whole breadth of the Indian transmission in China but also had been enriched significantly by the interpretations of Chinese thought. T'ien-t'ai meditation recognized sudden realization and gradual ascent to enlightenment.[44] Tao-hsin likewise included both ways. In his treatise we find the earliest written proof of the suddenness of the enlightenment experience. Chappell translates a remarkable passage, expressly attributed to Tao-hsin:

> Neither by [trying to] meditate on the Buddha, nor by [trying to] grab hold of the mind, nor by seeing the mind, nor by analyzing the mind, nor by reflection, nor by discernment, nor by dispersing confusion, but through identification with the natural rhythms of things. Don't force anything to go. Don't force anything to stay. Finally abiding in the one sole purity, the mind spontaneously becomes lucid and pure.[45]

The two important expressions in the passage are read in the original as *chih-ren-yün* 直任運 (Jpn., *shin ninnen*) and *tzu* 自 (Jpn., *ji*, also read in Japanese *mizukara* or *onozukara*). Yanagida explains the expression *ren-yün* by paraphrasing it to mean "giving oneself over to the course of heaven and earth." He alludes to Lao-tzu and Chuang-tzu, in whom this same combination of glyphs appears.[46] The following term *tzu* (literally, "of itself") is also to be read Taoistically. Chappell renders it "spontaneously." A bit later the text mentions that for one who has been enlightened the Dharma eye opens spontaneously.[47] Tao-hsin closes his comments on the fifth Dharma gate with the assertion that practitioners "enter into the gate of meditation *without delay*."[48] Yanagida translates this latter phrase as "quickly," which accords with the meaning of the Chinese glyph.[49] It is worth noting that the passages that treat the suddenness of enlightenment go together with explanations of the doctrine of *śūnyatā*. Obviously there is some connection between this doctrine and the idea of sudden enlightenment.

In comparison with the rich and close relation of Tao-hsin to the founder of T'ien-t'ai and his writings, textual evidence of his adherence to the Bodhidharma tradition is rather weak. Earlier we remarked the use of the same glyph for entrance (*ju, nyū*) in the titles of the Bodhidharma treatise and Tao-hsin's *Fundamental Expedient Teachings for Reposing the Mind That Attains Enlightenment*. The second compound in Tao-hsin's title, *an-hsin* (Jpn., *anjin*), also occupies a prominent place in the Bodhidharma treatise. In his text Tao-hsin praises the inexhaustible fullness of the mind that has reached satisfaction (*an-hsin*).[50] When he recognizes T'an-lin's identification of the mysterious *pi-kuan*, the highest Mahāyāna meditation, with *an-hsin*, further ties in the relationship come to light. Less reliable is the connection that the *Ch'üan fa-pao chi*, which carries no weight in the Bodhidharma treatise, draws to the founder of Chinese Zen when it suggests a line of tradition from Bodhidharma and Hui-k'o through Seng-ts'an to Tao-hsin and points in its biographical sketch of the latter to Seng-ts'an as one of his teachers.[51] The history of Zen remains somewhat tangled here.

The same may be said regarding the significance of the *Laṅkāvatāra Sūtra* in the early period of Chinese Zen. It is mentioned only once in the part of the chronicle attributed to Tao-hsin—in the opening lines, where it is referred to as "foundational for the First Principle." If the arguments for the gradual ascent to enlightenment in Tao-hsin's text cover a wide range, this is attributed to the influence of T'ien-t'ai. Most notable is the passage that contains the famous comparison of gradual ascent with shooting a bow. Chappell translates it as follows:

> Like a man who is studying archery, first he shoots with great license, but then he hits the bull's eye with a small leeway [of error]. First he hits something big, next he hits something small, then he hits a hair, and then he divides a hair into 100 parts and hits a hundredth of a hair. Next, the last arrow hits the end of the previous arrow. A succession of arrows do not allow the arrows to drop [to the ground]. It is like a man who practices the Way. Moment after moment he dwells in his mind. Thought after thought continuously without even a short interval in awareness he practices correct awareness without interruption and correct awareness in the present.[52]

The glyph 次 that Chappell renders as *next* and *then* appears seven times in the passage. The comparison of practice with shooting a bow has its own history in East Asia. Yanagida cites striking passages from the *prajñāpāramitā* literature and alludes to T'ien-t'ai writings.[53] The metaphor accommodates the kind of step-by-step progress in practice that Tao-hsin recommends for the calming of the mind:

> If you achieve a calm mind and do not have the mind which clings to objectified phenomena, then your mind gradually becomes tranquil and stable and step by step eliminates the various passions. Therefore, you finally do not create new [illusions] and it can be said that you are free.[54]

The Chinese compound that Chappell translates once as *gradually* and then as *step by step* 随分 (Chin., *sui-fen*; Jpn., *zuibun*) would be transposed in modern Japanese to *shidai ni*. Shen-hui, the chief opponent from the Southern school, criticizes the so-called calming of the mind 住心 (Chin., *chu-hsin*; Jpn., *jūshin*) that occurs at the beginning of this passage, seeing in it an expression of the doctrine of gradual enlightenment that was attributed to the Northern school.[55] Practice over an extended period is a commendable "expedient" (Skt., upāya; Chin., fang-pien; Jpn., hōben). Expedients are important to Tao-hsin since, as the text states, "the cultivation of the way involves expedient aids."[56] In Tao-hsin's view, the expedients are useful means that can lead to enlightenment. The Southern school of Hui-neng takes the radical position that the expedients useful to practice are a function of enlightenment.

The recitation of the name of the Buddha (Chin., nien-fo; Jpn., nenbutsu) is also an expedient, and one which found its way into Zen through Tao-hsin. The Fourth Patriarch lived on East Mountain close to Lu-shan, famous in Buddhist history for the Amithāba (Jpn., Amida) cult that was flourishing at the time. It was through him that the practice of the nenbutsu became widespread.[57]

Tao-hsin cites the sūtras of Amida Buddhism and refers to the "pure land" in which believers of this Buddha aspire to be reborn. But he does not associate the nenbutsu with the veneration of Amida. Clarifying the nature of the practice, he cites the Daibongyō 大品經: "'No object of thought' means to be thinking of Buddha."[58] According to this definition, the nenbutsu would be a kind of objectless meditation. In Tao-hsin's text, the nenbutsu leads to the Mahāyāna doctrine of the identity of mind and Buddha. The text answers the question of the significance of meditation without an object 無所念 (Chin., wu-suo-nien; Jpn., mushonen):

It means the mind which is "thinking on Buddha" is called thinking on no object. Apart from mind, there is no Buddha at all. Apart from Buddha, there is no mind at all. Thinking on Buddha is identical to the thinking mind. To seek the mind means to seek for the Buddha.[59]

It seems that Tao-hsin had become acquainted with the nenbutsu during his stay in the temple monastery of Ta-lin and had taken it up in his practice of meditation.[60] For him it touched on the fundamental principles of the wisdom sūtras. The Ch'üan fu-pao chi mentions the practice of the nenbutsu by his disciples Hung-jen and Shen-hsiu.

Tao-hsin's Zen rests on the core teaching of Mahāyāna, the Mādhyamika doctrine of the emptiness (śūnyatā) of all things (dharma), which enlightenment recognizes when it grasps the essence of reality. The Fourth Patriarch was not content with transmitting this doctrine to his disciples, but gave perplexing, concrete instructions as to how the goal can be reached. His text represents the oldest version of a manual of Zen meditation of the sort later composed by the Chinese master Tsung-tse 宗賾 during the Sung period and by Dōgen in Japan during the Kamakura period.[61] Tao-hsin's guide offers, as the Japanese Buddhist historian Sekiguchi asserts, "the first example of a Ch'an description of meditation technique."[62]

In Tao-hsin's text we find two practical guides to meditation. In the first section he recommends looking at body and mind, the five skandha or elements of existence, the four elements, the six sense organs, the three poisons, and all dharmas in order to grasp that all is empty, without coming to be or passing away, identical and without duality.[61] Still more concrete is a second guide whose wording can be rendered:

> When you first begin practicing, sitting meditation (Chin., tso-ch'an; Jpn., zazen) and viewing the mind (Chin., k'an-hsin; Jpn., kanshin), go off by yourself and sit in one place. First make your body erect and sit correctly. Make your clothes roomy and loosen your belt. Relax your body and loosen your limbs. Massage yourself seven or eight times. Expel completely the air in your belly. Through the natural flow you will obtain your true nature, clear and empty, quiet and pure. The body and mind being harmonized, the spirit is able to be peaceful. Then obscure and mysterious, the inner breath is clear and cool. Slowly, slowly you collect your mind and your spiritual path becomes clear and keen.[64]

One who practices in this way realizes that the nature of mind is one with the Buddha-nature and identical with the original mind. Even when he is giving practical guidance, there is more involved here for Tao-hsin than mere technique. Making his own the same love of negation found in prajñāpāramitā literature, he stresses: "The basis of our method is no-method."[65] Tao-hsin enjoins zealous practice

> without interval both day and night, whether walking, staying, sitting or lying down, always practice this contemplation![66]

> Work hard! Work hard![67]

The true Buddhist disciple "constantly dwells in meditation."[68] Such admonitions are repeated again and again. The disciples are told to dedicate themselves with all their energies to practice. The text paints the mood of intense discipline carried on in the monastery of many a Zen master. In this respect one may compare the Japanese master Dōgen with the old masters of East Mountain.

HUNG-JEN (601–651), THE FIFTH PATRIARCH

As the chronicles attest, Tao-hsin gathered about himself a considerable band of listeners, but only the names of a few disciples remain in the recorded tradition.[69] After his death the robe fell on the shoulders of his chief disciple Hung-jen, who had lived with him from the first days on Mt Shuan-feng (624). What had begun as an insignificant place of practice and later developed into a monastic community, was destined in time to become one of the most outstanding centers of Chinese Buddhism. It is hardly possible to separate the special role of Tao-hsin and Hung-jen from this course of events. Of the two, Hung-jen was the stronger personality and there is more historical material and persuasive evidence concerning him.[70] He stepped completely into the footsteps of his master and brought the work to full bloom. The rich fruits were visible in the following generation of "Ten Great Disciples."

The main substance of biographical reports on Hung-jen are found in the two chronicles *Ch'üan fa-pao chi* and *Leng-ch'ieh shih-tzu chi*. Legendary elements embellish the story of his childhood years with his mother, whom he served with filial piety. At the age of seven or twelve he set out for the path of homelessness. Tao-hsin was appointed his instructor, and it seems that Hung-jen was with his teacher already from the time of the latter's stay in Chi-chou and the monastery of Ta-lin. As patriarch he settled with his community on the eastern peak of the mountain. The sources name his school and that of Tao-hsin as the "schools" or "doctrines" of East Mountain.

The bonds between the two patriarchs Tao-hsin and Hung-jen are apparent when one analyzes the works that have come to be ascribed to them. Only one copy remains of Tao-hsin's text, which is included in the *Leng-ch'ieh shih-tzu chi*, and that copy cannot be dated precisely. The writings of Hung-jen, transcribed by his disciples, are also undated and have come down in a later handwriting.

On the basis of these materials, McRae has gone to great pains to produce a new edition. His assessment of the handwriting, and the publication and title of the work, yield the following picture: Hung-jeng's text was published in Korea in 1570 under the title *The Treatise on the Supreme Vehicle* (Chin., *Tsui-shang sheng lun*; Jpn., *Saijōjōron*), was reprinted several times (for the first time in Japan in 1716), and was taken up in an anthology. The text first discovered in Tun-huang was published in Peking in 1931, where D. T. Suzuki came upon it, later to publish a facsimile edition in Japan (1935). The text appeared in Peking under the title *Treatise on the One Vehicle of Manifesting One's Own Mind* 一乘顯自心論 (Chin., *I-sheng hsien tzu-hsin lun*; Jpn., *Ichijō kenjishinron*). Another Tun-huang text ended up in the library of Ryūkoku University in Kyoto. Suzuki discovered three more Tun-huang manuscripts in England (S–2669, S–3558, S–4064) and published the manuscripts known to him (without consulting the Ryūkoku manuscript) in 1951 in *Zen shisōshi kenkyū II*. (This edition also appears in volume 2 of Suzuki's *Zenshū* [Collected Works, 1968, pp. 303–91]. The remaining manuscripts were discovered by Yanagida. The text was taken into the Taishō edition (no. 2011, vol. 48). The title is generally given as *Treatise on the Essentials of Cultivating the Mind* (Chin., *Hsiu-hsin yao lun*; Jpn., *Shūshin'yō-ron*).[71]

On the basis of handwriting data and other indications, McRae came to the view that Hung-jen's text is the older. He places its composition around the end of the seventh century, and reckons the text of Tao-hsin to stem from the early years of the following century. The dating of the two manuscripts is unclear. The numerous manuscripts of Hung-jen's text attest to the wide circulation and popularity it enjoyed in China at the time. For several centuries the *Hsiu-hsin yao lun* stood as the standard work on East Mountain teaching. McRae's view is thus solidly based. It is clear that similarities between the two writings appear not only in the basic traits of their contents but also in the manner of expression and use of words.[72]

The literal meaning of the central term of the treatise, *shou-hsin* 守心 (Jpn., *shushin*) or "guarding the mind," calls to mind the ancient Buddhist meditation practice of attentiveness. In Hung-jen it is to be understood in the Mahāyāna context as the central doctrine of the identity of mind and Buddha. The true mind is identical with self-nature, Dharma-nature, Buddha-nature. Just as the "Dharma sun" appears bright and pure to the original mind, "it does not generate false thoughts and extinguishes the illusion of personal possession."[73] It is all a matter of letting the sun appear completely. This happens through "maintaining awareness of the mind."[74]

The relationship of the key word *shou-hsin* to Tao-hsin's *shou-i* is obvious. The question of independence is answered differently, depending on when one dates the composition of the texts. The incomparable value of mindfulness appears in a passage of the treatise of Hung-jen, in which three essential traits or fruits of this endeavor are presented:

> Maintaining awareness of the mind is the fundamental basis of *nirvāṇa*, the essential gateway for entering the path, the basic principle of the entire Buddhist canon.[75]

The passages that follow make it clear that present attentiveness is the core of the Way.

The metaphors of sun and mirror, which belong together and express the same thing, play an important role in Hung-jen's treatise. Both metaphors assert that the originally pure mind, like the unhindered shining sun and the unsullied mirror become covered over and sullied in the existence of sentient beings in this world of becoming (*saṃsāra*), with its ignorance, appetites, and delusions. After a few brief introductory remarks, Hung-jen's treatise opens with a passage containing the metaphor of sun and clouds, which is related to a quotation from a Buddhist text of undetermined origin in which the Buddha nature in sentient beings is likened to the sun, "essentially bright, perfect, and complete."[76] Hung-jen relates the comparison to the mind, which he sees as identical to the Buddha nature:

> The sun's light is not destroyed, but merely deflected by the clouds and mists. The pure mind possessed by all sentient beings is also like this, in simply being covered by the layered clouds of discriminative thinking, false thoughts, and ascriptive views. If one can just distinctly maintain [awareness of] the mind and not produce false thought then the Dharma sun of *nirvāṇa* will be naturally manifest. Therefore, it is known that one's own mind is inherently pure.[77]

The final line emphasizes the core of the metaphor. Like the sun, the mind is "inherently pure."

In another passage of the treatise the metaphor of sun and clouds is related to that of the mirror. Since the mind is clouded by delusions like the sun by clouds, one needs practice, which consists in "maintaining awareness of the mind. By just distinctly maintaining awareness of the True Mind, the doubts of false thoughts will go away and the sun of wisdom will appear." This occurrence, as the passage thereafter makes plain, can be understood "according to the metaphor of polishing a mirror. When the dust is gone, the Nature naturally becomes manifest."[78]

The metaphor of the mirror, classical in Chinese literature since the time of Lao-tzu, resounds also in Tao-hsin's text. The practicer, after long and intensive meditation, comes to the insight, as it is said, that "one's own body is like the moon [reflected] in the water, or like an image in a mirror."[79] Both images have enjoyed resilience through the centuries in Zen literature. The enlightenment verses attributed to Shen-hsiu and Hui-neng in the *Platform Sūtra* illustrate the differing evaluations and interpretations of the metaphor of the mirror that were a point of contention between the Northern and Southern schools during the eighth century.

In Hung-jen's treatise the metaphors do not concern ascetic practice but rather attention to the originally pure mind. This also holds for the richly informative passages in the sections on Guṇabhadra and Hui-k'o in the *Leng-ch'ieh shih-tzu chi*, in which the fateful term "polishing the mirror" appears: "It is like the polishing of a bronze mirror: When the dust is completely gone from the surface of the mirror, the mirror is naturally bright and pure."[80] McRae adds the explanation: "The brightness of the mirror and the existence of dust on its surface are of two fundamentally different layers of reality. The mirror is not really affected by the dust."[81] Hung-jen's treatise, like the early *Leng-ch'ieh shih-tzu chi* chronicle, can be considered representative of the standpoint of the Northern school.

Like Tao-hsin, Hung-jen enjoins his disciples to zealous practice and gives concrete instructions for Zen meditation. He commends to the beginner a method drawn from one of the Amida sūtras:

> Sit properly with the body erect, closing the eyes and mouth. Look straight ahead with the mind, visualizing a sun at an appropriate distance away. Maintain the image continuously without stopping. Regulate your breath so that it does not sound alternately coarse and fine, as this can make one sick.[82]

The method of visual concentration, a favorite in Amida Buddhism, did not secure a lasting place in Zen Buddhism.

Hung-jen warns against going astray, against "sensory perceptions" and "restricted breathing," against illusions, and above all against anything that "leads to the activation of discriminative thinking, which constitutes a defiled state of mind."[83] A method of meditation that gently and naturally calms the mind safeguards against these pitfalls:

> View your own consciousness tranquilly and attentively, so that you can see how it is always moving, like flowing water or a glittering mirage. After you have perceived this consciousness, simply continue to view it gently and naturally, without [the consciousness assuming any fixed position] inside or outside of yourself. Do this tranquilly and attentively, until its fluctuations dissolve into peaceful stability. This flowing consciousness will disappear like a gust of wind.[84]

This guidance shows the high degree of refinement of the psychological understanding of Zen meditation in the early period. Still, despite his lenient character, Hung-jen demands of his disciples the engagement of all their strength. Time and again he reiterates, "Make effort! Make effort!"[85] The conviction of the mind's original purity and the demand for greater effort in practice may appear contradictory. The experience of this basic tension is the starting point of the spiritual way of the great Japanese master Dōgen, who was tormented by the question, "Why painful practice if all sentient beings possess the Buddha nature?" There is no theoretical answer to this question. The answer is simple: practice. Hung-jen's treatise manifests this insight.

Aside from the *Hsiu-hsin yao lun*, the most valuable source for the Zen teaching of Hung-jen, there is a rather long entry on the Fifth Patriarch in the *Leng-ch'ieh shih-tzu chi*, whose editor, Ching-chüeh, was a disciple of Hsüan-tse, a member of the most intimate circle of Hung-jen's disciples, and who is an important witness for the Zen of East Mountain. Ching-chüeh's report relies on the *Leng-ch'ieh jen-fa chih*, a treatise of his teacher that is no longer extant but which he cites. No mention is made of the *Hsiu-hsin yao lun*. The justification may perhaps lie in the first lines of the entry, which answer the question of why Hung-jen had preferred solitariness in the mountains to life in the cities. He replies that in the heights of the mountains and the depths of the valleys the mind comes equally of itself to calm. Just as trees blossom and bring forth fruit, so has Hung-jen through the practice of *zazen* opened up the flowers of enlightenment:

> The great master Hung-jen practiced *zazen* quietly and purely. He did not compose any writings but taught deep principles with words and transmitted these to people in silence. Those who still claim that Hung-jen had taught his method of *zazen* in a book are in error.[86]

Ching-chüeh's entry is interesting on several counts. He emphasizes the meaning of his teacher Hsüan-tse, whom the patriarch had entrusted with the construction of a mausoleum before his death and whom he had charged, together with Shen-hsiu, with the task of diffusing the *Laṅkāvatāra Sūtra*.[87] The account of the expiration of Hung-jen is also the classical source concerning the ten disciples, who are named expressly.[88] After his death he was honored with a portrait and the verses of well-known artists.

In the *Leng-ch'ieh shih-tzu chi* there follows one final section of great interest. Throughout his life the great master used a particular form of question to teach, which D. T. Suzuki called "pointing at things and asking meanings" 指事問義 (Chin., *chih-shih wen-i*; Jpn., *shiji mongi*). Two examples may be adduced:

> There is a single little house filled with crap and weeds and dirt—What is it? If you sweep out all the crap and weeds and dirt and clean it all up so there is not a single thing left inside, then what is it?[89]

The *Leng-ch'ieh shih-tzu chi* also ascribes such questions to Guṇabhadra, Bodhidharma, and Shen-hsiu. Guṇabhadra's questions follow a quotation from the

Laṅkāvatāra Sūtra. In his explanatory remarks, Yanagida reminds us of the passage in this sūtra that contains the 108 questions of the bodhisattva Mahātmati.[90] D. T. Suzuki saw in the *shiji mongi* the first beginnings of the kōan. In this regard, Yanagida notes that the *Leng-ch'ieh shih-tzu chi* only presents the questions of masters without the replies of the disciples, while in the bodhisattva treatise the disciples put questions that are answered by the master.[91] Both examples of kōan-like questions are worthy of note, although kōan in the proper sense of the term only appear in the latter half of the eighth century.

The Zen doctrine of East Mountain contains a wealth of theoretical insights and practical instructions that press towards further development. Absent are the signs of an acute tension like that in the confrontation between the Southern and Northern schools based on the dichotomy between "sudden" and "gradual" enlightenment, which would become virulent in the next century. But the seeds of the coming conflict are already recognizable.

THE NORTHERN SCHOOL

FROM EAST MOUNTAIN TO THE NORTHERN SCHOOL

The Northern school of Zen is not a clearly defined, institutionally identifiable entity in Chinese Buddhism. The designation was coined to set it off against the Southern school when one of the third-generation disciples of Hung-jen took the offensive against Hung-jen's successor Shen-hsiu (60?–706) and his following. In the mouths of its opponents, the term *Northern school* carried the pejorative sense of a "branch line of Bodhidharma Zen" or even of a "heresy." Adherents of the so-called Northern school did not use the name to characterize themselves.[92] In these circumstances, it is difficult to pinpoint the beginning of the Northern school. Yanagida sees East Mountain as the historical locus of the outbreak of a new movement in Chinese Buddhism. In his view the Northern school was comprised of "all those disciples who broke off from the Dharma gate of East Mountain to Ch'ang-an and Lo-yang."[93] The Zen method of the Northern school was a further development of that of East Mountain and the *Shushin'yō-ron* was its foundation.[94]

Hung-jen had assembled about himself on East Mountain a large group of disciples, ten of whom were particularly eminent.[95] It seems that after the death of the master harmony among the disciples broke down. Differences and factions are mentioned in the sources that have come down to us, but it is hard to be certain about details. Fa-ju (638–689), a pioneer of the Northern school, is referred to in the earliest written documents of the age. Two texts apparently composed shortly after his death—the epitaph of an anonymous author and a text entitled *The Deeds and Conduct of Fa-ju* (Chin., *Fa-ju Ch-an-shih hsing-chuan*; Jpn., *Hōnyo zenji gyōjō*), also anonymous—show broad agreement in content, which suggests mutual dependence but does not permit us to say which of the two is earlier.[96] Both texts contain the generational line that ties the Zen patriarchs of East Mountain to Bodhidharma. Moreover, both stress the direct transmission of the mind, outside of the scriptures. And both cite the same text from the introduction of Hui-yüan (334–416) to the meditation sūtra of Dharmatrāta (Chin., *Ta-mo-to-lo ch'an ching*; Jpn., *Datsumatara zengyō*, T. 618), which testifies to the transmission of mind from Buddha to Ānanda to Dharmatrāta and Buddhasena, and can be understood as an intimation of the Zen doctrine of the transmission of the lamp.[97] We may note in passing that in reference to the legend of the smiling disciple, the early generational list from the Northern school mentions the Buddha's beloved disciple Ānanda, while that of the Southern school mentions Kāśyapa.

The *Den hōbōki* chronicle uses these two early texts as a basis for its biographical treatment of Fa-ju, and accords him high praise as the pioneer of the Northern school.[98] His first teacher is listed as Hui-ming, disciple of Fa-min 法敏 (597–645) of the Mādhyamika school, a figure well known for his ascetical rigors. Reports have it that Hui-ming sent Fa-ju to Hung-jen, where he stayed until the latter's death sixteen years later. On East Mountain Fa-ju received the seal of Dharma successor and hence can be considered as a legitimate heir of the fifth patriarch. The text of the *Hōnyo zenji gyōjō* notes that he achieved enlightenment in "sudden entry in the One Vehicle."[99] Curiously, the term "sudden" (Chin., *tun*; Jpn., *ton*) is used here to characterize the experience of a master of the Northern school.

Fa-ju escaped into the solitude of Sung Mountain to avoid assuming a high administrative post in the capital city after the death of the emperor Kao-tsung 高宗 (683). During the three final years of his life he devoted himself fully and without distraction to the spread of the doctrine and practice of Zen. In the monastery of Shōrin-ji, famous for its association with Bodhidharma and Hui-k'o, he gathered about himself a large number of disciples, whom he asked Shen-hsiu to join before his death.

The few extant sources depict Fa-ju as a significant figure in early Chinese Zen, but the period of his activity was too brief to leave a strong mark. One reason that later chronicles do not mention his name may be that in attacking the supposedly deviant line, Shen-hui concentrated his attention on Shen-hsiu and his disciples.

The fortunes of the Northern school took their first turn for the better when the disciples of Hung-jen accepted an invitation to the imperial court. The appearance of the eminent masters Lao-an 老安 (or Hui-an 慧安) and Shen-hsiu in the capital (ca. 700 and 701) excited attention. Both were commended with honor by the empress Wu and were held in high esteem both by the court and the people—not least because of their advanced age. Lao-an's date of birth is uncertain, but he seems to have lived a full hundred years.[100] His miraculous powers further enhanced his already enchanting figure. Among typical Zen sayings of his that have been transmitted is the following: "If you drive a nail into a mirror, it makes a sound. Is there also a sound before you strike?" Both before and after his stay in the capital he worked in the monastery of Yü-ch'uan ssu (Jpn., Gyokusen-ji). The names of several of his disciples have come down to us, among them Tao-shun 道俊, who likewise was invited to the imperial court (707 or 708),[101] and Chih-t'a 智達 (or Hui-t'a 慧達), a persuasive advocate of sudden enlightenment.

Shen-hsiu, the noted leader of Zen disciples in the cities, was showered with distinctions. In general, the time in which he worked was an auspicious one. After an ascent marred by intrigue and shady power struggles, the empress Wu assumed the throne and ruled from 690–705. She promoted Buddhism vigorously and drew important Buddhists of all schools to her court, where she had them retranslate Buddhist texts like the *Avatamsaka Sūtra*, the *Laṅkāvatāra Sūtra*, the *Vimalakīrti Sūtra*, and the *Ta-cheng ch'i-hsin lun* (Jpn., *Daijōkishinron*). She also lavished material riches on them. Bodhidharma Zen flourished as its adherents rushed in great numbers from East Mountain to the capital cities of Ch'ang-an and Lo-yang. As Yanagida remarks, "The Zen school that had begun as an unaccustomed novelty in Chinese Buddhism won a position as the Buddhism of the new age."[102]

SHEN-HSIU

The life of Shen-hsiu reached its peak in his call to the imperial court and in his work as a teacher in the capital cities of Lo-yang and Ch'ang-an. The biographical sources, above all the epitaph of the famous literary figure Ch'ang Yüeh[103] (apparently composed some three years after his death), and the reports of the *Den hōbōki* and *Ryōga shikiji* chronicles that rely on it, depict graphically the solemn entry in imperial litters into the eastern capital of Lo-yang; the uncommon reverence of the empress Wu (who prostrated herself and touched her head to the ground) and of the high aristocracy throughout the capital city; and the participation of the people. Apparently this esteem was less religious than political, a recognition of the support that Buddhism had given to the so-called Chou revolution that brought the empress Wu to the heights of her power.[104]

Shen-hsiu's life, as he himself assures us, contained little of note.[105] At the age of thirteen he helped the poor and sick. In wanderings to temple sites he met a well-intentioned friend (*kalyāna mitra*), who advised him to enter the monkhood. In the year 625 he took the monastic vows at the temple of T'ien-kung ssu 大宮寺 (Jpn., Tengū-ji) in Lo-yang. A gap in his biography follows as the next years were taken up with travels and residence in temples, which further enhanced his reputation. Although he was already beyond his prime when he heard of the meditation Buddhism being practiced on East Mountain (651 or 656), he went there and was accepted by Hung-jen into the circle of disciples. He passed his days and nights in fervent meditation. So completely did he master the Way that after six years, as his epitaph has it, "the Dharma of East Mountain was full in Shen-hsiu."[106] After being named Dharma heir, he took tearful leave of the East Mountain. A gap of fifteen years follows.[107] Between 676 and 679 his name appears in the monks' register at the temple of Gyokusen-ji not far from Lo-yang, where, at the wish of respected monks, he was installed with great solemnity. He spent the final decade of the century in this monastery. Numerous disciples gathered around him and large numbers of people streamed in to hear him discourse.[108] His hermitage "Gate of Liberation," located near Gyokusen-ji where the master spent

most of his time and which he later handed over to the temple, became the center of the Zen school.

Regarding Shen-hsiu's inner, spiritual progress the sources have little to say. His ascetical path is described as one of gradual practice, but details of his enlightenment experience are hidden from us.[109] His epitaph summarizes the content of his teachings thus: After calming the thoughts and conceptions of the mind and strenuous concentration

> there is no longer any difference between "profane" and "sacred," no "before" or "after" in ascetical endeavors. With the entry into samādhi all objects vanish; with the achievement of wisdom all things are the same.[110]

The epitaph also suggests that Shen-hsiu held the Laṅkāvatāra Sūtra in special reverence and recommended it to his disciples. His relationship to the Laṅkāvatāra Sūtra also seems to be behind his choice of the name "Gate of Liberation," as the expression appears in the the sūtra. Furthermore, the chronicle of the Laṅkā masters contains the words of admonition that Hung-jen directed to Hsüan-tse and Shen-hsiu shortly before his death, entrusting the spread of the Laṅkāvatāra Sūtra to him and to Shen-hsiu.[111] But the report is erroneous. Shen-hsiu was not present at Hung-jen's death, and there is no clear indication that he had any particular relationship to this sūtra. In his teachings several Mahāyāna sūtras are mentioned. A not particularly credible episode has him giving precedence to the prajñāpāramitā sūtras in a dialogue with the empress Wu:

> The empress asked, "The doctrine that you are transmitting, to which school does it belong?"
> Answer: "It is the doctrine of the East Mountain of Chi-chou that I have received and pass on."
> Question: "On which sūtras do you rely?"
> Answer: "On the doctrine of the samādhi of one practice (ichigyō sanmai) of the Monjūsetsuhannya Sūtra."
> Empress Wu: "As for way of practice, it does not surpass the Dharma gate of East Mountain."[112]

The chronicle stresses that this transmission did not rest on writings and words but was oral.

The doctrine of the Northern school, whose most illustrious representative was Shen-hsiu, cannot be understood without a thoroughgoing study of the available documents. These writings are too numerous and too broad in scope to be assessed adequately in the space of this brief supplement. Two findings, however, should be singled out as having clearly emerged from the industrious research carried out in the United States. First, the Northern school, which for a long time after the introduction of Zen to the West remained in the shadows of Zen studies, is now seen to be an important branch of Chinese Zen Buddhism, and one deeply imbued with the spirit of Bodhidharma. Second, differences in emphasis exist between the Northern school and other lines of Zen that have occasionally flared up into heated confrontations, but these differences only make sense when seen in the full context of Zen Buddhism.

Several works and collections trace their origins to Shen-hsiu. The closest relationship to him can be claimed for the *Kuan-hsin lun* 觀心論 (Jpn., *Kanjinron*), which is identical to the *P'o-hsiang lun* 破相論 (Jpn., *Hasōron*) attributed to Bodhidharma and is preserved in several manuscripts.[113] The text was apparently composed by Shen-hsiu during his stay in Gyokusen-ji prior to his being summoned to the capital city and was perhaps stimulated by a work with the same title by Chih-i, founder of the Tendai school. Shen-hsiu's text relies on the doctrine of his master Hung-jen and shows considerable agreement with the latter's positions in the *Shushin'yō-ron*. The very title contains the motif of "seeing of mind," which recalls key expressions of the patriarchs of East Mountain: "preserving the one" (Tao-hsin) and "preserving the mind" (Hung-jen). The mind, like Buddha nature and Buddha mind, Dharma-nature and thusness, is the central reality of Mahāyāna Buddhism. Shen-hsiu's view is rooted in Mahāyāna doctrine, and his Zen interpretation relies on the sūtras. In the *Kanjinron*, for example, he cites sūtras of various orientations: the ancient Buddhist *Bathhouse Sūtra* 温室經 (Jpn., *Onshitsukyō*; Chin., *Wen-shih ching*), the *Mahāparinirvāṇa Sūtra*, the *Vimalakīrti Sūtra* inspired by the spirit of the wisdom sūtras, and the *Daśabhūmika Sūtra*, which is included in the Yogācāra tradition. Other Mahāyāna writings are mentioned in the corpus that stems from Shen-hsiu. Indeed, doctrine is emphasized so much more than practice that Shen-hsiu can be seen as an early forerunner of Tsung-mi, whose studies led him to the important thesis that doctrine and meditation are one (Chin., *chiao-ch'an i-chih*; Jpn., *kyōzen itchi*).[114] Shen-hsiu's eclecticism does not permit us to locate him in one of the doctrinal traditions of Mahāyāna. The most important points of contact with his thinking are found in Tendai and Kegon.

Shen-hsiu's leitmotif resounds full and strong in the opening lines of his *Kanjinron*, a work constructed in a question-and-answer genre. To the first question, which asks what is most necessary in the search for enlightenment, he replies with the title of his work: to see or behold the mind is to embrace all the practices of Zen. The request in the second question for further teaching occasions a lengthy statement that stresses the central importance of the mind:

> Of the myriad dharmas, mind is the most basic. All the various dharmas are simply the products of the mind. If one can comprehend the mind, then the myriad practices will all be accomplished.[115]

The fundamental meaning of mind is a reality for all beings. Shen-hsiu compares it to a tree whose branches, flowers, and fruit depend on the root. Two kinds of functions 起用 (Chin., *ch'i-yung*; Jpn., *kiyō*) must be distinguished for the mind—that of "pure mind" 淨心 (Chin., *ching-hsin*; Jpn., *jōshin*) and that of "defiled mind" 染心 (Chin., *jan-hsin*; Jpn., *senshin*):

> The Pure Mind is the mind of untainted Suchness 無漏眞如 (Chin., *wu-lou chen-ju*; Jpn., *muro shinnyo*). The defiled mind is the mind of tainted igno-

rance.... One who is himself enlightened to Suchness is unaffected by defilements and is called a sage. [Such a one] is eventually able to distantly transcend suffering and to realize the joy of nirvāṇa. One who acts in accord with the defiled is subject to its attachments and obscurations and is called an ordinary person. [Such a one] sinks helplessly within the triple realm and is subject to various kinds of suffering. Why is this? Because the defiled mind obstructs the essence of Suchness.[116]

The distinction between the pure and the defiled mind corresponds to the dual aspect of Suchness in the Treatise on the Awakening of Faith in Mahāyāna, whose influence on Shen-hsiu is unmistakable.[117]

In the Kanjinron metaphors and symbolic interpretations take up a disproportionate amount of space.[118] Shen-hsiu considers the six sense organs, the three poisons, the six virtues, and the like as symbols of spiritual advance on the path of enlightenment. He also views religious works such as the construction of temples, the casting of statues, the painting of images of the Buddha, the burning of incense and offering of flowers, and even the calling on the name of the Buddha—the nenbutsu already zealously practiced on East Mountain—as symbols of the spiritual life. Similarly, the utensils mentioned in the Bathhouse Sūtra are seen as symbols. Shen-hsiu takes the interpretative technique over from Tendai and puts it to the service of Zen.[119]

At the close of the treatise, Shen-hsiu takes up the thesis formulated at the outset, that all beholding of the mind leads to the goal of full enlightenment. He stresses, "The mind is the gateway to transcendence, the ford to liberation (nirvāṇa)."[120] And a few lines later:

If you only concentrate the mind and illuminate your inner [being], then with the enlightened contemplation constantly brilliant, you will extirpate the three poisons and block out the six bandits.... [You will] transcend the unenlightened state to the state of the sage.... Enlightenment is in an instant.[121]

Although there are passages in the treatise that assume a gradual process to the experience of enlightenment, this final statement contains the Chinese glyphs that point to suddenness.[122]

The dating of a group of Tun-huang texts that deal with the five upāya or skillful means (Chin., fang-pien; Jpn., hōben) is uncertain.[123] The oldest of these texts seems to have originated in the circle of Shen-hsiu's disciples and provide important insight into his teachings.[124] If it is surprising that the early Mahāyāna idea of upāya found its way into Zen teachings, one should remember that the concept also gained a new meaning in the process. Upāya in Zen is no longer a merely provisional aid or artifice. Since means and end are joined together, upāya is the same as enlightenment and thus belongs to the realm of what is final, unconditioned, and absolute, as the title of the important Mahāyāna text, The Gate of the Unborn Upāya, makes clear.[125] The Unborn is indestructible, released from the samsaric cycle of rebirths. The realization of the first upāya in the Comprehensive Explanation of the Essence of Buddhahood takes place through a stepping beyond into the transcendent. *Upāya* is referred to in the *Treatise on the Awakening of Faith in Mahāyāna* and said to mean

> that the essence of the mind transcends thoughts. The characteristic of the transcendence of thoughts is equivalent to the realm of space which pervades everywhere. The one characteristic of the *dharmadhātu* is the universally same *dharmakāya* of the *Tathāgata*. Inherent enlightenment is preached in relation to the *dharmakāya*.[126]

The *upāya* texts take over this central statement. The *Treatise* represents pure Mahāyāna doctrine. Mind is the final reality, as the above quotation indicates, identical with the Dharma-body of the Buddha. The *Treatise* likes to characterize it as "Suchness" 眞如 (Skt., *tathatā*; Chin., *chen-ju*; Jpn., *shinnyo*) and leaves no room for duality. Nevertheless, important expressions used in the *upāya* texts can lead to misunderstanding. The *Treatise* refers to enlightenment as *chüeh* 覺 (Jpn., *kaku*) and distinguishes between what it calls "inherent (or original) enlightenment" 本覺 (Chin., *pen-chüeh*; Jpn., *hongaku*) and "beginning (or temporal) enlightenment" 始覺 (Chin., *shih-chüeh*; Jpn., *shikaku*). The progressive process that comes into the picture after one has resolved to reach full enlightenment takes place through a "breaking away from thought" 惟念 (Chin., *li-nien*; Jpn., *rinen*).

The ambiguity of the term *rinen*, which appears frequently in the writings of the Northern school, admits of a variety of interpretations. Not uncommonly, a dualistic interpretation is possible. A detailed study by Robert Zeuschner has revealed no less than five possible meanings of the word.[127] In some contexts, meanings, ideas, and thought are separated from mind and not identical with it, which seems to argue for a dualistic reading. Such a view, Zeuschner concludes, "would justify Shen-hui's criticisms" and not necessarily imply "a deliberate misrepresentation."[128]

The orientation to the goal of enlightenment that characterizes Shen-hsiu's Zen doctrine argues against the dualistic interpretation. The *upāya* writings demand of the practitioner the observance of the *vinaya* vows and the practice of sitting meditation, and they encourage the calling of the name of the Buddha (nenbutsu) in a meditative sense.[129] But these are preparatory steps. The cleaning of all defilements takes place "in a moment."[130] Enlightenment consists in a "seeing of mind" whose "universal sameness" alone is real. Asked what he sees when he sees purity, the enlightened one replies, "I see no thing."[131] The seeing of enlightenment is without object.

Like *rinen*, the "seeing of purity" can also be presented variously. Shen-hui's attack is directed against views that he takes to be dualistic. According to these views, he says, purity stands objectified over against the mind like defiled thoughts and representations. On this point of contention against the Northern school Tsung-mi, Shen-hui's successor in the patriarchate of the Hotse school (Jpn., Kataku), has attracted considerable attention, not only among the Chinese Zen masters[132] but also among modern, Japanese scholars like D. T. Suzuki well acquainted with the Tun-huang manuscripts.[133] His writings interpret the Zen practice of the Northern school in the sense of Shen-hsiu's legendary verses in the *Platform Sūtra*, which liken the mind to a mirror that must be constantly polished. But the classical mirror metaphor can be interpreted in another way. In the concluding section of his book, McRae explains the original meaning of the metaphor and the verse of the *Platform Sūtra* by recalling a passage of Shen-hsiu's *Kanjinron* that speaks of a lamp and its flame:

> Further, lamps of eternal brightness are none other than the truly enlightened mind. When one's wisdom is bright and distinct, it is likened to a lamp.... The augmentation of moral disciple is taken as the addition of oil. For wisdom to be bright and penetrating is likened to the lamp's flame [or brightness]. If one constantly burns such a lamp of truly suchlike true enlightenment, its illumination will destroy all the darkness of ignorance and stupidity.[134]

The passage does not talk of the continued removal of specks of dust; moral preparation and sitting are, like oil, "additions." The mirror is the symbol of the mind that lights up by itself, that brightens everything and penetrates everything. One *upāya* text contains the following question-answer play on this image:

> *When viewing, what things do you view?*
> —Viewing, viewing, no thing is viewed.
> *Who views?*
> —The enlightened mind views.[135]

There is no distinction here between subject and object. The mind is "purity." "In purity, there is not a single thing."[136]

THE NORTHERN SCHOOL AFTER SHEN-HSIU

The splendid burial ceremony of the hundred-year-old Shen-hsiu marked the high point of the Northern school that revered him as its founder. The power-hungry empress Wei, who was as devoted to Buddhism as the empress Wu had been, took the occasion to place the full pomp of the imperial court at the service of the Buddhists.[137] There followed several years of political unrest, which came to an end with the ascent to the throne of the emperor Hsüan-tsung 玄宗 (ruled 713–755). The young emperor, who attributed deteriorating conditions in the kingdom to the excessive power of the Buddhist monasteries, took repressive measures. A number of restrictive edicts were imposed on all Buddhist schools. The emperor professed to the ancient Chinese principle of the equality of the three great religions—Confucianism, Taoism, and Buddhism—but showed favoritism towards Taoism, whose cultivation of longevity he held in high esteem. The history of the Northern school after Shen-hsiu must be seen against this political backdrop.

After Shen-hsiu's death at Tengū-ji, the focal point of the Northern school shifted to the capital cities and their surrounding areas, especially the monasteries on Mount Sung. There the master's two chief disciples, P'u-chi (651–739) and I-fu (658–736), remained until the latter took up residence in the western capital of Ch'ang-an, while the former stayed behind in the mountainous solitude around the eastern capital of Lo-yang. I-fu fostered ties with the imperial court.[118] In his youth he had intended to practice Zen meditation with Fa-ju, but because of the master's premature death he had to abandon his plan and enter into discipleship under Shen-hsiu. He practiced for ten years in Gyokusen-ji and then accompanied the master to the imperial court in Lo-yang (701), where he remained until the latter's death. He became the most important representative of the next generation of the Northern school in the region around Ch'ang-an. At first he lived on Mount Chung-nan. Later he settled in the monastery of Tz'u-en ssu 慈恩寺 (Jpn., Jion-ji), located in the capital city (722). Three years later he took up the invitation of the emperor to accompany him to Lo-yang, where he joined P'u-chi in Fu-hsien ssu 福先寺 (Jpn., Fukusen-ji) for two years (725–727). The final years of his life were spent in Ch'ang-an. Emperor Hsüan-tsung gave him the posthumous title of master of the "Great Knowledge" 大智 (Chin., Ta-chih; Jpn., Daichi).

The young Buddhist monk I-hsing 一行 (685–727), an intermittent student of P'u-chi, who is reckoned as a member of the Northern school of Zen, enjoyed higher imperial favor. His fame, however, spread farther than this school and he became one of the most outstanding Buddhists of his age. Besides him only two other Buddhist monks—the great pilgrim to India and translator Hsüan-tsang (602–664) and Shen-hsiu—are accorded biographies in the official annals of the T'ang dynasty. The development of the religiously searching, highly gifted I-hsing leads from meditative Zen through the strict rule of the *vinaya* and the multi-dimensional tendencies of Tendai towards esoteric elements that had been brought to Ch'ang-an (716) by the Indian Śubhakarasimha (637–735). I-hsing became the student of the newcomer and contributed greatly to the recognition, spread, and adaptation to Chinese thought of the new branch of the Buddha religion. His inclination to Taoism, which he shared with many contemporaries and not a few monks of the Northern school—among them I-fu—directed him naturally towards esoteric doctrines and rites. He composed a commentary on the *Mahāvairocana Sūtra*, which Śubhakarasimha had translated into the vernacular with Chinese assistance. More than his Buddhist image and activity, I-hsing's uncommon knowledge of astronomy and the natural sciences served to win him the favor and friendship of the emperor. At thirty-four years of age he was called to the imperial court and became an esteemed adviser in important matters of state. The emperor, according to one report, bestowed on him the title of "Heavenly Master." In Chinese Tantrism he ranks as the sixth patriarch.

The figure of I-hsing stands out against a backdrop of the ever-increasing ambitions of powerful court officials, who alternatively played the role of protector and adversary of the Buddhist monks.[139] The Northern school of Zen was as closely bound to the political events of the age as it was to its intellectual and cultural climate. So attractive a personality as I-hsing must have impressed and influenced his fellow monks.

Of Ching-hsien 景賢 (660–723), another of the disciples of Shen-hsiu, we know that he sought instruction on tantric meditation from Śubhakarasimha.[140] These discussions stimulated his writing, which show the approximation of Zen to the esoteric. The contacts continued. I-hsing and also I-fu became students of the Indian Tantric master Vajrabodhi when the latter visited Ch'ang-an.

P'u-chi, the head of the Northern school after Shen-hsiu's death, is depicted in the sources as an imposing presence, turned in on himself, unapproachable, highly cultivated, and of wide-reaching influence:

> The distinguished persons of the age and the common folk strove for the honor to greet him, but he always kept a strong, silent mien and seldom showed himself kindly disposed towards those who visited him. This made him all the more highly regarded.[141]

Honored by all, he spent his final years in the two capital cities. The epitaph composed about him by the man of letters Li-yung 李邕, whom he had befriended, bestows praise on him effusively, but through Li-yung, a motley personality, he fell into questionable company.[142] Given his distinguished style of life and his closeness to the political events of the time, P'u-chi's image exhibits weak points that came to light after his death.

P'u-chi's biography recounts the story of a young lad drawn to the monastic life by a love of meditation and study. He studied the *Lotus Sūtra*, Yogācāra texts, and the *Daijōkishinron*. Under the direction of the important *vinaya* master Hung-ching 弘景 (634–712) he entered more deeply into the monastic rule. With the death of the master he joined the circle of Shen-hsiu's disciples, still aspiring to learn Zen meditation from Fa-ju. His practice was so successful that after five years the master handed over to him the *Viśesacintibrahma-paripṛcchā Sūtra* and the *Laṅkāvatāra Sūtra*, wherein he was able to find the essence of Zen. After two more years he left the monastery of Gyokusen-ji in possession of the enlightenment certificate of Shen-hsiu and took himself to Mount Sung, where between 701 and 705 his name appears in the register of monks of Sung-yüeh ssu 崇岳寺 (Jpn., Sūgaku-ji).

In the year 725 P'u-chi moved to the capital of Lo-yang, where he lived first in Ching-ai ssu 敬愛寺 (Jpn., Keiai-ji) and later in Hsing-t'ang ssu 興唐寺 (Jpn., Kōtō-ji). There he was able to carry on his teaching successfully among the upper crust of society. In the monastery young monks entrusted themselves to his direction.[143] His own practice brought him a profound respect for the monastic rule, and through him the ancient Buddhist *vinaya* took a strong hold in the Northern school.[144] He transmitted to his disciples the fundamental teachings of Mahāyāna and made them intimate with the sūtras, above all with the *Laṅkāvatāra Sūtra* and the *Daijōkishinron*.

In meditation P'u-chi carried ahead the style of the masters of East Mountain and Shen-hsiu, as the epitaph testifies:

> By concentrating the mind on a single locus, one ceases thinking about the myriad conditions. One may achieve penetration in an instant, or one may

achieve gradually realization over [a period of] months and years—but [in either case] one illuminates the essence of Buddhahood.[145]

As the passage shows, P'u-chi was familiar, like his predecessors, with both sudden and gradual enlightenment.

THE DECLINE OF THE NORTHERN SCHOOL

The story of the decline of the Northern school is bound up with the attacks of Shen-hui at the "Great Dharma Gathering" in the monastery of Ta-yün ssu (Jpn., Daiun-ji) in Hua-t'ai (732). For some time, these attacks were seen as the principal cause of the ensuing decline, but recent research leads us to other conclusions. Careful study of the Tun-huang texts indicates that the Dharma gathering of Hua-t'ai was not—as reports from his school lead us to believe—the resounding success Shen-hui had hoped for. The writings of the Northern school do not report the event. Nor is anything said of the position that the two living principal disciples of Shen-hsiu, P'u-chi and I-fu, took towards the attacks of Shen-hui. Neither are any grievous losses to the Northern school recorded in the years immediately following the gathering.

The two main points of Shen-hui's attack have to do with the correct genealogical lines and the suddenness of enlightenment. On neither point can the Northern school be shown to be in aberration. Rather, the two points of contention illumine Zen's situation at the close of the early period. The interest in genealogy is part of all Chinese Buddhism, but in no school is it so marked and so essential as in Zen, where it is a matter of the direct transmission of the mind of the founder Śākyamuni. The oldest listings were mentioned in the epitaph for Fa-ju and in the *Den hōbōki* chronicle; both belong to the Northern school, which cannot be accused of any lack of attention to the importance of transmission. To be sure, the school makes no pretension to the type of linear transmission espoused by Shen-hui. Perhaps there was even something like a "horizontal succession" after Hung-jen's death, from Shen-hsiu to Lao-an and Hsüan-tse.[146] The title of patriarch does not appear in the lists of the early period.

At the Great Dharma Gathering, Shen-hui claimed the title of Sixth Patriarch for Hui-neng (638–713), who had already been dead for almost twenty years. Perhaps he was more concerned with laying claim himself to the title of Seventh Patriarch. In any case, his attack was directed against P'u-chi, who was held in far higher esteem that Shen-hui in the capital of Lo-yang. The dispute was not settled at the Great Dharma Gathering but smouldered for many years thereafter. In the end Hui-neng went down in Zen history as "Sixth Patriarch." The spiritual transmission from master to disciple became a central dogma of Zen.

The simplicity of the slogan, "Suddenness of the South, Gradualness of the North," which expresses the second point of contention that Shen-hui raised against the Northern school, can easily obscure the complexity of the problem. Whether the freeing experience is gained suddenly or gradually, and just what suddenness and gradualness mean in the context of practice, was a matter of bitter controversy in Chinese Buddhism during the fourth and fifth centuries. Never fully resolved, it remained a particularly vital issue in the Zen school even after the clash between the Southern and Northern schools abated, flaring up again during the Sung period in the conflict between kōan Zen and the Zen of silent enlightenment. It is in this that it has come down to us in the present.

Several elements need to be distinguished here. The dispute is not primarily about enlightenment but about practice, practice both before and after enlightenment. That the experience of enlightenment itself takes place suddenly is not contended. What Shen-hui rejects is progressive practice prior to enlightenment (the "mirror-wiping" of Shen-hsiu's legendary enlightenment verses in the *Platform Sūtra*), which he characterizes as inconsistent with the Mahāyāna metaphysic. If specks of dust, which symbolize thoughts and passions, must be constantly wiped away from the mirror-mind, this would give a reality to delusions which they do not possess, since like all dharmas in the world of appearances they are "empty" (*śūnya*). The originally pure mind awakens spontaneously in enlightenment, without needing to be preceded by practice.

Shen-hui likewise rejects as inconsistent with the Mahāyāna metaphysic all talk of "seeing the mind" and "purity," since such talk makes mind and purity objects and thus introduces a duality into reality. Mahāyāna allows no subject-object duality to taint the original purity of mind and, Shen-hui's attacks notwithstanding, the Northern school maintains this basic Mahāyāna line on non-duality.[147]

The ambiguity of the idea of *upāya*, so highly treasured by the Northern school and yet violently attacked by Shen-hui, in no small way aggravates the judgment of the controversy between North and South. In the title of the important treatise, *The Gate of the [Five] Unborn Upāya*, attributed to Shen-hsiu, *upāya* is called "unborn" in the sense of the Mahāyāna metaphysic. This qualification invokes a passage in the *Vimalakīrti Sūtra* in which *upāya* is described as something acquired through wisdom (*prajñā*).[148] At the same time, the application of means implies a mediation. Mediated enlightenment does not take place immediately and spontaneously, and therefore not suddenly either.[149] Shen-hui argues sharply against the use of means since these appear to exclude sudden enlightenment.

The ambiguity of means suggested in the *Vimalakīrti Sūtra* is confirmed in late writings of the Northern school, which vouch for the suddenness of enlightenment but at the same time concede an important place to *upāya*. Thus, for instance, we read in the *Chen-tsung lun* 眞宗論 (Jpn., *Shinshūron*):

> The World Renowned One did not speak a single word and did not explain a single method. Just as a good doctor explains what medicines can heal what illnesses, but does not prescribe these medicines when there is no illness.[150]

Shen-hsui insists that no medicines are necessary since the originally pure mind is completely sound. Yet the protagonist of suddenness recommends "means" that aid to a first awakening if sudden enlightenment is impossible.[151] Classical Zen masters also recommend the use of skillful means on the way to enlightenment.[152] The tension between the sudden and the gradual is rooted in human nature and is everywhere perceived in different forms. It seems difficult, if not impossible, to draw a clear line doctrinally between Zen schools. The undeniable distinction between the Northern and Southern schools lay above all in the sociopolitical realm.[153] The rhetorical power of the phrase "Suddenness of the South, Gradualness of the North" has helped to keep it alive down through the centuries.[154]

For the decline of the Northern school the sociopolitical and rhetorical-polemical factors are at least as important as the conflict over doctrine. The general attack of Shen-hui at the Great Dharma Gathering of Hua-t'ai, which focused on genealogy and doctrine, in no way damaged the the flourishing Northern school. P'u-chi and I-fu had high standing at the imperial court, as had the masters of the founding generation, Shen-hsiu, Lao-an, and Shen-hui before them. Shen-hui wanted to assume the position of the Northern school masters at the court and, beyond this, to be recognized as the seventh Chinese patriarch of Zen, a dignity that P'u-chi not only contested during life but also after his death in the epitaphs dedicated to him.[155] Shen-hui strengthened his attacks after the death of P'u-chi (739) and continued them undiminished until his own death.

During the second half of the eighth century the situation of Zen in China worked against the Northern school. The close ties to the imperial court no longer carried great influence but gradually came to be seen as a weakness. Disgusted with political disorders, the people came more and more to favor the rough climate of the countryside. The Northern school that had come to full bloom in the atmosphere of the court had already cooperated in the spread of Zen in the provinces, but now new schools came to the forefront. The Northern school was no longer, as it had been at the beginning of the century, the main force. Among the many names of masters from the Northern school who were known during the time span from 150 years after the death of P'u-chi until the dissolving of the school, there is no outstanding charismatic personality.[156] The creative power of the Northern school was spent. On the one hand, the distinctive style that had been cultivated in the imperial court and alienated Zen from the ordinary folk, and on the other the lack of great masters during the final years contributed to this overall decline.[157]

The Li-tai fa-pao-chi (Jpn., Reikidai hōbōki) and Pao-lin chuan (Jpn., Hōrinden) chronicles, as well as the writings of Tsung-mi, provide information on the development of Chinese Zen during the eighth century. It is worth noting that Shen-hui, who had stirred so much unrest, finds little place in the overall picture. His school "opened the following age," as Faure rightly notes, "but was not part of its mainstream."[158] The Szechwan and Oxhead schools enjoyed a brief period of flowering and influenced the development of Zen. Both schools advocated the suddenness of enlightenment.[159]

The Szechwan (or Pao-t'ang) school was from its beginnings marked by Mādhyamika philosophy. Its best-known master, Wu-chu, had a large circle of disciples. He took a radical view, defending the suddenness of enlightenment and rejecting rites and asceticism to the point of antinomianism. The *Rekidai hōbōki* seems to stem from an adherent of this school.[160]

The Oxhead school traces its origins—though without proof—to the early period of Zen. It stands close to the Southern school, and one of its disciples is mentioned in the editorship of the *Platform Sūtra*. This sūtra, the sūtra of the Sixth Patriarch, became the Magna Carta of classical Chinese Zen. It lifted the Sixth Patriarch, Hui-neng, out of historical darkness and made him into an ideal Zen personality. The school of Ma-tsu Tao-i became the foundational source of a new age, the "Golden Age of Zen." The Chinese chronicle of the Sung period describes for posterity the scene that at the time presented itself in the surrounding countryside of Kiangsi and Hunan:

> Westward from the river Ma-tsu is the master, southward from the lake Shih-t'ou is the master. People go back and forth between them incessantly. He who has not seen these great masters is regarded an ignoramus.[161]

The great figures of Ma-tsu and Shih-t'ou, of Pai-chang and Huang-po, of Chao-chou and Lin-chi, of Lung-tan and Te-shan, that step out of the chronicles and kōan collections, fascinated D. T. Suzuki and his western audience. This Zen has earned for itself an abiding place in the spiritual history of humanity.

NOTES

1. On the early phase of Buddhist meditation in China, see the opening pages of the contribution by Whalen W. Lai, "T'an-ch'ien and the Early Ch'an Tradition: Translation and Analysis of the Essay 'Wang-shih fei-lun'," in W. Lai and Lewis R. Lancaster, eds., *Early Ch'an in China and Tibet* (Berkeley Buddhist Studies Series, 1983).
2. See the contribution of Jan Yün-hua, "Seng-ch'ou's Method of Dhyāna," Lai and Lancaster, *Early Ch'an in China and Tibet*, 51–63.
3. W. Lai, "T'an-ch'ien and the Early Ch'an Tradition," 65–87.
4. T. 2060, 596b.
5. Cited by Jan Yün-hua, "Seng-ch'ou's Method of Dhyāna," 56. The declarations on Seng-ch'ou follow this essay. The author gives as his sources the biography in the *Hsü Kao seng chuan* of Tao-hsüan (596–661) and five unedited manuscripts in the collection of Paul Pelliot in Paris, which he describes. The citation is from ms. 1.
6. Jan Yüan-hua, "Seng-ch'ou's Method of Dhyāna," 59; citation from ms. 2.
7. Jan Yüan-hua, "Seng-ch'ou's Method of Dhyāna," 60; citation from ms. 2.
8. Jan Yüan-hua, "Seng-ch'ou's Method of Dhyāna," 61; citation from ms. 2.
9. Yanagida Seizan cites and explains the passage from the *Zoku kōsōden* in section 15, "Bodhidharma and Seng-ch'ou" of his *Goroku no rekishi* 語録の歴史 (311–7), in *Tōhō gakuhō* 東方学報 57 (1985): 211–663. See also his *Daruma* in vol. 16 of a series entitled The Human Intellectual Heritage (Tokyo: Kodansha, 1981), 137–8. See also Faure, *Le Traité de Bodhidharma* (Editions Le Mail, 1986), 15, 18.
10. See also Whalen W. Lai in *Early Ch'an in China and Tibet*.
11. Cited in Lai, "T'an-ch'ien and the Early Ch'an Tradition," 73.

12. See Yanagida, *Goroku no rekishi*, 290; *Daruma no goroku*, 7.

13. See Yanagida, *Goroku no rekishi*, 278. The text was first discovered by D. T. Suzuki in 1936 in the National Library of Peking (no. 99) and named by him *The Long Scroll of the Treatise of the Two Entrances*. Two years later he discovered the same text in the Stein Collection in the British Museum of London (no. 2715). The Tun-huang text is older than the reproduction in Tao-hsüan's historical work (T. 2060, 50.551c), according to Yanagida (300, 279). This text has been translated into modern Japanese by Yanagida and published with ample commentary under the title *The Record of Daruma* (Zen no shoki I, Zen no goroku 1 [Tokyo, 1965]). John McRae, in his book *The Northern School and the Formation of Early Ch'an Buddhism* (Honolulu, 1986), gives an English translation of the treatise and the accompanying letters (102–6). He alludes to the English translation and commentary of John Alexander Jorgensen, *The Earliest Texts of Ch'an Buddhism: The Long Scroll* (M. A. Dissertation, Australian National University, 1979). Bernard Faure has done a French translation in *Le Traité de Bodhidharma*.

14. See Yanagida, *Goroku no rekishi*, 307 and 293, 601–2; *Daruma*, 100, 105.

15. See Yanagida, *Goroku no rekishi*, 302–3; *Daruma*, 140, 142. Cf. McRae, *The Northern School*, 112–5; and Faure, *Le Traité de Bodhidharma*, 28–32.

16. The apocryphal sūtra composed later than the Bodhidharma treatise, **Vajrasamādhi Sūtra* (金剛三昧經 T. 273; Chin., *Chin-kang san-mei ching*; Jpn., *Kongōsammaikyō*) reads *chiao-kuan* 覺觀 (Jpn., *kakkan*) instead of *pi-kuan* (Jpn., *hekikan*). See Yanagida, *Goroku no rekishi*, 303. The expression *chiao-kuan* appears also in the *Vimalakīrti Sūtra* (T. 475, 14.540a8; see *Daruma*, 146.

17. See Young-ho Kim, *Tao-sheng's Commentary on the Lotus Sūtra* (New York, 1990), 33.

18. See Yanagida, *Daruma*, 147–55. Yanagida points to the difference from early Buddhist doctrine and stresses its novelty. See also his *Goroku no rekishi*, 305ff.

19. See Yanagida, *Daruma no goroku*, 9ff. The treatise of Bodhidharma is the oldest source of the dialogue genre; see *Daruma*, 107.

20. Yanagida, *Daruma*, 107–8.

21. Yanagida, *Daruma*, 108–9.

22. See the introduction to Yanagida, *Daruma no goroku*, 13–4.

23. The text is given in Yanagida's *Daruma no goroku*, 31. His Japanese reading of the phrase is *oshie ni yorite shū o satori* 教に藉りて宗を悟り (33).

24. See Yanagida, *Daruma*, 143.

25. See Yanagida, *Goroku no rekishi*, 308, 310–1. D. T. Suzuki divides the Tun-huang text of the Bodhidharma treatise in three parts of 101 numbers. Part I (1–11) contains the treatise of the two entrances and four practices as well as two letters; part II (12–67) contains the first appendix (Jpn., *zatsuron* 雜論); and part III (68–101) the second appendix. Yanagida's translated and edited text appears in *Daruma no goroku*. In addition, there are still more recently discovered texts of small compass (appendix 2 in Yanagida's text), which Bernard Faure has likewise translated in his *Le Traité de Bodhidharma* as "Mélanges" (36–7).

26. See Yanagida, *Goroku no rekishi*, 271, 325; Faure, *Le Traité de Bodhidharma*, 79.

27. Yanagida, *Goroku no rekishi*, 325; and the complete section on Yüan, 323–30.

28. See Yanagida, *Goroku no rekishi*, 344ff; see also the section on the "Mélanges" in Faure, *Le Traité de Bodhidharma*, 53–63.

29. T. 2060, 50.552b. An English translation appears in Isshū Miura and Ruth Fuller Sasaki, Zen Dust (New York, 1966), 373. Faure speaks of various currents in his introduction to the Bodhidharma treatise (Le Traité de Bodhidharma, 48–9). David Chappell refers to "two strands of Bodhidharma influence" in his essay "The Teachings of the Fourth Ch'an Patriarch," in Lai and Lancaster, Early Ch'an in China and Tibet, 92.

30. Yanagida, Goroku no rekishi, 285.

31. Yanagida, Goroku no rekishi, 285–6.

32. The composition of the Ryōga shikiji (T. 2837) is dated 716 (Yanagida and Hu Shih) and 720 (Yin-shun); see Chappell, "The Teachings of the Fourth Ch'an Patriarch," 94. The Den hōbōki (T. 2838) is dated 713 by Yampolsky (Lai and Lancaster, Early Ch'an in China and Tibet, 6). In Goroku no rekishi, Yanagida refers to the Den hōbōki as "the oldest historical chronicle of the Zen school" (8) and the Ryōga shikiji as "the first historical book of the Zen school" (284). Later he notes that it is not clear which of the works is older than the other (319).

33. The Bodhidharma treatise is said to be "replete with errors" and to contain "presumably partial, provisional teachings." See the translation of the work by McRae in The Northern School, 255–69; citations, 257, 259.

34. On the following see the section on Early Ch'an Lineage in Chappell, "The Teachings of the Fourth Ch'an Patriarch," 93ff; see also McRae, The Northern School, 79–85.

35. T. 2837, 85.1286c–1289b. English translation by Chappell, "The Teachings of the Fourth Ch'an Patriarch," 107–29. The Ryōga shikiji was edited and translated into modern Japanese by Yanagida in Shoki no zenshi I, Zen no goroku 2 (Tokyo, 1971); he attributes the text to Tao-hsin. For Yanagida, the text is based on what "Tao-hsin himself had said" (190), but this does not exclude transmission and transcription in his circle of disciples. The date is uncertain.

36. Translation by Chappell, "The Teachings of the Fourth Ch'an Patriarch," 114, 118.

37. Yanagida, Goroku no rekishi, 124; the text appears on 112.

38. McRae, The Northern School, 138ff, 322. Chappell translates the phrase as "unified mindfulness without deviation" ("The Teachings of the Fourth Ch'an Patriarch," 99–100). That Tao-hsin criticized Lao-tzu and Chuang-tzu (McRae, 120; Chappell, 100) does not contradict the strong influence of Taoism on Chinese Zen. Yanagida treats the historical background of the expression in a lengthy note (Goroku no rekishi, 234–5).

39. Biographical information on Tao-hsin can be found in the historical work of Tao-hsüan (T. 2060, 50.605b; English translation in McRae, The Northern School, 31–2) and in the Den hōbōki (edited with commentary by Yanagida in Shoki no zenshi I, Zen no goroku 2:327–435; English translation, McRae, 255–69; biography of Tao-hsin, 261ff). McRae compares the two biographies, showing where they concur and diverge from one another. The Den hōbōki omits the period in Ta-lin temple, but both biographies report his entry into the monastery at 7 years of age and his time in a monastery on Mount Chi-chou. From the Ta-lin monastery he moved to East Mountain in 624.

40. English translation by Chappell, "The Teachings of the Fourth Patriarch," 107.

41. See Chappell, "The Teachings of the Fourth Patriarch," 121.

42. See Faure, La volonté d'orthodoxie, 76. He deals with Ch'an and T'ien-t'ai on 75–9.

43. On the *Treatise on the Awakening of Faith* (T. 1666) and Ch'an, see Faure, *La volonté d'orthodoxie*, 59ff.

44. Faure sees the *Makashikan* (T. 1911) as favoring sudden enlightenment, and the *Hsiao-chih-kuan* 修習止觀坐禪要法 (Jpn., *Shujūshishikan zazenhōyō* or *Shōshikan* 小止觀, T. 1915) as for gradual enlightenment. *La volonté d'orthodoxie*, 76.

45. Chappell, "The Teachings of the Fourth Patriarch," 110.

46. See Yanagida's commentary in *Zen no goroku* 2:210.

47. English translation by Chappell, "The Teachings of the Fourth Patriarch," 110, 113.

48. Chappell, "The Teachings of the Fourth Patriarch," 114.

49. Chappell, "The Teachings of the Fourth Patriarch," 229.

50. English translation, Chappell, "The Teachings of the Fourth Patriarch," 109.

51. See the English translation of the *Den hōbōki* by McRae (*The Northern School*), the genealogy (257), and Seng-ts'an, the teacher of Tao-hsin (262).

52. English translation, Chappell, "The Teachings of the Fourth Patriarch," 116–7.

53. The metaphor appears already in Lieh-tzu 列子. A lengthy quotation from the *Monjusetsuhannya Sūtra* (Chin., *Wen-shu shuo ching*, T. 232) demonstrates progressive ascetic practice. The comparison with arrows shot one after the other into the air appears in Tendai texts. See Yanagida's commentary, *Zen no goroku* 2:246–7.

54. English translation, Chappell, "The Teachings of the Fourth Patriarch," 118.

55. See Yanagida, *Zen no goroku* 2:254. The *Dayōkishinron* likewise teaches gradual enlightenment, as Yanagida's quotations show.

56. English translation, Chappell, "The Teachings of the Fourth Patriarch," 119. Yanagida observes in a note that bodily *zazen* is a skillful means (*hōben*) for spiritual *zazen* (*Zen no goroku*, 259). Like the *samādhi* of the one practice, it is found in the realm of non-differentiation and inconceivablity (cf. Chappell, 107). According to the *Den hōbōki*, Bodhidharma instructed his disciple Hui-k'o secretly with the aid of skillful means that cannot be spoken with words (see Yanagida, 355–6; English translation in McRae, *The Northern School*, 259).

57. Cf. Faure, *La volonté d'orthodoxie*, 79ff.

58. Also called the *Makahannyakyō* (T. 1509), cited in Yanagida, *Zen no goroku* 2:196.

59. Chappell, "Teachings of the Fourth Ch'an Patriarch," 108. See also p. 114: "You should know that the Buddha is identical to your mind."

60. In the monastery of Ta-lin he met Shan-fu 善伏 (d. 660), who had studied Amidist meditation with Hui-chao 慧超 (546–622), a disciple of Chih-i. See Faure, *La volonté d'orthodoxie*, 75.

61. See Carl Bielefeldt, *Dōgen's Manuals of Zen Meditation* (Berkeley, 1988), 83ff.

62. Sekiguchi Shindai, *Tendai shikan no kenkyū* (Tokyo, 1969), 346. Cited in Bielefeldt, *Dōgen's Manuals*, 86.

63. Translation by Chappell, "Teachings of the Fourth Ch'an Patriarch," 112, 117.

64. Translation by Chappell, "Teachings of the Fourth Ch'an Patriarch," 119.

65. Translation by Chappell, "Teachings of the Fourth Ch'an Patriarch," 120.

66. Translation by Chappell, "Teachings of the Fourth Ch'an Patriarch," 118.

67. Translation by Chappell, "Teachings of the Fourth Ch'an Patriarch," 119.

68. Translation by Chappell, "Teachings of the Fourth Ch'an Patriarch," 113. A similar admonition to zeal in practice is put in the mouth of Tao-hsin in the *Den hōbōki*. For the

text, see *Shoki no zenshi I, Zen no goroku 2*, 380.1. I have rendered the passage following Yanagida's citation of it in *Shoki zenshūshisho no kenkyū* (Kyoto, 1967), 100. The third sentence must read "sit in meditation for three or five years ..." This, according to Yanagida, is "the oldest proof for the practice of meditation in the seated position."

69. Fa-hsien (577–633), who came from Tendai, Shan-fu (d. 660), a student of Mādhyamika, and perhaps also Hsüan-shuang 玄爽 (d. 652), are mentioned as disciples of Tao-hsin.

70. McRae (*The Northern School*, 40–1) gives a list of reasons for preferring the importance of Hung-jen.

71. See McRae, *The Northern School*, 284, and on the text, 35. See also 309–12. The edited text appears at the end of the book (1–16, Chinese numbering), and its translation on 121–32. An earlier English translation by W. Pachow appeared in the pages of the *University of Ceylon Review* 21/1 (1963):47–62, which was reprinted in the author's *Chinese Buddhism: Aspects of Interaction and Reinterpretation* (Lanham, Md.: University Press of America, 1980), 35–54.

72. See the admittedly tentative interpretation of McRae, *The Northern School*, 119, 120.

73. See McRae, *The Northern School*, 123. In the corresponding notes McRae notes that this formula appears nine times in the text (n. 60, 315).

74. This is how McRae translates the core term. "According to a more liberal interpretation," he adds, it means "to maintain constant, undiscriminating awareness of the absolute mind or Buddha nature within oneself" (*The Northern School*, 136).

75. Translation by McRae, *The Northern School*, 124.

76. Translation by McRae, *The Northern School*, 121. On this quotation, see 313–4. This is the oldest example of the metaphor in Zen literature.

77. Translation by McRae, *The Northern School*, 122.

78. Translation by McRae, *The Northern School*, 125.

79. Translation by Chappell, "Teachings of the Fourth Ch'an Patriarch," 118. Compare Yanagida, *Zen no goroku* 2:249, 252.

80. For the text on Guṇabhadra, see Yanagida's *Zen no goroku* 2:112. Translation by McRae, *The Northern School*, 134. For the text in the section on Hui-k'o, see *Zen no goroku* 2:146–7. Yanagida adds a note in the section on Guṇabhadra that the use of the metaphor relies on the *Laṅkāvatāra Sūtra*, in which mention is made of the sudden appearance of self-nature (116).

81. Translation by McRae, *The Northern School*, 135.

82. Translation by McRae, *The Northern School*, 127.

83. Translation cited by McRae, *The Northern School*, 128, 130.

84. Translation by McRae, *The Northern School*, 130.

85. The phrase appears no less than nine times in the brief treatise.

86. Yanagida, *Zen no goroku* 2:268–9. The *Ryōga shikiji* often stresses the ineffability of the experience. Yanagida writes: "It is worth noting that even though Hsüan-tse considered Hung-jen's writings on the Zen Way to be apocryphal, his disciple Ching-chüeh does not even mention the text of the *Shushinyō-ron* but cites from the book" (272). The *Ryōga shikiji*, like the *Den hōbōki*, mentions the physical work of Hung-jen that is also brought forth in later chronicles.

87. Yanagida, *Zen no goroku* 2:273.

88. Yanagida, *Zen no goroku* 2:273. This is the only mention of Hui-neng in a writing of the Northern school.

89. Translation by McRae, *The Northern School*, 92.

90. Yanagida, *Zen no goroku* 2:125.

91. Yanagida, *Goroko no rekishi*, 352; cf. *Zen no goroku* 2:125.

92. The only exception is the *Ta-cheng pei-pien lun* 大乘北宗論 (Jpn., *Daijōhokushūron*); see Yanagida, *Goroku no rekishi*, 356, n. 9.

93. Yanagida, *Zen no goroku* 2:15.

94. Yanagida, *Goroku no rekishi*, 356.

95. The figure ten, as Yanagida notes, is not necessarily historical, but follows the number of disciples of Śākyamuni and Confucius. Hui-neng, according to the *Platform Sūtra*, also had ten disciples. See *Zen no goroku* 2:15 *et passim*.

96. Yanagida has edited the text and added a commentary in an appendix to his *Shoki zenshūshisho no kenkyū*, 487–96; on Fa-ju see 35–46 and McRae, *The Northern School*, 85–6.

97. Compare McRae, *The Northern School*, 80ff, and Yanagida, *Shoki zenshōshisho no kenkyū*, 37ff.

98. English translation by McRae, *The Northern School*, 255–69; on Fa-ju, see 264–5.

99. See the text edited by Yanagida, *Shoki zenshūshisho no kenkyū*.

100. On Lao-an and his disciples, see McRae, *The Northern School*, 56–9. The birth date is given differently in the chronicles; the dating 584–709 appears frequently.

101. See McRae, *The Northern School*, 39. After the death of Shen-hsiu in 706, Hung-jen's disciples Fa-hsien 法顯 (643–720) and Hsüan-tse (see p. 318 in text) were invited to the court (McRae, 59–60).

102. Yanagida, *Zen no goroku* 2:17.

103. The epitaph, the only extant source, has been edited and commented on by Yanagida in his *Shoki zenshūshisho no kenkyū*, 497–516. On the two chronicles, see also notes 32, 35, 39 above. McRae mentioned, aside from a memorial for the throne, an anonymous inscription, entries in later writings, and so forth. *The Northern School*, 45–6.

104. Yanagida writes: "The foundation of the so-called Northern school was certainly a fruit of the Wu-Chou revolution" (*Shoki zenshūshisho no kenkyū*, 45).

105. On the following, see McRae, *The Northern School*, 45–56; Faure, *La volonté d'orthodoxie*, 25–33. The birth date is unknown. All sources concur in the declaration that Shen-hsiu reached an age of over 100 years.

106. Yanagida, *Shoki zenshūshisho no kenkyū*, 498.

107. The *Den hōbōki* reports the banishment of Shen-hsiu, during which time he wore lay clothes and lived in the monastery of T'ien-chü ssu 天居寺 (Jpn., Tenko-ji). Yanagida notes that this report is unclear (Yanagida, *Zen no goroku* 2:401–2).

108. According to the *Den hōbōki*, Shen-hsiu began his teaching after the death of Fa-ju (689).

109. See *Den hōbōki* in Yanagida, *Zen no goroku* 2:396.

110. Yanagida, *Shoki zenshūshisho no kenkyū*, 499.

111. See note 87 above.

112. *Ryōga shikiji* in Yanagida, *Zen no goroku* 2:298. The *Monjusetsuhannya Sūtra* belongs to the literature of the wisdom sūtras; see note 53 above.

113. On the transmission of the text in seven Tun-huang manuscripts, see McRae, *The Northern School*, 325. The text was edited by D. T. Suzuki in comparative printing with five manuscripts. See *Suzuki Daisetsu zenshū* 鈴木大拙全集 (Tokyo, 1983), 29:144–97. On ascertaining the authorship of Shen-hsiu and the identification of the writing with the *Hasōron* of Bodhidharma, see Yanagida, *Goroku no rekishi*, 263ff, 269.

114. Cf. Faure, *La volonté d'orthodoxie*, 67.

115. Translation by McRae, *The Northern School*, 207. Cf. Faure, *La volonté d'orthodoxie*, 60.

116. Translation by McRae, *The Northern School*, 208.

117. See Faure, *La volonté d'orthodoxie*, 60.

118. More than half of the text, which consists of sixteen questions and answers. See especially the detailed replies to questions 12 and 13 in *Suzuki Daisetsu zenshū*, 29:167–88.

119. On the method, which is called "contemplative analysis" 觀心釋 (Chin., *kuan-hsin shih*; Jpn., *kanjinshaku*), see the detailed treatment of McRae, *The Northern School*, 198–207.

120. Translation by McRae, *The Northern School*, 201, slightly modified. The final word 解脱, read *gedatsu* in Japanese (Chin., *chieh-t'o*), indicates in Buddhism the final liberation, namely *nirvāṇa*.

121. Translation by McRae, *The Northern School*, 201.

122. *Suzuki Daisetsu zenshū* 29:194.

123. In note 161 (*The Northern School*, 327–30), McRae reports on the seven manuscripts found in Tun-huang. See also editions in Ui Hakuju, *Zenshūshi kenkyū* 禅宗史研究 I (1939), 447–518; *Suzuki Daisetsu zenshū* 3:153–235. McRae follows in his translation selected portions of the editions of Suzuki (171–96). The related text of the *Treatise on Perfect Illumination* 圓明論 (Chin., *Yüan-ming lun*; Jpn., *Enmyōron*), which was likewise found in Tun-Huang, has been edited for the first time by McRae (18–44) and translated into English (149–71).

124. Yanagida gives as writings of Shen-hsiu the *Kanjinron* and the *Ta-ch'eng wu-sheng fa-pien men* 大乗無生方便門 (Jpn., *Daijōmushōhōbenmon*, T. 2834; see also his *Shoki zenshūshisho no kenkyū*, 256), and calls them "a summary of the Zen of the Northern school"(*Goroku no rekishi*, 266). Suzuki remarks in the introduction to his edition that the *upāya* texts originated after Shen-hsiu (*Zenshū* 3:141). McRae cites the view of the Japanese scholar Takeda Tadashi to the effect that the *upāya* texts "existed in basic form during Shen-hsui's life and that any variations or additions occurred within twenty years or so after his death" (*The Northern School*, 330). The treatise on perfect illumination, in his view, was "probably taken from a lecture or lectures of Shen-hsiu or another prominent Northern school figure" (149).

125. *Daijōmushōhōbenmon*; see note 124 above.

126. Translation by McRae, *The Northern School*, 175; cited from the *Daijōkishinron* (Skt., *Mahāyānaśraddhotpāda Śāstra*), T. 1666. The first *upāya* embraces in content the four following, which are called "Opening the Gates of Wisdom and Sagacity," "Manifesting the Inconceivable Dharma," "Elucidation of the True Nature of the Dharmas," and "The Naturally Unobstructed Path of Emancipation." The corresponding sūtras are the *Lotus Sūtra, Vimalakīrti Sūtra, Viśesacintibrahma Śāstra, and the Avataṃsaka Sūtra*. See McRae, 219; Faure, *La volonté d'orthodoxie*, 61.

127.   Robert B. Zeuschner, "The Concept of *li-nien* in the Northern Line of Ch'an Buddhism," in Lai and Lancaster, *Early Ch'an in China and Tibet*, 131–48.

128.   Zeuschner, "The Concept of *li-nien*," 145–6.

129.   The text is included in *Suzuki Daisetsu zenshū* 3:168. Translation by McRae, *The Northern School*, 172.

130.   *Suzuki Daisetsu zenshū* 3:168. The text here uses the classical expression *tun-wu* (Jpn., *tongo*).

131.   *Suzuki Daisetsu zenshū* 3:169; McRae, *The Northern School*, 173.

132.   On the critique of Shen-hsiu's teachings in the *upāya* treatises by masters of the Southern school (Ma-tsu, Lin-chi, Pai-chang), see Yanagida, *Goroku no rekishi*, 266–9.

133.   Compare Suzuki's introduction to the *upāya* texts. In his critique he follows that of Tsung-mi, who accused Shen-hsiu and the Northern school of denying the identity of enlightenment and defilements (*Zenshū* 3:141–8).

134.   Translation by McRae, *The Northern School*, 235.

135.   Translation by McRae, *The Northern School*, 238.

136.   Translation by McRae, *The Northern School*, 173–4. The text appears in *Suzuki Daisetsu zenshū* 3:190.

137.   The emperors Chung-tsung 中宗 (ruled 705–710) and Jui-tsung 睿宗 (ruled 710–712) fought during the years of unrest from 705 to 712 against the claim to power of the empress Wei, without being able to exercise their imperial authority completely.

138.   After the death of Shen-hsiu, Lao-an and Hsüan-tse held influential positions at the court. The report that shortly after Shen-hsiu's death P'u-chi refused a position at court is uncertain. See McRae, *The Northern School*, 67, 295 n. 173. Emperor Hsüan-tsung kept his distance from the two chief disciples P'u-chi and I-fu. See Faure, *La volonté d'orthodoxie*, 91. On the biography of I-fu, cf. the section in McRae, 64–5.

139.   Faure describes the political scene and the ambitious utilitarianism of high officials whose fate is intertwined with that of the Northern school. See *La volonté d'orthodoxie*, 91ff.

140.   On the following, compare the section on Tantrism in Faure, *La volonté d'orthodoxie*, 101–5.

141.   Cited from the "Ancient Annals of the T'ang" (945) by Faure, *La volonté d'orthodoxie*, 129.

142.   See Faure, *La volonté d'orthodoxie*, 93, 122 n. 36.

143.   The number of disciples given in the sources is not reliable, but one should consider that "P'u-chi taught an exceptionally large number of disciples during the more than three decades of his teaching career....Sixty-three were major disciples who had 'ascended into the hall' ...." McRae, *The Northern School*, 67.

144.   See the essay of Shiina Kōyū 椎名宏雄, "Hokushūzen ni okeru kairitsu no mondai" 北宗禅における戒律の問題, *Shūkyō kenkyū* 宗教研究, 11(1969):135–59.

145.   Cited in McRae, *The Northern School*, 324 n. 153.

146.   See McRae, *The Northern School*, 60.

147.   See the text to notes 80 and 81 for Hung-jen and to notes 134–6 for Shen-hsiu.

148.   See the quotation in B. Faure, *The Rhetoric of Immediacy: A Cultural Critique of Ch'an/Zen Buddhism* (Princeton University Press, 1991), 63.

149. Faure distinguishes three orders of meaning in the term *sudden*: quick, absolute, and immediate. *Rhetoric of Immediacy*, 33; see also his *La volonté d'orthodoxie*, 170–6.

150. The full title of the work reads *Ta-ch'eng k'ai-hsin hsien-hsing tun-wu chen-tsung lun* 大乘開心顯性頓悟眞宗論 (Jpn., *Daijō kaishin kenshō tongo shinshūron*), T. 2835; the text is also to be found in *Suzuki Daisetsu zenshū* 3:321. Cf. Faure, *La volonté d'orthodoxie*, 175. Exemplary for the relationship of sudden enlightenment and the application of *upāya* is the treatise *Tun-wu ta-ch'eng cheng-li chüeh* (Jpn., *Tongo daijō shōriketsu*) by Mo-ho-yen, a Chinese member of the Northern school who advocated the standpoint of suddenness in the Council of Lhasa. For further details, see Luis O. Gomez, "The Direct and the Gradual Approaches of Zen Master Mahāyāna: Fragments of the teachings of Mo-ho-yen," Robert M. Gimello and Peter N. Gregory, eds., *Studies in Ch'an and Hua-yen* (Honolulu: University of Hawaii Press, 1983), 69–167, especially 89–103. Gomez shows how the "radical sudden enlightenment position" (89) of Mo-ho-yen also "made a major concession to the gradualists" (100) because of "the dialectical necessities and limitations of a sudden enlightenment position" (103). Compare the essay in the same volume by Jeffrey Broughton, "Early Ch'an Schools in Tibet," 1–68.

151. See Faure, *La volonté d'orthodoxie*, 175; cf. his *Rhetoric of Immediacy*, 36.

152. For example, Lin-chi. See Faure, *Rhetoric of Immediacy*, 36. Wu-chu (714–774) and his school (the Szechwan or Pao-t'ang school) are known for a radical rejection of all means. The school is described by Tsung-mi in the *Ch'an-yüan chu-ch'üan-chi tu-hsü* (Jpn., *Zengen-shosenshū-tojo*); the text can be found in Kamata Shigeo, ed., *Zen no goroku 9* (Tokyo, 1971). A lengthy citation also appears in Broughton, "Early Ch'an Schools in Tibet," 38–40.

153. Faure, *Rhetoric of Immediacy*, 38–9.

154. Faure speaks of the "rhetorical emphasis on sudden," *Rhetoric of Immediacy*, 39–40.

155. McRae translates sections from two epitaphs in *The Northern School*, 65.

156. The names of at least 125 masters of the Northern school after Shen-hsiu have come down to us. The school was numerically at its strongest during the second half of the eighth century. See McRae, *The Northern School*, 70.

157. In his investigation of the decline of the Northern school, McRae attributes great significance to "the school's close identification with the imperial court" (242). He takes this "identification" as an "obstacle to the school's continued success" (243) and notes that "an inescapable consequence" was "a taint of scholasticism" (245).

158. Faure, *La volonté d'orthodoxie*, 116.

159. In the Northern school, Lao-an's disciple Chih-ta (or Hui-ta) treats the suddenness of enlightenment. See Faure, "Le Maître de dhyāna Chih-ta et le 'subtisme' de l'école du Nord," *Cahiers d'Extrême Asie* 2 (1986):123–31. See also McRae, *The Northern School*, 58.

160. The chronicle has been edited by Yanagida and translated into modern Japanese with a commentary in *Shoki no zenshi II, Zen no goroku* 3 (Tokyo, 1976). See also his essay, "The Li-tai fa-pao chi and the Ch'an Doctrine of Sudden Awakening," in Lai and Lancaster, *Early Ch'an in China and Tibet*, 13–49.

161. Translation by Ruth Fuller Sasaki in H. Dumoulin and R. Sasaki, *The Development of Chinese Zen after the Sixth Patriarch* (New York, 1954), 6, 46.

Appendices

Appendix 1
Abbreviations

AM	*Asia Major*
AMG	*Annales du museé Guimet*, Paris
AS	*Asiatische Studien*, Bern
Bi-yän-lu I–III	W. Gundert, *Bi-yän-lu: Meister Yüan-Wu's Niederschrift der Smaragdenen Felswand*, 3 vols. (Munich, 1964–1973)
Ch'en, *Buddhism in China*	Kenneth K. S. Ch'en, *Buddhism in China: A Historical Survey* (Princeton, 1964)
Chin.	Chinese
Chinese Philosophy II	Fung Yu-lan, *A History of Chinese Philosophy*, vol. 2 (Princeton, 1953)
Chūgoku zenshūshi	Yanagida Seizan, *Chūgoku zenshūshi* [History of the Zen School in China], vol. 3 of *Zen no rekishi* [History of Zen], edited by D. T. Suzuki and K. Nishitani (Tokyo, 1974), pp. 1–108
EB	*The Eastern Buddhist*, Kyoto
Enō kenkyū	*Enō kenkyū* [Studies on Hui-neng: Foundational Studies on the Life and Sources of Hui-neng], edited by the Association for Zen Research in Komazawa University (Tokyo, 1978)
Entretiens de Lin-tsi	*Entretiens de Lin-tsi*, translated with a commentary by Paul Demiéville (Paris, 1972)
Essays I–III	D. T. Suzuki, *Essays in Zen Buddhism*, edited by Christmas Humphreys, 3 vols. (London, 1970)
JA	*Journal Asiatique*, Paris
JAOS	*Journal of the American Oriental Society*
Jpn.	Japanese

Kōsōden

Biographies of Eminent Monks (Kao-seng chuan). T. 2059, vol. 50, Nj. 1490

MN

Monumenta Nipponica, Tokyo

Mochizuki, Bukkyō daijiten

Mochizuki Shinkō, Bukkyō daijiten [Cyclopedia of Buddhism] (Tokyo, 1932–1936), 10 vols.

MS

Monumenta Serica, St. Augustin

Mumonkan

Mumonkan: Die Schranke ohne Tor. Meister Wu-men's Sammlung der achtundvierzig Kōan, with new translation and commentary (Mainz, 1975). English quotations in the text are based on Shibayama Zenkei, Zen Comments on the Mumonkan (New York, 1974)

Nj.

A Catalogue of the Chinese Translation of the Buddhist Canon of the Buddhists in China and Japan, compiled by Nanjō Bunyū (Oxford, 1883; reprint, Tokyo, 1929)

NOAG

Nachrichten der Deutschen Gesellschaft für Natur- und Völderkunde Ostasiens

Record of Lin-chi

The Recorded Sayings of Ch'an Master Lin-chi Hui-chao of Chen Prefecture, translated by Ruth Fuller Sasaki (Kyoto, 1975)

Rinzairoku

Rinzairoku [Discourses of Lin-chi], with an introduction and commentary by Yanagida Seizan, in Butten kōza [Lectures on Buddhism], vol. 30 (Tokyo, 1972)

S

Saeculum: Jahrbuch für Universalgeschichte, Freiburg im Breisgau and Munich

Shoki

Yanagida Seizan, Shoki zenshū shisho no kenkyū [Researches in the Early History of the Zen School] (Kyoto, 1967)

SK

Shūkyō kenkyū [Religious Studies], Tokyo

Skt.

Sanskrit

Sōdai jugaku	Kusumoto Bun'yū, Sōdai jugaku no zenshisō kenkyū [Studies on Zen Thought in Confucianism during the Sung Period] (Nagoya, 1980)
Sō kōsoden	Biographies of Eminent Monks Compiled during the Sung Period (Sung kao-seng chuan). T. 2060, vol. 50
SPSR	The Social and Political Science Review
T.	Taishō shinshū daizōkyō [Taishō Tripiṭaka in Chinese], edited by J. Takakusu, K. Watanabe, G. Ono, et al. (Tokyo, 1922–1933), 85 vols. Citations to the Taishō Tripiṭaka are followed by the catalog number of the specific text cited and the volume in which it appears.
The Development of Chinese Zen	H. Dumoulin, The Development of Chinese Zen after the Sixth Patriarch, in the Light of the Mumonkan, translated and annotated by Ruth Fuller Sasaki (New York, 1953)
TP	T'oung pao, Leiden
Yampolsky	Philip Yampolsky, The Platform Sūtra of the Sixth Patriarch: The Text of the Tun-huang Manuscript with Translation, Introduction, and Notes (New York, 1967)
Z.	Dainihon zokuzōkyō (Kyoto, 1905–1912), 75 vols.
Zen Dust	Isshū Miura and Ruth Fuller Sasaki, Zen Dust: The History of the Kōan and Kōan Study in Rinzai Zen (New York, 1966)
Zengaku daijiten	Zengaku daijiten [Cyclopedia of Zen], edited by Komazawa University (Tokyo, 1978), 3 vols.
Zengaku jiten	Zengaku jiten [Dictionary of Zen], edited by Jimbō Nyoten and Inoue Jisaku (Kyoto, 1944)
Zenshūshi I–III	Ui Hakuju, Zenshūshi kenkyū [Studies in the History of Zen] (Tokyo, 1939–1943), 3 vols.

ZMR	*Zeitschrift für Missionswissenschaft und Religionswissenschaft,* Münster
Zoku kōsōden	*Further Biographies of Eminent Monks.* T. 2060, vol. 50; Nj. 1493
ZB	*Zen bunka* [*Zen Culture*], Kyoto

Chronological Table

Han Dynasty		206 BCE–220 CE
Western (Former) Han	206 BCE–8 CE	
Eastern (Later) Han	25–220	
Three Kingdoms Period		220–265
Wei (north)	220–265	
Shu (southwest)	221–263	
Wu (southeast)	222–280	
Chin Dynasty		265–420
Western Chin	265–317	
Eastern Chin	317–420	
Southern and Northern Dynasties (Nan-pei-ch'ao)		420–581
Sui Dynasty		581–618
T'ang Dynasty		618–907
An Lu-shan Rebellion	756–763	
persecution of Buddhism	841–846	
Five Dynasties		907–960
Sung Dynasty		960–1279
Northern Sung	960–1127	
Southern Sung	1127–1279	
Yuan Dynasty (Mongol rule)		1271–1368
Ming Dynasty		1368–1644
Ching Dynasty (Manchu rule)		1644–1911

Chinese Characters

Amida 阿彌陀

anjin hōmon 安心法門

An Lu-shan 安錄山

anroku (hsing-lu) 行錄

Anseikō, *see* An Shih-kao

An Shih-kao (Anseikō) 安正高

Banshō Gyōshū, *see* Wan-sung Hsing-hsiu

Baso shikeroku (Ma-tsu ssu-chia lu) 馬祖四家錄

Benshū-ron (Pien-tsung lun) 辯宗論

betsugo (pieh-yü) 別語

biwa 琵琶

bodai (p'u-t'i) = bodhi 菩提

Bodaidaruma (P'u-t'i-ta-mo Bodhidharma) 菩提達磨

Bodaidaruma nanshū tei zehi ron 菩提達摩南宗定是非論

bonbu (pṛthagjana) 凡夫

buji (wu shih) 無事

buji no hito 無事の人

Bukka Engo zenji hekiganroku (Fo-kuo yüan-wu ch'an-shih pi-yen lu) 佛果圜悟禪師碧巖錄

Bukka zenji, *see* Fo-kuo ch'an-shih

Bushū Sōzan Honjaku zenji goroku (Fu-chou Ts'ao-shan Pen-chi ch'an-shih yü-lu) 撫州曹山本寂禪師語錄

Busshinron no tenkai 佛身論の展開

busshō 佛性

Butsudabaddara (Buddhabhadra) 佛陀跋陀羅

Butten 佛典

Butten kōza 佛典講座

Ch'an, *see* Zen

Ch'ang-ch'ing Hui-leng (Chōkei Eryō) 長慶慧稜

Chang Ming-yüan 張明遠

Chang Tsai 張載

Ch'ang Yüeh 張說

Ch'an-men shih-tzu ch'eng-hsi-t'u, *see* Zemmon shishi shōshūzu

ch'an-na, *see* zenna

ch'an-shih, *see* zenji

Ch'an-yüan chu-ch'üan-chi tu-hsü, *see* Zengen-shosenshū-tojo

Chao-chou Ts'ung-shen (Jōshū Jūshin) 趙州從諗

Chao K'uang-yin 趙匡胤

Chao-lun (Jōron) 肇論

Chao Meng-fu 趙孟頫

Chen-chou Lin-chi Hui-chao ch'an-shih yü-lu, *see* Chinjū Rinzai Eshō zenji goroku

Chen Ch'u-chang 陳楚璋

Ch'eng Hao 程顥

Ch'eng I 程頤

chen-jen, *see* shinnin

Chen-ju-yüan, *see* Shinnyo-in

Ch'eng-kuan (Chōkan) 澄觀

Chen-tsung 眞宗

Ch'en Tsun-su 陳尊宿

chi (chih) 智

ch'i, see ki

Chiang Shen 蔣伸

Chia-t'ai p'u-teng lu, see Katai futōroku

chieh-wen, see kitsumon

Chien-chung ching-kuo hsü-teng lu,
    see Kenchū seikoku zokutōroku

Chien-nü 倩女

chieshō 智慧性

Chigi, see Chih-i

Chigon, see Chih-yen

chih, see chi

Chih-ch'ang (Chijō) 智常

Chih-ch'e (Shitetsu) 志徹

Chih-ch'eng (Shisei) 志誠

Chih-chih-ssu, see Seishi-ji

Chih-hsien (Chisen) 智詵

Chih-i (Chigi) 智顗

Chih-men Kuang-tsu (Chimon Kōso)
    智門光祚

Chih Min-tu 支愍度

Chih-tao (Shidō) 志道

Chih Tun (Shiton) 支遁

Chih-t'ung (Shitsū) 志通

Chih-wei (Chii) 智威

Chih-weng (Jikiō) 直翁

Chih-yao (Chiyaku) 智藥

Chih-yen (Chigon) 智巖

Chii, see Chih-wei

Chijō, see Chih-ch'ang

Chimon Kōso, see Chih-men Kuang-tsu

Ching 靜

Ch'ing 清

Ch'ing-chü (Seikyo) 清居

Ching-chüeh (Jōkaku) 淨覺

Ching-shan (Kinzan) 徑山

Ching-te ch'uan-teng lu, see Keitoku
    dentōroku

ching-tso, see seiza

Ching-t'u, see Jōdo

Ch'ing-yüan Hsing-ssu (Seigen Gyōshi) 青原行思

Chinjū Rinzai Eshō zenji goroku
    (Chen-chou Lin-chi Hui-chao
    ch'an-shih yü-lu) 鎮州臨濟慧照禪師語錄

Ch'in-liang-ssu, see Seiryōji

Chisen, see Chih-hsien

Ch'i-sung (Kaisū) 契嵩

Chi-tsang (Kichizō) 吉藏

ch'iung-ch'an-k'o, see kyūzenkaku

Chiyaku, see Chih-yao

Chi-yin Hui-hung (Jakuon Ekō) 寂音慧洪

Chodang chip, see Sodōshū

Chōkan, see Ch'eng-kuan

Chōkei Eryō, see Ch'ang-ching Hui-leng

Chou Tun-i 周敦頤

Chuan-fa cheng-tsung-chi, see Dembō
    shōjūki

Chuan fa-pao chi, see Den hōbōki

Chuang-tzu 莊子

Ch'üan T'ang wen 全唐文

Ch'üan Te-yü 權德輿

Ch'u-chi 處寂

Chü-chih (Gutei) 俱胝

Chūhō Myōhon, see Chung-feng Ming-
    pen

Chu Hsi 朱熹

Chūkō-ji (Chung-yü-ssu) 中興寺

Chün-ch'en wu-wei, see Kunshin goi

Chung-feng Ming-pen (Chūhō Myōhon)
    中峰明本

Chung-tsung 中宗

Ch'ung-yüan 崇遠

Chung-yung, see Chūyō

Chung-yü-ssu, see Chūkō-ji

Chū-ron 中論

Chūyō (Chung-yung) 中庸

Daiampanshuikyō 大安般守意經
    (Ta-an-pan-shou-i-ching)

Daian-ji (Ta-an-ssu) 大安寺
daianjin 大安心
Daiba 提婆
Daibon-ji (Ta-fan-ssu) 大梵寺
Daichijushō zenji (Ta-chih shou-sheng
    ch'an-ssu) 大智壽聖禪寺
Daie Sōkō, see Ta-hui Tsung-kao
daifunshi 大憤志
daigijō 大疑情
Daigu, see Ta-yü
daihōe 大法會
Daijō bosatsudō no kenkyū
    大乘菩薩道の研究
Daijōdaigishō (Ta-sheng ta-i-chang)
    大乘大義章
Daijō kishinron (Ta-sheng ch'i-hsin lun)
    大乘起信論
Daikan zenji, see Ta-chien ch'an-shih
daiki daiyū (ta-chi ta-yung) 大機大用
Daiō kokushi 大應國師
Dairin-ji (Ta-lin-ssu) 大林寺
daisen 大仙
daishinkon 大信根
daishu (ta-chu) 大珠
dairoku 大德
Daitoku-ji 大德寺
Daitsū zenji 大通禪師
Daiun-ji (Ta-yün-ssu) 大雲寺
Darumatara zengyō (Ta-mo-to-lo
    ch'an-ching) 達磨多羅禪經
Dazai Shundai 太宰春臺
Den hōbōki (Chuan fa-pao chi) 傳法寶紀
Dembōin (Ch'uan-fa-yüan) 傳法院
Dembō shōjūki (Chuan-fa cheng-tsung-
    chi) 傳法正宗記
dō (tao) 道
Dōfuku, see Tao-fu
dōgen 道眼
Dōgen, see Tao-yüan

dōgen bunmyō 道眼分明
Dōgen Kigen 道元希玄
Dōgo Enchi, see Tao-wu Yüan-chih
Dōiku, see Tao-yü
Dōitsu, see Tao-i
Dōkin, see Tao-chin
dokusan 獨參
dōnin 道人
Dōrin, see Tao-lin
dōryū 道流
Dōsen, see Tao-hsüan
Dōshin, see Tao-hsin
Dōshō, see Tao-sheng
Dōtokukyō (Tao-te-ching) 道德經

c 慧

Echū, see Hui-chung
Edo 江戶
Eikaku Genken, see Yung-chüeh
    Yüan-hsien
Einei-ji (Yung-ning-ssu) 永寧寺
Eisai, see Myōan Eisai
Eka, see Hui-k'o
Ekan, see Hui-kuan
Ekikyō (I-ching) 易經
Eman, see Hui-man
Emyō, see Hui-ming
en (yüan) 圓
Engakkyō, see Engakukyō
engaku 圓覺
Engakukyō (Yüan-chüeh ching) 圓覺經
Engakukyō daishoshō (Yüan-chüeh ching
    ta-shu ch'ao) 圓覺經大疏鈔
Engaku Sōen, see Yüan-chüeh Tsung-yen
engi 緣起
Engo Kokugon, see Yüan-wu K'o-ch'in
Enkei Kōmon, see Yen-ch'i Kuang-wen

Enni Ben'en 圓爾辦圓

Ennin 圓仁

Enō, see Hui-neng

Enryōroku (Wan-ling lu) 宛陵錄

ensō (yüan-hsiang) 圓相

erh-chung-ju, see nishu'nyū

Eshō zenji, see Hui-chao ch'an-shih

Fa-chen 法珍

Fa-chih (Hōji) 法持

Fa-chin (Hōkin) 法欽

Fa-ch'üan-ssu, see Hōsen-ji

Fa-ch'ung (Hōchū) 法沖

Fa-hai 法海

Fa-hsing-ssu, see Hosshō-ji

Fa-ju (Hō'nyo) 法如

Fa-jung (Hōyū) 法融

Fa-lang (Hōrō) 法朗

Fang Kuan 房琯

Fa-ta (Hōtatsu) 法達

Fa-t'ai 法汰

Fa-ts'ai 法才

Fa-tsang (Hōzō) 法藏

Fa-yen Wen-i (Hōgen Bun'eki) 法眼文益

Fa-yüan 法瑗

Feng-hsüeh Yen-chao (Fūketsu Enshō)
   風穴延沼

Feng-Tzu-chen 馮子振

Fen-yang Shan-chao (Fun'yō Zenshō)
   汾陽善昭

Fo-chao Te-kuang (Busshō Tokkō)
   佛照德光

Fo-kuo ch'an-shih (Bukka zenji) 佛果禪師

Fo-kuo Wei-po 佛國惟白

Fo-kuo Yüan-wu ch'an-shih Pi-yen
   lu, see Bukka Engo zenji Hekiganroku

Fo-t'u-teng 佛圖澄

Fu-chou T's'ao-shan Pen-chi ch'an-shih
   yü-lu, see Bushū Sōzan Honjaku zenji
   goroku

Fuketsu Enshō, see Feng-hsüeh Yen-chao

funi daidō 不二大道

Fun'yōroku (Fen-yang lu) 汾陽錄

Fun'yō Zenshō, see Fen-yang Shan-chao

Furoku: Daruma no zempō to shisō
   oyobi sono ta
   附錄、達摩の禪法と思想及其他

furuku yori 古くより

fuzoku 付囑

gakudōnin 學道人

gakunin 學人

gakusha 學者

Gantō Zenkatsu, see Yen-t'ou Ch'üan-huo

Gatsurin Shikan, see Yüeh-lin Shih-kuan

gengaku (hsüan-hsüeh) 玄學

Genjō, see Hsüan-tsang

Gennin-ron (Yüan-jen lun) 原人論

Gensha shibi, see Hsüan-sha shih-pei

gidan 疑團

Godaishūshō 五大宗匠

goi (wu-wei) 五位

Goi kenketsu (Wu-wei hsien-chüeh)
   五位顯訣

Goi shiketsu (Wu-wei chih-chüeh)
   五位旨訣

Goke goroku (Wu-chia yü-lu) 五家語錄

Goke sanshōyōromon 五家參詳要路門

Goke shōjūsan (Wu-chia cheng-tsung
   tsan) 五家正宗贊

Goshin, see Wu-chen

Goso Hōen, see Wu-tsu Fa-yen

Goso Hōen goroku (Wu-tsu Fa-yen
   yü-lu) 五祖法演語錄

Gotō egen (Wu-teng hui-yüan) 五燈會元

Gotō gentō (Wu-teng yen-t'ung) 五燈嚴統

Gotōroku (Wu-teng lu) 五燈錄

gozan jissetsu (jūsatsu) 五山十刹

Gozu (Niu-t'ou) 牛頭

gudō 求道

guhō nyūsō 求法入宋

Guṇabhadra 求那跋陀羅

Gunin, see Hung-jen

Gutei, see Chü-chih

Gyokusen-ji (Yü-ch'uan-ssu) 玉泉寺

Gyosen goroku (Yü-hsüan yü-lu)
  御選語錄

hadaka no hito 裸の人

hahaji 波波地

Hakuin Ekaku 白隱慧鶴

Han 漢

Hang-chou T'ien-lung (Kōshū Tenryū)
  杭州天龍

hannya sammai 般若三昧

Han-shan (Kanzan) 寒山

Han-shan Te-ch'ing 憨山德淸

Han Yü 韓愈

happu 八不

hasō 破相

Heian 平安

Hekiganroku (Pi-yen lu) 碧巖錄

hekikan (pi-kuan) 壁觀

hen 偏

henchūshi 偏中至

henchūshō 偏中正

Hiei 比叡

ho, see katsu

Hoan Sosen, see P'o-an Tsu-hsien

hōben 方便

Hōchū, see Fa-ch'ung

Hōgen Bun'eki, see Fa-yen Wen-i

Ho Hung-ching 何弘敬

Hōji, see Fa-chih

Hōkin, see Fa-chin

hokkai 法界

hokkai engi 法界緣起

Hō koji goroku (P'ang chü-shih yü-lu)
  龐居士語錄

Hokushū 北宗

Hōkyō zammai (Pao-ching san-mei) 寶鏡三昧

hommu (pen-wu) 本無

honshō 本性

hontai 本體

Hō'nyo, see Fa-ju

Hō'nyo zenji gyōjō 法如禪師行狀

Hōrinden (Pao-lin chuan) 寶林傳

Hōrin-ji 寶林寺

Hōrō, see Fa-lang

Hōsen-ji (Fa-ch'üan-ssu) 法泉寺

Ho-shan Wu-yin (Kazan Muin) 禾山無殷

hosshin 法身

hosshō 法性

Hosshō-ji (Fa-hsing-ssu) 法性寺

hossō 法相

Hōtatsu, see Fa-ta

Hotei, see Pu-t'ai

Hotōha 保唐派

Hotō-ji (Pao-t'ang-ssu) 保唐寺

Ho-tse Shen-hui (Kataku Jinne) 荷澤神會

Ho-tse-ssu, see Kataku-ji

Hōyū, see Fa-jung

Hōzō, see Fa-tsang

Hōzō-ron (Pao-tsang lun) 寶藏論

Hsiang Hsiu 向秀

Hsiang-yen Chih-hsien (Kyōgen Chikan)
  香嚴智閑

Hsieh Liang-tso 謝良佐

Hsieh Ling-yün 謝靈運

hsin, see shin

hsing, see shō

Hsing-hua Ts'un-chiang, *see* Kōke Zonshō

hsing-lu, *see* anroku

Hsing-t'ao 行韜

Hsin-hsin-ming, *see* Shinjinmei

hsin hsüeh, *see* shingaku

Hsi-sou Shao-t'an (Kisō Shōdon)
　希叟紹曇

Hsi-t'ang Chih-ts'ang 西堂智藏

Hsiu-hsin-yao lun, *see* Shūshinyō-ron

hsüan-hsüeh, *see* gengaku

Hsüan-kao 玄高

Hsüan-lang 玄朗

Hsüan-sha shih-pei (Gensha shibi)
　玄沙師備

Hsüan-shih 宣什

Hsüan-su 玄素

Hsüan-tsang (Genjō) 玄奘

Hsüan-tse 玄賾

Hsüeh-feng I-ts'un (Seppō Gison)
　雪峯義存

Hsüeh-tou Ch'ung-hsien (Setchō Jūken)
　雪竇重顯

Hsü kao-seng-chuan, *see* Zoku kōsōden

Hsü-t'ang Chih-yü (Kidō Chigu) 虚堂智愚

Hsü-t'ang ho-shang yü-lu, *see* Kidō oshō
　goroku

Huang-lung Hui-nan (Ōryō Enan)
　黃龍慧南

Huang-mei-shan (Ōbaizan) 黃梅山

Huang-po Hsi-yüan (Ōbaku Kiun)
　黃蘗希運

Huan Hsüan 桓玄

Hua-t'ai 滑臺

Hua-yen, *see* Kegon

Hu Chi-hsi 胡籍溪

Hu-ch'iu Shao-lung (Kukyū Jōryū) 虎丘紹隆

Hui-an 慧安

Hui-chao ch'an-shih (Eshō zenji) 慧照禪師

Hui-chi 惠紀

Hui-chung (Echū) 慧忠

Hui-jui 慧叡

Hui-k'o (Eka) 慧可

Hui-kuan (Ekan) 慧觀

Hui-man (Eman) 慧滿

Hui-ming (Emyō) 惠明

Hui-neng (Enō) 慧能

Hui-t'ang Tsu-hsin (Maidō Soshin)
　晦堂祖心

Hui-yen 慧嚴

Hui-yen Chih-chao (Maigan Chishō)
　晦巖智昭

Hui-yüan 慧遠

Hung-cheng (Kōsei) 宏正

Hung-chih ch'an-shih kuang-lu,
　see Wanshi zenji kōroku

Hung-chih Cheng-chüeh (Wanshi
　Shōgaku) 宏智正覺

Hung-jen (Kōnin, Gunin) 弘忍

Hu Shih 胡適

Hyakujō Ekai, *see* Pai-chang Huai-hai

Hyakujō shingi (Pai-chang
　ch'ing-kuei) 百丈清規

Hyakuron 百論

ichigyō sammai 一行三昧

I-ching, *see* Ekikyō

I-fu 義福

Igyō, *see* Kuei-yang

Igyōshū 潙仰宗

ikka myōju 一顆明珠

in (yin) 陰

Indara, *see* Yin-t'o-lo

inka 印可

Isan Reiyū, *see* Kuei-shan Ling-yu

I-shan I-ning (Issan Ichinei) 一山一寧

ishin denshin 以心傳心

Issan Ichinei, *see* I-shan I-ning

Jakuon Ekō, *see* Chi-yin Hui-hung
jazen 邪禪
Jen-t'ien yen-mu, *see* Ninden gammoku
ji (shih) 事
Jichiroku (Tzu-chih lu) 自知錄
Jikiō, *see* Chih-weng
Jinne goroku (Shen-hui yü-lu) 神會語錄
Jinshū, *see* Shen-hsiu
jinzū 神通
jisan 自贊
jishō 自性
Jitoku, *see* Tzu-te

Jittoku, *see* Shih-te
Jizō (Ksitigarbha) 地藏
jō 定
Jōdo (Ching-t'u) 淨土
Jōjitsu 成實
Jōjitsu-ron 成實論
Jō-jōza, *see* Ting Shang-tso
Jōkaku, *see* Ching-chüeh
Jō-ron, *see* Chao-lun
Jōshū Jūshin, *see* Chao-chou Ts'ung-shen
Jōshū Shinsai zenji goroku
 趙州眞際禪師語錄
juko (sung ku) 頌古
Juko hyakusoku (Sung-ku pai-tse)
 頌古百則
Ju-min (Nyobin) 如敏
Jūnimon-ron 十二門論

Kaifuku Dōnei, *see* K'ai-fu Tao-ning
K'ai-fu Tao-ning (Kaifuku Dōnei)
 開福道寧
K'ai-hsi Tao-ch'ien 開善道謙
Kaisū, *see* Ch'i-sung
Kakuan Shion, *see* Kuo-an Shih-yuan
kakubutsu (ko wu) 格物
kakugi (ko-i) 格義

Kamakura 鎌倉
kamben 勘辨
kan 關
K'an-hua ch'an, *see* Kanna-zen
K'ang Seng-hui 康僧會
kanjō 看淨
Kanna-zen (K'an-hua ch'an) 看話禪
Kannon (Avalokiteśvara) 觀音
kanshin 看心
Kanshin-ron (Kuan-hsin lun) 觀心論
Kanzan, *see* Han-shan
Kao-feng Yüan-miao (Kōhō Gemmyō)
 高峰原妙
Kao-seng-chuan, *see* Kōsōden
kappatsu patchi
 活撥撥地、活潑潑地、活鱍鱍地
kasso 活祖
Katai futōroku (Chia-t'ai p'u-teng lu)
 嘉泰普燈錄
Kataku-ji (Ho-tse-ssu) 荷澤寺
Kataku Jinne, *see* Ho-tse Shen-hui
Katakushū 荷澤宗
katsu (ho) 喝
Kegon (Hua-yen) 華嚴
Keihō Shūmitsu, *see* Kuei-feng Tsung-mi
Keitoku dentōroku (Ching-te
 ch'uan-teng lu) 景德傳燈錄
Kenchō-ji 建長寺
Kenchū seikoku zokutōroku
 (Chien-chung ching-kuo hsü-teng lu)
 建中靖國續燈錄
kenchushi 兼中至
kenchūtō 兼中到
kenshō 見性
Kessan Muin, *see* Ho-shan Wu-yin
ki (ch'i) 氣
Kichijō-ji 吉祥寺
Kichizō, *see* Chi-tsang
Kidō Chigu, *see* Hsü-t'ang Chih-yü

Lin-chi-yüan, see Rinzai-in
Ling-chao 靈昭
Ling-ch'üan-yüan, see Reisen-in
Ling-mo 靈默
Ling-shu-yüan, see Reiju-in
Ling-yüan 靈源
Li-tai fa-pao-chi, see Rekidai hōbōki
Li Tsun-hsü 李遵勗
Li Tung 李侗 , see also Li Yen-p'ing
Liu (Ryū) 劉
Liu Chih-lüeh 劉至略
Liu I-min 劉遺民
Liu Pai-shui 劉白水
Liu P'ing-shan 劉屏山
Liu Tsung-yüan 柳宗元
Li Yao-fu 李堯夫
Li Yen-p'ing 李延平, see also Li Tung
Lo-fu-shan, see Rafuzan
Lohan, see Rakan
Lo-han Kuei-ch'en (Rakan Keichin)
　羅漢桂琛
Lo-p'u Yüan-an (Rakuho Gen'an)
　樂普元安
Lo Ts'ung-yen 羅從彦
Lo-yang ch'ih-lan-chi, see Rakuyō garanki
Lu 廬
Lu Chiu-yüan 陸九淵
　see also Lu Hsiang-shan
lüeh-chuan, see ryakuden
Lu Hsiang-shan 陸象山
　see also Lu Chiu-yüan
lun, see ron
Lung-hsing-ssu, see Ryūkō-ji
Lung-t'an 龍潭
Lun-yü, see Rongo
Lü Ta-lin 呂大臨

Ma Fang 馬防
Maidō Soshin, see Hui-t'ang Tsu-hsin

Maigan Chishō, see Hui-yen Chih-chao
makyō 魔境
Ma-tsu ssu-chia lu, see Baso shike roku
Ma-tsu Tao-i 馬祖道一
Meng-tzu 孟子
Mi-an Hsien-chieh (Mittan Kanketsu)
　密菴咸傑
Miao-hsieh (Myōkyō) 妙叶
Mikkyo 密敎
Ming (Myō) 明
Ming-tao 明道
Miroku (Maitreya) 彌勒
Mittan Kanketsu, see Mi-an Hsien-chieh
Mo-chao ch'an, see Mokushō-zen
Mo-chao ming, see Mokushōmei
Mokkei, see Mu-ch'i
Mokushōmei (Mo-chao ming) 默照銘
Mokushō-zen (Mo-chao ch'an) 默照禪
mondō 問答
Monju (Mañjuśrī) 文殊
mōsō 妄想
mu (wu) 無
Mu-ch'i (Mokkei) 牧谿
muge 無礙
mui (wu-wei) 無爲
muju 無住
Mujū, see Wu-chu
Mumon Ekai, see Wu-men Hui-k'ai
Mumonkan (Wu-men kuan) 無門關
munen (wu-nien) 無念
Muromachi 室町
mushin (wu-hsin) 無心
musō 無相
Myō, see Ming
Myōan Eisai 明菴榮西
Myōkyō, see Miao-hsieh
Myōshin-ji 妙心寺
myōu 妙有

Nāgārjuna, see Ryūju

Nampo Jōmyō 南浦紹明

Nan-ch'üan P'u-yüan (Nansen Fugan) 南泉普願

Nangaku Ejō, see Nan-yüeh Huai-jang

Nan'in Egyō, see Nan-yüan Hui-yung

Nansen Fugen, see Nan-ch'üan P'u-yüan

Nanshūtongyō saijō daijō makahannya-haramitsukyō: Rokuso Enō daishi Shōshū Daibon-ji ni oite sehō suru no dankyō (Nan-tsung tun-chiao tsui-shang ta-sheng mo-ho-po-jo po-lo-mi ching: Liu-tsu Hui-neng ta-shih yü Shao-chou Ta-fan-ssu shih-fa t'an-ching)

南宗頓教最上大乘摩訶般若波羅密經、六祖惠能大師於韶州大梵寺施法檀經

Nan-ton Hoku-zen 南頓北漸

Nan-tsung tun-chiao tsui-shang ta-sheng mo-ho-po-jo po-lo-mi ching: Liu-tsu Hui-neng ta-shih yü Shao-chou Ta-fan-ssu shih-fa t'an-ching, see Nanshūtongyō saijō daijō makahannya-haramitsukyō: Rokuso Enō daishi Shōshū Daibon-ji ni oite sehō suru no dankyō

Nan-yang Hui-chung 南陽慧忠

Nan-yüan Hui-yung (Nan'in Egyō) 南院慧顒

Nan-yüeh Huai-jang (Nangaku Ejō) 南嶽懷讓

Nara 奈良

nehan (nirvāna) 涅槃

nembutsu (nien-fo) 念佛

Nenko hyakusoku (Nien-ku pai-tse) 拈古百則

Nichiren 日蓮

nien-fo, see nembutsu

Nien-ku pai-tse, see Nenko hyakusoku

Niu-t'ou, see Gozu

Ninden gammoku (Jen-t'ien yen-mu) 人天眼目

nindengyō 人天教

nishu'nyū (erh-chung-ju) 二種入

Nyobin, see Ju-min

Nyoraizen 如來禪

Ōbaizan, see Huang-mei-shan

Ōbaku Kiun, see Huang-po Hsi-yüan

Ogyū Sorai 荻生徂徠

Ōmori Sōgen 大森曹玄

Ōryō Enan, see Huang-lung Hui-nan

Pai-chang ch'ing-kuei, see Hyakujō shingi

Pai-chang Huai-hai (Hyakujō Ekai) 百丈懷海

P'ang chü-shih yü-lu, see Hō koji goroku

P'ang Yün 龐蘊

Pao-chih ho-shang 寶誌和尙

Pao-ching san-mei, see Hōkyō zammai

Pao-lin chuan, see Hōrinden

Pao-shou Yen-chao 保壽延沼

Pao-t'ang-ssu, see Hotō-ji

Pao-tsang lun, see Hōzō-ron

pen-wu, see hommu

pieh-yü, see betsugo

Pien-tsung lun, see Benshū-ron

pi-kuan, see hekikan

Pi-yen lu, see Hekiganroku

P'o-an Tsu-hsien (Hoan Sosen) 破庵祖先

P'u-chi 普寂

P'u-hua 普化

Pu-tai (Hotei) 布袋

p'u-t'i, see bodai

P'u-t'i-ta-mo, see Bodaidaruma

Rafuzan (Lo-fu-shan) 羅浮山

Rajū (Kumārajīva) 羅什

Rakan (Lohan) 羅漢

Rakan Keichin, see Lo-han Kuei-ch'en

Rakudōka 樂道歌

Rakuho Gen'an, see Lo-p'u Yüan-an

Rakuyō garanki (Lo-yang ch'ih-lan-chi) 洛陽伽藍記

Reiju-in (Ling-shu-yüan) 靈樹院

Reisen-in (Ling-ch'üan-yüan) 靈泉院

Rekidai hōbōki (Li-tai fa-pao-chi) 歷代法寶記

Renchi Shukō, see Lien-chi Chih-hung

resso-zō 列祖像

ri (li) 理

rigaku (li hsüeh) 理學

ri hokkai 理法界

riji muge (li-shih wu-ai) hokkai 理事無礙法界

Rinzai Eshō goroku (Lin-chi Hui-chao yü-lü) 臨濟慧照語錄

Rinzai Gigen, see Lin-chi I-hsüan

Rinzai-in (Lin-chi-yüan) 臨濟院

Rinzairoku 臨濟錄

Risshū 律宗

Ritsu 律

ron (lun) 論

Rongo (Lun-yü) 論語

ryakuden (lüeh-chuan) 略傳

Ryōga Butsujinhō shi 楞伽佛人法志

Ryōga shijiki (Leng-ch'ieh shih-tzu chi) 楞伽師資記

Ryōkai, see Liang Kai

Ryū, see Liu

Ryūju (Nāgārjuna) 龍樹

Ryūkō-ji (Lung-hsing-ssu) 龍興寺

Saichō 最澄

Saijōjō busshō-ka 最上乘佛性歌

Saijōjō-ron (Tsui-shang-ch'en lun) 最上乘論

sambō 三寶

san 贊　(讚)

Sandōkai (Ts'an-t'ung-chi) 參同契

sange 懺悔

sangen 三玄

sankan 三關

sanku 三句

sankyō itchi 三教一致

sankyōzu 三教圖

San-lun tsung, see Sanronshū

Sannei, see Tsan-ning

Sanron 三論

Sanronshū (San-lun tsung) 三論宗

San-sheng, Hui-jan (Sanshō E'nen) 三聖慧然

Sanshō E'nen, see San-sheng Hui-jang

san-t'ai 三臺

sanyō 三要

sanzen 參禪

satori 悟り

Seigen Gyōshi, see Ch'ing-yüan Hsing-ssu

Seikyo, see Ch'ing-chü

Seiryō-ji (Ch'ing-liang-ssu) 清涼寺

Seishi-ji (Chih-chih-ssu) 制旨寺

seiza (ching-tso) 靜坐

Sekisō Soen, see Shih-shuang Ch'u-yuan

Sekitō Kisen, see Shih-t'ou

Seng-chao 僧肇

Seng-ch'üan 僧詮

Seng-fu 僧副

Seng-lang 僧朗

Seng-na 僧那

Seng-ts'an 僧璨

Senni gedō 先尼外道

Seppō Gison, see Hsüeh-feng I-ts'un

Setchō Jūken, see Hsüeh-tou ch'ung-hsien

Shao Hsiu 紹修

Shao-lin-ssu, see Shōrin-ji

Shao Yung 邵雍

Shen-hsiu (Jinshū) 神秀

Shen-hui, *see* Ho-tse Shen-hui

Shen-hui yü-lu, *see* Jinne goroku

Shidō, *see* Chih-tao

shih, *see* ji

Shih-shuang Ch'u-yüan (Sekisō Soen)
 石霜楚圓

Shih-te (Jittoku) 拾得

Shih-t'ou Hsi-ch'ien (Sekitō Kisen)
 石頭希遷

shikan (chih-kuan) 止觀

shikatsu (ssu-ho) 四喝

Shike goroku (Ssu-chia yü-lu) 四家語錄

shikishin 色身

shiku fumbetsu (ssu-chü fen-pieh)
 四句分別

shin (hsin) 心

shingaku (hsin hsüeh) 心學

Shingon 眞言

Shinjinmei (Hsin-hsin-ming) 信心銘

shinkū 眞空

shinnin (chen-jen) 眞人

Shinnyoin (Chen-ju-yüan) 眞如院

Shinzoku Tōshi no keifu 新続灯史の系譜

shiryōken (ssu-liao-chien) 四料簡

Shisei, *see* Chih-ch'eng

shishōyū 四照用

Shitetsu, *see* Chih-ch'e

Shiton, *see* Chih Tun

Shitsū, *see* Chih-t'ung

shō (hsing) 性

shō 正

shōchūhen 正中偏

shōchūrai 正中來

Shōdōka 證道歌

shōgo 證悟

shōjō 小乘

Shōrin-ji (Shao-lin-ssu) 少林寺

Shōshitsu Rokumon 小室六門

Shōtoku Taishi 聖德太子

Shou-shan Sheng-nien (Shuzan Shōnen) 首山省念

Shōyōan 從容庵

Shōyōroku (Ts'ung-jung lu) 從容錄

Shuan-fen-shan (Sōhōzan) 雙峰山

Shūbun 周文

Shūhō, *see* Tsung-po

shukke 出家

Shūmon jikki-ron 宗門十規論

Shūmon rentō eyō (Tsung-men lien-teng
 hui-yao) 宗門聯燈會要

Shushi gorui 朱子語類

Shūshinyō-ron (Hsiu-hsin-yao lun) 修心要論

Shuzan Shōnen, *see* Shou-shan Sheng-
 nien

Sōanka (Ts'ao-an-ko) 草庵歌

sobutsu 祖佛

sōdō 僧堂

Sodōshū (Tsu-t'ang chi) 祖堂集

Soeishū 祖英集

Sōkei, *see* Ts'ao-ch'i

Sōkei daishi betsuden 曹溪大師別傳

Sō kōsōden (Sung kao-seng-chuan)
 宋高僧傳

sokushin sokubutsu 卽心卽佛

Soshizen (Tsu-shih ch'an) 祖師禪

Sotei Jion (Tsu-t'ing shih-yüan) 祖庭事苑

Sōtō (Ts'ao-tung) 曹洞

Sōzan Honjaku, *see* Ts'ao-shan

Ssu-chia yü-lu, *see* Shike goroku

ssu-chü fen-pieh, *see* shiku fumbetsu

ssu-ho, *see* shikatsu

ssu-liao-chien, *see* shiryōken

Sūgyōroku (Tsung-ching lu) 宗鏡錄

Sui 隋

suimōken 吹毛劍

Sung 宋

Sung kao-seng-chuan, *see* Sō kōsōden

sung-ku, *see* juko

Sung-ku pai-tse, *see* Juko hyakusoku

Sung Yün 宋雲

sūsokkan 數息觀

Su-tsung 肅宗

Suzuki, Daisetsu Teitarō 鈴木大拙貞太郎

Ta-an-pan-shou-i-ching,
    see Daiampanshuikyō

Ta-an-ssu, *see* Daian-ji

t'a-chi, *see* tōki

Ta-chien ch'an-shih (Daikan zenji)
    大鑑禪師

Ta-chih shou-sheng ch'an-ssu,
    see Daichijushō-zenji

ta-chi ta-yung, *see* daiki daiyū

ta-chu, *see* daishu

Ta-chüeh 大覺

Ta-chu Hui-hai 大珠慧海

Ta-fan-ssu, *see* Daibon-ji

Ta-hui Tsung-kao (Daie Sōkō) 大慧宗杲

tai (t'i) 體

t'ai-chi, *see* taikyoku

taikyoku (t'ai-chi) 太極

Tai-tsung 代宗

Ta-kuei 大潙

Ta-lin-ssu, *see* Dairin-ji

Ta-mo-to-lo ch'an-ching, *see* Darumatara
    zengyō

T'ang 唐

Tangen Ōshin, *see* Tan-yüan Ying-chen

T'an-lin 曇林

tantō choku'nyū 單刀直入

Tan-yüan Ying-chen (Tangen Ōshin)
    耽源應眞

tao, *see* dō

Tao-an 道安

Tao-chin (Dōkin) 道欽

Tao-fu (Dōfuku) 道副

Tao-hsin (Dōshin) 道信

Tao-hsüan (Dōsen) 道宣

Tao-i (Dōitsu) 道一

Tao-lin (Dōrin) 道林

Tao-sheng (Dōshō) 道生

Tao-te-ching, *see* Dōtokukyō

Tao-ts'an 道燦

Tao-wu Yüan-chih (Dōgo Enchi)
    道悟圓智

Tao-yu 道猷

Tao-yü (Dōiku) 道育

Tao-yüan (Dōgen) 道原

Ta-sheng ch'i-hsin lun, *see* Daijō kishin-
    ron

Ta-sheng ta-i-chang, *see* Daijōdaigishō

Ta-yü (Daigu) 大愚

Ta-yün-ssu, *see* Daiun-ji

te, *see* toku

Te-ch'ing (Tokusei) 德清

Te-i (Tokui) 德異

teishō 提唱

ten (t'ien) 天

Tendai 天台

Tendai Tokushō, *see* T'ien-t'ai Te-shao

Tendō Nyojo, *see* T'ien-t'ung Ju-ching

Tennō Dōgo, *see* T'ien-huang Tao-wu

Tenryū-ji 天龍寺

Tenshō kōtōroku (T'ien-sheng
    kuang-teng lu) 天聖廣燈錄

Te-shan Hsüan-chien (Tokusan Senkan)
    德山宣鑑

tesson 姪孫

t'i, *see* tai

t'ien, *see* ten

T'ien-huang Tao-wu (Tennō Dōgo)
    天皇道悟

T'ien-sheng kuang-teng lu, *see* Tenshō
    kōtōroku

T'ien-t'ai Chih-i 天台智顗

T'ien-t'ai Te-shao (Tendai Tokushō)
　天台德韶

T'ien-t'ung Cheng-chüeh 天童正覺

T'ien-t'ung Ju-ching (Tendō Nyojō)
　天童如淨

Ting Shang-tso (Jō jōza) 定上座

Tōfuku-ji 東福寺

tōki (t'a-chi) 塔記

toku (te) 德

Tokui, see Te-i

Tokusan Senkan, see Te-shan Hsüan-
　chien

Tokusei, see Te-ch'ing

ton (tun) 頓

Tongo nyūdō yōmon-ron (Tun-wu ju-tao
　yao-men lun) 頓悟入道要門論

Tongo saijōjō-ron 頓悟最上乘論

Tonkō shutsudo rokuso dankyō
　敦煌出土六祖壇經

Tōrei Enji 東嶺圓慈

Tōrin Jōsō, see Tung-lin Ch'ang-tsung

tōshi 燈史

Tosotsu Jūetsu, see Tou-shuai Ts'ung-yüeh

Tou-shuai Ts'ung-yüeh (Tosotsu Jūetsu)
　兜率從悦

Tōzan Ryōkai, see Tung-shan Liang-chieh

Tōzan Ryōkai zenji goroku (Tung-shan
　Liang-chieh ch'an-shih yü-lu)
　洞山良价禪師語錄

Tōzan Shusho, see Tung-shan Shou-ch'u

Tsan-ning (Sannei) 贊寧

Ts'an-t'ung-chi, see Sandōkai

Ts'ao-an-ko, see Sōanka

Ts'ao-chi (Sōkei) 曹溪

Ts'ao-shan Pen-chi (Sōzan Honjaku)
　曹山本寂

Ts'ao-tung, see Sōtō

tso-ch'an, see zazen

Tsui-shang-ch'eng lun, see Saijōjō-ron

Tsung-chih 總持

Tsung-ching lu, see Sūgyōroku

Ts'ung-jung lu see Shōyōroku

Tsung-men lien-teng hui-yao, see Shūmon
　rentō eyō

Tsung-mi, see Kuei-feng Tsung-mi

Tsung-pao (Shūhō) 宗寶

Tsu-shih ch'an, see Soshizen

Tsu-t'ang chi, see Sodōshū

Tsu-t'ing shih-yüan, see Sotei Jion

Tu Fei 杜朏

Tu Fu 杜甫

tun, see ton

Tung-lin Ch'ang-tsung (Tōrin Jōsō)
　東林常總

Tung-shan Liang-chieh (Tōzan Ryōkai)
　洞山良价

Tung-shan Liang-chieh ch'an-shih yü-lu,
　see Tōzan Ryōkai zenji goroku

Tung-shan Shou-ch'u (Tōzan Shusho)
　洞山守初

Tun-huang 敦煌

Tun-wu ju-tao yao-men lun, see Tongo
　nyūdō yōmon-ron

Tu-shun 杜順

Tzu-chih lu, see Jichiroku

Tzu-te (Jitoku) 自得

u (yu) 有

Ui Hakuju 宇井伯壽

Ummon Bun'en, see Yün-men Wen-yen

Ummon Kyōshin zenji kōroku (Yün-men
　K'uang-chen ch'an-shih kuang-lu)
　雲門匡眞禪師廣錄

Ummon oshō kōroku (Yün-men ho-shang
　kuang-lu) 雲門和尚廣錄

Ummonroku (Yün-men lu) 雲門錄

Ungan Donjō, see Yün-yen T'an-sheng

Ungo Dōyō, see Yün-chü Tao-ying

Wang Shao-i 王紹懿

Wang Shou-jen 王守仁

Wang Wei 王維

Wang Yang-ming 王陽明

Wan-ling lu, see Enryōroku

Wanshi Shōgaku, see Hung-chih Cheng-chüeh

Wanshi zenji kōroku (Hung-chih ch'an-shih kuang-lu) 宏智禪師廣錄

Wan-sung Hsing-hsiu (Banshō Gyōshū) 萬松行秀

watō 話頭

Wei Ch'u 韋璩

Wu 武

wu, see mu

Wu-chen (Goshin) 悟眞

Wu-chia cheng-tsung tsan, see Goke shōjūsan

Wu-chia yü-lu, see Goke goroku

Wu-chu (Mujū) 無住

Wu-chun Shih-fan (Bujun Shihan) 無準師範

Wu-hsiang 無相

wu-hsin, see mushin

Wu-men Hui-k'ai (Mumon Ekai) 無門慧開

Wu-men Kuan, see Mumonkan

wu-nien, see munen

wu-shih, see buji

Wu-teng hui-yüan, see Gotō egen

Wu-teng lu, see Gotōroku

Wu-teng yen-t'ung, see Gotō gentō

Wu-tsu Fa-yen (Goso Hōen) 五祖法演

Wu-tsu Fa-yen yü-lu, see Goso Hōen goroku

Wu-tsung 武宗

wu-wei, see mui

wu-wei, see goi

Wu-wei chih-chüeh, see Goi shiketsu

Wu-wei hsien-chüeh, see Goi kenketsu

Yakusan Igen, see Yüeh-shan Wei-yen

Yanagida Seizan 柳田聖山

yang, see yō

Yang Chien 楊簡

Yang-ch'i Fang-hui (Yōgi Hōe) 楊岐方會

Yang Hsüan-chih 楊衒之

Yang-shan Hui-chi (Kyōzan Ejaku) 仰山慧寂

Yang Shih 楊時

Yen-ch'i Huang-wen (Enkei Kōmon) 偃谿黃聞

Yen Hui 顏回

Yen-t'ou Ch'üan-huo (Gantō Zenkatsu) 巖頭全豁

yin, see in

Yin-t'o-lo (Indara) 因陀羅

Yin-tsung 印宗

yō (yang) 陽

yō (yung) 用

Yōgi Hōe, see Yang-ch'i Fang-hui

Yōka Genkaku, see Yung-chia Hsüan-chüeh

Yōmyō Enju, see Yung-ming Yen-shou

yu, see u

yüan, see en

Yüan 元

Yüan 遠

Yüan-chüeh ching, see Engakukyō

Yüan-chüeh ching ta-shu ch'ao, see Engakukyō Daishoshō

Yüan-chüeh Tsung-yen (Engaku Sōen) 圓覺宗演

yüan-hsiang, *see* ensō

Yüan-jen-lun, *see* Gennin-ron

Yüan-wu K'o-ch'in (Engo Kokugon)
圜悟克勤

Yü-ch'uan-ssu, *see* Gyokusen-ji

Yüeh-lin Shih-kuan (Gatsurin Shikan)
月林師觀

Yüeh-shan Wei-yen (Yakusan Igen)
藥山惟儼

Yü-hsüan yü-lu, *see* Gyosen goroku

yuishiki 唯識

Yün 筠

Yün-chü Tao-ying (Ungo Dōyō)
雲居道膺

yung, *see* yō

Yung-cheng 雍正

Yung-chia Hsüan-chüeh (Yōka Genkaku)
永嘉玄覺

Yung-chüeh Yüan-hsien (Eikaku Genken)
永覺元賢

Yung-ming Yen-shou (Yōmyō Enju)
永明延壽

Yung-ning-ssu, *see* Ei'nei-ji

Yün-men ho-shang kuang-lu, *see* Ummon Oshō kōroku

Yün-men K'uang-chen ch'an-shih kuang-lu, *see* Ummon Kyōshin zenji kōroku

Yün-men lu, *see* Ummonroku

Yün-men Wen-yen (Ummon Bun'en)
雲門文偃

Yün-yen T'an-sheng (Ungan Donjō)
雲巖曇晟

Yü Ti 干頎

Yu Tso 游酢

zazen (tso-ch'an) 坐禪

zazengi 坐禪儀

Zemmon shishi shōshūzu (Ch'an-men shih-tzu ch'eng-hsi-t'u) 禪門師資承襲圖

Zen (Ch'an) 禪

zenchishiki 善知識

Zengen-shosenshū-tojo (Ch'an-yüan chu-ch'üan-chi tu-hsü) 禪源諸詮集都序

Zengyō 禪經

zenji (ch'an-shih) 禪師

zenjō 禪定

Zenjō itchi 禪淨一致

zenkiga 禪機畫

Zenki no jidai 禪機の時代

zenna (ch'an-na) 禪那

Zen-no-shinzui—Mumonkan
禪の心髓、無門關

Zoku kōsōden (Hsü kao-seng-chuan)
續高僧傳

Genealogical Tables

Table I: *From Bodhidharma to Hui-neng and his disciples*

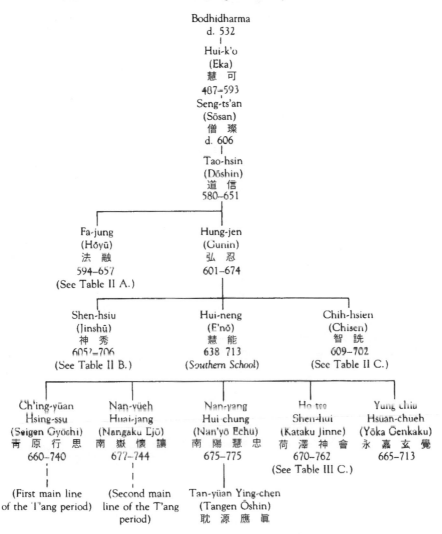

Bodhidharma
d. 532

Hui-k'o
(Eka)
慧 可
487–593

Seng-ts'an
(Sōsan)
僧 璨
d. 606

Tao-hsin
(Dōshin)
道 信
580–651

Fa-jung
(Hōyū)
法 融
594–657
(See Table II A.)

Hung-jen
(Gunin)
弘 忍
601–674

Shen-hsiu
(Jinshū)
神 秀
605?–706
(See Table II B.)

Hui-neng
(E'nō)
慧 能
638–713
(Southern School)

Chih-hsien
(Chisen)
智 詵
609–702
(See Table II C.)

Ch'ing-yüan
Hsing-ssu
(Seigen Gyōshi)
青 原 行 思
660–740

(First main line
of the T'ang period)

Nan-yüeh
Huai-jang
(Nangaku Ljō)
南 嶽 懷 讓
677–744

(Second main
line of the T'ang
period)

Nan-yang
Hui-chung
(Nan'yō Echu)
南 陽 慧 忠
675–775

Tan-yüan Ying-chen
(Tangen Ōshin)
耽 源 應 真

Ho-tse
Shen-hui
(Kataku Jinne)
荷 澤 神 會
670–762
(See Table III C.)

Yung-chia
Hsüan-chueh
(Yōka Genkaku)
永 嘉 玄 覺
665–713

Table II: *Collateral Lines of the Early Period*

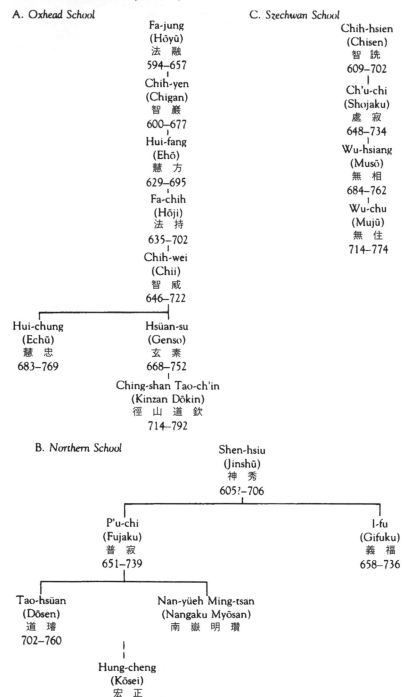

A. *Oxhead School*

Fa-jung
(Hōyū)
法 融
594–657

Chih-yen
(Chigan)
智 巖
600–677

Hui-fang
(Ehō)
慧 方
629–695

Fa-chih
(Hōji)
法 持
635–702

Chih-wei
(Chii)
智 威
646–722

Hui-chung
(Echū)
慧 忠
683–769

Hsüan-su
(Genso)
玄 素
668–752

Ching-shan Tao-ch'in
(Kinzan Dōkin)
徑 山 道 欽
714–792

C. *Szechwan School*

Chih-hsien
(Chisen)
智 詵
609–702

Ch'u-chi
(Shojaku)
處 寂
648–734

Wu-hsiang
(Musō)
無 相
684–762

Wu-chu
(Mujū)
無 住
714–774

B. *Northern School*

Shen-hsiu
(Jinshū)
神 秀
605?–706

P'u-chi
(Fujaku)
普 寂
651–739

I-fu
(Gifuku)
義 福
658–736

Tao-hsüan
(Dōsen)
道 璿
702–760

Nan-yüeh Ming-tsan
(Nangaku Myōsan)
南 嶽 明 瓚

Hung-cheng
(Kōsei)
宏 正

Table III: *Main Lines of the T'ang Period*

A. *First Main Line*

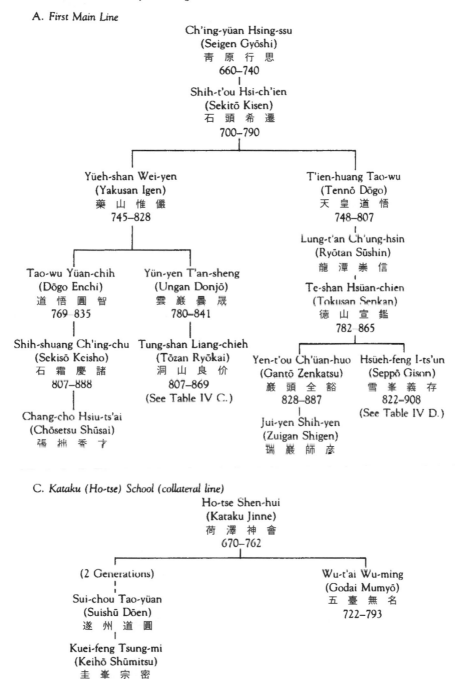

Ch'ing-yüan Hsing-ssu
(Seigen Gyōshi)
青 原 行 思
660–740

Shih-t'ou Hsi-ch'ien
(Sekitō Kisen)
石 頭 希 遷
700–790

Yüeh-shan Wei-yen
(Yakusan Igen)
藥 山 惟 儼
745–828

T'ien-huang Tao-wu
(Tennō Dōgo)
天 皇 道 悟
748–807

Lung-t'an Ch'ung-hsin
(Ryōtan Sūshin)
龍 潭 崇 信

Te-shan Hsüan-chien
(Tokusan Senkan)
德 山 宣 鑑
782 865

Tao-wu Yüan-chih
(Dōgo Enchi)
道 悟 圓 智
769 835

Yün-yen T'an-sheng
(Ungan Donjō)
雲 巖 曇 晟
780–841

Shih-shuang Ch'ing-chu
(Sekisō Keisho)
石 霜 慶 諸
807–888

Tung-shan Liang-chieh
(Tōzan Ryōkai)
洞 山 良 价
807–869
(See Table IV C.)

Yen-t'ou Ch'üan-huo
(Gantō Zenkatsu)
巖 頭 全 豁
828–887

Hsüeh-feng I-ts'un
(Seppō Gison)
雪 峯 義 存
822–908
(See Table IV D.)

Chang-cho Hsiu-ts'ai
(Chōsetsu Shūsai)
張 拙 秀 才

Jui-yen Shih-yen
(Zuigan Shigen)
瑞 巖 師 彥

C. *Kataku (Ho-tse) School (collateral line)*

Ho-tse Shen-hui
(Kataku Jinne)
荷 澤 神 會
670–762

(2 Generations)

Sui-chou Tao-yüan
(Suishū Dōen)
遂 州 道 圓

Kuei-feng Tsung-mi
(Keihō Shūmitsu)
圭 峯 宗 密
780–841

Wu-t'ai Wu-ming
(Godai Mumyō)
五 臺 無 名
722–793

B. *Second Main Line*

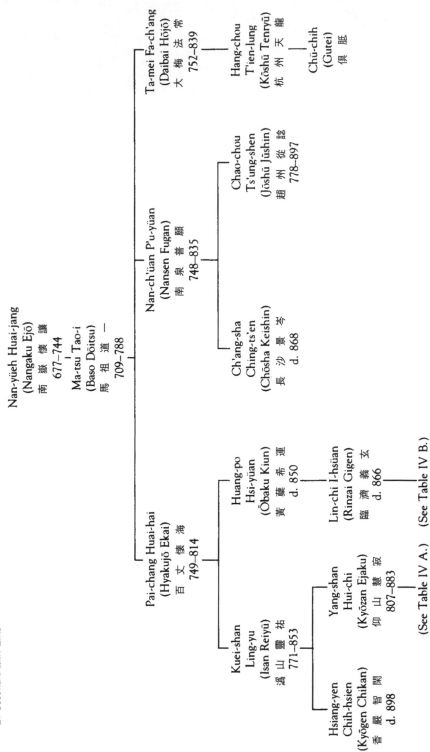

Table IV: *The·Five Houses*

A. *House of Igyō (Kuei-yang)*

Kuei-shan Ling-yu
(Isan Reiyū)
潙 山 靈 祐
771–853

Yang-shan Hui-chi
(Kyōzan Ejaku)
仰 山 慧 寂
807–883
Nan-t'a Kuang-yung
(Nantō Kōyū)
南 塔 光 涌
850–938

Pa-chiao Hui-ch'ing
(Bashō Esei)
芭 蕉 慧 清
Hsing-yang Ch'ing-jang
(Kōyō Shinjō)
興 陽 清 讓

Hsiang-yen Chih-hsien
(Kyōgen Chikan)
香 嚴 智 閑
d. 898

B. *House of Rinzai (Lin-chi)*

Lin-chi I-hsüan
(Rinzai Gigen)
臨 濟 義 玄
d. 866
Hsing-hua Ts'ung-chiang
(Kōke Zonshō)
興 化 存 奬
830–888
Nan-yüan Hui-yung
(Nan'in Egyō)
南 院 慧 顒
d. 930
Feng-hsüeh Yen-chao
(Fuketsu Enshō)
風 穴 延 沼
896–973
Shou-chan Sheng-nien
(Shuzan Shōnen)
首 山 省 念
926–993
Fen-yang Shan-chao
(Fun'yō Zenshō)
汾 陽 善 昭
942–1024
Shih-shuang Ch'u-yüan
(Sekisō Soen)
石 霜 楚 圓
986–1039

Yang-ch'i Fang-hui
(Yōgi Hōe)
楊 岐 方 會
992–1049
(See Table V A. 1–3)

Huang-lung Hui-nan
(Ōryō E'nan)
黃 龍 慧 南
1002–1069
(See Table V B.)

C. *House of Sōtō (Ts'ao-tung)*

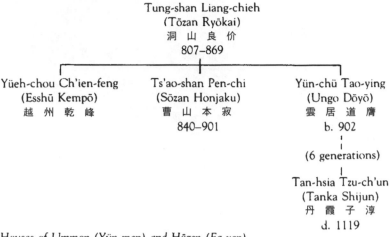

Tung-shan Liang-chieh
(Tōzan Ryōkai)
洞 山 良 价
807–869

Yüeh-chou Ch'ien-feng
(Esshū Kempō)
越 州 乾 峰

Ts'ao-shan Pen-chi
(Sōzan Honjaku)
曹 山 本 寂
840–901

Yün-chü Tao-ying
(Ungo Dōyō)
雲 居 道 膺
b. 902

(6 generations)

Tan-hsia Tzu-ch'un
(Tanka Shijun)
丹 霞 子 淳
d. 1119

D. *Houses of Ummon (Yün-men) and Hōgen (Fa-yen)*

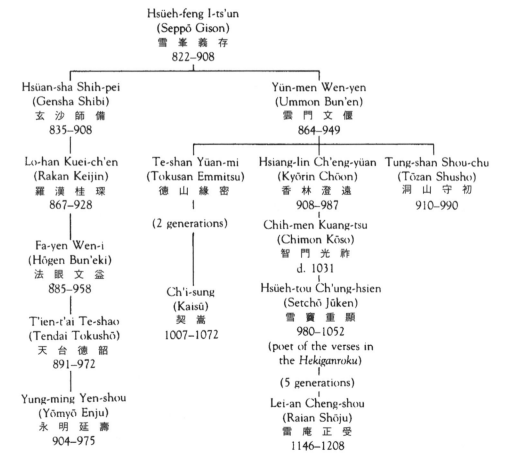

Hsüeh-feng I-ts'un
(Seppō Gison)
雪 峯 義 存
822–908

Hsüan-sha Shih-pei
(Gensha Shibi)
玄 沙 師 備
835–908

Lo-han Kuei-ch'en
(Rakan Keijin)
羅 漢 桂 琛
867–928

Fa-yen Wen-i
(Hōgen Bun'eki)
法 眼 文 益
885–958

T'ien-t'ai Te-shao
(Tendai Tokushō)
天 台 德 韶
891–972

Yung-ming Yen-shou
(Yōmyō Enju)
永 明 延 壽
904–975

Yün-men Wen-yen
(Ummon Bun'en)
雲 門 文 偃
864–949

Te-shan Yüan-mi
(Tokusan Emmitsu)
德 山 緣 密

(2 generations)

Ch'i-sung
(Kaisū)
契 嵩
1007–1072

Hsiang-lin Ch'eng-yüan
(Kyōrin Chōon)
香 林 澄 遠
908–987

Chih-men Kuang-tsu
(Chimon Kōso)
智 門 光 祚
d. 1031

Hsüeh-tou Ch'ung-hsien
(Setchō Jūken)
雪 竇 重 顯
980–1052
(poet of the verses in
the *Hekiganroku*)

(5 generations)

Lei-an Cheng-shou
(Raian Shōju)
雷 庵 正 受
1146–1208

Tung-shan Shou-chu
(Tōzan Shusho)
洞 山 守 初
910–990

Table V: *The Rinzai (Lin-chi) School during the Sung Period*

A. *Line of Yōgi (Yang-ch'i)*

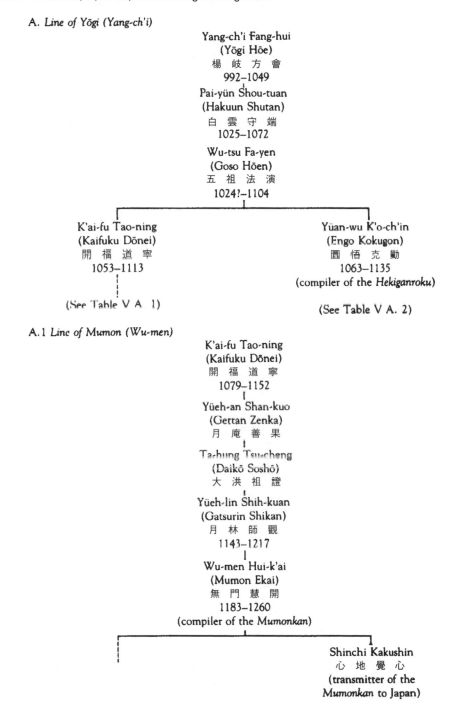

Yang-ch'i Fang-hui
(Yōgi Hōe)
楊 岐 方 會
992–1049

Pai-yün Shou-tuan
(Hakuun Shutan)
白 雲 守 端
1025–1072

Wu-tsu Fa-yen
(Goso Hōen)
五 祖 法 演
1024?–1104

K'ai-fu Tao-ning
(Kaifuku Dōnei)
開 福 道 寧
1053–1113

(See Table V A 1)

Yüan-wu K'o-ch'in
(Engo Kokugon)
圜 悟 克 勤
1063–1135
(compiler of the *Hekiganroku*)

(See Table V A. 2)

A.1 *Line of Mumon (Wu-men)*

K'ai-fu Tao-ning
(Kaifuku Dōnei)
開 福 道 寧
1079–1152

Yüeh-an Shan-kuo
(Gettan Zenka)
月 庵 善 果

Ta-hung Tsu-cheng
(Daikō Soshō)
大 洪 祖 證

Yüeh-lin Shih-kuan
(Gatsurin Shikan)
月 林 師 觀
1143–1217

Wu-men Hui-k'ai
(Mumon Ekai)
無 門 慧 開
1183–1260
(compiler of the *Mumonkan*)

Shinchi Kakushin
心 地 覺 心
(transmitter of the
Mumonkan to Japan)

A.2 *Line of Engo (Yüan-wu)*

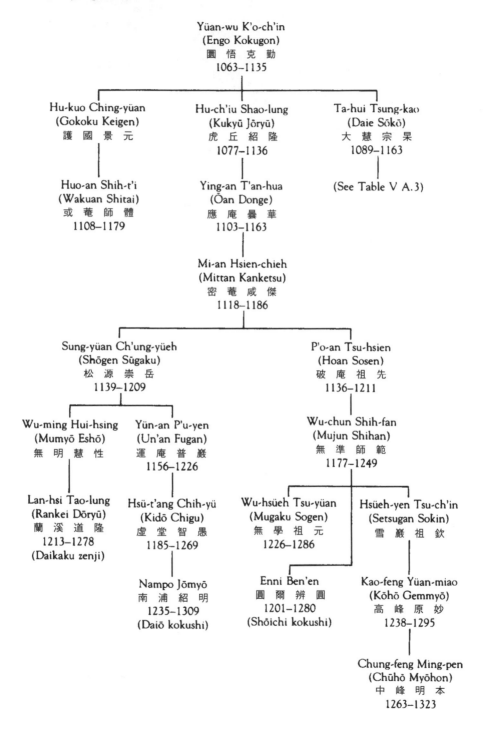

Yüan-wu K'o-ch'in
(Engo Kokugon)
圜 悟 克 勤
1063–1135

Hu-kuo Ching-yüan
(Gokoku Keigen)
護 國 景 元

Hu-ch'iu Shao-lung
(Kukyū Jōryū)
虎 丘 紹 隆
1077–1136

Ta-hui Tsung-kao
(Daie Sōkō)
大 慧 宗 杲
1089–1163

Huo-an Shih-t'i
(Wakuan Shitai)
或 菴 師 體
1108–1179

Ying-an T'an-hua
(Ōan Donge)
應 庵 曇 華
1103–1163

(See Table V A.3)

Mi-an Hsien-chieh
(Mittan Kanketsu)
密 菴 咸 傑
1118–1186

Sung-yüan Ch'ung-yüeh
(Shōgen Sūgaku)
松 源 崇 岳
1139–1209

P'o-an Tsu-hsien
(Hoan Sosen)
破 庵 祖 先
1136–1211

Wu-ming Hui-hsing
(Mumyō Eshō)
無 明 慧 性

Yün-an P'u-yen
(Un'an Fugan)
運 庵 普 巖
1156–1226

Wu-chun Shih-fan
(Mujun Shihan)
無 準 師 範
1177–1249

Lan-hsi Tao-lung
(Rankei Dōryū)
蘭 溪 道 隆
1213–1278
(Daikaku zenji)

Hsü-t'ang Chih-yü
(Kidō Chigu)
虛 堂 智 愚
1185–1269

Wu-hsüeh Tsu-yüan
(Mugaku Sogen)
無 學 祖 元
1226–1286

Hsüeh-yen Tsu-ch'in
(Setsugan Sokin)
雪 巖 祖 欽

Nampo Jōmyō
南 浦 紹 明
1235–1309
(Daiō kokushi)

Enni Ben'en
圓 爾 辨 圓
1201–1280
(Shōichi kokushi)

Kao-feng Yüan-miao
(Kōhō Gemmyō)
高 峰 原 妙
1238–1295

Chung-feng Ming-pen
(Chūhō Myōhon)
中 峰 明 本
1263–1323

A.3 *Line of Daie (Ta-hui)*

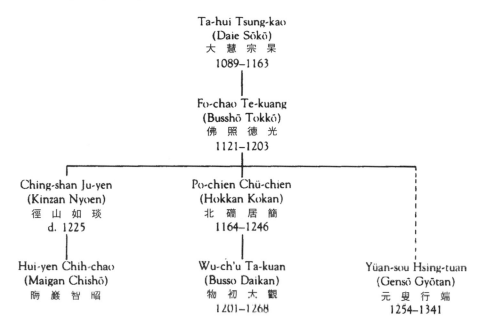

Ta-hui Tsung-kao
(Daie Sōkō)
大 慧 宗 杲
1089–1163

Fo-chao Te-kuang
(Busshō Tokkō)
佛 照 德 光
1121–1203

Ching-shan Ju-yen
(Kinzan Nyoen)
徑 山 如 琰
d. 1225

Po-chien Chü-chien
(Hokkan Kokan)
北 磵 居 簡
1164–1246

Hui-yen Chih-chao
(Maigan Chishō)
晦 巖 智 昭

Wu-ch'u Ta-kuan
(Busso Daikan)
物 初 大 觀
1201–1268

Yüan-sou Hsing-tuan
(Gensō Gyōtan)
元 叟 行 端
1254–1341

B. *Line of Ōryō (Huang-lung)*

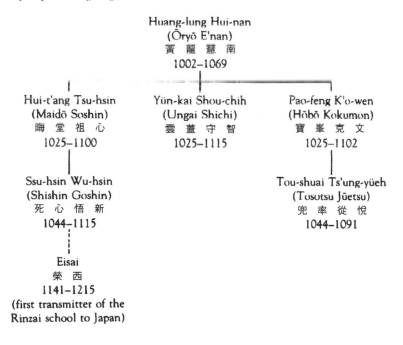

Huang-lung Hui-nan
(Ōryō E'nan)
黃 龍 慧 南
1002–1069

Hui-t'ang Tsu-hsin
(Maidō Soshin)
晦 堂 祖 心
1025–1100

Yün-kai Shou-chih
(Ungai Shichi)
雲 蓋 守 智
1025–1115

Pao-feng K'o-wen
(Hōbō Kokumon)
寶 峯 克 文
1025–1102

Ssu-hsin Wu-hsin
(Shishin Goshin)
死 心 悟 新
1044–1115

Tou-shuai Ts'ung-yüeh
(Tosotsu Jūetsu)
兜 率 從 悅
1044–1091

Eisai
榮 西
1141–1215
(first transmitter of the
Rinzai school to Japan)

Table VI: *The Sōtō (Ts'ao-tung) School during the Sung Period*

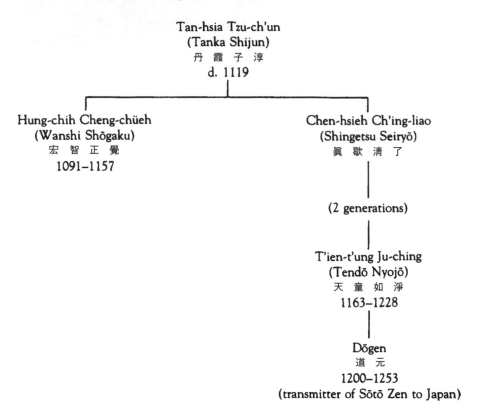

Tan-hsia Tzu-ch'un
(Tanka Shijun)
丹 霞 子 淳
d. 1119

Hung-chih Cheng-chüeh
(Wanshi Shōgaku)
宏 智 正 覺
1091–1157

Chen-hsieh Ch'ing-liao
(Shingetsu Seiryō)
眞 歇 淸 了

(2 generations)

T'ien-t'ung Ju-ching
(Tendō Nyojō)
天 童 如 淨
1163–1228

Dōgen
道 元
1200–1253
(transmitter of Sōtō Zen to Japan)

Indexes

Index of Names and Titles

Index of Terms and Subjects